Key Popu
Vita, Statistics

Local and Health Authority Areas

Population and vital statistics by area of
usual residence in the United Kingdom, 2016

Provisional Long Term International Migration
(LTIM) estimates, year ending Dec 2017*

Series VS No 39, PPI No. 35

Data for 2016, 2017*

Key Population and Vital Statistics
Series VS No.39, PPI No. 35

Contents	Page No.

Key Population and Vital Statistics
Series VS No.39, PPI No. 35

Statistical bulletin

Population estimates for the UK, England and Wales, Scotland and Northern Ireland: mid-2016

National and subnational mid-year population estimates for the UK and its constituent countries by administrative area, age, sex and components of population change.

Contact:
Neil Park
pop.info@ons.gsi.gov.uk
+44 (0)1329 444661

Release date:
22 June 2017

Next release:
June 2018

Table of contents

1 . Main points

- The population of the UK at 30 June 2016 is estimated to be 65,648,000 people.

- Over the year to mid-2016, the number of people resident in the UK increased by 0.8% (538,000), this growth rate is similar to the average annual growth rate since 2005.

- The population increase of the UK reflected increases of 193,000 people through natural change (35.8% of the total increase), 336,000 through net international migration (62.4% of the total increase) and an increase of 9,500 people in the armed forces population based in the UK.

- The UK population continues to age, but at a slower rate than recent years with only a small change to the proportion aged 65 and over (18.0% in mid-2016 compared with 17.9% in mid-2015) and an unchanged median age of 40.

- The annual population growth varied across the UK – in England it was 0.9%, Wales 0.5%, Scotland 0.6% and Northern Ireland 0.6%.

2 . Statistician's comment

"The population of the UK continued to grow in the year to mid-2016 at a similar rate to that seen over recent years. Net international migration continued to be the main driver, but there was also an increase in births and fewer deaths than last year.

"Population growth was not evenly distributed however, with London's growth rate more than twice that in Wales, Scotland, Northern Ireland, and the three northern English regions."

Neil Park, Head of Population Estimates Unit, Office for National Statistics

3 . Things you need to know about this release

These are the official population estimates for the UK as at 30 June 2016 and therefore reflect the size of the UK population around the time of the EU referendum (23 June 2016). They are based on the census and are updated annually to account for population change during the period from 1 July to 30 June. The two main contributors to population change are natural change (births minus deaths) and net migration (the difference between long-term moves into and out of the UK or local areas).

Information about the quality, including strengths and limitations, of the estimates published in this release can be found in the Quality and Methodology Information (QMI) reports for population estimates and for internal migration estimates. Some of the administrative data used in estimating international immigration for local authorities (LA) in England and Wales were not available at the time of production of the mid-2016 population estimates. Further details are provided in the QMI, including an assessment of the likely impact based on the impact of the same methods being used in 2015.

This release includes national and subnational population estimates for England and Wales, Scotland, and Northern Ireland. This statistical bulletin also covers the mid-2016 internal migration estimates for England and Wales.

4 . UK population continues to grow at 0.8% per year

The population of the UK was 65.6 million (65,648,000) in mid-2016, with a 95% confidence interval of plus or minus 0.2%. In the year to mid-2016, the population of the UK increased by 0.8%, consistent with the rate of population growth in the period since 2005, which varied between 0.6% and 0.8%. Figure 1 shows how UK population growth has varied since 1944.

Figure 1: Annual population change for the UK, mid-1944 to mid-2016

Figure 1: Annual population change for the UK, mid-1944 to mid-2016

Source: Office for National Statistics, National Records of Scotland, Northern Ireland Statistics and Research Agency

Notes:

1. At mid-1947 and mid-1952 population estimates changed in the way home armed forces resident in the UK and UK armed forces posted abroad were included or excluded. Population estimates back to 1838 are available in the supporting information tables.

In the year to mid-2016, the UK population increased by 538,000 people. In numerical terms this is the largest increase in population since the year to mid-1947 when the population increased by 551,000. Over the last 10 years, annual population change for the UK has been, on average, 482,000. There are differences between the methods and definitions used to calculate population estimates during the 1940s and now that affect the direct comparability of population estimates from these periods.

In the 11 years between mid-2005 and mid-2016, the population of the UK increased by just over 5 million people; the previous increase of 5 million took 35 years (between mid-1970 to mid-2005) and the 5 million before that were added over a 17-year period between mid-1953 and mid-1970.

5 . UK population grew by 538,000 in the year to mid-2016

At the national level population change can be split into natural change (births minus deaths), net international migration (immigration minus emigration) and other change, which at the national level reflects changes due to armed forces personnel moving into or out of the UK.

Figure 2 shows that while natural change has increased, net international migration remains the largest component of population change. Overall, natural change accounted for 35.8% of the population change, net international migration for 62.4% and other changes 1.8%.

Figure 2: Population change for the UK, mid-1992 onwards

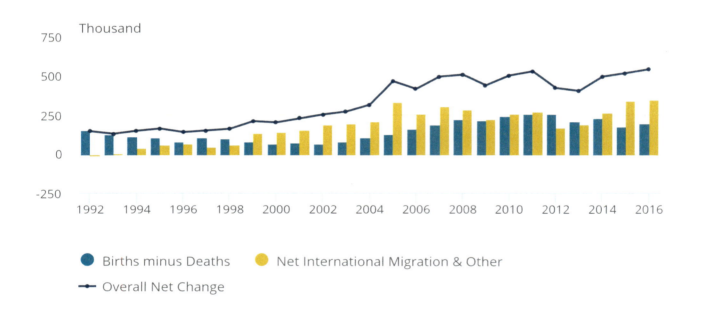

Figure 2: Population change for the UK, mid-1992 onwards

Source: Office for National Statistics, National Records of Scotland, Northern Ireland Statistics and Research Agency

Notes:

1. Figures may not add exactly due to rounding.

2. Other changes comprises changes to the size of armed forces stationed in the UK and other special population adjustments; and is combined with net international migration for the purposes of this graph.

Population change due to natural change, was 193,000 in mid-2016 (or 0.3% of the mid-2015 population), an increase of 21,000 on the previous year. It remains below the level of the peak seen between 2008 and 2014, but above the levels seen between 1992 and 2008. Figure 2 shows that natural change and overall change are slightly higher than in the year to mid-2015. Other changes increased, reflecting changes to armed forces personnel based in the UK; net international migration remained at a similar level to mid-2015.

Births and deaths

In the year to mid-2016, there were 781,000 births (an increase of 0.7% on the previous year) and 588,000 deaths (a decrease of 2.6%). Further analysis of fertility in the UK will be published by the Office for National Statistics (ONS) in July 2017.

The decrease in deaths is partly a result of the winter period 2015 to 2016 excess winter mortality significantly decreasing from the winter period 2014 to 2015. Further analysis from ONS has suggested that this was due mainly to the most prevalent strain of the flu virus impacting younger people rather than older people, who are more at risk.

Decreases in mortality over recent years have resulted in increasing life expectancies in the UK and a narrowing of the gap in life expectancies between men and women. This reflects a fall in the proportions of males who smoke or hold a higher-risk occupation. This is one reason why the ratio of males to females in the UK population has continued to increase. There are now 98 men for every 100 women, compared with 95 men per 100 women in mid-2005. The other main reason for the increase in this ratio is that net international migration results in more men residing in the UK as they tend to migrate to the UK more than women.

International migration

Net international migration in the year to mid-2016 was at a similar level to that seen in mid-2015, at 336,000 or 0.5% of the mid-2015 population. Compared with mid-2015, there were 13,000 more immigrants and 13,000 more emigrants. Analysis of the International Passenger Survey (IPS) data, that form the basis of these estimates, showed that these changes were not statistically significant. It showed that net migration remained around record levels, but it was stable compared with recent years; while immigration levels were among the highest estimates recorded.

In addition to the direct impact of migration on the size of the population, current and past international migration also has indirect effects on the size of the population as it changes the numbers of births and deaths in the UK. A fuller assessment of the indirect effect of migration on the size of the population would consider:

- births to, and deaths of, people who had migrated to the UK

- births to, and deaths of, people who emigrated from the UK (and who would have given birth, or died, in the UK had they not emigrated)

- how to account for births to, and deaths of, UK-born people who had emigrated and subsequently returned to the UK

- how to account for births to, and deaths of, UK-born people who had parents (or grandparents) who were themselves immigrants

Some additional information for England and Wales can be obtained in Parents' Country of Birth 2015, this showed that in the calendar year 2015, of all births in England and Wales 27.5% were to mothers born outside of the UK. Background information on the UK population, its size, characteristics and the causes of population change is available in the Overview of the UK Population: March 2017.

Other changes

Other changes, comprising changes to the size of the armed forces stationed in the UK and other special population adjustments, tend to have small effects on the national population but can have a larger impact at a local level. In the year to mid-2016, the UK population increased by 9,500 due to other changes, compared with an increase of 5,800 in the year to mid-2015. This reflects trends such as the return of British Armed Forces based in Germany.

6 . Population of England reaches 55 million

Table 1 shows that, of the four countries of the UK, England's population grew the fastest to mid-2016, over both a 1-year period and a 10-year period, and has exceeded 55 million for the first time.

Table 1: Population growth for UK countries, mid-2016

	Population mid-2016	Share of UK population	Increase on mid-2015	Percentage change since mid-2015	Percentage change since mid-2006
England	55,268,100	84.2%	481,800	0.9%	8.4%
Wales	3,113,200	4.7%	14,100	0.5%	4.3%
Scotland	5,404,700	8.2%	31,700	0.6%	5.3%
Northern Ireland	1,862,100	2.8%	10,500	0.6%	6.8%
UK	65,648,100	100.0%	538,100	0.8%	7.9%

Source: Office for National Statistics, National Records of Scotland, Northern Ireland Statistics and Research Agency

Notes:

1. Figures may not add exactly due to rounding.

While the population in England grew faster than the rest of the UK, population growth at the regional level varied from 1.3% in London to 0.5% in the North East. The datasets accompanying this release, for example Table MYE3, provide population estimates for the four UK countries, regions and counties of England, and for local and unitary authorities across the UK.

Comparing the mid-2016 and mid-2015 population estimates at the local authority level demonstrates that population trends vary across the UK. These include:

- the total population grew in 364 local authorities in the year to mid-2016, compared with 350 to mid-2015

- while the 26 local authorities showing population decreases to mid-2016 were spread throughout England, Wales and Scotland, 17 of these were in coastal areas

- of the 14 authorities showing population increases of 2% or above, 8 of these were in London

Five of these local authorities are in Inner London – Westminster, Camden, City of London, Islington and Haringey; the other three a block in East London – Tower Hamlets, Newham, and Barking and Dagenham. This growth pattern is consistent with the Office for National Statistics (ONS) Analysis of City Regions based on mid-2015 population estimates. This shows that while city regions have grown faster than the rest of the UK since 2011, the drivers of growth in each city region vary. London is growing faster than the others, because of its young age structure and attractiveness to international migrants.

7 . UK population continues to age

Returning to the overall UK population, its composition is determined by the pattern of births, deaths and migration that have taken place in previous years. The pyramid in Figure 3a shows some important trends in the age structure of the UK, comparing the population at mid-2016 and 10 years previously.

The proportion of the population aged 65 and over reached 18.0% in mid-2016, representing a rise of 0.1 percentage points on mid-2015. On this measure the rapid ageing of the population seen between 2009 and 2015 may be temporarily slowing as relatively smaller cohorts turn age 65. By contrast, the large peak of people born in the year to mid-1947 means that there is a large cohort now aged 69.

Figure 3a: Population pyramid for the UK, mid-2016, single year of age 0 to 89

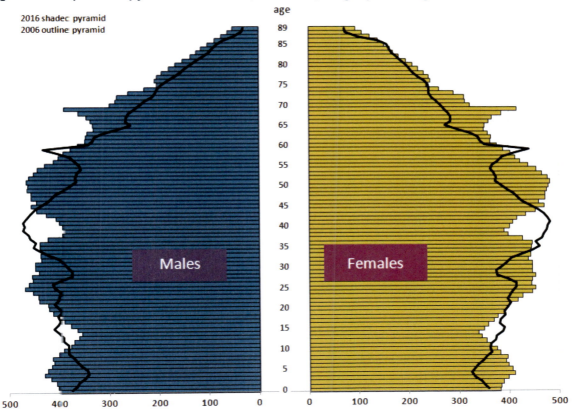

Population (thousands)

Source: Office for National Statistics, National Records of Scotland, Northern Ireland Statistics and Research Agency

Notes:

1. Data for those aged 90 and over has been excluded from this population pyramid.

The effects of international immigration to the UK since mid-2006 are visible in the pyramid. For most ages, the peaks and troughs present in the pyramid in mid-2006 are visible in the mid-2016 data, shifted by 10 years. However, the profile of the mid-2016 pyramid is wider and flatter, especially for those aged 20 to 37 in mid-2016 (who were 10 to 27 in mid-2006). Such a change can only be generated by new population being added through net international migration.

The peaks and troughs in younger populations result in a mid-2016 population of 0 to 10 year olds that is 13.0% higher than this age group in mid-2006 (1.0 million more people). However, there are 16.3% fewer 11 to 18 year olds in the mid-2016 population (1.1. million fewer people).

The population pyramid in Figure 3b is interactive, allowing you to compare the population structures of different areas and over time. An interactive pyramid that can be customised further is available as part of the Population Estimates Analysis Tool.

Figure 3b: Interactive population pyramids

These pyramids show that areas located near one another can have very different population structures. For example, Ceredigion's population pyramid has a very different shape from neighbouring Powys, with a peak of people around their early 20s, reflecting the presence of a large student population in Ceredigion. Some urban areas such as Manchester and London authorities show a different pattern again, with high proportions of people in their 20s and 30s.

As part of this release a time series of median age by local authority (MYE6) has been published. Median age is the age that divides a population into two numerically equal groups – that is, half the people are younger than this age and half are older. Median age provides a useful summary measure of the age structure of the population. These show:

- median age in the UK has remained unchanged for 2 years, at 40 years old

- age structures vary across the UK – Northern Ireland still has a relatively young age structure, with 16.0% of the population being aged 65 and over, and a median age of 38.3

- age structures vary subnationally – London has a notably young age structure, with 11.6% of its population aged 65 and over (Tower Hamlets showing the lowest proportion at 6.0%) and a median age of 34.8; the South West, by contrast, has 21.6% of its population aged 65 and over (33.3% in West Somerset), and a median age of 43.6

8 . Growth in population aged under 65 is highest in London

In addition to looking at older age groups, population estimates are often used alongside population projections to understand demand for education services or the structure of the working-age population. In mid-2016, 18.8% of the UK population were aged 0 to 15 and 63.1% aged 16 to 64, with the remaining 18.0% being aged 65 and over. Figures 4a to 4c show the growth in population over 5 years for the four countries of the UK and the regions of England, by the three main broad age groups.

Figure 4a: Change in population for ages 0 to 15

UK countries and regions of England, mid-2011 to mid-2016

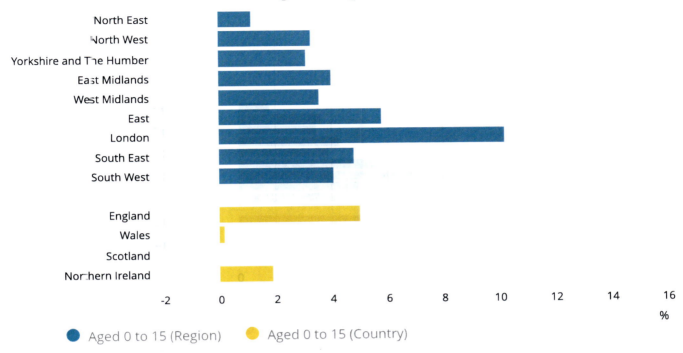

Figure 4a: Change in population for ages 0 to 15

UK countries and regions of England, mid-2011 to mid-2016

Aged 0 to 15 (Region)   Aged 0 to 15 (Country)

Source: Office for National Statistics, National Records of Scotland, Northern Ireland Statistics and Research Agency

Figure 4b: Change in population for ages 16 to 64

UK countries and regions of England, mid-2011 to mid-2016

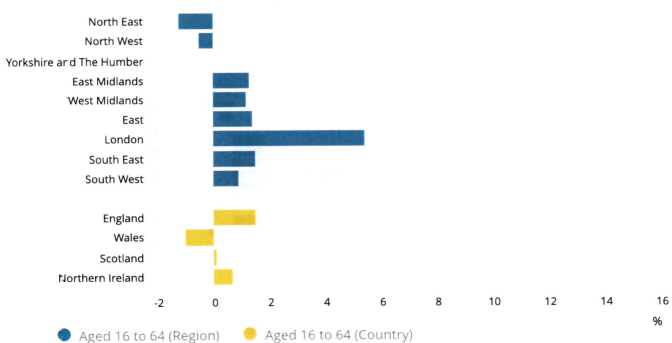

Figure 4b: Change in population for ages 16 to 64

UK countries and regions of England, mid-2011 to mid-2016

Aged 16 to 64 (Region)   Aged 16 to 64 (Country)

Source: Office for National Statistics, National Records of Scotland, Northern Ireland Statistics and Research Agency

Figure 4c: Change in population for ages 65 and over

UK countries and regions of England, mid-2011 to mid-2016

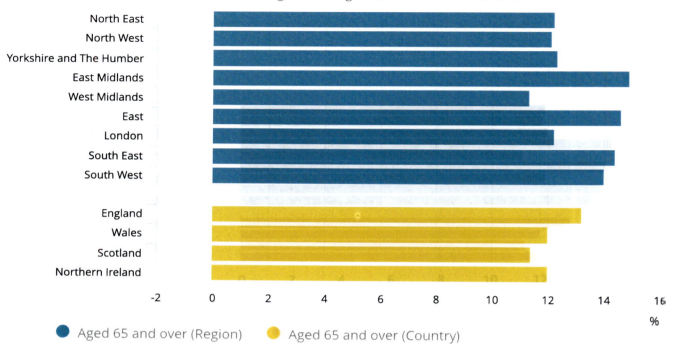

Figure 4c: Change in population for ages 65 and over

UK countries and regions of England, mid-2011 to mid-2016

● Aged 65 and over (Region)   ● Aged 65 and over (Country)

Source: Office for National Statistics, National Records of Scotland, Northern Ireland Statistics and Research Agency

These figures show that while the population aged 65 and over is growing across the UK and across the regions of England at a similar rate, growth rates in the younger groups are much lower. They are also less even – while the proportions of people aged 0 to 15 and 16 to 64 have grown in England and Northern Ireland since mid-2011, growth in these groups has been small or negative in Wales and Scotland.

Within England, a clear regional difference can be seen. London had the highest growth in both the young and working age groups, and has the highest number and proportion of people in each of these age groups of any region. This reflects the particular drivers of population change in London, notably:

- a young age structure, which produces large numbers of births,

- relatively high net international migration of predominantly working age people

- net internal migration inwards of young working age adults

- net outwards internal migration of those aged 30 and over

9 . Drivers of population change vary across the UK

Changes in local populations can be driven by a variety of components – including international migration, internal migration, births and deaths. Interactive population maps are available in Figure 5 for viewing the mid-2016 population estimates overall change and changes in its components.

To use this interactive tool select a local authority to view the population change and the components of change in the mid-2016 population estimates. The components of change maps compare each driver of change to the mid-2015 population total for each area. Other changes (for example, in special populations such as prisoners) are included in the datasets that accompany this bulletin, but are not presented in Figure 5.

Figure 5: Map of population change mid-2015 to mid-2016 and main components of change, local authorities in UK

Internal migration changes are commented on further in section 10, where maps separating in-and-out migration are available. The following demonstrate examples of patterns that can be observed in the remaining components.

Subnational population growth

In the 12 months to mid-year 2016, many parts of London experienced relatively high levels of population growth while growth across the rest of the UK and particularly in coastal areas, was lower (as described in section 4).

A number of authorities in Northamptonshire, Leicestershire and Lincolnshire also had relatively high population growth. As a result, population growth in the East Midlands was faster in the year to mid-2016 than the previous year and the fastest of the English regions outside London. The other maps show a variety of drivers for population change in these areas.

Subnational international migration

Certain urban areas have high net international migration, despite being surrounded by areas that have negative rates. These include areas home to higher education institutions, such as Southampton, Exeter, Newcastle, Ceredigion, Edinburgh and Glasgow. The Migration Statistics Quarterly Bulletin showed, however, that student international immigration decreased significantly in the year to June 2016 and student areas in general have received a smaller share of immigration in the mid-2016 estimates.

The high-growth areas of London show the highest levels of net international migration and negative net internal migration. This pattern can be seen in other areas where migrants initially settle, such as Oxford or Boston, but subsequently move onto another local authority. Another explanation for the negative net-internal migration in London is that many parents with young children move out of London.

Subnational natural change (births minus deaths)

The younger age-structures of places like London, Northern Ireland, Manchester and Birmingham tend to lead to higher numbers of births than deaths, resulting in relatively high levels of positive natural change.

Around a third of local authority areas showed negative natural change, reflecting older age structures. Negative natural change can be seen in clusters all around the coastlines of England, Wales and Scotland. These areas are typically part of the "Rural coastal and amenity" sub-group in the 2011 local authority classification and as shown by Table MYE6 many have high median ages.

Population change for groups of areas can be explored using classifications, such as the rural-urban classification and the 2011 local authority classification. The datasets accompanying this release (such as Table MYE3) allow groups of areas to be explored through data on English regions; we welcome your feedback on other ways you would like to see the data published.

10 . Moves between local authorities in England and Wales similar to last year

Sections 10, 11 and 12 replace the previous internal migration annual publication for England and Wales. Internal migration is a component used in the production of the mid-2016 population estimates for England and Wales. Estimates of internal migration moves for areas within Northern Ireland are produced by the Northern Ireland Statistics and Research Agency (NISRA); estimates of internal migration moves for areas within Scotland are produced by National Records of Scotland (NRS). A comparison of ONS's, NISRA's and NRS's methods is available.

In the 12-month period between July 2015 and June 2016, an estimated 2.85 million people moved between local authorities in England and Wales. This is the same level as shown in the previous two 12-month periods.

The following comparisons consider internal migration at regional and local authority level. There are several other factors that will influence total population change in an area, including births, deaths and international migration. This means that total population change will not necessarily be in the same direction as net internal migration.

The two regions with the highest numbers of moves in and moves out were London and the South East although they also have the largest populations. To take account of the effect of population size we look at the number of moves per 1,000 population.

The South West had the highest rate of inflows (26.8 moves per 1,000 population (mid-2015)) and London had the highest rate of outflows (33.6 moves per 1,000 population (mid-2015)) (Figure 6).

Apart from London with a net outflow of 10.8 per 1,000 population (mid-2015), all other regions, Wales, Northern Ireland and Scotland had net inflows, with the highest rate in the South West (5.5 per 1,000 population (mid-2015)).

Previous years' internal migration estimates show that this general pattern of a large net outflow from London and a large net inflow to other parts of southern and eastern England has existed for a number of years.

Figure 6: Internal migration moves per 1,000 population (mid-2015), including cross-border moves, year ending June 2016

UK constituent countries and English regions

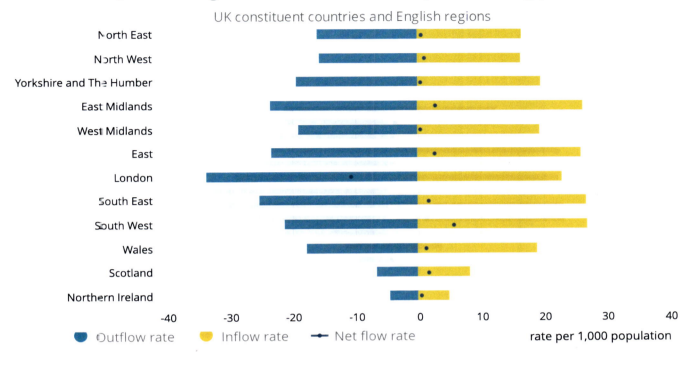

Figure 6: Internal migration moves per 1,000 population (mid-2015), including cross-border moves, year ending June 2016

UK constituent countries and English regions

Source: Office for National Statistics, National Records of Scotland, Northern Ireland Statistics and Research Agency

Figure 7: Maps of inflow, outflow and net flow per 100 population (mid-2015), between local authorities in England and Wales, year ending June 2016

In total there were 223 local authorities with more people moving in than out, of which 93 had a net inflow of more than 5 per 1,000 population (mid-2015) and 25 had a net inflow of more than 10 per 1,000 population. Many of those were in regions that also had a higher net inflow: South West, East of England, South East and East Midlands. However, there were still local authorities within these regions that had a net outflow, demonstrating there is considerable within-region variation.

Conversely, there were 125 local authorities with more people moving out than in, of which 50 had a net outflow of more than 5 per 1,000 population (mid-2015) and 25 had a net outflow of more than 10 per 1,000 population. London had a particular concentration of local authorities with high net outflows, reflecting the high net outflow for the London region overall. An important explanation for this is that many parents with young children move out of London. London is also the most common region of first residence for international migrants to the UK and some of these may later move to other regions, potentially also with children. Similar factors may also contribute to the high net outflows from many provincial cities.

11 . Impact of cross-border migration on the population of England and Wales

Cross-border moves are where people move, in either direction, between England and Wales (combined) and Northern Ireland and Scotland.

Figure 8: England and Wales (combined) cross-border moves to and from Northern Ireland and Scotland, years ending June 2002 to June 2016

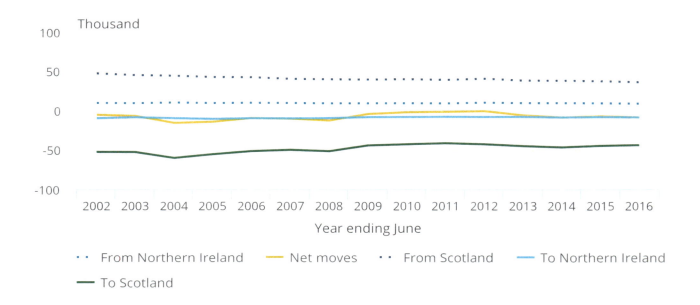

Figure 8: England and Wales (combined) cross-border moves to and from Northern Ireland and Scotland, years ending June 2002 to June 2016

Source: Office for National Statistics, National Records of Scotland, Northern Ireland Statistics and Research Agency

As with the previous year, more people moved out of England and Wales than into England and Wales (a net flow of negative 8,800). Flow levels were largest for people aged 19 to 29. Net flows to Scotland (from England and Wales) were highest for people aged 19 to 21 and net flows from Scotland (to England and Wales) were highest for people aged 23 to 25. Conversely, net flows to Northern Ireland were highest for people aged 22 to 23 and net flows from Northern Ireland highest for people aged 19 to 21 (Figure 8).

12 . Characteristics of movers in England and Wales by age, sex and area

Most moves occur in early adulthood with the peak age for movers being 19, the main age at which people leave home for study. There is another smaller peak at age 22; in many cases this will reflect graduates leaving university, moving for employment, further study or returning to their home address.

Levels of moves remain comparatively high for those aged in their 20s and 30s but gradually decline with age. This may reflect people becoming more settled in their employment, in an area or in relationships, or because they have school-age children.

However, from those aged in their late 70s onwards, the proportion of people moving rises slightly. There are many reasons why people of this age may wish to move, including being closer to their family, downsizing, or to access support and care.

In the London region, outflows were 7,800 higher than inflows for people aged 19, a peak in net outflows despite large numbers moving into London. This is likely to be driven by young adults moving in and out of London for higher education. The number of people moving into London outnumbered the number of people moving out of London for people in their early to mid 20s. The peak occurred at age 23 and is likely to be driven by young adults seeking work in London, potentially after they graduated from university. Otherwise, there is a net outflow for all other ages from London, which is highest – after aged 19 – for people in their 30s and 40s along with young children.

A way of considering the age and sex profile of movers is to consider how it compares with the age and sex profile of the general population. For the total number of internal migration moves the sex ratio is fairly neutral; in the year to June 2016 around 1.4 million (48%) of moves were by males and 1.5 million (52%) were by females.

Figure 9: Population pyramids showing movers into local authorities in England and Wales (including moves from Northern Ireland and Scotland), year ending June 2016, and the total population of England and Wales, mid-2016

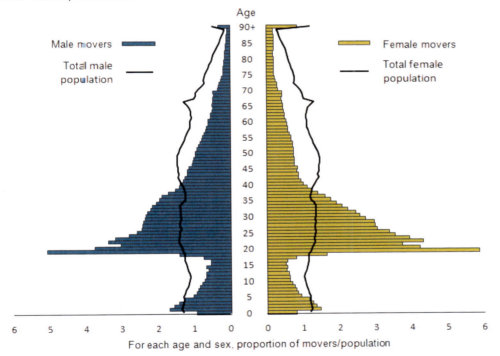

For each age and sex, proportion of movers/population

Source: Office for National Statistics, National Records of Scotland, Northern Ireland Statistics and Research Agency

Notes:

1. Data represent proportion of each sex that have that age.

2. "Age" is age at mid-2016.

In Figure 9 where the solid pyramid (moves) is wider than the outline pyramid (population), people at that age have a higher propensity to move. This applies to very young children and adults aged between 19 and their late 30s. For all other ages the outline pyramid is wider than the solid pyramid indicating people who have a lower propensity to move.

13 . UK has third highest population in Europe

The Overview of the UK Population: March 2017 presents charts illustrating how the UK population compares with the other 32 member states of the European Union (EU) and the European Free Trade Association. It shows that, using a 1 January 2016 population estimate, the UK was estimated to have the third largest population and the fourth highest population density. Further comparisons using 2015 data are available from UK Perspectives 2016: The UK in a European context.

The size of the UK population living in EU countries has been analysed in What information is there on British migrants living in Europe?: Jan 2017 using the 2010 to 2011 round of European censuses. This shows that around 900,000 UK citizens are long-term residents of other EU countries, with large populations living in Spain, France, Ireland and Germany.

Data are available on the EU-born population living in the UK. The Office for National Statistics (ONS) Population of the UK by Country of Birth and Nationality: 2015 shows that in 2015 there were 3.2 million non-UK born residents born in the EU. This compares with 5.4 million non-UK born residents born outside of the EU.

14 . Links to related statistics and how to find data

The mid-year population estimates are essential building blocks for a wide range of National Statistics. Table 2 illustrates the wide variety of related products and a number of tables and online sources for obtaining population estimates data.

Table 2: Where to find data on...

UK mid-year pop estimates – in more detail	Local authority single-year of age estimates	Interactive population pyramids, or tables MYE2 and MYEB2
	Time series data	Table MYEB2 or NOMIS
	Previous mid-year estimates series	ONS archive website
	Components of population change for local authorities	Tables MYE2 and MYEB2
	Other local authority-based geographies	Regions and counties are available in MYE2 and MYE3; others can be obtained via the open geography portal
	Small areas and geographies built from them - Clinical Commissioning Groups, Parliamentary Constituencies, national parks	Small area population estimates or NOMIS

Similar data – but not UK mid-year population estimates	Median ages	Table MYE 6
	Population density	Table MYE 5
	Census estimates	2011 Census – UK LA statistics
	Forward in time - population projections	England and Wales: National population projections table of contents; Comparing Subnational Population Projections to MYEs 2015
	Going beyond age 90 - estimates of the very old	ONS ageing statistics
	Calendar year population estimates	Eurostat
	Population eligible to vote	Electoral statistics for the UK: 2016
	Household estimates	Families and households in the UK: 2016
Specific countries or themes	Wales's population estimates	Welsh Government
	Scotland's population estimates	National Records Scotland
	Northern Ireland's population estimates	Northern Ireland Statistics and Research Agency
	Births	Published separately for England and Wales, Scotland and Northern Ireland
	Deaths	Published separately for England and Wales, Scotland and Northern Ireland
	Internal migration	Internal migration tables
	International migration	Migration Statistics Quarterly Report
		Local Area Migration Indicators, UK
	Characteristics of the population	Population of the UK by Country of Birth and Nationality: 2015
		Sexual identity, UK: 2015
		Population estimates by marital status and living arrangements, England and Wales: 2002 to 2015

Corresponding estimates for small areas (super output areas, wards, Parliamentary Constituencies, health areas and national parks) will be released later in 2017. Estimates of the very old (including centenarians) will be released in September 2017.

The ONS Census Transformation Programme will be publishing an administrative data research update in the autumn of 2017. Part of this update will include a set of research outputs, derived from administrative data, covering numbers in the population by age and sex for each local authority in England and Wales.

You should be aware that the mid-year population estimates will continue to remain the official population estimates for England and Wales, carrying the National Statistics accreditation. Benefits delivered from ongoing administrative data research will be used to better understand the current population estimates process and drive potential improvements wherever possible.

15 . What has changed in this publication?

An important change in this release is that it combines commentary previously published separately as Internal migration, England and Wales and Population Estimates for UK, England and Wales, Scotland and Northern Ireland. This reflects the importance of internal migration as a component of the population estimates and the benefits of using the two publications together.

Further changes compared with last year's releases include:

- the availability of estimates of median age by local authority for England and Wales, as dataset Table MYE6

- the separation of the smaller publication dataset tables and the larger, machine-readable "detailed time series" dataset tables into two separate files

- the availability of interactive graphs and maps within the bulletin itself

Methods changes for this year are described in the Methodology Guide for mid-2016 UK Population Estimates (England and Wales). We welcome your comments on the usefulness and presentation of the population estimates in this release. Please contact the population estimates team using the email address pop.info@ons.gsi.gov.uk

16 . Upcoming changes to this bulletin

A number of changes to methods will be introduced to the mid-2017 estimates to be published in June 2018. A back-series of estimates, for mid-2012 to mid-2016, using these new methods will be published in summer 2018. Further details can be found in the Methodology Guide for mid-2016 UK Population Estimates (England and Wales).

17 . Quality and methodology

The Population estimates Quality and Methodology Information report and Internal migration Quality and Methodology Information report contain important information on:

- the strengths and limitations of the data and how it compares with related data

- uses and users of the data

- how the output was created

- the quality of the output including the accuracy of the data

Mid-year population estimates relate to the usually resident population. They account for long-term international migrants but not for short-term. This approach is consistent with the standard UN definition for population estimates, which is based upon the concept of usual residence and includes people who reside, or intend to reside, in the country for at least 12 months, whatever their nationality.

Mid-year population estimates are compiled to provide information about the size of the population and how it changes over time. This information is used for planning services, managing the economy and in the calculation of rates where a population denominator is required, such as social and economic indicators.

Net international migration estimates quoted in this report include net flows of asylum seekers and refugees where applicable. Other changes include moves of armed forces personnel at home and overseas.

Measures of statistical uncertainty are available for the years mid-2012 to mid-2015.

Methods guides, which detail the data sources and methodology used to produce the mid-year population estimates are available for the UK countries:

- England and Wales Methodology Guide for mid-2016 UK Population Estimates (England and Wales)

- Internal migration methodology

- Northern Ireland Methodology Report

- Scotland Mid-Year Population Estimates for Scotland: Methodology Guide 2016

Further information and research is published on the population statistics research page. Revisions policies for population statistics include the mid-year estimates. It explains how revisions to statistics are categorised and implemented by ONS, including revisions following a census.

Maps for administrative areas

Map 1: UK counties and unitary authorities, 2017

Map 2: England and Wales: NHS regions, NHS region local offices, clinical commissioning groups and local health boards, 2017

Map 3: London region: London Boroughs, 2017

UK: Counties and Unitary Authorities[1], 2017

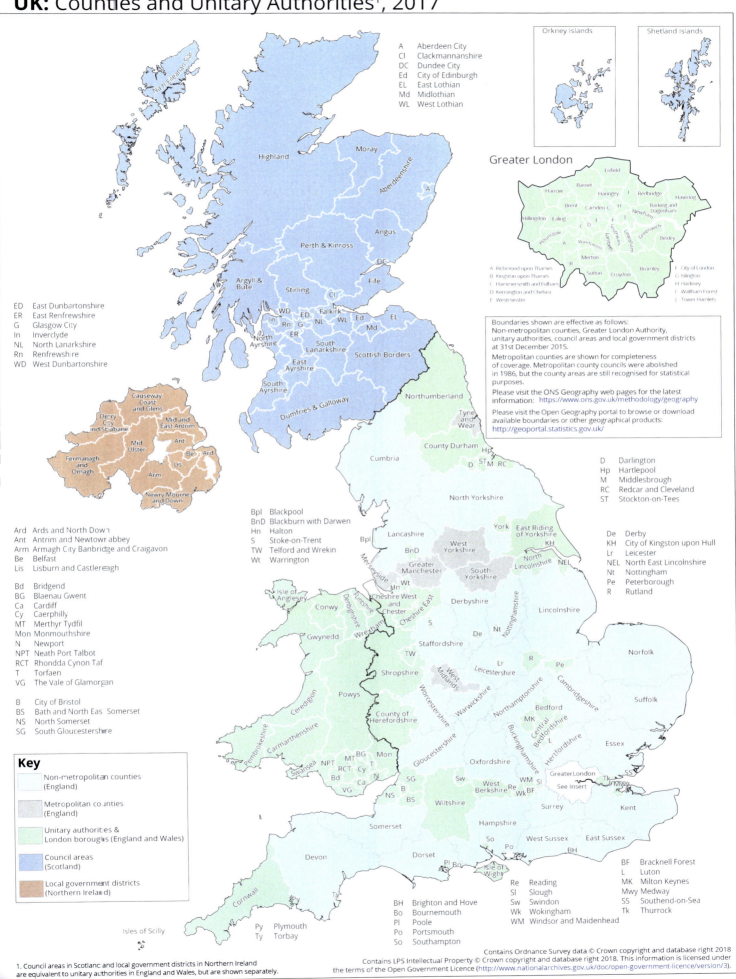

A   Aberdeen City
CI   Clackmannanshire
DC   Dundee City
Ed   City of Edinburgh
EL   East Lothian
Md   Midlothian
WL   West Lothian

Orkney Islands

Shetland Islands

Greater London

A   Richmond upon Thames
B   Kingston upon Thames
C   Hammersmith and Fulham
D   Kensington and Chelsea
E   Westminster
F   City of London
G   Islington
H   Hackney
I   Waltham Forest
J   Tower Hamlets

Boundaries shown are effective as follows:
Non-metropolitan counties, Greater London Authority,
unitary authorities, council areas and local government districts
at 31st December 2015.

Metropolitan counties are shown for completeness
of coverage. Metropolitan county councils were abolished
in 1986, but the county areas are still recognised for statistical
purposes.

Please visit the ONS Geography web pages for the latest
information: https://www.ons.gov.uk/methodology/geography

Please visit the Open Geography portal to browse or download
available boundaries or other geographical products:
http://geoportal.statistics.gov.uk/

ED   East Dunbartonshire
ER   East Renfrewshire
G   Glasgow City
In   Inverclyde
NL   North Lanarkshire
Rn   Renfrewshire
WD   West Dunbartonshire

D   Darlington
Hp   Hartlepool
M   Middlesbrough
RC   Redcar and Cleveland
ST   Stockton-on-Tees

Ard Ards and North Down
Ant Antrim and Newtownabbey
Arm Armagh City Banbridge and Craigavon
Be   Belfast
Lis Lisburn and Castlereagh

Bpl Blackpool
BnD Blackburn with Darwen
Hn   Halton
S   Stoke-on-Trent
TW   Telford and Wrekin
Wt   Warrington

De   Derby
KH   City of Kingston upon Hull
Lr   Leicester
NEL North East Lincolnshire
Nt   Nottingham
Pe   Peterborough
R   Rutland

Bd   Bridgend
BG   Blaenau Gwent
Ca   Cardiff
Cy   Caerphilly
MT   Merthyr Tydfil
Mon Monmouthshire
N   Newport
NPT Neath Port Talbot
RCT Rhondda Cynon Taf
T   Torfaen
VG   The Vale of Glamorgan

B   City of Bristol
BS   Bath and North East Somerset
NS   North Somerset
SG   South Gloucestershire

Key

- Non-metropolitan counties (England)
- Metropolitan counties (England)
- Unitary authorities & London boroughs (England and Wales)
- Council areas (Scotland)
- Local government districts (Northern Ireland)

BH   Brighton and Hove
Bo   Bournemouth
Pl   Poole
Po   Portsmouth
So   Southampton

Py   Plymouth
Ty   Torbay

Re   Reading
Sl   Slough
Sw   Swindon
Wk   Wokingham
WM   Windsor and Maidenhead

BF   Bracknell Forest
L   Luton
MK   Milton Keynes
Mwy Medway
SS   Southend-on-Sea
Tk   Thurrock

Contains Ordnance Survey data © Crown copyright and database right 2018
Contains LPS Intellectual Property © Crown copyright and database right 2018. This information is licensed under
the terms of the Open Government Licence (http://www.nationalarchives.gov.uk/doc/open-government-licence/version/3).

1. Council areas in Scotland and local government districts in Northern Ireland
are equivalent to unitary authorities in England and Wales, but are shown separately.

Office for National Statistics

Produced by ONS Geography
GIS & Mapping Unit

23

England and Wales: NHS regions, NHS region local offices, clinical commissioning groups and local health boards, 2017

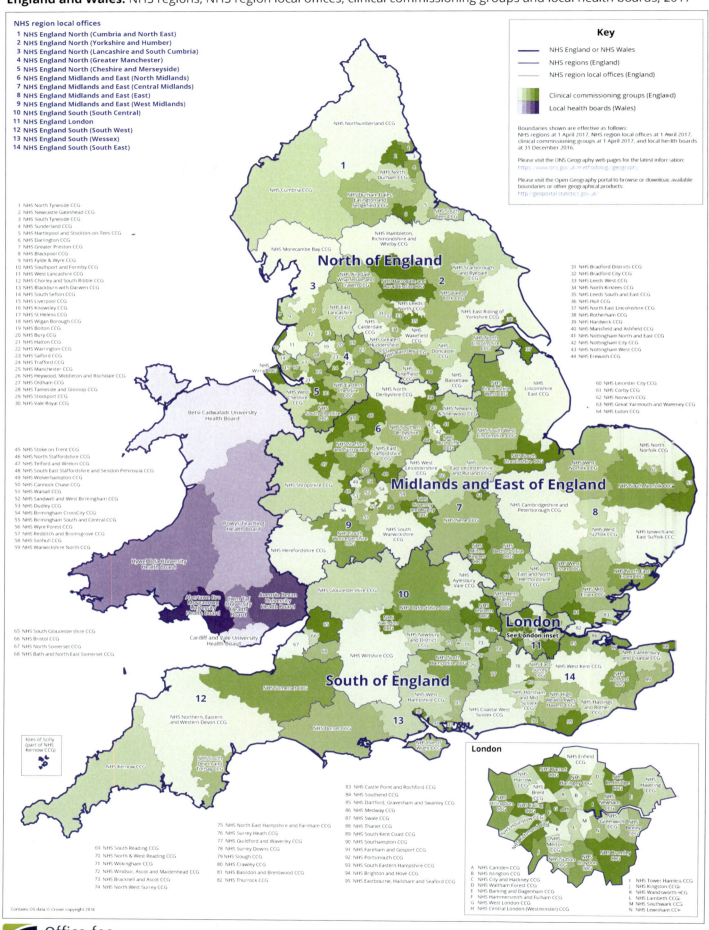

NHS region local offices
1 NHS England North (Cumbria and North East)
2 NHS England North (Yorkshire and Humber)
3 NHS England North (Lancashire and South Cumbria)
4 NHS England North (Greater Manchester)
5 NHS England North (Cheshire and Merseyside)
6 NHS England Midlands and East (North Midlands)
7 NHS England Midlands and East (Central Midlands)
8 NHS England Midlands and East (East)
9 NHS England Midlands and East (West Midlands)
10 NHS England South (South Central)
11 NHS England London
12 NHS England South (South West)
13 NHS England South (Wessex)
14 NHS England South (South East)

1 NHS North Tyneside CCG
2 NHS Newcastle Gateshead CCG
3 NHS South Tyneside CCG
4 NHS Sunderland CCG
5 NHS Hartlepool and Stockton-on-Tees CCG
6 NHS Darlington CCG
7 NHS Greater Preston CCG
8 NHS Blackpool CCG
9 NHS Fylde & Wyre CCG
10 NHS Southport and Formby CCG
11 NHS West Lancashire CCG
12 NHS Chorley and South Ribble CCG
13 NHS Blackburn with Darwen CCG
14 NHS South Sefton CCG
15 NHS Liverpool CCG
16 NHS Knowsley CCG
17 NHS St Helens CCG
18 NHS Wigan Borough CCG
19 NHS Bolton CCG
20 NHS Bury CCG
21 NHS Halton CCG
22 NHS Warrington CCG
23 NHS Salford CCG
24 NHS Trafford CCG
25 NHS Manchester CCG
26 NHS Heywood, Middleton and Rochdale CCG
27 NHS Oldham CCG
28 NHS Tameside and Glossop CCG
29 NHS Stockport CCG
30 NHS Vale Royal CCG

45 NHS Stoke on Trent CCG
46 NHS North Staffordshire CCG
47 NHS Telford and Wrekin CCG
48 NHS South East Staffordshire and Seisdon Peninsula CCG
49 NHS Wolverhampton CCG
50 NHS Cannock Chase CCG
51 NHS Walsall CCG
52 NHS Sandwell and West Birmingham CCG
53 NHS Dudley CCG
54 NHS Birmingham CrossCity CCG
55 NHS Birmingham South and Central CCG
56 NHS Wyre Forest CCG
57 NHS Redditch and Bromsgrove CCG
58 NHS Solihull CCG
59 NHS Warwickshire North CCG

65 NHS South Gloucestershire CCG
66 NHS Bristol CCG
67 NHS North Somerset CCG
68 NHS Bath and North East Somerset CCG

69 NHS South Reading CCG
70 NHS North & West Reading CCG
71 NHS Wokingham CCG
72 NHS Windsor, Ascot and Maidenhead CCG
73 NHS Bracknell and Ascot CCG
74 NHS North West Surrey CCG

75 NHS North East Hampshire and Farnham CCG
76 NHS Surrey Heath CCG
77 NHS Guildford and Waverley CCG
78 NHS Surrey Downs CCG
79 NHS Slough CCG
80 NHS Crawley CCG
81 NHS Basildon and Brentwood CCG
82 NHS Thurrock CCG

31 NHS Bradford Districts CCG
32 NHS Bradford City CCG
33 NHS Leeds West CCG
34 NHS North Kirklees CCG
35 NHS Leeds South and East CCG
36 NHS Hull CCG
37 NHS North East Lincolnshire CCG
38 NHS Rotherham CCG
39 NHS Hardwick CCG
40 NHS Mansfield and Ashfield CCG
41 NHS Nottingham North and East CCG
42 NHS Nottingham West CCG
43 NHS Nottingham West CCG
44 NHS Erewash CCG

60 NHS Leicester City CCG
61 NHS Corby CCG
62 NHS Norwich CCG
63 NHS Great Yarmouth and Waveney CCG
64 NHS Luton CCG

83 NHS Castle Point and Rochford CCG
84 NHS Southend CCG
85 NHS Dartford, Gravesham and Swanley CCG
86 NHS Medway CCG
87 NHS Swale CCG
88 NHS Thanet CCG
89 NHS South Kent Coast CCG
90 NHS Southampton CCG
91 NHS Fareham and Gosport CCG
92 NHS Portsmouth CCG
93 NHS South Eastern Hampshire CCG
94 NHS Brighton and Hove CCG
95 NHS Eastbourne, Hailsham and Seaford CCG

A NHS Camden CCG
B NHS Islington CCG
C NHS City and Hackney CCG
D NHS Waltham Forest CCG
E NHS Barking and Dagenham CCG
F NHS Hammersmith and Fulham CCG
G NHS West London CCG
H NHS Central London (Westminster) CCG
I NHS Tower Hamlets CCG
J NHS Kingston CCG
K NHS Wandsworth CCG
L NHS Lambeth CCG
M NHS Southwark CCG
N NHS Lewisham CCG

Key

— NHS England or NHS Wales
— NHS regions (England)
— NHS region local offices (England)

Clinical commissioning groups (England)
Local health boards (Wales)

Boundaries shown are effective as follows:
NHS regions at 1 April 2017, NHS region local offices at 1 April 2017, clinical commissioning groups at 1 April 2017, and local health boards at 31 December 2016.

Please visit the ONS Geography web pages for the latest information:
https://www.ons.gov.uk/methodology/geography

Please visit the Open Geography portal to browse or download available boundaries or other geographical products:
http://geoportal.statistics.gov.uk/

Contains OS data © Crown copyright 2018

Office for National Statistics

Produced by ONS Geography
GIS & Mapping Unit

London region: London boroughs, 2017

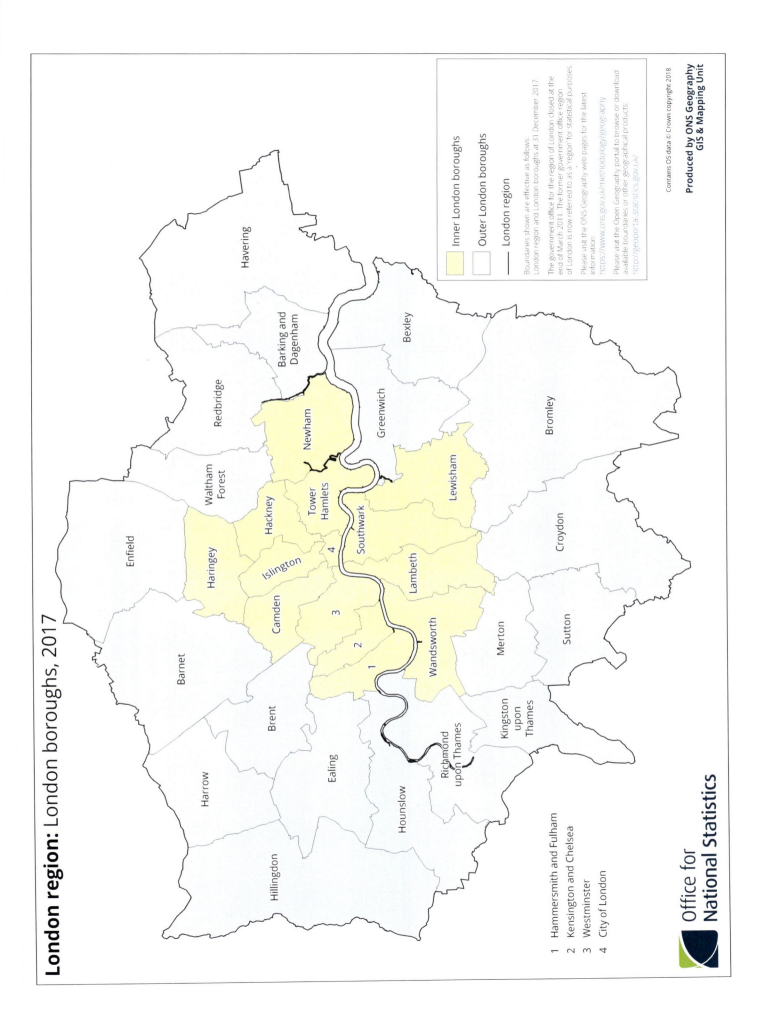

Inner London boroughs

Outer London boroughs

London region

Boundaries shown are effective as follows:
London region and London boroughs at 31 December 2017.

The government office for the region of London closed at the end of March 2011. The former government office region of London is now referred to as a 'region' for statistical purposes.

Please visit the ONS Geography web pages for the latest information:
https://www.ons.gov.uk/methodology/geography

Please visit the Open Geography portal to browse or download available boundaries or other geographical products.
http://geoportal.statistics.gov.uk/

Contains OS data © Crown copyright 2018

Produced by ONS Geography
GIS & Mapping Unit

1 Hammersmith and Fulham
2 Kensington and Chelsea
3 Westminster
4 City of London

Office for
National Statistics

25

Section 1 Mid-2016 Population Estimates for the United Kingdom

MYE1: Population estimates: Summary for the UK, mid-2016

MYE2: Population estimates: Persons / males / females - by selected age groups and sex
for local authorities in the UK, mid-2016

MYE3: Components of population change for local authorities in the UK, mid-2016

MYE4: Population estimates: Summary for the UK, mid-1971 to mid-2016

The following data can be found on the accompanying CD-ROM:

Population estimates and components of population change.

Detailed time-series 2001 - 2016 by sex and age for the UK and local authorities.

MYEB	Information note
MYEB1	Detailed population estimates series, UK(2001-2016)
MYEB2	Detailed components of change series, England and Wales (2001-2016)
MYEB3	Summary Components of change series, UK (2001-2016)

Office for National Statistics

Notes and definitions

1. Estimates are presented both rounded to the nearest hundred and unrounded. Unrounded estimates are published to enable and encourage further calculations and analysis. However, the estimates should not be taken to be accurate to the level of detail provided. More information on the accuracy of the estimates is available in the
Quality and Methodology document (QMI).

2. The estimates are produced using a variety of data sources and statistical models, including some statistical disclosure control methods, and small estimates should not be taken to refer to particular individuals.

3. The estimated resident population of an area includes all those people who usually live there, regardless of nationality. Arriving international migrants are included in the usually resident population if they remain in the UK for at least a year. Emigrants are excluded if they remain outside the UK for at least a year. This is consistent with the United Nations definition of a long-term migrant. Armed forces stationed outside of the UK are excluded. Students are taken to be usually resident at their term time address.

4. Population estimates for local authorities in England and Wales for mid-2012 to mid-2016 have been revised. Estimates for 2001-2011 are unchanged.

5. Where subnational level data appears, the population estimates reflect boundaries in place as of the reference year.

6. Where data appears for age 90 please note this is for ages 90 and above.

MYE3
7. Internal migration is defined as residential moves between different local authorities (LAs) in the UK, including those that cross the boundaries between the four UK nations: England, Wales, Scotland and Northern Ireland.

8. Internal migration figures for Northern Ireland include flows to and from the Isle of Man. This means that net internal migration at UK level will not sum to zero.

9. Other changes presented in this table comprise changes to the size of armed forces stationed in the UK and other special population adjustments. At geographies higher than local authority, adjustments due to rounding may also be included. This means that other changes at local authority level may not sum to other changes at national level.

MYE5

10. The population density estimates and area measurements are displayed rounded to the nearest integer though calculations have been performed on the unrounded data.

11. Standard Area Measurements (SAM) data used reflect the position as at 31 December 2016. Land area measurements have been used in compiling these population density figures. Information on this is available from the **ONS Geoportal.**

12. The area measurements are a definitive set derived from boundaries maintained by Ordnance Survey and Ordnance Survey of Northern Ireland. The current measurements may differ from those published previously in tables, publications, or other statistical outputs, even allowing for boundary changes or changes to the physical structure of the land because of improvements to the source of the data.

Further advice on the appropriate use of these data can be obtained by emailing pop.info@ons.gsi.gov.uk or phoning +44 (0) 1329 444661 and asking to speak to a statistician.

Data supplier:
Population Estimates Unit
Population Statistics Division
Office for National Statistics
Segensworth Road
FAREHAM
PO15 5RR
Tel: +44 (0)1329 444661
Email: pop.info@ons.gov.uk

Release number: MYE11
Date published: 22 March 2018

MYE1: Population estimates: Summary for the UK, mid-2016

Country / Code	K02000001 UNITED KINGDOM	K03000001 GREAT BRITAIN	K04000001 ENGLAND AND WALES	E92000001 ENGLAND	W92000004 WALES	S92000003 SCOTLAND	N92000002 NORTHERN IRELAND
All People	65,648,100	63,785,900	58,381,200	55,268,100	3,113,200	5,404,700	1,862,100
Males	32,377,700	31,462,500	28,835,000	27,300,900	1,534,000	2,627,500	915,200
Females	33,270,400	32,323,500	29,546,300	27,967,100	1,579,100	2,777,200	946,900
Age Groups							
0-4	4,014,300	3,889,500	3,602,300	3,429,000	173,300	287,200	124,800
5-9	4,037,500	3,909,900	3,611,100	3,428,300	182,800	298,900	127,500
10-14	3,625,100	3,511,800	3,237,400	3,070,300	167,100	274,400	113,300
15-19	3,778,900	3,660,600	3,361,900	3,179,400	182,500	298,700	118,400
20-24	4,253,800	4,135,000	3,771,000	3,560,000	211,100	364,000	118,700
25-29	4,510,600	4,386,600	4,012,500	3,811,600	200,900	374,100	124,000
30-34	4,408,200	4,284,300	3,932,400	3,749,600	182,800	351,900	123,800
35-39	4,179,500	4,060,000	3,732,200	3,557,000	175,200	327,800	119,600
40-44	4,174,100	4,053,900	3,716,300	3,535,300	181,000	337,600	120,200
45-49	4,619,100	4,488,600	4,096,300	3,883,100	213,300	392,300	130,500
50-54	4,632,000	4,501,100	4,094,400	3,873,100	221,400	406,700	130,800
55-59	4,066,700	3,950,900	3,580,100	3,377,700	202,400	370,800	115,800
60-64	3,534,200	3,437,300	3,115,800	2,931,000	184,800	321,600	96,900
65-69	3,636,500	3,547,000	3,229,500	3,032,100	197,400	317,500	89,500
70-74	2,852,100	2,775,500	2,536,500	2,381,300	155,200	239,000	76,600
75-79	2,154,500	2,099,000	1,912,200	1,796,000	116,100	186,800	55,500
80-84	1,606,700	1,567,000	1,430,600	1,345,400	85,200	136,400	39,700
85-89	993,000	969,300	891,300	840,200	51,000	78,000	23,700
90 and over	571,200	558,500	517,400	487,800	29,600	41,100	12,700

Figures may not add exactly due to rounding.

MYE2: Population estimates: Persons by selected age groups for local authorities in the UK, mid-2016

Thousands

| Code | Name | All ages | Age groups (years) | | | | | | | | | | | | | | | | | | |
			0-4	5-9	10-14	15-19	20-24	25-29	30-34	35-39	40-44	45-49	50-54	55-59	60-64	65-69	70-74	75-79	80-84	85-89	90
K02000001	**UNITED KINGDOM**	65,648.1	4,014.3	4,037.5	3,625.1	3,778.9	4,253.8	4,510.6	4,408.2	4,179.5	4,174.1	4,619.1	4,632.0	4,066.7	3,534.2	3,636.5	2,852.1	2,154.5	1,606.7	993.0	571.2
K03000001	**GREAT BRITAIN**	63,785.9	3,889.5	3,909.9	3,511.8	3,660.6	4,135.0	4,386.6	4,284.3	4,060.0	4,053.9	4,488.6	4,501.1	3,950.9	3,437.3	3,547.0	2,775.5	2,099.0	1,567.0	969.3	558.5
K04000001	**ENGLAND AND WALES**	58,381.2	3,602.3	3,611.1	3,237.4	3,361.9	3,771.0	4,012.5	3,932.4	3,732.2	3,716.3	4,096.3	4,094.4	3,580.1	3,115.8	3,229.5	2,536.5	1,912.2	1,430.6	891.3	517.4
E92000001	**ENGLAND**	55,268.1	3,429.0	3,428.3	3,070.3	3,179.4	3,560.0	3,811.6	3,749.6	3,557.0	3,535.3	3,883.1	3,873.1	3,377.7	2,931.0	3,032.1	2,381.4	1,796.5	1,345.4	840.2	487.8
E12000001	**NORTH EAST**	2,636.6	148.4	153.0	139.1	151.5	185.8	173.2	162.6	150.2	154.0	181.4	194.1	179.1	156.7	160.5	119.9	94.9	69.6	40.9	21.7
E06000047	County Durham	521.8	27.9	29.4	26.6	30.0	37.0	31.2	30.7	28.5	30.0	37.5	39.6	35.8	32.3	33.8	26.0	19.7	13.7	8.0	4.2
E06000005	Darlington	106.3	6.4	6.5	6.1	5.9	5.5	6.5	6.5	6.5	6.7	7.7	8.0	7.1	6.1	6.3	4.9	4.0	2.9	1.7	1.0
E06000001	Hartlepool	92.8	5.5	5.9	5.2	5.5	5.7	6.1	5.7	5.0	5.3	6.5	7.1	6.4	5.4	5.5	3.9	3.3	2.6	1.4	0.8
E06000002	Middlesbrough	140.3	9.8	9.3	8.1	9.0	12.2	10.5	9.2	7.7	7.8	8.6	9.5	8.8	7.5	6.9	5.1	4.3	3.2	1.9	0.9
E06000057	Northumberland	317.4	15.1	16.8	16.7	16.6	15.1	16.6	16.4	16.8	18.3	22.4	25.0	24.5	22.4	24.1	18.2	13.5	9.7	5.8	3.3
E06000003	Redcar and Cleveland	135.5	7.7	7.8	7.3	7.5	7.8	8.1	7.6	7.0	7.5	9.4	10.4	9.4	8.4	9.1	7.3	5.8	3.9	2.3	1.3
E06000004	Stockton-on-Tees	196.0	12.1	12.9	11.3	11.3	12.3	12.8	13.0	11.7	11.8	13.8	14.4	13.1	11.2	10.9	8.1	6.4	4.8	2.8	1.4
E11000007	Tyne and Wear (Met County)	1,126.4	63.8	64.4	57.7	65.8	90.2	81.6	73.5	67.1	66.5	75.6	79.9	74.0	63.5	63.7	46.4	38.1	28.8	17.0	8.9
E08000037	Gateshead	202.6	11.3	11.7	10.4	11.6	12.4	13.6	14.3	12.9	12.3	14.0	14.7	13.4	11.1	11.8	8.9	7.6	5.6	3.1	1.7
E08000021	Newcastle upon Tyne	293.7	17.1	16.8	14.3	20.0	39.7	27.0	20.3	16.6	15.9	16.7	17.5	16.0	13.6	13.2	9.3	7.7	6.1	3.8	2.2
E08000022	North Tyneside	203.6	11.5	11.8	11.0	10.6	10.1	12.0	13.1	13.5	13.4	14.7	15.6	14.1	12.5	12.6	9.2	7.2	5.6	3.4	1.8
E08000023	South Tyneside	149.2	8.5	8.4	7.8	8.1	8.7	9.5	9.1	8.5	8.6	10.5	11.7	11.0	9.3	9.3	6.7	5.5	4.1	2.5	1.4
E08000024	Sunderland	277.3	15.5	15.6	14.3	15.4	19.3	19.5	16.7	15.6	16.3	19.6	20.5	19.6	17.0	16.9	12.3	10.0	7.4	4.1	1.8
E12000002	**NORTH WEST**	7,224.0	443.2	443.4	402.2	420.7	477.5	492.9	467.5	431.1	443.1	510.3	516.5	457.4	396.3	414.7	317.5	245.6	177.6	107.1	59.4
E06000008	Blackburn with Darwen	148.5	11.0	11.1	10.3	9.9	9.2	10.0	10.7	9.7	9.6	10.4	9.6	8.5	7.4	7.1	5.0	3.8	2.7	1.6	0.8
E06000009	Blackpool	140.0	8.5	7.9	7.5	7.9	8.2	8.9	8.1	7.5	8.2	10.4	10.9	9.4	8.0	8.6	6.9	5.4	3.9	2.3	1.4
E06000049	Cheshire East	377.3	20.5	21.6	20.6	20.4	18.2	18.7	19.8	21.0	24.5	29.1	29.9	26.1	22.8	25.7	20.3	15.2	11.2	7.2	4.3
E06000050	Cheshire West and Chester	335.7	18.9	18.9	17.9	18.7	20.0	18.9	19.0	18.8	21.2	24.7	25.7	22.7	20.1	21.9	16.9	13.2	9.3	5.8	3.3
E06000006	Halton	127.3	7.9	8.4	7.5	7.3	7.4	8.2	8.2	7.5	8.2	9.0	9.1	8.5	7.8	8.0	5.3	3.9	2.8	1.5	0.8
E06000007	Warrington	209.0	12.5	12.9	11.9	11.7	11.2	13.2	13.4	13.1	14.2	16.1	16.4	13.4	11.3	11.8	9.4	7.3	4.8	2.8	1.5
E10000006	Cumbria	498.8	24.9	26.4	25.6	26.3	25.7	26.2	26.1	25.6	28.8	37.1	39.3	36.5	33.1	36.6	28.3	21.8	15.5	9.5	5.6
E07000026	Allerdale	97.1	4.7	5.3	5.0	5.2	4.8	5.0	5.0	5.0	5.5	7.5	7.6	7.1	6.5	7.3	5.5	4.3	3.0	1.8	1.1
E07000027	Barrow-in-Furness	67.5	3.8	3.8	3.6	3.8	3.9	4.1	3.8	3.5	4.0	5.1	5.3	4.6	4.1	4.5	3.6	2.8	1.8	1.0	0.6
E07000028	Carlisle	108.4	6.2	6.1	5.7	5.6	6.6	6.2	6.4	6.1	6.6	7.8	8.1	7.8	6.6	7.0	5.3	4.2	3.1	1.9	1.1
E07000029	Copeland	69.3	3.7	3.7	3.5	3.5	3.7	4.0	3.9	3.6	4.1	5.1	5.6	5.2	4.6	4.9	3.6	2.9	2.0	1.1	0.7
E07000030	Eden	52.6	2.3	2.6	2.6	2.7	2.3	2.5	2.4	2.5	2.9	4.0	4.3	4.0	3.8	4.2	3.3	2.5	1.7	1.1	0.7
E07000031	South Lakeland	103.8	4.2	4.9	5.2	5.4	4.4	4.5	4.6	5.0	5.8	7.6	8.3	7.9	7.5	8.6	6.9	5.2	3.8	2.6	1.5
E11000001	Greater Manchester (Met County)	2,780.8	187.5	184.0	162.2	164.7	196.9	214.1	201.9	180.8	174.5	193.2	187.9	160.8	135.7	139.2	105.6	81.0	57.2	34.3	19.2
E08000001	Bolton	283.5	19.5	19.4	17.2	17.3	17.1	19.1	18.6	17.2	18.2	20.5	19.6	17.0	14.7	15.6	11.9	8.9	6.0	3.6	2.0
E08000002	Bury	188.5	12.3	12.5	11.4	10.7	10.0	12.1	12.2	11.7	12.1	14.0	13.8	11.9	10.1	10.8	8.3	6.3	4.3	2.5	1.5
E08000003	Manchester	541.3	39.3	35.2	28.9	35.7	68.4	63.6	51.1	39.2	30.9	30.3	27.5	22.6	18.3	16.3	11.3	9.3	6.9	4.1	2.4
E08000004	Oldham	232.3	16.9	17.0	15.7	15.0	13.9	16.0	15.6	14.3	14.2	16.3	15.4	13.5	11.7	11.9	9.1	7.0	4.6	2.8	1.6
E08000005	Rochdale	216.4	15.2	15.0	13.2	13.3	13.1	15.0	14.4	13.6	13.6	15.3	14.7	13.3	11.7	11.4	8.4	6.3	4.5	2.7	1.5
E08000006	Salford	248.1	17.6	16.2	13.3	13.6	18.8	22.5	21.7	16.8	14.9	16.0	15.9	13.8	11.0	11.3	8.5	6.7	4.8	2.9	1.8
E08000007	Stockport	289.8	18.1	18.1	16.4	15.8	14.1	17.0	17.7	18.5	18.8	21.2	21.6	19.0	16.5	17.1	13.4	10.7	8.2	5.1	2.7
E08000008	Tameside	223.1	14.7	14.4	12.6	12.4	12.8	15.1	14.7	13.5	14.0	16.5	16.8	14.5	12.1	12.8	9.7	7.2	4.9	2.8	1.6
E08000009	Trafford	234.2	15.0	16.4	15.1	13.3	10.6	12.9	15.3	16.7	16.9	17.7	17.7	14.5	11.9	11.9	9.2	7.5	5.8	3.9	2.1

MYE2: Population estimates: Persons by selected age groups for local authorities in the UK, mid-2016

Thousands

Code	Name	All ages	Age groups (years)																		
			0-4	5-9	10-14	15-19	20-24	25-29	30-34	35-39	40-44	45-49	50-54	55-59	60-64	65-69	70-74	75-79	80-84	85-89	90
E08000010	Wigan	323.5	18.8	19.9	18.3	17.8	18.1	20.8	20.7	19.3	21.0	25.5	24.6	20.7	17.8	20.1	15.9	11.1	7.1	4.1	2.1
E10000017	Lancashire	1,195.4	68.4	71.6	65.9	70.9	77.9	72.7	68.8	65.8	72.2	85.3	86.9	78.1	69.3	75.5	59.1	44.3	32.2	19.5	11.0
E07000117	Burnley	87.5	5.9	5.9	5.1	5.0	5.1	5.8	5.8	5.2	5.2	6.1	5.9	5.6	4.9	5.3	3.9	2.8	2.0	1.3	0.7
E07000118	Chorley	114.3	6.6	6.8	6.3	6.0	5.7	7.0	7.2	7.0	8.0	8.8	8.7	7.5	6.6	7.5	5.7	4.0	2.6	1.4	0.9
E07000119	Fylde	78.2	3.4	4.1	3.9	3.9	3.1	3.6	3.9	3.8	4.4	5.6	6.3	5.9	5.3	6.0	5.1	3.8	3.0	1.9	1.1
E07000120	Hyndburn	80.4	5.5	5.3	4.8	4.7	4.7	5.3	5.1	4.7	5.0	5.9	5.5	4.8	4.3	4.7	3.7	2.6	1.9	1.1	0.6
E07000121	Lancaster	141.7	7.8	7.6	6.9	10.0	14.9	8.6	7.7	7.3	7.6	9.2	9.7	8.7	7.7	8.5	6.8	5.2	3.9	2.4	1.3
E07000122	Pendle	90.5	6.3	6.3	5.4	5.1	4.7	6.0	6.3	5.6	5.5	6.1	5.9	5.7	5.1	5.5	4.0	2.9	2.1	1.4	0.7
E07000123	Preston	141.0	9.2	9.2	7.9	9.2	14.2	11.0	9.3	8.6	8.5	9.4	9.3	8.0	6.6	6.4	4.7	3.9	3.1	1.7	1.0
E07000124	Ribble Valley	58.9	2.6	3.3	3.5	3.7	2.5	2.8	2.6	2.8	3.7	4.7	5.0	4.4	3.8	4.2	3.4	2.4	1.9	1.1	0.7
E07000125	Rossendale	69.8	4.2	4.5	4.2	3.8	3.5	4.2	4.2	4.2	4.7	5.5	5.3	4.7	4.2	4.4	3.1	2.0	1.5	0.9	0.6
E07000126	South Ribble	110.1	6.2	6.6	6.1	6.0	5.4	6.6	6.5	6.2	7.3	8.2	8.5	7.2	6.6	7.1	5.6	4.3	2.9	1.8	1.0
E07000127	West Lancashire	113.1	5.7	6.3	6.1	7.7	8.6	6.2	5.3	5.2	6.6	8.0	8.6	7.7	6.8	7.5	6.1	4.6	3.3	1.9	1.0
E07000128	Wyre	110.0	5.0	5.6	5.6	5.9	5.4	5.5	5.1	5.2	5.9	7.7	8.3	7.9	7.3	8.4	7.2	5.8	4.2	2.6	1.4
E11000002	Merseyside (Met County)	1,411.2	83.1	80.6	72.7	82.9	102.7	102.2	91.5	81.3	81.6	95.0	100.8	93.3	80.7	80.3	60.8	49.6	37.9	22.5	11.6
E08000011	Knowsley	148.0	9.8	9.3	8.4	9.0	9.5	10.3	9.4	8.1	8.3	10.2	11.3	10.8	8.7	7.7	5.5	4.8	3.8	2.2	0.9
E08000012	Liverpool	487.6	29.3	26.1	22.5	31.0	52.6	45.0	38.1	31.5	26.9	30.0	31.0	28.3	24.2	22.4	15.9	13.4	10.5	6.0	2.9
E08000014	Sefton	274.9	14.7	15.3	14.2	15.0	14.3	16.3	14.8	14.0	15.7	19.0	21.1	20.3	17.6	17.9	14.3	12.0	9.5	5.8	3.1
E08000013	St. Helens	178.5	10.4	10.5	9.5	9.9	10.0	11.5	11.0	10.0	11.3	13.0	13.2	11.8	10.5	11.5	9.0	6.9	4.7	2.6	1.3
E08000015	Wirral	322.2	19.0	19.4	18.1	18.0	16.3	19.0	18.2	17.8	19.4	22.9	24.2	22.2	19.7	20.8	16.1	12.4	9.4	6.0	3.3
E12000003	YORKSHIRE AND THE HUMBER	5,425.4	331.2	335.0	303.5	322.6	385.4	365.1	344.2	321.1	332.0	380.3	378.9	339.8	296.9	308.5	237.3	182.5	135.3	80.9	45.0
E06000011	East Riding of Yorkshire	337.8	16.0	18.0	17.5	18.7	15.5	15.3	15.6	17.0	20.6	24.9	26.7	24.5	23.0	26.8	20.5	15.6	11.3	6.5	3.6
E06000010	Kingston upon Hull, City of	260.0	17.8	16.6	13.8	14.6	22.4	23.1	19.3	15.9	16.0	16.7	17.2	15.3	12.8	12.6	8.7	7.1	5.4	3.2	1.5
E06000012	North East Lincolnshire	159.8	9.8	10.0	9.1	8.8	9.0	10.9	9.8	8.7	9.4	11.2	11.7	10.5	9.3	9.6	7.3	6.0	4.5	2.7	1.5
E06000013	North Lincolnshire	170.8	9.5	10.6	9.6	9.3	8.9	10.2	10.4	9.5	10.2	12.4	13.0	11.8	10.7	11.1	8.5	6.3	4.6	2.7	1.6
E06000014	York	206.9	10.2	10.9	9.6	13.7	22.7	15.8	13.2	12.2	12.0	13.6	13.4	11.8	10.3	11.1	8.8	6.9	5.3	3.4	2.0
E10000023	North Yorkshire	609.5	30.5	33.3	32.6	33.4	27.3	32.8	30.8	31.1	35.9	45.0	48.4	44.5	40.4	44.0	35.0	26.2	19.3	12.0	7.0
E07000163	Craven	56.3	2.5	2.9	3.0	3.1	2.3	2.6	2.4	2.7	3.2	4.2	4.5	4.3	4.2	4.4	3.6	2.5	2.0	1.3	0.8
E07000164	Hambleton	90.6	4.4	4.8	4.7	4.8	3.8	4.7	4.3	4.4	5.1	6.7	7.6	6.7	6.2	6.9	5.6	4.2	3.0	1.9	1.0
E07000165	Harrogate	159.8	8.0	9.3	9.3	9.4	5.9	7.9	8.2	8.8	10.3	12.4	13.0	11.4	9.8	10.5	8.4	6.7	5.0	3.2	2.1
E07000166	Richmondshire	53.9	2.9	2.9	2.7	3.2	3.4	4.5	3.4	2.8	3.0	3.8	3.7	3.6	3.2	3.5	2.7	2.0	1.4	0.8	0.4
E07000167	Ryedale	53.9	2.4	2.7	2.7	3.0	2.5	2.5	2.4	2.4	2.9	3.9	4.4	4.1	3.9	4.3	3.5	2.5	1.9	1.2	0.6
E07000168	Scarborough	108.2	5.3	5.5	5.4	5.4	5.5	5.7	5.2	4.8	5.8	7.2	8.1	8.1	7.8	8.7	6.9	5.3	3.8	2.4	1.3
E07000169	Selby	86.9	4.9	5.2	4.8	4.6	4.0	5.0	5.0	5.0	5.7	6.8	7.1	6.3	5.4	5.7	4.3	2.9	2.1	1.3	0.7
E11000003	South Yorkshire (Met County)	1,385.4	82.7	84.4	75.9	83.0	109.0	99.0	89.1	81.3	83.1	97.6	95.3	85.7	73.5	74.5	60.3	46.2	33.9	19.9	11.2
E08000016	Barnsley	241.8	14.6	14.4	13.0	13.2	14.1	15.6	15.6	13.8	14.8	18.3	18.0	16.5	14.2	14.3	11.6	8.4	6.0	3.6	1.9
E08000017	Doncaster	307.4	18.7	19.5	17.2	16.8	17.3	20.9	20.6	18.2	18.7	21.5	22.4	20.5	17.9	17.9	13.7	10.6	8.0	4.6	2.4
E08000018	Rotherham	262.1	16.0	16.4	15.0	15.0	14.7	16.6	16.1	14.7	16.1	19.3	19.2	17.5	15.1	15.6	12.8	9.6	6.6	3.8	2.2
E08000019	Sheffield	574.1	33.4	34.1	30.7	38.1	62.9	45.9	36.8	34.6	33.5	38.4	35.6	31.2	26.3	26.7	22.3	17.6	13.3	8.0	4.7
E11000006	West Yorkshire (Met County)	2,295.0	154.6	151.1	135.5	141.0	170.6	158.0	156.1	145.6	144.8	158.9	153.2	135.6	116.8	118.8	88.1	68.3	50.9	30.4	16.6
E08000032	Bradford	532.5	40.9	40.7	37.4	35.3	32.7	35.5	37.4	36.0	34.4	35.0	33.1	30.6	26.3	24.8	16.9	14.3	10.9	6.5	3.7
E08000033	Calderdale	209.1	13.1	13.3	12.2	12.1	11.0	12.6	12.7	12.8	13.6	16.0	15.9	13.9	12.0	12.5	9.3	6.7	4.7	3.0	1.7
E08000034	Kirklees	435.2	28.1	28.8	26.6	26.6	28.3	28.3	27.8	27.3	28.0	31.7	29.9	26.4	22.9	24.3	18.1	13.6	9.6	5.9	3.1
E08000035	Leeds	781.1	51.6	48.1	41.0	49.0	80.0	59.5	55.9	50.2	47.6	50.6	49.0	42.2	36.0	37.2	27.9	22.3	17.3	10.3	5.4
E08000036	Wakefield	337.1	20.9	20.2	18.3	18.1	18.7	22.1	22.4	19.3	21.3	25.6	25.1	22.5	19.5	20.0	15.9	11.5	8.3	4.7	2.7

MYE2: Population estimates: Persons by selected age groups for local authorities in the UK, mid-2016

Thousands

Code	Name	All ages	0-4	5-9	10-14	15-19	20-24	25-29	30-34	35-39	40-44	45-49	50-54	55-59	60-64	65-69	70-74	75-79	80-84	85-89	90
E12000004	EAST MIDLANDS	4,725.4	278.5	284.2	258.3	280.1	322.0	299.8	287.5	277.5	294.3	338.9	341.9	300.1	266.7	282.2	221.3	160.4	117.5	72.5	41.6
E06000015	Derby	256.2	17.5	17.8	15.1	15.9	19.0	19.4	17.7	16.2	15.8	17.5	17.0	14.1	11.9	11.9	9.6	7.5	6.1	4.0	2.2
E06000016	Leicester	349.5	26.1	24.1	21.0	23.8	38.4	31.3	26.8	23.5	20.8	20.1	19.4	18.1	15.5	13.0	9.0	7.4	5.6	3.6	2.2
E06000018	Nottingham	324.8	21.3	19.5	16.6	25.3	50.0	29.4	23.0	19.9	17.9	18.6	17.9	15.1	12.7	11.6	8.3	6.8	5.4	3.4	2.0
E06000017	Rutland	38.9	1.8	1.9	2.2	2.6	1.9	2.0	1.9	2.1	2.3	2.8	2.8	2.6	2.5	2.8	2.4	1.7	1.2	0.8	0.5
E10000007	Derbyshire	786.7	41.2	43.6	41.8	43.2	41.6	44.8	43.7	43.5	50.0	61.6	62.3	54.5	49.1	52.8	42.0	29.6	21.3	12.8	7.5
E07000032	Amber Valley	124.8	6.4	6.7	6.5	6.7	6.4	6.8	6.8	7.0	8.2	9.9	9.8	8.6	8.0	8.9	6.8	4.6	3.3	2.0	1.3
E07000033	Bolsover	78.2	4.4	4.4	4.2	4.3	4.5	4.7	4.9	4.3	4.9	6.3	5.9	5.3	4.6	4.8	4.1	2.8	2.0	1.1	0.7
E07000034	Chesterfield	104.5	5.6	5.8	5.1	5.7	6.1	6.4	6.2	6.0	6.7	7.9	8.0	7.2	6.3	6.7	5.2	3.9	2.8	1.8	1.1
E07000035	Derbyshire Dales	71.5	2.9	3.5	3.9	3.9	3.0	3.0	2.9	3.1	4.2	5.5	6.1	5.5	5.2	6.0	4.7	3.3	2.4	1.5	0.9
E07000036	Erewash	115.1	6.6	6.7	6.1	6.1	6.4	7.4	6.7	6.7	7.4	9.0	9.1	7.5	6.4	6.9	5.6	4.2	3.2	1.9	1.2
E07000037	High Peak	91.7	4.6	5.1	4.9	5.2	5.1	5.1	4.9	4.9	5.7	7.3	7.6	6.8	5.8	6.2	4.7	3.2	2.3	1.4	0.8
E07000038	North East Derbyshire	100.5	4.8	5.3	5.1	5.2	5.2	5.2	5.1	5.1	6.1	7.6	7.7	7.2	6.7	7.4	6.3	4.5	3.1	1.8	1.0
E07000039	South Derbyshire	100.4	5.8	6.1	5.9	6.0	5.0	6.0	6.2	6.4	6.9	8.1	7.8	6.4	6.0	6.1	4.6	3.1	2.2	1.4	0.6
E10000018	Leicestershire	680.5	36.8	39.4	37.3	41.0	44.2	38.1	38.5	38.6	43.1	51.1	51.3	44.7	39.9	43.0	33.6	24.2	17.9	11.2	6.5
E07000129	Blaby	97.6	5.5	5.9	5.5	5.5	4.9	5.7	6.0	5.7	6.4	7.4	7.3	6.5	5.6	6.1	4.8	3.6	2.7	1.6	0.9
E07000130	Charnwood	177.4	9.5	9.8	8.9	12.1	18.6	11.3	10.8	10.0	10.4	12.0	11.9	10.5	9.6	9.9	7.7	5.7	4.3	2.7	1.6
E07000131	Harborough	90.3	4.7	5.5	5.5	5.2	3.9	4.3	4.2	5.0	6.1	7.5	7.4	6.3	5.5	6.0	4.8	3.4	2.5	1.9	0.9
E07000132	Hinckley and Bosworth	109.9	6.1	6.2	6.0	5.9	5.1	6.3	6.2	6.5	7.0	8.4	8.4	7.5	6.9	7.7	5.8	4.1	2.9	1.9	1.0
E07000133	Melton	51.0	2.7	2.9	2.8	2.8	2.4	2.7	2.6	2.7	3.1	4.1	4.4	3.6	3.3	3.6	2.7	1.9	1.4	0.8	0.5
E07000134	North West Leicestershire	98.4	5.3	5.9	5.7	5.5	5.2	5.5	5.6	5.7	6.8	7.9	7.7	6.5	5.9	6.3	5.1	3.3	2.3	1.4	0.9
E07000135	Oadby and Wigston	56.0	3.0	3.2	3.0	4.0	4.1	2.4	3.1	3.1	3.3	3.9	4.1	3.7	3.1	3.3	2.7	2.3	1.9	1.2	0.7
E10000019	Lincolnshire	744.8	40.6	40.8	37.7	41.9	42.8	42.3	41.4	39.3	42.9	51.9	55.0	50.3	46.8	52.9	43.4	31.2	22.2	13.7	7.7
E07000136	Boston	67.7	4.4	4.0	3.4	3.5	3.6	4.6	4.7	4.0	4.0	4.4	4.6	4.2	4.0	4.3	3.5	2.6	1.9	1.2	0.7
E07000137	East Lindsey	138.7	6.4	6.8	6.5	7.0	5.9	6.6	5.9	5.8	7.0	9.1	10.3	10.3	10.5	12.8	10.8	7.4	5.1	3.0	1.6
E07000138	Lincoln	97.4	5.9	5.2	4.3	7.1	12.9	7.7	7.0	5.8	5.2	5.7	6.0	5.3	4.5	4.5	3.4	2.6	2.0	1.4	0.8
E07000139	North Kesteven	113.6	6.0	6.3	6.1	6.2	5.2	6.3	6.4	6.1	6.9	8.7	8.8	7.5	6.7	7.9	6.7	5.2	3.4	2.0	1.2
E07000140	South Holland	92.5	5.1	5.0	4.6	4.9	4.4	5.3	5.2	5.0	5.6	6.4	6.9	6.1	5.7	6.7	5.3	4.2	3.0	1.9	1.1
E07000141	South Kesteven	140.9	7.8	8.4	7.9	7.9	6.3	7.3	7.5	7.9	8.8	10.6	10.9	10.0	8.8	9.7	7.9	5.4	3.9	2.5	1.5
E07000142	West Lindsey	93.9	5.0	5.1	5.0	5.3	4.5	4.6	4.6	4.7	5.3	6.9	7.5	6.9	6.4	7.1	5.8	4.0	2.9	1.7	0.8
E10000021	Northamptonshire	732.5	47.5	48.9	43.2	41.9	44.5	43.7	47.1	46.9	50.0	54.8	54.3	45.8	40.3	42.9	32.0	22.0	15.9	9.9	5.9
E07000150	Corby	68.3	5.1	5.1	4.0	3.8	3.6	4.7	5.5	4.8	4.4	4.8	5.0	4.3	3.5	3.2	2.4	1.8	1.2	0.7	0.3
E07000151	Daventry	81.1	4.2	4.9	4.8	4.6	3.8	4.2	4.0	4.4	5.3	6.7	6.8	5.8	5.2	5.6	4.3	2.8	2.0	1.2	0.7
E07000152	East Northamptonshire	91.4	5.0	5.6	5.5	5.7	4.2	4.7	4.9	5.2	6.2	7.3	7.0	6.1	5.5	6.2	4.6	3.1	2.2	1.4	0.9
E07000153	Kettering	98.9	6.5	6.6	6.0	5.3	5.0	6.0	6.2	6.3	6.9	7.6	7.2	5.9	5.3	6.0	4.5	3.0	2.2	1.4	1.0
E07000154	Northampton	224.5	16.5	15.7	12.8	13.0	15.3	15.5	17.4	16.2	15.5	15.0	15.2	12.5	10.7	10.9	7.9	5.7	4.3	2.7	1.6
E07000155	South Northamptonshire	89.9	4.9	5.7	5.5	5.1	3.7	4.2	4.2	5.2	6.4	7.5	7.4	6.4	5.5	6.1	4.6	3.1	2.2	1.4	0.8
E07000156	Wellingborough	78.4	5.3	5.3	4.6	4.5	3.8	4.4	4.9	4.8	5.2	5.9	5.6	4.9	4.5	4.8	3.8	2.5	1.8	1.1	0.7
E10000024	Nottinghamshire	811.5	45.7	48.1	43.4	44.5	44.5	48.8	47.4	47.6	51.6	60.4	62.0	54.9	48.2	51.2	41.1	29.9	21.8	13.2	7.2
E07000170	Ashfield	124.5	7.5	7.6	6.9	7.0	7.0	8.2	7.6	7.3	7.9	9.5	9.4	8.1	7.1	7.3	6.2	4.4	2.9	1.6	0.9
E07000171	Bassetlaw	115.2	6.4	6.5	6.1	6.5	6.1	6.3	6.3	6.2	7.1	8.7	9.2	8.2	7.3	7.8	6.2	4.4	3.1	1.9	1.0
E07000172	Broxtowe	112.1	6.2	6.4	5.5	6.0	6.2	7.6	6.7	6.2	7.2	8.1	8.3	7.3	6.4	7.2	5.6	4.2	3.1	1.9	1.1
E07000173	Gedling	116.7	6.4	6.9	6.2	6.4	6.0	6.9	6.8	7.2	7.5	8.8	8.8	7.9	7.0	7.4	5.6	4.5	3.4	2.0	1.0
E07000174	Mansfield	107.9	6.7	6.5	5.6	5.7	6.3	7.2	7.1	6.5	6.6	7.7	8.2	7.4	6.3	6.2	5.1	3.6	2.7	1.6	0.9
E07000175	Newark and Sherwood	119.8	6.5	7.1	6.5	6.6	6.5	6.8	6.4	6.5	7.4	9.0	9.3	8.3	7.4	8.1	6.5	4.7	3.2	2.0	1.1
E07000176	Rushcliffe	115.2	5.9	7.2	6.6	6.3	5.9	7.1	6.1	7.1	7.9	8.7	8.9	7.6	6.8	7.2	5.8	4.2	3.3	2.1	1.3

MYE2: Population estimates: Persons by selected age groups for local authorities in the UK, mid-2016

Thousands

Code	Name	All ages	0-4	5-9	10-14	15-19	20-24	25-29	30-34	35-39	40-44	45-49	50-54	55-59	60-64	65-69	70-74	75-79	80-84	85-89	90
E12000005	**WEST MIDLANDS**	5,810.8	365.8	366.8	336.8	350.5	392.6	396.0	370.9	348.5	357.7	404.9	401.6	347.6	309.5	316.5	262.5	197.5	144.7	89.3	50.6
E06000019	Herefordshire, County of	189.5	9.6	10.4	9.8	9.9	8.8	11.0	10.6	10.3	10.6	13.3	14.4	13.2	12.7	13.5	11.1	8.1	6.1	3.8	2.2
E06000051	Shropshire	314.4	15.0	16.9	16.7	17.6	15.5	17.2	16.4	16.4	18.3	23.0	24.5	22.1	20.7	22.3	18.7	13.7	9.8	6.1	3.6
E06000021	Stoke-on-Trent	253.7	17.9	16.5	14.1	14.5	18.0	18.8	17.6	15.2	15.3	17.2	16.9	15.1	13.6	13.6	10.6	7.9	5.6	3.4	1.7
E06000020	Telford and Wrekin	173.7	11.2	11.7	10.4	10.8	11.3	10.8	11.5	10.7	11.2	12.9	12.5	10.4	9.5	9.5	7.4	5.4	3.5	2.0	1.1
E10000028	Staffordshire	866.4	45.0	48.5	46.4	48.7	49.9	52.1	49.0	48.2	54.4	65.3	66.0	58.0	52.2	56.6	46.9	34.1	23.6	13.9	7.8
E07000192	Cannock Chase	98.5	5.5	5.8	5.4	5.5	5.7	6.3	6.3	5.8	6.5	7.8	7.8	6.3	5.6	5.7	4.8	3.4	2.2	1.4	0.8
E07000193	East Staffordshire	116.9	7.4	7.2	6.8	6.5	6.5	7.3	7.3	7.1	7.3	8.7	8.8	7.7	6.5	6.7	5.5	4.0	3.0	1.8	0.9
E07000194	Lichfield	102.8	5.1	5.7	5.6	5.6	5.0	5.3	5.3	5.7	6.6	7.7	8.0	6.9	6.3	7.3	6.6	4.6	2.9	1.7	1.0
E07000195	Newcastle-under-Lyme	128.1	6.3	6.8	6.5	8.0	10.3	8.9	7.5	7.0	7.6	9.0	9.1	8.2	7.3	8.0	6.2	4.7	3.5	2.1	1.1
E07000196	South Staffordshire	111.2	5.0	5.5	5.6	6.1	5.8	6.3	5.4	5.5	6.7	8.4	9.0	8.1	7.2	8.0	6.7	5.1	3.5	2.0	1.2
E07000197	Stafford	133.7	6.7	7.5	6.8	7.1	7.7	8.1	7.4	7.5	8.3	10.1	10.2	9.0	8.1	8.8	7.5	5.5	3.7	2.3	1.3
E07000198	Staffordshire Moorlands	98.2	4.3	5.2	5.2	5.3	4.7	4.9	4.6	4.8	6.1	7.8	7.8	6.9	6.6	7.6	6.0	4.4	3.0	1.8	1.0
E07000199	Tamworth	77.0	4.7	5.0	4.4	4.5	4.2	5.0	5.1	4.7	5.2	5.7	5.4	4.8	4.6	4.6	3.6	2.4	1.7	0.9	0.5
E10000031	Warwickshire	559.0	31.5	32.8	30.3	31.2	31.7	34.1	32.7	33.1	36.0	40.9	41.8	36.2	32.0	34.3	29.2	20.8	15.0	9.6	5.7
E06000218	North Warwickshire	63.2	3.3	3.5	3.4	3.4	3.1	3.6	3.5	3.3	4.0	4.9	5.1	4.6	4.0	4.3	3.5	2.4	1.6	1.0	0.6
E06000219	Nuneaton and Bedworth	127.7	8.0	8.1	7.0	7.1	7.1	8.1	8.3	7.8	8.0	9.2	9.4	8.0	7.3	7.7	6.2	4.4	3.1	1.8	0.9
E07000220	Rugby	105.3	6.6	6.8	6.1	6.2	5.0	6.2	7.0	6.9	7.2	7.7	7.8	6.5	5.5	5.8	5.1	3.7	2.6	1.7	1.1
E07000221	Stratford-on-Avon	123.3	6.0	6.5	6.6	6.5	5.0	5.9	5.7	6.2	7.6	9.2	9.9	8.9	8.0	9.0	8.0	5.7	4.2	2.7	1.6
E07000222	Warwick	139.5	7.6	7.9	7.3	8.0	11.5	10.3	8.2	8.9	9.2	9.8	9.7	8.2	7.2	7.6	6.4	4.6	3.5	2.3	1.5
E11000005	West Midlands (Met County)	2,870.6	203.5	196.8	177.7	185.5	226.5	219.1	200.9	181.8	175.4	189.5	181.9	154.3	132.5	127.6	106.6	84.6	64.3	40.0	22.1
E08000025	Birmingham	1,128.1	85.9	81.7	74.9	80.4	104.4	92.5	82.2	74.9	68.2	69.4	65.6	55.4	46.8	42.0	33.7	27.2	21.6	13.7	7.6
E08000026	Coventry	353.2	23.7	23.0	18.9	23.0	39.4	33.9	26.6	21.9	20.4	21.0	19.8	17.3	14.7	14.2	12.1	9.3	6.9	4.4	2.7
E08000027	Dudley	317.6	19.4	19.4	18.5	18.1	17.8	19.5	19.6	18.5	19.4	23.7	22.8	19.2	17.7	18.4	16.1	12.3	9.0	5.4	2.7
E08000028	Sandwell	322.6	24.5	23.2	20.5	19.5	20.0	23.0	24.2	21.5	21.0	22.5	21.3	17.7	14.9	14.0	11.9	9.5	6.9	4.2	2.4
E08000029	Solihull	212.2	12.5	13.1	12.6	12.5	10.7	12.1	11.5	12.1	13.1	15.7	16.2	13.9	11.7	12.9	10.9	8.0	6.2	4.2	2.4
E08000030	Walsall	278.9	19.4	19.1	17.4	17.0	16.9	19.1	18.6	16.6	16.9	19.3	18.9	16.2	14.1	14.1	12.0	9.8	7.2	4.1	2.2
E08000031	Wolverhampton	258.0	18.2	17.4	14.8	15.1	17.2	18.9	18.2	16.3	16.5	17.9	17.2	14.7	12.6	12.1	9.9	8.4	6.4	4.0	2.2
E10000034	Worcestershire	583.5	32.1	33.2	31.5	32.2	31.0	33.0	32.2	32.8	36.4	42.8	43.6	38.3	36.4	39.5	31.9	22.8	16.8	10.7	6.4
E07000234	Bromsgrove	96.8	5.1	5.6	5.4	5.2	4.7	5.2	4.9	5.4	6.4	7.4	7.6	6.5	6.0	6.2	5.3	3.9	3.0	2.0	1.2
E07000235	Malvern Hills	76.6	3.4	3.8	4.1	4.3	3.3	3.4	3.0	3.5	4.2	5.4	6.1	5.7	5.4	6.1	5.1	3.8	2.9	1.9	1.2
E07000236	Redditch	85.1	5.6	5.5	4.9	4.7	4.4	5.7	6.0	5.9	5.6	5.9	5.7	5.3	5.2	5.2	3.8	2.4	1.6	1.1	0.6
E07000237	Worcester	101.9	6.2	6.1	5.5	6.3	8.4	7.4	6.9	6.5	6.7	7.2	7.0	5.8	5.2	5.1	4.0	3.0	2.3	1.4	0.9
E07000238	Wychavon	123.1	6.3	6.6	6.6	6.5	5.3	5.9	6.0	6.3	7.4	9.4	9.8	8.7	8.4	9.3	7.4	5.4	3.9	2.5	1.5
E07000239	Wyre Forest	100.0	5.6	5.6	5.0	5.2	4.9	5.5	5.4	5.2	6.1	7.5	7.3	6.3	6.2	7.6	6.4	4.3	3.0	1.8	1.1
E12000006	**EAST**	6,129.0	379.0	383.6	343.0	344.6	345.7	383.0	386.6	386.7	397.0	437.7	439.2	381.7	336.4	360.0	285.0	211.7	163.4	104.1	60.5
E06000055	Bedford	168.8	11.3	11.1	10.1	10.2	9.3	9.8	11.1	11.5	11.3	12.3	12.2	10.4	8.8	9.0	6.9	5.1	4.1	2.7	1.5
E06000056	Central Bedfordshire	276.7	17.7	17.8	15.8	14.7	13.6	17.3	18.1	18.7	19.0	20.7	21.4	18.2	15.3	15.8	12.1	8.5	6.4	3.7	2.0
E06000032	Luton	215.9	18.1	16.7	14.2	13.2	14.6	18.0	19.0	16.0	13.8	13.3	13.2	10.8	8.8	7.6	5.8	5.2	4.0	2.3	1.2
E06000031	Peterborough	196.7	16.3	14.3	11.6	10.9	11.0	15.0	15.9	14.4	13.2	13.2	12.5	11.0	9.3	8.8	6.6	5.0	4.1	2.6	1.4
E06000033	Southend-on-Sea	180.6	11.5	11.4	9.9	9.9	9.5	10.7	11.8	12.3	13.1	13.1	12.8	11.0	9.5	10.2	8.2	6.0	4.7	3.3	2.1
E06000034	Thurrock	168.4	12.9	12.6	10.5	9.8	9.5	11.4	12.7	12.5	12.4	12.4	11.5	9.1	7.9	7.9	5.6	4.0	2.9	1.9	1.0
E10000003	Cambridgeshire	644.6	38.5	39.0	35.1	37.6	42.8	41.7	40.3	41.9	42.6	46.4	45.9	39.4	35.0	36.8	28.9	20.9	15.6	10.2	6.1
E07000008	Cambridge	124.6	7.0	6.8	5.6	9.3	19.2	11.7	9.1	8.5	7.1	7.2	6.8	5.6	5.0	4.5	3.5	2.7	2.3	1.6	1.2
E07000009	East Cambridgeshire	88.2	5.5	5.9	5.2	4.6	3.7	4.7	5.4	6.0	6.3	6.7	6.5	5.6	4.9	5.3	4.2	3.0	2.3	1.5	0.8

MYE2: Population estimates: Persons by selected age groups for local authorities in the UK, mid-2016

Thousands

Code	Name	All ages	0-4	5-9	10-14	15-19	20-24	25-29	30-34	35-39	40-44	45-49	50-54	55-59	60-64	65-69	70-74	75-79	80-84	85-89	90
														Age groups (years)							
E07000010	Fenland	99.6	6.0	5.5	5.0	5.5	5.3	6.0	5.9	5.3	5.9	7.0	7.3	6.4	6.3	6.8	5.4	4.0	3.0	2.0	1.1
E07000011	Huntingdonshire	176.1	10.6	10.4	9.7	9.6	8.2	11.1	10.8	11.2	11.8	13.4	13.5	11.7	10.1	11.0	8.6	6.0	4.1	2.5	1.5
E07000012	South Cambridgeshire	156.0	9.5	10.3	9.5	8.6	6.4	8.1	9.2	10.8	11.5	12.1	11.7	10.1	8.7	9.2	7.2	5.1	3.9	2.6	1.5
E10000012	Essex	1,457.9	86.5	87.9	81.5	82.0	80.4	88.0	85.0	87.6	93.3	106.7	106.7	93.5	82.7	90.6	72.2	52.7	40.7	25.4	14.6
E07000066	Basildon	183.8	12.8	12.0	10.9	10.5	10.2	12.3	12.3	12.2	12.1	13.3	12.9	11.4	9.4	9.7	7.5	5.7	4.5	2.7	1.4
E07000067	Braintree	151.2	8.7	9.8	8.8	8.5	7.3	8.7	9.0	9.0	10.1	11.7	11.5	9.7	8.9	9.6	7.2	5.0	3.7	2.4	1.5
E07000068	Brentwood	76.8	4.5	4.3	4.4	4.3	3.9	4.5	4.5	4.9	5.0	5.8	6.1	5.0	4.1	4.4	3.6	2.8	2.4	1.6	1.0
E07000069	Castle Point	89.8	4.5	4.7	4.7	5.1	4.9	4.8	4.4	4.5	5.3	6.4	6.5	6.0	5.6	6.9	5.7	4.2	3.0	1.6	0.9
E07000070	Chelmsford	174.2	10.2	10.6	10.1	9.5	9.4	11.1	11.3	11.3	12.0	12.9	12.6	10.8	9.5	10.2	8.0	5.8	4.6	2.9	1.6
E07000071	Colchester	187.6	11.7	11.3	9.9	11.2	15.2	14.4	12.5	12.0	12.1	12.9	12.5	10.4	9.2	10.3	7.9	5.7	4.3	2.6	1.5
E07000072	Epping Forest	129.9	8.1	7.7	7.1	6.9	6.9	7.9	7.6	8.4	8.5	9.8	10.0	8.5	7.2	7.4	6.1	4.4	3.5	2.4	1.5
E07000073	Harlow	85.9	6.7	6.1	4.9	4.8	4.8	5.9	6.5	6.1	5.5	5.8	5.9	5.3	4.4	3.8	2.9	2.4	2.1	1.4	0.6
E07000074	Maldon	63.4	3.0	3.4	3.3	3.6	2.9	3.0	2.6	3.2	3.9	5.0	5.1	4.7	4.5	5.0	4.0	2.7	1.9	1.1	0.6
E07000075	Rochford	85.7	4.1	4.9	4.7	4.9	4.4	4.5	4.1	4.6	5.6	6.7	6.7	5.8	5.2	6.0	4.8	3.6	2.7	1.6	0.9
E07000076	Tendring	143.4	7.2	7.5	7.1	7.6	6.8	6.8	5.9	6.1	7.3	9.3	10.1	9.8	9.8	12.3	10.5	7.8	5.8	3.6	2.2
E07000077	Uttlesford	86.3	5.1	5.5	5.5	5.1	3.8	4.2	4.3	5.3	5.9	7.0	6.9	6.0	4.9	5.2	4.1	2.8	2.2	1.4	0.9
E10000015	Hertfordshire	1,176.4	76.7	79.3	69.4	67.1	64.3	74.0	78.2	82.9	83.4	86.5	86.4	72.2	58.7	58.1	45.5	35.3	28.8	18.5	10.9
E07000095	Broxbourne	96.9	6.4	6.3	5.6	5.7	5.2	6.3	6.3	6.5	6.3	7.3	7.0	6.0	4.8	5.0	4.0	3.3	2.6	1.6	0.8
E07000096	Dacorum	152.4	9.8	10.3	8.6	8.4	7.4	9.7	10.3	10.6	10.8	11.2	11.4	10.0	8.3	7.7	5.9	4.4	3.7	2.5	1.5
E07000242	East Hertfordshire	146.1	8.6	9.4	8.9	8.6	6.8	8.0	8.4	9.9	11.0	11.7	11.9	9.6	7.7	8.0	6.0	4.5	3.6	2.2	1.2
E07000098	Hertsmere	103.7	6.9	7.2	6.3	5.9	5.2	6.3	6.6	6.8	7.1	7.4	7.7	6.4	5.3	5.4	4.4	3.2	2.7	1.8	1.1
E07000099	North Hertfordshire	132.7	8.4	8.6	7.5	7.1	6.0	7.5	8.6	9.4	9.7	10.0	10.0	8.3	6.9	7.3	5.8	4.4	3.6	2.2	1.4
E07000240	St Albans	147.0	10.1	11.1	9.6	8.1	5.9	8.0	9.0	11.1	11.9	11.3	10.6	8.6	7.2	7.1	5.7	4.4	3.5	2.3	1.4
E07000243	Stevenage	87.3	6.0	6.0	4.9	4.8	5.1	6.4	6.6	6.0	5.5	6.2	6.7	5.5	4.2	3.9	3.0	2.4	2.0	1.3	0.6
E07000102	Three Rivers	92.7	5.7	6.3	5.7	5.4	4.2	5.3	5.4	6.5	6.7	7.0	7.1	5.9	4.8	4.9	3.8	3.0	2.5	1.6	1.0
E07000103	Watford	96.6	7.3	6.9	5.8	5.2	5.0	7.4	8.7	8.4	7.3	6.8	6.2	5.1	4.1	3.6	2.9	2.3	1.8	1.2	0.7
E07000241	Welwyn Hatfield	121.0	7.5	7.2	6.4	7.9	13.5	9.0	8.4	7.8	7.1	7.5	7.8	6.8	5.5	5.1	4.1	3.4	2.9	1.9	1.2
E10000020	Norfolk	891.7	47.7	49.3	44.2	48.4	52.4	52.3	50.9	47.4	51.0	60.2	62.6	57.3	55.0	63.6	52.0	38.6	29.3	18.7	10.7
E07000143	Breckland	137.1	7.6	7.9	6.9	7.2	6.9	7.9	7.8	7.2	7.8	9.3	10.0	8.8	8.5	10.0	8.2	6.2	4.5	2.8	1.7
E07000144	Broadland	127.4	6.1	6.8	6.5	6.9	5.6	5.9	6.2	6.8	8.0	9.6	9.8	8.7	8.2	9.6	7.7	5.9	4.5	2.9	1.6
E07000145	Great Yarmouth	99.0	5.6	5.7	5.1	5.6	5.5	6.0	5.7	4.9	5.3	6.6	7.0	6.4	6.2	7.1	5.9	4.2	3.1	2.0	1.1
E07000146	King's Lynn and West Norfolk	151.8	8.6	8.5	7.5	7.7	7.1	8.7	8.5	7.7	8.3	10.1	10.8	10.0	9.8	11.4	9.5	7.1	5.3	3.3	1.8
E07000147	North Norfolk	103.6	4.2	4.7	4.6	4.8	4.3	4.5	4.4	4.3	5.0	6.6	7.3	7.7	8.0	9.7	8.1	5.9	4.7	3.1	1.7
E07000148	Norwich	139.9	8.6	7.9	6.3	8.7	17.3	13.0	11.4	9.2	8.1	8.3	7.7	6.7	6.0	6.2	4.7	3.7	2.9	2.0	1.3
E07000149	South Norfolk	133.0	7.0	7.8	7.3	7.5	5.5	6.4	6.9	7.4	8.4	9.7	9.9	9.0	8.2	9.6	7.9	5.7	4.3	2.7	1.5
E10000029	Suffolk	751.2	41.8	44.3	40.9	40.6	38.3	44.8	43.4	41.5	44.3	52.9	53.9	48.9	45.5	51.7	41.2	30.3	22.9	15.0	9.0
E07000200	Babergh	90.3	4.3	5.0	5.2	4.9	3.9	4.3	4.0	4.4	5.5	6.8	7.0	6.2	5.9	7.0	5.7	4.0	2.9	1.9	1.2
E07000201	Forest Heath	63.3	5.1	4.1	3.0	3.0	4.3	5.6	5.2	3.8	3.2	3.6	4.0	3.6	3.2	3.6	2.7	2.0	1.6	1.0	0.6
E07000202	Ipswich	138.5	9.6	8.9	7.6	7.8	8.9	10.9	10.8	9.5	8.8	9.4	9.0	8.0	7.0	6.8	5.0	3.9	3.1	2.2	1.2
E07000203	Mid Suffolk	100.7	4.8	5.7	7.6	5.5	4.5	5.1	5.1	5.3	6.1	7.5	7.8	7.2	6.7	7.6	6.0	4.2	3.0	1.9	1.1
E07000204	St Edmundsbury	113.4	6.2	6.9	6.2	6.0	5.8	7.1	7.2	6.5	6.9	8.4	8.2	6.9	6.4	7.4	6.1	4.6	3.3	2.2	1.3
E07000205	Suffolk Coastal	127.8	5.7	7.1	7.1	7.2	5.2	5.6	5.3	6.2	7.4	9.1	9.8	9.4	8.7	10.3	8.1	5.9	4.7	3.1	1.9
E07000206	Waveney	117.2	6.2	6.6	6.0	6.2	5.8	6.2	5.8	5.8	6.4	7.9	8.1	7.7	7.5	9.0	7.6	5.6	4.3	2.8	1.7

MYE2: Population estimates: Persons by selected age groups for local authorities in the UK, mid-2016

Thousands

Code	Name	All ages	0-4	5-9	10-14	15-19	20-24	25-29	30-34	35-39	40-44	45-49	50-54	55-59	60-64	65-69	70-74	75-79	80-84	85-89	90
E12000007	LONDON	8,769.7	634.4	578.8	487.1	467.7	565.8	823.5	861.1	757.5	632.2	592.2	546.6	447.6	354.8	314.9	236.2	187.2	141.8	88.1	52.2
E09000007	Camden	249.2	14.4	14.4	12.3	12.9	22.3	28.6	25.6	21.3	17.7	16.0	13.7	11.4	9.6	9.1	7.2	5.2	3.7	2.4	1.6
E09000001	City of London	7.2	0.4	0.4	0.3	0.2	0.4	0.4	0.5	0.5	0.5	0.6	0.6	0.5	0.5	0.5	0.3	0.3	0.3	0.1	0.1
E09000012	Hackney	273.1	20.9	17.8	15.3	13.6	16.4	33.6	38.2	28.4	19.3	16.3	14.3	10.9	8.4	6.6	4.6	3.6	2.7	1.5	0.9
E09000013	Hammersmith and Fulham	181.8	11.5	10.7	8.2	7.6	13.4	21.1	20.8	16.6	14.4	12.5	11.0	8.5	6.7	6.1	4.5	3.6	2.4	1.5	0.8
E09000014	Haringey	272.1	19.2	16.7	15.6	15.2	17.4	26.1	28.8	26.5	21.1	19.2	17.3	13.0	10.1	8.6	6.0	4.9	3.4	1.9	1.0
E09000019	Islington	232.1	13.3	11.8	9.9	11.4	25.1	31.5	29.5	20.1	15.0	13.8	13.0	9.8	7.6	6.6	4.8	3.8	2.6	1.6	0.9
E09000020	Kensington and Chelsea	156.8	8.7	8.4	7.4	6.5	9.2	12.9	14.7	14.9	12.2	11.4	10.8	9.1	7.4	7.5	5.9	4.2	2.7	1.7	1.2
E09000022	Lambeth	323.1	20.4	18.0	15.4	14.3	21.6	47.0	42.8	30.3	22.5	20.5	19.6	14.6	10.5	8.2	5.9	4.9	3.5	2.2	1.2
E09000023	Lewisham	298.9	22.7	20.1	16.0	15.1	19.1	28.5	31.2	28.9	23.0	21.1	19.6	14.9	10.6	8.7	5.7	5.3	3.9	2.4	1.4
E09000025	Newham	344.5	29.5	23.6	20.3	20.6	27.5	40.9	41.2	29.8	22.7	21.1	17.7	14.6	10.8	8.2	6.3	4.7	3.2	1.7	1.0
E09000028	Southwark	311.7	21.6	18.7	15.0	14.8	24.3	39.3	36.2	28.3	22.2	20.9	19.1	15.6	10.5	8.1	5.9	4.6	3.3	2.0	1.2
E09000030	Tower Hamlets	300.9	22.3	19.0	16.5	15.9	26.6	44.1	41.4	29.8	20.4	16.0	12.5	10.2	8.1	5.8	4.0	3.5	2.6	1.6	0.7
E09000032	Wandsworth	321.5	22.7	18.5	13.5	12.4	19.6	41.8	45.9	32.9	24.0	19.7	16.8	13.1	10.5	9.6	6.9	5.7	3.9	2.4	1.4
E09000033	Westminster	242.0	13.7	13.2	10.8	11.5	16.6	23.4	28.0	23.5	18.8	16.7	14.6	11.9	10.2	9.0	6.9	5.4	3.9	2.5	1.4
E09000002	Barking and Dagenham	208.2	20.0	19.3	14.6	13.1	13.3	16.5	17.6	16.4	14.9	13.7	12.2	9.6	7.2	5.9	4.4	3.6	2.8	1.9	1.2
E09000003	Barnet	384.8	27.1	27.0	23.2	20.7	22.3	30.8	32.4	30.8	27.8	26.9	24.3	20.5	16.8	16.1	12.8	9.3	7.7	5.0	3.4
E09000004	Bexley	245.1	16.2	16.5	14.7	14.6	14.8	17.3	16.1	16.6	15.8	17.7	17.7	15.0	11.6	11.5	9.1	7.7	6.0	3.9	2.2
E09000005	Brent	326.4	25.2	21.3	18.8	18.5	20.6	29.1	31.8	26.7	22.8	21.1	20.4	18.2	14.4	11.6	8.7	7.1	5.4	3.1	1.6
E09000006	Bromley	327.6	21.7	21.4	18.9	17.5	15.2	20.0	21.7	25.0	23.7	25.1	24.1	19.9	15.9	16.9	13.2	10.1	8.3	5.5	3.3
E09000008	Croydon	383.3	28.7	27.7	23.7	22.8	20.3	27.7	30.0	29.4	26.7	27.1	28.4	22.4	18.1	15.5	11.6	9.2	7.2	4.2	2.5
E09000009	Ealing	344.8	26.3	24.0	19.9	18.6	19.3	28.1	30.7	29.6	26.3	24.4	22.0	18.2	15.7	13.0	9.4	7.8	5.9	3.3	2.1
E09000010	Enfield	332.1	25.1	25.0	21.3	20.2	20.3	25.5	26.4	24.7	22.4	23.6	22.5	18.4	14.1	12.3	10.2	8.1	6.1	3.7	2.2
E09000011	Greenwich	279.1	22.5	19.8	16.0	15.3	18.6	25.2	25.8	25.8	20.8	19.1	16.9	13.8	10.5	9.3	6.8	5.2	3.9	2.3	1.5
E09000015	Harrow	248.7	17.9	16.1	14.5	14.4	13.5	18.6	19.7	19.4	16.9	16.3	16.1	14.7	12.7	11.1	8.7	7.0	5.5	3.3	2.0
E09000016	Havering	253.4	17.0	15.6	14.2	14.4	14.9	17.7	17.3	16.6	15.6	17.2	17.6	16.1	12.9	13.3	10.4	8.3	7.0	4.7	2.5
E09000017	Hillingdon	299.9	23.0	21.0	17.4	18.1	21.4	23.0	23.9	23.8	20.5	19.9	19.2	16.2	13.0	11.7	9.1	7.3	5.9	3.5	1.9
E09000018	Hounslow	268.3	21.3	18.7	14.8	14.3	15.6	22.3	25.7	24.2	20.4	17.6	16.6	14.1	11.6	10.0	7.3	5.8	4.2	2.4	1.3
E09000021	Kingston upon Thames	173.7	11.7	11.6	9.4	9.3	13.0	13.3	14.1	14.5	13.5	12.2	11.0	9.2	7.5	7.3	5.5	4.0	3.1	2.1	1.4
E09000024	Merton	206.7	16.0	13.8	10.8	9.9	10.7	16.6	20.2	20.1	15.9	14.6	13.4	10.7	8.7	7.9	5.6	4.8	3.5	2.3	1.3
E09000026	Redbridge	301.3	23.1	21.7	19.7	18.5	18.0	24.4	25.8	25.1	21.5	19.6	18.3	15.8	13.0	11.3	8.3	6.6	5.2	3.3	2.0
E09000027	Richmond upon Thames	195.2	13.5	14.1	11.2	9.5	8.1	10.5	14.1	16.9	17.3	15.6	14.2	11.4	9.4	9.5	7.0	5.0	3.7	2.6	1.8
E09000029	Sutton	201.9	14.2	13.8	11.8	11.2	9.8	12.6	15.0	16.2	15.5	15.5	14.6	11.7	9.5	9.2	7.2	5.4	4.4	2.8	1.6
E09000031	Waltham Forest	274.2	22.5	19.0	15.7	14.6	16.5	25.1	27.9	24.0	20.2	19.4	16.8	13.6	10.6	8.8	6.5	5.2	4.0	2.4	1.5
E12000008	SOUTH EAST	9,030.3	542.4	567.7	512.0	527.8	544.6	545.2	550.7	573.2	595.1	653.2	656.0	565.5	486.1	515.2	411.2	304.6	234.1	152.6	93.0
E06000036	Bracknell Forest	119.7	7.7	8.5	7.1	7.4	6.1	7.6	8.6	9.1	9.0	9.3	9.1	7.6	6.0	5.4	4.0	3.0	2.2	1.3	0.8
E06000043	Brighton and Hove	287.2	14.7	14.6	13.5	17.6	32.0	26.6	21.8	20.5	20.3	20.9	19.9	14.6	11.7	11.6	8.7	6.7	5.3	3.7	2.4
E06000046	Isle of Wight	140.3	6.7	6.9	6.9	7.7	6.6	6.8	6.6	6.6	7.6	9.8	10.4	9.9	9.9	11.4	9.7	6.5	4.9	3.2	2.1
E06000035	Medway	277.0	18.7	18.1	16.6	17.1	18.6	20.1	18.7	17.9	17.7	19.8	19.5	17.0	14.0	14.3	10.7	7.7	5.5	3.2	1.7
E06000042	Milton Keynes	266.2	20.1	20.9	16.9	14.8	13.2	17.3	21.3	22.1	19.9	18.8	17.5	15.4	13.4	12.3	8.3	6.0	4.0	2.6	1.5
E06000044	Portsmouth	213.3	13.4	13.1	11.1	13.8	24.8	17.9	15.9	13.1	12.7	13.6	13.4	11.6	9.0	9.1	7.1	5.3	4.1	2.6	1.8
E06000038	Reading	162.7	12.3	11.0	8.5	9.5	14.4	14.0	14.2	13.5	11.1	10.5	9.8	7.9	6.3	5.9	4.5	3.6	2.8	1.8	1.1
E06000039	Slough	147.7	13.2	12.7	10.1	8.7	7.9	10.6	13.6	14.0	11.3	9.8	8.5	7.2	6.0	4.7	3.1	2.6	2.0	1.2	0.7
E06000045	Southampton	250.4	16.4	14.8	11.7	17.2	33.7	22.6	19.0	16.6	14.4	13.9	14.4	12.4	10.3	10.1	7.9	5.8	4.5	3.1	1.8
E06000037	West Berkshire	158.6	9.5	10.4	9.7	9.7	7.4	8.4	9.0	9.8	11.3	12.7	12.4	10.6	9.1	9.3	7.2	5.0	3.6	2.2	1.3

35

MYE2: Population estimates: Persons by selected age groups for local authorities in the UK, mid-2016

Thousands

Code	Name	All ages	0-4	5-9	10-14	15-19	20-24	25-29	30-34	35-39	40-44	45-49	50-54	55-59	60-64	65-69	70-74	75-79	80-84	85-89	90
E06000040	Windsor and Maidenhead	149.7	9.0	9.8	9.5	9.0	6.1	8.4	9.4	10.4	11.0	11.8	11.2	9.2	7.7	7.9	6.5	4.9	3.8	2.5	1.6
E06000041	Wokingham	163.1	10.1	11.6	10.5	9.5	7.5	8.1	9.2	11.6	12.4	12.8	12.4	10.6	8.5	8.7	7.0	5.1	3.9	2.3	1.4
E10000002	Buckinghamshire	533.1	33.2	36.0	33.2	31.1	26.1	28.9	30.3	34.6	36.9	40.8	40.2	34.7	29.0	29.1	23.6	17.8	13.9	8.5	5.1
E07000004	Aylesbury Vale	192.7	12.5	13.2	11.6	11.3	9.7	11.6	12.1	13.1	13.5	14.8	14.6	12.5	10.3	10.3	7.7	5.6	4.2	2.5	1.5
E07000005	Chiltern	95.2	5.2	6.7	6.4	5.6	3.7	4.0	3.8	5.5	6.7	7.4	7.6	6.8	5.4	5.6	4.8	3.8	3.0	1.8	1.2
E07000006	South Bucks	69.8	4.1	4.5	4.1	3.7	3.1	3.5	3.7	4.2	4.4	5.5	5.4	4.9	4.0	4.0	3.2	2.8	2.2	1.5	0.9
E07000007	Wycombe	175.4	11.4	11.6	11.1	10.5	9.6	9.8	10.6	11.8	12.3	13.1	12.5	10.5	9.3	9.2	7.9	5.6	4.5	2.6	1.5
E10000011	East Sussex	549.6	27.9	30.8	29.1	30.4	26.3	27.2	27.2	27.8	31.7	38.9	41.4	37.4	35.1	40.7	33.0	24.1	18.9	13.0	8.6
E07000061	Eastbourne	103.0	5.8	5.6	5.1	5.8	5.8	5.5	6.0	5.9	6.1	6.8	7.0	6.4	5.9	7.0	5.6	4.4	3.6	2.8	1.8
E07000062	Hastings	92.9	5.7	5.6	5.0	5.5	5.3	5.9	5.6	5.3	5.6	6.9	7.0	6.1	5.4	5.9	4.3	2.9	2.2	1.5	1.1
E07000063	Lewes	101.6	4.9	5.9	5.6	5.6	4.5	4.9	5.0	5.2	6.1	7.4	7.7	6.9	6.5	7.3	5.9	4.5	3.6	2.4	1.6
E07000064	Rother	94.0	3.9	4.8	4.5	4.8	4.0	3.9	3.5	3.8	4.7	6.1	7.1	6.7	6.8	8.6	7.0	5.2	4.0	2.8	1.9
E07000065	Wealden	158.1	7.5	8.9	8.9	8.7	6.7	7.0	7.1	7.6	9.2	11.7	12.6	11.3	10.5	12.0	10.1	7.0	5.5	3.5	2.2
E10000014	Hampshire	1,365.1	76.9	82.5	76.4	77.3	69.3	76.8	76.1	79.9	89.3	100.3	104.4	91.7	78.7	85.5	69.4	51.4	39.0	25.1	15.1
E07000084	Basingstoke and Deane	175.2	11.5	11.7	10.0	9.7	8.4	10.6	12.0	12.1	12.4	13.6	13.6	11.2	9.1	9.4	7.4	5.2	3.7	2.2	1.3
E07000085	East Hampshire	118.7	6.2	7.0	7.0	7.0	5.2	5.4	5.2	6.2	7.7	9.2	9.7	8.8	7.4	8.1	6.6	4.7	3.6	2.3	1.4
E07000086	Eastleigh	129.5	7.6	8.3	7.4	7.1	6.4	8.2	7.9	8.5	8.6	9.4	9.6	8.5	7.5	7.6	5.8	4.5	3.3	2.2	1.2
E07000087	Fareham	115.8	5.7	6.3	6.2	6.6	6.0	6.2	6.1	6.3	7.3	8.7	9.0	8.1	6.9	7.7	6.5	4.8	3.8	2.3	1.3
E07000088	Gosport	85.5	5.0	5.4	4.8	5.0	5.0	5.5	5.5	4.9	5.3	6.0	6.2	5.7	4.7	5.2	4.0	2.9	2.3	1.4	0.8
E07000089	Hart	94.9	5.5	6.4	5.9	5.3	3.8	5.1	5.0	6.1	7.4	7.5	7.5	6.0	5.0	5.6	4.6	3.4	2.4	1.4	0.9
E07000090	Havant	123.9	6.6	7.1	6.7	7.2	6.8	7.1	6.6	6.1	6.8	8.7	9.2	8.7	7.6	8.2	6.9	5.3	4.1	2.7	1.5
E07000091	New Forest	179.5	8.2	9.5	9.1	9.1	7.8	8.5	7.7	8.4	10.2	12.2	13.7	12.7	12.1	14.1	11.8	8.9	7.2	5.0	3.3
E07000092	Rushmoor	96.1	6.8	6.0	5.2	5.3	5.8	7.5	7.4	7.2	7.2	7.2	7.0	5.6	4.3	4.3	3.3	2.5	1.6	1.0	0.7
E07000093	Test Valley	122.8	7.1	7.6	6.9	6.6	5.7	6.6	6.4	7.0	8.3	9.3	9.8	8.4	7.2	8.0	6.5	4.5	3.5	2.1	1.2
E07000094	Winchester	123.1	6.6	7.3	7.1	8.5	8.3	6.0	6.1	7.1	8.1	8.5	9.1	7.9	6.9	7.4	6.0	4.6	3.5	2.5	1.4
E10000016	Kent	1,540.4	91.8	96.6	89.3	92.5	91.4	90.2	89.6	90.7	96.6	111.5	112.3	96.7	85.4	94.5	74.7	54.2	40.8	26.5	15.2
E07000105	Ashford	125.9	8.1	8.4	7.8	7.5	6.4	7.2	7.3	7.4	8.1	9.7	9.5	7.7	6.7	7.7	6.1	4.2	3.0	1.9	1.2
E07000106	Canterbury	162.5	7.6	8.2	8.2	12.2	21.4	10.9	8.3	7.6	8.1	9.7	10.1	9.1	8.6	9.8	7.8	5.8	4.3	3.0	1.9
E07000107	Dartford	105.1	7.6	7.2	6.3	5.7	5.5	7.6	8.4	8.0	7.4	7.8	7.3	6.0	4.9	4.6	3.6	2.8	2.3	1.4	0.8
E07000108	Dover	114.6	6.1	6.5	6.2	6.5	5.9	6.0	6.0	5.9	6.6	8.1	8.8	8.1	7.6	8.4	6.6	4.6	3.4	2.2	1.2
E07000109	Gravesham	106.2	7.3	7.1	6.5	6.4	5.9	7.1	7.0	6.8	6.9	7.8	7.6	6.4	5.3	5.4	4.3	3.4	2.7	1.6	0.8
E07000110	Maidstone	165.7	10.3	10.5	9.4	9.3	8.7	10.2	10.6	10.4	10.8	12.3	12.2	10.4	8.9	9.8	7.7	5.7	4.3	2.6	1.4
E07000111	Sevenoaks	119.0	7.2	8.0	7.1	6.6	5.1	5.9	5.9	7.4	8.0	9.0	9.1	7.8	6.8	7.7	6.0	4.4	3.5	2.3	1.2
E07000112	Shepway	111.0	5.8	6.3	5.7	6.1	5.5	6.2	5.7	5.9	6.5	8.1	8.3	7.5	6.9	8.3	6.4	4.7	3.4	2.3	1.5
E07000113	Swale	144.9	9.2	9.6	8.5	8.7	8.1	8.6	8.8	8.5	8.9	10.3	10.8	9.3	8.2	9.1	7.0	4.9	3.4	2.1	1.1
E07000114	Thanet	140.8	8.4	8.6	7.8	8.3	7.8	7.6	7.6	7.4	7.8	9.3	9.8	9.1	8.7	10.0	8.0	5.7	4.2	2.9	1.7
E07000115	Tonbridge and Malling	127.3	7.6	8.3	8.2	8.1	6.1	6.7	6.9	7.8	9.1	10.0	9.8	8.2	6.8	7.2	5.9	4.4	3.4	1.9	1.0
E07000116	Tunbridge Wells	117.4	6.6	7.9	7.5	7.2	4.9	6.3	7.1	7.6	8.5	9.3	9.0	7.3	6.1	6.6	5.2	3.7	3.0	2.2	1.3
E10000025	Oxfordshire	678.5	40.4	41.9	37.6	40.9	49.7	43.9	45.3	43.6	43.2	47.5	48.0	40.9	34.6	36.3	29.2	21.9	16.6	10.6	6.4
E07000177	Cherwell	146.6	9.3	9.8	8.4	8.2	7.0	8.7	10.4	10.1	10.0	10.9	11.1	9.2	7.7	8.1	6.2	4.7	3.5	2.2	1.2
E07000178	Oxford	155.3	9.0	8.8	7.8	11.6	25.9	14.0	12.6	10.3	8.1	8.2	8.1	6.7	5.7	5.4	4.3	3.2	2.6	1.7	1.2
E07000179	South Oxfordshire	139.2	8.2	8.7	8.0	7.8	6.1	7.4	7.9	8.4	9.5	10.9	10.7	9.3	7.8	8.3	7.1	5.3	3.9	2.4	1.5
E07000180	Vale of White Horse	128.7	7.6	7.9	7.4	7.5	5.8	7.2	7.9	8.2	8.5	9.4	9.6	8.6	7.2	7.7	6.1	4.6	3.5	2.3	1.4
E07000181	West Oxfordshire	108.7	6.2	6.7	6.0	5.8	4.8	6.4	6.5	6.6	7.1	8.1	8.4	7.1	6.1	6.8	5.6	4.0	3.1	2.0	1.2
E10000030	Surrey	1,181.0	72.5	76.6	68.6	68.4	63.9	65.4	67.1	79.8	84.6	88.7	88.7	74.7	62.0	63.8	51.7	39.0	31.6	20.7	13.3
E07000207	Elmbridge	136.1	9.7	10.1	8.7	7.5	5.1	5.7	7.0	10.0	10.9	11.1	10.7	8.6	6.9	6.9	5.5	4.3	3.5	2.4	1.7

MYE2: Population estimates: Persons by selected age groups for local authorities in the UK, mid-2016

Thousands

Code	Name	All ages	0-4	5-9	10-14	15-19	20-24	25-29	30-34	35-39	40-44	45-49	50-54	55-59	60-64	65-69	70-74	75-79	80-84	85-89	90
E07000208	Epsom and Ewell	79.0	5.1	5.1	4.8	4.8	4.1	4.1	4.6	5.6	5.9	5.9	5.9	4.9	4.0	4.4	3.3	2.6	2.0	1.3	0.8
E07000209	Guildford	146.8	8.0	8.8	8.0	9.3	14.0	11.4	9.1	9.2	9.7	9.8	9.9	8.4	7.2	7.2	5.6	4.3	3.4	2.2	1.4
E07000210	Mole Valley	87.3	4.4	5.2	5.1	5.1	3.6	3.9	3.9	5.0	5.7	6.9	7.1	6.3	5.3	5.5	4.8	3.6	2.9	1.9	1.2
E07000211	Reigate and Banstead	145.3	9.7	9.7	8.4	7.8	6.4	8.2	9.1	10.8	10.6	10.9	11.1	9.0	7.5	7.8	6.0	4.4	3.7	2.5	1.7
E07000212	Runnymede	86.4	4.9	4.9	4.3	5.5	8.4	6.4	5.0	5.3	5.8	5.8	6.0	5.1	4.2	4.2	3.5	2.6	2.2	1.4	0.9
E07000213	Spelthorne	98.9	6.5	6.1	5.3	5.1	4.8	5.9	6.4	7.3	6.8	7.4	7.5	6.4	5.1	5.2	4.3	3.5	2.7	1.7	1.0
E07000214	Surrey Heath	88.7	5.0	5.6	5.4	5.1	4.1	4.7	4.8	5.6	6.4	7.2	7.1	5.9	4.9	4.8	4.1	3.1	2.5	1.5	0.9
E07000215	Tandridge	86.5	5.0	5.4	5.0	4.9	3.7	4.5	4.5	5.5	5.8	6.7	6.9	5.8	5.0	5.2	4.3	3.1	2.4	1.7	1.0
E07000216	Waverley	124.6	7.2	8.2	7.7	8.0	5.5	5.0	5.9	7.5	9.0	9.6	9.3	8.1	6.8	7.5	6.4	4.8	3.9	2.6	1.7
E07000217	Woking	101.4	7.1	7.3	5.9	5.2	4.2	5.8	6.8	8.0	8.1	7.5	7.2	6.2	5.1	5.0	3.8	2.9	2.4	1.7	1.0
E10000032	West Sussex	846.9	47.9	50.7	45.8	45.3	40.0	44.7	47.6	51.4	54.2	61.8	62.4	55.4	49.6	54.7	45.1	34.0	26.7	18.5	11.1
E07000223	Adur	63.6	3.8	3.8	3.3	3.3	2.9	3.2	3.5	3.9	4.3	4.7	4.6	4.0	3.7	4.2	3.5	2.7	2.1	1.4	0.8
E07000224	Arun	157.3	8.0	8.2	7.4	7.5	7.3	7.8	7.7	7.9	8.6	10.7	11.1	10.3	10.0	12.4	10.7	8.3	6.3	4.3	2.6
E07000225	Chichester	119.1	5.8	6.4	6.0	6.5	6.8	5.5	5.3	5.8	6.7	8.0	8.9	8.3	7.7	8.8	7.5	5.8	4.6	3.0	1.9
E07000226	Crawley	111.5	8.3	8.0	6.5	6.1	6.0	8.2	9.4	9.3	8.0	7.9	7.3	6.4	5.2	4.6	3.2	2.5	2.1	1.6	0.8
E07000227	Horsham	138.5	7.2	8.2	8.2	8.1	6.1	6.5	6.7	8.0	8.9	10.7	11.2	9.9	8.4	9.0	7.4	5.5	4.2	2.8	1.6
E07000228	Mid Sussex	147.5	8.6	9.6	8.7	8.3	5.9	7.5	8.5	9.7	10.5	11.5	11.2	9.5	8.4	8.8	7.2	4.9	4.0	2.9	1.7
E07000229	Worthing	109.2	6.0	6.5	5.7	5.6	5.0	6.0	6.5	6.9	7.3	8.2	8.1	6.9	6.1	6.8	5.6	4.3	3.4	2.6	1.8
E12000009	SOUTH WEST	5,517.0	306.2	315.8	288.3	313.9	340.5	332.9	318.4	311.1	330.1	384.2	398.3	358.9	327.5	359.1	290.3	211.6	161.2	104.8	63.8
E06000022	Bath and North East Somerset	186.9	9.6	10.2	9.4	13.5	20.9	12.2	9.8	9.6	10.7	12.2	12.6	11.0	9.8	10.3	8.4	6.4	4.9	3.3	2.0
E06000028	Bournemouth	193.7	11.4	10.4	8.3	11.2	18.1	13.3	14.4	14.0	12.3	12.6	12.5	10.8	9.3	10.1	7.8	6.0	5.1	3.7	2.5
E06000023	Bristol, City of	456.0	30.7	27.6	22.3	26.4	48.6	48.6	39.6	32.6	27.3	26.2	25.7	21.8	18.7	18.0	13.6	10.6	8.3	5.4	3.6
E06000052	Cornwall	555.1	29.3	30.1	28.5	31.1	30.2	27.3	27.5	28.9	32.2	38.7	40.8	38.8	37.0	42.7	34.1	23.4	17.3	10.9	6.3
E06000053	Isles of Scilly	2.3	0.1	0.1	0.1	0.1	0.1	0.1	0.1	0.1	0.2	0.1	0.2	0.2	0.2	0.2	0.2	0.1	0.1	0.1	0.0
E06000024	North Somerset	211.7	11.9	12.5	11.5	11.2	9.6	10.5	11.3	12.2	13.4	15.6	15.7	13.6	12.8	14.7	12.3	8.9	6.8	4.2	2.8
E06000026	Plymouth	262.4	15.8	15.2	13.1	15.9	25.0	18.7	17.8	15.0	14.8	17.2	17.3	16.1	13.4	14.1	11.5	8.6	6.6	3.9	2.3
E06000029	Poole	150.7	8.4	8.8	7.9	8.3	7.4	8.6	9.2	9.3	9.2	10.8	11.1	9.5	8.7	9.7	7.8	5.9	4.8	3.4	1.9
E06000025	South Gloucestershire	276.7	16.2	17.1	15.1	16.3	17.4	17.1	17.7	17.6	17.7	20.7	21.0	17.0	14.4	15.0	12.8	9.5	7.3	4.4	2.4
E06000030	Swindon	218.6	15.1	14.5	12.4	12.2	11.1	14.3	15.7	15.4	16.0	16.7	16.3	13.8	11.4	10.6	8.1	6.0	4.5	2.9	1.6
E06000027	Torbay	134.4	7.4	7.1	6.7	6.9	6.5	7.0	6.7	6.3	7.3	9.3	10.1	9.4	8.9	10.3	8.6	6.2	4.8	3.0	2.0
E06000054	Wiltshire	492.2	28.2	30.9	28.6	28.1	23.3	27.5	27.7	27.4	31.8	37.1	37.7	33.2	29.2	31.0	25.0	18.1	13.7	8.7	5.2
E10000008	Devon	778.8	38.3	41.7	39.2	42.9	44.9	42.5	38.8	39.3	43.1	53.0	57.2	53.6	51.2	58.2	47.4	34.0	25.7	17.1	10.7
E07000040	East Devon	140.3	6.5	7.3	7.0	7.2	5.5	6.3	6.0	6.4	7.6	9.4	9.9	9.5	9.7	11.6	10.1	7.6	5.9	4.1	2.6
E07000041	Exeter	127.5	6.6	6.6	5.4	8.9	17.7	11.5	8.9	7.6	7.1	7.4	7.5	6.4	5.7	5.9	4.5	3.7	2.8	2.0	1.3
E07000042	Mid Devon	79.9	4.3	4.8	4.6	4.6	3.5	3.9	4.1	4.1	4.8	5.9	6.0	5.5	5.3	5.7	4.5	3.3	2.4	1.6	0.9
E07000043	North Devon	94.6	4.9	5.3	5.0	5.0	4.4	5.1	4.7	4.9	5.4	6.7	7.1	6.7	6.1	7.0	5.9	4.2	3.1	2.0	1.3
E07000044	South Hams	84.8	3.6	4.4	4.4	4.4	3.3	3.7	3.6	3.8	4.5	5.9	6.9	6.7	6.4	7.3	5.9	3.9	3.0	1.8	1.1
E07000045	Teignbridge	129.9	6.5	6.8	6.6	6.7	5.6	6.4	6.2	6.6	7.2	9.2	10.3	9.4	9.0	10.2	8.3	5.7	4.3	3.0	1.9
E07000046	Torridge	67.0	3.3	3.5	3.4	3.4	2.9	3.2	2.9	3.2	3.6	4.7	5.1	5.1	5.0	5.8	4.5	3.1	2.3	1.4	0.8
E07000047	West Devon	54.7	2.5	2.9	2.8	2.9	2.0	2.5	2.3	2.6	3.0	3.8	4.5	4.2	4.0	4.6	3.8	2.5	1.9	1.2	0.7
E10000009	Dorset	422.9	19.1	21.9	21.8	22.7	17.6	19.9	18.0	19.8	23.0	28.7	31.6	30.2	28.9	34.8	29.2	21.3	16.7	11.1	6.6
E07000048	Christchurch	49.6	2.2	2.5	2.5	2.5	2.0	2.2	2.1	2.4	2.7	3.3	3.5	3.2	3.0	4.0	3.7	2.8	2.4	1.6	1.0
E07000049	East Dorset	89.1	3.8	4.6	4.4	4.4	3.6	3.7	3.4	3.8	4.7	6.0	6.6	6.4	6.1	7.8	6.6	5.1	4.0	2.6	1.6
E07000050	North Dorset	70.9	3.4	3.9	3.9	4.3	3.0	3.7	3.4	3.7	4.0	4.8	5.3	5.0	4.7	5.4	4.4	3.0	2.4	1.6	0.9
E07000051	Purbeck	46.3	2.1	2.5	2.4	2.4	2.1	2.3	2.1	2.2	2.6	3.1	3.5	3.4	3.2	3.8	3.1	2.2	1.7	1.1	0.6

MYE2: Population estimates: Persons by selected age groups for local authorities in the UK, mid-2016 *Thousands*

Code	Name	All ages	0-4	5-9	10-14	15-19	20-24	25-29	30-34	35-39	40-44	45-49	50-54	55-59	60-64	65-69	70-74	75-79	80-84	85-89	90
E07000052	West Dorset	101.5	4.3	4.9	5.3	5.4	3.8	4.4	3.9	4.3	5.4	6.8	7.9	7.5	7.4	8.8	7.4	5.4	4.2	2.8	1.7
E07000053	Weymouth and Portland	65.4	3.3	3.5	3.3	3.6	3.1	3.6	3.2	3.3	3.6	4.7	4.9	4.7	4.5	5.0	4.0	2.8	2.1	1.4	0.8
E10000013	Gloucestershire	623.1	35.1	36.1	33.5	35.9	33.7	35.6	35.7	35.8	39.4	46.1	47.2	41.9	37.6	39.5	31.6	23.5	17.3	11.1	6.7
E07000078	Cheltenham	117.2	6.7	6.5	6.1	7.2	8.1	8.2	8.5	7.8	7.4	7.8	8.2	7.0	6.1	6.3	5.0	4.0	3.1	2.1	1.4
E07000079	Cotswold	86.1	3.9	4.6	4.5	4.6	4.2	3.6	3.7	4.2	5.3	6.6	7.0	6.4	6.0	6.3	5.3	3.8	3.0	1.9	1.2
E07000080	Forest of Dean	85.4	4.2	4.5	4.3	5.3	4.5	4.1	3.8	3.9	5.0	6.4	6.8	6.2	6.0	6.5	5.1	3.6	2.5	1.5	1.0
E07000081	Gloucester	128.4	9.1	8.2	7.2	7.6	8.0	8.9	9.1	8.3	8.2	9.4	9.3	7.9	6.5	6.4	5.1	3.7	2.8	1.8	1.0
E07000082	Stroud	117.5	6.1	6.9	6.7	6.5	5.2	5.8	5.7	6.4	7.9	9.2	9.2	8.4	7.6	8.2	6.3	4.7	3.4	2.1	1.1
E07000083	Tewkesbury	88.5	5.2	5.3	4.7	4.6	3.8	4.9	4.9	5.3	5.6	6.6	6.7	6.0	5.5	5.8	4.7	3.7	2.6	1.7	1.0
E10000027	Somerset	551.4	29.6	31.4	29.8	31.1	26.1	29.9	28.4	27.7	31.6	39.2	41.4	38.2	36.0	39.9	31.9	23.1	17.4	11.7	7.2
E07000187	Mendip	113.1	6.0	6.5	6.5	7.1	5.2	5.8	5.5	5.8	6.8	8.6	8.9	7.9	7.3	7.9	6.1	4.4	3.4	2.1	1.3
E07000188	Sedgemoor	121.3	6.8	7.0	6.6	6.9	6.0	6.6	6.3	6.0	6.9	8.8	9.4	8.5	7.9	8.6	6.8	5.0	3.5	2.4	1.4
E07000189	South Somerset	166.5	8.9	9.5	8.9	9.1	7.8	9.1	8.7	8.3	9.6	11.6	12.1	11.4	10.9	12.4	10.0	7.3	5.3	3.6	2.2
E07000190	Taunton Deane	116.0	6.6	6.8	6.3	6.4	5.6	7.0	6.6	6.3	6.9	8.2	8.4	7.7	7.2	7.6	6.1	4.5	3.6	2.6	1.6
E07000191	West Somerset	34.5	1.4	1.5	1.5	1.6	1.5	1.4	1.4	1.2	1.4	2.0	2.6	2.7	2.8	3.4	2.8	2.0	1.6	1.0	0.6
W92000004	WALES	3,113.2	173.3	182.8	167.1	182.5	211.1	200.9	182.8	175.2	181.0	213.3	221.4	202.4	184.8	197.4	155.2	116.1	85.2	51.0	29.6
W06000001	Isle of Anglesey	69.7	3.8	4.0	3.5	3.5	3.3	3.9	3.5	3.5	3.8	4.7	4.9	5.0	4.8	5.5	4.4	3.2	2.2	1.4	0.8
W06000002	Gwynedd	123.3	6.3	6.9	6.4	7.7	10.7	7.7	6.0	5.9	6.6	7.8	8.3	7.9	7.4	8.2	6.8	4.9	3.8	2.5	1.4
W06000003	Conwy	116.8	5.7	6.1	5.8	6.2	5.4	6.1	5.5	5.6	6.2	7.9	8.7	8.3	7.7	9.1	7.4	5.7	4.5	2.9	1.8
W06000004	Denbighshire	95.0	5.3	5.7	5.2	5.3	5.0	5.4	4.5	4.6	5.5	6.6	7.1	6.4	6.1	7.1	5.6	4.2	2.9	1.8	0.9
W06000005	Flintshire	154.6	8.4	9.6	8.7	8.6	8.2	9.7	8.9	8.7	9.6	11.6	11.6	10.1	9.2	10.5	7.9	5.9	3.9	2.2	1.3
W06000006	Wrexham	135.4	8.1	8.8	7.7	7.5	7.4	8.6	8.6	8.1	8.5	9.8	9.7	8.5	8.0	8.4	6.5	4.6	3.4	2.1	1.1
W06000023	Powys	132.3	6.1	6.9	6.8	7.4	6.1	6.7	5.7	5.9	7.1	9.2	10.3	9.7	9.7	10.6	8.6	6.2	4.7	2.8	1.8
W06000008	Ceredigion	73.7	3.2	3.5	3.4	4.7	9.0	3.6	2.8	3.1	3.4	4.4	4.9	4.9	4.9	5.5	4.3	3.1	2.3	1.5	0.9
W06000009	Pembrokeshire	124.2	6.2	7.1	6.6	7.0	6.3	7.0	5.9	6.0	6.5	8.3	9.3	8.6	8.5	9.4	7.6	5.6	4.3	2.5	1.5
W06000010	Carmarthenshire	185.8	9.8	10.8	10.1	10.2	10.0	10.6	9.7	9.6	10.4	12.5	13.9	13.0	12.5	13.1	10.7	7.8	5.7	3.4	2.0
W06000011	Swansea	244.5	13.2	13.4	12.8	15.4	21.7	17.0	15.0	14.2	14.3	15.8	16.1	14.9	13.5	14.2	11.2	8.7	6.8	4.0	2.3
W06000012	Neath Port Talbot	141.7	7.7	7.9	7.5	8.0	7.8	8.5	9.0	8.6	8.6	9.9	10.4	9.9	9.0	9.1	7.0	5.3	3.8	2.4	1.3
W06000013	Bridgend	143.4	8.1	8.2	7.8	8.2	7.7	9.0	8.8	8.8	9.2	10.5	10.7	9.5	8.5	8.9	7.1	5.5	3.8	2.2	1.1
W06000014	Vale of Glamorgan	128.9	7.1	7.9	7.2	7.6	6.7	7.2	7.1	7.9	8.2	9.2	9.3	8.8	8.1	8.2	6.6	4.9	3.4	2.2	1.3
W06000015	Cardiff	361.2	22.5	22.1	18.4	23.7	42.5	31.5	27.1	23.1	21.0	21.5	21.6	19.5	16.4	15.5	11.3	9.1	7.2	4.5	2.8
W06000016	Rhondda Cynon Taf	238.2	14.1	14.6	13.2	14.0	15.9	16.7	14.8	14.1	14.2	16.7	16.7	15.0	13.3	14.5	11.2	8.2	5.8	3.2	1.9
W06000024	Merthyr Tydfil	59.7	3.7	3.7	3.2	3.4	3.6	4.2	4.2	3.5	3.4	4.2	4.3	4.0	3.4	3.5	2.6	2.1	1.4	0.8	0.5
W06000018	Caerphilly	180.5	10.5	11.2	10.4	10.4	10.5	11.6	11.5	11.1	11.1	13.1	12.9	11.6	10.5	11.1	8.6	6.3	4.4	2.3	1.2
W06000019	Blaenau Gwent	69.6	3.8	4.0	3.5	4.0	4.3	4.9	4.3	3.9	4.1	5.3	5.2	4.6	4.0	4.3	3.5	2.6	1.8	0.9	0.6
W06000020	Torfaen	92.0	5.3	5.6	5.1	5.4	5.4	6.1	5.6	5.1	5.1	6.5	6.8	6.2	5.4	5.8	4.5	3.3	2.5	1.4	0.9
W06000021	Monmouthshire	93.3	4.3	5.0	5.0	5.3	4.4	4.6	4.1	4.5	5.3	7.2	8.0	6.7	6.3	6.9	5.5	4.0	3.1	1.9	1.1
W06000022	Newport	149.5	9.9	9.8	8.7	9.0	9.3	10.3	10.0	9.5	8.9	10.6	10.6	9.3	7.5	8.0	6.2	4.9	3.6	2.1	1.2

MYE2: Population estimates: Persons by selected age groups for local authorities in the UK, mid-2016

Thousands

Code	Name	All ages	Age groups (years)																		
			0-4	5-9	10-14	15-19	20-24	25-29	30-34	35-39	40-44	45-49	50-54	55-59	60-64	65-69	70-74	75-79	80-84	85-89	90
S92000003	SCOTLAND	5,404.7	287.2	298.9	274.4	298.7	364.0	374.1	351.9	327.8	337.6	392.3	406.7	370.8	321.6	317.5	239.0	186.8	136.4	78.0	41.1
S12000033	Aberdeen City	229.8	12.2	11.1	9.1	11.5	21.2	24.7	20.2	16.1	14.1	14.3	14.8	13.6	11.8	11.1	7.7	6.4	5.0	3.1	1.6
S12000034	Aberdeenshire	262.2	15.0	16.5	14.6	14.2	13.5	13.8	15.9	16.9	18.2	20.4	20.6	18.2	16.5	16.3	11.5	8.6	6.0	3.5	1.9
S12000041	Angus	116.5	5.8	6.2	6.1	6.5	6.3	5.9	6.3	6.3	7.1	8.3	9.1	8.4	7.7	8.4	6.3	4.9	3.5	2.1	1.2
S12000035	Argyll and Bute	87.1	3.8	4.3	4.3	4.8	4.9	4.4	3.9	4.2	5.0	6.2	7.0	6.7	6.3	6.9	5.3	4.1	2.8	1.6	0.9
S12000036	City of Edinburgh	507.2	26.5	25.7	21.0	25.1	45.6	53.4	45.4	37.3	32.8	32.4	32.3	29.2	24.4	23.5	16.8	13.7	10.9	7.0	3.9
S12000005	Clackmannanshire	51.4	2.9	2.9	2.7	2.9	3.0	2.7	2.8	2.9	3.3	4.2	4.1	3.7	3.2	3.4	2.5	1.8	1.1	0.7	0.3
S12000006	Dumfries and Galloway	149.5	6.8	7.8	7.5	7.7	7.8	7.5	7.3	6.9	8.1	10.8	12.1	11.4	10.9	11.3	9.1	7.0	5.1	2.9	1.5
S12000042	Dundee City	148.3	8.0	7.6	6.9	8.8	14.2	13.9	10.6	8.3	7.6	9.1	9.9	9.6	7.6	7.8	5.7	4.9	3.9	2.4	1.2
S12000008	East Ayrshire	122.2	6.7	6.8	6.4	6.7	7.2	7.3	7.0	6.8	7.7	9.5	9.7	8.8	7.7	7.8	5.9	4.5	3.1	1.7	0.9
S12000045	East Dunbartonshire	107.5	5.5	6.1	6.0	6.2	6.2	5.3	4.9	5.6	6.5	8.0	8.7	8.2	7.0	6.9	5.4	4.6	3.4	2.0	1.0
S12000010	East Lothian	104.1	5.7	6.4	5.7	5.8	6.1	5.3	5.5	5.9	6.8	8.1	8.3	7.7	6.3	6.4	4.9	3.8	2.8	1.6	0.8
S12000011	East Renfrewshire	93.8	5.3	6.2	6.0	5.9	5.3	4.5	4.1	5.3	6.0	7.0	7.3	6.7	5.8	5.4	4.2	3.5	2.8	1.6	0.9
S12000014	Falkirk	159.4	8.7	9.5	8.6	8.7	9.1	9.2	9.9	10.1	11.2	12.7	12.5	10.9	9.3	9.6	7.0	5.5	3.9	2.0	1.1
S12000015	Fife	370.3	19.8	21.3	19.3	21.1	24.4	21.6	21.1	21.3	23.0	27.4	27.8	25.9	22.7	23.9	18.2	13.4	9.6	5.5	3.0
S12000046	Glasgow City	615.1	34.9	31.3	26.7	33.1	56.0	64.4	54.6	43.2	37.3	41.2	42.1	37.0	29.6	25.8	19.0	16.0	12.3	6.9	3.7
S12000017	Highland	234.8	11.7	13.0	12.7	12.8	11.8	12.3	13.3	13.2	14.2	17.1	18.6	17.6	16.3	16.2	12.3	9.0	6.6	3.9	2.0
S12000018	Inverclyde	79.2	3.8	4.2	4.0	4.4	4.8	4.6	4.5	4.3	4.6	5.9	6.7	6.2	5.0	5.0	3.9	3.0	2.2	1.3	0.7
S12000019	Midlothian	88.6	5.7	5.4	4.9	5.0	5.0	5.1	5.4	5.5	5.6	6.6	6.7	6.2	5.3	5.5	4.1	3.0	2.1	1.2	0.6
S12000020	Moray	96.1	4.8	5.5	5.1	5.5	5.5	5.5	5.7	5.2	6.1	7.3	7.3	6.6	6.1	6.2	4.8	3.7	2.7	1.6	0.8
S12000013	Na h-Eileanan Siar	26.9	1.2	1.4	1.4	1.3	1.2	1.2	1.3	1.4	1.6	2.1	2.1	2.0	2.0	2.1	1.5	1.3	0.9	0.5	0.3
S12000021	North Ayrshire	135.9	6.8	7.5	7.3	7.8	8.1	7.4	6.9	6.8	8.1	10.0	10.8	10.0	9.1	9.4	7.3	5.5	3.9	2.0	1.1
S12000044	North Lanarkshire	339.4	19.0	20.7	19.7	20.3	20.8	20.8	21.7	21.5	22.7	26.3	26.5	23.1	19.7	18.6	14.0	10.9	7.5	3.8	1.7
S12000023	Orkney Islands	21.9	1.0	1.2	1.1	1.1	1.1	1.2	1.1	1.1	1.3	1.6	1.8	1.7	1.5	1.5	1.3	1.0	0.6	0.4	0.2
S12000024	Perth and Kinross	150.7	7.2	7.9	7.7	8.5	8.3	7.9	8.6	8.2	8.8	10.9	12.0	10.8	10.1	10.3	8.0	6.3	4.7	2.9	1.6
S12000038	Renfrewshire	175.9	9.3	9.6	9.2	9.9	10.9	11.3	10.9	10.3	10.7	13.5	14.1	13.0	10.5	10.3	7.8	6.2	4.5	2.5	1.3
S12000026	Scottish Borders	114.5	5.8	6.0	6.0	6.1	5.6	4.9	5.3	5.4	6.9	8.8	9.4	8.9	8.2	8.8	6.7	5.1	3.5	2.1	1.1
S12000027	Shetland Islands	23.2	1.3	1.4	1.3	1.3	1.3	1.4	1.3	1.4	1.5	1.7	1.8	1.6	1.5	1.5	1.1	0.8	0.5	0.3	0.2
S12000028	South Ayrshire	112.5	5.2	5.8	5.6	6.1	6.0	5.7	5.4	5.6	6.5	8.0	8.8	8.6	8.0	8.3	6.8	5.1	3.7	2.1	1.2
S12000029	South Lanarkshire	317.1	17.0	17.8	16.7	17.7	18.4	17.7	18.8	19.3	20.6	24.6	25.2	23.6	20.4	18.9	14.4	11.2	8.2	4.5	2.2
S12000030	Stirling	93.8	4.4	4.9	5.1	6.5	7.9	6.2	4.8	5.0	5.6	6.9	7.2	6.3	5.4	5.5	4.2	3.4	2.4	1.3	0.7
S12000039	West Dunbartonshire	89.9	4.9	5.2	4.7	4.9	5.7	5.8	5.7	5.1	5.2	6.7	7.3	6.7	5.7	5.3	3.9	3.0	2.2	1.2	0.6
S12000040	West Lothian	180.1	10.6	11.8	10.8	10.5	10.6	10.9	11.7	11.5	12.7	14.5	14.1	12.1	9.8	9.7	7.3	5.4	3.5	1.8	0.9
N92000002	NORTHERN IRELAND	1,862.1	124.8	127.5	113.3	118.4	118.7	124.0	123.8	119.6	120.2	130.5	130.8	115.8	96.9	89.5	76.6	55.5	39.7	23.7	12.7
N09000001	Antrim and Newtownabbey	141.0	9.2	9.9	8.8	8.9	8.5	8.8	9.0	9.4	9.5	10.1	10.1	8.7	7.3	6.9	5.9	4.3	3.0	1.8	0.9
N09000011	Ards and North Down	159.6	9.1	10.0	9.2	9.1	8.0	9.0	9.2	9.5	10.2	11.6	11.6	10.9	9.7	10.2	8.8	5.6	4.0	2.5	1.4
N09000002	Armagh City, Banbridge & Craigavon	210.3	15.4	15.6	13.4	12.9	12.4	14.4	14.4	14.1	14.0	14.8	14.5	12.6	10.3	9.6	8.3	6.0	4.1	2.4	1.3
N09000003	Belfast	339.6	23.0	21.9	18.4	22.2	29.2	26.7	26.0	22.5	20.3	21.3	22.4	20.3	16.0	13.6	12.0	9.4	7.3	4.7	2.5
N09000004	Causeway Coast and Glens	143.5	8.8	9.3	8.7	9.4	9.1	8.5	8.4	8.6	9.3	10.5	10.5	9.3	8.0	7.5	6.6	4.8	3.2	1.9	1.0
N09000005	Derry City and Strabane	150.1	10.6	10.6	9.5	10.6	9.7	10.0	9.9	9.3	9.8	11.1	10.9	9.0	7.6	7.0	5.6	4.0	2.7	1.4	0.7
N09000006	Fermanagh and Omagh	115.8	7.7	8.2	7.6	7.6	6.3	7.3	7.4	7.5	7.6	8.0	8.1	7.4	6.6	5.9	4.7	3.4	2.4	1.5	0.8
N09000007	Lisburn and Castlereagh	141.2	8.9	9.4	8.2	8.4	7.9	8.7	9.3	9.3	9.2	10.4	10.7	9.3	7.4	6.9	6.2	4.7	3.4	2.0	1.0
N09000008	Mid and East Antrim	137.8	8.1	8.5	8.2	8.3	8.0	8.4	8.2	8.2	8.8	10.4	10.4	9.1	7.9	7.5	6.6	4.7	3.4	2.1	1.1
N09000009	Mid Ulster	145.4	10.9	11.0	9.7	9.4	9.1	10.4	10.4	10.0	10.0	9.8	9.4	8.2	6.9	6.2	5.2	3.7	2.6	1.6	0.9
N09000010	Newry, Mourne and Down	177.8	13.0	13.2	11.6	11.8	10.6	11.8	11.7	11.2	11.3	12.5	12.3	10.9	9.3	8.2	6.7	4.9	3.6	2.0	1.1

MYE2: Population estimates: Males by selected age groups for local authorities in the UK, mid-2016

Thousands

Code	Name	All ages	0-4	5-9	10-14	15-19	20-24	25-29	30-34	35-39	40-44	45-49	50-54	55-59	60-64	65-69	70-74	75-79	80-84	85-89	90
K02000001	UNITED KINGDOM	32,377.7	2,057.9	2,066.9	1,856.6	1,939.6	2,176.4	2,274.8	2,199.3	2,080.1	2,068.9	2,277.0	2,281.8	2,007.2	1,731.3	1,764.1	1,360.3	989.4	694.0	380.5	171.7
K03000001	GREAT BRITAIN	31,462.5	1,993.9	2,001.6	1,798.5	1,878.6	2,115.5	2,213.0	2,138.5	2,022.2	2,010.2	2,213.3	2,217.3	1,950.2	1,683.0	1,720.6	1,324.1	964.3	677.5	372.0	168.1
K04000001	ENGLAND AND WALES	28,835.0	1,846.3	1,849.4	1,658.1	1,726.0	1,933.8	2,026.9	1,966.2	1,860.9	1,845.3	2,023.8	2,019.9	1,769.5	1,526.6	1,567.1	1,212.2	881.8	621.3	343.7	156.1
E92000001	ENGLAND	27,300.9	1,757.6	1,755.7	1,572.4	1,631.8	1,824.1	1,924.2	1,874.9	1,773.8	1,756.4	1,919.8	1,911.6	1,670.4	1,436.6	1,470.6	1,137.4	827.8	584.2	324.0	147.4
E12000001	NORTH EAST	1,294.0	76.6	78.5	71.4	77.6	95.9	87.6	79.9	73.7	75.1	88.3	94.8	87.6	76.7	77.8	57.6	43.1	29.9	15.5	6.4
E06000047	County Durham	256.4	14.4	15.1	13.6	15.4	18.9	15.5	15.3	13.9	14.6	18.5	19.6	17.3	15.8	16.5	12.6	9.1	6.0	3.1	1.3
E06000005	Darlington	51.8	3.3	3.3	3.2	3.0	2.7	3.2	3.1	3.2	3.2	3.8	4.0	3.4	3.1	3.1	2.4	1.8	1.3	0.6	0.3
E06000001	Hartlepool	45.3	2.8	3.0	2.7	2.8	2.9	3.0	2.7	2.4	2.6	3.1	3.5	3.2	2.6	2.7	1.9	1.4	1.1	0.5	0.2
E06000002	Middlesbrough	69.3	5.1	4.7	4.1	4.6	6.5	5.5	4.5	3.7	3.9	4.1	4.6	4.3	3.6	3.4	2.4	1.9	1.4	0.7	0.2
E06000057	Northumberland	155.0	7.8	8.7	8.6	8.6	8.0	8.3	7.9	8.3	8.9	10.7	12.1	11.8	10.9	11.6	8.9	6.3	4.3	2.3	1.0
E06000003	Redcar and Cleveland	65.8	4.0	4.0	3.8	3.8	4.1	3.9	3.6	3.3	3.6	4.5	5.1	4.6	4.0	4.4	3.5	2.7	1.7	0.9	0.4
E06000004	Stockton-on-Tees	96.5	6.3	6.5	5.8	5.9	6.5	6.5	6.3	5.6	5.7	6.8	6.9	6.4	5.5	5.3	3.9	2.9	2.0	1.1	0.4
E11000007	Tyne and Wear (Met County)	553.9	32.9	33.2	29.6	33.5	46.3	41.8	36.5	33.3	32.5	36.9	39.1	36.6	31.1	30.9	21.9	16.9	12.1	6.3	2.5
E08000037	Gateshead	99.7	5.9	5.9	5.2	6.0	6.5	6.6	7.1	6.5	6.1	6.9	7.2	6.7	5.5	5.7	4.2	3.5	2.4	1.2	0.5
E08000021	Newcastle upon Tyne	148.4	8.8	8.7	7.4	10.1	20.4	14.8	10.6	8.4	8.1	8.5	8.6	8.1	6.8	6.6	4.5	3.4	2.6	1.5	0.7
E08000022	North Tyneside	98.4	5.9	6.2	5.7	5.5	5.1	5.7	6.1	6.7	6.5	7.1	7.6	6.8	6.1	6.0	4.3	3.1	2.3	1.2	0.5
E08000023	South Tyneside	72.2	4.3	4.3	4.0	4.1	4.5	4.8	4.3	4.1	4.1	5.1	5.7	5.4	4.6	4.5	3.1	2.5	1.7	0.9	0.3
E08000024	Sunderland	135.2	8.0	8.0	7.4	7.9	9.7	9.9	8.3	7.6	7.8	9.4	10.0	9.7	8.3	8.1	5.7	4.4	3.0	1.5	0.5
E12000002	NORTH WEST	3,563.2	227.3	227.0	206.5	215.6	243.1	249.1	232.8	214.2	218.4	251.3	253.6	226.2	195.9	203.6	152.3	112.7	75.8	40.5	17.5
E06000008	Blackburn with Darwen	74.4	5.7	5.6	5.3	5.2	4.9	4.9	5.3	5.0	4.8	5.3	4.8	4.3	3.7	3.6	2.4	1.8	1.2	0.6	0.2
E06000009	Blackpool	69.2	4.4	4.1	3.8	4.0	4.1	4.5	4.0	3.8	4.1	5.1	5.6	4.8	4.0	4.2	3.4	2.5	1.6	0.9	0.4
E06000049	Cheshire East	184.9	10.6	11.2	10.5	10.4	9.4	9.5	9.5	10.2	12.0	14.1	14.8	12.9	11.3	12.5	9.8	7.1	4.9	2.8	1.3
E06000050	Cheshire West and Chester	163.7	9.8	9.6	9.1	9.5	10.0	9.2	9.2	9.1	10.3	12.0	12.5	11.0	9.9	10.7	8.2	6.1	4.0	2.3	1.0
E06000006	Halton	62.2	4.1	4.2	3.8	3.7	3.7	4.0	4.0	3.6	3.9	4.5	4.5	4.1	3.8	4.0	2.6	1.8	1.1	0.6	0.3
E06000007	Warrington	103.7	6.4	6.5	6.2	6.1	5.9	6.7	6.7	6.4	7.2	7.9	8.3	6.7	5.6	5.7	4.5	3.3	2.2	1.0	0.4
E10000006	Cumbria	246.0	12.8	13.6	13.2	13.5	13.7	13.3	12.9	12.6	13.9	18.0	19.4	18.2	16.4	18.2	14.0	10.4	6.8	3.6	1.6
E07000026	Allerdale	47.9	2.3	2.7	2.6	2.7	2.6	2.6	2.5	2.4	2.6	3.7	3.8	3.5	3.2	3.6	2.7	2.1	1.3	0.7	0.3
E07000027	Barrow-in-Furness	33.3	1.9	1.9	1.9	1.9	2.0	2.1	1.9	1.7	1.9	2.5	2.6	2.3	2.0	2.2	1.8	1.3	0.8	0.4	0.2
E07000028	Carlisle	52.9	3.2	3.1	2.9	2.7	3.2	3.0	3.1	3.1	3.3	3.8	4.0	3.9	3.3	3.4	2.6	1.9	1.3	0.7	0.4
E07000029	Copeland	34.8	1.9	1.9	1.8	1.8	2.1	2.0	1.9	1.8	1.9	2.5	2.8	2.6	2.3	2.5	1.9	1.4	0.9	0.4	0.2
E07000030	Eden	26.1	1.2	1.4	1.4	1.4	1.3	1.4	1.2	1.2	1.4	1.9	2.1	2.0	1.9	2.1	1.7	1.2	0.8	0.4	0.2
E07000031	South Lakeland	51.0	2.2	2.6	2.7	2.9	2.5	2.4	2.2	2.4	2.7	3.6	4.0	3.8	3.7	4.3	3.4	2.5	1.7	1.0	0.4
E11000001	Greater Manchester (Met County)	1,379.8	95.8	94.2	83.3	84.9	100.0	108.3	100.7	90.5	86.9	95.9	92.7	80.3	67.8	68.5	50.1	36.9	24.2	12.9	5.8
E08000001	Bolton	140.4	10.0	9.9	8.9	9.2	8.8	9.4	9.2	8.5	8.9	10.2	9.6	8.3	7.3	7.6	5.7	4.2	2.6	1.3	0.7
E08000002	Bury	92.4	6.4	6.4	5.9	5.5	5.3	5.9	5.8	5.7	5.9	6.8	6.8	5.8	4.9	5.3	4.0	2.8	1.8	1.0	0.5
E08000003	Manchester	274.0	20.2	17.9	14.7	18.0	33.7	33.6	26.9	20.9	16.0	15.5	13.5	11.4	9.3	8.2	5.1	4.1	2.8	1.4	0.7
E08000004	Oldham	114.3	8.6	8.5	8.2	7.8	7.1	7.9	7.6	6.9	7.2	8.2	7.4	6.7	5.7	5.7	4.1	3.2	1.9	1.0	0.5
E08000005	Rochdale	106.4	7.8	7.7	6.8	6.9	6.8	7.3	7.0	6.5	6.6	7.5	7.2	6.5	5.8	5.6	4.0	2.9	1.9	1.0	0.5
E08000006	Salford	125.0	8.9	8.4	6.8	6.9	9.6	11.6	11.2	8.8	7.5	8.0	8.2	7.1	5.6	5.6	4.1	3.1	2.0	1.1	0.5
E08000007	Stockport	141.9	9.1	9.4	8.5	8.1	7.2	8.3	8.3	9.1	9.2	10.3	10.7	9.5	8.3	8.4	6.3	4.9	3.6	2.0	0.8
E08000008	Tameside	109.5	7.4	7.3	6.4	6.3	6.6	7.2	6.9	6.6	6.9	8.1	8.4	7.4	6.1	6.3	4.7	3.2	2.1	1.0	0.5
E08000009	Trafford	114.6	7.7	8.3	7.7	6.9	5.7	6.5	7.3	8.0	8.2	8.6	8.6	7.2	6.0	5.8	4.3	3.3	2.5	1.4	0.6

MYE2: Population estimates: Males by selected age groups for local authorities in the UK, mid-2016

Thousands

Code	Name	All ages	0-4	5-9	10-14	15-19	20-24	25-29	30-34	35-39	40-44	45-49	50-54	55-59	60-64	65-69	70-74	75-79	80-84	85-89	90
											Age groups (years)										
E08000010	Wigan	161.3	9.7	10.4	9.4	9.3	9.3	10.5	10.3	9.6	10.5	12.7	12.4	10.3	8.8	9.9	7.8	5.3	3.1	1.6	0.6
E10000017	Lancashire	590.0	34.9	36.8	34.0	36.5	40.1	36.9	34.0	32.4	35.7	42.1	43.0	38.4	34.2	37.0	28.7	20.7	14.0	7.4	3.2
E07000117	Burnley	43.2	3.0	3.0	2.7	2.6	2.7	2.8	2.9	2.5	2.6	3.1	2.9	2.8	2.5	2.6	1.9	1.3	0.8	0.5	0.2
E07000118	Chorley	57.3	3.4	3.5	3.3	3.1	2.9	3.6	3.6	3.5	4.1	4.4	3.0	3.8	3.3	3.7	2.9	1.9	1.2	0.5	0.3
E07000119	Fylde	38.2	1.7	2.1	2.0	2.1	1.7	1.9	2.0	1.9	2.2	2.8	3.0	2.9	2.6	2.9	2.5	1.7	1.3	0.7	0.3
E07000120	Hyndburn	39.7	2.7	2.7	2.6	2.4	2.4	2.6	2.5	2.3	2.5	3.0	2.7	2.4	2.2	2.4	1.8	1.2	0.8	0.5	0.2
E07000121	Lancaster	69.7	4.0	4.0	3.6	5.0	7.7	4.5	3.7	3.6	3.7	4.5	4.6	4.2	3.8	4.2	3.3	2.5	1.7	0.9	0.4
E07000122	Pendle	44.8	3.3	3.2	2.7	2.6	2.4	3.0	3.2	2.9	2.8	3.0	2.9	2.8	2.5	2.8	2.0	1.4	0.9	0.5	0.2
E07000123	Preston	71.4	4.7	4.8	4.1	4.7	7.2	5.8	4.8	4.5	4.4	4.8	4.8	4.0	3.4	3.2	2.3	1.8	1.3	0.6	0.3
E07000124	Ribble Valley	28.9	1.3	1.7	1.8	1.9	1.4	1.5	1.2	1.3	1.8	2.3	2.5	2.2	1.9	2.0	1.6	1.1	0.8	0.4	0.2
E07000125	Rossendale	34.4	2.2	2.3	2.2	1.9	1.8	2.0	2.0	2.0	2.3	2.7	2.7	2.3	2.1	2.2	1.5	1.0	0.7	0.3	0.2
E07000126	South Ribble	53.8	3.2	3.4	3.0	3.1	2.8	3.2	3.2	3.0	3.6	4.0	4.2	3.5	3.3	3.4	2.7	2.0	1.2	0.7	0.3
E07000127	West Lancashire	55.0	2.9	3.2	3.2	3.8	4.2	3.3	2.5	2.5	3.1	3.9	4.2	3.8	3.2	3.5	2.9	2.2	1.4	0.7	0.3
E07000128	Wyre	53.6	2.6	2.9	2.9	3.2	2.8	2.8	2.4	2.6	2.8	3.7	4.1	3.8	3.6	4.1	3.5	2.7	1.9	1.0	0.4
E11000002	Merseyside (Met County)	689.2	42.9	41.2	37.2	41.9	51.3	51.8	46.4	40.6	39.5	46.3	48.1	45.4	39.2	39.2	28.6	22.1	15.8	8.4	3.3
E08000011	Knowsley	70.5	5.1	4.8	4.2	4.5	4.8	4.9	4.4	3.7	3.8	4.7	5.3	5.2	4.2	3.7	2.5	2.1	1.5	0.8	0.3
E08000012	Liverpool	242.7	15.0	13.4	11.5	15.2	25.6	23.7	20.6	16.8	13.5	15.1	14.6	13.7	11.9	11.1	7.6	6.0	4.4	2.2	0.9
E08000014	Sefton	132.4	7.6	7.9	7.3	7.7	7.4	8.3	7.3	6.8	7.3	9.2	10.1	9.8	8.5	8.7	6.5	5.2	3.9	2.1	0.9
E08000013	St. Helens	87.7	5.3	5.3	4.9	5.2	5.0	5.6	5.4	4.9	5.6	6.3	6.6	5.9	5.2	5.6	4.3	3.2	2.1	1.0	0.4
E08000015	Wirral	155.9	9.9	9.9	9.3	9.3	8.4	9.4	8.7	8.5	9.3	11.0	11.5	10.7	9.5	10.2	7.6	5.5	3.9	2.3	0.9
E12000003	**YORKSHIRE AND THE HUMBER**	2,678.2	169.5	171.4	154.8	164.4	197.0	185.1	170.7	160.0	165.4	188.5	188.5	168.3	146.8	150.6	113.1	83.1	57.5	30.3	13.3
E06000011	East Riding of Yorkshire	165.7	8.4	9.2	8.9	9.7	8.6	7.7	7.7	8.1	10.0	12.2	13.3	12.2	11.1	13.1	9.9	7.3	4.9	2.6	1.1
E06000010	Kingston upon Hull, City of	130.9	9.2	8.6	7.1	7.6	11.4	11.9	9.7	8.3	8.3	8.4	8.6	7.6	6.5	6.3	4.1	3.2	2.3	1.2	0.5
E06000012	North East Lincolnshire	78.5	4.9	5.2	4.6	4.5	4.6	5.4	4.8	4.3	4.8	5.5	5.8	5.2	4.6	4.7	3.5	2.6	2.0	1.0	0.4
E06000013	North Lincolnshire	84.6	4.8	5.4	4.9	4.7	4.7	5.1	5.2	4.8	5.1	6.1	6.5	5.9	5.3	5.6	4.1	3.0	2.0	1.1	0.4
E06000014	York	101.4	5.3	5.6	4.9	6.5	11.2	8.4	6.8	6.1	6.0	6.6	6.6	5.9	5.0	5.2	4.1	3.1	2.2	1.2	0.6
E10000023	North Yorkshire	300.5	15.7	17.2	16.7	18.0	14.6	17.6	15.5	15.3	17.3	21.8	23.6	22.0	19.8	21.5	16.8	11.9	8.4	4.6	2.0
E07000163	Craven	27.3	1.3	1.5	1.6	1.6	1.2	1.3	1.1	1.3	1.5	2.1	2.1	2.1	2.1	2.1	1.7	1.2	0.8	0.5	0.2
E07000164	Hambleton	44.5	2.2	2.4	2.4	2.5	2.0	2.6	2.2	2.2	2.4	3.2	3.7	3.3	3.0	3.4	2.7	1.9	1.3	0.7	0.3
E07000165	Harrogate	78.1	4.1	4.7	4.7	5.3	2.8	4.1	4.1	4.3	5.0	6.0	6.4	5.7	4.8	5.1	4.0	3.0	2.2	1.2	0.6
E07000166	Richmondshire	29.1	1.5	1.5	1.5	1.9	2.3	3.1	2.0	1.6	1.6	1.9	1.9	1.8	1.6	1.7	1.3	1.0	0.6	0.3	0.1
E07000167	Ryedale	26.4	1.3	1.4	1.3	1.6	1.3	1.2	1.1	1.2	1.4	1.9	2.1	2.0	1.9	2.2	1.7	1.1	0.9	0.5	0.2
E07000168	Scarborough	52.6	2.7	2.8	2.8	2.8	2.9	2.9	2.6	2.3	2.8	3.5	3.9	3.9	3.8	4.2	3.3	2.4	1.6	0.9	0.4
E07000169	Selby	42.7	2.5	2.7	2.4	2.4	2.1	2.4	2.4	2.5	2.7	3.3	3.5	3.2	2.6	2.8	2.1	1.3	0.9	0.5	0.2
E11000003	South Yorkshire (Met County)	686.1	42.2	43.3	38.7	42.3	56.2	49.7	44.2	40.8	41.4	48.6	47.8	42.8	36.3	36.5	28.8	21.2	14.3	7.5	3.5
E08000016	Barnsley	119.3	7.3	7.5	6.6	6.7	7.1	7.6	7.7	6.7	7.3	9.2	9.0	8.2	7.1	7.1	5.6	3.9	2.6	1.3	0.6
E08000017	Doncaster	152.5	9.6	9.9	8.7	8.6	9.0	10.5	10.5	9.4	9.5	10.6	11.2	10.3	8.8	8.7	6.7	4.7	3.4	1.7	0.7
E08000018	Rotherham	129.0	8.0	8.4	7.6	7.7	7.6	8.1	7.8	7.1	7.9	9.7	9.8	8.7	7.5	7.7	6.1	4.5	2.8	1.4	0.6
E08000019	Sheffield	285.4	17.2	17.5	15.8	19.3	32.5	23.4	18.3	17.6	16.7	19.0	17.9	15.6	12.8	13.0	10.4	8.1	5.6	3.1	1.5
E11000006	West Yorkshire (Met County)	1,130.4	79.1	77.0	69.0	71.1	85.7	79.3	76.7	72.3	72.6	79.3	76.1	66.7	58.1	57.8	41.7	30.8	21.3	11.0	4.8
E08000032	Bradford	262.5	20.6	20.8	19.0	18.0	16.8	17.4	18.2	18.3	17.6	17.3	16.1	14.8	13.2	12.1	7.9	6.4	4.5	2.4	1.1
E08000033	Calderdale	102.6	6.8	6.7	6.2	6.2	6.2	6.2	6.2	6.3	6.7	8.0	8.0	6.9	6.1	6.1	4.5	3.1	1.9	1.0	0.5
E08000034	Kirklees	215.7	14.4	14.6	13.5	13.5	14.8	14.3	13.8	13.5	14.0	16.1	14.9	13.2	11.5	11.8	8.6	6.2	4.1	2.1	0.9
E08000035	Leeds	383.7	26.5	24.6	21.0	24.2	39.1	30.8	27.6	24.9	23.8	25.1	24.4	20.5	17.6	17.9	13.1	9.9	7.2	3.8	1.6
E08000036	Wakefield	165.9	10.7	10.3	9.4	9.2	9.5	10.7	11.0	9.4	10.5	12.8	12.7	11.3	9.7	9.9	7.6	5.4	3.6	1.7	0.7

MYE2: Population estimates: Males by selected age groups for local authorities in the UK, mid-2016

Thousands

Code	Name	All ages	0-4	5-9	10-14	15-19	20-24	25-29	30-34	35-39	40-44	45-49	50-54	55-59	60-64	65-69	70-74	75-79	80-84	85-89	90
E12000004	EAST MIDLANDS	2,335.3	142.3	145.2	131.9	143.5	166.7	151.4	141.8	137.3	145.5	167.1	169.2	148.9	131.7	138.5	107.4	75.0	51.7	27.9	12.4
E06000015	Derby	127.1	8.8	9.1	7.9	8.2	10.0	9.9	8.8	7.9	7.9	8.7	8.4	7.1	5.8	5.7	4.5	3.4	2.6	1.5	0.6
E06000016	Leicester	174.4	13.3	12.2	10.7	12.2	19.3	15.9	13.5	12.2	10.6	9.9	9.7	8.9	7.8	6.5	4.3	3.2	2.4	1.3	0.6
E06000018	Nottingham	164.4	10.8	10.1	8.6	12.5	25.4	15.6	12.2	10.7	9.3	9.3	9.0	7.6	6.2	6.1	4.0	3.0	2.3	1.3	0.5
E06000017	Rutland	20.0	0.9	1.0	1.1	1.4	1.1	1.2	1.1	1.1	1.2	1.4	1.4	1.3	1.2	1.4	1.1	0.8	0.6	0.3	0.2
E10000007	Derbyshire	386.7	21.0	22.3	21.3	22.2	21.3	22.4	21.3	20.9	24.6	30.4	30.9	27.3	24.4	26.0	20.4	13.9	9.2	4.9	2.2
E07000032	Amber Valley	61.3	3.3	3.4	3.4	3.4	3.2	3.4	3.3	3.3	4.0	4.9	4.9	4.3	4.0	4.4	3.3	2.2	1.4	0.8	0.4
E07000033	Bolsover	38.6	2.2	2.3	2.1	2.2	2.3	2.4	2.4	2.2	2.4	3.1	3.0	2.6	2.3	2.4	2.0	1.3	0.9	0.4	0.2
E07000034	Chesterfield	51.3	2.8	2.9	2.6	3.0	3.1	3.1	3.2	2.9	3.3	3.9	4.0	3.6	3.2	3.3	2.5	1.8	1.2	0.6	0.3
E07000035	Derbyshire Dales	35.2	1.4	1.8	2.0	2.0	1.6	1.7	1.4	1.5	2.1	2.7	3.0	2.8	2.6	2.9	2.3	1.5	1.1	0.5	0.3
E07000036	Erewash	56.4	3.4	3.5	3.1	3.1	3.2	3.6	3.1	3.2	3.6	4.4	4.6	3.8	3.2	3.3	2.7	2.0	1.4	0.7	0.3
E07000037	High Peak	45.2	2.4	2.6	2.5	2.7	2.6	2.7	2.4	2.3	2.8	3.7	3.8	3.4	3.0	3.1	2.2	1.5	1.0	0.5	0.2
E07000038	North East Derbyshire	49.1	2.4	2.7	2.5	2.6	2.7	2.6	2.5	2.4	3.0	3.7	3.8	3.6	3.3	3.6	3.0	2.2	1.4	0.7	0.4
E07000039	South Derbyshire	49.6	3.0	3.1	3.1	3.1	2.6	2.9	3.0	3.1	3.4	4.1	3.8	3.2	2.9	3.0	2.3	1.5	0.9	0.5	0.2
E10000018	Leicestershire	336.8	18.9	20.2	19.2	21.6	24.1	18.7	18.3	18.7	21.2	25.2	25.3	22.4	19.9	21.1	16.3	11.4	7.9	4.3	1.9
E07000129	Blaby	47.8	2.9	3.0	2.9	2.9	2.6	2.7	2.8	2.8	3.1	3.7	3.6	3.3	2.7	2.9	2.3	1.6	1.2	0.6	0.2
E07000130	Charnwood	89.4	4.9	5.0	4.6	6.6	10.7	5.7	5.2	4.9	5.3	5.9	5.9	5.3	4.8	4.9	3.6	2.7	1.9	1.1	0.5
E07000131	Harborough	44.7	2.4	2.8	2.8	2.8	2.1	2.2	2.0	2.4	3.0	3.7	3.7	3.2	2.7	3.0	2.4	1.6	1.1	0.6	0.3
E07000132	Hinckley and Bosworth	54.2	3.1	3.2	3.1	3.1	2.6	3.1	3.0	3.2	3.5	4.2	4.2	3.7	3.4	3.8	2.8	1.9	1.3	0.7	0.3
E07000133	Melton	25.0	1.4	1.5	1.4	1.4	1.2	1.4	1.2	1.3	1.5	2.0	2.2	1.7	1.7	1.8	1.3	0.9	0.6	0.3	0.2
E07000134	North West Leicestershire	48.8	2.7	3.0	2.9	2.9	2.6	2.7	2.7	2.8	3.4	3.9	3.9	3.3	3.1	3.1	2.5	1.6	1.0	0.5	0.2
E07000135	Oadby and Wigston	27.0	1.5	1.6	1.5	2.1	2.4	0.9	1.5	1.5	1.6	1.9	2.0	1.9	1.5	1.6	1.2	1.0	0.8	0.4	0.2
E10000019	Lincolnshire	364.4	20.7	20.8	19.1	21.0	22.0	21.6	20.4	19.1	20.9	25.0	26.7	24.3	22.6	26.0	21.5	14.9	10.1	5.5	2.4
E07000136	Boston	33.5	2.2	2.1	1.7	1.8	1.9	2.4	2.4	2.0	2.0	2.1	2.2	2.1	1.9	2.1	1.7	1.2	0.8	0.5	0.2
E07000137	East Lindsey	67.7	3.2	3.4	3.3	3.5	3.2	3.4	2.9	2.8	3.3	4.3	4.9	4.9	5.0	6.3	5.4	3.5	2.4	1.3	0.5
E07000138	Lincoln	48.1	3.1	2.8	2.2	3.3	6.3	4.0	3.7	2.9	2.7	2.9	2.9	2.6	2.2	2.2	1.7	1.1	0.8	0.5	0.2
E07000139	North Kesteven	55.5	3.0	3.1	3.1	3.1	2.7	3.2	3.2	3.0	3.4	4.2	4.3	3.6	3.3	3.8	3.3	2.5	1.6	0.8	0.4
E07000140	South Holland	45.4	2.5	2.7	2.3	2.5	2.2	2.6	2.6	2.4	2.7	3.2	3.4	3.1	2.8	3.3	2.6	2.0	1.4	0.8	0.3
E07000141	South Kesteven	68.2	4.0	4.2	3.9	3.9	3.3	3.6	3.5	3.7	4.2	5.1	5.3	4.8	4.3	4.7	3.8	2.6	1.7	1.0	0.5
E07000142	West Lindsey	45.9	2.6	2.6	2.5	2.7	2.3	2.3	2.1	2.2	2.5	3.3	3.6	3.3	3.1	3.6	2.9	1.9	1.4	0.7	0.3
E10000021	Northamptonshire	361.8	24.3	25.0	21.7	21.5	20.5	21.7	22.8	23.4	24.6	27.1	27.1	22.8	19.8	20.5	15.7	10.5	7.3	3.8	1.7
E07000150	Corby	33.6	2.6	2.6	2.0	1.9	1.8	2.3	2.6	2.5	2.2	2.4	2.5	2.1	1.7	1.5	1.1	0.8	0.5	0.3	0.1
E07000151	Daventry	40.5	2.2	2.4	2.5	2.4	2.1	2.3	2.0	2.1	2.6	3.2	3.4	2.9	2.6	2.7	2.1	1.3	0.9	0.5	0.2
E07000152	East Northamptonshire	45.2	2.5	2.9	2.8	3.0	2.1	2.3	2.3	2.5	3.0	3.6	3.6	3.0	2.7	3.0	2.3	1.5	1.1	0.5	0.3
E07000153	Kettering	48.6	3.3	3.4	3.0	2.7	2.6	3.0	3.1	3.1	3.4	3.7	3.6	3.0	2.6	2.8	2.2	1.4	1.0	0.5	0.3
E07000154	Northampton	111.3	8.5	8.0	6.3	6.5	7.7	7.8	8.6	8.4	7.9	7.6	7.6	6.1	5.1	5.3	3.8	2.7	1.9	1.0	0.5
E07000155	South Northamptonshire	44.2	2.5	2.9	2.8	2.7	2.0	2.1	2.0	2.4	3.0	3.6	3.6	3.2	2.8	2.9	2.3	1.5	1.0	0.6	0.2
E07000156	Wellingborough	38.4	2.7	2.7	2.3	2.3	2.0	2.1	2.3	2.4	2.5	2.9	2.8	2.4	2.2	2.3	1.9	1.2	0.8	0.4	0.2
E10000024	Nottinghamshire	399.7	23.5	24.5	22.3	22.9	23.0	24.4	23.3	23.4	25.3	29.9	30.7	27.3	23.9	25.2	19.7	14.0	9.5	5.0	2.3
E07000170	Ashfield	61.1	3.9	3.8	3.5	3.6	3.5	3.9	3.7	3.5	3.8	4.6	4.7	4.1	3.5	3.6	3.0	2.1	1.3	0.6	0.3
E07000171	Bassetlaw	57.2	3.2	3.2	3.1	3.4	3.3	3.2	3.2	3.1	3.4	4.3	4.6	4.1	3.7	3.8	3.0	2.1	1.4	0.8	0.3
E07000172	Broxtowe	55.6	3.2	3.3	2.8	3.1	3.9	3.9	3.6	3.4	3.6	4.1	4.0	3.6	3.2	3.5	2.7	2.0	1.3	0.8	0.4
E07000173	Gedling	56.8	3.3	3.6	3.2	3.3	3.0	3.4	3.2	3.5	3.7	4.3	4.3	3.9	3.4	3.6	2.6	2.0	1.4	0.8	0.3
E07000174	Mansfield	53.1	3.4	3.3	2.9	2.9	3.2	3.6	3.5	3.2	3.3	3.8	4.0	3.7	3.1	3.1	2.4	1.7	1.2	0.6	0.3
E07000175	Newark and Sherwood	59.1	3.4	3.6	3.3	3.4	3.3	3.4	3.2	3.2	3.6	4.5	4.6	4.1	3.6	4.0	3.2	2.2	1.5	0.7	0.3
E07000176	Rushcliffe	56.8	3.1	3.7	3.5	3.3	3.0	3.0	2.9	3.4	3.9	4.2	4.4	3.9	3.3	3.5	2.7	1.9	1.5	0.8	0.4

MYE2: Population estimates: Males by selected age groups for local authorities in the UK, mid-2016

Thousands

Code	Name	All ages	0-4	5-9	10-14	15-19	20-24	25-29	30-34	35-39	40-44	45-49	50-54	55-59	60-64	65-69	70-74	75-79	80-84	85-89	90
E12000005	**WEST MIDLANDS**	2,878.1	188.0	188.0	172.4	180.5	201.7	201.4	185.8	172.9	178.5	200.7	198.7	172.6	152.8	154.6	126.0	91.5	62.9	34.4	14.8
E06000019	Herefordshire, County of	93.9	5.0	5.4	5.0	5.0	4.7	5.8	5.5	5.2	5.3	6.5	7.2	6.5	6.1	6.6	5.4	3.9	2.8	1.5	0.6
E06000051	Shropshire	156.1	7.8	8.6	8.4	9.0	8.4	9.3	8.5	8.2	9.0	11.6	12.3	10.9	10.1	10.8	9.0	6.4	4.4	2.4	1.0
E06000021	Stoke-on-Trent	126.9	9.2	8.4	7.2	7.5	9.1	9.6	9.0	7.8	7.8	8.8	8.6	7.6	6.8	6.6	5.2	3.6	2.4	1.3	0.5
E06000020	Telford and Wrekin	86.3	5.7	6.0	5.1	5.5	5.9	5.5	5.7	5.4	5.7	6.6	6.3	5.1	4.7	4.6	3.5	2.5	1.5	0.8	0.3
E10000028	Staffordshire	431.0	23.2	24.7	24.0	25.3	26.6	27.3	24.5	24.0	27.0	32.7	32.8	28.8	25.6	27.7	22.8	16.0	10.3	5.3	2.3
E07000192	Cannock Chase	48.8	2.8	2.9	2.8	2.8	3.0	3.1	3.1	2.9	3.2	3.9	3.9	3.2	2.7	2.8	2.4	1.5	1.0	0.5	0.2
E07000193	East Staffordshire	58.6	3.8	3.6	3.5	3.3	3.4	3.8	3.7	3.7	3.7	4.4	4.4	3.9	3.2	3.3	2.6	1.8	1.3	0.7	0.3
E07000194	Lichfield	51.1	2.6	2.9	2.9	3.0	2.8	2.7	2.7	2.7	3.3	3.8	4.0	3.5	3.0	3.5	3.2	2.1	1.3	0.7	0.3
E07000195	Newcastle-under-Lyme	63.7	3.2	3.5	3.3	4.1	5.3	4.7	3.7	3.5	3.8	4.5	4.5	4.1	3.6	3.9	3.1	2.2	1.5	0.8	0.3
E07000196	South Staffordshire	55.4	2.5	2.8	2.9	3.2	3.2	3.5	2.8	2.8	3.3	4.2	4.4	4.0	3.5	3.9	3.2	2.5	1.5	0.8	0.3
E07000197	Stafford	67.3	3.5	3.8	3.5	3.7	4.4	4.5	3.8	3.7	4.1	5.0	5.1	4.4	4.0	4.3	3.6	2.6	1.7	0.9	0.4
E07000198	Staffordshire Moorlands	48.4	2.2	2.7	2.6	2.8	2.4	2.5	2.3	2.3	3.0	3.9	3.9	3.4	3.3	3.7	3.0	2.1	1.4	0.7	0.3
E07000199	Tamworth	37.8	2.4	2.6	2.3	2.4	2.1	2.5	2.4	2.3	2.5	2.9	2.6	2.3	2.2	2.2	1.8	1.1	0.7	0.3	0.1
E10000031	Warwickshire	276.6	16.1	16.7	15.6	16.1	16.6	17.7	16.1	16.4	17.8	20.1	20.8	18.2	15.8	16.7	14.2	9.8	6.6	3.7	1.7
E07000218	North Warwickshire	31.2	1.7	1.7	1.8	1.8	1.6	1.8	1.7	1.6	2.0	2.4	2.5	2.3	2.0	2.1	1.8	1.1	0.7	0.4	0.2
E07000219	Nuneaton and Bedworth	62.7	4.1	4.1	3.5	3.6	3.7	3.9	4.0	3.9	4.0	4.6	4.7	4.0	3.6	3.7	3.0	2.0	1.3	0.7	0.3
E07000220	Rugby	52.5	3.3	3.4	3.2	3.2	2.7	3.1	3.3	3.4	3.6	3.9	3.9	3.3	2.7	2.8	2.5	1.8	1.1	0.7	0.3
E07000221	Stratford-on-Avon	60.2	3.0	3.5	3.3	3.4	2.6	3.1	2.8	3.1	3.6	4.4	4.8	4.4	4.0	4.3	3.9	2.7	1.9	1.0	0.5
E07000222	Warwick	70.0	3.9	4.0	3.8	4.2	6.0	5.8	4.2	4.5	4.6	4.8	4.9	4.2	3.5	3.7	3.0	2.1	1.6	0.9	0.4
E11000005	West Midlands (Met County)	1,420.0	104.6	101.2	91.1	95.3	114.5	109.7	100.7	90.0	88.1	93.5	89.1	76.6	65.7	62.0	50.4	38.4	27.4	15.3	6.6
E08000025	Birmingham	557.7	44.2	42.2	38.5	40.8	51.6	46.3	41.4	37.0	34.1	34.1	32.0	27.1	23.4	20.1	15.8	12.2	9.3	5.2	2.3
E08000026	Coventry	178.2	12.3	12.0	9.6	12.0	20.7	17.8	14.0	11.1	10.3	10.5	9.8	8.7	7.2	6.9	5.7	4.3	3.0	1.7	0.8
E08000027	Dudley	155.8	9.9	9.9	9.4	9.3	9.0	9.5	9.6	9.0	9.7	11.8	11.3	9.6	8.7	9.0	7.8	5.7	3.8	2.1	0.8
E08000028	Sandwell	159.9	12.6	11.8	10.6	10.3	10.3	11.5	11.7	10.7	10.8	11.0	10.3	8.9	7.5	6.9	5.6	4.3	2.9	1.6	0.6
E08000029	Solihull	103.2	6.4	6.7	6.6	6.5	5.5	6.1	5.6	5.7	6.3	7.6	7.9	6.9	5.6	6.3	5.2	3.6	2.5	1.6	0.7
E08000030	Walsall	137.1	9.9	9.8	8.9	8.7	8.4	9.2	9.2	8.3	8.5	9.7	9.3	8.0	7.0	6.9	5.5	4.5	3.0	1.5	0.7
E08000031	Wolverhampton	128.0	9.3	8.8	7.6	7.8	8.9	9.4	9.2	8.2	8.5	8.9	8.4	7.3	6.2	5.9	4.7	3.8	2.8	1.5	0.7
E10000034	Worcestershire	287.3	16.4	17.1	16.1	16.7	16.0	16.6	15.8	16.0	17.8	20.9	21.6	19.0	17.9	19.6	15.5	10.8	7.6	4.1	1.8
E07000234	Bromsgrove	47.7	2.6	2.9	2.7	2.8	2.4	2.7	2.4	2.6	3.1	3.6	3.7	3.2	3.0	3.1	2.5	1.9	1.3	0.8	0.3
E07000235	Malvern Hills	37.4	1.7	2.0	2.1	2.2	1.7	1.7	1.4	1.7	2.0	2.6	3.0	2.9	2.6	3.0	2.5	1.8	1.4	0.7	0.4
E07000236	Redditch	42.3	2.8	2.9	2.5	2.4	2.3	2.9	2.9	3.0	2.8	2.9	2.9	2.5	2.5	2.6	1.9	1.1	0.7	0.4	0.2
E07000237	Worcester	50.3	3.2	3.1	2.8	3.1	4.2	3.7	3.4	3.3	3.3	3.6	3.6	2.9	2.6	2.5	1.9	1.4	1.0	0.5	0.2
E07000238	Wychavon	60.3	3.2	3.4	3.3	3.3	2.8	3.0	2.9	3.0	3.6	4.5	4.8	4.3	4.1	4.6	3.7	2.6	1.8	1.0	0.4
E07000239	Wyre Forest	49.3	2.8	2.9	2.6	2.7	2.6	2.7	2.7	2.5	3.1	3.6	3.6	3.1	3.0	3.7	3.1	2.0	1.4	0.7	0.3
E12000006	**EAST**	3,021.3	194.0	196.7	176.2	177.3	178.2	193.6	190.7	190.3	196.5	216.3	217.0	189.5	163.8	173.6	137.1	98.8	72.2	40.8	18.8
E06000055	Bedford	83.6	5.8	5.7	5.2	5.4	5.0	4.9	5.4	5.5	5.6	6.2	6.0	5.2	4.3	4.4	3.3	2.4	1.7	1.0	0.5
E06000056	Central Bedfordshire	136.8	9.1	9.1	8.1	7.7	7.1	8.6	8.8	8.9	9.4	10.2	10.6	9.2	7.5	7.7	5.8	4.0	2.9	1.5	0.7
E06000032	Luton	109.2	9.3	8.7	7.3	6.6	7.5	9.4	9.9	8.3	7.1	6.7	6.5	5.5	4.4	3.7	2.7	2.5	1.8	0.9	0.4
E06000031	Peterborough	98.5	8.4	7.4	5.9	5.6	5.7	7.8	8.0	7.3	6.8	6.7	6.1	5.3	4.4	4.4	3.1	2.3	1.8	1.0	0.4
E06000033	Southend-on-Sea	88.5	5.8	5.8	5.1	5.0	4.8	5.2	5.8	6.1	6.3	6.5	6.5	5.6	4.7	4.8	3.8	2.8	2.0	1.2	0.6
E06000034	Thurrock	83.1	6.7	6.3	5.4	5.0	4.8	5.4	6.0	6.0	6.2	6.3	5.9	4.6	4.0	3.9	2.7	1.8	1.2	0.7	0.3
E10000003	Cambridgeshire	322.5	19.6	20.1	18.2	19.4	22.4	22.3	20.3	21.0	21.4	23.1	22.9	19.8	17.0	18.0	14.2	9.8	7.0	4.0	1.9
E07000008	Cambridge	64.7	3.6	3.5	2.9	4.7	10.3	7.2	5.1	4.5	3.5	3.8	3.5	2.8	2.4	2.2	1.6	1.2	1.0	0.6	0.4
E07000009	East Cambridgeshire	43.6	2.8	3.1	2.8	2.4	2.0	2.3	2.5	2.9	3.2	3.3	3.2	2.8	2.4	2.6	2.1	1.5	1.0	0.6	0.2

MYE2: Population estimates: Males by selected age groups for local authorities in the UK, mid-2016

Thousands

Code	Name	All ages	Age groups (years)																		
			0-4	5-9	10-14	15-19	20-24	25-29	30-34	35-39	40-44	45-49	50-54	55-59	60-64	65-69	70-74	75-79	80-84	85-89	90
E07000010	Fenland	49.2	3.1	2.8	2.6	2.8	2.7	3.1	2.9	2.6	3.0	3.4	3.7	3.2	3.1	3.3	2.7	1.9	1.3	0.8	0.3
E07000011	Huntingdonshire	88.0	5.5	5.4	5.1	5.1	4.1	5.7	5.4	5.5	6.0	6.7	6.7	5.9	5.0	5.4	4.3	2.8	1.9	1.0	0.5
E07000012	South Cambridgeshire	77.1	4.7	5.4	4.9	4.4	3.3	4.1	4.5	5.3	5.8	5.8	5.8	5.1	4.2	4.5	3.6	2.4	1.8	1.0	0.5
E1000012	Essex	713.2	44.5	45.0	42.0	42.5	41.5	43.9	41.3	42.4	45.5	52.2	52.2	46.2	40.2	43.1	34.3	24.2	17.9	9.9	4.4
E07000066	Basildon	89.3	6.4	6.2	5.6	5.4	5.1	6.0	5.8	5.9	5.9	6.6	6.3	5.6	4.5	4.6	3.5	2.5	1.9	1.1	0.4
E07000067	Braintree	74.3	4.5	5.0	4.5	4.5	3.8	4.2	4.4	4.3	5.0	5.8	5.6	4.8	4.4	4.5	3.5	2.4	1.6	0.9	0.5
E07000068	Brentwood	37.3	2.4	2.2	2.2	2.2	2.0	2.3	2.1	2.3	2.4	2.8	3.0	2.5	2.0	2.1	1.7	1.2	1.0	0.6	0.3
E07000069	Castle Point	43.7	2.3	2.3	2.4	2.6	2.0	2.3	2.2	2.2	2.5	3.1	3.2	3.1	2.7	3.2	2.7	1.9	1.3	0.7	0.3
E07000070	Chelmsford	86.2	5.3	5.4	5.2	5.0	4.7	5.6	5.7	5.5	6.1	6.4	6.2	5.3	4.7	4.8	3.8	2.6	2.1	1.2	0.5
E07000071	Colchester	93.2	5.9	5.9	5.1	5.8	8.0	7.3	6.3	6.0	6.1	6.4	6.1	5.2	4.5	4.8	3.8	2.6	1.9	1.0	0.5
E07000072	Epping Forest	62.8	4.1	3.9	3.6	3.5	3.6	3.9	3.6	4.0	4.1	4.7	4.8	4.2	3.5	3.6	2.9	2.0	1.5	1.0	0.4
E07000073	Harlow	41.7	3.5	3.1	2.6	2.5	2.5	2.8	3.1	3.1	2.7	2.8	2.9	2.5	2.1	1.8	1.3	1.0	0.8	0.5	0.2
E07000074	Maldon	31.3	1.6	1.7	1.7	1.9	1.5	1.5	1.2	1.5	1.9	2.4	2.6	2.4	2.2	2.5	1.9	1.3	0.9	0.4	0.2
E07000075	Rochford	41.9	2.1	2.5	2.4	2.5	2.3	2.3	2.0	2.2	2.7	3.2	3.3	2.9	2.5	2.9	2.2	1.7	1.2	0.6	0.3
E07000076	Tendring	69.0	3.7	3.8	3.7	3.9	3.5	3.5	2.8	2.8	3.4	4.5	4.8	4.7	4.6	5.7	5.0	3.7	2.6	1.5	0.7
E07000077	Uttlesford	42.4	2.6	2.9	2.8	2.7	2.0	2.1	2.0	2.5	2.8	3.5	3.4	3.0	2.5	2.6	2.0	1.3	1.0	0.5	0.3
E1000015	Hertfordshire	576.1	39.2	40.6	35.5	34.4	32.4	36.5	37.5	40.4	40.9	42.5	42.8	36.0	29.1	27.8	21.5	15.9	12.4	7.1	3.4
E07000095	Broxbourne	46.9	3.3	3.2	2.9	3.0	2.7	3.2	2.9	3.1	3.0	3.5	3.3	2.9	2.3	2.4	1.9	1.5	1.1	0.6	0.2
E07000096	Dacorum	74.9	5.0	5.3	4.5	4.2	3.7	4.8	5.0	5.2	5.4	5.6	5.6	4.9	4.2	3.7	2.8	2.0	1.6	0.9	0.5
E07000242	East Hertfordshire	71.6	4.4	4.8	4.5	4.4	3.4	3.9	4.0	4.8	5.4	5.7	6.0	4.8	3.9	3.8	2.9	2.1	1.6	0.9	0.4
E07000098	Hertsmere	49.9	3.5	3.7	3.2	3.1	2.6	3.0	3.1	3.3	3.3	3.5	3.7	3.1	2.6	2.5	2.0	1.4	1.1	0.7	0.4
E07000099	North Hertfordshire	65.1	4.4	4.4	3.8	3.6	3.1	3.7	4.1	4.6	4.8	4.9	5.0	4.2	3.4	3.5	2.8	2.0	1.6	0.8	0.4
E07000240	St Albans	71.9	5.1	5.7	4.9	4.1	2.9	3.9	4.2	5.3	5.9	5.7	5.3	4.3	3.6	3.3	2.7	2.1	1.6	0.9	0.5
E07000243	Stevenage	43.0	3.0	3.1	2.6	2.6	2.6	3.1	3.2	3.0	2.7	3.0	3.3	2.8	2.2	1.9	1.4	0.8	0.8	0.5	0.2
E07000102	Three Rivers	45.1	2.9	3.2	2.9	2.8	2.1	2.6	2.5	3.1	3.3	3.5	3.5	2.9	2.3	2.4	1.8	1.3	1.1	0.6	0.3
E07000103	Watford	47.8	3.7	3.5	3.0	2.7	2.5	3.5	4.2	4.2	3.7	3.4	3.2	2.6	2.0	1.7	1.3	1.0	0.7	0.4	0.2
E07000241	Welwyn Hatfield	59.8	3.9	3.7	3.2	3.9	6.9	4.7	4.2	3.9	3.4	3.8	3.7	3.4	2.8	2.5	1.9	1.5	1.2	0.8	0.4
E10000020	Norfolk	438.3	24.3	25.3	22.8	24.6	26.6	26.6	25.5	23.7	25.3	29.7	30.8	28.0	26.3	30.8	25.6	18.4	13.2	7.4	3.3
E07000143	Breckland	68.2	3.9	4.1	3.6	3.7	3.7	4.1	4.0	3.6	3.9	4.6	5.0	4.4	4.1	4.8	4.1	2.9	2.1	1.2	0.5
E07000144	Broadland	62.2	3.1	3.5	3.3	3.5	3.0	3.0	3.0	3.3	3.9	4.7	4.9	4.2	3.9	4.7	3.7	2.9	2.0	1.1	0.5
E07000145	Great Yarmouth	48.9	2.9	2.9	2.6	2.9	2.9	3.1	2.9	2.5	2.7	3.2	3.4	3.1	3.1	3.6	2.9	2.0	1.4	0.8	0.3
E07000146	King's Lynn and West Norfolk	74.4	4.4	4.3	3.9	3.9	3.8	4.5	4.2	3.8	4.1	5.0	5.3	4.8	4.7	5.4	4.6	3.4	2.4	1.3	0.6
E07000147	North Norfolk	50.4	2.1	2.4	2.4	2.4	2.2	2.3	2.3	2.1	2.5	3.2	3.5	3.7	3.8	4.7	4.0	2.8	2.2	1.2	0.5
E07000148	Norwich	69.5	4.4	4.0	3.2	4.2	8.2	6.6	5.9	4.8	4.3	4.3	4.0	3.4	2.9	2.9	2.2	1.7	1.2	0.8	0.4
E07000149	South Norfolk	64.8	3.5	4.0	3.8	3.9	2.8	3.0	3.3	3.6	4.0	4.7	4.8	4.4	4.0	4.7	3.9	2.8	2.0	1.1	0.5
E10000029	Suffolk	371.5	21.3	22.7	20.8	21.0	20.4	23.0	22.3	20.7	22.0	26.3	26.6	24.1	21.8	25.0	19.9	14.5	10.3	6.0	2.9
E07000200	Babergh	44.0	2.2	2.6	2.6	2.6	2.0	2.2	1.9	2.1	2.8	3.3	3.5	3.0	2.8	3.4	2.7	1.9	1.3	0.8	0.4
E07000201	Forest Heath	32.1	2.6	2.1	1.5	1.5	2.4	3.1	2.7	2.0	1.6	1.8	2.1	1.8	1.5	1.8	1.3	1.0	0.7	0.4	0.2
E07000202	Ipswich	69.4	4.9	4.6	4.0	4.1	4.6	5.3	5.7	4.9	4.4	4.9	4.5	3.9	3.4	3.3	2.4	1.8	1.4	0.9	0.4
E07000203	Mid Suffolk	49.8	2.5	2.9	2.9	2.8	2.4	2.6	2.6	2.5	3.0	3.8	3.8	3.5	3.3	3.8	3.0	2.0	1.4	0.8	0.4
E07000204	St Edmundsbury	56.9	3.2	3.5	3.2	3.1	3.2	3.8	4.0	3.4	3.5	4.2	4.0	3.4	3.0	3.5	2.9	2.2	1.5	0.9	0.4
E07000205	Suffolk Coastal	62.4	2.9	3.6	3.6	3.6	2.8	2.9	2.7	3.0	3.6	4.4	4.8	4.6	4.2	5.0	3.9	2.8	2.2	1.2	0.6
E07000206	Waveney	56.8	3.1	3.4	3.0	3.2	3.1	3.0	2.8	2.8	3.1	3.9	3.9	3.7	3.5	4.4	3.7	2.7	1.9	1.1	0.5

Thousands

Code	Name	All ages	0-4	5-9	10-14	15-19	20-24	25-29	30-34	35-39	40-44	45-49	50-54	55-59	60-64	65-69	70-74	75-79	80-84	85-89	90
E12000007	LONDON	4,369.2	324.9	296.1	248.9	240.8	283.2	408.2	443.1	390.3	321.4	296.2	268.2	220.8	171.6	149.8	108.8	84.5	61.5	34.3	16.5
E09000007	Camden	125.4	7.3	7.4	6.2	6.6	11.1	14.4	13.5	11.4	8.8	8.2	6.9	5.8	4.8	4.3	3.3	2.3	1.6	1.0	0.5
E09000001	City of London	4.0	0.2	0.2	0.2	0.1	0.2	0.2	0.4	0.3	0.3	0.4	0.3	0.3	0.2	0.2	0.2	0.1	0.1	0.1	0.0
E09000012	Hackney	136.0	10.6	9.0	7.8	7.0	7.7	15.3	19.9	15.4	9.8	8.1	6.9	5.3	4.1	3.1	2.1	1.7	1.2	0.6	0.3
E09000013	Hammersmith and Fulham	89.8	5.8	5.4	4.1	3.8	6.7	10.4	10.9	8.7	7.4	6.1	5.4	4.0	2.9	2.7	2.1	1.6	1.0	0.6	0.3
E09000014	Haringey	136.9	9.8	8.4	8.0	7.9	8.8	13.4	15.1	14.2	11.0	9.7	8.5	6.1	4.7	3.9	2.7	2.3	1.5	0.7	0.3
E09000019	Islington	116.8	6.9	6.0	5.0	5.6	12.0	15.0	16.0	11.1	7.9	7.2	6.5	4.7	3.7	3.1	2.2	1.8	1.1	0.7	0.3
E09000020	Kensington and Chelsea	78.4	4.4	4.4	3.9	3.3	4.9	6.5	7.7	8.0	6.1	5.8	5.1	4.4	3.4	3.1	2.6	2.0	1.4	0.8	0.4
E09000022	Lambeth	162.3	10.5	9.2	7.8	7.4	9.7	22.2	23.7	16.1	11.9	10.5	9.7	7.0	5.0	3.9	2.6	2.2	1.5	0.9	0.4
E09000023	Lewisham	147.3	11.7	10.4	8.1	7.6	9.1	13.9	15.6	14.9	11.5	10.6	9.4	7.2	4.9	4.2	2.9	2.3	1.7	0.9	0.4
E09000025	Newham	181.9	15.1	12.2	10.2	10.6	14.3	23.4	24.1	16.4	12.3	11.1	8.8	7.2	5.1	3.8	2.5	2.2	1.4	0.7	0.3
E09000028	Southwark	155.4	11.0	9.6	7.6	7.5	11.3	18.7	19.0	14.8	11.6	10.9	9.4	7.6	5.1	3.9	2.7	2.1	1.4	0.8	0.4
E09000030	Tower Hamlets	157.0	11.3	9.7	8.4	8.1	13.0	22.1	22.6	16.4	11.5	9.1	6.8	5.6	4.1	2.8	1.9	1.6	1.2	0.6	0.2
E09000032	Wandsworth	155.1	11.6	9.5	6.9	6.2	8.4	18.1	22.8	17.0	12.2	9.6	8.3	6.5	4.9	4.5	3.1	2.5	1.7	0.9	0.4
E09000033	Westminster	126.1	6.9	6.8	5.5	6.2	9.0	12.3	15.4	13.3	10.1	8.9	7.6	5.7	4.8	4.3	3.3	2.5	1.8	1.1	0.5
E09000002	Barking and Dagenham	102.2	10.3	9.9	7.6	6.7	6.9	8.2	8.3	7.8	7.2	6.6	5.8	4.9	3.5	2.8	2.0	1.5	1.1	0.7	0.3
E09000003	Barnet	189.8	14.0	13.8	11.9	10.8	11.3	15.7	16.2	15.6	13.8	13.1	11.6	10.0	8.1	7.6	5.8	4.1	3.3	2.0	1.1
E09000004	Bexley	118.3	8.3	8.4	7.6	7.5	7.3	8.4	7.6	7.9	7.6	8.3	8.5	7.5	5.7	5.5	4.2	3.3	2.5	1.4	0.6
E09000005	Brent	166.0	12.9	10.9	9.7	9.7	11.1	15.3	17.1	14.0	11.5	10.5	10.0	9.0	7.2	5.6	4.0	3.3	2.4	1.2	0.5
E09000006	Bromley	157.4	11.2	10.9	9.7	9.1	7.5	9.4	10.3	11.8	11.4	12.1	11.6	9.8	7.6	7.9	6.1	4.4	3.5	2.1	1.0
E09000008	Croydon	186.1	14.7	14.1	12.0	11.7	10.3	13.1	14.1	14.8	13.1	12.9	13.8	11.0	8.6	7.4	5.3	4.1	3.2	1.7	0.8
E09000009	Ealing	173.4	13.6	12.3	10.2	9.6	10.0	14.3	15.9	15.3	13.2	12.5	10.9	9.0	7.5	6.4	4.3	3.7	2.5	1.3	0.7
E09000010	Enfield	162.0	12.9	12.8	11.0	10.5	10.6	12.3	12.4	11.9	10.8	11.4	10.7	9.1	6.7	5.9	4.7	3.6	2.6	1.4	0.6
E09000011	Greenwich	140.2	11.5	10.2	8.1	7.8	9.6	12.9	12.8	13.5	10.8	9.4	8.3	7.0	5.1	4.6	3.1	2.3	1.7	0.9	0.5
E09000015	Harrow	124.0	9.1	8.2	7.5	7.8	7.0	9.7	10.0	10.0	8.6	7.9	7.8	7.1	6.3	5.3	4.0	3.3	2.5	1.3	0.7
E09000016	Havering	121.7	8.6	8.0	7.2	7.4	7.5	8.5	8.3	7.9	7.6	8.2	8.5	8.0	6.4	6.4	4.7	3.3	2.8	1.7	0.7
E09000017	Hillingdon	150.2	11.9	10.7	9.0	9.4	11.4	11.8	11.8	11.9	10.4	9.9	9.4	8.1	6.5	5.6	4.3	3.4	2.6	1.4	0.7
E09000018	Hounslow	136.1	11.0	9.6	7.5	7.4	8.1	11.4	13.3	12.8	10.8	8.8	8.4	7.0	5.8	4.9	3.4	2.7	1.9	0.9	0.4
E09000021	Kingston upon Thames	85.4	5.9	5.9	4.7	4.5	6.3	6.6	7.1	7.2	6.7	6.1	5.4	4.6	3.7	3.5	2.6	1.8	1.3	0.8	0.4
E09000024	Merton	101.8	8.1	7.1	5.5	5.1	5.5	8.0	10.1	10.1	7.9	7.2	6.5	5.2	4.1	3.7	2.6	2.2	1.5	0.9	0.5
E09000026	Redbridge	151.1	12.0	11.1	10.3	9.6	9.2	12.7	13.2	12.7	10.9	9.8	8.9	7.9	6.4	5.5	3.9	3.1	2.3	1.2	0.7
E09000027	Richmond upon Thames	94.9	6.8	7.2	5.7	4.8	3.9	5.0	6.8	8.2	8.6	7.7	7.0	5.6	4.5	4.5	3.3	2.2	1.6	0.9	0.5
E09000029	Sutton	98.5	7.4	7.1	6.0	5.9	5.0	5.9	6.9	7.8	7.7	7.6	7.1	5.9	4.7	4.3	3.3	2.4	1.8	1.1	0.5
E09000031	Waltham Forest	137.8	11.5	9.8	8.0	7.5	8.6	13.0	14.4	12.2	10.4	9.8	8.2	6.6	5.0	4.3	2.9	2.4	1.7	1.0	0.4
E12000008	SOUTH EAST	4,449.2	278.0	291.3	262.7	271.6	281.9	277.1	271.0	280.6	293.4	322.5	325.8	280.7	238.5	248.4	195.6	140.2	102.1	59.5	28.3
E06000036	Bracknell Forest	59.5	4.0	4.3	3.6	3.9	3.2	3.8	4.2	4.2	4.6	4.6	4.6	3.8	3.0	2.7	1.9	1.4	1.0	0.5	0.3
E06000043	Brighton and Hove	144.3	7.5	7.5	6.9	8.7	15.8	14.0	11.7	10.5	10.4	10.7	10.0	7.3	5.8	5.9	4.2	3.1	2.2	1.4	0.7
E06000046	Isle of Wight	68.6	3.5	3.6	3.6	4.0	3.5	3.5	3.3	3.3	3.6	4.6	5.1	4.8	4.7	5.6	4.7	3.1	2.2	1.2	0.6
E06000035	Medway	137.3	9.6	9.3	8.3	9.0	9.3	10.1	9.3	8.8	8.8	9.9	9.8	8.4	7.0	6.9	5.1	3.6	2.4	1.2	0.6
E06000042	Milton Keynes	131.9	10.3	10.6	8.7	7.6	6.9	8.2	10.5	11.1	10.0	9.4	8.6	7.7	6.5	5.9	4.0	2.6	1.7	1.0	0.4
E06000044	Portsmouth	108.6	6.8	6.7	5.7	7.2	13.7	9.5	8.2	6.9	6.5	6.9	6.7	5.9	4.4	4.4	3.4	2.4	1.8	1.0	0.5
E06000038	Reading	82.1	6.3	5.7	4.3	4.7	7.1	7.1	7.4	7.0	5.8	5.4	5.0	4.1	3.3	2.9	2.1	1.6	1.2	0.9	0.5
E06000039	Slough	74.3	6.8	6.5	5.2	4.5	4.1	5.2	6.5	7.2	6.1	5.1	4.3	3.6	3.1	2.3	1.4	1.2	0.8	0.4	0.2
E06000045	Southampton	127.8	8.5	7.7	6.0	8.8	17.9	12.0	9.9	8.6	7.7	7.1	7.4	6.3	5.2	4.9	3.8	2.6	1.9	1.2	0.6
E06000037	West Berkshire	78.6	4.8	5.3	4.9	5.0	3.9	4.2	4.4	4.7	5.5	6.4	6.3	5.4	4.5	4.5	3.5	2.4	1.6	0.9	0.4

Age groups (years)

MYE2: Population estimates: Males by selected age groups for local authorities in the UK, mid-2016

Thousands

Code	Name	All ages	Age groups (years)																		
			0-4	5-9	10-14	15-19	20-24	25-29	30-34	35-39	40-44	45-49	50-54	55-59	60-64	65-69	70-74	75-79	80-84	85-89	90
E06000040	Windsor and Maidenhead	74.3	4.6	5.1	5.0	5.0	3.0	4.3	4.5	5.1	5.5	5.1	5.7	4.6	3.7	3.8	3.1	2.2	1.7	1.0	0.5
E06000041	Wokingham	80.4	5.2	6.0	5.3	4.9	3.9	4.2	4.3	5.5	6.1	6.3	6.2	5.4	4.2	4.2	3.2	2.4	1.7	0.9	0.4
E10000002	Buckinghamshire	261.4	16.9	18.4	17.0	16.2	13.4	13.9	14.6	16.7	18.3	19.9	20.3	17.3	14.4	14.0	11.2	8.1	6.1	3.2	1.5
E07000004	Aylesbury Vale	95.3	6.4	6.7	6.0	6.1	5.0	5.5	5.9	6.4	6.7	7.3	7.3	6.3	5.1	5.0	3.7	2.6	1.9	0.9	0.4
E07000005	Chiltern	46.2	2.6	3.5	3.3	2.9	1.9	2.0	1.8	2.6	3.3	3.6	3.8	3.4	2.6	2.7	2.3	1.7	1.3	0.7	0.4
E07000006	South Bucks	33.7	2.1	2.3	2.1	1.9	1.5	1.7	1.8	2.0	2.1	2.7	2.7	2.5	2.1	1.9	1.5	1.2	0.9	0.6	0.2
E07000007	Wycombe	86.2	5.8	5.9	5.6	5.3	5.0	4.7	5.2	5.7	6.2	6.4	6.5	5.1	4.6	4.4	3.8	2.6	2.0	1.0	0.5
E10000011	East Sussex	266.0	14.3	16.1	14.9	15.5	13.8	13.6	13.4	13.3	15.2	18.9	20.3	18.2	16.6	19.3	15.7	11.0	8.2	4.9	2.6
E07000061	Eastbourne	49.9	2.9	3.0	2.6	3.0	3.1	2.8	3.0	2.9	2.9	3.4	3.4	3.1	2.7	3.3	2.6	2.0	1.5	1.0	0.6
E07000062	Hastings	45.5	2.9	2.9	2.6	2.8	2.7	2.8	2.8	2.7	2.9	3.4	3.5	2.9	2.6	2.9	2.1	1.4	0.9	0.6	0.3
E07000063	Lewes	49.4	2.6	3.1	2.9	2.9	2.4	2.4	2.5	2.4	2.9	3.6	3.8	3.4	3.1	3.5	2.7	2.0	1.5	0.9	0.5
E07000064	Rother	45.1	2.1	2.4	2.3	2.5	2.2	2.0	1.7	1.8	2.2	3.0	3.5	3.2	3.2	4.0	3.4	2.4	1.8	1.1	0.6
E07000065	Wealden	76.1	3.8	4.7	4.5	4.4	3.6	3.5	3.4	3.5	4.3	5.6	6.1	5.6	5.0	5.6	4.8	3.2	2.5	1.4	0.7
E10000014	Hampshire	668.8	39.2	42.2	39.4	40.1	35.7	39.0	37.2	38.5	43.2	48.9	51.2	45.7	38.5	41.1	33.0	23.7	17.3	9.9	4.7
E07000084	Basingstoke and Deane	86.8	6.0	6.0	5.1	5.0	4.3	5.2	5.8	5.9	6.2	6.8	6.8	5.7	4.5	4.6	3.5	2.4	1.7	0.9	0.4
E07000085	East Hampshire	57.4	3.2	3.5	3.6	3.5	2.7	2.7	2.6	2.8	3.6	4.4	4.6	4.4	3.7	3.9	3.2	2.1	1.6	0.9	0.4
E07000086	Eastleigh	63.5	3.8	4.2	3.9	3.7	3.3	4.0	3.8	4.0	4.2	4.7	4.6	4.2	3.7	3.6	2.8	2.1	1.5	0.9	0.4
E07000087	Fareham	56.8	2.9	3.2	3.2	3.5	3.3	3.2	3.0	3.1	3.5	4.2	4.4	4.1	3.3	3.7	3.1	2.2	1.7	0.9	0.4
E07000088	Gosport	42.6	2.5	2.8	2.5	2.6	2.7	2.9	2.8	2.5	2.6	2.9	3.1	2.9	2.3	2.6	1.9	1.3	1.0	0.6	0.2
E07000089	Hart	47.2	2.8	3.3	3.0	2.8	2.0	2.9	2.5	3.0	3.6	3.8	3.8	3.0	2.4	2.6	2.1	1.6	1.1	0.6	0.3
E07000090	Havant	60.0	3.4	3.7	3.4	3.7	3.5	3.5	3.2	2.9	3.3	4.0	4.4	4.2	3.7	3.9	3.2	2.4	1.8	1.1	0.5
E07000091	New Forest	86.4	4.2	4.8	4.7	4.7	4.1	4.4	3.6	4.0	4.7	5.8	6.6	6.2	5.8	6.7	5.6	4.1	3.2	2.0	1.0
E07000092	Rushmoor	48.4	3.5	3.0	2.8	2.7	3.1	3.9	3.8	3.6	3.6	3.6	3.5	2.9	2.1	2.1	1.6	1.2	0.7	0.4	0.2
E07000093	Test Valley	59.9	3.6	3.8	3.5	3.3	2.9	3.3	3.1	3.4	4.0	4.5	4.8	4.2	3.5	3.9	3.1	2.1	1.6	0.8	0.4
E07000094	Winchester	59.8	3.3	3.8	3.7	4.4	3.8	3.1	3.0	3.3	4.0	4.2	4.4	4.0	3.4	3.6	2.9	2.1	1.5	0.9	0.4
E10000016	Kent	755.7	47.0	49.6	46.0	47.0	47.0	45.2	43.4	43.9	47.0	55.0	56.0	47.8	41.8	45.8	35.7	25.2	17.7	10.2	4.5
E07000105	Ashford	61.2	4.1	4.2	4.0	3.7	3.3	3.5	3.4	3.4	3.9	4.7	4.8	3.9	3.3	3.7	2.9	1.9	1.3	0.7	0.4
E07000106	Canterbury	79.7	3.9	4.3	4.3	6.0	11.0	6.0	4.1	3.6	3.8	4.7	5.0	4.4	4.1	4.7	3.6	2.7	1.8	1.2	0.6
E07000107	Dartford	51.6	3.9	3.6	3.2	2.9	2.8	3.5	4.1	4.0	3.7	3.9	3.7	3.0	2.5	2.2	1.7	1.3	1.0	0.5	0.3
E07000108	Dover	56.4	3.1	3.3	3.1	3.3	3.1	3.0	2.9	4.0	3.2	4.1	4.4	4.0	3.7	4.1	3.2	2.2	1.5	0.8	0.4
E07000109	Gravesham	52.5	3.6	3.6	3.4	3.4	2.9	3.4	3.5	3.3	3.4	3.9	3.8	3.3	2.6	2.6	2.1	1.5	1.2	0.7	0.3
E07000110	Maidstone	81.9	5.3	5.4	4.9	4.9	4.6	5.1	5.1	5.1	5.3	6.1	6.1	5.2	4.3	4.8	3.8	2.6	1.9	1.0	0.4
E07000111	Sevenoaks	57.7	3.6	4.2	3.6	3.3	2.5	3.0	2.9	3.5	3.8	4.3	4.6	3.8	3.4	3.6	2.8	2.0	1.5	0.9	0.3
E07000112	Shepway	54.8	2.9	3.2	3.0	3.1	2.9	3.1	2.9	3.0	3.2	4.1	4.2	3.7	3.3	4.1	3.1	2.2	1.5	0.9	0.5
E07000113	Swale	71.6	4.8	4.9	4.4	4.5	4.3	4.3	4.2	4.1	4.4	5.0	5.4	4.6	4.1	4.4	3.4	2.4	1.5	0.8	0.3
E07000114	Thanet	68.2	4.4	4.4	4.1	4.4	4.1	3.7	3.6	3.5	3.7	4.4	4.8	4.4	4.1	4.9	3.8	2.6	1.8	1.1	0.5
E07000115	Tonbridge and Malling	62.3	3.9	4.3	4.2	4.1	3.0	3.3	3.2	3.7	4.4	4.9	4.8	4.1	3.4	3.5	2.8	2.0	1.5	0.8	0.3
E07000116	Tunbridge Wells	57.9	3.4	4.0	3.8	3.5	2.5	3.2	3.6	3.9	4.3	4.7	4.5	3.6	3.0	3.2	2.5	1.8	1.3	0.8	0.4
E10000025	Oxfordshire	338.0	20.9	21.4	19.1	20.9	26.5	23.7	22.9	22.0	21.1	23.4	23.7	20.2	17.0	17.7	13.8	10.1	7.5	4.3	2.0
E07000177	Cherwell	72.7	4.8	5.0	4.2	4.1	3.8	4.5	5.2	5.1	4.8	5.4	5.5	4.6	3.9	3.9	3.0	2.1	1.6	0.9	0.4
E07000178	Oxford	79.1	4.7	4.5	4.0	5.8	13.6	8.0	6.5	5.5	4.0	4.1	4.0	3.3	2.8	2.7	2.0	1.4	1.1	0.7	0.4
E07000179	South Oxfordshire	68.6	4.2	4.5	4.0	4.0	3.3	4.0	3.9	4.1	4.6	5.3	5.2	4.6	3.8	4.0	3.3	2.5	1.8	1.0	0.4
E07000180	Vale of White Horse	64.1	3.9	4.1	3.9	4.0	3.1	3.7	4.0	4.1	4.2	4.7	4.8	4.2	3.6	3.9	2.9	2.2	1.6	0.9	0.4
E07000181	West Oxfordshire	53.6	3.2	3.4	3.1	2.9	2.6	3.5	3.3	3.3	3.4	3.9	4.1	3.5	2.9	3.3	2.6	1.9	1.3	0.8	0.4
E10000030	Surrey	580.0	37.0	39.4	34.9	35.0	32.5	33.3	32.4	38.7	41.9	43.8	44.2	37.1	30.7	30.6	24.5	17.9	13.7	8.2	4.2
E07000207	Elmbridge	65.9	4.8	5.2	4.5	3.9	2.6	2.8	3.2	4.7	5.3	5.4	5.3	4.1	3.4	3.2	2.6	1.9	1.5	0.9	0.5

MYE2: Population estimates: Males by selected age groups for local authorities in the UK, mid-2016

Thousands

Code	Name	All ages	0-4	5-9	10-14	15-19	20-24	25-29	30-34	35-39	40-44	45-49	50-54	55-59	60-64	65-69	70-74	75-79	80-84	85-89	90
E07000208	Epsom and Ewell	38.3	2.6	2.6	2.4	2.4	1.9	2.0	2.1	2.7	2.9	2.9	3.0	2.4	1.9	2.1	1.5	1.1	0.9	0.5	0.3
E07000209	Guildford	73.6	4.1	4.6	4.0	4.8	7.3	6.1	4.8	4.6	5.0	4.9	4.9	4.2	3.5	3.5	2.7	2.0	1.5	0.9	0.4
E07000210	Mole Valley	42.7	2.3	2.7	2.5	2.6	1.9	1.9	1.9	2.3	2.7	3.4	3.5	3.2	2.6	2.7	2.2	1.6	1.3	0.8	0.4
E07000211	Reigate and Banstead	71.0	4.9	5.0	4.2	3.9	3.2	4.1	4.3	5.3	5.3	5.4	5.6	4.5	3.7	3.7	2.9	2.0	1.5	1.0	0.5
E07000212	Runnymede	42.1	2.4	2.6	2.2	2.6	3.9	3.2	2.5	2.6	2.9	2.8	3.0	2.6	2.1	2.0	1.7	1.1	1.0	0.6	0.3
E07000213	Spelthorne	48.7	3.3	3.2	2.7	2.7	2.5	2.9	3.1	3.6	3.4	3.5	3.8	3.3	2.6	2.5	2.0	1.6	1.2	0.6	0.3
E07000214	Surrey Heath	44.0	2.6	2.8	2.8	2.6	2.2	2.4	2.4	2.8	3.1	3.6	3.6	3.0	2.4	2.3	2.0	1.5	1.0	0.6	0.3
E07000215	Tandridge	42.2	2.6	2.8	2.5	2.5	1.9	2.3	2.1	2.6	2.8	3.2	3.5	2.8	2.5	2.5	1.9	1.5	1.0	0.7	0.3
E07000216	Waverley	60.9	3.7	4.2	4.1	4.3	3.0	2.6	2.8	3.4	4.4	4.8	4.5	4.0	3.3	3.6	3.0	2.2	1.7	1.0	0.5
E07000217	Woking	50.6	3.7	3.8	3.1	2.7	2.1	2.9	3.3	4.1	4.2	3.8	3.6	3.2	2.6	2.5	1.8	1.4	1.1	0.6	0.4
E10000032	West Sussex	411.7	24.7	26.2	23.7	23.6	20.7	22.2	23.1	24.7	26.1	30.5	30.5	26.9	24.0	25.9	21.3	15.4	11.5	7.3	3.4
E07000223	Adur	31.0	2.0	2.0	1.7	1.7	1.5	1.6	1.7	1.8	2.0	2.3	2.3	1.9	1.8	1.9	1.7	1.2	0.9	0.6	0.3
E07000224	Arun	75.3	4.0	4.3	3.8	3.8	3.8	3.9	3.8	3.8	4.1	5.2	5.3	4.9	4.7	5.8	5.1	3.8	2.7	1.7	0.8
E07000225	Chichester	57.5	3.0	3.3	3.1	3.4	3.6	2.8	2.6	2.7	3.1	3.9	4.2	3.9	3.8	4.0	3.6	2.7	2.1	1.2	0.5
E07000226	Crawley	55.8	4.4	4.2	3.4	3.2	3.1	4.0	4.6	4.7	4.1	4.1	3.7	3.2	2.6	2.2	1.5	1.1	0.8	0.6	0.3
E07000227	Horsham	67.4	3.7	4.2	4.2	4.1	3.1	3.3	3.2	3.7	4.3	5.2	5.4	4.9	4.1	4.4	3.5	2.5	1.8	1.1	0.5
E07000228	Mid Sussex	72.1	4.4	4.8	4.5	4.5	3.0	3.7	4.1	4.6	5.0	5.6	5.6	4.7	4.1	4.3	3.4	2.2	1.7	1.2	0.5
E07000229	Worthing	52.7	3.1	3.4	3.0	2.9	2.6	2.9	3.1	3.3	3.5	4.1	4.0	3.4	2.9	3.2	2.6	1.9	1.4	1.0	0.4
E12000009	SOUTH WEST	2,712.3	157.1	161.6	147.6	160.6	176.3	170.7	159.2	154.3	162.3	188.8	195.7	175.9	158.9	173.7	139.7	99.0	70.7	40.9	19.3
E06000022	Bath and North East Somerset	92.1	4.9	5.2	4.9	6.8	10.7	6.4	5.0	4.7	5.2	6.0	6.1	5.4	4.8	5.0	4.0	2.9	2.2	1.3	0.6
E06000028	Bournemouth	97.5	5.8	5.3	4.3	5.7	9.1	7.0	7.4	7.4	6.5	6.7	6.4	5.4	4.6	4.9	3.8	2.8	2.2	1.4	0.8
E06000023	Bristol, City of	228.3	15.7	14.2	11.3	13.2	23.9	25.1	20.6	17.2	14.0	13.4	12.8	10.7	9.3	8.9	6.6	4.9	3.5	2.1	1.0
E06000052	Cornwall	269.5	14.9	15.5	14.6	15.9	15.4	13.8	13.3	14.1	15.4	18.3	19.7	18.8	17.8	20.6	16.5	11.0	7.7	4.3	1.8
E06000053	Isles of Scilly	1.2	0.1	0.1	0.1	0.0	0.1	0.1	0.1	0.1	0.1	0.1	0.1	0.1	0.1	0.1	0.1	0.0	0.0	0.0	0.0
E06000024	North Somerset	103.1	6.1	6.6	5.9	5.7	5.0	5.2	5.4	5.9	6.6	7.6	7.9	6.6	6.2	7.0	6.0	4.1	2.9	1.7	0.8
E06000026	Plymouth	130.5	8.1	7.8	6.7	8.1	13.3	9.9	9.1	7.5	7.3	8.2	8.5	8.1	6.5	6.8	5.6	3.9	2.8	1.5	0.8
E06000029	Poole	74.0	4.3	4.6	4.0	4.2	3.8	4.4	4.6	4.7	4.6	5.4	5.5	4.7	4.1	4.6	3.7	2.8	2.0	1.3	0.6
E06000025	South Gloucestershire	137.3	8.3	8.7	7.7	8.5	9.3	8.4	8.9	8.7	8.8	10.3	10.4	8.6	7.1	7.3	6.1	4.4	3.2	1.8	0.7
E06000030	Swindon	109.0	7.7	7.4	6.4	6.1	5.6	6.9	7.7	7.8	8.3	8.6	8.2	7.0	5.7	5.2	3.8	2.8	2.0	1.2	0.5
E06000027	Torbay	65.2	3.7	3.6	3.4	3.6	3.4	3.5	3.3	2.9	3.6	4.5	4.9	4.6	4.4	4.9	4.2	2.9	2.1	1.1	0.6
E06000054	Wiltshire	243.3	14.6	15.7	14.6	14.3	12.7	14.7	14.1	13.4	15.2	18.1	18.7	16.4	14.3	15.1	11.9	8.5	6.1	3.4	1.6
E10000008	Devon	379.9	19.8	21.5	20.2	22.0	23.6	22.2	19.1	19.2	20.8	25.6	27.7	25.8	24.4	28.2	22.9	15.8	11.4	6.6	3.2
E07000040	East Devon	67.8	3.4	3.7	3.6	3.8	3.0	3.3	2.9	3.1	3.6	4.5	4.7	4.5	4.5	5.6	4.8	3.5	2.6	1.6	0.9
E07000041	Exeter	63.2	3.4	3.4	2.8	4.3	8.9	6.3	4.6	3.9	3.7	3.7	3.6	3.1	2.7	2.7	2.1	1.6	1.2	0.7	0.3
E07000042	Mid Devon	39.0	2.2	2.5	2.4	2.4	1.8	1.8	2.0	1.9	2.3	2.9	2.9	2.7	2.6	2.9	2.3	1.5	1.0	0.6	0.3
E07000043	North Devon	46.4	2.5	2.7	2.6	2.6	2.4	2.7	2.3	2.4	2.6	3.3	3.5	3.2	2.9	3.4	2.8	1.9	1.4	0.8	0.4
E07000044	South Hams	41.1	1.8	2.3	2.2	2.3	1.9	2.0	1.7	1.8	2.2	2.7	3.2	3.2	3.1	3.6	2.8	1.9	1.4	0.7	0.4
E07000045	Teignbridge	62.9	3.3	3.6	3.4	3.5	2.9	3.2	3.0	3.3	3.4	4.4	5.0	4.5	4.3	4.9	4.0	2.6	1.9	1.1	0.5
E07000046	Torridge	32.8	1.8	1.8	1.7	1.8	1.5	1.6	1.5	1.5	1.7	2.3	2.5	2.4	2.4	2.8	2.2	1.5	1.0	0.5	0.2
E07000047	West Devon	26.8	1.3	1.5	1.5	1.5	1.1	1.3	1.2	1.2	1.4	1.9	2.2	2.1	1.9	2.2	1.9	1.2	0.8	0.5	0.2
E10000009	Dorset	206.4	9.8	11.1	11.3	11.9	9.6	10.6	8.6	9.8	11.2	13.9	15.5	14.6	13.8	16.5	14.1	10.0	7.4	4.5	2.1
E07000048	Christchurch	23.9	1.1	1.3	1.4	1.3	1.1	1.1	1.0	1.1	1.3	1.6	1.7	1.5	1.4	1.9	1.7	1.3	1.1	0.6	0.3
E07000049	East Dorset	42.9	1.9	2.3	2.2	2.3	1.9	1.9	1.6	1.8	2.3	2.9	3.2	3.1	2.9	3.6	3.2	2.4	1.8	1.1	0.5
E07000050	North Dorset	35.4	1.7	2.0	2.0	2.4	1.7	2.1	1.7	2.0	1.9	2.4	2.6	2.4	2.2	2.6	2.1	1.5	1.1	0.6	0.3
E07000051	Purbeck	22.9	1.1	1.2	1.3	1.3	1.2	1.2	1.1	1.2	1.3	1.4	1.7	1.7	1.5	1.8	1.5	1.1	0.8	0.4	0.2

MYE2: Population estimates: Males by selected age groups for local authorities in the UK, mid-2016 *Thousands*

Code	Name	All ages	Age groups (years)																	
			0-4	5-9	10-14	15-19	20-24	25-29	30-34	35-39	40-44	45-49	50-54	55-59	60-64	65-69	70-74	75-79	80-84	85-89	90
E07000052	West Dorset	48.9	2.2	2.5	2.7	2.8	2.0	2.3	1.8	2.0	2.6	3.2	3.8	3.6	3.5	4.2	3.5	2.5	1.8	1.1	0.5
E07000053	Weymouth and Portland	32.4	1.7	1.8	1.7	1.8	1.7	1.9	1.5	1.7	1.8	2.3	2.5	2.3	2.2	2.4	2.0	1.3	0.9	0.6	0.2
E10000013	Gloucestershire	305.4	18.0	18.4	17.0	18.3	17.2	17.5	17.6	17.8	19.7	23.1	23.0	20.6	18.5	19.0	15.0	11.1	7.5	4.3	2.0
E07000078	Cheltenham	57.3	3.4	3.4	3.1	3.4	3.8	4.1	4.4	4.0	3.8	4.0	3.9	3.5	2.9	3.0	2.3	1.8	1.3	0.8	0.4
E07000079	Cotswold	41.7	2.0	2.3	2.3	2.4	2.2	1.8	1.8	2.0	2.5	3.2	3.9	3.1	2.9	3.0	2.5	1.8	1.3	0.8	0.4
E07000080	Forest of Dean	42.0	2.1	2.3	2.2	2.8	2.4	2.1	1.9	1.9	2.4	3.2	3.4	3.1	2.9	3.2	2.5	1.8	1.1	0.6	0.3
E07000081	Gloucester	63.3	4.7	4.1	3.6	3.9	4.2	4.2	4.4	4.1	4.2	4.7	4.6	3.9	3.2	3.1	2.4	1.7	1.2	0.7	0.3
E07000082	Stroud	57.8	3.1	3.6	3.5	3.4	2.7	2.9	2.8	3.2	3.9	4.6	4.5	4.1	3.8	3.9	3.1	2.2	1.5	0.8	0.3
E07000083	Tewkesbury	43.3	2.7	2.7	2.4	2.4	1.9	2.4	2.4	2.6	2.8	3.3	3.3	2.9	2.6	2.8	2.3	1.7	1.1	0.6	0.3
E10000027	Somerset	269.5	15.1	16.0	15.2	16.0	13.7	15.0	14.3	13.3	15.1	19.0	20.2	18.8	17.6	19.6	15.4	10.9	7.7	4.6	2.1
E07000187	Mendip	55.1	3.0	3.3	3.3	3.7	2.8	2.8	2.7	2.7	3.2	4.1	4.4	3.8	3.6	3.9	2.9	2.1	1.5	0.8	0.4
E07000188	Sedgemoor	59.6	3.5	3.6	3.4	3.6	3.1	3.3	3.1	2.9	3.3	4.3	4.6	4.2	3.9	4.2	3.3	2.4	1.6	0.9	0.4
E07000189	South Somerset	81.9	4.5	4.9	4.4	4.7	4.1	4.6	4.5	4.1	4.6	5.8	5.8	5.7	5.3	6.1	4.8	3.5	2.4	1.5	0.6
E07000190	Taunton Deane	56.4	3.4	3.4	3.2	3.2	3.0	3.5	3.3	3.0	3.3	3.9	4.1	3.8	3.5	3.8	2.9	2.0	1.6	1.0	0.5
E07000191	West Somerset	16.6	0.7	0.8	0.8	0.8	0.8	0.8	0.7	0.6	0.6	1.0	1.2	1.3	1.3	1.6	1.4	1.0	0.7	0.4	0.2
W92000004	WALES	1,534.0	88.7	93.7	85.7	94.2	109.7	102.7	91.3	87.1	88.9	104.0	108.3	99.0	90.0	96.6	74.8	54.0	37.1	19.7	8.7
W06000001	Isle of Anglesey	34.3	1.9	2.1	1.8	1.8	1.7	2.0	1.7	1.8	1.9	2.3	2.4	2.5	2.4	2.7	2.1	1.6	1.0	0.5	0.2
W06000002	Gwynedd	61.1	3.2	3.5	3.3	3.9	5.5	4.0	3.1	3.0	3.3	3.8	4.1	3.9	3.6	4.2	3.4	2.3	1.6	0.9	0.4
W06000003	Conwy	56.9	2.9	3.1	3.0	3.2	2.8	3.1	2.7	2.8	3.0	3.8	4.2	4.0	3.7	4.4	3.6	2.6	2.0	1.1	0.6
W06000004	Denbighshire	46.8	2.7	2.9	2.7	2.8	2.7	2.8	2.3	2.1	2.6	3.2	3.4	3.2	3.0	3.5	2.7	2.0	1.3	0.7	0.3
W06000005	Flintshire	76.3	4.4	4.9	4.4	4.5	4.4	4.9	4.5	4.3	4.7	5.6	5.6	5.0	4.5	5.2	3.8	2.8	1.8	0.9	0.4
W06000006	Wrexham	67.5	4.2	4.5	4.0	4.0	4.0	4.3	4.3	4.1	4.3	4.7	4.9	4.2	3.9	4.1	3.2	2.2	1.5	0.8	0.3
W06000023	Powys	65.5	3.2	3.5	3.5	3.9	3.3	3.6	2.9	2.9	3.4	4.5	5.1	4.7	4.8	5.3	4.2	3.1	2.1	1.1	0.5
W06000008	Ceredigion	36.9	1.6	1.8	1.8	2.4	5.2	1.9	1.3	1.6	1.7	2.2	2.3	2.4	2.4	2.8	2.1	1.5	1.0	0.6	0.3
W06000009	Pembrokeshire	61.0	3.2	3.6	3.5	3.7	3.3	3.6	3.0	2.9	3.0	4.1	4.5	4.2	4.2	4.6	3.6	2.8	1.9	1.0	0.5
W06000010	Carmarthenshire	90.9	5.0	5.5	5.3	5.4	5.0	5.3	4.8	4.4	5.0	6.1	6.8	6.1	6.1	6.4	5.3	3.8	2.6	1.4	0.6
W06000011	Swansea	122.1	6.9	7.0	6.6	8.2	12.1	8.9	7.8	7.3	7.0	7.8	8.0	7.1	6.5	6.7	5.2	3.8	2.9	1.5	0.7
W06000012	Neath Port Talbot	69.6	4.0	4.1	3.8	4.1	4.1	4.2	4.5	4.4	4.2	4.9	5.1	4.8	4.4	4.4	3.4	2.4	1.6	0.9	0.3
W06000013	Bridgend	71.1	4.2	4.3	4.0	4.3	4.2	4.6	4.6	4.5	4.6	5.1	5.2	4.7	4.0	4.3	3.4	2.4	1.6	0.8	0.3
W06000014	Vale of Glamorgan	62.7	3.6	4.1	3.7	3.9	3.5	3.8	3.7	3.9	4.0	4.3	4.4	4.2	3.9	3.9	3.1	2.2	1.5	0.8	0.3
W06000015	Cardiff	178.3	11.6	11.3	9.3	11.7	20.9	16.4	14.0	11.6	10.7	10.6	10.5	9.5	8.1	7.6	5.3	3.9	2.9	1.6	0.8
W06000016	Rhondda Cynon Taf	116.8	7.1	7.5	6.7	7.1	8.2	8.3	7.1	6.9	6.9	8.2	8.2	7.4	6.5	7.1	5.4	3.8	2.5	1.2	0.5
W06000024	Merthyr Tydfil	29.3	1.9	1.9	1.7	1.7	1.8	2.1	2.0	1.8	1.6	2.0	2.1	2.0	1.7	1.7	1.3	1.0	0.6	0.3	0.1
W06000018	Caerphilly	88.4	5.3	5.8	5.4	5.4	5.2	5.8	5.5	5.3	5.5	6.4	6.5	5.7	5.1	5.4	4.2	2.9	1.8	0.9	0.4
W06000019	Blaenau Gwent	34.3	1.9	2.1	1.8	2.0	2.1	2.4	2.1	2.0	2.1	2.6	2.6	2.3	2.0	2.2	1.7	1.2	0.8	0.4	0.1
W06000020	Torfaen	44.8	2.7	2.9	2.6	2.7	2.7	3.0	2.7	2.5	2.5	3.2	3.4	3.1	2.6	2.8	2.1	1.5	1.1	0.6	0.3
W06000021	Monmouthshire	46.0	2.2	2.5	2.6	2.8	2.4	2.5	2.0	2.1	2.5	3.5	3.9	3.3	3.0	3.4	2.7	1.9	1.4	0.7	0.3
W06000022	Newport	73.5	5.1	5.0	4.4	4.7	4.7	5.1	4.8	4.8	4.4	5.2	5.1	4.7	3.7	3.9	2.9	2.3	1.6	0.8	0.3

MYE2: Population estimates: Males by selected age groups for local authorities in the UK, mid-2016

Thousands

Code	Name	All ages	0-4	5-9	10-14	15-19	20-24	25-29	30-34	35-39	40-44	45-49	50-54	55-59	60-64	65-69	70-74	75-79	80-84	85-89	90
S92000003	SCOTLAND	2,627.5	147.5	152.3	140.4	152.6	181.7	186.1	172.3	161.3	164.9	189.4	197.4	180.7	156.4	153.5	111.9	82.5	56.2	28.3	12.0
S12000033	Aberdeen City	114.1	6.2	5.6	4.6	5.5	10.1	13.1	10.5	8.5	7.3	7.3	7.3	6.8	6.0	5.4	3.6	2.7	2.0	1.0	0.4
S12000034	Aberdeenshire	130.4	7.7	8.5	7.5	7.6	7.2	7.1	7.7	8.4	9.1	9.9	10.1	9.1	8.2	8.2	5.5	4.0	2.7	1.3	0.6
S12000041	Angus	56.8	3.0	3.1	3.1	3.4	3.3	3.0	3.1	3.0	3.4	4.0	4.6	4.0	3.7	4.1	3.0	2.2	1.5	0.8	0.3
S12000035	Argyll and Bute	43.3	1.9	2.2	2.2	2.6	3.0	2.5	2.0	2.1	2.4	3.0	3.4	3.2	3.1	3.4	2.6	1.8	1.2	0.6	0.2
S12000036	City of Edinburgh	246.8	13.6	13.0	10.9	12.6	20.8	26.0	22.4	18.9	16.8	16.3	16.2	14.3	12.1	11.2	7.7	5.9	4.5	2.4	1.2
S12000005	Clackmannanshire	25.2	1.5	1.4	1.4	1.5	1.6	1.3	1.4	1.4	1.6	2.1	2.0	1.8	1.6	1.6	1.2	0.8	0.5	0.2	0.1
S12000006	Dumfries and Galloway	72.5	3.5	3.9	3.9	4.0	4.0	3.7	3.5	3.3	3.9	5.1	5.9	5.6	5.3	5.7	4.3	3.3	2.3	1.1	0.5
S12000042	Dundee City	71.4	4.1	3.9	3.6	4.2	6.9	7.0	5.3	4.0	3.7	4.5	4.7	4.6	3.7	3.7	2.7	2.2	1.5	0.9	0.4
S12000008	East Ayrshire	59.3	3.5	3.5	3.2	3.5	3.7	3.6	3.4	3.2	3.7	4.5	4.7	4.3	3.7	3.8	2.8	2.1	1.3	0.6	0.2
S12000045	East Dunbartonshire	52.0	2.7	3.1	3.2	3.3	3.3	2.8	2.4	2.6	3.1	3.7	4.2	3.9	3.4	3.3	2.5	2.0	1.5	0.7	0.3
S12000010	East Lothian	49.8	2.9	3.3	3.0	2.9	3.0	2.6	2.5	2.7	3.4	3.7	4.1	3.7	3.0	3.0	2.3	1.7	1.2	0.6	0.3
S12000011	East Renfrewshire	44.6	2.7	3.2	3.0	3.1	2.8	2.2	1.9	2.4	2.9	3.2	3.5	3.2	2.8	2.5	1.8	1.5	1.1	0.6	0.3
S12000014	Falkirk	78.0	4.5	4.8	4.4	4.6	4.7	4.5	4.7	5.0	5.4	6.3	6.2	5.4	4.4	4.7	3.3	2.4	1.7	0.8	0.3
S12000015	Fife	179.6	10.2	10.9	9.9	10.7	12.0	10.5	10.2	10.3	11.2	13.4	13.3	12.8	11.0	11.5	8.6	6.1	4.1	2.0	0.9
S12000046	Glasgow City	299.0	17.8	15.9	13.7	16.7	27.1	31.8	27.9	22.2	18.7	19.9	20.0	17.6	14.4	12.5	8.8	6.5	4.5	2.2	1.0
S12000017	Highland	114.8	6.0	6.7	6.4	6.8	6.2	6.2	6.5	6.5	6.7	8.2	9.1	8.7	8.0	8.0	6.0	4.1	2.8	1.5	0.6
S12000018	Inverclyde	37.8	2.0	2.2	2.1	2.3	2.4	2.3	2.2	2.0	2.1	2.7	3.3	3.0	2.4	2.4	1.8	1.3	0.8	0.4	0.2
S12000019	Midlothian	42.6	2.9	2.7	2.5	2.5	2.5	2.5	2.5	2.6	2.7	3.1	3.2	2.9	2.6	2.6	1.9	1.3	0.9	0.5	0.2
S12000020	Moray	47.7	2.5	2.9	2.6	2.9	3.0	2.9	2.8	2.6	3.0	3.7	3.6	3.3	3.0	2.9	2.3	1.7	1.1	0.6	0.3
S12000013	Na h-Eileanan Siar	13.3	0.6	0.8	0.7	0.7	0.7	0.6	0.6	0.7	0.8	1.1	1.0	1.0	1.0	1.1	0.7	0.6	0.4	0.2	0.1
S12000021	North Ayrshire	64.7	3.5	3.8	3.7	4.0	4.1	3.6	3.2	3.2	3.7	4.6	5.1	4.8	4.3	4.5	3.4	2.5	1.6	0.7	0.3
S12000044	North Lanarkshire	164.2	9.8	10.5	10.1	10.4	10.8	10.2	10.4	10.4	11.0	12.7	12.9	11.1	9.4	8.9	6.3	4.7	3.0	1.3	0.5
S12000023	Orkney Islands	10.9	0.5	0.6	0.6	0.6	0.6	0.6	0.5	0.5	0.6	0.8	0.9	0.9	0.8	0.8	0.6	0.5	0.3	0.1	0.1
S12000024	Perth and Kinross	74.0	3.7	4.1	3.9	4.4	4.4	4.0	4.2	4.2	4.2	5.2	5.9	5.3	5.0	5.0	3.8	2.9	2.1	1.1	0.5
S12000038	Renfrewshire	84.7	4.8	4.8	4.6	5.1	5.5	5.7	5.4	4.9	5.0	6.3	6.8	6.4	5.1	4.8	3.6	2.7	1.8	0.9	0.4
S12000026	Scottish Borders	55.5	2.9	3.1	3.1	3.1	2.8	2.5	2.4	2.6	3.3	4.2	4.7	4.3	4.0	4.3	3.2	2.3	1.5	0.9	0.3
S12000027	Shetland Islands	11.8	0.7	0.7	0.7	0.7	0.7	0.7	0.7	0.7	0.8	0.8	0.9	0.8	0.8	0.8	0.5	0.4	0.2	0.1	0.0
S12000028	South Ayrshire	53.7	2.7	3.0	2.8	3.1	3.0	2.8	2.5	2.7	3.0	3.8	4.2	4.1	3.8	4.0	3.2	2.3	1.6	0.8	0.4
S12000029	South Lanarkshire	153.0	8.9	9.0	8.4	9.1	9.4	8.7	8.9	9.3	10.1	12.0	12.1	11.4	9.8	9.0	6.8	4.8	3.3	1.6	0.6
S12000030	Stirling	45.1	2.2	2.5	2.7	3.2	3.9	3.0	2.3	2.3	2.7	3.3	3.5	3.1	2.6	2.7	1.9	1.5	1.0	0.5	0.2
S12000039	West Dunbartonshire	42.7	2.5	2.7	2.4	2.5	2.9	2.9	2.7	2.4	2.4	3.1	3.5	3.2	2.8	2.4	1.8	1.2	0.9	0.4	0.2
S12000040	West Lothian	88.3	5.5	6.1	5.4	5.3	5.5	5.4	5.6	5.6	6.2	7.0	6.9	6.0	4.7	4.7	3.4	2.5	1.5	0.7	0.3
N92000002	NORTHERN IRELAND	915.2	64.0	65.2	58.2	61.0	61.0	61.8	60.7	57.9	58.7	63.7	64.4	57.0	48.3	43.4	36.2	25.1	16.5	8.6	3.6
N09000001	Antrim and Newtownabbey	68.5	4.7	5.1	4.5	4.5	4.4	4.3	4.3	4.4	4.5	4.8	5.0	4.2	3.6	3.3	2.8	1.9	1.3	0.6	0.2
N09000011	Ards and North Down	77.3	4.7	5.1	4.7	4.8	4.1	4.4	4.4	4.5	4.8	5.5	5.6	5.3	4.8	4.9	4.3	2.6	1.7	0.9	0.4
N09000002	Armagh City, Banbridge & Craigavon	104.3	7.8	8.0	6.8	6.7	6.4	7.3	7.1	7.0	6.9	7.3	7.3	6.3	5.1	4.6	3.9	2.7	1.7	0.9	0.4
N09000003	Belfast	164.4	11.8	11.3	9.4	11.3	14.7	13.0	12.8	10.8	9.9	10.3	10.7	9.7	7.9	6.4	5.4	4.0	2.8	1.6	0.7
N09000004	Causeway Coast and Glens	71.2	4.6	4.8	4.5	4.8	4.6	4.3	4.2	4.2	4.6	5.2	5.3	4.7	4.0	3.7	3.2	2.2	1.4	0.7	0.3
N09000005	Derry City and Strabane	73.7	5.4	5.4	4.9	5.5	4.9	4.9	4.8	4.4	4.7	5.4	5.3	4.4	3.7	3.5	2.7	1.9	1.2	0.6	0.2
N09000006	Fermanagh and Omagh	58.0	3.9	4.2	3.9	3.9	3.4	3.7	3.7	3.7	3.8	3.9	4.1	3.7	3.3	3.0	2.3	1.6	1.0	0.6	0.2
N09000007	Lisburn and Castlereagh	69.2	4.7	4.8	4.3	4.3	4.2	4.3	4.6	4.5	4.5	5.0	5.2	4.5	3.6	3.3	2.9	2.1	1.4	0.7	0.3
N09000008	Mid and East Antrim	67.5	4.1	4.3	4.2	4.2	4.2	4.3	3.9	3.9	4.3	5.1	5.1	4.6	3.9	3.6	3.1	2.2	1.4	0.7	0.3
N09000009	Mid Ulster	73.0	5.6	5.6	4.9	4.9	4.7	5.3	5.3	5.0	5.0	5.0	4.8	4.1	3.5	3.0	2.5	1.8	1.1	0.6	0.2
N09000010	Newry, Mourne and Down	88.1	6.7	6.7	6.0	6.1	5.4	5.9	5.7	5.5	5.6	6.1	6.2	5.4	4.6	4.0	3.2	2.3	1.5	0.8	0.3

MYE2: Population estimates: Females by selected age groups for local authorities in the UK, mid-2016

Thousands

Code	Name	All ages	0-4	5-9	10-14	15-19	20-24	25-29	30-34	35-39	40-44	45-49	50-54	55-59	60-64	65-69	70-74	75-79	80-84	85-89	90
														Age groups (years)							
K02000001	UNITED KINGDOM	33,270.4	1,956.4	1,970.6	1,768.4	1,839.4	2,077.3	2,235.8	2,208.9	2,099.4	2,105.2	2,342.2	2,350.2	2,059.5	1,802.9	1,872.5	1,491.8	1,165.1	912.7	612.5	399.5
K03000001	GREAT BRITAIN	32,323.5	1,895.7	1,908.3	1,713.3	1,781.9	2,019.5	2,173.6	2,145.8	2,037.8	2,043.7	2,275.3	2,283.8	2,000.7	1,754.3	1,826.4	1,451.4	1,134.7	889.5	597.3	390.4
K04000001	ENGLAND AND WALES	29,546.3	1,756.0	1,761.7	1,579.3	1,635.9	1,837.3	1,985.6	1,966.2	1,871.3	1,871.0	2,072.5	2,074.5	1,810.6	1,589.2	1,662.4	1,324.3	1,030.4	809.2	547.6	361.3
E92000001	ENGLAND	27,967.1	1,671.4	1,672.6	1,497.8	1,547.6	1,735.9	1,887.4	1,874.7	1,783.2	1,778.8	1,963.3	1,961.5	1,707.2	1,494.4	1,561.5	1,243.8	968.2	761.1	516.2	340.5
E12000001	NORTH EAST	1,342.6	71.8	74.5	67.7	73.9	89.9	85.6	82.8	76.5	78.9	93.1	99.2	91.5	80.1	82.7	62.3	51.9	39.8	25.3	15.3
E06000047	County Durham	265.3	13.5	14.4	13.0	14.6	18.0	15.7	15.4	14.6	15.4	19.0	20.0	18.4	16.5	17.3	13.4	10.6	7.8	4.9	2.9
E06000005	Darlington	54.5	3.1	3.2	2.9	2.9	2.8	3.4	3.4	3.3	3.5	3.9	4.1	3.7	3.1	3.3	2.5	2.2	1.7	1.1	0.7
E06000001	Hartlepool	47.6	2.7	2.9	2.6	2.7	2.8	3.1	3.0	2.7	2.7	3.4	3.6	3.2	2.8	2.8	2.0	1.9	1.5	0.9	0.5
E06000002	Middlesbrough	71.0	4.7	4.6	4.0	4.4	5.7	5.0	4.7	4.0	3.9	4.5	4.9	4.5	3.9	3.5	2.7	2.3	1.9	1.2	0.6
E06000057	Northumberland	162.5	7.3	8.1	8.1	8.0	7.1	8.3	8.6	8.6	9.3	11.7	13.0	12.7	11.5	12.5	9.3	7.2	5.4	3.5	2.3
E06000003	Redcar and Cleveland	69.7	3.7	3.8	3.5	3.7	3.7	4.1	4.0	3.7	4.0	4.9	5.4	4.8	4.4	4.7	3.8	3.1	2.2	1.4	0.9
E06000004	Stockton-on-Tees	99.5	5.8	6.3	5.5	5.4	5.8	6.3	6.7	6.0	6.1	7.0	7.4	6.7	5.7	5.6	4.2	3.5	2.7	1.7	1.0
E11000007	Tyne and Wear (Met County)	572.5	30.9	31.2	28.1	32.2	43.9	39.8	37.0	33.7	34.0	38.7	40.8	37.4	32.4	32.9	24.5	21.2	16.7	10.7	6.3
E08000037	Gateshead	103.0	5.5	5.8	5.2	5.6	5.9	7.0	7.2	6.3	6.2	7.2	7.5	6.8	5.7	6.1	4.7	4.1	3.2	1.9	1.2
E08000021	Newcastle upon Tyne	145.3	8.3	8.1	6.9	9.9	19.3	12.2	9.7	8.2	7.8	8.2	8.9	8.0	6.8	6.6	4.8	4.4	3.5	2.4	1.5
E08000022	North Tyneside	105.2	5.6	5.6	5.3	5.1	5.0	6.3	6.9	6.8	6.9	7.6	8.0	7.3	6.4	6.6	4.9	4.1	3.3	2.2	1.3
E08000023	South Tyneside	76.9	4.1	4.1	3.8	4.0	4.2	4.8	4.8	4.4	4.5	5.5	6.0	5.6	4.8	4.7	3.5	3.1	2.4	1.6	1.0
E08000024	Sunderland	142.1	7.5	7.6	6.9	7.5	9.6	9.6	8.4	8.0	8.5	10.2	10.5	9.8	8.7	8.9	6.6	5.5	4.4	2.6	1.3
E12000002	NORTH WEST	3,660.8	215.9	216.4	195.7	205.2	234.4	243.8	234.8	216.9	224.7	259.0	262.9	231.2	200.4	211.1	165.3	132.9	101.8	66.6	41.9
E06000008	Blackburn with Darwen	74.0	5.4	5.5	5.1	4.7	4.3	5.0	5.4	4.8	4.8	5.1	4.8	4.2	3.7	3.5	2.6	2.0	1.5	1.0	0.6
E06000009	Blackpool	70.8	4.2	3.9	3.7	3.9	4.1	4.4	4.1	3.7	4.1	5.2	5.3	4.6	4.0	4.4	3.5	2.9	2.3	1.5	1.0
E06000049	Cheshire East	192.4	9.8	10.4	10.1	10.0	8.8	9.2	10.3	10.8	12.5	15.1	15.1	13.2	11.5	13.2	10.5	8.1	6.3	4.5	3.0
E06000050	Cheshire West and Chester	172.0	9.1	9.2	8.8	9.2	10.0	9.6	9.8	9.7	10.9	12.7	13.2	11.7	10.2	11.2	8.7	7.1	5.3	3.5	2.3
E06000006	Halton	65.1	3.8	4.2	3.7	3.6	3.6	4.2	4.1	3.9	4.3	4.6	4.7	4.4	4.1	4.1	2.7	2.1	1.7	0.9	0.5
E06000007	Warrington	105.2	6.0	6.3	5.8	5.6	5.3	6.5	6.8	6.7	7.0	8.2	8.1	6.6	5.7	6.1	5.0	4.0	2.7	1.7	1.1
E10000006	Cumbria	252.8	12.1	12.7	12.4	12.8	12.0	12.8	13.2	13.0	15.0	19.1	19.8	18.3	16.7	18.4	14.3	11.5	8.7	5.9	3.9
E07000026	Allerdale	49.2	2.4	2.6	2.4	2.5	2.2	2.4	2.5	2.6	2.9	3.9	3.9	3.6	3.3	3.7	2.7	2.2	1.7	1.1	0.7
E07000027	Barrow-in-Furness	34.2	1.9	1.9	1.7	1.9	1.8	2.0	1.9	1.7	2.1	2.6	2.6	2.3	2.1	2.2	1.8	1.5	1.0	0.6	0.4
E07000028	Carlisle	55.5	3.0	3.0	2.8	2.9	3.4	3.2	3.3	3.1	3.3	3.9	4.1	3.9	3.4	3.5	2.8	2.2	1.8	1.2	0.8
E07000029	Copeland	34.5	1.8	1.8	1.7	1.7	1.6	2.0	1.9	1.8	2.1	2.6	2.8	2.5	2.2	2.4	1.8	1.5	1.1	0.7	0.4
E07000030	Eden	26.6	1.1	1.2	1.3	1.3	1.0	1.1	1.2	1.3	1.5	2.1	2.2	2.0	1.9	2.1	1.7	1.3	0.9	0.7	0.5
E07000031	South Lakeland	52.8	2.0	2.3	2.5	2.5	1.9	2.1	2.3	2.6	3.1	4.0	4.3	4.0	3.8	4.3	3.5	2.7	2.2	1.6	1.0
E11000001	Greater Manchester (Met County)	1,401.0	91.7	89.8	78.9	79.8	96.9	105.8	101.2	90.2	87.6	97.3	95.1	80.6	67.9	70.7	55.5	44.1	33.0	21.5	13.4
E08000001	Bolton	143.1	9.6	9.5	8.3	8.1	8.2	9.7	9.4	8.7	9.2	10.3	10.0	8.7	7.4	8.0	6.1	4.8	3.4	2.2	1.3
E08000002	Bury	96.1	6.0	6.1	5.4	5.1	4.8	6.2	6.3	6.0	6.2	7.2	7.0	6.1	5.2	5.5	4.3	3.5	2.6	1.5	1.0
E08000003	Manchester	267.3	19.1	17.2	14.2	17.6	34.7	29.9	24.2	18.4	14.9	14.8	14.0	11.2	9.0	8.0	6.2	5.3	4.1	2.7	1.7
E08000004	Oldham	118.1	8.3	8.4	7.6	7.2	6.8	8.1	8.0	7.3	7.0	8.0	8.1	6.8	6.0	6.2	4.9	3.8	2.7	1.7	1.1
E08000005	Rochdale	109.9	7.4	7.3	6.4	6.4	6.3	7.7	7.4	7.1	6.9	7.8	7.5	6.9	5.9	5.8	4.3	3.4	2.7	1.7	1.1
E08000006	Salford	123.1	8.7	7.7	6.5	6.7	9.2	10.9	10.4	8.0	7.4	8.0	7.8	6.7	5.3	5.7	4.5	3.6	2.8	1.8	1.3
E08000007	Stockport	148.0	9.0	8.7	7.8	7.7	6.9	8.8	9.3	9.5	9.5	10.8	11.0	9.5	8.2	8.7	7.1	5.8	4.6	3.1	1.9
E08000008	Tameside	113.6	7.3	7.1	6.3	6.0	6.3	7.9	7.8	6.8	7.1	8.4	8.5	7.1	6.0	6.5	5.0	4.0	2.8	1.8	1.1
E08000009	Trafford	119.6	7.3	8.1	7.4	6.4	5.0	6.4	8.0	8.7	8.7	9.1	9.1	7.3	5.9	6.1	4.9	4.2	3.3	2.4	1.5

MYE2: Population estimates: Females by selected age groups for local authorities in the UK, mid-2016

Thousands

Code	Name	All ages	0-4	5-9	10-14	15-19	20-24	25-29	30-34	35-39	40-44	45-49	50-54	55-59	60-64	65-69	70-74	75-79	80-84	85-89	90
																Age groups (years)					
E08000010	Wigan	162.2	9.1	9.6	8.9	8.5	8.8	10.3	10.4	9.7	10.6	12.8	12.2	10.3	9.0	10.1	8.1	5.9	4.0	2.5	1.5
E10000017	Lancashire	605.4	33.5	34.8	31.9	34.4	37.9	35.8	34.8	33.3	36.5	43.2	43.9	39.7	35.1	38.5	30.4	23.6	18.2	12.1	7.8
E07000117	Burnley	44.3	2.9	2.8	2.4	2.3	2.5	3.0	2.9	2.7	2.6	3.0	3.0	2.8	2.4	2.8	2.0	1.5	1.1	0.8	0.6
E07000118	Chorley	57.0	3.2	3.3	3.0	2.9	2.8	3.4	3.6	3.4	3.8	4.5	4.3	3.7	3.3	3.8	2.8	2.1	1.5	0.9	0.7
E07000119	Fylde	39.9	1.7	2.1	1.9	1.8	1.4	1.8	1.9	1.9	2.2	2.8	3.2	3.0	2.7	3.1	2.6	2.1	1.7	1.2	0.8
E07000120	Hyndburn	40.7	2.8	2.6	2.3	2.3	2.3	2.7	2.6	2.4	2.5	2.9	2.8	2.5	2.2	2.3	1.9	1.4	1.1	0.7	0.4
E07000121	Lancaster	72.0	3.8	3.7	3.3	5.0	7.1	4.1	4.0	3.7	3.9	4.7	5.0	4.6	4.0	4.3	3.5	2.7	2.2	1.4	1.0
E07000122	Pendle	45.7	3.1	3.0	2.7	2.5	2.4	3.0	3.2	2.8	2.8	3.1	3.0	2.9	2.6	2.8	2.0	1.5	1.2	0.9	0.5
E07000123	Preston	69.7	4.5	4.4	3.9	4.5	7.0	5.2	4.4	4.1	4.1	4.6	4.5	4.0	3.3	3.2	2.4	2.1	1.7	1.1	0.7
E07000124	Ribble Valley	29.9	1.2	1.6	1.7	1.7	1.1	1.4	1.4	1.5	1.9	2.4	2.5	2.2	1.9	2.2	1.7	1.3	1.0	0.7	0.5
E07000125	Rossendale	35.4	2.1	2.2	2.0	1.9	1.7	2.2	2.2	2.1	2.4	2.8	2.6	2.4	2.2	2.2	1.6	1.1	0.9	0.6	0.4
E07000126	South Ribble	56.3	3.0	3.2	3.0	2.9	2.6	3.4	3.3	3.2	3.7	4.2	4.3	3.7	3.3	3.7	2.9	2.3	1.6	1.1	0.7
E07000127	West Lancashire	58.1	2.8	3.0	2.9	3.8	4.4	2.9	2.7	2.8	3.5	4.1	4.4	3.9	3.5	3.9	3.2	2.4	1.8	1.2	0.7
E07000128	Wyre	56.4	2.4	2.7	2.7	2.7	2.6	2.7	2.7	2.7	3.1	4.0	4.3	4.1	3.7	4.3	3.7	3.1	2.3	1.6	1.0
E11000002	Merseyside (Met County)	722.0	40.3	39.4	35.6	41.1	51.4	50.3	45.2	40.6	42.0	48.7	52.7	47.9	41.5	41.1	32.2	27.6	22.2	14.0	8.3
E08000011	Knowsley	77.5	4.7	4.5	4.1	4.5	4.8	5.5	5.0	4.4	4.5	5.5	6.0	5.5	4.5	4.0	3.0	2.7	2.3	1.3	0.7
E08000012	Liverpool	244.9	14.3	12.7	11.0	15.9	27.0	21.3	17.5	14.7	13.4	14.9	16.4	14.6	12.3	11.3	8.3	7.4	6.1	3.7	2.0
E08000014	Sefton	142.4	7.1	7.4	7.0	7.3	6.8	8.0	7.5	7.2	8.3	9.8	11.1	10.5	9.1	9.2	7.8	6.8	5.6	3.7	2.2
E08000013	St. Helens	90.8	5.0	5.2	4.6	4.7	5.0	5.9	5.6	5.0	5.7	6.7	6.6	5.9	5.3	6.0	4.7	3.7	2.7	1.6	0.9
E08000015	Wirral	166.4	9.2	9.5	8.9	8.7	7.9	9.6	9.5	9.3	10.1	11.8	12.6	11.5	10.3	10.6	8.4	6.9	5.5	3.7	2.4
E12000003	**YORKSHIRE AND THE HUMBER**	**2,747.2**	161.7	163.6	148.7	158.2	188.3	180.0	173.5	161.1	166.6	191.8	190.4	171.5	150.0	158.0	124.2	99.4	77.8	50.6	31.7
E06000011	East Riding of Yorkshire	172.1	7.6	8.8	8.7	9.1	7.0	7.6	7.9	8.9	10.7	12.7	13.4	12.3	11.9	13.8	10.6	8.4	6.4	3.9	2.5
E06000010	Kingston upon Hull, City of	129.2	8.7	8.0	6.7	7.0	10.9	11.2	9.6	7.6	7.7	8.2	8.6	7.7	6.4	6.3	4.5	3.9	3.1	2.0	1.1
E06000012	North East Lincolnshire	81.3	4.9	4.9	4.5	4.3	4.3	5.5	5.0	4.4	4.7	5.8	6.0	5.3	4.6	4.8	3.8	3.3	2.5	1.7	1.0
E06000013	North Lincolnshire	86.2	4.7	5.2	4.6	4.6	4.2	5.2	5.2	4.7	5.1	6.3	6.4	5.9	5.4	5.6	4.4	3.3	2.6	1.7	1.2
E06000014	York	105.6	5.0	5.3	4.7	7.1	11.5	7.4	6.4	6.1	6.0	7.0	6.8	6.0	5.3	5.9	4.7	3.8	3.1	2.1	1.4
E10000023	North Yorkshire	309.0	14.8	16.2	15.9	15.4	12.7	15.2	15.2	15.7	18.6	23.2	24.7	22.5	20.6	22.5	18.2	14.3	10.9	7.4	4.9
E07000163	Craven	29.1	1.2	1.4	1.4	1.5	1.1	1.2	1.2	1.4	1.7	2.2	2.4	2.2	2.1	2.3	1.9	1.4	1.2	0.8	0.6
E07000164	Hambleton	46.1	2.2	2.3	2.3	2.3	1.8	2.1	2.1	2.2	2.7	3.5	3.9	3.4	3.1	3.5	2.9	2.3	1.7	1.1	0.7
E07000165	Harrogate	81.7	3.9	4.5	4.6	4.2	3.1	3.8	4.1	4.6	5.3	6.4	6.6	5.8	5.0	5.4	4.4	3.7	2.9	2.0	1.5
E07000166	Richmondshire	24.8	1.4	1.4	1.3	1.2	1.1	1.4	1.4	1.3	1.4	1.9	1.9	1.8	1.6	1.8	1.4	1.0	0.8	0.5	0.3
E07000167	Ryedale	27.5	1.2	1.3	1.3	1.4	1.2	1.3	1.2	1.2	1.6	2.1	2.2	2.1	2.0	2.1	1.8	1.4	1.0	0.7	0.4
E07000168	Scarborough	55.6	2.6	2.7	2.6	2.6	2.8	2.8	2.6	2.5	3.0	3.7	4.2	4.2	4.0	4.5	3.6	2.9	2.2	1.5	0.9
E07000169	Selby	44.3	2.4	2.5	2.4	2.3	1.9	2.6	2.6	2.6	2.9	3.5	3.6	3.1	2.7	2.9	2.2	1.6	1.2	0.8	0.5
E11000003	South Yorkshire (Met County)	699.3	40.5	41.1	37.2	40.7	52.8	49.3	44.9	40.5	41.6	49.0	47.4	42.9	37.1	38.0	31.5	25.0	19.6	12.4	7.8
E08000016	Barnsley	122.6	7.3	6.9	6.4	6.5	6.9	7.9	7.9	7.1	7.4	9.1	9.1	8.3	7.1	7.2	6.0	4.5	3.4	2.3	1.3
E08000017	Doncaster	154.8	9.0	9.6	8.5	8.1	8.4	10.4	10.1	8.8	9.1	10.9	11.2	10.3	9.0	9.2	7.0	5.8	4.6	2.8	1.7
E08000018	Rotherham	133.2	8.0	7.9	7.4	7.3	7.1	8.5	8.3	7.6	8.3	9.6	9.4	8.8	7.6	7.9	6.7	5.1	3.8	2.4	1.6
E08000019	Sheffield	288.7	16.3	16.6	14.9	18.7	30.4	22.4	18.6	17.0	16.8	19.4	17.7	15.5	13.5	13.7	11.8	9.6	7.7	4.9	3.2
E11000006	West Yorkshire (Met County)	1,164.6	75.5	74.2	66.5	70.0	84.9	78.7	79.4	73.2	72.2	79.6	77.1	68.9	58.7	61.0	46.4	37.5	29.6	19.4	11.8
E08000032	Bradford	270.1	20.3	19.9	18.5	17.4	15.9	18.1	19.1	17.7	16.8	17.7	17.1	15.8	13.2	12.6	9.0	7.9	6.4	4.1	2.6
E08000033	Calderdale	106.4	6.3	6.6	6.1	5.9	6.5	6.5	6.5	6.5	6.9	8.0	7.0	7.0	6.0	6.4	4.8	3.6	2.8	2.0	1.3
E08000034	Kirklees	219.6	13.7	14.2	13.1	13.1	13.5	14.0	14.0	13.8	13.9	15.6	15.0	13.2	11.4	12.5	9.5	7.4	5.5	3.7	2.2
E08000035	Leeds	397.3	25.1	23.6	20.0	24.8	40.9	28.7	28.3	25.2	23.8	25.5	24.6	21.6	18.4	19.4	14.8	12.4	10.1	6.5	3.8
E08000036	Wakefield	171.2	10.2	9.9	8.9	8.9	9.2	11.5	11.4	9.9	10.8	12.8	12.4	11.2	9.8	10.2	8.3	6.2	4.8	3.0	1.9

MYE2: Population estimates: Females by selected age groups for local authorities in the UK, mid-2016

Thousands

Code	Name	All ages	Age groups (years)																			
			0-4	5-9	10-14	15-19	20-24	25-29	30-34	35-39	40-44	45-49	50-54	55-59	60-64	65-69	70-74	75-79	80-84	85-89	90
E12000004	EAST MIDLANDS	2,390.1	136.2	139.1	126.3	136.6	155.3	148.4	145.7	140.2	148.7	171.8	172.7	151.2	135.0	143.7	114.0	85.4	65.8	44.6	29.2
E06000015	Derby	129.1	8.7	8.7	7.2	7.7	9.0	9.5	8.9	8.3	7.9	8.8	8.6	7.0	6.0	6.2	5.0	4.1	3.5	2.5	1.6
E06000016	Leicester	175.1	12.8	11.9	10.3	11.6	19.1	15.4	13.2	11.3	10.2	10.2	9.6	9.1	7.7	6.5	4.7	4.2	3.3	2.3	1.5
E06000018	Nottingham	160.4	10.5	9.4	8.0	12.8	24.7	13.9	10.8	9.2	8.6	9.2	8.9	7.5	6.5	5.5	4.4	3.8	3.2	2.2	1.4
E06000017	Rutland	19.0	0.9	1.0	1.0	1.2	0.8	0.8	0.8	1.0	1.1	1.4	1.4	1.3	1.3	1.4	1.2	0.9	0.7	0.5	0.4
E10000007	Derbyshire	400.0	20.2	21.3	20.5	21.0	20.3	22.4	22.4	22.6	25.5	31.2	31.4	27.2	24.7	26.8	21.6	15.7	12.1	8.0	5.3
E07000032	Amber Valley	63.5	3.1	3.3	3.1	3.3	3.2	3.5	3.6	3.6	4.1	4.9	4.9	4.3	4.0	4.5	3.5	2.4	1.9	1.3	0.9
E07000033	Bolsover	39.6	2.2	2.2	2.1	2.1	2.1	2.4	2.5	2.1	2.5	3.2	3.0	2.6	2.3	2.4	2.1	1.5	1.1	0.7	0.5
E07000034	Chesterfield	53.3	2.8	2.9	2.5	2.7	3.0	3.3	3.0	3.1	3.4	4.0	4.0	3.6	3.1	3.4	2.7	2.1	1.6	1.1	0.8
E07000035	Derbyshire Dales	36.3	1.4	1.7	1.9	1.9	1.4	1.4	1.5	1.6	2.2	2.8	3.1	2.8	2.7	3.0	2.3	1.8	1.4	0.9	0.6
E07000036	Erewash	58.7	3.1	3.2	3.0	3.0	3.1	3.8	3.6	3.5	3.8	4.6	4.6	3.7	3.3	3.6	2.9	2.2	1.8	1.2	0.8
E07000037	High Peak	46.5	2.3	2.5	2.4	2.6	2.5	2.4	2.5	2.6	2.9	3.7	3.9	3.5	2.9	3.1	2.5	1.8	1.3	0.8	0.6
E07000038	North East Derbyshire	51.4	2.4	2.5	2.6	2.6	2.5	2.6	2.6	2.7	3.1	4.0	3.9	3.6	3.4	3.8	3.3	2.4	1.7	1.1	0.6
E07000039	South Derbyshire	50.8	2.8	3.0	2.8	2.8	2.4	3.1	3.2	3.3	3.5	4.1	4.0	3.2	3.0	3.0	2.3	1.6	1.3	0.9	0.4
E10000018	Leicestershire	343.7	17.9	19.3	18.1	19.4	20.0	19.4	20.1	19.9	21.9	25.9	26.0	22.3	20.0	21.9	17.3	12.8	10.0	6.9	4.6
E07000129	Blaby	49.8	2.6	3.0	2.7	2.7	2.3	2.9	3.2	2.9	3.3	3.7	3.7	3.2	2.8	3.1	2.5	2.0	1.5	1.0	0.6
E07000130	Charnwood	88.0	4.6	4.8	4.3	5.5	7.9	5.6	5.6	5.1	5.2	6.1	6.0	5.3	4.8	5.0	4.0	3.0	2.4	1.7	1.1
E07000131	Harborough	45.5	2.2	2.7	2.6	2.5	1.8	2.1	2.2	2.6	3.1	3.8	3.8	3.1	2.8	3.1	2.4	1.8	1.4	1.0	0.7
E07000132	Hinckley and Bosworth	55.7	2.9	3.0	2.9	2.8	2.5	3.2	3.3	3.3	3.6	4.3	4.3	3.8	3.5	3.9	3.0	2.2	1.6	1.1	0.7
E07000133	Melton	26.0	1.3	1.5	1.4	1.4	1.2	1.3	1.3	1.4	1.6	2.1	2.2	1.8	1.6	1.8	1.4	0.9	0.8	0.5	0.3
E07000134	North West Leicestershire	49.6	2.6	2.9	2.7	2.6	2.6	2.8	2.9	2.9	3.4	3.9	3.8	3.3	2.9	3.2	2.6	1.7	1.3	0.9	0.7
E07000135	Oadby and Wigston	28.9	1.5	1.6	1.5	1.9	1.7	1.5	1.6	1.6	1.7	2.0	2.2	1.8	1.6	1.7	1.5	1.2	1.1	0.7	0.5
E10000019	Lincolnshire	380.4	19.9	19.9	18.7	20.9	20.8	20.7	21.0	20.2	22.0	26.9	28.4	26.0	24.2	27.0	21.9	16.4	12.1	8.2	5.3
E07000136	Boston	34.2	2.2	1.9	1.7	1.7	1.6	2.2	2.3	2.0	2.0	2.3	2.4	2.2	2.1	2.1	1.7	1.4	1.1	0.7	0.5
E07000137	East Lindsey	71.1	3.2	3.3	3.2	3.4	2.7	3.3	3.0	3.0	3.7	4.8	5.4	5.5	5.3	6.5	5.3	3.8	2.7	1.8	1.1
E07000138	Lincoln	49.3	2.9	2.4	2.1	3.8	6.6	3.6	3.3	2.9	2.5	2.9	3.1	2.7	2.3	2.3	1.8	1.4	1.2	0.8	0.6
E07000139	North Kesteven	58.1	3.0	3.2	3.0	3.1	2.5	3.0	3.2	3.1	3.5	4.6	4.5	3.9	3.4	4.1	3.4	2.7	1.8	1.2	0.8
E07000140	South Holland	47.1	2.6	2.4	2.3	2.4	2.1	2.6	2.7	2.5	2.9	3.2	3.5	3.1	3.0	3.4	2.7	2.2	1.7	1.1	0.7
E07000141	South Kesteven	72.7	3.7	4.2	3.9	3.9	3.0	3.7	4.0	4.1	4.6	5.5	5.6	5.2	4.6	5.0	4.0	2.8	2.2	1.5	1.1
E07000142	West Lindsey	48.0	2.4	2.5	2.4	2.6	2.2	2.2	2.5	2.5	2.8	3.6	3.6	3.6	3.3	3.5	2.9	2.0	1.5	1.0	0.6
E10000021	Northamptonshire	370.6	23.3	23.9	21.4	20.4	19.0	22.0	24.3	23.5	25.4	27.7	27.1	23.1	20.4	22.4	16.3	11.5	8.7	6.1	4.2
E07000150	Corby	34.7	2.5	2.5	2.0	1.9	1.8	2.4	2.9	2.3	2.2	2.3	2.5	2.2	1.8	1.7	1.3	1.0	0.7	0.4	0.2
E07000151	Daventry	40.6	2.0	2.4	2.3	2.2	1.7	2.0	2.0	2.3	2.8	3.5	3.4	2.8	2.6	2.9	2.1	1.4	1.0	0.7	0.5
E07000152	East Northamptonshire	46.2	2.5	2.7	2.7	2.7	2.0	2.4	2.6	2.8	3.2	3.7	3.5	3.1	2.8	3.2	2.3	1.6	1.2	0.9	0.6
E07000153	Kettering	50.3	3.2	3.2	2.9	2.7	2.4	3.1	3.2	3.2	3.5	3.8	3.6	2.9	2.7	3.2	2.3	1.6	1.2	0.9	0.7
E07000154	Northampton	113.2	8.0	7.7	6.5	6.4	7.6	7.7	8.8	7.8	7.7	7.4	7.6	6.3	5.6	5.7	4.1	3.1	2.4	1.7	1.1
E07000155	South Northamptonshire	45.6	2.4	2.7	2.7	2.4	1.7	2.1	2.3	2.9	3.4	3.9	3.7	3.2	2.7	3.2	2.3	1.6	1.2	0.8	0.6
E07000156	Wellingborough	40.0	2.6	2.6	2.3	2.2	1.7	2.3	2.6	2.4	2.7	3.0	2.8	2.5	2.3	2.6	1.9	1.3	1.0	0.7	0.5
E10000024	Nottinghamshire	411.7	22.2	23.7	21.1	21.6	21.5	24.4	24.1	24.2	26.2	30.5	31.3	27.6	24.3	26.1	21.4	16.0	12.3	8.1	5.0
E07000170	Ashfield	63.4	3.6	3.8	3.4	3.4	3.5	4.3	3.9	3.8	4.1	4.8	4.7	4.0	3.6	3.7	3.2	2.4	1.7	1.0	0.6
E07000171	Bassetlaw	58.0	3.2	3.2	3.0	3.1	2.9	3.1	3.0	3.2	3.6	4.4	4.6	4.1	3.6	4.0	3.2	2.3	1.8	1.1	0.7
E07000172	Broxtowe	56.5	3.0	3.1	2.7	2.9	3.0	3.7	3.5	3.3	3.6	4.0	4.3	3.7	3.2	3.8	2.9	2.2	1.7	1.1	0.7
E07000173	Gedling	59.9	3.1	3.3	3.0	3.1	2.9	3.5	3.6	3.7	3.9	4.5	4.5	4.1	3.6	3.8	3.0	2.4	1.9	1.2	0.7
E07000174	Mansfield	54.8	3.3	3.3	2.7	2.8	3.2	3.6	3.6	3.3	3.3	3.9	4.1	3.7	3.1	3.1	2.7	1.9	1.6	1.1	0.6
E07000175	Newark and Sherwood	60.7	3.2	3.5	3.2	3.2	3.2	3.3	3.2	3.3	3.8	4.5	4.7	4.2	3.8	4.1	3.4	2.5	1.8	1.2	0.8
E07000176	Rushcliffe	58.4	2.9	3.5	3.2	3.1	3.0	2.9	3.2	3.7	4.0	4.5	4.4	3.8	3.4	3.6	3.0	2.2	1.9	1.3	0.9

MYE2: Population estimates: Females by selected age groups for local authorities in the UK, mid-2016

Thousands

Code	Name	All ages	Age groups (years)																		
			0-4	5-9	10-14	15-19	20-24	25-29	30-34	35-39	40-44	45-49	50-54	55-59	60-64	65-69	70-74	75-79	80-84	85-89	90+
E12000005	WEST MIDLANDS	2,922.6	177.7	170.0	184.4	170.0	191.0	194.6	185.2	175.6	179.1	204.2	202.9	175.0	156.8	162.4	136.5	106.0	81.8	54.9	35.9
E06000019	Herefordshire, County of	95.6	4.6	5.1	4.7	4.9	4.2	5.2	5.1	5.2	5.4	6.8	7.2	6.8	6.6	6.9	5.8	4.2	3.4	2.3	1.5
E06000051	Shropshire	158.3	7.3	8.2	8.3	8.6	7.1	7.9	7.8	8.2	9.3	11.4	12.2	11.2	10.6	11.6	9.7	7.3	5.4	3.6	2.6
E06000021	Stoke-on-Trent	126.8	8.7	8.2	6.9	7.0	8.9	9.2	8.7	7.4	7.5	8.4	8.3	7.5	6.8	7.0	5.4	4.3	3.3	2.1	1.2
E06000020	Telford and Wrekin	87.4	5.4	5.8	5.3	5.3	5.4	5.3	5.7	5.4	5.5	6.4	6.2	5.4	4.9	4.9	3.8	2.8	2.0	1.2	0.8
E10000028	Staffordshire	435.5	21.8	23.8	22.4	23.3	23.3	24.8	24.5	24.2	27.3	32.6	33.2	29.2	26.6	28.9	24.0	18.1	13.3	8.6	5.5
E07000192	Cannock Chase	49.7	2.7	2.8	2.6	2.7	3.2	3.2	3.2	2.9	3.2	3.9	3.9	3.1	2.9	2.9	2.4	1.9	1.3	0.9	0.5
E07000193	East Staffordshire	58.4	3.6	3.5	3.3	3.1	3.0	3.5	3.6	3.4	3.6	4.3	4.4	3.8	3.2	3.4	2.8	2.2	1.7	1.1	0.7
E07000194	Lichfield	51.8	2.5	2.8	2.7	2.6	2.3	2.5	2.7	3.0	3.3	3.9	4.0	3.4	3.2	3.7	3.4	2.4	1.6	1.0	0.7
E07000195	Newcastle-under-Lyme	64.5	3.1	3.3	3.2	3.9	5.0	4.1	3.8	3.5	3.9	4.5	4.6	4.1	3.8	4.1	3.1	2.6	2.0	1.3	0.8
E07000196	South Staffordshire	55.8	2.4	2.7	2.7	3.0	2.6	2.8	2.6	2.8	3.4	4.2	4.5	4.1	3.7	4.1	3.5	2.7	2.0	1.2	0.8
E07000197	Stafford	66.4	3.2	3.7	3.3	3.4	3.3	3.6	3.6	3.8	4.2	5.1	5.1	4.5	4.1	4.5	3.9	2.9	2.0	1.4	0.9
E07000198	Staffordshire Moorlands	49.8	2.1	2.6	2.5	2.5	2.3	2.4	2.3	2.5	3.1	3.9	3.9	3.5	3.3	3.9	3.0	2.3	1.7	1.1	0.7
E07000199	Tamworth	39.2	2.3	2.4	2.1	2.2	2.1	2.6	2.7	2.4	2.6	2.8	2.8	2.5	2.3	2.3	1.8	1.3	1.0	0.6	0.4
E10000031	Warwickshire	282.4	15.4	16.1	14.8	15.1	15.1	16.5	16.6	16.7	18.2	20.8	21.0	18.1	16.1	17.6	15.1	11.0	8.4	5.9	4.1
E07000218	North Warwickshire	32.0	1.6	1.7	1.6	1.6	1.5	1.8	1.8	1.8	2.0	2.5	2.5	2.3	2.0	2.2	1.7	1.3	0.9	0.6	0.4
E07000219	Nuneaton and Bedworth	65.0	3.9	4.0	3.5	3.5	3.4	4.2	4.3	3.9	4.0	4.6	4.7	4.0	3.7	3.9	3.2	2.4	1.8	1.1	0.7
E07000220	Rugby	52.8	3.2	3.4	2.9	3.0	2.3	3.1	3.6	3.5	3.6	3.8	3.9	3.1	2.8	2.9	2.6	1.9	1.4	1.0	0.8
E07000221	Stratford-on-Avon	63.1	3.0	3.1	3.2	3.1	2.4	2.8	2.9	3.2	4.1	4.8	5.1	4.6	4.0	4.6	4.1	2.9	2.3	1.7	1.2
E07000222	Warwick	69.5	3.7	3.9	3.5	3.8	5.5	4.6	3.9	4.4	4.5	5.0	4.8	4.1	3.7	3.9	3.3	2.5	2.0	1.5	1.0
E11000005	West Midlands (Met County)	1,450.5	98.9	95.6	86.6	90.2	112.0	109.4	100.3	91.8	87.3	96.0	92.8	77.7	66.7	65.7	56.3	46.2	37.0	24.7	15.5
E08000025	Birmingham	570.4	41.8	39.5	36.4	39.6	52.8	46.2	40.8	38.0	34.0	35.3	33.6	28.2	23.4	21.9	17.9	15.0	12.4	8.4	5.3
E08000026	Coventry	175.0	11.5	11.0	9.4	11.1	18.7	16.2	12.7	10.8	10.1	10.5	10.0	8.5	7.5	7.3	6.3	5.1	3.9	2.7	1.8
E08000027	Dudley	161.7	9.5	9.5	9.1	8.7	8.7	10.0	10.1	9.5	9.8	11.9	11.5	9.6	8.9	9.4	8.3	6.6	5.2	3.3	1.9
E08000028	Sandwell	162.7	11.8	11.4	9.9	9.2	9.7	11.6	12.5	10.8	10.2	11.4	10.9	8.7	7.5	7.1	6.3	5.2	4.0	2.6	1.7
E08000029	Solihull	108.9	6.0	6.4	6.0	6.0	5.3	6.0	6.0	6.4	6.8	8.1	8.4	7.0	6.0	6.6	5.7	4.4	3.6	2.6	1.7
E08000030	Walsall	141.8	9.4	9.3	8.5	8.3	8.5	9.9	9.3	8.3	8.4	9.7	9.5	8.2	7.0	7.2	6.5	5.3	4.2	2.6	1.6
E08000031	Wolverhampton	130.0	8.8	8.5	7.3	7.3	8.3	9.4	8.9	8.1	8.0	9.1	8.8	7.4	6.4	6.1	5.2	4.6	3.7	2.5	1.6
E10000034	Worcestershire	296.2	15.6	16.1	15.4	15.6	15.0	16.4	16.5	16.8	18.6	21.9	22.0	19.3	18.5	19.9	16.4	12.0	9.2	6.5	4.7
E07000234	Bromsgrove	49.0	2.5	2.7	2.6	2.4	2.2	2.5	2.5	2.8	3.2	3.8	3.9	3.2	3.0	3.1	2.8	2.0	1.7	1.3	0.9
E07000235	Malvern Hills	39.2	1.6	1.9	2.0	2.1	1.6	1.6	1.6	1.9	2.2	2.8	3.1	2.8	2.8	3.1	2.7	2.0	1.5	1.1	0.8
E07000236	Redditch	42.8	2.7	2.6	2.4	2.3	2.1	2.8	3.1	2.9	2.8	3.0	2.9	2.7	2.7	2.6	1.9	1.2	0.9	0.6	0.5
E07000237	Worcester	51.6	3.0	3.0	2.7	3.2	3.7	3.7	3.5	3.2	3.4	3.6	3.4	2.9	2.6	2.6	1.7	1.7	1.3	0.9	0.6
E07000238	Wychavon	62.9	3.1	3.3	3.3	3.2	2.5	2.9	3.1	3.3	3.8	4.9	5.0	4.4	4.2	4.7	3.7	2.8	2.1	1.5	1.1
E07000239	Wyre Forest	50.7	2.7	2.7	2.4	2.5	2.3	2.8	2.7	2.7	3.1	3.9	3.7	3.2	3.2	3.9	3.3	2.3	1.6	1.1	0.8
E12000006	EAST	3,107.7	185.0	187.0	166.8	167.3	167.5	189.4	195.9	196.4	200.5	221.4	222.2	192.2	172.6	186.4	147.9	112.9	91.3	63.3	41.8
E06000055	Bedford	85.3	5.5	5.4	4.8	4.8	4.3	5.0	5.8	6.0	5.7	6.2	6.2	5.2	4.5	4.6	3.6	2.7	2.4	1.6	1.1
E06000056	Central Bedfordshire	139.9	8.7	8.7	7.8	7.0	6.5	8.7	9.3	9.7	9.6	10.5	10.8	9.1	7.8	8.1	6.2	4.4	3.5	2.2	1.3
E06000032	Luton	106.7	8.8	8.0	6.8	6.6	7.2	8.6	9.1	7.8	6.7	6.6	6.7	5.3	4.4	3.9	3.1	2.8	2.2	1.4	0.8
E06000031	Peterborough	98.2	7.8	6.9	5.7	5.3	5.3	7.2	8.0	7.1	6.3	6.5	6.4	5.4	4.9	4.5	3.4	2.6	2.3	1.6	0.9
E06000033	Southend-on-Sea	92.1	5.7	5.6	4.8	4.9	4.7	5.5	6.0	6.2	6.4	6.6	6.3	5.4	4.8	5.3	4.4	3.2	2.7	2.1	1.5
E06000034	Thurrock	85.3	6.2	6.3	5.1	4.8	4.7	6.0	6.7	6.5	6.2	6.2	5.6	4.5	3.9	4.0	3.0	2.2	1.7	1.1	0.7
E10000003	Cambridgeshire	322.1	18.9	18.9	16.9	18.2	20.4	19.3	20.1	20.9	21.2	23.3	23.0	19.6	17.9	18.8	14.7	11.1	8.6	6.2	4.2
E07000008	Cambridge	59.9	3.4	3.3	2.8	4.6	8.9	4.6	4.0	4.0	3.5	3.4	3.3	2.8	2.6	2.3	1.8	1.5	1.3	1.0	0.8
E07000009	East Cambridgeshire	44.6	2.7	2.8	2.4	2.2	1.7	2.5	2.9	3.1	3.1	3.4	3.3	2.8	2.6	2.7	2.1	1.5	1.2	0.9	0.6

Thousands

MYE2: Population estimates: Females by selected age groups for local authorities in the UK, mid-2016

Code	Name	All ages	0-4	5-9	10-14	15-19	20-24	25-29	30-34	35-39	40-44	45-49	50-54	55-59	60-64	65-69	70-74	75-79	80-84	85-89	90
E07000010	Fenland	50.4	2.9	2.7	2.5	2.7	2.6	2.9	3.0	2.6	2.9	3.6	3.6	3.2	3.3	3.5	2.7	2.1	1.7	1.2	0.8
E07000011	Huntingdonshire	88.1	5.1	5.1	4.6	4.5	4.0	5.4	5.4	5.7	5.8	6.7	6.8	5.8	5.1	5.6	4.3	3.2	2.3	1.5	1.1
E07000012	South Cambridgeshire	79.0	4.7	5.0	4.6	4.2	3.2	4.0	4.7	5.5	5.7	6.2	5.9	5.0	4.4	4.7	3.7	2.8	2.1	1.5	1.0
E10000012	Essex	744.7	41.9	42.9	39.5	39.5	38.9	44.1	43.8	45.2	47.8	54.5	54.6	47.3	42.5	47.6	37.8	28.5	22.7	15.5	10.1
E07000066	Basildon	94.5	6.3	5.8	5.3	5.2	5.0	6.3	6.5	6.3	6.2	6.7	6.7	5.8	4.9	5.1	4.0	3.2	2.6	1.7	1.0
E07000067	Braintree	76.9	4.1	4.8	4.3	4.0	3.5	4.5	4.6	4.7	5.1	5.9	5.9	4.9	4.5	5.1	3.7	2.6	2.0	1.5	1.1
E07000068	Brentwood	39.5	2.1	2.1	2.2	2.1	1.9	2.2	2.3	2.5	2.6	3.0	3.1	2.5	2.1	2.2	1.9	1.5	1.4	1.0	0.6
E07000069	Castle Point	46.0	2.1	2.4	2.3	2.5	2.3	2.4	2.3	2.3	2.7	3.3	3.3	3.0	3.0	3.7	3.0	2.3	1.7	1.0	0.6
E07000070	Chelmsford	88.0	4.8	5.2	4.9	4.5	4.6	5.5	5.6	5.8	6.0	6.5	6.4	5.4	4.8	5.4	4.2	3.1	2.5	1.7	1.1
E07000071	Colchester	94.4	5.9	5.4	4.8	5.4	7.2	7.1	6.2	6.0	6.0	6.5	6.4	5.3	4.8	5.5	4.1	3.0	2.4	1.6	1.1
E07000072	Epping Forest	67.1	4.0	3.7	3.4	3.4	3.4	4.0	4.0	4.4	4.4	5.1	5.2	4.3	3.7	3.8	3.2	2.4	2.0	1.5	1.0
E07000073	Harlow	44.1	3.2	3.0	2.4	2.3	2.3	3.1	3.5	3.0	2.9	3.0	3.0	2.7	2.2	2.0	1.6	1.4	1.3	0.9	0.5
E07000074	Maldon	32.2	1.5	1.6	1.6	1.7	1.4	1.5	1.4	1.7	2.1	2.6	2.5	2.4	2.3	2.5	2.0	1.4	1.0	0.7	0.4
E07000075	Rochford	43.8	2.0	2.4	2.3	2.4	2.2	2.2	2.1	2.4	2.9	3.5	3.3	2.9	2.7	3.1	2.6	1.9	1.5	1.0	0.6
E07000076	Tendring	74.3	3.5	3.7	3.4	3.6	3.3	3.3	3.1	3.3	3.8	4.8	5.3	5.1	5.2	6.5	5.5	4.1	3.2	2.2	1.5
E07000077	Uttlesford	43.9	2.5	2.7	2.7	2.4	1.8	2.1	2.3	2.8	3.1	3.5	3.6	3.0	2.5	2.6	2.1	1.5	1.2	0.9	0.6
E10000015	Hertfordshire	600.3	37.6	38.7	33.9	32.6	31.9	37.5	40.7	42.5	42.5	44.0	43.6	36.2	29.6	30.3	24.0	19.4	16.4	11.3	7.5
E07000095	Broxbourne	50.0	3.2	3.1	2.7	2.7	2.5	3.2	3.3	3.4	3.3	3.8	3.7	3.1	2.5	2.6	2.1	1.9	1.5	1.0	0.5
E07000096	Dacorum	77.5	4.8	5.0	4.2	4.2	3.7	4.9	5.3	5.4	5.4	5.7	5.8	5.0	4.1	4.0	3.1	2.5	2.1	1.5	1.0
E07000242	East Hertfordshire	74.5	4.2	4.6	4.4	4.2	3.4	4.1	4.4	5.1	5.6	6.0	5.9	4.8	3.8	4.1	3.2	2.4	2.0	1.3	0.9
E07000098	Hertsmere	53.8	3.4	3.5	3.1	2.8	2.6	3.3	3.5	3.5	3.8	3.9	3.9	3.3	2.7	2.9	2.3	1.8	1.6	1.1	0.8
E07000099	North Hertfordshire	67.6	4.0	4.2	3.7	3.5	2.9	3.8	4.5	4.8	4.9	5.1	5.0	4.1	3.5	3.8	3.0	2.4	2.0	1.3	1.0
E07000240	St Albans	75.1	5.0	5.4	4.6	4.0	3.0	4.1	4.7	5.8	6.0	5.6	5.3	4.3	3.7	3.8	3.0	2.4	1.9	1.4	1.0
E07000243	Stevenage	44.3	3.0	2.9	2.4	2.2	2.5	3.3	3.4	3.0	2.8	3.2	3.3	2.7	2.0	2.0	1.6	1.4	1.2	0.8	0.4
E07000102	Three Rivers	47.5	2.8	3.1	2.8	2.6	2.1	2.7	2.9	3.4	3.4	3.6	3.6	3.0	2.5	2.6	2.0	1.7	1.4	1.0	0.7
E07000103	Watford	48.8	3.7	3.4	2.8	2.5	2.5	3.8	4.5	4.2	3.6	3.4	2.9	2.5	2.0	1.9	1.5	1.2	1.0	0.7	0.5
E07000241	Welwyn Hatfield	61.2	3.6	3.5	3.2	4.0	6.6	4.3	4.1	3.9	3.7	3.7	4.1	3.4	2.7	2.6	2.2	1.9	1.7	1.2	0.8
E10000020	Norfolk	453.4	23.4	23.9	21.4	23.8	25.7	25.7	25.4	23.7	25.7	30.5	31.8	29.3	28.7	32.8	26.5	20.2	16.1	11.3	7.4
E07000143	Breckland	68.9	3.7	3.8	3.3	3.5	3.3	3.8	3.8	3.5	3.9	4.8	5.0	4.4	4.5	5.2	4.1	3.2	2.4	1.6	1.2
E07000144	Broadland	65.2	3.0	3.2	3.2	3.4	2.6	3.0	3.3	3.5	4.1	4.9	4.9	4.5	4.3	5.0	3.9	3.1	2.5	1.8	1.1
E07000145	Great Yarmouth	50.1	2.7	2.8	2.5	2.7	2.6	2.8	2.8	2.4	2.7	3.4	3.6	3.2	3.2	3.6	3.0	2.2	1.7	1.2	0.8
E07000146	King's Lynn and West Norfolk	77.4	4.2	4.2	3.6	3.8	3.3	4.2	4.3	3.8	4.3	5.2	5.5	5.3	5.1	6.0	4.9	3.7	2.9	2.0	1.2
E07000147	North Norfolk	53.2	2.1	2.3	2.2	2.3	2.1	2.2	2.1	2.2	2.5	3.4	3.8	4.0	4.2	5.0	4.1	3.1	2.5	1.8	1.2
E07000148	Norwich	70.4	4.2	3.8	3.0	4.5	9.1	6.4	5.5	4.4	3.8	3.9	3.8	3.3	3.2	3.2	2.5	2.0	1.7	1.3	0.9
E07000149	South Norfolk	68.2	3.6	3.8	3.5	3.6	2.7	3.4	3.6	3.9	4.4	5.0	5.1	4.6	4.2	4.9	4.0	2.9	2.4	1.6	1.0
E10000029	Suffolk	379.7	20.5	21.6	20.1	19.6	17.9	21.8	21.2	20.8	22.4	26.6	27.2	24.9	23.6	26.6	21.2	15.8	12.6	9.0	6.2
E07000200	Babergh	46.2	2.1	2.4	2.6	2.4	1.9	2.1	2.1	2.3	2.8	3.5	3.5	3.2	3.1	3.6	3.0	2.1	1.6	1.1	0.8
E07000201	Forest Heath	31.2	2.5	2.0	1.5	1.5	1.9	2.5	2.5	1.8	1.6	1.8	2.0	1.8	1.7	1.8	1.4	1.0	0.8	0.6	0.4
E07000202	Ipswich	69.1	4.7	4.3	3.6	3.7	4.3	5.6	5.1	4.7	4.4	4.5	4.5	4.1	3.6	3.5	2.5	2.1	1.8	1.3	0.9
E07000203	Mid Suffolk	50.9	2.3	2.8	2.8	2.7	2.1	2.5	2.5	2.8	3.1	3.8	4.0	3.7	3.4	3.9	3.0	2.2	1.7	1.1	0.7
E07000204	St Edmundsbury	56.5	3.0	3.4	3.0	2.8	2.6	3.3	3.3	3.1	3.5	4.2	4.1	3.5	3.3	3.8	3.2	2.4	1.8	1.3	0.9
E07000205	Suffolk Coastal	65.5	2.8	3.5	3.5	3.6	2.4	2.6	2.7	3.2	3.8	4.7	5.0	4.7	4.6	5.3	4.2	3.2	2.6	1.8	1.3
E07000206	Waveney	60.3	3.1	3.3	3.0	3.0	2.8	3.2	3.0	3.0	3.3	4.1	4.2	3.9	4.0	4.7	3.9	2.9	2.4	1.7	1.1

MYE2: Population estimates: Females by selected age groups for local authorities in the UK, mid-2016

Thousands

Code	Name	All ages	Age groups (years)																		
			0-4	5-9	10-14	15-19	20-24	25-29	30-34	35-39	40-44	45-49	50-54	55-59	60-64	65-69	70-74	75-79	80-84	85-89	90
E12000007	LONDON	1,100.6	309.6	282.7	238.1	226.9	282.5	415.3	418.0	367.2	310.8	296.0	278.4	226.9	183.2	165.1	127.4	102.8	80.3	53.7	35.7
E09000007	Camden	123.7	7.1	7.0	6.1	6.4	11.1	14.2	12.0	9.8	0.0	7.9	6.8	5.5	4.8	4.8	3.9	2.9	2.1	1.5	1.1
E09000001	City of London	3.3	0.2	0.2	0.1	0.1	0.3	0.2	0.2	0.2	0.3	0.3	0.3	0.2	0.2	0.3	0.1	0.1	0.1	0.1	0.0
E09000012	Hackney	137.3	10.2	8.9	7.5	6.6	8.8	18.2	18.3	13.0	9.5	8.1	7.4	5.6	4.3	3.6	2.5	1.9	1.4	0.9	0.6
E09000013	Hammersmith and Fulham	92.0	5.7	5.3	4.1	3.8	6.7	10.7	9.9	7.9	7.0	6.4	5.7	4.4	3.8	3.4	2.4	2.0	1.3	0.9	0.5
E09000014	Haringey	135.2	9.5	8.3	7.6	7.3	8.6	12.7	13.7	12.4	10.2	9.5	8.8	6.9	5.4	4.7	3.3	2.7	1.9	1.2	0.7
E09000019	Islington	115.3	6.4	5.8	4.9	5.8	13.1	16.5	13.5	9.0	7.2	6.6	6.5	5.1	4.0	3.4	2.6	2.0	1.5	1.0	0.6
E09000020	Kensington and Chelsea	78.3	4.3	4.0	3.5	3.2	4.3	6.3	7.1	6.9	6.1	5.5	5.6	4.7	4.0	4.2	3.3	2.2	1.3	1.0	0.8
E09000022	Lambeth	160.8	9.8	8.8	7.6	7.0	11.8	24.8	19.1	14.2	10.5	10.0	9.9	7.5	5.5	4.3	3.3	2.2	2.0	1.0	0.8
E09000023	Lewisham	151.6	11.1	9.7	7.9	7.5	10.1	14.7	15.6	14.0	11.5	10.5	10.3	7.7	5.7	4.5	3.4	2.7	2.2	1.3	0.8
E09000025	Newham	162.7	14.4	11.4	10.1	9.9	13.1	17.5	17.2	13.4	10.3	10.0	8.8	7.4	5.6	4.4	3.1	2.5	1.7	1.0	0.6
E09000028	Southwark	156.3	10.6	9.1	7.4	7.3	12.9	20.6	17.2	13.6	10.6	10.0	9.7	8.0	5.3	4.2	3.2	2.5	1.9	1.3	0.8
E09000030	Tower Hamlets	143.9	11.0	9.2	8.1	7.8	13.6	21.9	18.8	13.4	8.9	6.9	5.6	4.6	4.1	3.1	2.1	1.9	1.4	0.9	0.5
E09000032	Wandsworth	166.4	11.1	9.0	6.6	6.2	11.3	23.7	23.1	15.9	11.9	10.1	8.6	6.6	5.6	5.1	3.8	3.2	2.3	1.4	1.0
E09000033	Westminster	115.9	6.8	6.4	5.3	5.4	7.6	11.1	12.5	10.2	8.7	7.8	7.0	6.2	5.4	4.7	3.6	2.9	2.1	1.4	0.8
E09000002	Barking and Dagenham	106.0	9.7	9.4	7.0	6.4	6.4	8.3	9.3	8.6	7.7	7.1	6.3	4.8	3.6	3.1	2.4	2.1	1.7	1.2	0.9
E09000003	Barnet	195.0	13.2	13.2	11.3	10.0	11.1	15.1	16.2	15.2	14.0	13.8	12.7	10.5	8.7	8.4	7.0	5.1	4.4	3.1	2.3
E09000004	Bexley	126.8	7.9	8.1	7.1	7.1	7.5	8.9	8.6	8.7	8.2	9.4	9.1	7.5	5.9	6.0	5.0	4.4	3.5	2.5	1.6
E09000005	Brent	160.4	12.3	10.4	9.1	8.9	9.6	13.8	14.7	12.7	11.2	10.5	10.4	9.2	7.2	6.0	4.7	3.8	3.0	1.9	1.1
E09000006	Bromley	170.2	10.5	10.6	9.2	8.4	7.7	10.6	11.5	13.2	12.3	12.9	12.5	10.1	8.3	9.0	7.1	5.7	4.8	3.4	2.3
E09000008	Croydon	197.2	13.9	13.7	11.7	11.1	10.0	14.6	15.9	15.2	13.6	14.2	14.6	11.4	9.5	8.2	6.3	5.1	4.0	2.5	1.7
E09000009	Ealing	171.4	12.7	11.7	9.8	9.0	9.3	13.9	14.9	14.4	13.0	11.9	11.1	9.2	8.1	6.6	5.1	4.2	3.3	2.0	1.3
E09000010	Enfield	170.1	12.2	12.1	10.4	9.6	9.7	13.2	14.0	12.8	11.7	12.2	11.8	9.3	7.4	6.4	5.5	4.5	3.5	2.2	1.5
E09000011	Greenwich	138.9	11.0	9.6	7.8	7.5	9.0	12.3	13.0	12.3	10.0	9.6	8.6	6.8	5.4	4.7	3.6	2.9	2.2	1.4	1.1
E09000015	Harrow	124.7	8.8	8.0	7.0	6.6	6.5	8.9	9.8	9.4	8.4	8.5	8.6	7.6	6.5	5.8	4.7	3.8	3.0	2.0	1.3
E09000016	Havering	131.7	8.4	7.6	7.0	7.1	7.4	9.2	9.0	8.7	8.0	9.0	9.1	8.1	6.6	7.0	5.7	4.8	4.2	3.0	1.8
E09000017	Hillingdon	149.7	11.1	10.3	8.4	8.7	10.0	11.2	12.1	11.8	10.1	10.0	9.8	8.1	6.5	6.1	4.8	3.9	3.3	2.1	1.3
E09000018	Hounslow	132.2	10.4	9.1	7.2	6.8	7.5	10.8	12.4	11.5	9.6	8.8	8.2	7.1	5.9	5.2	3.9	3.1	2.3	1.5	0.9
E09000021	Kingston upon Thames	88.3	5.8	5.7	4.7	4.8	6.7	6.7	7.0	7.3	6.8	6.1	5.5	4.6	3.8	3.8	2.8	2.2	1.8	1.3	1.0
E09000024	Merton	104.9	7.8	6.7	5.3	4.8	5.2	8.6	10.1	10.0	7.9	7.4	6.9	5.5	4.5	4.2	3.0	2.6	2.0	1.4	0.9
E09000026	Redbridge	150.2	11.2	10.7	9.4	8.9	8.8	11.7	12.6	12.4	10.6	9.8	9.4	7.9	6.6	5.8	4.5	3.6	2.9	2.1	1.4
E09000027	Richmond upon Thames	100.3	6.7	6.8	5.5	4.7	4.2	5.5	7.3	8.7	8.7	7.9	7.1	5.8	4.8	5.0	3.7	2.7	2.2	1.6	1.3
E09000029	Sutton	103.4	6.8	6.7	5.8	5.3	4.8	6.7	8.1	8.4	7.8	7.9	7.4	5.9	4.8	4.9	3.9	3.0	2.5	1.7	1.1
E09000031	Waltham Forest	136.4	10.9	9.2	7.6	7.1	7.9	12.2	13.6	11.8	9.8	9.6	8.6	7.0	5.6	4.5	3.5	2.8	2.3	1.4	1.1
E12000008	SOUTH EAST	4,581.1	264.4	276.4	249.3	256.2	262.7	268.2	279.7	292.6	301.7	330.7	330.2	284.9	247.7	266.7	215.6	164.4	132.0	93.1	64.7
E06000036	Bracknell Forest	60.3	3.7	4.2	3.5	3.5	2.9	3.8	4.4	4.9	4.4	4.6	4.5	3.8	2.9	2.8	2.1	1.6	1.3	0.8	0.5
E06000043	Brighton and Hove	142.9	7.2	7.2	6.6	9.0	16.2	12.5	10.2	10.0	9.9	10.2	10.0	7.3	5.9	5.7	4.5	3.6	3.0	2.3	1.7
E06000046	Isle of Wight	71.7	3.2	3.3	3.4	3.7	3.1	3.3	3.3	3.3	3.9	5.2	5.3	5.1	5.2	5.8	5.0	3.4	2.8	2.0	1.5
E06000035	Medway	139.6	9.1	8.8	8.3	8.2	9.3	10.0	9.3	9.1	8.8	9.9	9.8	8.6	7.0	7.4	5.5	4.1	3.1	2.0	1.3
E06000042	Milton Keynes	134.4	9.8	10.2	8.2	7.1	6.2	9.0	10.8	11.0	9.9	9.4	8.9	7.7	6.9	6.4	4.3	3.3	2.3	1.6	1.1
E06000044	Portsmouth	104.8	6.5	6.4	5.3	6.6	11.0	8.3	7.7	6.3	6.2	6.8	6.8	5.7	4.5	4.7	3.7	2.9	2.3	1.7	1.2
E06000038	Reading	80.6	5.9	5.4	4.1	4.8	7.3	6.9	6.8	6.5	5.3	5.1	4.8	3.8	3.1	3.0	2.4	2.0	1.6	1.1	0.7
E06000039	Slough	73.4	6.4	6.2	5.0	4.2	3.8	5.4	7.1	6.9	5.2	4.7	4.2	3.6	2.9	2.3	1.6	1.4	1.2	0.8	0.5
E06000045	Southampton	122.6	7.9	7.2	5.6	8.4	15.8	10.5	9.1	8.0	6.7	6.8	7.1	6.1	5.1	5.2	4.1	3.1	2.6	1.9	1.3
E06000037	West Berkshire	79.9	4.7	5.1	4.8	4.7	3.4	4.1	4.6	5.1	5.8	6.3	6.1	5.2	4.6	4.8	3.7	2.6	2.0	1.3	0.9

MYE2: Population estimates: Females by selected age groups for local authorities in the UK, mid-2016

Thousands

Code	Name	All ages	Age groups (years)																		
			0-4	5-9	10-14	15-19	20-24	25-29	30-34	35-39	40-44	45-49	50-54	55-59	60-64	65-69	70-74	75-79	80-84	85-89	90
E06000040	Windsor and Maidenhead	75.3	4.3	4.8	4.5	4.0	3.1	4.1	4.9	5.3	5.5	6.5	5.5	4.6	3.9	3.9	3.4	2.7	2.2	1.5	1.1
E06000041	Wokingham	82.7	4.9	5.6	5.1	4.6	3.6	3.9	4.9	6.1	6.3	6.5	6.2	5.3	4.3	4.5	3.7	2.7	2.2	1.3	1.0
E10000002	Buckinghamshire	271.7	16.3	17.7	16.2	14.9	12.8	15.0	15.8	17.9	18.6	20.9	19.9	17.3	14.6	15.1	12.4	9.7	7.8	5.2	3.6
E07000004	Aylesbury Vale	97.4	6.1	6.5	5.6	5.2	4.6	6.1	6.3	6.7	6.7	7.5	7.3	6.2	5.2	5.3	4.1	3.0	2.3	1.6	1.1
E07000005	Chiltern	49.0	2.6	3.3	3.1	2.7	1.9	2.0	2.1	3.0	3.4	3.8	3.8	3.4	2.7	2.9	2.5	2.1	1.7	1.1	0.8
E07000006	South Bucks	36.1	2.0	2.2	2.0	1.8	1.6	1.8	2.0	2.2	2.3	2.8	2.7	2.4	2.0	2.1	1.8	1.6	1.2	1.0	0.6
E07000007	Wycombe	89.2	5.6	5.7	5.5	5.1	4.7	5.1	5.5	6.0	6.1	6.7	6.1	5.4	4.7	4.7	4.1	3.0	2.5	1.6	1.0
E10000011	East Sussex	283.6	13.6	14.7	14.2	14.8	12.5	13.6	13.8	14.6	16.5	20.0	21.1	19.2	18.5	21.3	17.3	13.1	10.7	8.1	6.0
E07000061	Eastbourne	53.1	3.0	2.6	2.6	2.8	2.7	2.6	3.0	3.0	3.1	3.4	3.6	3.3	3.2	3.7	3.0	2.4	2.1	1.7	1.2
E07000062	Hastings	47.5	2.8	2.7	2.4	2.7	2.7	3.1	2.8	2.7	2.8	3.5	3.5	3.3	2.8	3.0	2.2	1.6	1.2	1.0	0.8
E07000063	Lewes	52.3	2.3	2.8	2.7	2.7	2.1	2.4	2.5	2.8	3.3	3.8	3.9	3.5	3.4	3.7	3.2	2.4	2.1	1.5	1.2
E07000064	Rother	48.9	1.8	2.4	2.2	2.3	1.8	2.0	1.8	2.0	2.5	3.2	3.6	3.5	3.6	4.6	3.7	2.8	2.2	1.7	1.3
E07000065	Wealden	81.9	3.7	4.3	4.4	4.3	3.2	3.5	3.7	4.1	4.9	6.1	6.5	5.7	5.5	6.4	5.3	3.8	3.0	2.1	1.6
E10000014	Hampshire	696.3	37.7	40.3	36.9	37.3	33.6	37.8	38.9	41.4	46.1	51.4	53.2	46.0	40.1	44.4	36.4	27.7	21.7	15.2	10.4
E07000084	Basingstoke and Deane	88.4	5.6	5.7	4.9	4.7	4.1	5.4	6.2	6.2	6.3	6.9	6.8	5.6	4.5	4.9	3.8	2.8	2.1	1.3	0.9
E07000085	East Hampshire	61.3	3.0	3.5	3.4	3.5	2.5	2.7	2.7	3.4	4.0	4.8	5.1	4.4	3.7	4.2	3.4	2.6	2.0	1.4	1.0
E07000086	Eastleigh	66.1	3.8	4.0	3.5	3.4	3.1	4.2	4.1	4.4	4.5	4.7	4.9	4.3	3.8	3.9	3.1	2.4	1.8	1.3	0.8
E07000087	Fareham	59.0	2.9	3.1	3.0	3.1	2.7	3.0	3.1	3.1	3.9	4.5	4.7	4.1	3.5	4.0	3.5	2.6	2.1	1.4	0.9
E07000088	Gosport	42.9	2.4	2.6	2.3	2.4	2.3	2.6	2.8	2.4	2.7	3.1	3.1	2.8	2.4	2.6	2.1	1.5	1.3	0.9	0.6
E07000089	Hart	47.7	2.7	3.1	2.9	2.5	1.8	2.2	2.5	3.2	3.8	3.8	3.7	3.0	2.5	2.9	2.4	1.8	1.3	0.9	0.6
E07000090	Havant	63.9	3.2	3.4	3.3	3.5	3.3	3.6	3.4	3.1	3.6	4.7	4.7	4.5	3.9	4.3	3.6	2.9	2.3	1.6	1.0
E07000091	New Forest	93.1	4.0	4.6	4.4	4.3	3.8	4.1	4.1	4.4	5.4	6.4	7.1	6.5	6.3	7.4	6.2	4.8	4.0	3.0	2.3
E07000092	Rushmoor	47.7	3.3	3.0	2.5	2.6	2.7	3.6	3.6	3.6	3.6	3.5	3.5	2.7	2.2	2.2	1.7	1.4	0.9	0.7	0.5
E07000093	Test Valley	63.0	3.5	3.8	3.4	3.2	2.8	3.4	3.3	3.7	4.3	4.7	5.0	4.2	3.7	4.1	3.4	2.4	1.9	1.3	0.9
E07000094	Winchester	63.3	3.3	3.6	3.4	4.1	4.6	3.0	3.1	3.8	4.1	4.3	4.7	4.0	3.5	3.8	3.1	2.5	1.9	1.5	1.0
E10000016	Kent	784.7	44.8	47.0	43.3	45.5	44.4	44.9	46.3	46.8	49.5	56.5	56.4	48.9	43.6	48.8	39.0	29.1	23.1	16.2	10.7
E07000105	Ashford	64.7	3.9	4.2	3.8	3.8	3.1	3.7	3.9	3.9	4.2	5.0	4.8	3.8	3.4	4.0	3.2	2.2	1.7	1.2	0.8
E07000106	Canterbury	82.8	3.6	4.0	3.9	6.2	10.4	4.9	4.2	4.0	4.3	5.0	5.1	4.7	4.4	5.1	4.2	3.1	2.5	1.9	1.3
E07000107	Dartford	53.5	3.7	3.6	3.0	2.8	2.8	4.1	4.3	4.0	3.7	3.9	3.6	3.0	2.4	2.3	1.9	1.6	1.3	0.8	0.5
E07000108	Dover	58.2	3.0	3.1	3.0	3.2	2.8	2.9	3.1	3.0	3.4	4.0	4.5	4.1	3.8	4.3	3.4	2.4	1.9	1.3	0.9
E07000109	Gravesham	53.8	3.7	3.5	3.1	3.0	2.9	3.6	3.5	3.5	3.5	3.9	3.7	3.2	2.7	2.8	2.3	1.9	1.5	1.0	0.5
E07000110	Maidstone	83.8	5.0	5.1	4.6	4.4	4.1	5.1	5.5	5.3	5.5	6.2	6.1	5.2	4.6	5.0	3.9	3.1	2.4	1.6	1.0
E07000111	Sevenoaks	61.3	3.6	3.8	3.6	3.3	2.6	2.9	3.0	3.9	4.2	4.7	4.5	4.0	3.5	4.0	3.2	2.4	1.9	1.4	0.9
E07000112	Shepway	56.2	2.9	3.1	2.7	2.9	2.6	3.0	2.9	3.0	3.3	4.0	4.1	3.9	3.6	4.2	3.3	2.4	1.8	1.4	1.1
E07000113	Swale	73.3	4.5	4.6	4.1	4.2	3.8	4.3	4.6	4.4	4.5	5.3	5.4	4.6	4.1	4.7	3.6	2.6	1.9	1.3	0.8
E07000114	Thanet	72.7	4.1	4.2	3.7	3.9	3.8	3.9	4.1	3.9	4.1	4.9	5.0	4.7	4.6	5.2	4.2	3.1	2.4	1.8	1.2
E07000115	Tonbridge and Malling	65.0	3.7	4.0	4.0	3.9	3.1	3.4	3.7	4.2	4.7	5.1	5.0	4.1	3.3	3.7	3.2	2.4	1.8	1.1	0.7
E07000116	Tunbridge Wells	59.4	3.2	3.8	3.7	3.7	2.4	3.1	3.5	3.7	4.2	4.6	4.5	3.7	3.1	3.4	2.7	2.0	1.7	1.4	0.9
E10000025	Oxfordshire	340.4	19.5	20.6	18.5	20.0	23.2	20.2	22.4	21.6	22.2	24.1	24.3	20.7	17.6	18.6	15.4	11.7	9.1	6.3	4.4
E07000177	Cherwell	73.9	4.5	4.7	4.2	4.1	3.3	4.2	5.2	5.0	5.2	5.5	5.6	4.6	3.9	4.1	3.2	2.5	1.9	1.4	0.8
E07000178	Oxford	76.2	4.3	4.4	3.8	5.8	12.3	6.0	6.1	4.8	4.1	4.1	4.1	3.4	3.0	2.8	2.3	1.8	1.4	1.0	0.8
E07000179	South Oxfordshire	70.6	4.0	4.2	4.0	3.8	2.8	3.4	4.0	4.3	4.9	5.6	5.5	4.6	4.0	4.3	3.8	2.8	2.1	1.4	1.0
E07000180	Vale of White Horse	64.5	3.7	3.8	3.6	3.5	2.7	3.5	3.9	4.2	4.3	4.7	4.8	4.4	3.6	3.9	3.2	2.4	1.9	1.4	0.9
E07000181	West Oxfordshire	55.2	3.0	3.3	2.9	2.9	2.2	3.0	3.2	3.3	3.7	4.2	4.3	3.6	3.2	3.5	2.9	2.1	1.7	1.2	0.8
E10000030	Surrey	601.0	35.5	37.2	33.7	33.4	31.3	32.2	34.7	41.1	42.8	44.9	44.5	37.6	31.3	33.2	27.2	21.1	17.8	12.5	9.1
E07000207	Elmbridge	70.2	4.9	4.9	4.2	3.6	2.5	2.8	3.8	5.3	5.6	5.7	5.3	4.5	3.5	3.7	2.9	2.4	1.9	1.4	1.1

MYE2: Population estimates: Females by selected age groups for local authorities in the UK, mid-2016

Thousands

Code	Name	All ages	0-4	5-9	10-14	15-19	20-24	25-29	30-34	35-39	40-44	45-49	50-54	55-59	60-64	65-69	70-74	75-79	80-84	85-89	90
E07000208	Epsom and Ewell	40.7	2.5	2.5	2.4	2.4	2.2	2.1	2.4	2.9	2.9	3.0	3.0	2.5	2.1	2.3	1.8	1.4	1.1	0.8	0.5
E07000209	Guildford	73.3	3.9	4.2	4.0	4.6	6.7	5.3	4.3	4.6	4.8	4.9	5.0	4.3	3.6	3.7	2.9	2.3	1.9	1.3	1.0
E07000210	Mole Valley	44.6	2.1	2.5	2.6	2.4	1.7	1.9	2.0	2.7	3.0	3.5	3.5	3.1	2.7	2.9	2.5	1.9	1.6	1.1	0.8
E07000211	Reigate and Banstead	74.3	4.8	4.7	4.2	3.8	3.1	4.1	4.8	5.6	5.3	5.5	5.5	4.5	3.8	4.1	3.2	2.4	2.1	1.5	1.2
E07000212	Runnymede	44.3	2.5	2.3	2.1	2.9	4.4	3.2	2.5	2.7	3.0	3.0	3.0	2.6	2.1	2.2	1.8	1.4	1.3	0.9	0.6
E07000213	Spelthorne	50.1	3.2	3.0	2.5	2.4	2.4	3.0	3.3	3.7	3.4	3.9	3.8	3.1	2.5	2.7	2.3	1.9	1.6	1.0	0.6
E07000214	Surrey Heath	44.7	2.4	2.7	2.6	2.5	1.9	2.3	2.4	2.8	3.3	3.5	3.6	2.9	2.4	2.5	2.1	1.6	1.5	0.9	0.6
E07000215	Tandridge	44.3	2.4	2.7	2.5	2.5	1.8	2.2	2.4	2.9	3.0	3.5	3.4	3.0	2.5	2.7	2.3	1.6	1.4	1.0	0.7
E07000216	Waverley	63.6	3.5	4.0	3.7	3.7	2.5	2.4	3.1	4.1	4.6	4.8	4.8	4.0	3.5	3.9	3.4	2.6	2.2	1.6	1.2
E07000217	Woking	50.8	3.4	3.6	2.9	2.5	2.1	2.9	3.5	4.0	4.0	3.7	3.6	3.1	2.5	2.5	2.0	1.6	1.3	1.0	0.6
E10000032	West Sussex	435.2	23.2	24.5	22.1	21.7	19.3	22.5	24.6	26.7	28.1	31.3	31.9	28.4	25.6	28.8	23.8	18.5	15.3	11.3	7.8
E07000223	Adur	32.6	1.8	1.8	1.5	1.5	1.3	1.6	1.8	2.1	2.2	2.4	2.3	2.1	1.9	2.3	1.8	1.5	1.2	0.8	0.5
E07000224	Arun	82.0	4.0	3.9	3.6	3.6	3.6	3.9	4.0	4.1	4.5	5.5	5.8	5.4	5.3	6.6	5.6	4.5	3.6	2.6	1.8
E07000225	Chichester	61.7	2.8	3.1	2.9	3.1	3.2	2.7	2.7	3.1	3.5	4.1	4.7	4.3	4.0	4.7	4.0	3.1	2.6	1.8	1.3
E07000226	Crawley	55.8	3.9	3.9	3.1	2.9	2.9	4.3	4.8	4.5	3.9	3.9	3.6	3.3	2.6	2.4	1.6	1.3	1.3	1.0	0.5
E07000227	Horsham	71.1	3.5	3.9	4.0	3.9	3.0	3.2	3.5	4.2	4.6	5.5	5.8	5.0	4.3	4.6	3.9	2.9	2.4	1.7	1.1
E07000228	Mid Sussex	75.5	4.2	4.8	4.2	3.9	2.9	3.8	4.4	5.0	5.5	5.8	5.6	4.8	4.3	4.5	3.9	2.7	2.3	1.8	1.2
E07000229	Worthing	56.5	3.0	3.1	2.7	2.7	2.4	3.0	3.4	3.6	3.8	4.1	4.1	3.5	3.1	3.6	3.0	2.4	2.0	1.6	1.3
E12000009	SOUTH WEST	2,804.6	149.1	154.2	140.8	153.3	164.2	162.1	159.2	156.8	167.8	195.4	202.6	183.0	168.6	185.4	150.6	112.7	90.5	63.9	44.4
E06000022	Bath and North East Somerset	94.8	4.7	5.0	4.5	6.7	10.2	5.8	4.8	4.9	5.6	6.2	6.5	5.6	5.1	5.3	4.4	3.5	2.8	2.0	1.4
E06000028	Bournemouth	96.2	5.6	5.1	4.1	5.5	9.0	6.3	7.0	6.5	5.8	5.9	6.1	5.4	4.7	5.1	4.0	3.2	2.9	2.3	1.7
E06000023	Bristol, City of	227.7	15.0	13.5	11.1	13.3	24.7	23.5	19.0	15.4	13.3	12.8	12.9	11.1	9.5	9.1	7.1	5.7	4.9	3.4	2.6
E06000052	Cornwall	285.6	14.4	14.6	13.9	15.2	14.7	13.4	14.2	14.8	16.8	20.4	21.2	20.1	19.2	22.1	17.6	12.4	9.6	6.6	4.4
E06000053	Isles of Scilly	1.1	0.1	0.1	0.0	0.0	0.1	0.0	0.1	0.1	0.1	0.1	0.1	0.1	0.1	0.1	0.1	0.1	0.0	0.0	0.0
E06000024	North Somerset	108.6	5.8	6.0	5.6	5.5	4.7	5.3	5.9	6.3	6.8	7.9	7.9	7.1	6.7	7.7	6.3	4.8	3.9	2.6	2.0
E06000026	Plymouth	131.8	7.8	7.5	6.4	7.8	11.7	8.8	8.7	7.4	7.5	9.0	8.7	8.0	6.9	7.3	5.9	4.7	3.8	2.4	1.5
E06000029	Poole	76.7	4.1	4.2	3.9	4.1	3.7	4.2	4.6	4.7	4.6	5.3	5.6	4.9	4.5	5.1	4.0	3.1	2.7	2.1	1.3
E06000025	South Gloucestershire	139.4	8.0	8.4	7.4	7.7	8.1	8.7	8.7	8.9	8.9	10.5	10.6	8.4	7.3	7.7	6.6	5.1	4.1	2.6	1.6
E06000030	Swindon	109.5	7.3	7.1	6.0	6.1	5.5	7.4	8.0	7.6	7.8	8.1	8.0	6.8	5.7	5.5	4.2	3.2	2.5	1.8	1.1
E06000027	Torbay	69.2	3.6	3.5	3.2	3.3	3.2	3.5	3.4	3.4	3.7	4.8	5.2	4.7	4.6	5.4	4.4	3.3	2.7	1.9	1.4
E06000054	Wiltshire	248.9	13.6	15.2	14.0	13.8	10.6	12.7	13.6	14.0	16.6	19.0	19.0	16.7	14.9	15.9	13.0	9.6	7.5	5.3	3.7
E10000008	Devon	398.9	18.5	20.2	19.0	20.8	21.3	20.3	19.7	20.1	22.3	27.4	29.6	27.8	26.8	30.0	24.6	18.1	14.4	10.5	7.5
E07000040	East Devon	72.4	3.1	3.6	3.4	3.4	2.5	3.0	3.1	3.3	3.9	4.9	5.2	5.0	5.2	6.0	5.3	4.1	3.3	2.5	1.8
E07000041	Exeter	64.4	3.2	3.2	2.6	4.6	8.8	5.2	4.3	3.7	3.5	3.7	3.8	3.3	3.0	3.1	2.4	2.0	1.7	1.4	1.0
E07000042	Mid Devon	40.8	2.1	2.4	2.2	2.2	1.7	2.1	2.1	2.2	2.4	3.1	3.2	2.8	2.7	2.9	2.3	1.7	1.3	0.9	0.6
E07000043	North Devon	48.3	2.4	2.6	2.4	2.4	2.0	2.4	2.4	2.5	2.8	3.4	3.6	3.5	3.1	3.6	3.1	2.2	1.7	1.2	0.9
E07000044	South Hams	43.8	1.8	2.1	2.2	2.1	1.4	1.6	1.9	2.1	2.4	3.2	3.6	3.5	3.4	3.8	3.1	2.0	1.7	1.1	0.7
E07000045	Teignbridge	67.0	3.1	3.2	3.2	3.1	2.6	3.2	3.2	3.3	3.9	4.7	5.3	4.9	4.7	5.3	4.3	3.1	2.5	1.9	1.4
E07000046	Torridge	34.2	1.5	1.7	1.6	1.6	1.4	1.6	1.5	1.7	1.9	2.4	2.6	2.7	2.6	3.0	2.2	1.6	1.2	0.8	0.6
E07000047	West Devon	28.0	1.2	1.4	1.3	1.4	0.9	1.2	1.2	1.4	1.6	2.0	2.3	2.2	2.1	2.4	1.9	1.3	1.0	0.7	0.5
E10000009	Dorset	216.5	9.3	10.8	10.5	10.8	8.0	9.3	9.4	10.0	11.8	14.8	16.1	15.6	15.1	18.3	15.2	11.3	9.3	6.6	4.4
E07000048	Christchurch	25.7	1.0	1.2	1.2	1.2	0.9	1.1	1.1	1.2	1.4	1.7	1.7	1.7	1.6	2.2	1.9	1.5	1.3	1.0	0.7
E07000049	East Dorset	46.2	1.9	2.3	2.2	2.1	1.7	1.8	1.8	2.0	2.5	3.1	3.4	3.3	3.2	4.2	3.4	2.7	2.2	1.5	1.0
E07000050	North Dorset	35.5	1.7	1.9	1.9	1.9	1.3	1.6	1.8	1.7	2.1	2.4	2.6	2.5	2.4	2.8	2.3	1.6	1.3	1.0	0.7
E07000051	Purbeck	23.4	1.0	1.2	1.1	1.2	0.9	1.0	1.1	1.1	1.3	1.6	1.7	1.8	1.7	2.0	1.6	1.1	0.9	0.6	0.4

MYE2: Population estimates: Females by selected age groups for local authorities in the UK, mid-2016

Thousands

Code	Name	All ages	Age groups (years)																		
			0-4	5-9	10-14	15-19	20-24	25-29	30-34	35-39	40-44	45-49	50-54	55-59	60-64	65-69	70-74	75-79	80-84	85-89	90
E07000052	West Dorset	52.6	2.1	2.4	2.5	2.6	1.8	2.1	2.1	2.2	2.8	3.5	4.1	3.9	3.9	4.5	3.9	2.9	2.4	1.7	1.1
E07000053	Weymouth and Portland	33.1	1.6	1.7	1.6	1.8	1.4	1.7	1.6	1.7	1.8	2.4	2.4	2.4	2.3	2.6	2.0	1.4	1.2	0.8	0.5
E10000013	Gloucestershire	317.7	17.1	17.7	16.5	17.6	16.5	18.1	18.0	18.0	19.7	23.0	24.2	21.3	19.1	20.5	16.6	12.4	9.8	6.8	4.7
E07000078	Cheltenham	59.9	3.3	3.2	3.0	3.8	4.3	4.1	4.1	3.7	3.6	3.8	4.2	3.5	3.1	3.3	2.7	2.1	1.8	1.3	1.0
E07000079	Cotswold	44.5	1.9	2.3	2.2	2.2	2.0	1.8	1.9	2.2	2.7	3.4	3.6	3.3	3.1	3.3	2.8	2.1	1.7	1.1	0.8
E07000080	Forest of Dean	43.4	2.1	2.2	2.1	2.6	2.1	2.0	2.0	2.0	2.6	3.2	3.5	3.2	3.1	3.3	2.6	1.9	1.4	0.9	0.7
E07000081	Gloucester	65.0	4.4	4.1	3.6	3.7	3.8	4.7	4.7	4.1	4.0	4.7	4.7	4.0	3.2	3.3	2.8	2.0	1.6	1.1	0.7
E07000082	Stroud	59.7	2.9	3.3	3.2	3.1	2.5	2.9	2.9	3.3	4.0	4.6	4.8	4.2	3.8	4.3	3.3	2.5	1.9	1.3	0.8
E07000083	Tewkesbury	45.2	2.5	2.6	2.2	2.1	1.9	2.6	2.6	2.7	2.8	3.3	3.4	3.1	2.9	3.0	2.5	1.9	1.5	1.0	0.7
E10000027	Somerset	282.0	14.4	15.4	14.6	15.1	12.4	14.9	14.2	14.5	16.5	20.1	21.2	19.4	18.4	20.3	16.5	12.2	9.7	7.0	5.1
E07000187	Mendip	58.1	2.9	3.2	3.1	3.4	2.4	3.0	2.8	3.1	3.6	4.5	4.5	4.1	3.7	4.1	3.2	2.3	1.9	1.3	1.0
E07000188	Sedgemoor	61.7	3.3	3.5	3.2	3.3	2.9	3.3	3.1	3.1	3.6	4.5	4.7	4.3	4.0	4.3	3.5	2.6	1.9	1.4	1.0
E07000189	South Somerset	84.6	4.4	4.7	4.4	4.4	3.6	4.5	4.1	4.3	5.0	5.8	6.3	5.7	5.6	6.3	5.1	3.8	3.0	2.1	1.6
E07000190	Taunton Deane	59.6	3.2	3.3	3.1	3.2	2.6	3.5	3.3	3.3	3.7	4.2	4.4	3.9	3.7	3.8	3.2	2.5	2.0	1.6	1.1
E07000191	West Somerset	17.9	0.6	0.8	0.7	0.8	0.7	0.7	0.7	0.7	0.8	1.1	1.3	1.4	1.5	1.7	1.4	1.0	0.9	0.6	0.5
W92000004	WALES	1,579.1	84.6	89.1	81.5	88.3	101.4	98.2	91.5	88.1	92.1	109.3	113.0	103.4	94.8	100.9	80.4	62.2	48.1	31.4	20.9
W06000001	Isle of Anglesey	35.4	1.9	1.9	1.7	1.7	1.5	1.9	1.8	1.7	1.9	2.4	2.5	2.5	2.4	2.8	2.3	1.7	1.3	0.9	0.6
W06000002	Gwynedd	62.2	3.1	3.4	3.1	3.8	5.2	3.7	2.9	2.9	3.4	4.0	4.0	4.0	3.8	4.0	3.4	2.6	2.2	1.6	1.0
W06000003	Conwy	60.0	2.8	3.0	2.8	3.0	2.6	3.0	2.8	2.8	3.2	4.2	4.5	4.3	4.1	4.6	3.7	3.1	2.6	1.8	1.3
W06000004	Denbighshire	48.2	2.6	2.8	2.4	2.5	2.3	2.7	2.2	2.4	2.9	3.4	3.6	3.3	3.1	3.6	2.9	2.2	1.6	1.1	0.6
W06000005	Flintshire	78.4	4.1	4.7	4.3	4.1	3.8	4.8	4.4	4.5	4.9	6.0	6.0	5.1	4.7	5.4	4.1	3.1	2.1	1.3	0.9
W06000006	Wrexham	67.9	4.0	4.3	3.7	3.5	3.4	4.3	4.3	3.9	4.2	5.1	4.8	4.3	4.1	4.3	3.3	2.4	1.9	1.2	0.8
W06000023	Powys	66.8	2.9	3.4	3.4	3.5	2.8	3.1	2.8	3.0	3.7	4.7	5.2	5.0	4.9	5.3	4.4	3.2	2.6	1.7	1.3
W06000008	Ceredigion	36.8	1.6	1.8	1.6	2.3	3.8	1.7	1.4	1.5	1.7	2.2	2.6	2.5	2.5	2.7	2.2	1.6	1.3	0.9	0.6
W06000009	Pembrokeshire	63.2	3.1	3.5	3.2	3.3	3.0	3.4	3.0	3.1	3.5	4.2	4.8	4.4	4.4	4.8	4.0	2.9	2.4	1.5	1.1
W06000010	Carmarthenshire	94.8	4.8	5.3	4.9	4.8	4.9	5.3	4.9	5.2	5.4	6.4	7.2	6.8	6.4	6.7	5.4	4.0	3.1	2.0	1.4
W06000011	Swansea	122.4	6.3	6.4	6.2	7.1	9.7	8.1	7.2	6.9	7.3	7.9	8.2	7.8	7.1	7.5	6.0	4.8	3.9	2.5	1.6
W06000012	Neath Port Talbot	72.1	3.8	3.9	3.7	3.9	3.7	4.2	4.5	4.2	4.4	5.0	5.4	5.0	4.6	4.7	3.7	2.9	2.2	1.5	0.9
W06000013	Bridgend	72.3	4.0	3.9	3.8	3.9	3.5	4.4	4.2	4.3	4.6	5.4	5.5	4.8	4.4	4.6	3.7	3.0	2.1	1.3	0.8
W06000014	Vale of Glamorgan	66.2	3.5	3.9	3.6	3.6	3.3	3.5	3.5	4.0	4.2	4.9	4.9	4.6	4.2	4.3	3.5	2.7	1.9	1.4	1.0
W06000015	Cardiff	182.9	11.0	10.8	9.1	12.0	21.6	15.1	13.2	11.5	10.3	10.8	11.1	9.9	8.3	7.9	6.0	5.2	4.3	2.9	1.9
W06000016	Rhondda Cynon Taf	121.4	7.0	7.1	6.5	6.9	7.6	8.5	7.7	7.1	7.3	8.5	8.5	7.7	6.8	7.4	5.8	4.5	3.3	2.0	1.4
W06000024	Merthyr Tydfil	30.4	1.8	1.8	1.5	1.7	1.8	2.1	2.2	1.7	1.8	2.1	2.2	2.0	1.7	1.8	1.4	1.1	0.8	0.5	0.3
W06000018	Caerphilly	92.0	5.2	5.5	5.0	5.1	5.2	5.9	6.0	5.7	5.7	6.7	6.4	5.9	5.4	5.7	4.5	3.4	2.5	1.4	0.9
W06000019	Blaenau Gwent	35.3	1.9	1.9	1.8	2.0	2.2	2.5	2.1	2.0	2.0	2.7	2.6	2.3	2.0	2.2	1.8	1.4	1.0	0.6	0.4
W06000020	Torfaen	47.2	2.6	2.7	2.5	2.7	2.7	3.1	2.9	2.7	2.7	3.3	3.4	3.1	2.8	3.0	2.3	1.8	1.5	0.9	0.6
W06000021	Monmouthshire	47.2	2.0	2.5	2.4	2.6	2.0	2.1	2.1	2.4	2.8	3.7	4.0	3.4	3.3	3.5	2.8	2.1	1.6	1.2	0.8
W06000022	Newport	76.0	4.8	4.8	4.3	4.3	4.6	5.2	5.3	4.7	4.5	5.5	5.5	4.7	3.8	4.1	3.3	2.6	2.1	1.3	0.8

MYE2: Population estimates: Females by selected age groups for local authorities in the UK, mid-2016

Thousands

Code	Name	All ages	0-4	5-9	10-14	15-19	20-24	25-29	30-34	35-39	40-44	45-49	50-54	55-59	60-64	65-69	70-74	75-79	80-84	85-89	90
S92000003	SCOTLAND	2,777.2	139.7	146.6	134.0	146.0	182.3	188.0	179.6	166.5	172.7	202.8	209.3	190.1	165.1	164.1	127.2	104.3	80.2	49.7	29.1
S12000033	Aberdeen City	115.7	6.0	5.5	4.4	6.0	11.2	11.6	9.7	7.6	6.8	7.1	7.5	6.8	5.8	5.6	4.1	3.7	3.0	2.0	1.1
S12000034	Aberdeenshire	131.8	7.3	8.0	7.2	6.7	6.4	6.8	8.2	8.5	9.1	10.5	10.5	9.1	8.3	8.1	5.9	4.6	3.4	2.2	1.3
S12000041	Angus	59.8	2.8	3.1	3.0	3.0	3.0	2.9	3.2	3.3	3.7	4.3	4.6	4.3	4.0	4.3	3.3	2.6	2.0	1.3	0.9
S12000035	Argyll and Bute	43.8	1.9	2.1	2.0	2.2	1.9	1.9	1.9	2.1	2.5	3.2	3.6	3.4	3.2	3.5	2.7	2.2	1.6	1.0	0.6
S12000036	City of Edinburgh	260.4	12.9	12.7	10.1	12.5	24.8	27.5	23.0	18.4	16.1	16.1	16.1	14.9	12.3	12.3	9.2	7.9	6.5	4.6	2.8
S12000005	Clackmannanshire	26.2	1.3	1.4	1.3	1.4	1.4	1.4	1.5	1.5	1.7	2.1	2.1	1.9	1.7	1.8	1.3	1.0	0.7	0.4	0.2
S12000006	Dumfries and Galloway	77.0	3.3	3.9	3.6	3.7	3.8	3.8	3.8	3.6	4.3	5.7	6.2	5.8	5.6	5.7	4.8	3.7	2.9	1.8	1.0
S12000042	Dundee City	76.8	3.9	3.7	3.3	4.6	7.4	6.9	5.4	4.3	4.0	4.6	5.2	4.9	3.9	4.1	3.1	2.8	2.4	1.5	0.8
S12000008	East Ayrshire	62.9	3.2	3.3	3.2	3.3	3.5	3.7	3.6	3.5	4.0	5.0	5.0	4.5	3.9	4.0	3.1	2.4	1.8	1.0	0.6
S12000045	East Dunbartonshire	55.5	2.7	3.0	2.9	2.9	2.8	2.5	2.4	3.0	3.4	4.3	4.5	4.3	3.7	3.6	2.9	2.6	2.0	1.2	0.7
S12000010	East Lothian	54.3	2.8	3.1	2.7	2.9	3.1	2.8	3.0	3.2	3.5	4.4	4.2	3.9	3.3	3.4	2.6	2.1	1.6	1.0	0.6
S12000011	East Renfrewshire	49.2	2.6	3.0	3.0	2.8	2.5	2.2	2.2	2.9	3.2	3.8	3.9	3.4	3.0	2.9	2.3	1.9	1.7	1.1	0.7
S12000014	Falkirk	81.4	4.1	4.7	4.2	4.1	4.5	4.6	5.2	5.1	5.8	6.4	6.3	5.5	4.8	4.9	3.7	3.1	2.2	1.3	0.8
S12000015	Fife	190.8	9.6	10.4	9.4	10.4	12.4	11.1	10.9	11.0	11.8	14.0	14.5	13.2	11.7	12.4	9.5	7.4	5.5	3.5	2.1
S12000046	Glasgow City	316.0	17.1	15.4	12.9	16.5	28.9	32.6	26.7	21.0	18.5	21.2	22.1	19.4	15.2	13.3	10.3	9.5	7.9	4.8	2.8
S12000017	Highland	119.9	5.7	6.3	6.3	6.0	5.6	6.2	6.8	6.7	7.5	9.0	9.6	8.9	8.3	8.2	6.4	5.0	3.8	2.4	1.4
S12000018	Inverclyde	41.3	1.8	2.0	2.0	2.1	2.4	2.3	2.2	2.2	2.5	3.2	3.4	3.2	2.6	2.6	2.1	1.7	1.4	0.9	0.5
S12000019	Midlothian	46.0	2.8	2.7	2.3	2.5	2.5	2.7	2.9	2.9	2.9	3.5	3.5	3.2	2.7	2.9	2.2	1.7	1.2	0.7	0.4
S12000020	Moray	48.4	2.3	2.7	2.5	2.6	2.5	2.6	2.9	2.6	3.1	3.6	3.7	3.3	3.1	3.2	2.6	2.0	1.6	1.0	0.5
S12000013	Na h-Eileanan Siar	13.6	0.6	0.6	0.7	0.7	0.6	0.6	0.7	0.7	0.8	1.0	1.1	1.0	1.0	1.0	0.8	0.7	0.6	0.3	0.2
S12000021	North Ayrshire	71.2	3.3	3.7	3.6	3.8	4.0	3.8	3.7	3.7	4.4	5.4	5.7	5.2	4.8	4.9	3.9	3.1	2.3	1.3	0.8
S12000044	North Lanarkshire	175.1	9.2	10.1	9.6	10.0	10.1	10.6	11.3	11.1	11.7	13.6	13.7	12.0	10.3	9.7	7.6	6.2	4.5	2.5	1.2
S12000023	Orkney Islands	11.0	0.4	0.6	0.6	0.5	0.5	0.6	0.6	0.6	0.7	0.8	0.9	0.8	0.8	0.8	0.7	0.5	0.3	0.2	0.1
S12000024	Perth and Kinross	76.7	3.4	3.8	3.8	4.0	3.9	3.9	4.4	4.0	4.6	5.8	6.0	5.5	5.1	5.3	4.3	3.4	2.6	1.8	1.1
S12000038	Renfrewshire	91.2	4.5	4.8	4.5	4.8	5.5	5.6	5.5	5.3	5.7	7.2	7.3	6.6	5.5	5.5	4.2	3.5	2.7	1.6	0.9
S12000026	Scottish Borders	59.0	2.9	3.0	2.9	3.0	2.8	2.5	2.8	2.8	3.7	4.6	4.8	4.5	4.1	4.4	3.5	2.8	2.0	1.2	0.8
S12000027	Shetland Islands	11.4	0.6	0.6	0.6	0.7	0.6	0.7	0.6	0.7	0.7	0.8	0.9	0.8	0.7	0.7	0.6	0.4	0.3	0.2	0.1
S12000028	South Ayrshire	58.8	2.5	2.8	2.8	2.9	3.0	2.9	2.9	3.0	3.4	4.2	4.6	4.5	4.2	4.3	3.6	2.8	2.2	1.3	0.9
S12000029	South Lanarkshire	164.1	8.2	8.8	8.3	8.6	9.0	9.0	9.9	10.0	10.5	12.7	13.1	12.2	10.6	9.9	7.6	6.3	4.9	3.0	1.6
S12000030	Stirling	48.7	2.2	2.4	2.5	3.3	4.0	3.3	2.5	2.6	3.0	3.6	3.7	3.2	2.7	2.8	2.3	1.9	1.4	0.8	0.5
S12000039	West Dunbartonshire	47.1	2.4	2.5	2.3	2.4	2.8	2.9	3.0	2.7	2.8	3.7	3.8	3.5	3.0	2.8	2.1	1.8	1.3	0.8	0.5
S12000040	West Lothian	91.9	5.1	5.7	5.3	5.2	5.1	5.5	6.1	5.8	6.5	7.5	7.2	6.1	5.1	5.1	3.9	2.9	2.0	1.1	0.6
N92000002	NORTHERN IRELAND	946.9	60.7	62.3	55.2	57.4	57.8	62.2	63.1	61.6	61.5	66.8	66.4	58.8	48.6	46.1	40.3	30.4	23.2	15.2	9.2
N09000001	Antrim and Newtownabbey	72.5	4.5	4.9	4.3	4.3	4.2	4.5	4.8	5.0	5.0	5.3	5.1	4.4	3.7	3.6	3.1	2.4	1.7	1.1	0.7
N09000011	Ards and North Down	82.2	4.4	4.9	4.5	4.3	3.8	4.6	4.8	5.0	5.4	6.1	6.1	5.7	4.9	5.4	4.6	3.0	2.3	1.6	1.1
N09000002	Armagh City, Banbridge & Craigavon	105.9	7.6	7.6	6.5	6.2	5.9	7.1	7.3	7.1	7.1	7.5	7.3	6.2	5.1	5.0	4.3	3.3	2.4	1.5	0.9
N09000003	Belfast	175.1	11.1	10.6	9.0	10.9	14.5	13.7	13.2	11.7	10.4	11.0	11.8	10.6	8.1	7.2	6.6	5.4	4.6	3.1	1.8
N09000004	Causeway Coast and Glens	72.4	4.2	4.5	4.2	4.6	4.5	4.2	4.2	4.4	4.8	5.4	5.3	4.6	4.0	3.7	3.4	2.6	1.8	1.2	0.7
N09000005	Derry City and Strabane	76.4	5.2	5.2	4.6	5.1	4.8	5.1	5.1	4.9	5.1	5.7	5.6	4.6	3.9	3.5	2.9	2.1	1.5	0.9	0.5
N09000006	Fermanagh and Omagh	57.8	3.8	3.9	3.7	3.6	3.0	3.5	3.7	3.8	3.8	4.0	4.0	3.7	3.2	2.9	2.4	1.8	1.3	0.9	0.6
N09000007	Lisburn and Castlereagh	72.0	4.3	4.6	4.0	4.0	3.6	4.4	4.7	4.8	4.7	5.4	5.5	4.8	3.8	3.5	3.3	2.6	2.0	1.2	0.7
N09000008	Mid and East Antrim	70.3	3.9	4.2	4.1	4.0	3.9	4.1	4.2	4.3	4.6	5.3	5.2	4.5	4.0	3.9	3.4	2.6	2.0	1.4	0.8
N09000009	Mid Ulster	72.4	5.3	5.4	4.8	4.5	4.4	5.1	5.1	5.0	5.0	4.8	4.6	4.1	3.4	3.1	2.7	2.0	1.5	1.0	0.6
N09000010	Newry, Mourne and Down	89.7	6.3	6.5	5.6	5.7	5.1	6.0	6.0	5.7	5.7	6.4	6.1	5.5	4.6	4.2	3.5	2.6	2.0	1.3	0.8

MYE3: Components of population change for local authorities in the UK, mid-2016

Code	Name	Estimated Population mid-2015	Births	Deaths	Births minus Deaths	Internal Migration Inflow	Internal Migration Outflow	Internal Migration Net	International Migration Inflow	International Migration Outflow	International Migration Net	Other	Estimated Population mid-2016
K02000001	UNITED KINGDOM	65,110,034	780,983	588,143	192,840	-	-	-13	649,550	313,899	335,651	9,542	65,648,054
K03000001	GREAT BRITAIN	63,258,413	756,604	572,802	183,802	-	-	-13	636,552	302,359	334,193	9,522	63,785,917
K04000001	ENGLAND AND WALES	57,885,413	701,348	516,725	184,623	43,889	52,695	-8,806	596,152	284,859	311,293	8,694	58,381,217
E92000001	ENGLAND	54,786,327	668,063	484,202	183,861	95,356	107,541	-12,185	579,326	277,709	301,617	8,447	55,268,067
E12000001	NORTH EAST	2,624,579	28,582	27,392	1,190	43,090	42,072	1,018	15,292	6,001	9,291	511	2,636,589
E06000047	County Durham	519,347	5,341	5,501	-160	17,232	15,935	1,297	2,168	937	1,231	61	521,776
E06000005	Darlington	105,998	1,198	1,152	46	3,712	3,652	60	335	181	154	69	106,327
E06000001	Hartlepool	92,498	1,071	1,004	67	2,341	2,257	84	276	82	194	2	92,845
E06000002	Middlesbrough	139,310	1,883	1,411	472	6,013	6,714	-701	1,625	391	1,234	11	140,326
E06000057	Northumberland	316,453	2,869	3,511	-642	9,854	8,669	1,185	452	220	232	216	317,444
E06000003	Redcar and Cleveland	135,324	1,411	1,533	-122	4,105	4,080	25	353	89	264	5	135,496
E06000004	Stockton-on-Tees	195,128	2,243	1,882	361	6,287	6,574	-287	1,093	378	715	41	195,958
E11000007	Tyne and Wear (Met County)	1,120,521	12,566	11,398	1,168	29,203	29,848	-645	8,990	3,723	5,267	106	1,126,417
E08000037	Gateshead	201,724	2,241	2,137	104	7,612	7,685	-73	1,196	352	844	29	202,628
E08000021	Newcastle upon Tyne	290,764	3,422	2,525	897	19,074	20,039	-965	5,425	2,442	2,983	34	293,713
E08000022	North Tyneside	202,725	2,261	2,148	113	7,381	7,084	297	730	310	420	20	203,575
E08000023	South Tyneside	148,495	1,741	1,668	73	3,777	3,300	477	281	132	149	0	149,194
E08000024	Sunderland	276,813	2,901	2,920	-19	6,774	7,155	-381	1,358	487	871	23	277,307
E12000002	NORTH WEST	7,175,178	86,624	69,861	16,763	117,264	111,647	5,617	55,689	30,039	25,650	753	7,223,961
E06000008	Blackburn with Darwen	147,856	2,188	1,260	928	4,617	5,653	-1,036	1,077	385	692	22	148,462
E06000009	Blackpool	140,162	1,672	1,857	-185	7,747	7,996	-249	618	364	254	1	139,983
E06000049	Cheshire East	375,722	3,890	3,810	80	14,810	13,687	1,123	1,749	1,434	315	63	377,303
E06000050	Cheshire West and Chester	333,949	3,573	3,413	160	14,332	13,002	1,330	1,370	1,049	321	-36	335,724
E06000006	Halton	126,719	1,530	1,189	341	3,543	3,557	-14	434	191	243	17	127,306
E06000007	Warrington	207,781	2,367	1,892	475	7,077	6,807	270	1,083	704	379	68	208,973
E10000006	Cumbria	498,581	4,806	5,430	-624	11,882	11,518	364	1,592	1,126	466	6	498,793
E07000026	Allerdale	96,756	882	1,098	-216	3,024	2,574	450	218	112	106	3	97,099
E07000027	Barrow-in-Furness	67,676	780	767	13	1,639	1,794	-155	126	72	54	-56	67,532
E07000028	Carlisle	108,109	1,243	1,107	136	3,638	3,536	102	374	368	6	35	108,388
E07000029	Copeland	69,688	714	743	-29	1,696	2,083	-387	73	56	17	17	69,306
E07000030	Eden	52,576	399	526	-127	2,265	2,123	142	194	149	45	6	52,642
E07000031	South Lakeland	103,776	788	1,189	-401	4,700	4,488	212	607	369	238	1	103,826
E11000001	Greater Manchester (Met County)	2,754,017	37,119	24,182	12,937	67,422	68,871	-1,449	30,298	15,240	15,058	281	2,780,844
E08000001	Bolton	281,828	3,838	2,571	1,267	8,666	9,430	-764	2,208	1,023	1,185	20	283,536
E08000002	Bury	187,788	2,423	1,912	511	7,189	7,478	-289	1,117	640	477	16	188,503
E08000003	Manchester	529,809	8,069	3,498	4,571	38,378	38,588	-210	15,169	8,024	7,145	4	541,319
E08000004	Oldham	230,197	3,323	2,127	1,196	6,619	7,375	-756	2,219	521	1,698	14	232,349
E08000005	Rochdale	214,314	2,980	1,993	987	7,171	7,218	-47	1,694	628	1,066	30	216,350
E08000006	Salford	245,186	3,670	2,122	1,548	13,068	13,532	-464	3,451	1,653	1,798	53	248,121
E08000007	Stockport	288,169	3,441	2,712	729	11,325	10,493	832	846	776	70	21	289,821
E08000008	Tameside	221,507	2,927	2,171	756	7,538	7,146	392	909	484	425	29	223,109
E08000009	Trafford	232,975	2,869	1,909	960	10,438	10,435	3	1,166	912	254	18	234,210
E08000010	Wigan	322,244	3,579	3,167	412	8,252	8,398	-146	1,519	579	940	76	323,526
E10000017	Lancashire	1,188,875	13,256	12,083	1,173	39,409	37,263	2,146	6,835	3,871	2,964	260	1,195,418

MYE3: Components of population change for local authorities in the UK, mid-2016

Code	Name	Estimated Population mid-2015	Births	Deaths	Births minus Deaths	Internal Migration Inflow	Internal Migration Outflow	Internal Migration Net	International Migration Inflow	International Migration Outflow	International Migration Net	Other	Estimated Population mid-2016
E07000117	Burnley	87,262	1,210	888	322	3,274	3,544	-270	389	211	178	4	87,496
E07000118	Chorley	112,000	1,243	1,011	232	5,429	4,461	968	201	158	43	60	114,266
E07000119	Fylde	77,490	645	1,028	-383	4,775	3,797	978	212	153	59	9	78,153
E07000120	Hyndburn	80,113	1,065	822	243	3,240	3,288	-48	221	141	80	4	80,392
E07000121	Lancaster	140,787	1,493	1,474	19	7,673	7,795	-122	2,114	1,090	1,024	15	141,723
E07000122	Pendle	89,925	1,277	829	448	2,943	3,413	-470	795	199	596	16	90,515
E07000123	Preston	140,685	1,884	1,184	700	8,247	9,259	-1,012	1,684	1,164	520	130	141,023
E07000124	Ribble Valley	58,519	456	570	-114	3,084	2,660	424	151	113	38	-3	58,864
E07000125	Rossendale	69,418	798	608	190	3,245	3,095	150	107	71	36	-7	69,787
E07000126	South Ribble	109,685	1,229	974	255	4,746	4,596	150	221	190	31	15	110,136
E07000127	West Lancashire	112,482	1,001	1,232	-231	6,027	5,468	559	509	264	245	6	113,061
E07000128	Wyre	109,546	955	1,463	-508	6,146	5,307	839	231	117	114	11	110,002
E11000002	Merseyside (Met County)	1,401,516	16,223	14,745	1,478	34,814	31,682	3,132	10,633	5,675	4,958	71	1,411,155
E08000011	Knowsley	147,262	1,918	1,518	400	5,792	5,579	213	251	135	116	10	148,001
E08000012	Liverpool	480,873	5,931	4,409	1,522	24,309	23,231	1,078	8,379	4,214	4,165	-33	487,605
E08000014	Sefton	274,089	2,818	3,186	-368	8,868	8,084	784	873	582	291	57	274,853
E08000013	St. Helens	177,592	1,991	1,907	84	5,353	4,749	604	434	237	197	3	178,480
E08000015	Wirral	321,700	3,565	3,725	-160	7,757	7,304	453	696	507	189	34	322,216
E12000003	**YORKSHIRE AND THE HUMBER**	5,390,211	64,030	50,997	13,033	105,286	104,157	1,129	40,702	21,196	19,506	1,491	5,425,370
E06000011	East Riding of Yorkshire	336,756	2,910	3,812	-902	14,713	13,043	1,670	885	653	232	48	337,804
E06000010	Kingston upon Hull, City of	258,587	3,552	2,490	1,062	8,980	9,936	-956	2,780	1,507	1,273	69	260,035
E06000012	North East Lincolnshire	159,971	1,877	1,691	186	3,862	4,550	-688	627	289	338	21	159,828
E06000013	North Lincolnshire	169,843	1,811	1,713	98	5,105	4,790	315	832	315	517	34	170,807
E06000014	York	205,784	2,006	1,806	200	13,029	13,118	-89	2,510	1,542	968	57	206,920
E10000023	North Yorkshire	606,017	5,718	6,457	-739	24,184	21,889	2,295	2,515	1,415	1,100	865	609,538
E07000163	Craven	55,826	451	662	-211	2,992	2,346	646	163	80	83	-1	56,343
E07000164	Hambleton	90,074	812	955	-143	4,225	3,741	484	255	130	125	51	90,591
E07000165	Harrogate	159,916	1,505	1,633	-128	6,639	6,623	16	869	604	265	-301	159,768
E07000166	Richmondshire	52,565	536	442	94	2,704	2,785	-81	290	103	187	1,111	53,876
E07000167	Ryedale	53,332	449	606	-157	2,864	2,291	573	209	83	126	-13	53,861
E07000168	Scarborough	108,089	996	1,353	-357	4,352	4,114	238	444	258	186	1	108,157
E07000169	Selby	86,215	969	806	163	4,393	3,974	419	285	157	128	17	86,942
E11000003	South Yorkshire (Met County)	1,375,457	16,028	12,973	3,055	35,386	35,474	-88	11,786	4,931	6,855	134	1,385,413
E08000016	Barnsley	239,855	2,763	2,389	374	6,935	6,282	653	1,318	361	957	8	241,847
E08000017	Doncaster	305,496	3,538	3,128	410	8,074	8,132	-58	2,166	715	1,451	75	307,374
E08000018	Rotherham	260,929	3,167	2,611	556	7,537	7,420	117	871	357	514	26	262,142
E08000019	Sheffield	569,177	6,560	4,845	1,715	24,229	25,029	-800	7,431	3,498	3,933	25	574,050
E11000006	West Yorkshire (Met County)	2,277,796	30,128	20,055	10,073	57,279	58,609	-1,330	18,767	10,544	8,223	263	2,295,025
E08000032	Bradford	529,879	7,986	4,441	3,545	14,352	17,083	-2,731	3,973	2,142	1,831	15	532,539
E08000033	Calderdale	207,832	2,433	1,944	489	7,127	6,812	315	744	333	411	22	209,069
E08000034	Kirklees	432,855	5,392	3,863	1,529	13,381	13,981	-600	2,885	1,460	1,425	27	435,236
E08000035	Leeds	773,213	10,273	6,585	3,688	38,149	37,749	400	9,590	5,993	3,597	189	781,087
E08000036	Wakefield	334,017	4,044	3,222	822	10,432	9,146	1,286	1,575	616	959	10	337,094

MYE3: Components of population change for local authorities in the UK, mid-2016

Code	Name	Estimated Population mid-2015	Births	Deaths	Births minus Deaths	Internal Migration Inflow	Internal Migration Outflow	Internal Migration Net	International Migration Inflow	International Migration Outflow	International Migration Net	Other	Estimated Population mid-2016
E12000004	EAST MIDLANDS	4,677,425	53,787	43,585	10,202	122,500	109,739	12,761	38,712	14,965	23,747	1,255	4,725,390
E06000015	Derby	253,875	3,312	2,245	1,067	10,827	10,967	-140	2,464	1,086	1,378	23	256,203
E06000016	Leicester	344,036	5,211	2,584	2,627	17,124	19,359	-2,235	7,908	2,857	5,051	34	349,513
E06000018	Nottingham	318,936	4,380	2,380	2,000	25,864	26,022	-158	7,019	3,113	3,906	95	324,779
E06000017	Rutland	38,352	344	351	-7	2,430	2,210	220	147	53	94	290	38,949
E06000007	Derbyshire	783,082	7,796	8,030	-234	26,055	23,157	2,898	1,610	822	788	200	786,734
E10000007	Derbyshire	124,188	1,215	1,274	-59	5,295	4,711	584	178	109	69	20	124,802
E07000032	Amber Valley	77,917	849	872	-23	3,775	3,684	91	339	102	237	3	78,225
E07000033	Bolsover	104,463	1,053	1,135	-82	3,586	3,589	-3	227	83	144	5	104,527
E07000034	Chesterfield	71,301	525	836	-311	3,192	2,863	329	141	77	64	94	71,477
E07000035	Derbyshire Dales	114,684	1,256	1,138	118	4,907	4,633	274	188	157	31	5	115,112
E07000036	Erewash	91,523	877	813	64	3,370	3,414	44	197	113	84	5	91,720
E07000037	High Peak	99,661	890	1,089	-199	3,634	3,634	902	131	59	72	14	100,450
E07000038	North East Derbyshire	99,345	1,131	873	258	5,466	4,789	677	209	122	87	54	100,421
E07000039	South Derbyshire	673,410	7,116	6,065	1,051	30,298	25,843	4,455	3,072	1,536	1,536	14	680,466
E10000018	Leicestershire	96,458	1,104	860	244	5,524	4,724	800	220	154	66	-6	97,562
E07000129	Blaby	175,167	1,880	1,410	470	11,401	10,511	890	1,592	731	861	-10	177,378
E07000130	Charnwood	89,144	845	789	56	5,085	4,152	933	249	135	114	4	90,251
E07000131	Harborough	108,603	1,151	1,043	108	5,375	4,320	1,055	296	190	106	9	109,881
E07000132	Hinckley and Bosworth	50,956	493	458	35	2,127	2,216	-89	136	95	41	24	50,967
E07000133	Melton	97,098	1,059	925	134	4,950	3,873	1,077	244	113	131	-4	98,436
E07000134	North West Leicestershire	55,984	584	580	4	4,437	4,648	-211	335	118	217	-3	55,991
E07000135	Oadby and Wigston	737,350	7,783	7,882	-99	27,695	24,482	3,213	5,350	1,514	3,836	511	744,811
E10000019	Lincolnshire	66,876	821	697	124	2,060	2,971	-911	1,733	208	1,525	95	67,709
E07000136	Boston	138,068	1,230	1,882	-652	6,947	5,863	1,084	363	122	241	2	138,743
E07000137	East Lindsey	96,641	1,277	863	414	8,212	8,486	-274	1,098	507	591	13	97,385
E07000138	Lincoln	112,186	1,137	1,064	73	6,439	5,406	1,033	254	107	147	205	113,644
E07000139	North Kesteven	91,245	982	1,046	-64	3,974	3,532	442	1,085	215	870	34	92,527
E07000140	South Holland	139,376	1,424	1,383	41	7,064	6,044	1,020	609	274	335	128	140,900
E07000141	South Kesteven	92,958	912	947	-35	5,536	4,717	819	208	81	127	34	93,903
E07000142	West Lindsey	722,167	9,113	6,113	3,000	24,480	22,256	2,224	7,639	2,563	5,076	-15	732,452
E10000021	Northamptonshire	66,887	971	578	393	2,519	2,220	299	927	202	725	-9	68,295
E07000150	Corby	79,795	797	681	116	3,971	3,971	934	403	165	238	15	81,098
E07000151	Daventry	90,074	949	813	136	5,039	4,080	959	456	230	226	-13	91,382
E07000152	East Northamptonshire	97,605	1,246	848	398	4,718	4,127	591	614	272	342	11	98,947
E07000153	Kettering	221,503	3,283	1,740	1,543	9,933	11,245	-1,312	4,057	1,301	2,756	9	224,499
E07000154	Northampton	89,106	859	718	141	5,439	4,927	512	275	148	127	-22	89,864
E07000155	South Northamptonshire	77,197	1,008	735	273	3,889	3,648	241	907	245	662	-6	78,367
E10000024	Nottinghamshire	806,217	8,732	7,935	797	30,314	28,030	2,284	3,503	1,421	2,082	103	811,483
E07000170	Ashfield	123,577	1,467	1,241	226	5,733	5,232	501	340	133	207	2	124,513
E07000171	Bassetlaw	114,689	1,252	1,205	47	4,130	4,009	121	512	137	375	-20	115,212
E07000172	Broxtowe	111,837	1,173	1,043	130	6,799	7,024	-225	635	341	294	80	112,116
E07000173	Gedling	116,142	1,287	1,120	167	5,931	5,588	343	250	172	78	16	116,746
E07000174	Mansfield	106,780	1,282	1,101	181	4,637	4,432	205	926	234	692	22	107,880
E07000175	Newark and Sherwood	118,695	1,198	1,192	6	6,164	5,324	840	494	193	301	6	119,848
E07000176	Rushcliffe	114,497	1,073	1,033	40	6,982	6,483	499	346	211	135	-3	115,168

MYE3: Components of population change for local authorities in the UK, mid-2016

Code	Name	Estimated Population mid-2015	Births	Deaths	Births minus Deaths	Internal Migration Inflow	Internal Migration Outflow	Internal Migration Net	International Migration Inflow	International Migration Outflow	International Migration Net	Other	Estimated Population mid-2016
E12000005	**WEST MIDLANDS**	5,755,032	70,820	53,493	17,327	110,942	109,246	1,696	54,885	19,608	35,277	1,441	5,810,773
E06000019	Herefordshire, County of	188,522	1,749	2,097	-348	6,689	6,404	285	1,486	448	1,038	35	189,532
E06000051	Shropshire	312,227	2,905	3,411	-506	12,126	10,134	1,992	1,126	644	482	197	314,392
E06000021	Stoke-on-Trent	251,746	3,502	2,451	1,051	9,300	10,092	-792	2,362	730	1,632	22	253,659
E06000020	Telford and Wrekin	171,677	2,082	1,422	660	6,817	6,126	691	1,054	411	643	56	173,727
E10000028	Staffordshire	862,166	8,591	8,365	226	28,537	27,395	1,142	3,446	1,457	1,989	907	866,430
E07000192	Cannock Chase	98,490	1,053	938	115	3,512	3,784	-272	225	77	148	32	98,513
E07000193	East Staffordshire	116,196	1,450	1,096	354	4,176	4,428	-252	1,013	373	640	-1	116,937
E07000194	Lichfield	102,566	930	1,037	-107	4,755	4,645	110	256	127	129	133	102,831
E07000195	Newcastle-under-Lyme	126,863	1,203	1,309	-106	7,166	6,221	945	704	299	405	19	128,126
E07000196	South Staffordshire	110,712	958	1,098	-140	5,408	4,875	533	156	76	80	-12	111,173
E07000197	Stafford	132,220	1,250	1,233	17	5,908	5,469	439	628	352	276	712	133,664
E07000198	Staffordshire Moorlands	98,011	813	1,038	-225	3,780	3,444	336	123	74	49	5	98,176
E07000199	Tamworth	77,108	934	616	318	2,259	2,956	-697	341	79	262	19	77,010
E10000031	Warwickshire	555,154	6,080	5,419	661	22,726	21,388	1,338	3,870	2,102	1,768	70	558,991
E07000218	North Warwickshire	62,765	665	722	-57	3,310	2,926	384	140	58	82	19	63,193
E07000219	Nuneaton and Bedworth	126,603	1,640	1,212	428	4,960	4,576	384	502	241	261	-2	127,674
E07000220	Rugby	104,455	1,264	969	295	4,416	4,385	31	979	445	534	-24	105,291
E07000221	Stratford-on-Avon	122,438	1,105	1,314	-209	6,470	5,797	673	775	370	405	38	123,345
E07000222	Warwick	138,893	1,406	1,202	204	7,749	7,883	-134	1,474	988	486	39	139,488
E11000005	West Midlands (Met County)	2,834,490	39,827	24,501	15,326	70,895	76,312	-5,417	38,518	12,513	26,005	147	2,870,551
E08000025	Birmingham	1,112,950	17,163	8,466	8,697	43,275	47,764	-4,489	17,719	6,879	10,840	79	1,128,077
E08000026	Coventry	344,288	4,555	2,755	1,800	17,042	17,543	-501	10,416	2,764	7,652	-24	353,215
E08000027	Dudley	316,331	3,725	3,062	663	9,328	9,299	29	928	394	534	1	317,558
E08000028	Sandwell	319,101	4,839	2,929	1,910	12,467	13,606	-1,139	3,447	719	2,728	31	322,631
E08000029	Solihull	210,834	2,295	1,975	320	9,708	9,037	671	621	303	318	23	212,166
E08000030	Walsall	275,880	3,789	2,731	1,058	10,305	9,566	739	1,668	471	1,197	13	278,887
E08000031	Wolverhampton	255,106	3,461	2,583	878	9,611	10,338	-727	3,719	983	2,736	24	258,017
E10000034	Worcestershire	579,050	6,084	5,827	257	20,029	17,572	2,457	3,023	1,303	1,720	7	583,491
E07000234	Bromsgrove	95,800	925	1,091	-166	5,479	4,485	994	174	86	88	54	96,770
E07000235	Malvern Hills	76,136	557	979	-422	4,439	3,819	620	329	116	213	8	76,555
E07000236	Redditch	84,821	1,101	679	422	2,600	3,181	-581	610	199	411	15	85,088
E07000237	Worcester	100,985	1,233	827	406	5,946	5,777	169	869	510	359	8	101,927
E07000238	Wychavon	121,709	1,166	1,160	6	6,308	5,336	972	824	283	541	-84	123,144
E07000239	Wyre Forest	99,599	1,102	1,091	11	3,601	3,318	283	217	109	108	6	100,007
E12000006	**EAST**	6,075,970	73,106	55,309	17,797	156,946	141,857	15,089	47,634	26,002	21,632	-1,483	6,129,005
E06000055	Bedford	166,376	2,215	1,439	776	8,290	7,300	990	1,816	1,181	635	37	168,814
E06000056	Central Bedfordshire	272,421	3,319	2,019	1,300	15,116	12,748	2,368	1,765	1,192	573	69	276,731
E06000032	Luton	213,581	3,613	1,409	2,204	8,361	11,158	-2,797	4,656	1,743	2,913	13	215,914
E06000031	Peterborough	193,657	3,149	1,476	1,673	7,979	8,623	-644	3,023	1,077	1,946	103	196,735
E06000033	Southend-on-Sea	179,234	2,292	1,897	395	8,069	7,424	645	879	558	321	11	180,606
E06000034	Thurrock	166,040	2,514	1,203	1,311	7,298	7,082	216	1,386	535	851	10	168,428
E10000003	Cambridgeshire	641,524	7,532	5,297	2,235	29,586	30,416	-830	7,749	5,946	1,803	-157	644,575
E07000008	Cambridge	125,105	1,418	868	550	13,448	14,928	-1,480	4,404	3,930	474	-14	124,635
E07000009	East Cambridgeshire	87,783	1,035	735	300	4,220	4,240	-20	625	380	245	-119	88,189
E07000010	Fenland	98,814	1,156	1,129	27	4,914	4,745	169	924	301	623	3	99,636
E07000011	Huntingdonshire	175,334	2,086	1,421	665	7,793	7,823	-30	828	651	177	-51	176,095

MYE3: Components of population change for local authorities in the UK, mid-2016

Code	Name	Estimated Population mid-2015	Births	Deaths	Births minus Deaths	Internal Migration Inflow	Internal Migration Outflow	Internal Migration Net	International Migration Inflow	International Migration Outflow	International Migration Net	Other	Estimated Population mid-2016
E07000012	South Cambridgeshire	154,488	1,837	1,144	693	9,803	9,272	531	968	684	284	24	156,020
E10000012	Essex	1,445,323	16,523	14,142	2,381	50,301	43,853	6,448	7,489	3,866	3,623	135	1,457,910
E07000066	Basildon	181,951	2,551	1,521	1,030	8,241	7,880	361	741	318	423	3	183,768
E07000067	Braintree	150,530	1,678	1,452	226	7,128	6,854	274	488	290	198	5	151,233
E07000068	Brentwood	76,403	855	751	104	4,285	4,154	131	336	206	130	1	76,769
E07000069	Castle Point	89,184	870	1,046	-176	4,267	3,612	655	161	75	86	3	89,752
E07000070	Chelmsford	172,719	1,927	1,420	507	8,686	8,223	463	1,012	610	402	106	174,197
E07000071	Colchester	184,916	2,248	1,619	629	10,555	9,706	849	2,350	1,180	1,170	69	187,633
E07000072	Epping Forest	129,274	1,626	1,257	369	7,278	7,381	-103	744	362	382	1	129,923
E07000073	Harlow	85,335	1,222	705	517	3,734	4,114	-380	708	316	392	3	85,867
E07000074	Maldon	62,824	576	626	-50	3,384	2,792	592	143	86	57	-5	63,418
E07000075	Rochford	85,192	754	829	-75	4,285	3,744	541	123	71	52	-2	85,708
E07000076	Tendring	141,790	1,293	2,185	-892	7,044	4,802	2,242	322	127	195	18	143,353
E07000077	Uttlesford	85,205	923	731	192	5,317	4,494	823	361	225	136	-67	86,289
E10000015	Hertfordshire	1,165,332	14,728	9,250	5,478	50,400	49,591	809	8,967	4,329	4,638	129	1,176,386
E07000095	Broxbourne	96,311	1,262	753	509	4,822	4,981	-159	535	319	216	4	96,881
E07000096	Dacorum	151,069	1,929	1,218	711	7,984	7,757	227	975	521	454	-16	152,445
E07000242	East Hertfordshire	144,488	1,636	1,043	593	8,096	7,613	483	905	346	559	7	146,130
E07000098	Hertsmere	103,157	1,333	880	453	6,743	7,035	-292	819	460	359	28	103,705
E07000099	North Hertfordshire	131,611	1,578	1,166	412	7,356	6,824	532	488	398	90	10	132,655
E07000240	St Albans	146,188	1,845	1,065	780	7,817	8,263	-446	907	412	495	8	147,025
E07000243	Stevenage	86,579	1,191	757	434	4,231	4,290	-59	525	204	321	10	87,285
E07000102	Three Rivers	91,797	1,068	759	309	5,721	5,352	369	415	273	142	59	92,676
E07000103	Watford	96,348	1,508	694	814	6,162	7,237	-1,075	1,294	817	477	13	96,577
E07000241	Welwyn Hatfield	117,784	1,378	915	463	9,693	8,464	1,229	2,104	579	1,525	6	121,007
E10000020	Norfolk	884,748	9,141	9,772	-631	27,414	22,538	4,876	6,097	3,114	2,983	-245	891,731
E07000143	Breckland	135,698	1,439	1,562	-123	6,956	5,684	1,272	800	377	423	-147	137,123
E07000144	Broadland	126,626	1,133	1,514	-381	6,595	5,514	1,081	232	156	76	0	127,402
E07000145	Great Yarmouth	98,615	1,071	1,141	-70	3,604	3,536	68	573	194	379	0	98,992
E07000146	King's Lynn and West Norfolk	151,261	1,641	1,770	-129	5,797	5,382	415	871	493	378	-128	151,797
E07000147	North Norfolk	103,252	763	1,398	-635	4,821	4,100	721	382	165	217	32	103,587
E07000148	Norwich	138,097	1,733	1,123	610	11,063	11,318	-255	2,897	1,477	1,420	-7	139,865
E07000149	South Norfolk	131,199	1,361	1,264	97	7,946	6,372	1,574	342	252	90	5	132,965
E10000029	Suffolk	747,734	8,080	7,405	675	23,676	20,668	3,008	3,807	2,461	1,346	-1,588	751,175
E07000200	Babergh	89,900	834	984	-150	4,828	4,464	364	252	147	105	31	90,250
E07000201	Forest Heath	63,676	1,029	510	519	3,622	2,951	671	434	509	-75	-1,493	63,298
E07000202	Ipswich	137,694	2,017	1,150	867	6,146	6,953	-807	1,574	803	771	-10	138,515
E07000203	Mid Suffolk	100,251	845	888	-43	5,389	4,940	449	224	131	93	-30	100,720
E07000204	St Edmundsbury	112,949	1,203	1,043	160	5,475	5,083	392	533	434	99	-211	113,389
E07000205	Suffolk Coastal	126,580	1,030	1,381	-351	6,407	5,132	1,275	491	293	198	134	127,836
E07000206	Waveney	116,684	1,122	1,449	-327	4,454	3,790	664	299	144	155	-9	117,167

MYE3: Components of population change for local authorities in the UK, mid-2016

Code	Name	Estimated Population mid-2015	Births	Deaths	Births minus Deaths	Internal Migration Inflow	Internal Migration Outflow	Internal Migration Net	International Migration Inflow	International Migration Outflow	International Migration Net	Other	Estimated Population mid-2016
E12000007	LONDON	8,666,930	129,847	48,513	81,334	198,327	291,629	-93,302	208,593	94,368	114,225	472	8,769,659
E09000007	Camden	243,837	2,756	1,131	1,625	20,300	23,452	-3,152	12,775	5,947	6,828	24	249,162
E09000001	City of London	6,687	58	42	16	745	809	-64	927	323	604	3	7,246
E09000012	Hackney	268,626	4,533	1,105	3,428	19,338	20,999	-1,661	5,583	2,752	2,831	15	273,239
E09000013	Hammersmith and Fulham	182,183	2,457	880	1,577	15,865	19,574	-3,709	5,565	3,904	1,661	71	181,783
E09000014	Haringey	268,251	4,147	1,201	2,946	21,313	24,701	-3,388	7,840	3,582	4,258	11	272,078
E09000019	Islington	227,507	2,922	1,005	1,917	20,649	22,654	-2,005	8,506	3,680	4,826	-190	232,055
E09000020	Kensington and Chelsea	158,589	1,764	841	923	9,934	13,818	-3,884	4,509	3,400	1,109	36	156,773
E09000022	Lambeth	320,736	4,410	1,451	2,959	32,031	34,447	-2,416	6,737	4,967	1,770	14	323,063
E09000023	Lewisham	294,999	4,803	1,496	3,307	22,916	24,809	-1,893	5,123	2,666	2,457	33	298,903
E09000025	Newham	336,254	6,211	1,294	4,917	19,553	27,349	-7,796	14,521	3,385	11,136	22	344,533
E09000028	Southwark	308,434	4,509	1,318	3,191	25,742	29,214	-3,472	8,294	4,801	3,493	9	311,655
E09000030	Tower Hamlets	293,828	4,597	1,095	3,502	22,197	25,228	-3,031	11,847	5,217	6,630	14	300,943
E09000032	Wandsworth	319,477	4,917	1,546	3,371	30,996	33,670	-2,674	6,445	5,186	1,259	64	321,497
E09000033	Westminster	238,047	2,656	1,142	1,514	16,564	21,932	-5,368	14,590	6,785	7,805	-24	241,974
E09000002	Barking and Dagenham	203,101	3,993	1,229	2,764	12,687	14,263	-1,576	4,689	799	3,890	3	208,182
E09000003	Barnet	378,778	5,330	2,394	2,936	22,812	24,591	-1,779	8,257	3,450	4,807	32	384,774
E09000004	Bexley	242,387	3,098	2,015	1,083	12,496	11,765	731	1,408	523	885	9	245,095
E09000005	Brent	323,443	5,236	1,712	3,524	18,066	26,022	-7,956	11,598	4,193	7,405	11	326,427
E09000006	Bromley	325,303	4,251	2,552	1,699	17,371	17,827	-456	1,936	936	1,000	34	327,580
E09000008	Croydon	380,070	5,913	2,433	3,480	20,656	23,458	-2,802	4,674	2,127	2,547	6	383,301
E09000009	Ealing	344,285	5,151	1,858	3,293	20,224	27,026	-6,802	8,788	4,755	4,033	-7	344,802
E09000010	Enfield	328,738	5,039	2,064	2,975	16,821	20,234	-3,413	5,142	1,317	3,825	2	332,127
E09000011	Greenwich	274,542	4,655	1,610	3,045	18,487	19,915	-1,428	4,747	1,952	2,795	185	279,139
E09000015	Harrow	246,818	3,661	1,489	2,172	13,277	17,436	-4,159	5,608	1,777	3,831	35	248,697
E09000016	Havering	249,375	3,447	2,286	1,161	12,340	10,637	1,703	1,750	613	1,137	-5	253,371
E09000017	Hillingdon	296,056	4,503	1,774	2,729	17,218	19,471	-2,253	5,566	2,230	3,336	31	299,899
E09000018	Hounslow	266,412	4,400	1,428	2,972	15,143	20,163	-5,020	6,294	2,427	3,867	39	268,270
E09000021	Kingston upon Thames	171,609	2,277	1,039	1,238	12,265	13,143	-878	3,486	1,719	1,767	-33	173,703
E09000024	Merton	205,965	3,362	1,203	2,159	14,818	17,693	-2,875	3,739	2,281	1,458	-1	206,706
E09000026	Redbridge	297,928	4,743	1,819	2,924	17,307	21,728	-4,421	6,620	1,733	4,887	10	301,328
E09000027	Richmond upon Thames	194,124	2,602	1,227	1,375	13,213	14,070	-857	2,106	1,567	539	6	195,187
E09000029	Sutton	199,870	2,684	1,431	1,253	13,101	10,766	335	1,232	749	483	4	201,945
E09000031	Waltham Forest	270,671	4,762	1,403	3,359	15,167	20,050	-4,883	7,691	2,625	5,066	9	274,222
E12000008	SOUTH EAST	8,949,392	102,826	79,017	23,809	238,756	225,097	13,659	79,278	38,103	41,175	2,312	9,030,347
E06000036	Bracknell Forest	119,205	1,448	700	748	6,071	6,870	-799	951	428	523	53	119,730
E06000043	Brighton and Hove	284,073	2,935	2,106	829	19,601	20,288	-687	5,806	2,865	2,941	17	287,173
E06000046	Isle of Wight	139,763	1,218	1,725	-507	4,611	3,844	767	409	182	227	14	140,264
E06000035	Medway	275,176	3,640	2,181	1,459	11,922	12,406	-484	1,640	911	729	77	276,957
E06000042	Milton Keynes	263,181	3,782	1,708	2,074	10,806	11,391	-585	2,854	1,279	1,575	-5	266,240
E06000044	Portsmouth	210,538	2,642	1,693	949	11,950	11,866	84	3,021	1,406	1,615	149	213,335
E06000038	Reading	161,701	2,532	1,057	1,475	11,558	14,048	-2,490	3,727	1,714	2,013	2	162,701
E06000039	Slough	146,038	2,652	845	1,807	6,902	8,502	-1,600	2,309	841	1,468	23	147,736
E06000045	Southampton	246,054	3,246	1,823	1,423	16,210	16,493	-283	5,836	2,685	3,151	32	250,377
E06000037	West Berkshire	157,460	1,761	1,191	570	8,242	8,144	98	868	463	405	43	158,576
E06000040	Windsor and Maidenhead	148,277	1,705	1,210	495	9,160	8,832	328	1,282	692	590	-1	149,689
E06000041	Wokingham	161,200	1,886	1,187	699	10,306	9,788	518	1,572	673	899	-229	163,087
E10000002	Buckinghamshire	527,114	6,183	4,037	2,146	24,682	22,843	1,839	4,047	2,324	1,723	234	533,056

MYE3: Components of population change for local authorities in the UK, mid-2016

Code	Name	Estimated Population mid 2015	Births	Deaths	Births minus Deaths	Internal Migration Inflow	Internal Migration Outflow	Internal Migration Net	International Migration Inflow	International Migration Outflow	International Migration Net	Other	Estimated Population mid 2016
E07000004	Aylesbury Vale	188,312	2,318	1,359	959	10,467	8,475	1,992	1,822	662	1,160	257	192,680
E07000005	Chiltern	94,662	910	771	139	5,368	5,134	234	430	258	172	-3	95,204
E07000006	South Bucks	69,307	767	660	107	4,803	4,556	247	443	306	137	11	69,809
E07000007	Wycombe	174,833	2,188	1,247	941	8,666	9,300	-634	1,352	1,098	254	-31	175,363
E10000011	East Sussex	545,021	5,102	6,411	-1,309	21,122	16,830	4,292	2,641	1,100	1,541	12	549,557
E07000061	Eastbourne	102,204	1,044	1,258	-214	5,913	5,373	540	804	338	466	7	103,003
E07000062	Hastings	91,937	1,083	1,001	82	4,535	4,045	490	607	228	379	15	92,903
E07000063	Lewes	100,898	864	1,094	-230	5,771	4,972	799	353	174	179	-15	101,631
E07000064	Rother	93,192	719	1,330	-611	5,899	4,706	1,193	320	135	185	7	93,966
E07000065	Wealden	156,790	1,392	1,728	-336	8,546	7,276	1,270	557	225	332	-2	158,054
E10000014	Hampshire	1,356,994	14,517	12,472	2,045	50,715	48,262	2,453	5,741	3,118	2,623	988	1,365,103
E07000084	Basingstoke and Deane	174,340	2,211	1,316	895	6,949	7,463	-514	986	539	447	58	175,226
E07000085	East Hampshire	118,694	1,051	1,179	-128	6,777	6,291	486	448	241	207	-554	118,705
E07000086	Eastleigh	128,977	1,467	1,018	449	6,329	6,308	21	350	248	102	-3	129,546
E07000087	Fareham	115,182	1,095	1,164	-69	5,721	5,238	483	324	179	145	77	115,818
E07000088	Gosport	84,757	932	805	127	3,613	3,341	272	222	119	103	233	85,492
E07000089	Hart	94,395	962	685	277	5,348	5,353	-5	413	154	259	-44	94,882
E07000090	Havant	123,122	1,336	1,324	12	5,793	5,160	633	293	140	153	-29	123,891
E07000091	New Forest	179,275	1,468	2,107	-639	7,689	7,218	471	622	269	353	69	179,529
E07000092	Rushmoor	95,166	1,413	702	711	5,408	6,402	-994	762	404	358	850	96,091
E07000093	Test Valley	121,352	1,373	1,101	272	6,897	6,018	879	518	318	200	120	122,823
E07000094	Winchester	121,734	1,209	1,071	138	9,295	8,574	721	803	507	296	211	123,100
E10000016	Kent	1,523,100	17,217	14,398	2,819	54,097	46,135	7,962	10,610	4,215	6,395	162	1,540,438
E07000105	Ashford	124,047	1,488	1,060	428	6,409	5,469	940	689	241	448	8	125,871
E07000106	Canterbury	159,663	1,370	1,548	-178	12,634	11,460	1,174	2,716	875	1,841	2	162,502
E07000107	Dartford	103,531	1,503	935	568	6,629	5,961	668	613	273	340	10	105,117
E07000108	Dover	113,446	1,158	1,252	-94	4,893	3,917	976	443	226	217	27	114,572
E07000109	Gravesham	105,715	1,380	850	530	4,501	5,036	-535	808	320	488	17	106,215
E07000110	Maidstone	164,019	1,974	1,430	544	8,195	7,903	292	1,566	689	877	-13	165,719
E07000111	Sevenoaks	118,165	1,243	1,007	236	6,753	6,491	262	557	229	328	20	119,011
E07000112	Shepway	109,838	1,106	1,283	-177	5,458	4,340	1,118	395	195	200	45	111,024
E07000113	Swale	142,465	1,798	1,271	527	6,470	5,176	1,294	840	246	594	37	144,917
E07000114	Thanet	139,822	1,628	1,696	-68	5,702	5,057	645	744	298	446	-17	140,828
E07000115	Tonbridge and Malling	125,779	1,373	1,020	353	7,750	6,834	916	486	241	245	12	127,305
E07000116	Tunbridge Wells	116,610	1,196	1,046	150	6,758	6,546	212	753	382	371	14	117,357
E10000025	Oxfordshire	673,590	7,819	5,312	2,507	31,068	33,086	-2,018	9,372	5,297	4,075	330	678,484
E07000177	Cherwell	145,554	1,871	1,181	690	7,068	7,360	-292	1,256	693	563	120	146,635
E07000178	Oxford	154,716	1,870	899	971	14,236	17,001	-2,765	5,822	3,458	2,364	6	155,292
E07000179	South Oxfordshire	138,177	1,556	1,187	369	8,062	7,892	170	783	446	337	103	139,156
E07000180	Vale of White Horse	126,534	1,410	1,004	406	8,258	7,071	1,187	927	419	508	18	128,653
E07000181	West Oxfordshire	108,609	1,112	1,041	71	4,739	5,057	-318	584	281	303	83	108,748
E10000030	Surrey	1,172,382	13,588	10,046	3,542	54,718	55,422	-704	10,902	5,476	5,426	310	1,180,956
E07000207	Elmbridge	135,398	1,694	1,025	669	7,660	8,195	-535	1,080	552	528	25	136,085
E07000208	Epsom and Ewell	78,459	919	620	299	5,096	5,094	2	539	319	220	19	78,999
E07000209	Guildford	145,056	1,551	1,080	471	10,228	10,801	-573	3,210	1,401	1,809	82	146,845
E07000210	Mole Valley	86,978	800	852	-52	4,860	4,704	156	451	272	179	-3	87,258
E07000211	Reigate and Banstead	143,794	1,790	1,349	441	8,165	7,742	423	844	434	410	216	145,284
E07000212	Runnymede	84,992	962	710	252	6,591	6,340	251	1,537	666	871	4	86,370

MYE3: Components of population change for local authorities in the UK, mid-2016

Code	Name	Estimated Population mid 2015	Births	Deaths	Births minus Deaths	Internal Migration Inflow	Internal Migration Outflow	Internal Migration Net	International Migration Inflow	International Migration Outflow	International Migration Net	Other	Estimated Population mid 2016
E07000213	Spelthorne	98,419	1,337	880	457	5,165	5,427	-262	669	353	316	-61	98,869
E07000214	Surrey Heath	88,385	947	750	197	5,222	5,249	-27	484	314	170	-20	88,705
E07000215	Tandridge	85,914	959	806	153	5,540	5,242	298	327	180	147	15	86,527
E07000216	Waverley	124,011	1,309	1,202	107	7,908	7,862	46	808	413	395	34	124,593
E07000217	Woking	100,976	1,320	772	548	5,426	5,909	-483	953	572	381	-1	101,421
E10000032	West Sussex	838,525	8,953	8,915	38	32,033	27,065	4,968	5,690	2,434	3,256	101	846,888
E07000223	Adur	63,526	684	715	-31	3,337	3,324	13	226	115	111	2	63,621
E07000224	Arun	155,798	1,573	2,197	-624	7,528	6,023	1,505	1,017	404	613	-5	157,287
E07000225	Chichester	117,784	998	1,402	-404	7,903	6,658	1,245	849	406	443	57	119,125
E07000226	Crawley	110,887	1,612	731	881	4,041	5,287	-1,246	1,581	565	1,016	8	111,546
E07000227	Horsham	136,258	1,322	1,256	66	7,925	6,145	1,780	655	259	396	23	138,523
E07000228	Mid Sussex	145,969	1,620	1,299	321	7,565	6,755	810	814	379	435	5	147,540
E07000229	Worthing	108,303	1,144	1,315	-171	5,691	4,830	861	548	306	242	11	109,246
E12000009	**SOUTH WEST**	5,471,610	58,441	56,035	2,406	146,834	116,686	30,148	38,541	27,427	11,114	1,695	5,516,973
E06000022	Bath and North East Somerset	184,287	1,874	1,700	174	13,907	12,540	1,367	2,867	1,767	1,100	18	186,946
E06000028	Bournemouth	191,673	2,234	1,996	238	15,108	14,562	546	3,808	2,650	1,158	38	193,653
E06000023	Bristol, City of	450,640	6,388	3,315	3,073	29,474	28,380	1,094	7,240	6,153	1,087	72	455,966
E06000052	Cornwall	550,283	5,377	6,094	-717	21,364	16,478	4,886	2,179	1,721	458	147	555,057
E06000053	Isles of Scilly	2,335	13	17	-4	178	185	-7	26	19	7	0	2,331
E06000024	North Somerset	209,941	2,248	2,369	-121	9,275	7,575	1,700	844	621	223	4	211,747
E06000026	Plymouth	261,386	3,106	2,438	668	13,031	13,421	-390	1,953	1,317	636	55	262,355
E06000029	Poole	150,005	1,612	1,659	-47	8,975	8,464	511	868	670	198	44	150,711
E06000025	South Gloucestershire	273,952	3,150	2,202	948	14,552	13,373	1,179	1,906	1,406	500	98	276,677
E06000030	Swindon	217,584	2,869	1,770	1,099	7,115	8,079	-964	1,972	1,104	868	-7	218,580
E06000027	Torbay	133,791	1,409	1,817	-408	6,358	5,509	849	485	293	192	-18	134,406
E06000054	Wiltshire	488,487	5,172	4,542	630	21,157	18,864	2,293	2,342	1,811	531	299	492,240
E10000008	Devon	772,406	7,135	8,852	-1,717	33,399	26,958	6,441	4,474	2,901	1,573	128	778,831
E07000040	East Devon	138,380	1,223	1,907	-684	8,316	5,848	2,468	428	294	134	-27	140,271
E07000041	Exeter	125,679	1,339	1,078	261	10,943	10,320	623	2,507	1,625	882	77	127,522
E07000042	Mid Devon	79,582	761	800	-39	4,280	4,061	219	275	183	92	26	79,880
E07000043	North Devon	94,162	909	1,087	-178	4,673	4,130	543	273	183	90	26	94,643
E07000044	South Hams	84,886	636	955	-319	4,904	4,759	145	291	187	104	18	84,834
E07000045	Teignbridge	128,903	1,169	1,549	-380	6,954	5,643	1,311	333	224	109	-26	129,917
E07000046	Torridge	66,312	635	816	-181	4,038	3,241	797	165	92	73	21	67,022
E07000047	West Devon	54,502	463	660	-197	3,308	2,973	335	202	113	89	13	54,742
E10000009	Dorset	420,847	3,490	5,166	-1,676	20,386	17,514	2,872	1,381	840	541	349	422,933
E07000048	Christchurch	49,211	381	689	-308	3,286	2,605	681	146	102	44	17	49,645
E07000049	East Dorset	88,711	656	1,145	-489	5,366	4,595	771	204	146	58	29	89,080
E07000050	North Dorset	70,607	621	695	-74	4,248	4,249	-1	302	157	145	238	70,915
E07000051	Purbeck	46,228	386	501	-115	2,565	2,493	72	144	79	65	91	46,341
E07000052	West Dorset	100,873	771	1,367	-596	6,375	5,260	1,115	380	252	128	-15	101,505
E07000053	Weymouth and Portland	65,217	675	769	-94	3,128	2,894	234	205	104	101	-11	65,447
E10000013	Gloucestershire	617,527	6,794	6,104	690	23,765	19,890	3,875	3,433	2,578	855	147	623,094
E07000078	Cheltenham	116,592	1,287	1,156	131	7,727	7,308	419	1,028	975	53	22	117,217
E07000079	Cotswold	85,548	747	879	-132	5,803	5,206	597	489	408	81	27	86,121
E07000080	Forest of Dean	84,576	813	903	-90	4,588	3,753	835	221	123	98	-8	85,411
E07000081	Gloucester	127,169	1,828	1,140	688	6,291	6,219	72	987	587	400	26	128,355

MYE3: Components of population change for local authorities in the UK, mid-2016

Code	Name	Estimated Population mid-2015	Births	Deaths	Births minus Deaths	Internal Migration Inflow	Internal Migration Outflow	Internal Migration Net	International Migration Inflow	International Migration Outflow	International Migration Net	Other	Estimated Population mid-2016
E07000082	Stroud	116,774	1,117	1,207	-90	5,781	5,059	722	307	256	51	15	117,472
E07000083	Tewkesbury	86,868	1,002	819	183	5,801	4,571	1,230	401	229	172	65	88,518
E10000027	Somerset	546,466	5,570	5,994	-424	21,808	17,912	3,896	2,763	1,576	1,187	321	551,446
E07000187	Mendip	112,056	1,109	1,159	-50	6,409	5,528	881	552	316	236	8	113,131
E07000188	Sedgemoor	120,141	1,319	1,194	125	5,737	4,942	795	545	289	256	28	121,345
E07000189	South Somerset	165,510	1,645	1,800	-155	7,537	6,913	624	808	484	324	223	166,526
E07000190	Taunton Deane	114,241	1,236	1,317	-81	6,357	4,932	1,425	707	387	320	64	115,969
E07000191	West Somerset	34,518	261	524	-263	2,010	1,839	171	151	100	51	-2	34,475
W92000004	**WALES**	3,099,086	33,285	32,523	762	58,654	55,275	3,379	16,826	7,150	9,676	247	3,113,150
W06000001	Isle of Anglesey	69,936	720	819	-99	2,197	2,391	-194	111	44	67	-45	69,665
W06000002	Gwynedd	122,635	1,222	1,362	-140	5,654	5,569	85	1,171	415	756	-13	123,323
W06000003	Conwy	116,450	1,083	1,480	-397	4,793	4,167	626	270	138	132	9	116,820
W06000004	Denbighshire	94,836	1,019	1,179	-160	4,394	4,201	193	217	105	112	3	94,984
W06000005	Flintshire	154,085	1,588	1,473	115	4,876	4,850	26	651	277	374	26	154,626
W06000006	Wrexham	135,418	1,487	1,321	166	3,864	4,236	-372	624	442	182	14	135,408
W06000023	Powys	132,730	1,089	1,541	-452	5,119	5,230	-111	333	183	150	20	132,337
W06000008	Ceredigion	74,211	593	763	-170	4,969	5,641	-672	553	261	292	4	73,665
W06000009	Pembrokeshire	123,671	1,136	1,438	-302	4,410	3,680	730	297	122	175	-37	124,237
W06000010	Carmarthenshire	185,247	1,884	2,253	-369	6,702	6,080	622	487	231	256	-2	185,754
W06000011	Swansea	242,316	2,528	2,610	-82	9,792	9,442	350	2,756	896	1,860	18	244,462
W06000012	Neath Port Talbot	140,946	1,505	1,590	-85	4,490	3,988	502	392	92	300	15	141,678
W06000013	Bridgend	142,259	1,537	1,510	27	4,656	3,803	853	427	156	271	-2	143,408
W06000014	Vale of Glamorgan	127,980	1,307	1,293	14	5,139	4,468	671	310	150	160	66	128,891
W06000015	Cardiff	357,496	4,556	2,760	1,796	20,099	21,019	-920	5,343	2,591	2,752	44	361,168
W06000016	Rhondda Cynon Taf	237,378	2,760	2,563	197	6,953	6,848	105	790	280	510	-11	238,179
W06000024	Merthyr Tydfil	59,247	735	619	116	1,594	1,436	158	243	69	174	19	59,714
W06000018	Caerphilly	180,168	2,091	1,758	333	4,636	4,782	-146	179	93	86	12	180,453
W06000019	Blaenau Gwent	69,547	727	784	-57	1,923	1,857	66	119	49	70	4	69,630
W06000020	Torfaen	91,767	1,028	959	69	2,532	2,449	83	117	51	66	9	91,994
W06000021	Monmouthshire	92,805	752	943	-191	4,549	4,096	453	263	103	160	49	93,276
W06000022	Newport	147,958	1,938	1,505	433	5,692	5,421	271	1,173	402	771	45	149,478
S92000003	**SCOTLAND**	5,373,000	55,256	56,077	-821	46,305	37,512	8,793	40,400	17,500	22,900	828	5,404,700
S12000033	Aberdeen City	230,350	2,556	2,116	440	8,148	11,591	-3,443	4,157	1,683	2,474	19	229,840
S12000034	Aberdeenshire	261,960	2,910	2,399	511	7,179	7,849	-670	978	662	316	73	262,190
S12000041	Angus	116,900	1,039	1,379	-340	3,565	3,570	-5	346	273	73	-108	116,520
S12000035	Argyll and Bute	86,890	702	1,093	-391	3,759	3,563	196	351	313	38	397	87,130
S12000036	City of Edinburgh	498,810	5,286	4,318	968	21,920	21,052	868	10,467	3,676	6,791	-267	507,170
S12000005	Clackmannanshire	51,360	535	551	-16	1,600	1,651	-51	157	94	63	-6	51,350
S12000006	Dumfries and Galloway	149,670	1,292	1,833	-541	3,544	3,162	382	340	328	12	-3	149,520
S12000042	Dundee City	148,210	1,541	1,696	-155	5,433	6,058	-625	1,439	637	802	38	148,270
S12000008	East Ayrshire	122,060	1,313	1,329	-16	3,272	3,083	189	152	114	-38	5	122,200
S12000045	East Dunbartonshire	106,960	968	1,097	-129	4,010	3,354	656	186	136	50	3	107,540
S12000010	East Lothian	103,050	1,090	1,027	63	3,550	2,879	671	455	166	289	17	104,090
S12000011	East Renfrewshire	92,940	891	848	43	3,897	3,129	768	179	128	51	8	93,810

MYE3: Components of population change for local authorities in the UK, mid-2016

Code	Name	Estimated Population mid-2015	Births	Deaths	Births minus Deaths	Internal Migration Inflow	Internal Migration Outflow	Internal Migration Net	International Migration Inflow	International Migration Outflow	International Migration Net	Other	Estimated Population mid-2016
S12000014	Falkirk	158,460	1,595	1,642	-47	4,166	3,381	785	383	228	155	27	159,380
S12000015	Fife	368,080	3,733	3,970	-237	9,353	8,787	566	2,051	1,009	1,042	879	370,330
S12000046	Glasgow City	606,340	7,041	6,262	779	23,504	23,476	28	11,462	3,527	7,935	-12	615,070
S12000017	Highland	234,110	2,242	2,472	-230	6,717	5,870	847	920	571	349	-306	234,770
S12000018	Inverclyde	79,500	688	985	-297	1,399	1,494	-95	131	92	39	13	79,160
S12000019	Midlothian	87,390	1,084	835	249	3,424	2,501	923	207	122	85	-37	88,610
S12000020	Moray	95,510	966	1,014	-48	3,242	2,769	473	321	241	80	55	96,070
S12000013	Na h-Eileanan Siar	27,070	229	336	-107	765	851	-86	72	53	19	4	26,900
S12000021	North Ayrshire	136,130	1,298	1,613	-315	3,558	3,453	105	184	224	-40	10	135,890
S12000044	North Lanarkshire	338,260	3,701	3,551	150	7,326	6,610	716	735	469	266	-2	339,390
S12000023	Orkney Islands	21,670	166	218	-52	806	586	220	52	49	3	9	21,850
S12000024	Perth and Kinross	149,930	1,338	1,621	-283	5,391	4,749	642	938	518	420	-29	150,680
S12000038	Renfrewshire	174,560	1,756	2,000	-244	5,358	4,256	1,102	804	292	512	0	175,930
S12000026	Scottish Borders	114,030	1,060	1,259	-199	4,079	3,392	687	315	312	3	9	114,530
S12000027	Shetland Islands	23,200	255	251	4	585	639	-54	91	52	39	11	23,200
S12000028	South Ayrshire	112,400	1,012	1,474	-462	3,530	3,022	508	256	218	38	-14	112,470
S12000029	South Lanarkshire	316,230	3,208	3,465	-257	8,525	7,561	964	640	507	133	30	317,100
S12000030	Stirling	92,830	830	915	-85	4,727	4,156	571	818	377	441	-7	93,750
S12000039	West Dunbartonshire	89,590	969	1,005	-36	2,362	2,160	202	194	108	86	18	89,860
S12000040	West Lothian	178,550	1,962	1,503	459	5,005	4,252	753	657	283	374	-6	180,130
N92000002	NORTHERN IRELAND	1,851,621	24,379	15,341	9,038	10,806	10,806	0	12,998	11,540	1,458	20	1,862,137
N09000001	Antrim and Newtownabbey	140,467	1,802	1,213	589	4,653	4,615	38	652	726	-74	12	141,032
N09000011	Ards and North Down	158,797	1,754	1,540	214	4,277	3,647	630	501	455	46	-94	159,593
N09000002	Armagh City, Banbridge & Craigavon	207,797	3,005	1,533	1,472	4,908	4,697	211	1,856	907	949	-169	210,260
N09000003	Belfast	338,907	4,563	3,086	1,477	15,519	16,502	-983	4,253	4,833	-580	758	339,579
N09000004	Causeway Coast and Glens	143,148	1,672	1,143	529	4,661	4,679	-18	650	907	-257	123	143,525
N09000005	Derry City and Strabane	149,473	2,071	1,137	934	3,338	3,842	-504	618	693	-75	314	150,142
N09000006	Fermanagh and Omagh	115,311	1,518	957	561	2,758	2,801	-43	688	564	124	-154	115,799
N09000007	Lisburn and Castlereagh	140,205	1,719	1,116	603	5,913	5,172	741	454	687	-233	-135	141,181
N09000008	Mid and East Antrim	137,145	1,538	1,280	258	3,559	3,515	44	948	396	552	-178	137,821
N09000009	Mid Ulster	144,002	2,172	1,001	1,171	3,411	3,485	-74	1,200	592	608	-318	145,389
N09000010	Newry, Mourne and Down	176,369	2,565	1,335	1,230	4,305	4,347	-42	1,178	780	398	-139	177,816

MYE4: Population estimates: Summary for the UK, mid-1971 to mid-2016

Thousands

Country Code/Year	K02000001 UNITED KINGDOM	K03000001 GREAT BRITAIN	K04000001 ENGLAND AND WALES	E92000001 ENGLAND	W92000004 WALES	S92000003 SCOTLAND	N92000002 NORTHERN IRELAND
Mid-2016	65,648.1	63,785.9	58,381.2	55,268.1	3,113.2	5,404.7	1,862.1
Mid 2015	65,110.0	63,258.4	57,885.4	54,786.3	3,099.1	5,373.0	1,851.6
Mid 2014	64,596.8	62,756.3	57,408.7	54,316.6	3,092.0	5,347.6	1,840.5
Mid 2013	64,105.7	62,275.9	56,948.2	53,865.8	3,082.4	5,327.7	1,829.7
Mid 2012	63,705.0	61,881.4	56,567.8	53,493.7	3,074.1	5,313.6	1,823.6
Mid 2011	63,285.1	61,470.8	56,170.9	53,107.2	3,063.8	5,299.9	1,814.3
Mid 2010	62,759.5	60,954.6	55,692.4	52,642.5	3,050.0	5,262.2	1,804.8
Mid 2009	62,260.5	60,467.2	55,235.3	52,196.4	3,038.9	5,231.9	1,793.3
Mid 2008	61,823.8	60,044.6	54,841.7	51,815.9	3,025.9	5,202.9	1,779.2
Mid 2007	61,319.1	59,557.4	54,387.4	51,381.1	3,006.3	5,170.0	1,761.7
Mid 2006	60,827.1	59,084.0	53,950.9	50,965.2	2,985.7	5,133.1	1,743.1
Mid 2005	60,413.3	58,685.5	53,575.3	50,606.0	2,969.3	5,110.2	1,727.7
Mid 2004	59,950.4	58,236.3	53,152.0	50,194.6	2,957.4	5,084.3	1,714.0
Mid 2003	59,636.7	57,931.7	52,863.2	49,925.5	2,937.7	5,068.5	1,704.9
Mid 2002	59,365.7	57,668.1	52,602.1	49,679.3	2,922.9	5,066.0	1,697.5
Mid 2001	59,113.0	57,424.2	52,360.0	49,449.7	2,910.2	5,064.2	1,688.8
Mid 2000	58,886.1	57,203.1	52,140.2	49,233.3	2,906.9	5,062.9	1,682.9
Mid 1999	58,684.4	57,005.4	51,933.5	49,032.9	2,900.6	5,072.0	1,679.0
Mid 1998	58,474.9	56,797.2	51,720.1	48,820.6	2,899.5	5,077.1	1,677.8
Mid 1997	58,314.2	56,643.0	51,559.6	48,664.8	2,894.9	5,083.3	1,671.3
Mid 1996	58,164.4	56,502.6	51,410.4	48,519.1	2,891.3	5,092.2	1,661.8
Mid 1995	58,024.8	56,375.7	51,272.0	48,383.5	2,888.5	5,103.7	1,649.1
Mid 1994	57,862.1	56,218.4	51,116.2	48,228.8	2,887.4	5,102.2	1,643.7
Mid 1993	57,713.9	56,078.3	50,985.9	48,102.3	2,883.6	5,092.5	1,635.6
Mid 1992	57,584.5	55,961.3	50,875.6	47,998.0	2,877.7	5,085.6	1,623.3
Mid 1991	57,438.7	55,831.4	50,748.0	47,875.0	2,873.0	5,083.3	1,607.3
Mid 1990	57,237.5	55,641.9	50,560.6	47,699.1	2,861.5	5,081.3	1,595.6
Mid 1989	57,076.5	55,486.0	50,407.8	47,552.7	2,855.2	5,078.2	1,590.4
Mid 1988	56,916.4	55,331.0	50,253.6	47,412.3	2,841.2	5,077.4	1,585.4
Mid 1987	56,804.0	55,222.0	50,123.0	47,300.4	2,822.6	5,099.0	1,582.0
Mid 1986	56,683.8	55,110.3	49,998.6	47,187.6	2,810.9	5,111.8	1,573.5
Mid 1985	56,554.0	54,988.6	49,860.7	47,057.4	2,803.4	5,127.9	1,565.4
Mid 1984	56,409.3	54,852.0	49,713.1	46,912.4	2,800.7	5,138.9	1,557.3
Mid 1983	56,315.7	54,765.1	49,617.0	46,813.7	2,803.3	5,148.1	1,550.6
Mid 1982	56,290.7	54,746.2	49,581.6	46,777.3	2,804.3	5,164.5	1,544.5
Mid 1981	56,357.5	54,814.5	49,634.3	46,820.8	2,813.5	5,180.2	1,543.0
Mid 1980	56,329.7	54,796.9	49,603.0	46,787.2	2,815.8	5,193.9	1,532.8
Mid 1979	56,240.1	54,711.8	49,508.2	46,698.1	2,810.1	5,203.6	1,528.3
Mid 1978	56,178.0	54,654.8	49,442.5	46,638.2	2,804.3	5,212.3	1,523.2
Mid 1977	56,189.9	54,666.6	49,440.4	46,639.8	2,800.6	5,226.2	1,523.3
Mid 1976	56,216.1	54,692.6	49,459.2	46,659.9	2,799.3	5,233.4	1,523.5
Mid 1975	56,225.7	54,702.2	49,469.8	46,674.4	2,795.4	5,232.4	1,523.5
Mid 1974	56,235.6	54,708.7	49,467.9	46,682.7	2,785.2	5,240.8	1,526.9
Mid 1973	56,222.9	54,692.9	49,459.0	46,686.2	2,772.8	5,233.9	1,530.0
Mid 1972	56,096.7	54,557.7	49,327.1	46,571.9	2,755.2	5,230.6	1,539.0
Mid 1971	55,928.0	54,387.6	49,152.0	46,411.7	2,740.3	5,235.6	1,540.4

Figures may not add exactly due to rounding.

Section 2 Population Density and Median Age

MYE5: Population estimates: Population density for the local authorities in the UK, mid-2001 to mid-2016

MYE6: Median age of population for local authorities in the UK, mid-2001 to mid-2016

MYE5: Population estimates: Population density for the local authorities in the UK, mid-2001 to mid-2016

Abbreviation: Est. Pop. (Estimated Population)

Thousands

Code	Name	Area (sq km)	2009 Est Pop: mid-2009	2009 people /km²	2010 Est Pop: mid-2010	2010 people /km²	2011 Est Pop: mid-2011	2011 people /km²	2012 Est Pop: mid-2012	2012 people /km²	2013 Est Pop: mid-2013	2013 people /km²	2014 Est Pop: mid-2014	2014 people /km²	2015 Est Pop: mid-2015	2015 people /km²	2016 Est Pop: mid-2016	2016 people /km²
K02000001	UNITED KINGDOM	242,545	62,260.5	256	62,759.5	258	63,285.1	260	63,705.0	263	64,105.7	264	64,596.8	266	65,110.0	268	65,648.1	271
K03000001	GREAT BRITAIN	228,957	60,467.2	264	60,954.6	266	61,470.8	268	61,881.4	270	62,275.9	272	62,756.3	274	63,258.4	276	63,785.9	279
K04000001	ENGLAND AND WALES	151,046	55,235.3	366	55,692.4	369	56,170.9	372	56,567.8	375	56,948.2	377	57,408.7	380	57,885.4	383	58,381.2	387
E92000001	ENGLAND	130,310	52,196.4	401	52,642.5	404	53,107.2	408	53,493.7	411	53,865.8	413	54,316.6	417	54,786.3	420	55,268.1	424
E12000001	NORTH EAST	8,574	2,575.4	300	2,586.9	302	2,596.4	303	2,602.4	304	2,610.6	304	2,618.7	305	2,624.6	306	2,636.6	307
E06000047	County Durham	2,226	507.3	228	510.6	229	513.0	230	514.3	231	515.9	232	517.6	233	519.3	233	521.8	234
E06000005	Darlington	197	104.4	530	105.0	533	105.6	536	105.5	534	105.7	535	105.9	536	106.0	537	106.3	538
E06000001	Hartlepool	94	91.5	974	91.8	976	92.1	980	92.3	986	92.7	990	92.6	990	92.5	989	92.8	992
E06000002	Middlesbrough	54	137.3	2,542	137.7	2,549	138.4	2,562	138.7	2,574	138.9	2,578	139.0	2,579	139.3	2,585	140.3	2,604
E06000057	Northumberland	5,014	314.5	63	315.5	63	316.3	63	316.5	63	316.4	63	316.8	63	316.5	63	317.4	63
E06000003	Redcar and Cleveland	245	135.9	555	135.4	553	135.2	552	135.0	551	135.0	551	135.1	552	135.3	553	135.5	553
E06000004	Stockton-on-Tees	205	190.0	927	190.9	931	191.8	936	192.5	939	193.4	944	194.4	949	195.1	952	196.0	956
E11000007	Tyne and Wear (Met County)	540	1,094.6	2,027	1,100.0	2,037	1,104.1	2,045	1,107.7	2,051	1,112.6	2,060	1,117.3	2,069	1,120.5	2,075	1,126.4	2,086
E08000037	Gateshead	142	197.5	1,391	198.7	1,400	200.3	1,411	200.3	1,407	200.1	1,406	200.8	1,410	201.7	1,417	202.6	1,423
E08000021	Newcastle upon Tyne	113	273.4	2,420	276.7	2,449	279.1	2,470	281.9	2,485	285.8	2,519	288.3	2,541	290.8	2,563	293.7	2,589
E08000022	North Tyneside	82	199.0	2,427	200.2	2,441	201.2	2,454	201.4	2,447	202.2	2,456	202.9	2,464	202.7	2,463	203.6	2,473
E08000023	South Tyneside	64	148.5	2,320	148.5	2,320	148.2	2,315	148.3	2,303	148.4	2,304	148.6	2,307	148.5	2,306	149.2	2,317
E08000024	Sunderland	137	276.2	2,016	276.0	2,014	275.3	2,010	275.8	2,006	276.1	2,009	276.8	2,014	276.8	2,014	277.3	2,018
E12000002	NORTH WEST	14,107	6,986.2	495	7,019.9	498	7,056.0	500	7,084.5	502	7,103.5	504	7,133.0	506	7,175.2	509	7,224.0	512
E06000008	Blackburn with Darwen	137	146.2	1,067	147.0	1,073	147.7	1,078	147.9	1,079	147.8	1,078	147.4	1,076	147.9	1,079	148.5	1,083
E06000009	Blackpool	35	142.6	4,074	142.8	4,079	142.1	4,059	142.0	4,075	141.6	4,063	140.9	4,043	140.2	4,022	140.0	4,017
E06000049	Cheshire East	1,166	368.0	316	369.1	317	370.7	318	372.4	319	373.0	320	374.6	321	375.7	322	377.3	323
E06000050	Cheshire West and Chester	917	329.1	359	329.6	359	329.5	359	330.2	360	331.1	361	332.3	362	333.9	364	335.7	366
E06000006	Halton	79	123.6	1,565	124.8	1,580	125.7	1,591	125.8	1,590	126.1	1,594	126.5	1,600	126.7	1,602	127.3	1,610
E06000007	Warrington	181	200.1	1,105	201.3	1,112	202.7	1,120	203.8	1,128	205.2	1,136	206.7	1,144	207.8	1,150	209.0	1,157
E10000006	Cumbria	6,767	500.8	74	500.2	74	499.8	74	499.2	74	498.5	74	498.4	74	498.6	74	498.8	74
E07000026	Allerdale	1,242	96.4	78	96.3	78	96.4	78	96.3	78	96.3	78	96.5	78	96.8	78	97.1	78
E07000027	Barrow-in-Furness	78	69.8	895	69.4	890	69.1	885	68.5	878	67.9	871	67.8	869	67.7	868	67.5	866
E07000028	Carlisle	1,039	107.0	103	107.0	103	107.5	103	107.9	104	108.0	104	108.1	104	108.1	104	108.4	104
E07000029	Copeland	732	70.7	97	70.6	96	70.6	96	70.3	96	70.1	96	69.9	95	69.7	95	69.3	95
E07000030	Eden	2,142	52.6	25	52.7	25	52.5	25	52.7	25	52.7	25	52.6	25	52.6	25	52.6	25
E07000031	South Lakeland	1,534	104.4	68	104.1	68	103.7	68	103.5	68	103.6	68	103.5	67	103.8	68	103.8	68
E11000001	Greater Manchester (Met County)	1,276	2,639.8	2,069	2,661.8	2,086	2,685.4	2,105	2,701.4	2,117	2,713.6	2,127	2,730.1	2,140	2,754.0	2,158	2,780.8	2,179
E08000001	Bolton	140	273.0	1,950	275.2	1,965	277.3	1,981	279.1	1,996	280.3	2,005	280.8	2,009	281.8	2,016	283.5	2,028
E08000002	Bury	99	183.9	1,857	184.8	1,866	185.4	1,873	186.2	1,872	186.5	1,875	187.3	1,883	187.8	1,888	188.5	1,895
E08000003	Manchester	116	483.8	4,171	492.6	4,247	502.9	4,335	510.5	4,414	513.7	4,442	518.8	4,486	529.8	4,581	541.3	4,681
E08000004	Oldham	142	222.8	1,569	223.8	1,576	225.2	1,586	225.7	1,586	227.0	1,594	228.2	1,603	230.2	1,617	232.3	1,632

MYE5: Population estimates: Population density for the local authorities in the UK, mid-2001 to mid-2016

Abbreviation: Est. Pop. (Estimated Population)

Thousands

Code	Name	Area (sq km)	Est Pop: mid-2009	people /km²	Est Pop: mid-2010	people /km²	Est Pop: mid-2011	people /km²	Est Pop: mid-2012	people /km²	Est Pop: mid-2013	people /km²	Est Pop: mid-2014	people /km²	Est Pop: mid-2015	people /km²	Est Pop: mid-2016	people /km²
E08000005	Rochdale	158	210.2	1,331	210.8	1,334	211.9	1,341	211.9	1,340	212.1	1,342	213.0	1,347	214.3	1,355	216.4	1,368
E08000006	Salford	97	228.9	2,360	231.8	2,390	234.5	2,417	236.9	2,438	238.7	2,456	241.5	2,485	245.2	2,523	248.1	2,553
E08000007	Stockport	126	282.3	2,240	282.6	2,243	283.3	2,248	283.8	2,251	284.9	2,260	286.4	2,272	288.2	2,286	289.8	2,299
E08000008	Tameside	103	217.4	2,111	218.8	2,124	219.7	2,133	220.2	2,135	220.5	2,138	220.7	2,139	221.5	2,147	223.1	2,163
E08000009	Trafford	106	223.1	2,104	225.2	2,125	227.1	2,142	228.3	2,153	230.1	2,170	232.3	2,191	233.0	2,197	234.2	2,209
E08000010	Wigan	188	314.4	1,672	316.3	1,682	318.1	1,692	318.7	1,694	319.8	1,700	321.1	1,706	322.2	1,713	323.5	1,719
E10000017	Lancashire	2,903	1,164.1	401	1,167.6	402	1,171.6	404	1,175.4	405	1,178.6	406	1,182.6	407	1,188.9	409	1,195.4	412
E07000117	Burnley	111	87.0	784	86.9	783	87.0	784	87.1	787	86.8	784	87.2	788	87.3	788	87.5	791
E07000118	Chorley	203	105.7	521	106.4	524	107.6	530	109.1	538	110.5	545	111.6	550	113.0	557	114.3	563
E07000119	Fylde	166	75.4	454	75.6	455	76.1	458	76.1	459	76.5	462	77.1	465	77.5	467	78.2	471
E07000120	Hyndburn	73	81.0	1,110	80.9	1,108	80.5	1,103	80.2	1,098	80.0	1,095	80.2	1,098	80.1	1,097	80.4	1,101
E07000121	Lancaster	576	136.0	236	137.1	238	137.8	239	139.3	242	139.8	243	140.2	243	140.8	244	141.7	246
E07000122	Pendle	169	89.3	528	89.2	528	89.6	530	89.5	529	90.0	531	89.7	529	89.9	531	90.5	534
E07000123	Preston	142	138.0	972	138.8	978	140.1	986	140.5	987	140.0	984	139.9	983	140.7	989	141.0	991
E07000124	Ribble Valley	583	57.0	98	57.2	98	57.3	98	57.6	99	57.9	99	58.1	100	58.5	100	58.9	101
E07000125	Rossendale	138	67.5	489	67.8	491	68.1	493	68.3	495	68.7	498	69.1	501	69.4	503	69.8	506
E07000126	South Ribble	113	108.6	961	108.8	963	109.2	966	109.0	965	109.0	965	109.1	966	109.7	971	110.1	975
E07000127	West Lancashire	347	110.6	319	110.8	319	110.6	319	110.9	320	111.2	321	111.8	323	112.5	324	113.1	326
E07000128	Wyre	282	108.1	382	107.9	381	107.7	381	107.8	382	108.2	383	108.6	385	109.5	388	110.0	390
E11000002	Merseyside (Met County)	647	1,371.8	2,127	1,375.9	2,133	1,380.8	2,141	1,386.4	2,144	1,388.1	2,146	1,393.5	2,155	1,401.5	2,167	1,411.2	2,182
E08000011	Knowsley	87	147.1	1,690	146.4	1,683	145.9	1,677	145.9	1,687	146.1	1,689	146.4	1,693	147.3	1,702	148.0	1,711
E08000012	Liverpool	112	457.5	4,085	461.4	4,120	465.7	4,158	470.2	4,204	471.8	4,219	474.6	4,243	480.9	4,300	487.6	4,360
E08000014	Sefton	155	274.2	1,792	273.8	1,790	274.0	1,791	273.8	1,767	273.4	1,764	273.9	1,767	274.1	1,768	274.9	1,773
E08000013	St. Helens	136	175.3	1,289	175.2	1,288	175.4	1,290	176.1	1,292	176.2	1,292	177.2	1,299	177.6	1,302	178.5	1,309
E08000015	Wirral	157	317.8	2,024	319.1	2,032	319.8	2,037	320.4	2,040	320.7	2,042	321.5	2,047	321.7	2,048	322.2	2,052
E12000003	**YORKSHIRE AND THE HUMBER**	15,405	5,223.3	339	5,254.8	341	5,288.2	343	5,316.9	345	5,337.9	346	5,360.1	348	5,390.2	350	5,425.4	352
E06000011	East Riding of Yorkshire	2,405	332.7	138	333.6	139	334.7	139	335.9	140	336.1	140	337.2	140	336.8	140	337.8	140
E06000010	Kingston upon Hull, City of	71	256.1	3,607	256.2	3,608	256.1	3,607	257.0	3,597	257.2	3,600	257.4	3,603	258.6	3,619	260.0	3,639
E06000012	North East Lincolnshire	192	158.7	827	159.0	828	159.7	832	159.8	833	160.0	834	160.0	834	160.0	834	159.8	833
E06000013	North Lincolnshire	846	165.6	196	166.5	197	167.5	198	168.4	199	168.7	199	169.2	200	169.8	201	170.8	202
E06000014	York	272	192.4	707	195.1	717	197.8	727	199.6	734	202.1	743	203.7	749	205.8	757	206.9	761
E10000023	North Yorkshire	8,038	596.4	74	599.0	75	601.2	75	603.5	75	604.7	75	604.7	75	606.0	75	609.5	76
E07000163	Craven	1,177	55.3	47	55.4	47	55.5	47	55.5	47	55.6	47	55.8	47	55.8	47	56.3	48
E07000164	Hambleton	1,311	88.6	68	89.1	68	89.6	68	89.8	68	90.0	69	89.9	69	90.1	69	90.6	69
E07000165	Harrogate	1,308	156.5	120	157.5	120	158.7	121	159.4	122	159.7	122	159.6	122	159.9	122	159.8	122
E07000166	Richmondshire	1,319	52.4	40	52.9	40	53.3	40	53.8	41	53.9	41	52.8	40	52.6	40	53.9	41
E07000167	Ryedale	1,507	52.2	35	51.9	34	51.9	34	52.2	35	52.3	35	52.8	35	53.3	35	53.9	36

MYE5: Population estimates: Population density for the local authorities in the UK, mid-2001 to mid-2016

Abbreviation: Est. Pop. (Estimated Population)

Thousands

Code	Name	Area (sq km)	Est Pop: mid-2016	people /km²	Est Pop: mid-2015	people /km²	Est Pop: mid-2014	people /km²	Est Pop: mid-2013	people /km²	Est Pop: mid-2012	people /km²	Est Pop: mid-2011	people /km²	Est Pop: mid-2010	people /km²	Est Pop: mid-2009	people /km²
E07000168	Scarborough	816	108.2	132	108.1	132	108.2	132	108.3	133	108.7	133	108.7	133	109.0	133	108.9	133
E07000169	Selby	599	86.9	145	86.2	144	85.6	143	84.9	142	84.2	140	83.5	139	83.2	139	82.4	138
E11000003	South Yorkshire (Met County)	1,552	1,385.4	893	1,375.5	886	1,366.1	880	1,358.5	876	1,352.4	872	1,343.8	866	1,332.9	859	1,323.9	853
E08000016	Barnsley	329	241.8	735	239.9	729	238.0	723	235.8	717	233.8	710	231.9	705	230.1	699	229.0	696
E08000017	Doncaster	568	307.4	541	305.5	538	304.4	536	303.7	535	302.9	533	302.5	533	301.3	530	300.2	528
E08000018	Rotherham	287	262.1	915	260.9	911	260.3	908	258.8	903	258.4	902	257.7	898	256.9	895	256.3	893
E08000019	Sheffield	368	574.1	1,560	569.2	1,547	563.5	1,531	560.2	1,523	557.3	1,515	551.8	1,499	544.6	1,480	538.4	1,463
E11000006	West Yorkshire (Met County)	2,029	2,295.0	1,131	2,277.8	1,122	2,261.8	1,115	2,250.6	1,109	2,240.4	1,104	2,227.4	1,098	2,212.6	1,090	2,197.6	1,083
E08000032	Bradford	366	532.5	1,453	529.9	1,446	527.6	1,440	525.9	1,435	524.4	1,431	523.1	1,429	518.0	1,415	512.4	1,400
E08000033	Calderdale	364	209.1	574	207.8	571	207.0	569	206.1	566	205.2	564	204.2	561	203.0	558	202.1	555
E08000034	Kirklees	409	435.2	1,065	432.9	1,059	430.0	1,052	427.8	1,047	425.3	1,041	423.0	1,034	418.3	1,023	414.8	1,014
E08000035	Leeds	552	781.1	1,416	773.2	1,401	765.4	1,387	760.9	1,379	757.6	1,373	750.7	1,360	747.6	1,354	743.9	1,348
E08000036	Wakefield	339	337.1	995	334.0	986	331.7	980	329.8	974	327.9	968	326.4	963	325.6	960	324.5	957
E12000004	EAST MIDLANDS	15,623	4,725.4	302	4,677.4	299	4,637.4	297	4,598.5	294	4,567.8	292	4,537.4	290	4,507.1	288	4,471.7	286
E06000015	Derby	78	256.2	3,283	253.9	3,254	252.3	3,233	251.3	3,221	250.6	3,211	248.9	3,192	247.0	3,167	244.0	3,128
E06000016	Leicester	73	349.5	4,766	344.0	4,691	338.5	4,615	334.6	4,563	332.1	4,528	329.6	4,515	324.9	4,451	319.7	4,380
E06000018	Nottingham	75	324.8	4,353	318.9	4,275	314.4	4,214	310.7	4,164	308.5	4,134	303.9	4,052	299.8	3,997	294.8	3,931
E06000017	Rutland	382	38.9	102	38.4	100	38.3	100	37.8	99	37.1	97	37.6	98	37.7	99	37.4	98
E10000007	Derbyshire	2,547	786.7	309	783.1	307	780.4	306	776.6	305	773.7	304	770.7	303	767.9	302	764.3	300
E07000032	Amber Valley	265	124.8	470	124.2	468	124.1	467	123.6	466	122.8	463	122.5	462	122.1	461	121.5	459
E07000033	Bolsover	160	78.2	488	77.9	486	77.2	482	76.8	479	76.5	477	76.0	475	75.7	473	75.2	470
E07000034	Chesterfield	66	104.5	1,583	104.5	1,582	104.3	1,580	104.1	1,576	103.8	1,572	103.8	1,573	103.4	1,567	103.0	1,561
E07000035	Derbyshire Dales	792	71.5	90	71.3	90	71.4	90	71.4	90	71.4	90	71.1	90	71.0	90	70.7	89
E07000036	Erewash	110	115.1	1,050	114.7	1,046	114.2	1,041	113.2	1,033	112.8	1,029	112.2	1,020	111.7	1,016	111.3	1,012
E07000037	High Peak	539	91.7	170	91.5	170	91.4	170	91.2	169	91.2	169	91.0	169	91.1	169	91.0	169
E07000038	North East Derbyshire	276	100.5	364	99.7	362	99.4	361	99.3	360	99.3	360	99.1	359	98.8	358	98.5	357
E07000039	South Derbyshire	338	100.4	297	99.3	294	98.4	291	97.1	287	95.9	284	94.9	281	94.1	278	93.0	275
E10000018	Leicestershire	2,083	680.5	327	673.4	323	666.7	320	660.9	317	656.2	315	651.2	313	646.3	310	642.3	308
E07000129	Blaby	130	97.6	748	96.5	739	95.8	735	95.1	729	94.6	725	94.1	724	93.9	723	93.5	719
E07000130	Charnwood	279	177.4	636	175.2	628	172.5	618	170.0	609	168.4	603	165.9	595	164.3	589	162.3	582
E07000131	Harborough	592	90.3	153	89.1	151	87.9	149	87.4	148	86.4	146	85.7	145	84.8	143	84.1	142
E07000132	Hinckley and Bosworth	297	109.9	370	108.6	365	107.6	362	106.5	358	106.0	356	105.3	355	104.7	353	104.5	352
E07000133	Melton	481	51.0	106	51.0	106	51.0	106	50.9	106	50.8	105	50.5	105	50.1	104	49.5	103
E07000134	North West Leicestershire	279	98.4	352	97.1	348	95.7	343	94.7	339	94.0	336	93.7	336	93.2	334	92.7	332
E07000135	Oadby and Wigston	24	56.0	2,380	56.0	2,380	56.1	2,383	56.3	2,392	56.1	2,385	56.0	2,332	55.2	2,299	55.6	2,317
E10000019	Lincolnshire	5,937	744.8	125	737.4	124	731.9	123	724.5	122	719.2	121	714.8	120	711.8	120	705.6	119
E07000136	Boston	365	67.7	186	66.9	183	66.5	182	65.8	180	64.9	178	64.6	177	64.5	177	63.4	174

MYE5: Population estimates: Population density for the local authorities in the UK, mid-2001 to mid-2016

Abbreviation: Est. Pop. (Estimated Population)

Code	Name	Area (sq km)	2016 Est Pop: mid-2016	2016 people /km²	2015 Est Pop: mid-2015	2015 people /km²	2014 Est Pop: mid-2014	2014 people /km²	2013 Est Pop: mid-2013	2013 people /km²	2012 Est Pop: mid-2012	2012 people /km²	2011 Est Pop: mid-2011	2011 people /km²	2010 Est Pop: mid-2010	2010 people /km²	2009 Est Pop: mid-2009	2009 people /km²
E07000137	East Lindsey	1,765	138.7	79	138.1	78	137.7	78	136.8	78	136.7	77	136.7	77	137.3	78	137.1	78
E07000138	Lincoln	36	97.4	2,729	96.6	2,708	95.9	2,687	95.4	2,672	94.5	2,649	93.1	2,586	92.2	2,561	90.8	2,523
E07000139	North Kesteven	922	113.6	123	112.2	122	111.2	121	109.9	119	109.3	118	108.5	118	107.5	117	106.5	115
E07000140	South Holland	751	92.5	123	91.2	122	90.4	120	89.2	119	88.5	118	88.4	118	87.9	117	87.0	116
E07000141	South Kesteven	943	140.9	149	139.4	148	138.3	147	136.6	145	135.2	143	134.1	142	133.1	141	132.2	140
E07000142	West Lindsey	1,156	93.9	81	93.0	80	91.9	80	90.8	79	90.1	78	89.4	77	89.4	77	88.6	77
E10000021	Northamptonshire	2,364	732.5	310	722.2	305	713.4	302	705.7	298	700.3	296	694.0	294	688.0	291	683.5	289
E07000150	Corby	80	68.3	851	66.9	833	65.5	815	64.2	800	63.1	786	61.6	770	60.1	752	59.0	738
E07000151	Daventry	663	81.1	122	79.8	120	78.9	119	78.5	118	78.2	118	78.1	118	77.7	117	77.7	117
E07000152	East Northamptonshire	510	91.4	179	90.1	177	89.0	175	88.1	173	87.4	171	86.9	170	86.3	169	85.9	168
E07000153	Kettering	233	98.9	424	97.6	418	96.9	415	95.8	410	94.9	406	93.8	403	92.9	399	92.1	395
E07000154	Northampton	81	224.5	2,779	221.5	2,742	218.4	2,704	215.9	2,673	214.3	2,653	212.5	2,623	210.1	2,594	207.9	2,566
E07000155	South Northamptonshire	634	89.9	142	89.1	141	88.2	139	87.3	138	86.3	136	85.4	135	85.6	135	85.7	135
E07000156	Wellingborough	163	78.4	481	77.2	473	76.4	469	75.9	466	76.1	467	75.6	464	75.2	461	75.1	461
E10000024	Nottinghamshire	2,085	811.5	389	806.2	387	801.6	385	796.4	382	790.2	379	786.8	377	783.6	376	780.1	374
E07000170	Ashfield	110	124.5	1,137	123.6	1,128	122.5	1,118	121.5	1,109	120.1	1,096	119.5	1,087	118.6	1,078	117.9	1,072
E07000171	Bassetlaw	638	115.2	181	114.7	180	114.3	179	113.7	178	113.2	178	113.0	177	112.9	177	112.6	176
E07000172	Broxtowe	80	112.1	1,400	111.8	1,396	111.5	1,392	111.1	1,387	110.6	1,380	109.7	1,372	109.3	1,366	109.2	1,365
E07000173	Gedling	120	116.7	973	116.1	968	115.8	965	115.0	958	114.1	951	113.7	948	113.1	942	112.7	939
E07000174	Mansfield	77	107.9	1,407	106.8	1,392	106.0	1,382	105.3	1,373	104.8	1,367	104.6	1,358	104.1	1,352	103.7	1,347
E07000175	Newark and Sherwood	651	119.8	184	118.7	182	117.9	181	116.9	179	115.9	178	115.0	177	114.6	176	113.9	175
E07000176	Rushcliffe	409	115.2	281	114.5	280	113.7	278	112.9	276	111.5	273	111.2	272	111.1	272	110.1	269
E12000005	**WEST MIDLANDS**	12,998	5,810.8	447	5,755.0	443	5,713.4	440	5,675.0	437	5,642.8	434	5,608.7	432	5,565.9	428	5,528.0	425
E06000019	Herefordshire, County of	2,180	189.5	87	188.5	86	187.7	86	186.4	86	185.2	85	183.6	84	182.9	84	182.4	84
E06000051	Shropshire	3,197	314.4	98	312.2	98	310.8	97	309.1	97	308.4	96	307.1	96	304.5	95	302.1	94
E06000021	Stoke-on-Trent	93	253.7	2,714	251.7	2,694	251.0	2,686	250.2	2,677	249.8	2,673	248.7	2,674	247.4	2,660	245.9	2,644
E06000020	Telford and Wrekin	290	173.7	598	171.7	591	169.8	585	168.6	581	167.8	578	166.8	575	165.6	571	164.9	569
E10000028	Staffordshire	2,620	866.4	331	862.2	329	859.9	328	856.8	327	852.0	325	849.5	324	845.3	323	841.3	321
E07000192	Cannock Chase	79	98.5	1,249	98.5	1,249	98.5	1,249	98.1	1,244	97.9	1,241	97.6	1,235	96.9	1,227	96.5	1,222
E07000193	East Staffordshire	387	116.9	302	116.2	300	115.7	299	114.9	297	114.5	296	113.9	294	113.0	292	112.0	289
E07000194	Lichfield	331	102.8	310	102.6	310	102.1	308	101.7	307	101.2	305	100.9	305	100.4	303	100.0	302
E07000195	Newcastle-under-Lyme	211	128.1	607	126.9	601	126.0	597	125.2	593	124.1	588	123.9	587	123.4	585	123.1	583
E07000196	South Staffordshire	407	111.2	273	110.7	272	110.7	272	110.3	271	108.4	266	108.3	266	108.1	265	107.6	264
E07000197	Stafford	598	133.7	223	132.2	221	132.0	221	132.0	221	131.6	220	130.9	219	130.0	217	129.0	216
E07000198	Staffordshire Moorlands	576	98.2	170	98.0	170	97.0	168	97.5	169	97.2	169	97.2	169	97.0	168	96.8	168
E07000199	Tamworth	31	77.0	2,496	77.1	2,499	77.0	2,497	77.1	2,499	77.1	2,499	76.9	2,480	76.6	2,470	76.3	2,400
E10000031	Warwickshire	1,975	559.0	283	555.2	281	552.5	280	549.5	278	548.3	278	546.6	277	544.2	276	542.1	274

MYE5: Population estimates: Population density for the local authorities in the UK, mid-2001 to mid-2016

Abbreviation: Est. Pop. (Estimated Population)

Thousands

Code	Name	Area (sq km)	2016		2015		2014		2013		2012		2011		2010		2009	
			Est Pop: mid-2016	people /km²	Est Pop: mid-2015	people /km²	Est Pop: mid-2014	people /km²	Est Pop: mid-2013	people /km²	Est Pop: mid-2012	people /km²	Est Pop: mid-2011	people /km²	Est Pop: mid-2010	people /km²	Est Pop: mid-2009	people /km²
E07000218	North Warwickshire	284	63.2	222	62.8	221	62.4	220	62.1	219	62.2	219	62.1	219	62.1	219	62.1	219
E07000219	Nuneaton and Bedworth	79	127.7	1,617	126.6	1,604	126.3	1,600	126.1	1,597	125.9	1,594	125.4	1,587	124.8	1,579	124.3	1,574
E07000220	Rugby	351	105.3	300	104.5	297	103.2	294	101.8	290	101.0	288	100.5	286	99.0	282	97.7	278
E07000221	Stratford-on-Avon	978	123.3	126	122.4	125	121.8	125	121.3	124	120.8	124	120.8	124	120.2	123	119.8	123
E07000222	Warwick	283	139.5	493	138.9	491	138.7	490	138.2	489	138.4	489	137.7	487	138.1	488	138.2	488
E11000005	West Midlands (Met County)	902	2,870.6	3,184	2,834.5	3,144	2,805.9	3,112	2,781.8	3,085	2,761.9	3,063	2,739.7	3,037	2,711.9	3,007	2,687.1	2,979
E08000025	Birmingham	268	1,128.1	4,213	1,113.0	4,156	1,101.5	4,113	1,092.2	4,079	1,085.2	4,052	1,074.3	4,009	1,061.1	3,959	1,050.1	3,918
E08000026	Coventry	99	353.2	3,581	344.3	3,490	335.0	3,396	328.4	3,330	322.5	3,270	316.9	3,201	311.7	3,148	307.4	3,105
E08000027	Dudley	98	317.6	3,242	316.3	3,229	315.7	3,222	314.4	3,209	313.6	3,201	313.3	3,197	312.2	3,186	311.1	3,174
E08000028	Sandwell	86	322.6	3,771	319.1	3,730	316.3	3,697	314.0	3,670	311.2	3,638	309.0	3,594	306.2	3,560	302.3	3,515
E08000029	Solihull	178	212.2	1,190	210.8	1,183	210.2	1,179	209.1	1,173	207.5	1,164	206.9	1,162	206.3	1,159	205.5	1,154
E08000030	Walsall	104	278.9	2,682	275.9	2,653	273.9	2,635	272.0	2,616	270.8	2,605	269.5	2,592	266.8	2,566	264.8	2,546
E08000031	Wolverhampton	69	258.0	3,716	255.1	3,674	253.3	3,647	251.7	3,625	251.1	3,616	249.9	3,589	247.6	3,589	246.0	3,565
E10000034	Worcestershire	1,741	583.5	335	579.1	333	576.0	331	572.6	329	569.3	327	566.6	325	564.1	324	562.3	323
E07000234	Bromsgrove	217	96.8	446	95.8	442	95.5	440	94.8	437	94.3	435	93.7	432	93.5	431	93.4	431
E07000235	Malvern Hills	577	76.6	133	76.1	132	76.2	132	75.6	131	75.1	130	74.7	129	74.5	129	74.1	128
E07000236	Redditch	54	85.1	1,568	84.8	1,563	84.5	1,558	84.5	1,558	84.4	1,557	84.3	1,561	83.6	1,548	83.1	1,539
E07000237	Worcester	33	101.9	3,063	101.0	3,035	100.7	3,027	100.4	3,016	99.6	2,994	98.7	2,990	97.7	2,959	97.1	2,943
E07000238	Wychavon	664	123.1	186	121.7	183	120.0	181	118.9	179	117.8	177	117.1	176	116.9	176	116.5	175
E07000239	Wyre Forest	195	100.0	512	99.6	510	99.0	507	98.5	504	98.1	502	98.0	503	97.9	502	98.0	503
E12000006	**EAST**	19,119	6,129.0	321	6,076.0	318	6,017.3	315	5,951.9	311	5,905.9	309	5,862.4	307	5,807.4	304	5,751.4	301
E06000055	Bedford	476	168.8	354	166.4	349	164.0	344	161.6	339	159.4	335	157.8	332	156.5	329	154.8	325
E06000056	Central Bedfordshire	716	276.7	387	272.4	381	267.8	374	263.8	369	259.6	363	255.6	357	252.5	353	250.3	350
E06000032	Luton	43	215.9	4,980	213.6	4,927	210.2	4,848	207.4	4,784	205.5	4,740	203.6	4,736	199.6	4,641	195.4	4,545
E06000031	Peterborough	343	196.7	573	193.7	564	190.5	555	188.4	549	186.6	543	184.5	538	181.8	530	179.0	522
E06000033	Southend-on-Sea	42	180.6	4,325	179.2	4,292	178.4	4,272	176.2	4,221	175.1	4,193	174.3	4,149	172.1	4,098	170.0	4,048
E06000034	Thurrock	163	168.4	1,030	166.0	1,016	163.8	1,002	161.3	987	159.8	978	158.3	971	156.6	961	155.0	951
E10000003	Cambridgeshire	3,046	644.6	212	641.5	211	635.2	209	628.9	206	625.9	205	622.3	204	614.9	202	606.2	199
E07000008	Cambridge	41	124.6	3,062	125.1	3,074	123.7	3,040	123.0	3,023	122.6	3,012	122.7	2,993	120.2	2,932	116.7	2,847
E07000009	East Cambridgeshire	651	88.2	135	87.8	135	87.0	134	85.9	132	85.2	131	84.2	129	83.3	128	82.4	127
E07000010	Fenland	546	99.6	182	98.8	181	97.6	179	96.6	177	96.0	176	95.5	175	95.1	174	94.4	173
E07000011	Huntingdonshire	906	176.1	194	175.3	193	173.9	192	172.1	190	171.2	189	170.0	188	168.4	186	167.1	184
E07000012	South Cambridgeshire	902	156.0	173	154.5	171	152.9	170	151.2	168	150.9	167	149.8	166	147.9	164	145.7	162
E10000012	Essex	3,464	1,457.9	421	1,445.3	417	1,433.3	414	1,417.6	409	1,407.1	406	1,396.6	403	1,388.9	401	1,379.5	398
E07000066	Basildon	110	183.8	1,670	182.0	1,654	180.7	1,642	178.5	1,622	176.5	1,605	175.0	1,591	173.8	1,580	173.1	1,573
E07000067	Braintree	612	151.2	247	150.5	246	150.1	245	149.2	244	148.4	243	147.5	241	146.0	239	144.6	236
E07000068	Brentwood	153	76.8	501	76.4	499	75.9	496	74.7	488	74.1	484	73.8	483	73.3	479	72.7	475

MYE5: Population estimates: Population density for the local authorities in the UK, mid-2001 to mid-2016

Abbreviation: Est. Pop. (Estimated Population)

Thousands

Code	Name	Area (sq km)	Est Pop: mid-2016	people /km²	Est Pop: mid-2015	people /km²	Est Pop: mid-2014	people /km²	Est Pop: mid-2013	people /km²	Est Pop: mid-2012	people /km²	Est Pop: mid-2011	people /km²	Est Pop: mid-2010	people /km²	Est Pop: mid-2009	people /km²
E07000069	Castle Point	45	89.8	1,991	89.2	1,979	88.9	1,973	88.6	1,966	88.2	1,957	88.0	1,955	88.1	1,958	88.1	1,958
E07000070	Chelmsford	339	174.2	514	172.7	510	171.6	506	170.3	503	169.4	500	168.5	497	167.4	494	166.2	490
E07000071	Colchester	329	187.6	570	184.9	562	181.0	550	178.0	541	176.2	535	173.6	528	171.7	522	169.0	514
E07000072	Epping Forest	339	129.9	383	129.3	381	128.5	379	127.0	375	126.0	372	124.9	368	124.2	366	123.8	365
E07000073	Harlow	31	85.9	2,812	85.3	2,794	84.6	2,771	83.4	2,732	82.8	2,712	82.2	2,651	81.5	2,629	80.7	2,604
E07000074	Maldon	359	63.4	177	62.8	175	62.8	175	62.2	173	61.9	173	61.7	172	61.8	172	61.8	172
E07000075	Rochford	169	85.7	506	85.2	503	84.8	500	84.0	495	83.9	495	83.3	493	83.4	494	83.1	492
E07000076	Tendring	338	143.4	424	141.8	420	140.4	416	139.0	412	138.4	410	138.1	408	139.1	411	139.6	413
E07000077	Uttlesford	641	86.3	135	85.2	133	84.1	131	82.7	129	81.2	127	80.0	125	78.6	123	76.8	120
E10000015	Hertfordshire	1,643	1,176.4	716	1,165.3	709	1,154.2	702	1,140.6	694	1,129.3	687	1,119.8	682	1,107.6	674	1,096.6	667
E07000095	Broxbourne	51	96.9	1,883	96.3	1,872	95.8	1,863	95.1	1,849	94.6	1,839	93.7	1,837	93.1	1,825	92.4	1,812
E07000096	Dacorum	212	152.4	717	151.1	711	149.5	704	148.1	697	146.7	691	145.3	685	143.7	678	142.2	671
E07000242	East Hertfordshire	476	146.1	307	144.5	304	142.8	300	140.9	296	139.4	293	138.2	290	136.9	288	136.0	286
E07000098	Hertsmere	101	103.7	1,025	103.2	1,020	102.5	1,014	101.4	1,003	100.9	998	100.4	994	99.4	984	98.6	977
E07000099	North Hertfordshire	375	132.7	353	131.6	351	130.9	349	129.2	344	128.3	342	127.5	340	126.3	337	125.3	334
E07000240	St Albans	161	147.0	912	146.2	907	145.2	901	143.5	890	142.1	882	141.2	877	139.5	867	137.9	856
E07000243	Stevenage	26	87.3	3,361	86.6	3,334	86.0	3,311	85.5	3,293	84.8	3,266	84.2	3,240	83.0	3,193	82.3	3,164
E07000102	Three Rivers	89	92.7	1,043	91.8	1,033	90.5	1,019	89.6	1,008	88.8	1,000	87.9	988	87.6	984	87.1	979
E07000103	Watford	21	96.6	4,507	96.3	4,496	95.6	4,459	93.9	4,382	91.9	4,290	90.7	4,317	88.6	4,218	86.5	4,118
E07000241	Welwyn Hatfield	130	121.0	934	117.8	909	115.3	890	113.4	875	111.7	862	110.7	852	109.6	843	108.4	834
E10000020	Norfolk	5,380	891.7	166	884.7	164	877.4	163	870.3	162	864.8	161	859.4	160	852.9	159	846.4	157
E07000143	Breckland	1,305	137.1	105	135.7	104	134.3	103	133.0	102	131.9	101	131.0	100	129.9	100	129.4	99
E07000144	Broadland	552	127.4	231	126.6	229	126.0	228	125.5	227	125.2	227	124.7	226	124.5	226	123.8	224
E07000145	Great Yarmouth	174	99.0	567	98.6	565	98.1	562	97.7	560	97.6	559	97.4	560	97.1	558	96.4	554
E07000146	King's Lynn and West Norfolk	1,439	151.8	105	151.3	105	150.2	104	149.2	104	148.6	103	147.9	103	147.1	102	146.4	102
E07000147	North Norfolk	962	103.6	108	103.3	107	102.9	107	102.1	106	101.8	106	101.7	106	100.8	105	100.6	104
E07000148	Norwich	39	139.9	3,584	138.1	3,539	136.6	3,500	135.1	3,462	133.9	3,430	132.2	3,389	130.9	3,357	129.2	3,313
E07000149	South Norfolk	908	133.0	146	131.2	145	129.3	142	127.7	141	126.0	139	124.5	137	122.6	135	120.5	133
E10000029	Suffolk	3,801	751.2	198	747.7	197	742.5	195	735.8	194	732.8	193	730.1	192	724.0	190	718.2	189
E07000200	Babergh	594	90.3	152	89.9	151	89.4	151	88.7	149	88.1	148	87.9	148	87.5	147	87.4	147
E07000201	Forest Heath	378	63.3	168	63.7	169	62.5	166	59.8	158	59.9	159	60.0	159	58.6	155	57.9	153
E07000202	Ipswich	40	138.5	3,505	137.7	3,484	136.4	3,452	135.6	3,431	135.1	3,417	133.7	3,429	131.7	3,378	129.3	3,316
E07000203	Mid Suffolk	871	100.7	116	100.3	115	99.6	114	98.4	113	97.8	112	97.1	111	96.2	110	95.3	109
E07000204	St Edmundsbury	657	113.4	173	112.9	172	112.4	171	111.9	170	111.6	170	111.4	170	110.0	167	108.4	165
E07000205	Suffolk Coastal	892	127.8	143	126.6	142	125.9	141	125.2	140	124.7	140	124.6	140	124.3	139	123.8	139
E07000206	Waveney	370	117.2	317	116.7	315	116.3	314	116.2	314	115.7	313	115.4	312	115.7	313	116.0	314

MYE5: Population estimates: Population density for the local authorities in the UK, mid-2001 to mid-2016

Abbreviation: Est. Pop. (Estimated Population)

Thousands

Code	Name	Area (sq km)	Est Pop: mid-2016	people /km²	Est Pop: mid-2015	people /km²	Est Pop: mid-2014	people /km²	Est Pop: mid-2013	people /km²	Est Pop: mid-2012	people /km²	Est Pop: mid-2011	people /km²	Est Pop: mid-2010	people /km²	Est Pop: mid-2009	people /km²
E12000007	**LONDON**	1,572	8,769.7	5,578	8,666.9	5,513	8,539.4	5,432	8,417.5	5,354	8,308.8	5,285	8,204.4	5,219	8,061.5	5,128	7,942.6	5,053
E09000007	Camden	22	249.2	11,435	243.8	11,191	236.0	10,832	230.5	10,578	224.8	10,317	220.1	10,004	214.7	9,760	212.9	9,678
E09000001	City of London	3	7.2	2,495	6.7	2,303	6.1	2,114	6.0	2,077	6.6	2,277	7.4	2,471	7.3	2,446	7.5	2,491
E09000012	Hackney	19	273.2	14,344	268.6	14,102	263.1	13,812	257.4	13,514	252.2	13,240	247.2	13,010	241.7	12,723	236.6	12,454
E09000013	Hammersmith and Fulham	16	181.8	11,086	182.2	11,110	181.7	11,080	181.4	11,064	182.1	11,106	182.4	11,403	180.8	11,303	180.1	11,257
E09000014	Haringey	30	272.1	9,192	268.3	9,063	264.4	8,933	261.0	8,819	257.9	8,713	255.5	8,518	252.7	8,425	249.8	8,327
E09000019	Islington	15	232.1	15,620	227.5	15,314	221.4	14,903	215.9	14,529	211.3	14,221	206.3	13,752	200.1	13,342	196.7	13,114
E09000020	Kensington and Chelsea	12	156.8	12,931	158.6	13,081	157.8	13,018	157.1	12,961	156.9	12,942	158.3	13,188	160.5	13,372	161.9	13,491
E09000022	Lambeth	27	323.1	12,050	320.7	11,963	316.6	11,810	312.7	11,664	309.4	11,539	304.5	11,277	297.7	11,024	294.1	10,891
E09000023	Lewisham	35	298.9	8,504	295.0	8,393	290.3	8,259	285.0	8,107	280.7	7,986	276.9	7,913	272.5	7,786	270.4	7,726
E09000025	Newham	36	344.5	9,517	336.3	9,288	328.1	9,062	321.5	8,880	316.3	8,737	310.5	8,624	299.2	8,310	286.4	7,957
E09000028	Southwark	29	311.7	10,798	308.4	10,686	302.8	10,492	298.7	10,348	293.4	10,167	288.7	9,956	283.8	9,785	281.1	9,694
E09000030	Tower Hamlets	20	300.9	15,210	293.8	14,850	284.6	14,383	273.6	13,828	263.6	13,323	256.0	12,801	248.5	12,426	240.5	12,025
E09000032	Wandsworth	34	321.5	9,383	319.5	9,324	316.5	9,238	313.1	9,138	309.5	9,033	307.7	9,050	302.6	8,901	299.3	8,804
E09000033	Westminster	21	242.0	11,261	238.0	11,079	229.9	10,699	225.3	10,486	223.7	10,413	219.6	10,456	217.2	10,342	217.0	10,332
E09000002	Barking and Dagenham	36	208.2	5,766	203.1	5,625	198.7	5,502	194.6	5,389	190.7	5,280	187.0	5,195	182.8	5,079	177.6	4,933
E09000003	Barnet	87	384.8	4,436	378.8	4,366	373.7	4,308	368.3	4,246	363.8	4,193	357.5	4,110	351.4	4,040	345.8	3,975
E09000004	Bexley	61	245.1	4,046	242.4	4,001	240.0	3,962	236.8	3,909	234.3	3,868	232.8	3,816	230.7	3,782	228.1	3,740
E09000005	Brent	43	326.4	7,551	323.4	7,481	320.1	7,404	317.1	7,335	314.6	7,277	312.2	7,262	304.8	7,088	298.1	6,933
E09000006	Bromley	150	327.6	2,182	325.3	2,167	321.6	2,142	318.2	2,119	314.0	2,092	310.6	2,070	308.6	2,057	306.9	2,046
E09000008	Croydon	86	383.3	4,431	380.1	4,394	377.1	4,359	373.6	4,320	369.2	4,268	364.8	4,242	358.0	4,162	352.8	4,102
E09000009	Ealing	56	344.8	6,208	344.3	6,198	343.0	6,175	342.1	6,159	340.3	6,127	339.3	6,059	334.1	5,966	330.0	5,892
E09000010	Enfield	81	332.1	4,109	328.7	4,067	324.4	4,013	320.3	3,963	317.3	3,925	313.9	3,876	307.6	3,798	302.0	3,728
E09000011	Greenwich	47	279.1	5,897	274.5	5,800	268.9	5,680	264.1	5,579	260.0	5,493	255.5	5,436	249.2	5,302	243.7	5,185
E09000015	Harrow	50	248.7	4,928	246.8	4,891	245.1	4,858	243.0	4,815	242.0	4,795	240.5	4,810	237.5	4,749	233.5	4,670
E09000016	Havering	112	253.4	2,255	249.4	2,220	246.0	2,190	242.1	2,155	239.7	2,134	237.9	2,124	236.2	2,109	234.1	2,090
E09000017	Hillingdon	116	299.9	2,592	296.1	2,559	291.4	2,518	286.0	2,472	281.2	2,430	275.5	2,375	269.5	2,323	265.7	2,290
E09000018	Hounslow	56	268.3	4,792	266.4	4,759	264.0	4,717	261.3	4,667	258.5	4,618	254.9	4,552	249.2	4,451	243.4	4,346
E09000021	Kingston upon Thames	37	173.7	4,662	171.6	4,606	168.4	4,520	165.7	4,446	163.2	4,380	160.4	4,336	158.6	4,288	157.3	4,252
E09000024	Merton	38	206.7	5,494	206.0	5,474	204.6	5,438	203.6	5,412	202.0	5,370	200.5	5,277	199.1	5,240	198.1	5,214
E09000026	Redbridge	56	301.3	5,341	297.9	5,281	293.9	5,208	288.9	5,120	284.6	5,045	281.4	5,025	275.1	4,912	270.4	4,829
E09000027	Richmond upon Thames	57	195.2	3,400	194.1	3,382	193.3	3,367	191.1	3,330	189.0	3,292	187.5	3,290	186.3	3,268	184.4	3,235
E09000029	Sutton	44	201.9	4,606	199.9	4,558	198.0	4,515	195.8	4,465	193.5	4,413	191.1	4,344	189.3	4,303	188.2	4,277
E09000031	Waltham Forest	39	274.2	7,066	270.7	6,975	267.8	6,901	265.7	6,845	262.5	6,763	259.7	6,660	254.0	6,513	248.1	6,363
E12000008	**SOUTH EAST**	19,073	9,030.3	473	8,949.4	469	8,874.0	465	8,793.2	461	8,724.9	457	8,652.8	454	8,577.8	450	8,490.9	445
E06000036	Bracknell Forest	109	119.7	1,095	119.2	1,090	118.0	1,079	116.5	1,065	115.1	1,052	113.7	1,043	112.9	1,036	111.9	1,027
E06000043	Brighton and Hove	83	287.2	3,469	284.1	3,431	280.7	3,390	278.0	3,358	275.7	3,331	273.0	3,289	269.5	3,247	265.6	3,200

MYE5: Population estimates: Population density for the local authorities in the UK, mid-2001 to mid-2016

Abbreviation: Est. Pop. (Estimated Population)

Thousands

Code	Name	Area (sq km)	Est Pop: mid-2009	people /km²	Est Pop: mid-2010	people /km²	Est Pop: mid-2011	people /km²	Est Pop: mid-2012	people /km²	Est Pop: mid-2013	people /km²	Est Pop: mid-2014	people /km²	Est Pop: mid-2015	people /km²	Est Pop: mid-2016	people /km²
E06000046	Isle of Wight	380	138.4	364	138.4	364	138.4	364	138.8	365	138.6	364	139.3	367	139.8	368	140.3	369
E06000035	Medway	194	260.2	1,341	262.7	1,354	264.9	1,365	268.1	1,385	270.7	1,399	273.2	1,412	275.2	1,422	277.0	1,431
E06000042	Milton Keynes	309	240.2	777	245.5	794	249.9	809	252.8	819	256.4	831	260.2	843	263.2	853	266.2	863
E06000044	Portsmouth	40	199.0	4,975	202.7	5,068	205.4	5,136	206.5	5,113	206.7	5,117	208.0	5,150	210.5	5,212	213.3	5,282
E06000038	Reading	40	152.3	3,808	154.3	3,857	155.3	3,883	156.8	3,881	158.6	3,926	160.3	3,967	161.7	4,003	162.7	4,027
E06000039	Slough	33	134.7	4,083	137.8	4,176	140.7	4,264	141.8	4,358	142.7	4,384	144.3	4,436	146.0	4,488	147.7	4,540
E06000045	Southampton	50	230.0	4,600	233.1	4,662	235.9	4,717	238.5	4,779	239.9	4,805	242.1	4,850	246.1	4,930	250.4	5,016
E06000037	West Berkshire	704	153.0	217	153.9	219	154.1	219	154.7	220	156.0	222	156.6	222	157.5	224	158.6	225
E06000040	Windsor and Maidenhead	197	142.4	723	144.0	731	145.1	737	145.7	742	146.3	744	147.5	751	148.3	755	149.7	762
E06000041	Wokingham	179	154.2	861	154.7	864	154.9	866	156.7	875	158.1	883	159.4	891	161.2	901	163.1	911
E10000002	Buckinghamshire	1,565	498.8	319	502.8	321	506.6	324	511.0	327	515.5	329	520.9	333	527.1	337	533.1	341
E07000004	Aylesbury Vale	903	171.4	190	172.9	191	174.9	194	177.6	197	180.9	200	184.2	204	188.3	209	192.7	213
E07000005	Chiltern	196	92.5	472	92.9	474	92.7	473	93.0	474	93.4	476	94.1	479	94.7	482	95.2	485
E07000006	South Bucks	141	66.0	468	66.7	473	67.1	476	67.5	478	68.1	482	68.7	486	69.3	491	69.8	494
E07000007	Wycombe	325	168.9	520	170.3	524	172.0	529	172.9	533	173.2	534	173.9	536	174.8	539	175.4	540
E10000011	East Sussex	1,709	520.4	304	523.7	306	527.2	308	531.1	311	534.9	313	540.5	316	545.0	319	549.6	322
E07000061	Eastbourne	44	98.2	2,232	98.5	2,239	99.3	2,257	99.9	2,262	100.4	2,273	101.3	2,295	102.2	2,314	103.0	2,333
E07000062	Hastings	30	89.3	2,976	89.6	2,987	90.2	3,006	90.4	3,041	90.9	3,058	91.4	3,074	91.9	3,093	92.9	3,126
E07000063	Lewes	292	96.1	329	97.1	332	97.6	334	98.7	338	99.6	341	100.4	344	100.9	345	101.6	348
E07000064	Rother	509	90.1	177	90.6	178	90.7	178	91.1	179	91.2	179	92.4	181	93.2	183	94.0	184
E07000065	Wealden	833	146.6	176	147.9	178	149.4	179	151.1	181	152.8	183	155.0	186	156.8	188	158.1	190
E10000014	Hampshire	3,679	1,301.7	354	1,312.3	357	1,322.1	359	1,331.4	362	1,340.2	364	1,349.6	367	1,357.0	369	1,365.1	371
E07000084	Basingstoke and Deane	634	164.1	259	166.4	262	168.6	266	170.7	269	172.1	271	173.4	274	174.3	275	175.2	276
E07000085	East Hampshire	514	114.3	222	115.4	224	116.0	226	116.6	227	117.4	228	118.0	229	118.7	231	118.7	231
E07000086	Eastleigh	80	122.4	1,530	124.2	1,553	125.9	1,573	126.8	1,589	127.8	1,602	128.9	1,616	129.0	1,617	129.5	1,624
E07000087	Fareham	74	110.8	1,498	111.4	1,505	111.9	1,513	112.9	1,521	113.9	1,534	114.7	1,545	115.2	1,551	115.8	1,560
E07000088	Gosport	25	82.0	3,278	82.3	3,292	82.7	3,307	83.3	3,284	83.5	3,294	84.3	3,326	84.8	3,342	85.5	3,371
E07000089	Hart	215	91.0	423	91.3	425	91.7	426	92.2	428	93.0	432	93.7	435	94.4	439	94.9	441
E07000090	Havant	55	119.4	2,171	120.1	2,184	120.8	2,196	121.3	2,190	121.7	2,197	122.3	2,209	123.1	2,223	123.9	2,237
E07000091	New Forest	753	175.4	233	176.3	234	176.8	235	177.5	236	178.2	237	179.0	238	179.3	238	179.5	238
E07000092	Rushmoor	39	92.6	2,374	93.4	2,395	94.4	2,419	94.8	2,428	94.9	2,430	95.2	2,439	95.2	2,437	96.1	2,461
E07000093	Test Valley	628	115.3	184	115.8	184	116.7	186	117.3	187	118.8	189	119.8	191	121.4	193	122.8	196
E07000094	Winchester	661	114.5	173	115.8	175	116.8	177	118.1	179	119.0	180	120.3	182	121.7	184	123.1	186
E10000016	Kent	3,545	1,435.3	405	1,451.9	410	1,466.5	414	1,480.2	418	1,493.1	421	1,509.3	426	1,523.1	430	1,540.4	435
E07000105	Ashford	581	115.7	199	117.0	201	118.4	204	120.1	207	121.7	210	123.2	212	124.0	214	125.9	217
E07000106	Canterbury	309	146.4	474	148.7	481	150.6	487	153.2	496	154.9	502	157.0	508	159.7	517	162.5	526
E07000107	Dartford	73	95.3	1,305	96.3	1,320	97.6	1,337	98.9	1,359	100.4	1,380	102.0	1,402	103.5	1,423	105.1	1,445
E07000108	Dover	315	110.1	349	111.1	353	111.7	355	111.8	355	112.5	357	113.3	360	113.4	360	114.6	364

MYE5: Population estimates: Population density for the local authorities in the UK, mid-2001 to mid-2016

Abbreviation: Est. Pop. (Estimated Population)

Thousands

Code	Name	Area (sq km)	Est Pop: mid-2016	people /km²	Est Pop: mid-2015	people /km²	Est Pop: mid-2014	people /km²	Est Pop: mid-2013	people /km²	Est Pop: mid-2012	people /km²	Est Pop: mid-2011	people /km²	Est Pop: mid-2010	people /km²	Est Pop: mid-2009	people /km²
E07000109	Gravesham	99	106.2	1,073	105.7	1,068	104.8	1,058	103.4	1,044	102.6	1,036	101.8	1,028	101.1	1,021	100.2	1,012
E07000110	Maidstone	393	165.7	421	164.0	417	161.5	411	159.2	405	157.4	400	155.8	396	153.7	391	151.6	386
E07000111	Sevenoaks	369	119.0	322	118.2	320	117.6	319	116.9	317	116.3	315	115.4	313	114.5	310	113.8	308
E07000112	Shepway	357	111.0	311	109.8	308	109.3	306	108.8	305	108.6	304	108.2	303	107.0	300	105.7	296
E07000113	Swale	374	144.9	387	142.5	380	140.9	376	139.3	372	137.8	368	136.3	365	135.0	361	133.0	356
E07000114	Thanet	103	140.8	1,363	139.8	1,353	138.5	1,340	136.8	1,324	135.7	1,313	134.4	1,305	133.5	1,296	132.3	1,285
E07000115	Tonbridge and Malling	240	127.3	530	125.8	524	124.6	519	123.2	513	122.0	508	121.1	505	120.1	500	118.5	494
E07000116	Tunbridge Wells	331	117.4	354	116.6	352	116.5	352	116.1	350	115.8	349	115.2	348	114.0	345	112.8	341
E10000025	Oxfordshire	2,605	678.5	260	673.6	259	669.4	257	664.0	255	660.0	253	654.8	251	648.7	249	643.1	247
E07000177	Cherwell	589	146.6	249	145.6	247	144.5	245	143.8	244	142.9	243	142.3	242	141.3	240	140.3	238
E07000178	Oxford	46	155.3	3,405	154.7	3,393	154.7	3,392	152.4	3,342	151.5	3,322	150.2	3,266	147.9	3,215	145.5	3,163
E07000179	South Oxfordshire	679	139.2	205	138.2	204	137.5	203	136.3	201	135.7	200	135.0	199	133.9	197	133.5	197
E07000180	Vale of White Horse	578	128.7	223	126.5	219	124.6	216	123.5	214	122.7	212	121.9	211	120.8	209	120.0	208
E07000181	West Oxfordshire	714	108.7	152	108.6	152	108.1	151	107.9	151	107.2	150	105.4	148	104.7	147	103.8	145
E10000030	Surrey	1,663	1,181.0	710	1,172.4	705	1,164.1	700	1,154.1	694	1,144.0	688	1,135.4	683	1,125.8	677	1,113.7	670
E07000207	Elmbridge	95	136.1	1,432	135.4	1,424	134.8	1,419	133.5	1,404	132.2	1,391	131.4	1,383	130.9	1,378	130.0	1,368
E07000208	Epsom and Ewell	34	79.0	2,318	78.5	2,302	78.0	2,288	76.9	2,257	75.8	2,225	75.2	2,212	74.3	2,185	73.1	2,150
E07000209	Guildford	271	146.8	542	145.1	535	142.6	526	140.7	519	139.3	514	137.6	508	135.5	500	133.6	493
E07000210	Mole Valley	258	87.3	338	87.0	337	86.9	336	86.8	336	86.1	333	85.6	332	85.4	331	84.7	328
E07000211	Reigate and Banstead	129	145.3	1,125	143.8	1,113	142.9	1,106	140.9	1,091	139.8	1,082	138.4	1,073	136.7	1,060	134.9	1,046
E07000212	Runnymede	78	86.4	1,107	85.0	1,089	83.9	1,075	83.1	1,065	81.9	1,049	80.5	1,032	80.3	1,029	79.4	1,018
E07000213	Spelthorne	45	98.9	2,203	98.4	2,193	97.9	2,182	97.4	2,169	96.7	2,155	95.9	2,130	94.8	2,108	94.0	2,089
E07000214	Surrey Heath	95	88.7	933	88.4	929	87.8	923	87.1	916	86.7	912	86.4	909	85.8	904	85.1	896
E07000215	Tandridge	248	86.5	349	85.9	346	85.3	344	84.6	341	83.6	337	83.2	335	82.8	334	82.1	331
E07000216	Waverley	345	124.6	361	124.0	359	123.4	357	122.8	356	122.1	354	121.8	353	121.0	351	120.1	348
E07000217	Woking	64	101.4	1,595	101.0	1,588	100.6	1,582	100.4	1,578	99.8	1,569	99.5	1,555	98.2	1,534	96.6	1,509
E10000032	West Sussex	1,991	846.9	425	838.5	421	830.5	417	822.9	413	816.0	410	808.9	406	803.2	404	796.0	400
E07000223	Adur	42	63.6	1,517	63.5	1,515	63.3	1,509	62.6	1,493	62.0	1,478	61.3	1,460	61.2	1,458	61.0	1,453
E07000224	Arun	221	157.3	712	155.8	705	154.7	700	153.0	693	151.6	686	149.8	678	149.5	676	148.9	674
E07000225	Chichester	786	119.1	152	117.8	150	116.3	148	115.8	147	114.9	146	114.0	145	113.4	144	112.5	143
E07000226	Crawley	45	111.5	2,480	110.9	2,466	109.9	2,443	109.0	2,423	108.2	2,407	107.1	2,379	105.5	2,344	103.8	2,308
E07000227	Horsham	530	138.5	261	136.3	257	134.5	254	133.2	251	132.3	249	131.5	248	130.9	247	129.8	245
E07000228	Mid Sussex	334	147.5	442	146.0	437	144.7	433	143.0	428	141.3	423	140.2	420	138.9	416	137.2	411
E07000229	Worthing	33	109.2	3,359	108.3	3,330	107.3	3,299	106.4	3,272	105.8	3,252	105.0	3,281	103.8	3,243	102.8	3,213
E12000009	**SOUTH WEST**	23,837	5,517.0	231	5,471.6	230	5,423.3	228	5,377.7	226	5,339.7	224	5,300.8	222	5,261.3	221	5,226.8	219
E06000022	Bath and North East Somerset	346	186.9	540	184.3	533	181.2	524	179.5	519	177.2	512	175.5	507	174.3	504	173.4	501
E06000028	Bournemouth	46	193.7	4,194	191.7	4,151	189.6	4,107	187.9	4,069	186.3	4,034	183.5	3,988	179.3	3,898	174.3	3,788
E06000023	Bristol, City of	110	456.0	4,156	450.6	4,108	443.8	4,045	438.4	3,996	433.0	3,948	428.1	3,892	423.0	3,846	419.0	3,809

MYE5: Population estimates: Population density for the local authorities in the UK, mid-2001 to mid-2016

Abbreviation: Est. Pop. (Estimated Population)

Thousands

Code	Name	Area (sq km)	Est Pop mid-2009	2009 people /km²	Est Pop mid-2010	2010 people /km²	Est Pop mid-2011	2011 people /km²	Est Pop mid-2012	2012 people /km²	Est Pop mid-2013	2013 people /km²	Est Pop mid-2014	2014 people /km²	Est Pop mid-2015	2015 people /km²	Est Pop mid-2016	2016 people /km²
E06000052	Cornwall	3,546	526.4	148	529.8	149	533.8	151	538.2	152	541.7	153	546.0	154	550.3	155	555.1	157
E06000053	Isles of Scilly	16	2.3	141	2.2	139	2.2	139	2.3	139	2.3	139	2.3	140	2.3	143	2.3	143
E06000024	North Somerset	374	201.7	539	203.0	543	203.1	543	204.5	547	206.2	552	208.2	557	209.9	562	211.7	567
E06000026	Plymouth	80	253.1	3,164	254.2	3,178	256.6	3,207	257.7	3,229	258.6	3,239	260.5	3,263	261.4	3,274	262.4	3,286
E06000029	Poole	65	145.4	2,237	146.8	2,258	148.1	2,278	148.5	2,293	148.8	2,297	149.7	2,311	150.0	2,316	150.7	2,327
E06000025	South Gloucestershire	497	259.7	523	261.5	526	263.4	530	266.2	536	269.0	541	271.0	545	274.0	551	276.7	557
E06000030	Swindon	230	204.4	889	206.9	900	209.7	912	211.9	921	214.0	930	216.0	939	217.6	946	218.6	950
E06000027	Torbay	63	131.6	2,090	131.4	2,086	131.2	2,082	131.5	2,091	132.2	2,102	133.3	2,119	133.8	2,127	134.4	2,137
E06000054	Wiltshire	3,255	466.7	143	470.2	144	474.3	146	476.9	147	479.9	147	484.6	149	488.5	150	492.2	151
E10000008	Devon	6,564	741.0	113	743.9	113	747.7	114	753.1	115	757.9	115	764.7	116	772.4	118	778.8	119
E07000040	East Devon	814	132.4	163	132.7	163	133.3	164	134.4	165	135.0	166	136.5	168	138.4	170	140.3	172
E07000041	Exeter	47	114.4	2,434	115.7	2,462	117.1	2,491	119.0	2,530	121.0	2,573	123.0	2,615	125.7	2,672	127.5	2,711
E07000042	Mid Devon	913	77.0	84	77.4	85	77.9	85	78.4	86	78.7	86	79.3	87	79.6	87	79.9	88
E07000043	North Devon	1,086	93.0	86	93.3	86	94.0	87	93.8	86	93.8	86	94.0	87	94.2	87	94.6	87
E07000044	South Hams	886	83.4	94	83.5	94	83.6	94	83.7	94	84.1	95	84.4	95	84.9	96	84.8	96
E07000045	Teignbridge	674	124.5	185	124.4	185	124.3	184	125.0	186	126.1	187	127.4	189	128.9	191	129.9	193
E07000046	Torridge	984	63.5	65	63.7	65	64.0	65	64.8	66	65.1	66	65.7	67	66.3	67	67.0	68
E07000047	West Devon	1,160	52.9	46	53.3	46	53.7	46	53.9	46	54.0	47	54.3	47	54.5	47	54.7	47
E10000009	Dorset	2,542	410.8	162	412.0	162	413.8	163	415.0	163	417.0	164	418.5	165	420.8	166	422.9	166
E07000048	Christchurch	50	47.3	946	47.7	954	47.9	958	48.0	953	48.5	962	49.0	973	49.2	977	49.6	985
E07000049	East Dorset	354	87.0	246	87.2	246	87.3	247	87.7	248	87.9	248	88.2	249	88.7	250	89.1	251
E07000050	North Dorset	609	67.8	111	67.9	112	69.0	113	69.4	114	69.9	115	70.0	115	70.6	116	70.9	116
E07000051	Purbeck	404	45.1	112	45.2	112	45.2	112	45.3	112	45.4	112	45.7	113	46.2	114	46.3	115
E07000052	West Dorset	1,082	98.6	91	99.0	92	99.3	92	99.5	92	100.1	93	100.5	93	100.9	93	101.5	94
E07000053	Weymouth and Portland	42	65.0	1,549	65.0	1,548	65.1	1,551	65.0	1,557	65.2	1,560	65.1	1,557	65.2	1,561	65.4	1,567
E10000013	Gloucestershire	2,653	590.5	223	594.1	224	598.3	226	602.2	227	606.0	228	611.7	231	617.5	233	623.1	235
E07000078	Cheltenham	47	114.0	2,425	114.9	2,445	115.6	2,461	116.1	2,491	115.8	2,485	116.4	2,498	116.6	2,502	117.2	2,516
E07000079	Cotswold	1,165	82.8	71	82.6	71	83.2	71	83.6	72	84.3	72	84.9	73	85.5	73	86.1	74
E07000080	Forest of Dean	526	82.0	156	81.9	156	82.2	156	82.7	157	83.0	158	83.7	159	84.6	161	85.4	162
E07000081	Gloucester	41	119.3	2,911	120.7	2,943	121.9	2,974	123.4	3,043	124.5	3,071	125.7	3,099	127.2	3,136	128.4	3,165
E07000082	Stroud	461	111.9	243	112.5	244	113.1	245	113.4	246	114.1	248	115.3	250	116.8	253	117.5	255
E07000083	Tewkesbury	414	80.6	195	81.5	197	82.3	199	83.0	200	84.3	203	85.8	207	86.9	210	88.5	214
E10000027	Somerset	3,451	526.6	153	528.6	153	531.6	154	535.2	155	538.4	156	542.2	157	546.5	158	551.4	160
E07000187	Mendip	739	108.6	147	109.0	148	109.4	148	110.1	149	110.3	149	111.1	150	112.1	152	113.1	153
E07000188	Sedgemoor	564	112.9	200	113.8	202	114.9	204	116.1	206	117.4	208	119.0	211	120.1	213	121.3	215
E07000189	South Somerset	959	160.7	168	160.9	168	162.1	169	163.0	170	164.0	171	164.8	172	165.5	173	166.5	174
E07000190	Taunton Deane	462	109.3	237	109.9	238	110.6	239	111.4	241	112.2	243	112.9	244	114.2	247	116.0	251
E07000191	West Somerset	725	35.1	48	35.0	48	34.6	48	34.6	48	34.4	47	34.4	47	34.5	48	34.5	48

MYE5: Population estimates: Population density for the local authorities in the UK, mid-2001 to mid-2016

Abbreviation: Est. Pop. (Estimated Population)

Thousands

Code	Name	Area (sq km)	Est Pop: mid-2016	people /km²	Est Pop: mid-2015	people /km²	Est Pop: mid-2014	people /km²	Est Pop: mid-2013	people /km²	Est Pop: mid-2012	people /km²	Est Pop: mid-2011	people /km²	Est Pop: mid-2010	people /km²	Est Pop: mid-2009	people /km²
W92000004	**WALES**	20,736	3,113.2	150	3,099.1	149	3,092.0	149	3,082.4	149	3,074.1	148	3,063.8	148	3,050.0	147	3,038.9	147
W06000001	Isle of Anglesey	711	69.7	98	69.9	98	70.1	99	70.1	99	70.0	98	69.9	98	69.8	98	69.9	98
W06000002	Gwynedd	2,535	123.3	49	122.6	48	121.9	48	121.7	48	122.0	48	121.5	48	121.2	48	120.3	47
W06000003	Conwy	1,126	116.8	104	116.5	103	116.4	103	115.9	103	115.6	103	115.3	102	114.7	102	114.6	102
W06000004	Denbighshire	837	95.0	114	94.8	113	94.8	113	94.5	113	94.1	112	93.9	112	94.2	112	94.4	113
W06000005	Flintshire	437	154.6	353	154.1	352	153.8	352	153.2	350	152.8	349	152.7	349	152.1	348	152.0	348
W06000006	Wrexham	504	135.4	269	135.4	269	136.0	270	135.8	270	135.5	269	135.1	268	134.0	266	133.3	264
W06000023	Powys	5,181	132.3	26	132.7	26	132.8	26	132.8	26	133.0	26	133.1	26	132.9	26	133.1	26
W06000008	Ceredigion	1,786	73.7	41	74.2	42	75.1	42	75.8	42	75.9	43	75.3	42	75.2	42	74.6	42
W06000009	Pembrokeshire	1,619	124.2	77	123.7	76	123.8	76	123.4	76	123.1	76	122.6	76	122.0	75	121.6	75
W06000010	Carmarthenshire	2,370	185.8	78	185.2	78	185.0	78	184.7	78	184.3	78	184.0	78	183.0	77	182.8	77
W06000011	Swansea	380	244.5	644	242.3	638	241.0	635	240.1	632	239.5	631	238.7	628	237.3	625	235.6	620
W06000012	Neath Port Talbot	441	141.7	321	140.9	319	140.5	318	139.9	317	140.1	317	139.9	317	139.6	317	139.5	316
W06000013	Bridgend	251	143.4	572	142.3	567	141.3	564	140.5	561	139.8	557	139.4	555	138.5	552	137.8	549
W06000014	Vale of Glamorgan	331	128.9	389	128.0	387	128.0	387	127.4	385	127.0	384	126.7	383	126.4	382	126.2	381
W06000015	Cardiff	141	361.2	2,563	357.5	2,537	354.8	2,518	352.1	2,499	348.7	2,475	345.4	2,450	341.4	2,421	337.7	2,395
W06000016	Rhondda Cynon Taf	424	238.2	562	237.4	560	236.9	558	236.2	557	235.6	555	234.4	553	234.5	553	234.7	554
W06000024	Merthyr Tydfil	111	59.7	536	59.2	532	59.1	530	59.0	529	58.9	529	58.9	530	58.5	527	58.2	524
W06000018	Caerphilly	277	180.5	651	180.2	650	179.9	649	179.2	646	179.0	645	178.8	645	178.1	643	177.2	640
W06000019	Blaenau Gwent	109	69.6	640	69.5	640	69.7	641	69.8	642	69.8	642	69.8	640	69.8	640	69.9	641
W06000020	Torfaen	126	92.0	732	91.8	730	91.5	728	91.4	727	91.3	727	91.2	724	91.1	723	91.2	724
W06000021	Monmouthshire	849	93.3	110	92.8	109	92.5	109	92.2	109	91.7	108	91.5	108	91.0	107	90.6	107
W06000022	Newport	191	149.5	785	148.0	777	147.1	772	146.7	770	146.3	768	145.8	763	144.8	758	143.8	753
S92000003	**SCOTLAND**	77,911	5,404.7	69	5,373.0	69	5,347.6	69	5,327.7	68	5,313.6	68	5,299.9	68	5,262.2	68	5,231.9	67
S12000033	Aberdeen City	186	229.8	1,236	230.4	1,238	228.9	1,231	227.1	1,221	224.9	1,209	222.5	1,196	219.7	1,181	217.0	1,167
S12000034	Aberdeenshire	6,313	262.2	42	262.0	41	260.5	41	257.8	41	255.6	40	253.7	40	251.4	40	249.0	39
S12000041	Angus	2,182	116.5	53	116.9	54	116.7	54	116.3	53	116.2	53	116.2	53	115.4	53	114.8	53
S12000035	Argyll and Bute	6,909	87.1	13	86.9	13	87.7	13	88.1	13	86.9	13	88.9	13	88.6	13	89.5	13
S12000036	City of Edinburgh	263	507.2	1,928	498.8	1,897	492.6	1,873	487.5	1,853	482.6	1,835	477.9	1,817	469.9	1,787	463.2	1,761
S12000005	Clackmannanshire	159	51.4	323	51.4	323	51.2	322	51.3	323	51.3	323	51.5	324	51.3	323	51.3	323
S12000006	Dumfries and Galloway	6,427	149.5	23	149.7	23	150.0	23	150.3	23	150.8	23	151.4	24	151.1	24	151.2	24
S12000042	Dundee City	60	148.3	2,471	148.2	2,470	148.1	2,469	148.1	2,468	147.8	2,463	147.2	2,453	146.1	2,434	145.2	2,420
S12000008	East Ayrshire	1,262	122.2	97	122.1	97	122.1	97	122.4	97	122.7	97	122.7	97	122.4	97	122.1	97
S12000045	East Dunbartonshire	174	107.5	618	107.0	615	106.7	613	105.8	608	105.9	609	105.0	603	104.9	603	105.0	603
S12000010	East Lothian	679	104.1	153	103.1	152	102.1	150	101.4	149	100.9	149	99.9	147	99.1	146	98.3	145
S12000011	East Renfrewshire	174	93.8	539	92.9	534	92.4	531	91.5	526	91.0	523	90.8	522	90.4	520	90.0	517
S12000014	Falkirk	297	159.4	537	158.5	534	157.7	531	157.2	529	156.8	528	156.3	526	155.1	522	154.2	519

MYE5: Population estimates: Population density for the local authorities in the UK, mid-2001 to mid-2016

Abbreviation: Est. Pop. (Estimated Population)

Thousands

Code	Name	Area (sq km)	Est Pop: mid-2016	people /km²	Est Pop: mid-2015	people /km²	Est Pop: mid-2014	people /km²	Est Pop: mid-2013	people /km²	Est Pop: mid-2012	people /km²	Est Pop: mid-2011	people /km²	Est Pop: mid-2010	people /km²	Est Pop: mid-2009	people /km²
S12000015	Fife	1,325	370.3	279	368.1	278	367.3	277	366.9	277	366.2	276	365.3	276	362.6	274	361.4	273
S12000046	Glasgow City	175	615.1	3,515	606.3	3,465	599.6	3,427	596.5	3,409	595.1	3,400	593.1	3,389	586.5	3,351	581.6	3,324
S12000017	Highland	25,657	234.8	9	234.1	9	233.1	9	232.9	9	232.9	9	232.7	9	230.7	9	228.8	9
S12000018	Inverclyde	160	79.2	495	79.5	497	79.9	499	80.3	502	80.7	504	81.2	508	81.5	509	81.7	510
S12000019	Midlothian	354	88.6	250	87.4	247	86.2	244	84.7	239	84.2	238	83.5	236	82.4	233	81.9	231
S12000020	Moray	2,238	96.1	43	95.5	43	94.8	42	94.4	42	92.9	42	93.5	42	93.7	42	93.2	42
S12000013	Na h-Eileanan Siar	3,059	26.9	9	27.1	9	27.3	9	27.4	9	27.6	9	27.7	9	27.6	9	27.4	9
S12000021	North Ayrshire	885	135.9	154	136.1	154	136.5	154	136.9	155	137.6	155	138.1	156	137.8	156	137.8	156
S12000044	North Lanarkshire	470	339.4	722	338.3	720	338.0	719	337.8	719	337.9	719	337.7	719	336.3	715	335.2	713
S12000023	Orkney Islands	989	21.9	22	21.7	22	21.6	22	21.6	22	21.5	22	21.4	22	21.2	21	20.9	21
S12000024	Perth and Kinross	5,286	150.7	29	149.9	28	148.9	28	147.8	28	147.7	28	146.9	28	145.6	28	144.4	27
S12000038	Renfrewshire	261	175.9	674	174.6	669	174.2	668	173.9	666	174.3	668	174.7	669	173.7	666	173.0	663
S12000026	Scottish Borders	4,732	114.5	24	114.0	24	114.0	24	113.9	24	113.7	24	113.9	24	113.7	24	113.6	24
S12000027	Shetland Islands	1,468	23.2	16	23.2	16	23.2	16	23.2	16	23.2	16	23.2	16	23.1	16	22.8	16
S12000028	South Ayrshire	1,222	112.5	92	112.4	92	112.5	92	112.9	92	112.9	92	113.0	92	112.6	92	112.5	92
S12000029	South Lanarkshire	1,772	317.1	179	316.2	178	315.3	178	314.8	178	314.3	177	313.9	177	313.2	177	312.2	176
S12000030	Stirling	2,187	93.8	43	92.8	42	91.5	42	91.2	42	91.0	42	90.3	41	89.6	41	88.7	41
S12000039	West Dunbartonshire	159	89.9	565	89.6	563	89.7	564	89.8	565	90.3	568	90.6	570	90.8	571	91.1	573
S12000040	West Lothian	428	180.1	421	178.6	417	177.2	414	176.2	412	176.0	411	175.3	410	174.1	407	173.0	404
N92000002	NORTHERN IRELAND	13,588	1,862.1	137	1,851.6	136	1,840.5	135	1,829.7	135	1,823.6	134	1,814.3	134	1,804.8	133	1,793.3	132
N09000001	Antrim and Newtownabbey	572	141.0	247	140.5	246	140.0	245	139.5	244	139.2	243	138.7	242	138.0	241	137.4	240
N09000011	Ards and North Down	461	159.6	346	158.8	345	157.9	343	157.6	342	157.6	342	156.9	341	156.5	340	156.1	339
N09000002	Armagh City, Banbridge & Craigavon	1,337	210.3	157	207.8	155	205.7	154	203.8	152	202.4	151	200.3	150	198.2	148	196.2	147
N09000003	Belfast	132	339.6	2,573	338.9	2,558	336.8	2,543	335.1	2,530	334.0	2,521	333.9	2,520	333.5	2,517	331.8	2,504
N09000004	Causeway Coast and Glens	1,980	143.5	72	143.1	72	142.3	72	141.7	72	141.4	71	140.9	71	140.1	71	139.6	71
N09000005	Derry City and Strabane	1,238	150.1	121	149.5	121	149.2	120	148.6	120	148.6	120	148.2	120	148.1	120	148.1	120
N09000006	Fermanagh and Omagh	2,857	115.8	41	115.3	40	115.0	40	114.4	40	114.2	40	113.5	40	112.9	40	112.0	39
N09000007	Lisburn and Castlereagh	505	141.2	280	140.2	277	138.6	274	136.8	271	136.3	270	135.3	268	133.9	265	132.4	262
N09000008	Mid and East Antrim	1,046	137.8	132	137.1	131	136.6	131	136.0	130	135.8	130	135.4	129	135.2	129	134.8	129
N09000009	Mid Ulster	1,827	145.4	80	144.0	79	142.9	78	141.3	77	140.4	77	139.0	76	137.2	75	135.4	74
N09000010	Newry, Mourne and Down	1,633	177.8	109	176.4	108	175.4	107	174.8	107	173.7	106	172.3	106	171.1	105	169.7	104

MYE5: Population estimates: Population density for the local authorities in the UK, mid-2001 to mid-2016

Abbreviation: Est Pop (Estimated Population)

Thousands

Code	Name	Area (sq km)	Est Pop: mid-2008	people /km²	Est Pop: mid-2007	people /km²	Est Pop: mid-2006	people /km²	Est Pop: mid-2005	people /km²	Est Pop: mid-2004	people /km²	Est Pop: mid-2003	people /km²	Est Pop: mid-2002	people /km²	Est Pop: mid-2001	people /km²
K02000001	UNITED KINGDOM	242,545	61,823.8	254	61,319.1	252	60,827.1	250	60,413.3	248	59,950.4	246	59,636.7	245	59,365.7	244	59,113.0	243
K03000001	GREAT BRITAIN	228,957	60,044.6	262	59,557.4	260	59,084.0	258	58,685.5	256	58,236.3	254	57,931.7	253	57,668.1	252	57,424.2	251
K04000001	ENGLAND AND WALES	151,046	54,841.7	363	54,387.4	360	53,950.9	357	53,575.3	355	53,152.0	352	52,863.2	350	52,602.1	348	52,360.0	347
E92000001	ENGLAND	130,310	51,815.9	398	51,381.1	394	50,965.2	391	50,606.0	388	50,194.6	385	49,925.5	383	49,679.3	381	49,449.7	379
E12000001	NORTH EAST	8,574	2,569.3	300	2,562.0	299	2,552.6	298	2,547.1	297	2,540.5	296	2,540.5	296	2,540.6	296	2,540.1	296
E06000047	County Durham	2,226	505.6	227	503.0	226	499.3	224	497.2	223	495.1	222	493.9	222	493.5	222	493.7	222
E06000005	Darlington	197	103.7	526	102.6	521	101.5	515	100.3	509	99.3	504	98.9	502	98.5	500	97.9	497
E06000001	Hartlepool	94	91.4	972	91.0	968	90.8	966	90.5	962	90.3	961	90.1	959	90.0	957	90.2	959
E06000002	Middlesbrough	54	137.9	2,553	138.2	2,559	138.2	2,559	138.5	2,565	138.5	2,564	139.1	2,575	140.1	2,594	141.2	2,615
E06000057	Northumberland	5,014	314.1	63	313.0	62	311.4	62	310.8	62	310.1	62	309.4	62	308.5	62	307.4	61
E06000003	Redcar and Cleveland	245	136.5	557	136.9	559	137.6	562	138.2	564	138.6	566	138.6	566	138.5	565	139.2	568
E06000004	Stockton-on-Tees	205	189.0	922	187.9	917	187.3	914	186.4	909	185.7	906	185.7	906	184.9	902	183.8	897
E11000007	Tyne and Wear (Met County)	540	1,091.1	2,021	1,089.5	2,018	1,086.5	2,012	1,085.4	2,010	1,082.8	2,005	1,084.7	2,009	1,086.5	2,012	1,086.8	2,013
E08000037	Gateshead	142	196.1	1,381	194.9	1,373	193.6	1,363	192.9	1,358	192.3	1,354	192.1	1,353	191.6	1,349	191.2	1,346
E08000021	Newcastle upon Tyne	113	271.6	2,404	271.6	2,403	270.3	2,392	269.6	2,386	266.9	2,362	266.9	2,362	267.0	2,363	266.2	2,356
E08000022	North Tyneside	82	198.0	2,414	196.5	2,396	195.4	2,383	194.1	2,367	193.2	2,356	193.0	2,354	192.7	2,350	192.0	2,342
E08000023	South Tyneside	64	148.6	2,322	148.6	2,323	148.9	2,326	149.6	2,337	150.3	2,348	151.2	2,362	152.2	2,378	152.8	2,387
E08000024	Sunderland	137	276.8	2,021	277.8	2,028	278.4	2,032	279.2	2,038	280.1	2,045	281.5	2,055	283.0	2,066	284.6	2,077
E12000002	NORTH WEST	14,107	6,958.5	493	6,929.3	491	6,901.6	489	6,870.0	487	6,840.4	485	6,814.7	483	6,784.9	481	6,773.0	480
E06000008	Blackburn with Darwen	137	144.9	1,058	143.9	1,051	143.1	1,045	142.1	1,038	141.4	1,032	140.4	1,025	139.5	1,019	138.5	1,011
E06000009	Blackpool	35	142.9	4,083	143.6	4,104	143.7	4,107	143.7	4,105	143.1	4,090	142.7	4,076	142.2	4,062	142.3	4,065
E06000049	Cheshire East	1,166	367.2	315	365.0	313	362.0	311	359.8	309	357.4	306	355.5	305	353.3	303	352.1	302
E06000050	Cheshire West and Chester	917	329.4	359	329.4	359	328.4	358	327.2	357	325.5	355	324.4	354	322.7	352	322.2	351
E06000006	Halton	79	122.9	1,556	122.0	1,545	121.3	1,535	120.4	1,524	120.0	1,518	119.2	1,509	118.8	1,504	118.6	1,501
E06000007	Warrington	181	198.2	1,095	196.6	1,086	194.6	1,075	193.0	1,066	191.8	1,060	192.0	1,061	191.6	1,059	191.2	1,056
E10000006	Cumbria	6,767	500.9	74	500.8	74	498.8	74	497.0	73	494.9	73	491.3	73	488.7	72	487.8	72
E07000026	Allerdale	1,242	96.2	77	95.9	77	95.3	77	95.0	77	94.8	76	94.6	76	93.8	76	93.5	75
E07000027	Barrow-in-Furness	78	69.8	895	70.0	898	70.3	901	70.5	904	70.8	908	70.9	909	71.3	915	72.0	923
E07000028	Carlisle	1,039	107.2	103	107.3	103	106.7	103	105.6	102	104.4	100	102.8	99	101.7	98	100.8	97
E07000029	Copeland	732	70.8	97	70.7	97	70.3	96	69.9	95	69.8	95	69.3	95	69.1	94	69.3	95
E07000030	Eden	2,142	52.4	24	52.2	24	51.9	24	51.7	24	51.4	24	50.9	24	50.3	23	49.9	23
E07000031	South Lakeland	1,534	104.5	68	104.7	68	104.3	68	104.3	68	103.7	68	102.9	67	102.4	67	102.4	67
E11000001	Greater Manchester (Met County)	1,276	2,620.0	2,053	2,598.6	2,037	2,582.3	2,024	2,564.1	2,009	2,549.8	1,998	2,538.6	1,989	2,523.2	1,977	2,516.1	1,972
E08000001	Bolton	140	270.5	1,932	268.3	1,917	266.8	1,906	265.0	1,893	264.5	1,889	263.8	1,884	262.4	1,874	261.3	1,866
E08000002	Bury	99	183.0	1,848	182.7	1,846	181.8	1,836	181.0	1,829	181.0	1,828	181.4	1,832	181.1	1,829	180.7	1,825
E08000003	Manchester	116	477.4	4,116	470.5	4,056	463.7	3,998	455.7	3,929	444.9	3,836	436.7	3,765	428.2	3,692	422.9	3,646
E08000004	Oldham	142	221.9	1,563	220.7	1,554	220.0	1,550	219.3	1,544	219.0	1,542	218.5	1,539	218.5	1,538	218.5	1,539

MYE5: Population estimates: Population density for the local authorities in the UK, mid-2001 to mid-2016

Abbreviation: Est. Pop. (Estimated Population)

Thousands

Code	Name	Area (sq km)	Est Pop: mid-2008	people /km²	Est Pop: mid-2007	people /km²	Est Pop: mid-2006	people /km²	Est Pop: mid-2005	people /km²	Est Pop: mid-2004	people /km²	Est Pop: mid-2003	people /km²	Est Pop: mid-2002	people /km²	Est Pop: mid-2001	people /km²
E08000005	Rochdale	158	209.7	1,327	208.4	1,319	207.8	1,315	207.2	1,311	207.3	1,312	207.5	1,313	206.7	1,308	206.4	1,307
E08000006	Salford	97	226.8	2,338	223.5	2,304	221.9	2,288	219.5	2,263	217.9	2,247	217.3	2,240	216.3	2,230	217.0	2,237
E08000007	Stockport	126	281.5	2,234	281.0	2,230	280.5	2,226	281.2	2,232	282.4	2,241	282.9	2,245	283.5	2,250	284.6	2,258
E08000008	Tameside	103	216.4	2,101	214.8	2,085	214.2	2,079	213.5	2,073	213.7	2,074	213.5	2,073	213.2	2,070	213.1	2,069
E08000009	Trafford	106	220.9	2,084	219.4	2,069	217.4	2,051	215.4	2,032	214.1	2,020	213.0	2,010	211.1	1,991	210.2	1,983
E08000010	Wigan	188	312.0	1,659	309.4	1,646	308.0	1,638	306.1	1,628	305.0	1,622	303.8	1,616	302.3	1,608	301.5	1,603
E10000017	Lancashire	2,903	1,163.4	401	1,161.8	400	1,159.1	399	1,154.3	398	1,149.5	396	1,144.6	394	1,138.4	392	1,136.5	392
E07000117	Burnley	111	87.3	787	87.3	786	87.6	790	87.6	789	87.9	792	88.3	795	88.8	800	89.5	806
E07000118	Chorley	203	105.4	519	104.4	514	103.8	511	103.3	509	102.8	506	102.0	502	101.1	498	100.6	495
E07000119	Fylde	166	75.2	453	75.3	454	74.8	451	74.8	451	74.7	450	74.2	447	73.7	444	73.3	442
E07000120	Hyndburn	73	81.2	1,112	81.5	1,116	81.5	1,116	81.3	1,114	81.3	1,113	81.4	1,115	81.2	1,113	81.5	1,116
E07000121	Lancaster	576	135.8	236	136.2	237	136.7	237	136.8	237	135.5	235	134.6	234	133.6	232	134.0	233
E07000122	Pendle	169	89.0	527	88.8	526	88.8	525	88.3	523	88.3	523	88.6	524	88.8	526	89.3	528
E07000123	Preston	142	138.4	975	138.5	975	137.8	970	136.2	959	134.4	947	132.7	934	131.1	923	130.4	918
E07000124	Ribble Valley	583	57.2	98	57.0	98	56.7	97	56.4	97	56.1	96	55.4	95	54.7	94	54.1	93
E07000125	Rossendale	138	67.1	486	66.6	483	66.2	480	65.9	477	65.6	476	65.7	476	65.6	475	65.6	476
E07000126	South Ribble	113	107.8	954	107.1	948	106.5	943	105.8	936	105.6	934	105.1	931	104.5	925	103.9	920
E07000127	West Lancashire	347	110.7	319	110.7	319	110.3	318	109.8	316	109.6	316	109.3	315	108.8	313	108.5	313
E07000128	Wyre	282	108.2	382	108.5	383	108.4	383	108.2	382	107.8	381	107.2	379	106.4	376	105.8	374
E11000002	Merseyside (Met County)	647	1,368.8	2,122	1,367.5	2,120	1,368.2	2,121	1,368.4	2,122	1,367.0	2,119	1,366.0	2,118	1,366.5	2,119	1,367.8	2,121
E08000011	Knowsley	87	147.8	1,699	148.2	1,703	148.8	1,710	148.9	1,711	149.2	1,715	149.8	1,722	150.5	1,730	151.2	1,738
E08000012	Liverpool	112	454.5	4,058	453.6	4,050	453.1	4,045	452.3	4,038	448.1	4,001	445.0	3,973	443.8	3,962	441.9	3,945
E08000014	Sefton	155	274.7	1,796	275.1	1,798	275.9	1,803	277.0	1,810	278.9	1,823	279.9	1,829	280.9	1,836	282.9	1,849
E08000013	St. Helens	136	175.1	1,288	175.0	1,287	175.2	1,288	175.4	1,289	175.7	1,292	176.0	1,294	176.3	1,296	176.8	1,300
E08000015	Wirral	157	316.7	2,017	315.7	2,011	315.4	2,009	314.9	2,006	315.1	2,007	315.4	2,009	315.1	2,007	315.0	2,006
E12000003	**YORKSHIRE AND THE HUMBER**	15,405	5,198.7	337	5,164.1	335	5,134.0	333	5,108.4	332	5,063.2	329	5,026.3	326	5,000.1	325	4,976.6	323
E06000011	East Riding of Yorkshire	2,405	332.5	138	330.9	138	328.6	137	327.3	136	325.1	135	321.9	134	318.6	132	314.9	131
E06000010	Kingston upon Hull, City of	71	256.7	3,616	255.8	3,602	255.5	3,599	255.2	3,594	253.0	3,564	250.6	3,530	249.5	3,514	249.9	3,520
E06000012	North East Lincolnshire	192	158.7	827	158.6	826	158.6	826	158.7	827	158.5	826	158.4	825	158.0	823	158.0	823
E06000013	North Lincolnshire	846	164.5	194	162.8	192	161.2	191	159.7	189	158.2	187	156.2	185	154.2	182	153.0	181
E06000014	York	272	190.8	701	189.8	698	189.0	695	188.2	692	186.6	686	184.0	676	182.1	669	181.3	667
E10000023	North Yorkshire	8,038	595.0	74	591.2	74	587.3	73	584.0	73	580.0	72	576.1	72	573.2	71	570.1	71
E07000163	Craven	1,177	55.6	47	55.4	47	55.1	47	54.9	47	54.4	46	54.1	46	53.8	46	53.7	46
E07000164	Hambleton	1,311	88.5	67	87.7	67	87.0	66	86.0	66	85.6	65	85.3	65	84.8	65	84.2	64
E07000165	Harrogate	1,308	155.8	119	155.1	119	154.3	118	153.7	117	152.5	117	151.8	116	151.5	116	151.5	116
E07000166	Richmondshire	1,319	52.1	40	51.6	39	51.0	39	50.4	38	49.4	37	48.5	37	47.8	36	47.1	36
E07000167	Ryedale	1,507	52.1	35	52.1	35	51.9	34	51.9	34	51.6	34	51.2	34	50.8	34	50.9	34

MYE5: Population estimates: Population density for the local authorities in the UK, mid-2001 to mid-2016

Abbreviation: Est. Pop. (Estimated Population)

Code	Name	Area (sq km)	2008 Est Pop: mid-2008	2008 people /km²	2007 Est Pop: mid-2007	2007 people /km²	2006 Est Pop: mid-2006	2006 people /km²	2005 Est Pop: mid-2005	2005 people /km²	2004 Est Pop: mid-2004	2004 people /km²	2003 Est Pop: mid-2003	2003 people /km²	2002 Est Pop: mid-2002	2002 people /km²	2001 Est Pop: mid-2001	2001 people /km²
E07000168	Scarborough	816	109.0	133	108.8	133	108.7	133	108.8	133	108.5	133	107.9	132	107.2	131	106.2	130
E07000169	Selby	599	81.8	137	80.5	134	79.4	132	78.4	131	77.9	130	77.4	129	77.1	129	76.6	128
E11000003	South Yorkshire (Met County)	1,552	1,315.4	848	1,306.3	842	1,299.7	837	1,293.2	833	1,283.4	827	1,276.5	822	1,271.3	819	1,266.5	816
E08000016	Barnsley	329	227.8	692	226.0	687	224.4	682	222.6	677	221.2	672	220.2	669	218.9	665	218.1	663
E08000017	Doncaster	568	298.4	525	296.2	522	294.0	518	292.2	514	290.9	512	290.1	511	288.6	508	286.9	505
E08000018	Rotherham	287	255.3	889	254.2	886	253.6	884	252.7	880	251.7	877	250.9	874	249.6	870	248.3	865
E08000019	Sheffield	368	534.0	1,451	529.9	1,440	527.6	1,434	525.7	1,429	519.6	1,412	515.3	1,400	514.2	1,397	513.1	1,394
E11000006	West Yorkshire (Met County)	2,029	2,185.0	1,077	2,168.8	1,069	2,154.2	1,062	2,142.2	1,056	2,118.2	1,044	2,102.7	1,036	2,093.2	1,032	2,083.1	1,027
E08000032	Bradford	366	507.3	1,386	501.4	1,370	495.7	1,354	491.4	1,343	484.7	1,324	479.2	1,309	475.2	1,298	470.8	1,286
E08000033	Calderdale	364	201.0	552	199.3	547	197.8	543	196.3	539	195.0	536	194.0	533	193.2	531	192.4	529
E08000034	Kirklees	409	411.8	1,007	408.0	997	404.3	988	400.7	980	397.5	972	394.5	965	392.1	959	389.0	951
E08000035	Leeds	552	741.7	1,344	738.6	1,338	736.2	1,334	735.1	1,332	723.0	1,310	717.6	1,300	716.4	1,298	715.6	1,296
E08000036	Wakefield	339	323.3	954	321.7	949	320.3	945	318.8	940	318.0	938	317.5	936	316.3	933	315.4	930
E12000004	EAST MIDLANDS	15,623	4,441.1	284	4,404.8	282	4,366.7	280	4,329.1	277	4,291.5	275	4,255.1	272	4,221.8	270	4,189.6	268
E06000015	Derby	78	241.9	3,101	239.9	3,076	238.1	3,053	236.5	3,032	234.5	3,006	232.8	2,985	232.0	2,974	230.7	2,958
E06000016	Leicester	73	315.5	4,322	311.3	4,264	306.5	4,199	301.5	4,131	294.1	4,029	288.6	3,954	285.3	3,908	282.8	3,873
E06000018	Nottingham	75	290.8	3,877	288.2	3,842	286.5	3,819	284.8	3,798	279.6	3,728	275.5	3,674	271.8	3,624	268.9	3,586
E06000017	Rutland	382	37.5	98	37.1	97	36.5	96	36.1	95	35.6	93	35.6	93	35.3	92	34.6	91
E10000007	Derbyshire	2,547	761.2	299	756.6	297	752.6	296	749.0	294	745.5	293	742.2	291	738.4	290	734.9	289
E07000032	Amber Valley	265	121.2	457	120.4	454	120.0	453	119.2	450	118.4	447	117.9	445	117.3	443	116.6	440
E07000033	Bolsover	160	75.1	469	74.8	468	74.3	465	73.8	462	73.6	460	73.3	458	72.5	453	71.9	449
E07000034	Chesterfield	66	102.6	1,555	102.0	1,546	101.7	1,541	101.3	1,535	100.5	1,523	99.9	1,514	99.3	1,504	98.8	1,497
E07000035	Derbyshire Dales	792	70.5	89	69.9	88	69.5	88	69.5	88	69.5	88	69.4	88	69.4	88	69.4	88
E07000036	Erewash	110	110.8	1,007	110.2	1,002	110.0	1,000	110.1	1,001	110.1	1,001	110.1	1,001	110.3	1,002	110.1	1,001
E07000037	High Peak	539	90.9	169	90.6	168	90.1	167	89.6	166	89.3	166	89.2	165	89.3	166	89.4	166
E07000038	North East Derbyshire	276	98.3	356	98.1	355	97.7	354	97.7	354	97.5	353	97.1	352	96.9	351	96.9	351
E07000039	South Derbyshire	338	92.0	272	90.7	268	89.3	264	87.8	260	86.5	256	85.3	252	83.5	247	81.7	242
E10000018	Leicestershire	2,083	639.2	307	634.6	305	629.6	302	624.9	300	622.1	299	618.0	297	614.1	295	610.3	293
E07000129	Blaby	130	93.3	718	92.7	713	92.3	710	91.7	706	91.7	705	91.6	705	91.2	702	90.4	695
E07000130	Charnwood	279	160.5	575	158.7	569	157.2	563	155.8	558	154.7	555	153.7	551	153.4	550	153.6	550
E07000131	Harborough	592	83.4	141	82.6	140	81.5	138	80.5	136	79.9	135	79.1	134	78.2	132	76.8	130
E07000132	Hinckley and Bosworth	297	104.2	351	103.5	348	103.0	347	102.4	345	102.0	343	101.2	341	100.5	338	100.2	337
E07000133	Melton	481	49.3	102	49.2	102	48.7	101	48.6	101	48.6	101	48.4	101	48.1	100	47.9	100
E07000134	North West Leicestershire	279	92.3	331	91.5	328	90.4	324	89.6	321	88.8	318	87.8	315	86.8	311	85.7	307
E07000135	Oadby and Wigston	24	56.2	2,343	56.5	2,353	56.5	2,355	56.2	2,342	56.5	2,352	56.2	2,340	55.8	2,324	55.8	2,325
E10000019	Lincolnshire	5,937	700.8	118	693.7	117	685.4	115	677.3	114	672.4	113	663.2	112	655.6	110	647.6	109
E07000136	Boston	365	62.2	170	61.0	167	59.8	164	58.6	160	58.1	159	57.0	156	56.4	154	55.8	153

MYE5: Population estimates: Population density for the local authorities in the UK, mid-2001 to mid-2016

Abbreviation: Est. Pop. (Estimated Population)

Thousands

Code	Name	Area (sq km)	Est Pop: mid-2008	people /km²	Est Pop: mid-2007	people /km²	Est Pop: mid-2006	people /km²	Est Pop: mid-2005	people /km²	Est Pop: mid-2004	people /km²	Est Pop: mid-2003	people /km²	Est Pop: mid-2002	people /km²	Est Pop: mid-2001	people /km²
E07000137	East Lindsey	1,765	137.5	78	136.9	78	136.0	77	135.5	77	134.9	76	133.2	75	132.1	75	130.7	74
E07000138	Lincoln	36	90.2	2,506	89.9	2,496	89.4	2,484	88.6	2,461	87.7	2,437	86.4	2,400	85.7	2,380	85.6	2,377
E07000139	North Kesteven	922	105.5	114	103.8	113	102.3	111	100.7	109	99.9	108	98.6	107	96.9	105	94.4	102
E07000140	South Holland	751	86.0	114	84.5	113	83.2	111	81.7	109	80.8	108	79.3	106	77.9	104	76.7	102
E07000141	South Kesteven	943	131.2	139	130.2	138	129.0	137	127.7	135	127.1	135	126.2	134	125.5	133	124.9	132
E07000142	West Lindsey	1,156	88.3	76	87.3	76	85.9	74	84.6	73	83.8	72	82.5	71	81.1	70	79.6	69
E10000021	Northamptonshire	2,364	678.2	287	672.1	284	663.6	281	654.5	277	646.6	274	642.7	272	636.8	269	631.0	267
E07000150	Corby	80	57.9	724	56.8	710	55.4	693	54.5	681	53.8	672	53.5	669	53.4	668	53.4	668
E07000151	Daventry	663	77.1	116	77.0	116	76.5	115	75.7	114	75.1	113	74.7	113	73.3	111	72.0	109
E07000152	East Northamptonshire	510	85.6	168	84.8	166	83.3	163	81.9	161	80.9	159	79.9	157	78.1	153	76.8	151
E07000153	Kettering	233	91.2	391	89.9	386	88.0	378	86.6	372	85.6	368	84.6	363	83.2	357	82.3	353
E07000154	Northampton	81	205.6	2,538	203.0	2,506	200.4	2,474	196.8	2,430	194.7	2,404	194.8	2,405	194.4	2,401	194.4	2,399
E07000155	South Northamptonshire	634	85.8	135	85.9	136	85.5	135	84.9	134	83.3	131	82.2	130	81.3	128	79.5	125
E07000156	Wellingborough	163	75.1	461	74.7	459	74.5	457	74.0	454	73.2	449	73.0	448	73.0	448	72.5	445
E10000024	Nottinghamshire	2,085	776.1	372	771.3	370	767.8	368	764.5	367	761.0	365	756.4	363	752.6	361	748.8	359
E07000170	Ashfield	110	117.0	1,063	116.3	1,057	115.7	1,052	115.0	1,046	114.1	1,037	113.0	1,028	112.5	1,023	111.5	1,013
E07000171	Bassetlaw	638	112.1	176	111.3	174	110.9	174	110.5	173	110.0	172	109.3	171	108.5	170	107.8	169
E07000172	Broxtowe	80	108.7	1,359	108.3	1,353	108.3	1,353	108.3	1,354	108.1	1,351	107.8	1,348	107.8	1,348	107.5	1,344
E07000173	Gedling	120	112.3	936	111.9	933	111.7	931	111.9	933	111.8	932	111.7	931	111.9	933	111.8	932
E07000174	Mansfield	77	103.3	1,341	102.1	1,326	101.3	1,316	100.4	1,304	99.7	1,295	99.3	1,289	98.4	1,277	98.1	1,274
E07000175	Newark and Sherwood	651	113.3	174	112.5	173	111.5	171	110.6	170	109.8	169	108.4	166	107.0	164	106.4	163
E07000176	Rushcliffe	409	109.4	267	108.9	266	108.4	265	107.8	264	107.4	263	107.0	262	106.5	261	105.8	259
E12000005	**WEST MIDLANDS**	12,998	5,496.2	423	5,451.9	419	5,415.5	417	5,380.7	414	5,346.4	411	5,325.5	410	5,301.2	408	5,280.7	406
E06000019	Herefordshire, County of	2,180	181.8	83	179.9	83	178.1	82	176.6	81	176.0	81	175.6	81	175.3	80	174.9	80
E06000051	Shropshire	3,197	300.5	94	297.6	93	294.5	92	291.5	91	288.8	90	286.9	90	284.9	89	283.3	89
E06000021	Stoke-on-Trent	93	245.5	2,640	243.7	2,620	243.1	2,614	241.5	2,597	241.1	2,592	240.0	2,581	240.0	2,580	240.4	2,585
E06000020	Telford and Wrekin	290	164.1	566	163.4	563	162.7	561	161.5	557	160.6	554	159.8	551	159.4	550	158.6	547
E10000028	Staffordshire	2,620	838.1	320	833.1	318	827.3	316	822.7	314	818.6	312	815.2	311	810.2	309	807.2	308
E07000192	Cannock Chase	79	96.0	1,215	95.4	1,207	95.0	1,202	94.8	1,200	94.2	1,192	93.8	1,187	93.0	1,177	92.2	1,167
E07000193	East Staffordshire	387	111.2	287	109.8	284	108.5	280	107.6	278	106.8	276	106.1	274	104.5	270	103.9	269
E07000194	Lichfield	331	99.5	301	98.5	298	97.4	294	96.3	291	95.6	289	94.5	285	93.7	283	93.2	282
E07000195	Newcastle-under-Lyme	211	123.2	584	123.5	585	123.2	584	123.2	584	123.1	583	122.7	581	122.2	579	122.0	578
E07000196	South Staffordshire	407	107.5	264	107.1	263	106.7	262	106.4	261	106.3	261	106.3	261	106.0	260	105.9	260
E07000197	Stafford	598	128.3	215	127.1	212	125.6	210	124.4	208	123.2	206	122.4	205	121.4	203	120.7	202
E07000198	Staffordshire Moorlands	576	96.6	168	96.3	167	95.9	166	95.3	166	95.0	165	95.0	165	94.9	165	94.6	164
E07000199	Tamworth	31	75.8	2,446	75.4	2,432	75.1	2,422	74.7	2,410	74.4	2,401	74.5	2,405	74.5	2,404	74.6	2,406
E10000031	Warwickshire	1,975	539.4	273	534.4	271	529.1	268	523.7	265	518.6	263	515.1	261	510.7	259	506.2	256

MYE5: Population estimates: Population density for the local authorities in the UK, mid-2001 to mid-2016

Abbreviation: Est. Pop. (Estimated Population)

Thousands

Code	Name	Area (sq km)	Est Pop: mid-2001	people /km²	Est Pop: mid-2002	people /km²	Est Pop: mid-2003	people /km²	Est Pop: mid-2004	people /km²	Est Pop: mid-2005	people /km²	Est Pop: mid-2006	people /km²	Est Pop: mid-2007	people /km²	Est Pop: mid-2008	people /km²
E07000218	North Warwickshire	284	61.8	218	61.8	218	61.7	217	61.8	217	61.9	218	61.9	218	61.8	218	62.0	218
E07000219	Nuneaton and Bedworth	79	119.2	1,509	119.6	1,514	120.5	1,526	120.7	1,527	121.0	1,532	121.8	1,542	122.7	1,553	123.9	1,568
E07000220	Rugby	351	87.5	249	88.7	253	89.1	254	90.0	256	91.3	260	93.1	265	94.7	270	96.4	275
E07000221	Stratford-on-Avon	978	111.6	114	112.3	115	113.0	116	113.5	116	114.8	117	116.7	119	118.5	121	119.7	122
E07000222	Warwick	283	126.1	446	128.3	453	130.7	462	132.7	469	134.6	476	135.6	479	136.7	483	137.4	486
E11000005	West Midlands (Met County)	902	2,568.0	2,847	2,576.4	2,856	2,585.5	2,866	2,594.0	2,876	2,611.9	2,896	2,626.0	2,911	2,641.8	2,929	2,666.1	2,956
E08000025	Birmingham	268	984.6	3,674	990.4	3,695	996.4	3,718	1,002.4	3,740	1,014.7	3,786	1,020.8	3,809	1,029.0	3,840	1,039.0	3,877
E08000026	Coventry	99	302.8	3,059	301.3	3,043	300.7	3,037	298.2	3,012	298.4	3,014	300.1	3,032	301.4	3,045	305.2	3,083
E08000027	Dudley	98	305.1	3,113	305.6	3,119	305.6	3,118	306.2	3,124	307.0	3,133	307.8	3,141	308.7	3,150	310.4	3,167
E08000028	Sandwell	86	284.6	3,309	285.6	3,321	287.1	3,339	288.8	3,359	290.4	3,377	292.5	3,401	294.6	3,426	298.4	3,469
E08000029	Solihull	178	199.6	1,121	200.0	1,124	200.5	1,127	201.2	1,130	201.6	1,132	202.4	1,137	203.2	1,141	204.8	1,150
E08000030	Walsall	104	253.3	2,436	254.3	2,445	255.4	2,455	256.7	2,468	258.2	2,482	259.5	2,495	260.9	2,509	263.0	2,529
E08000031	Wolverhampton	69	238.0	3,450	239.1	3,465	239.9	3,476	240.6	3,486	241.6	3,502	242.9	3,520	243.9	3,535	245.3	3,556
E10000034	Worcestershire	1,741	542.2	311	544.5	313	547.3	314	548.7	315	551.3	317	554.7	319	558.0	321	560.8	322
E07000234	Bromsgrove	217	87.9	405	89.0	410	90.0	415	90.5	417	91.0	420	91.7	423	92.6	427	93.1	429
E07000235	Malvern Hills	577	72.2	125	72.7	126	72.9	126	73.2	127	73.4	127	73.7	128	74.0	128	74.2	129
E07000236	Redditch	54	78.8	1,459	79.1	1,464	79.5	1,472	79.7	1,475	80.1	1,484	81.1	1,501	81.8	1,514	82.7	1,532
E07000237	Worcester	33	93.4	2,829	93.4	2,832	93.9	2,845	93.8	2,844	94.5	2,863	95.0	2,880	95.5	2,895	96.4	2,922
E07000238	Wychavon	664	113.1	170	113.5	171	113.9	172	114.3	172	114.7	173	115.5	174	116.1	175	116.2	175
E07000239	Wyre Forest	195	96.9	497	96.8	497	97.1	498	97.2	499	97.6	500	97.7	501	98.0	503	98.1	503
E12000006	**EAST**	19,119	5,400.5	282	5,432.7	284	5,474.1	286	5,508.6	288	5,562.7	291	5,606.3	293	5,653.5	296	5,708.4	299
E06000055	Bedford	476	148.1	311	149.6	314	150.7	317	151.3	318	151.7	319	152.3	320	153.1	322	154.2	324
E06000056	Central Bedfordshire	716	234.0	327	236.3	330	238.5	333	240.4	336	242.1	338	244.4	341	246.8	345	249.0	348
E06000032	Luton	43	185.9	4,323	185.6	4,317	185.0	4,303	183.6	4,269	185.4	4,311	187.3	4,356	189.7	4,413	192.1	4,467
E06000031	Peterborough	343	157.4	459	158.8	463	160.8	469	163.5	477	167.2	488	169.9	495	172.4	503	176.0	513
E06000033	Southend-on-Sea	42	160.4	3,818	161.2	3,837	161.4	3,844	161.5	3,845	162.6	3,873	163.8	3,899	165.4	3,939	168.2	4,004
E06000034	Thurrock	163	143.3	879	144.7	888	146.0	896	147.1	902	148.6	911	150.2	922	151.7	931	153.6	943
E10000003	Cambridgeshire	3,046	554.7	182	558.9	183	568.7	187	574.4	189	583.7	192	588.9	193	594.3	195	600.8	197
E07000008	Cambridge	41	109.9	2,681	109.5	2,672	111.3	2,715	112.2	2,736	117.2	2,859	116.7	2,845	115.5	2,816	116.2	2,834
E07000009	East Cambridgeshire	651	73.4	113	74.3	114	77.4	119	76.0	117	77.2	119	78.4	120	79.9	123	81.0	124
E07000010	Fenland	546	83.7	153	84.7	155	86.3	158	88.0	161	89.0	163	90.6	166	92.7	170	93.7	172
E07000011	Huntingdonshire	906	157.2	173	158.5	175	159.6	176	162.7	180	162.8	180	163.9	181	164.8	182	166.3	184
E07000012	South Cambridgeshire	902	130.5	145	131.9	146	134.1	149	135.6	150	137.4	152	139.3	154	141.5	157	143.6	159
E10000012	Essex	3,464	1,312.6	379	1,319.1	381	1,326.1	383	1,334.6	385	1,345.2	388	1,354.3	391	1,362.9	393	1,373.2	396
E07000066	Basildon	110	165.9	1,508	166.7	1,516	167.1	1,519	167.8	1,526	168.9	1,536	170.0	1,545	170.9	1,554	172.4	1,567
E07000067	Braintree	612	132.5	216	134.3	219	135.8	222	137.4	225	139.2	227	140.9	230	142.3	233	143.9	235
E07000068	Brentwood	153	68.5	448	68.8	450	69.2	453	69.9	457	70.5	461	71.0	464	71.3	466	71.9	470

MYE5: Population estimates: Population density for the local authorities in the UK, mid-2001 to mid-2016

Abbreviation: Est. Pop. (Estimated Population)

Thousands

Code	Name	Area (sq km)	Est Pop: mid-2001	people /km² (2001)	Est Pop: mid-2002	people /km² (2002)	Est Pop: mid-2003	people /km² (2003)	Est Pop: mid-2004	people /km² (2004)	Est Pop: mid-2005	people /km² (2005)	Est Pop: mid-2006	people /km² (2006)	Est Pop: mid-2007	people /km² (2007)	Est Pop: mid-2008	people /km² (2008)
E07000069	Castle Point	45	86.7	1,926	86.9	1,930	87.2	1,939	87.2	1,938	87.5	1,944	87.6	1,946	87.8	1,951	88.0	1,956
E07000070	Chelmsford	339	157.3	464	158.7	468	160.4	473	162.5	479	163.6	483	163.9	483	164.4	485	165.0	487
E07000071	Colchester	329	156.0	474	156.1	474	157.2	478	158.7	482	162.0	493	163.8	498	165.7	504	167.9	510
E07000072	Epping Forest	339	121.0	357	121.5	358	121.4	358	121.5	358	121.7	359	122.5	361	122.9	362	123.4	364
E07000073	Harlow	31	78.8	2,542	78.3	2,527	78.1	2,520	78.0	2,517	78.4	2,528	78.7	2,539	79.2	2,554	79.9	2,578
E07000074	Maldon	359	59.6	166	59.8	166	60.0	167	60.3	168	60.7	169	61.0	170	61.4	171	61.7	172
E07000075	Rochford	169	78.7	465	79.3	469	79.5	470	80.1	474	80.8	478	81.5	482	82.3	487	83.1	491
E07000076	Tendring	338	138.8	411	139.3	412	139.9	414	140.3	415	140.3	415	140.4	415	140.5	416	140.4	415
E07000077	Uttlesford	641	69.0	108	69.5	108	70.3	110	70.9	111	71.6	112	72.9	114	74.2	116	75.5	118
E10000015	Hertfordshire	1,643	1,035.5	630	1,040.4	633	1,045.3	636	1,047.4	637	1,055.5	642	1,063.2	647	1,073.0	653	1,085.4	661
E07000095	Broxbourne	51	87.2	1,710	87.7	1,720	87.8	1,722	87.8	1,722	88.8	1,741	89.7	1,759	90.8	1,781	91.6	1,797
E07000096	Dacorum	212	137.8	650	138.1	652	138.4	653	138.4	653	138.6	654	139.0	656	139.5	658	140.8	664
E07000242	East Hertfordshire	476	129.1	271	130.0	273	130.3	274	130.5	274	131.1	275	132.1	277	133.4	280	134.8	283
E07000098	Hertsmere	101	94.5	935	94.3	934	94.4	935	93.8	929	94.3	934	95.2	943	96.3	953	97.6	967
E07000099	North Hertfordshire	375	117.1	312	118.0	315	119.1	318	120.1	320	120.8	322	121.9	325	123.0	328	124.4	332
E07000240	St Albans	161	129.2	802	130.4	810	131.2	815	131.3	815	132.0	820	133.3	828	134.3	834	136.1	845
E07000243	Stevenage	26	79.8	3,069	80.1	3,081	80.3	3,089	80.0	3,077	80.3	3,090	80.4	3,090	80.7	3,105	81.6	3,139
E07000102	Three Rivers	89	82.9	932	83.4	938	83.9	943	84.0	943	84.3	947	84.5	949	85.3	958	86.2	969
E07000103	Watford	21	80.4	3,828	80.2	3,818	80.6	3,840	81.1	3,862	82.1	3,911	82.1	3,912	82.9	3,948	84.8	4,037
E07000241	Welwyn Hatfield	130	97.6	750	98.1	755	99.2	763	100.5	773	103.2	794	105.1	808	106.7	821	107.4	826
E10000020	Norfolk	5,380	798.6	148	803.5	149	810.1	151	815.7	152	822.9	153	829.1	154	834.9	155	841.5	156
E07000143	Breckland	1,305	121.6	93	122.2	94	123.2	94	123.9	95	125.5	96	126.6	97	127.8	98	128.9	99
E07000144	Broadland	552	118.8	215	119.4	216	120.3	218	121.0	219	121.6	220	122.4	222	123.2	223	123.4	224
E07000145	Great Yarmouth	174	90.9	523	91.4	526	92.5	532	93.3	536	94.1	541	94.5	543	95.2	547	95.9	551
E07000146	King's Lynn and West Norfolk	1,439	135.6	94	136.8	95	138.3	96	139.6	97	141.0	98	142.8	99	144.3	100	145.6	101
E07000147	North Norfolk	962	98.5	102	98.7	103	99.1	103	99.4	103	99.6	103	99.9	104	100.3	104	100.9	105
E07000148	Norwich	39	122.4	3,138	122.4	3,138	123.0	3,153	123.9	3,176	125.6	3,221	126.8	3,251	126.9	3,255	128.0	3,283
E07000149	South Norfolk	908	110.8	122	112.5	124	113.7	125	114.5	126	115.4	127	116.1	128	117.1	129	118.8	131
E10000029	Suffolk	3,801	669.9	176	674.6	177	681.4	179	689.1	181	697.8	184	703.0	185	709.1	187	714.3	188
E07000200	Babergh	594	83.5	141	84.1	142	85.1	143	85.6	144	86.0	145	86.7	146	86.9	146	87.3	147
E07000201	Forest Heath	378	56.1	149	56.5	149	57.3	152	57.3	152	58.1	154	57.6	152	57.5	152	57.5	152
E07000202	Ipswich	40	117.2	3,004	117.8	3,021	119.2	3,057	121.2	3,107	124.0	3,180	124.8	3,199	125.5	3,217	127.4	3,266
E07000203	Mid Suffolk	871	87.0	100	87.7	101	88.3	101	89.5	103	90.8	104	92.1	106	93.8	108	94.6	109
E07000204	St Edmundsbury	657	98.3	150	99.5	151	100.7	153	102.2	156	103.3	157	104.9	160	106.1	162	107.5	164
E07000205	Suffolk Coastal	892	115.2	129	115.7	130	116.8	131	118.2	133	119.6	134	121.0	136	123.0	138	123.8	139
E07000206	Waveney	370	112.5	304	113.2	306	114.0	308	115.1	311	116.0	314	116.0	314	116.2	314	116.3	314

MYE5: Population estimates: Population density for the local authorities in the UK, mid-2001 to mid-2016

Abbreviation: Est. Pop. (Estimated Population)

Code	Name	Area (sq km)	Est Pop: mid-2001	people /km²	Est Pop: mid-2002	people /km²	Est Pop: mid-2003	people /km²	Est Pop: mid-2004	people /km²	Est Pop: mid-2005	people /km²	Est Pop: mid-2006	people /km²	Est Pop: mid-2007	people /km²	Est Pop: mid-2008	people /km²
E12000007	LONDON	1,572	7,322.4	4,658	7,376.7	4,693	7,394.8	4,704	7,432.7	4,728	7,519.0	4,783	7,597.8	4,833	7,693.5	4,894	7,812.2	4,970
E09000007	Camden	22	202.6	9,208	204.0	9,271	204.3	9,284	207.3	9,425	211.1	9,595	211.0	9,592	211.5	9,615	210.3	9,558
E09000001	City of London	3	7.4	2,453	7.3	2,427	7.1	2,372	7.1	2,373	7.1	2,377	7.3	2,418	7.6	2,536	7.4	2,476
E09000012	Hackney	19	207.2	10,908	211.0	11,103	212.4	11,179	213.6	11,241	216.5	11,395	220.2	11,589	224.5	11,815	231.0	12,160
E09000013	Hammersmith and Fulham	16	169.4	10,586	172.0	10,749	171.5	10,719	172.1	10,755	173.3	10,831	174.7	10,917	176.5	11,030	177.1	11,068
E09000014	Haringey	30	221.3	7,375	224.5	7,482	225.0	7,501	226.5	7,549	229.3	7,642	233.2	7,772	236.8	7,893	244.5	8,149
E09000019	Islington	15	179.4	11,959	180.1	12,008	180.9	12,060	180.8	12,055	183.5	12,232	185.3	12,352	188.6	12,576	192.1	12,806
E09000020	Kensington and Chelsea	12	162.2	13,517	163.8	13,652	165.3	13,772	165.8	13,813	168.4	14,031	165.2	13,770	162.9	13,574	162.6	13,548
E09000022	Lambeth	27	273.4	10,125	273.0	10,113	272.2	10,081	274.3	10,158	277.6	10,282	280.5	10,390	285.0	10,554	289.1	10,708
E09000023	Lewisham	35	254.3	7,267	253.7	7,247	251.9	7,198	252.5	7,213	254.9	7,284	258.0	7,371	261.2	7,463	266.5	7,615
E09000025	Newham	36	249.4	6,928	255.3	7,091	256.2	7,117	254.4	7,068	253.8	7,050	258.0	7,167	266.3	7,397	276.5	7,680
E09000028	Southwark	29	256.7	8,852	256.3	8,837	255.2	8,801	257.3	8,871	261.8	9,028	267.6	9,226	272.6	9,401	277.0	9,551
E09000030	Tower Hamlets	20	201.1	10,055	207.0	10,352	208.7	10,433	211.2	10,558	213.4	10,669	218.4	10,920	225.3	11,263	231.9	11,595
E09000032	Wandsworth	34	271.7	7,992	274.9	8,086	276.8	8,142	278.6	8,195	283.2	8,330	287.5	8,457	291.4	8,572	294.3	8,656
E09000033	Westminster	21	203.3	9,682	208.1	9,910	211.0	10,048	214.6	10,217	223.1	10,625	222.8	10,611	220.6	10,506	218.7	10,413
E09000002	Barking and Dagenham	36	165.7	4,602	166.4	4,621	166.2	4,617	165.6	4,600	166.3	4,619	167.2	4,643	169.0	4,695	172.5	4,790
E09000003	Barnet	87	319.5	3,672	320.6	3,685	321.8	3,699	323.7	3,721	327.5	3,765	330.8	3,802	334.8	3,849	339.2	3,899
E09000004	Bexley	61	218.8	3,586	219.1	3,592	220.0	3,607	220.9	3,622	222.4	3,646	223.3	3,660	224.6	3,682	226.7	3,716
E09000005	Brent	43	269.6	6,270	269.9	6,276	268.3	6,240	268.3	6,240	270.9	6,301	276.5	6,430	283.3	6,588	290.9	6,765
E09000006	Bromley	150	296.2	1,975	296.7	1,978	297.3	1,982	297.3	1,982	299.4	1,996	301.0	2,006	302.6	2,018	305.0	2,033
E09000008	Croydon	86	335.1	3,897	335.4	3,900	335.9	3,906	337.1	3,920	339.1	3,942	340.4	3,959	344.0	4,000	349.3	4,062
E09000009	Ealing	56	307.3	5,487	309.2	5,522	308.1	5,502	310.1	5,537	312.8	5,585	315.3	5,631	318.7	5,691	324.0	5,786
E09000010	Enfield	81	277.3	3,423	280.7	3,466	281.8	3,479	282.2	3,484	284.8	3,516	287.4	3,549	291.5	3,599	297.4	3,672
E09000011	Greenwich	47	217.5	4,627	221.5	4,712	224.3	4,772	227.2	4,834	230.5	4,904	234.0	4,979	236.5	5,033	239.7	5,101
E09000015	Harrow	50	210.0	4,201	212.3	4,247	213.7	4,275	216.3	4,325	221.1	4,422	223.6	4,473	226.4	4,527	229.6	4,591
E09000016	Havering	112	224.7	2,006	225.1	2,009	225.2	2,011	225.8	2,016	227.0	2,027	228.2	2,037	229.8	2,052	231.8	2,070
E09000017	Hillingdon	116	245.6	2,117	247.1	2,130	248.1	2,138	248.7	2,144	251.4	2,168	254.4	2,193	257.0	2,215	261.1	2,250
E09000018	Hounslow	56	216.0	3,857	216.9	3,873	216.5	3,866	219.4	3,919	223.8	3,996	228.1	4,074	233.5	4,169	237.9	4,248
E09000021	Kingston upon Thames	37	149.0	4,028	149.6	4,044	149.7	4,045	151.1	4,083	152.5	4,121	153.7	4,153	154.5	4,175	156.0	4,217
E09000024	Merton	38	191.1	5,029	190.6	5,015	189.3	4,982	188.9	4,971	190.6	5,015	192.5	5,066	194.3	5,112	195.9	5,154
E09000026	Redbridge	56	241.9	4,320	244.3	4,362	247.4	4,418	248.8	4,442	251.6	4,492	255.6	4,564	260.0	4,642	265.5	4,740
E09000027	Richmond upon Thames	57	174.3	3,058	175.4	3,078	177.2	3,108	179.3	3,146	181.5	3,184	182.5	3,202	182.4	3,200	182.9	3,209
E09000029	Sutton	44	181.5	4,124	181.3	4,120	181.3	4,120	181.1	4,116	182.1	4,139	182.9	4,156	184.2	4,186	185.9	4,224
E09000031	Waltham Forest	39	222.0	5,693	223.8	5,738	224.1	5,747	225.0	5,769	226.7	5,814	230.7	5,916	235.7	6,043	242.1	6,208
E12000008	SOUTH EAST	19,073	8,023.4	421	8,045.2	422	8,087.9	424	8,133.1	426	8,202.9	430	8,270.9	434	8,351.4	438	8,426.4	442
E06000036	Bracknell Forest	109	109.7	1,006	109.5	1,004	109.5	1,004	109.2	1,002	109.5	1,004	109.9	1,008	110.7	1,016	111.5	1,023
E06000043	Brighton and Hove	83	249.9	3,011	249.7	3,009	249.8	3,010	249.8	3,010	252.9	3,047	255.6	3,079	258.2	3,110	262.0	3,157

MYE5: Population estimates: Population density for the local authorities in the UK, mid-2001 to mid-2016

Abbreviation: Est. Pop. (Estimated Population)

Thousands

Code	Name	Area (sq km)	Est Pop: mid-2008	people /km²	Est Pop: mid-2007	people /km²	Est Pop: mid-2006	people /km²	Est Pop: mid-2005	people /km²	Est Pop: mid-2004	people /km²	Est Pop: mid-2003	people /km²	Est Pop: mid-2002	people /km²	Est Pop: mid-2001	people /km²
			2008		**2007**		**2006**		**2005**		**2004**		**2003**		**2002**		**2001**	
E06000046	Isle of Wight	380	138.7	365	138.3	364	137.7	362	137.2	361	135.9	358	134.8	355	133.9	352	132.9	350
E06000035	Medway	194	258.2	1,331	255.8	1,319	253.5	1,307	252.1	1,299	251.5	1,296	251.2	1,295	250.3	1,290	249.7	1,287
E06000042	Milton Keynes	309	235.6	763	231.0	748	227.2	735	223.5	723	219.5	710	217.6	704	215.1	696	212.7	688
E06000044	Portsmouth	40	196.0	4,901	194.9	4,873	196.0	4,899	196.3	4,908	193.5	4,837	190.3	4,757	188.5	4,712	188.0	4,701
E06000038	Reading	40	151.5	3,787	149.7	3,742	148.3	3,708	146.9	3,674	144.6	3,615	144.1	3,602	143.9	3,598	144.7	3,617
E06000039	Slough	33	131.5	3,983	128.0	3,879	125.2	3,794	122.9	3,723	120.8	3,662	120.9	3,663	120.9	3,664	120.6	3,654
E06000045	Southampton	50	228.4	4,569	227.2	4,544	226.7	4,534	226.7	4,533	223.6	4,472	222.0	4,440	220.5	4,409	219.5	4,391
E06000037	West Berkshire	704	152.0	216	150.1	213	148.1	210	146.5	208	145.1	206	144.3	205	143.9	204	144.5	205
E06000040	Windsor and Maidenhead	197	141.3	717	139.7	709	138.0	701	136.4	693	135.1	686	134.2	681	133.6	678	133.5	678
E06000041	Wokingham	179	153.2	856	152.1	850	150.5	841	149.6	836	149.0	832	148.8	831	149.4	835	150.3	840
E10000002	Buckinghamshire	1,565	496.4	317	493.5	315	489.3	313	485.5	310	482.1	308	480.2	307	478.8	306	479.1	306
E07000004	Aylesbury Vale	903	170.7	189	169.5	188	168.1	186	166.7	185	165.9	184	165.7	183	165.6	183	165.9	184
E07000005	Chiltern	196	92.5	472	92.2	471	91.5	467	90.6	462	90.1	460	89.5	457	89.0	454	89.2	455
E07000006	South Bucks	141	65.4	464	65.0	461	64.1	455	63.6	451	62.8	445	62.0	440	61.8	438	61.9	439
E07000007	Wycombe	325	167.8	516	166.8	513	165.7	510	164.6	507	163.4	503	163.0	501	162.4	500	162.1	499
E10000011	East Sussex	1,709	519.2	304	515.9	302	511.5	299	508.5	298	505.0	295	501.1	293	496.9	291	493.1	289
E07000061	Eastbourne	44	98.4	2,235	97.6	2,219	96.5	2,194	95.5	2,170	93.8	2,131	92.2	2,095	90.8	2,064	89.8	2,042
E07000062	Hastings	30	88.7	2,957	88.0	2,934	87.5	2,917	87.4	2,914	86.9	2,895	86.6	2,887	85.9	2,862	85.4	2,846
E07000063	Lewes	292	95.5	327	94.8	325	94.2	322	93.8	321	93.8	321	93.2	319	92.9	318	92.2	316
E07000064	Rother	509	90.1	177	89.3	175	88.2	173	87.7	172	87.2	171	86.7	170	86.2	169	85.5	168
E07000065	Wealden	833	146.5	176	146.2	176	145.1	174	144.1	173	143.4	172	142.4	171	141.2	169	140.2	168
E10000014	Hampshire	3,679	1,293.6	352	1,283.4	349	1,272.5	346	1,263.1	343	1,255.4	341	1,250.5	340	1,245.1	338	1,241.4	337
E07000084	Basingstoke and Deane	634	162.0	256	160.2	253	158.8	250	157.5	248	155.7	246	154.8	244	153.6	242	152.9	241
E07000085	East Hampshire	514	113.2	220	112.3	218	111.1	216	110.5	215	110.0	214	109.6	213	109.6	213	109.4	213
E07000086	Eastleigh	80	121.3	1,516	120.6	1,507	119.4	1,493	118.1	1,476	117.1	1,463	116.7	1,459	116.4	1,455	116.3	1,453
E07000087	Fareham	74	110.2	1,489	109.4	1,478	108.4	1,465	108.1	1,461	108.5	1,466	108.5	1,467	108.5	1,466	108.2	1,462
E07000088	Gosport	25	81.7	3,269	80.6	3,225	79.6	3,183	78.6	3,146	78.1	3,124	77.6	3,103	76.8	3,073	76.7	3,067
E07000089	Hart	215	90.6	421	89.9	418	88.9	413	87.5	407	86.4	402	85.2	396	84.2	392	83.6	389
E07000090	Havant	55	119.0	2,164	118.3	2,151	117.8	2,142	117.5	2,137	117.4	2,134	117.3	2,134	117.2	2,130	116.9	2,125
E07000091	New Forest	753	174.5	232	174.0	231	173.3	230	172.4	229	171.8	228	171.3	227	170.6	227	169.5	225
E07000092	Rushmoor	39	92.6	2,374	91.9	2,356	91.1	2,335	90.0	2,309	89.4	2,291	89.7	2,301	89.9	2,305	90.9	2,331
E07000093	Test Valley	628	115.1	183	114.4	182	113.5	181	112.8	180	112.0	178	111.3	177	110.4	176	110.0	175
E07000094	Winchester	661	113.3	171	111.8	169	110.6	167	109.9	166	109.2	165	108.5	164	107.8	163	107.3	162
E10000016	Kent	3,545	1,423.3	401	1,407.8	397	1,389.6	392	1,375.2	388	1,361.4	384	1,349.0	381	1,339.0	378	1,331.2	376
E07000105	Ashford	581	114.6	197	113.3	195	111.5	192	109.4	188	107.3	185	105.6	182	104.4	180	103.0	177
E07000106	Canterbury	309	146.1	473	145.2	470	143.5	464	141.9	459	140.6	455	138.6	449	136.5	442	135.4	438
E07000107	Dartford	73	93.9	1,287	92.2	1,264	91.2	1,249	90.0	1,233	88.3	1,209	87.0	1,192	86.4	1,184	86.0	1,177
E07000108	Dover	315	109.8	349	109.0	346	107.9	343	107.5	341	106.9	339	105.8	336	104.9	333	104.6	332

MYE5: Population estimates: Population density for the local authorities in the UK, mid-2001 to mid-2016
Abbreviation: Est. Pop. (Estimated Population)

Thousands

Code	Name	Area (sq km)	Est Pop: mid-2008	people /km²	Est Pop: mid-2007	people /km²	Est Pop: mid-2006	people /km²	Est Pop: mid-2005	people /km²	Est Pop: mid-2004	people /km²	Est Pop: mid-2003	people /km²	Est Pop: mid-2002	people /km²	Est Pop: mid-2001	people /km²
E07000109	Gravesham	99	99.4	1,004	98.5	995	97.6	986	96.9	979	95.9	969	95.6	965	95.4	964	95.8	968
E07000110	Maidstone	393	149.7	381	147.7	376	145.3	370	143.4	365	142.2	362	141.2	359	140.3	357	139.1	354
E07000111	Sevenoaks	369	113.3	307	113.1	307	112.5	305	111.3	302	110.0	298	109.3	296	109.1	296	109.2	296
E07000112	Shepway	357	104.8	294	103.9	291	102.5	287	101.5	284	99.9	280	98.5	276	97.2	272	96.3	270
E07000113	Swale	374	131.7	352	129.7	347	127.6	341	126.5	338	125.9	337	125.3	335	124.2	332	123.1	329
E07000114	Thanet	103	131.8	1,279	130.6	1,268	129.6	1,258	129.3	1,255	128.8	1,250	128.1	1,244	127.7	1,240	126.8	1,231
E07000115	Tonbridge and Malling	240	117.0	487	115.5	481	113.5	473	111.7	465	110.4	460	109.5	456	108.7	453	107.8	449
E07000116	Tunbridge Wells	331	111.3	336	108.9	329	107.1	323	105.9	320	105.1	318	104.4	315	104.2	315	104.0	314
E10000025	Oxfordshire	2,605	638.8	245	635.1	244	630.9	242	627.6	241	620.4	238	616.0	236	609.5	234	607.3	233
E07000177	Cherwell	589	139.4	237	138.1	234	137.2	233	135.9	231	134.9	229	134.0	227	132.6	225	132.0	224
E07000178	Oxford	46	144.4	3,140	144.2	3,135	144.5	3,142	145.4	3,161	141.6	3,078	139.9	3,042	136.6	2,970	135.5	2,946
E07000179	South Oxfordshire	679	132.6	195	131.6	194	130.7	192	130.1	192	129.4	191	128.9	190	128.8	190	128.3	189
E07000180	Vale of White Horse	578	119.3	206	119.0	206	118.2	205	117.4	203	116.5	202	116.1	201	115.6	200	115.8	200
E07000181	West Oxfordshire	714	103.0	144	102.2	143	100.3	140	98.9	138	98.0	137	97.1	136	96.0	134	95.7	134
E10000030	Surrey	1,663	1,104.2	664	1,095.6	659	1,082.8	651	1,071.8	644	1,065.1	640	1,062.8	639	1,059.5	637	1,060.2	638
E07000207	Elmbridge	95	129.9	1,367	129.8	1,366	128.8	1,355	127.3	1,340	125.7	1,323	125.0	1,316	123.8	1,303	122.7	1,292
E07000208	Epsom and Ewell	34	72.5	2,133	71.3	2,098	70.0	2,060	69.2	2,034	68.4	2,011	67.7	1,992	67.6	1,987	67.1	1,973
E07000209	Guildford	271	132.4	489	131.7	486	130.7	482	129.0	476	128.6	474	128.8	475	129.3	477	129.8	479
E07000210	Mole Valley	258	84.3	327	83.2	323	82.3	319	81.8	317	81.5	316	81.2	315	80.5	312	80.3	311
E07000211	Reigate and Banstead	129	132.9	1,030	131.2	1,017	129.2	1,001	127.8	990	127.2	986	126.7	982	126.3	979	126.7	982
E07000212	Runnymede	78	78.7	1,009	78.3	1,004	77.2	989	77.0	987	76.9	987	77.6	994	77.6	996	78.1	1,001
E07000213	Spelthorne	45	93.2	2,071	92.4	2,054	91.5	2,034	90.6	2,013	90.1	2,003	90.2	2,005	90.3	2,006	90.4	2,009
E07000214	Surrey Heath	95	84.3	888	84.2	886	83.3	877	82.3	867	81.6	859	80.9	852	80.4	846	80.3	845
E07000215	Tandridge	248	81.5	329	81.0	327	80.0	323	79.4	320	79.1	319	79.0	319	78.9	318	79.3	320
E07000216	Waverley	345	119.0	345	118.1	342	117.0	339	116.4	337	116.2	337	116.0	336	115.6	335	115.7	335
E07000217	Woking	64	95.5	1,493	94.4	1,475	92.8	1,451	91.1	1,423	89.8	1,403	89.6	1,401	89.3	1,395	89.9	1,405
E10000032	West Sussex	1,991	791.0	397	784.3	394	777.4	391	770.8	387	766.0	385	760.9	382	757.3	381	755.0	379
E07000223	Adur	42	60.7	1,446	60.6	1,442	60.3	1,437	59.8	1,424	60.0	1,428	60.0	1,428	60.1	1,430	59.7	1,422
E07000224	Arun	221	148.5	672	147.7	668	146.8	664	146.0	661	145.1	657	143.5	649	142.4	644	141.0	638
E07000225	Chichester	786	111.8	142	110.6	141	109.7	140	108.8	138	108.2	138	107.5	137	107.0	136	106.5	135
E07000226	Crawley	45	102.8	2,285	101.6	2,258	100.7	2,239	99.7	2,216	98.9	2,197	98.7	2,194	99.2	2,204	100.4	2,232
E07000227	Horsham	530	129.1	244	128.3	242	127.2	240	125.9	238	124.9	236	123.8	234	122.7	231	122.3	231
E07000228	Mid Sussex	334	135.7	406	134.0	401	132.1	395	130.5	391	129.5	388	128.6	385	127.7	382	127.4	381
E07000229	Worthing	33	102.4	3,199	101.5	3,172	100.6	3,145	100.1	3,127	99.5	3,108	98.8	3,087	98.2	3,070	97.7	3,052
E12000009	**SOUTH WEST**	23,837	5,205.0	218	5,170.5	217	5,119.8	215	5,086.1	213	5,038.3	211	5,006.7	210	4,976.1	209	4,943.4	207
E06000022	Bath and North East Somerset	346	173.6	502	172.6	499	171.2	495	171.3	495	170.6	493	170.4	492	169.8	491	169.2	489
E06000028	Bournemouth	46	172.0	3,739	170.1	3,698	166.7	3,624	166.0	3,609	163.9	3,564	164.2	3,570	164.6	3,578	163.6	3,556
E06000023	Bristol, City of	110	414.8	3,771	411.9	3,745	408.4	3,713	405.4	3,686	395.7	3,598	391.5	3,559	389.7	3,543	390.0	3,546

MYE5: Population estimates: Population density for the local authorities in the UK, mid-2001 to mid-2016

Abbreviation: Est. Pop. (Estimated Population)

Thousands

Code	Name	Area (sq km)	2001 Est Pop: mid-2001	2001 people /km²	2002 Est Pop: mid-2002	2002 people /km²	2003 Est Pop: mid-2003	2003 people /km²	2004 Est Pop: mid-2004	2004 people /km²	2005 Est Pop: mid-2005	2005 people /km²	2006 Est Pop: mid-2006	2006 people /km²	2007 Est Pop: mid-2007	2007 people /km²	2008 Est Pop: mid-2008	2008 people /km²
E06000052	Cornwall	3,546	499.9	141	504.6	142	508.6	143	511.8	144	515.1	145	518.0	146	522.0	147	525.0	148
E06000053	Isles of Scilly	16	2.1	134	2.2	136	2.2	135	2.2	138	2.2	138	2.3	142	2.3	143	2.3	146
E06000024	North Somerset	374	188.8	505	189.7	507	191.3	512	192.8	515	194.7	521	197.0	527	199.5	533	200.9	537
E06000026	Plymouth	80	241.0	3,012	242.6	3,032	243.4	3,042	244.0	3,050	247.5	3,094	249.2	3,115	251.2	3,140	252.5	3,156
E06000029	Poole	65	138.4	2,129	139.0	2,138	139.0	2,138	139.1	2,140	139.9	2,152	141.1	2,171	142.9	2,198	144.2	2,219
E06000025	South Gloucestershire	497	246.0	495	247.8	499	249.2	501	251.2	505	253.2	509	255.3	514	256.6	516	258.0	519
E06000030	Swindon	230	180.1	783	182.1	792	184.4	802	186.4	810	189.7	825	192.3	836	196.9	856	201.5	876
E06000027	Torbay	63	130.0	2,063	130.5	2,072	131.2	2,083	131.9	2,094	132.2	2,098	131.9	2,093	132.2	2,098	132.1	2,096
E06000054	Wiltshire	3,255	433.5	133	438.4	135	442.6	136	445.6	137	448.7	138	453.0	139	458.8	141	464.0	143
E10000008	Devon	6,564	705.6	107	709.9	108	714.1	109	718.8	110	725.6	111	729.6	111	736.3	112	739.9	113
E07000040	East Devon	814	125.7	154	126.6	155	127.2	156	128.4	158	129.8	159	130.6	160	132.0	162	132.6	163
E07000041	Exeter	47	111.2	2,366	110.6	2,354	111.1	2,363	110.7	2,355	113.0	2,404	113.1	2,407	114.1	2,428	114.2	2,429
E07000042	Mid Devon	913	69.9	77	70.7	77	71.5	78	72.6	80	73.3	80	74.1	81	75.6	83	76.4	84
E07000043	North Devon	1,086	87.7	81	88.5	81	89.6	82	90.4	83	91.1	84	91.7	84	92.4	85	92.8	85
E07000044	South Hams	886	81.9	92	82.1	93	82.0	93	82.1	93	82.5	93	83.0	94	83.4	94	83.5	94
E07000045	Teignbridge	674	121.2	180	121.8	181	122.4	182	123.0	182	123.5	183	123.5	183	124.1	184	124.4	185
E07000046	Torridge	984	59.1	60	59.8	61	60.7	62	61.5	62	62.0	63	62.6	64	63.1	64	63.5	65
E07000047	West Devon	1,160	48.9	42	50.0	43	49.7	43	50.1	43	50.5	44	50.8	44	51.7	45	52.6	45
E10000009	Dorset	2,542	391.5	154	395.6	156	398.7	157	400.8	158	403.4	159	405.9	160	409.6	161	411.0	162
E07000048	Christchurch	50	44.9	898	45.1	902	45.3	906	45.5	909	45.8	915	46.0	921	46.5	930	47.0	939
E07000049	East Dorset	354	83.9	237	84.8	240	85.3	241	85.9	243	86.0	243	86.1	243	86.9	246	87.2	246
E07000050	North Dorset	609	62.0	102	62.9	103	64.0	105	64.9	107	65.9	108	67.0	110	68.1	112	68.1	112
E07000051	Purbeck	404	44.4	110	44.6	110	44.3	110	44.4	110	44.6	110	44.8	111	45.1	112	45.2	112
E07000052	West Dorset	1,082	92.5	86	93.7	87	95.1	88	95.6	88	96.4	89	97.1	90	98.0	91	98.5	91
E07000053	Weymouth and Portland	42	63.8	1,518	64.5	1,535	64.7	1,541	64.5	1,536	64.8	1,543	64.8	1,543	65.0	1,547	65.0	1,549
E10000013	Gloucestershire	2,653	565.0	213	566.4	214	569.3	215	572.6	216	576.9	217	580.7	219	585.4	221	587.6	221
E07000078	Cheltenham	47	110.0	2,341	109.8	2,336	109.3	2,325	109.8	2,335	110.9	2,361	111.6	2,375	112.5	2,394	113.0	2,404
E07000079	Cotswold	1,165	80.4	69	80.5	69	81.2	70	81.8	71	82.2	71	82.6	71	83.2	71	83.0	71
E07000080	Forest of Dean	526	80.1	152	80.1	152	80.7	153	81.1	154	81.5	155	81.7	155	82.0	156	82.1	156
E07000081	Gloucester	41	109.9	2,682	110.6	2,697	111.5	2,721	112.6	2,746	113.9	2,777	115.3	2,812	117.2	2,859	118.4	2,888
E07000082	Stroud	461	108.1	234	108.2	235	108.8	236	109.5	237	110.1	239	110.5	240	111.1	241	111.4	242
E07000083	Tewkesbury	414	76.5	185	77.2	187	77.7	188	77.9	188	78.3	189	78.9	191	79.4	192	79.8	193
E10000027	Somerset	3,451	498.7	145	503.1	146	506.8	147	510.7	148	514.3	149	517.3	150	522.2	151	525.7	152
E07000187	Mendip	739	104.0	141	104.6	142	105.2	142	105.8	143	106.3	144	106.8	145	107.8	146	108.6	147
E07000188	Sedgemoor	564	106.0	188	107.1	190	107.8	191	108.8	193	109.7	195	110.7	196	112.1	199	112.9	200
E07000189	South Somerset	959	151.1	158	152.2	159	153.5	160	155.0	162	156.5	163	157.4	164	159.0	166	160.2	167
E07000190	Taunton Deane	462	102.6	222	104.1	225	105.2	228	105.9	229	106.8	231	107.4	232	108.2	234	108.8	236
E07000191	West Somerset	725	35.1	48	35.2	49	35.2	49	35.2	49	35.0	48	34.9	48	35.1	48	35.2	49

MYE5: Population estimates: Population density for the local authorities in the UK, mid-2001 to mid-2016

Abbreviation: Est. Pop. (Estimated Population)

Thousands

Code	Name	Area (sq km)	2008 Est Pop: mid-2008	2008 people /km²	2007 Est Pop: mid-2007	2007 people /km²	2006 Est Pop: mid-2006	2006 people /km²	2005 Est Pop: mid-2005	2005 people /km²	2004 Est Pop: mid-2004	2004 people /km²	2003 Est Pop: mid-2003	2003 people /km²	2002 Est Pop: mid-2002	2002 people /km²	2001 Est Pop: mid-2001	2001 people /km²
W92000004	**WALES**	20,736	3,025.9	146	3,006.3	145	2,985.7	144	2,969.3	143	2,957.4	143	2,937.7	142	2,922.9	141	2,910.2	140
W06000001	Isle of Anglesey	711	69.9	98	69.7	98	69.4	98	69.1	97	68.8	97	68.1	96	67.9	95	67.8	95
W06000002	Gwynedd	2,535	119.7	47	119.4	47	119.1	47	118.6	47	118.7	47	118.0	47	117.3	46	116.8	46
W06000003	Conwy	1,126	114.4	102	113.8	101	113.0	100	112.4	100	112.3	100	111.2	99	110.6	98	109.7	97
W06000004	Denbighshire	837	94.7	113	94.5	113	94.0	112	94.0	112	94.0	112	93.9	112	93.5	112	93.1	111
W06000005	Flintshire	437	151.5	347	150.8	345	150.1	344	149.9	343	149.7	343	149.2	341	148.9	341	148.6	340
W06000006	Wrexham	504	132.4	263	131.3	260	130.3	259	129.2	256	129.0	256	128.9	256	128.6	255	128.5	255
W06000023	Powys	5,181	132.9	26	132.0	25	131.0	25	130.2	25	129.6	25	128.3	25	127.1	25	126.4	24
W06000008	Ceredigion	1,786	75.0	42	75.3	42	75.3	42	75.5	42	75.8	42	75.6	42	75.5	42	75.4	42
W06000009	Pembrokeshire	1,619	121.1	75	119.6	74	118.3	73	117.2	72	116.4	72	115.1	71	114.1	71	113.1	70
W06000010	Carmarthenshire	2,370	182.5	77	181.3	77	179.5	76	178.2	75	177.5	75	176.1	74	174.6	74	173.7	73
W06000011	Swansea	380	234.1	616	232.5	612	230.8	607	229.3	604	228.2	600	226.4	596	224.8	591	223.5	588
W06000012	Neath Port Talbot	441	139.5	316	139.0	315	138.3	314	137.7	312	137.1	311	136.2	309	134.9	306	134.4	305
W06000013	Bridgend	251	137.2	547	135.9	542	134.2	535	132.9	529	131.9	526	131.0	522	129.7	517	128.7	513
W06000014	Vale of Glamorgan	331	125.7	380	124.7	377	123.6	374	122.9	371	122.1	369	121.0	365	120.3	363	119.3	360
W06000015	Cardiff	141	332.8	2,360	328.2	2,328	323.8	2,296	321.0	2,277	317.1	2,249	313.2	2,222	312.0	2,213	310.1	2,199
W06000016	Rhondda Cynon Taf	424	234.7	554	234.5	553	234.5	553	234.1	552	234.0	552	232.4	548	231.8	547	231.9	547
W06000024	Merthyr Tydfil	111	57.7	520	57.2	515	56.6	510	56.3	507	56.0	505	56.0	504	56.0	504	56.2	506
W06000018	Caerphilly	277	176.3	636	175.0	632	173.7	627	172.8	624	172.4	622	171.4	619	170.8	617	169.5	612
W06000019	Blaenau Gwent	109	69.8	641	69.7	639	69.6	639	69.2	635	69.2	635	69.2	635	69.5	637	70.0	642
W06000020	Torfaen	126	91.1	723	91.0	722	90.8	721	90.6	719	90.5	718	90.7	720	90.7	720	90.9	722
W06000021	Monmouthshire	849	90.1	106	89.6	106	89.1	105	88.6	104	87.8	103	86.6	102	85.4	101	85.0	100
W06000022	Newport	191	142.7	747	141.4	740	140.6	736	139.6	731	139.3	729	139.1	728	138.7	726	137.6	721
S92000003	**SCOTLAND**	77,911	5,202.9	67	5,170.0	66	5,133.1	66	5,110.2	66	5,084.3	65	5,068.5	65	5,066.0	65	5,064.2	65
S12000033	Aberdeen City	186	214.0	1,151	212.5	1,142	209.6	1,127	208.7	1,122	207.8	1,117	209.3	1,125	210.7	1,133	211.9	1,139
S12000034	Aberdeenshire	6,313	246.8	39	244.4	39	241.2	38	237.6	38	234.7	37	231.3	37	228.8	36	226.9	36
S12000041	Angus	2,182	114.5	52	113.5	52	112.5	52	111.3	51	110.2	50	108.7	50	108.8	50	108.4	50
S12000035	Argyll and Bute	6,909	89.9	13	90.8	13	90.9	13	90.4	13	90.6	13	90.9	13	91.0	13	91.3	13
S12000036	City of Edinburgh	263	458.5	1,743	456.0	1,734	452.1	1,719	449.5	1,709	445.9	1,695	445.3	1,693	447.5	1,701	449.0	1,707
S12000005	Clackmannanshire	159	51.2	322	50.6	318	49.5	312	49.2	309	48.7	306	48.1	303	48.1	303	48.1	302
S12000006	Dumfries and Galloway	6,427	151.0	23	150.4	23	149.8	23	149.6	23	148.7	23	147.9	23	147.7	23	147.8	23
S12000042	Dundee City	60	144.3	2,405	143.7	2,395	143.4	2,390	143.6	2,393	143.1	2,385	144.1	2,401	144.4	2,406	145.5	2,424
S12000008	East Ayrshire	1,262	121.6	96	121.0	96	120.5	95	120.3	95	120.2	95	119.9	95	119.9	95	120.3	95
S12000045	East Dunbartonshire	174	104.9	603	105.1	604	105.6	607	106.0	609	106.5	612	107.0	615	107.4	617	108.3	622
S12000010	East Lothian	679	97.5	144	95.6	141	93.9	138	92.7	137	92.2	136	91.6	135	91.1	134	90.2	133
S12000011	East Renfrewshire	174	89.9	516	89.8	516	89.8	516	89.9	517	89.8	516	89.9	516	89.9	517	89.4	514
S12000014	Falkirk	297	153.3	516	152.3	513	151.1	509	150.1	505	148.3	499	146.8	494	145.9	491	145.3	489

MYE5: Population estimates: Population density for the local authorities in the UK, mid-2001 to mid-2016

Abbreviation: Est. Pop. (Estimated Population)

Thousands

Code	Name	Area (sq km)	Est Pop: mid-2001	people /km²	Est Pop: mid-2002	people /km²	Est Pop: mid-2003	people /km²	Est Pop: mid-2004	people /km²	Est Pop: mid-2005	people /km²	Est Pop: mid-2006	people /km²	Est Pop: mid-2007	people /km²	Est Pop: mid-2008	people /km²
S12000015	Fife	1,325	349.8	264	350.7	265	351.4	265	353.1	266	355.5	268	357.3	270	358.8	271	360.1	272
S12000046	Glasgow City	175	578.7	3,307	576.5	3,294	572.3	3,270	569.6	3,255	569.2	3,253	568.5	3,248	571.8	3,267	576.2	3,293
S12000017	Highland	25,657	208.9	8	209.8	8	211.6	8	214.6	8	218.1	8	220.8	9	224.0	9	227.0	9
S12000018	Inverclyde	160	84.2	526	83.7	523	83.3	521	82.7	517	82.7	517	82.3	515	82.1	513	82.0	513
S12000019	Midlothian	354	81.0	229	80.9	228	80.3	227	80.2	227	80.1	226	80.0	226	80.4	227	81.5	230
S12000020	Moray	2,238	87.0	39	87.7	39	88.8	40	89.4	40	90.1	40	90.8	41	91.4	41	92.8	41
S12000013	Na h-Eileanan Siar	3,059	26.5	9	26.4	9	26.4	9	26.7	9	26.9	9	27.1	9	27.2	9	27.3	9
S12000021	North Ayrshire	885	135.8	153	135.9	154	136.3	154	136.5	154	136.7	154	136.8	155	137.4	155	137.9	156
S12000044	North Lanarkshire	470	321.2	683	322.5	686	323.7	689	325.4	692	327.1	696	328.7	699	331.2	705	333.3	709
S12000023	Orkney Islands	989	19.2	19	19.3	20	19.5	20	19.8	20	20.1	20	20.3	21	20.6	21	20.7	21
S12000024	Perth and Kinross	5,286	135.0	26	135.1	26	136.0	26	136.9	26	138.1	26	139.4	26	141.1	27	143.1	27
S12000038	Renfrewshire	261	172.9	662	172.3	660	171.6	657	171.5	657	171.4	657	171.3	656	171.9	658	172.6	661
S12000026	Scottish Borders	4,732	107.0	23	107.5	23	108.4	23	109.5	23	110.3	23	110.9	23	112.2	24	113.4	24
S12000027	Shetland Islands	1,468	22.0	15	22.0	15	22.0	15	22.1	15	22.3	15	22.2	15	22.4	15	22.5	15
S12000028	South Ayrshire	1,222	112.2	92	111.7	91	111.6	91	111.8	92	112.0	92	112.1	92	112.4	92	112.6	92
S12000029	South Lanarkshire	1,772	302.3	171	302.8	171	303.5	171	305.7	173	306.9	173	308.5	174	310.4	175	311.3	176
S12000030	Stirling	2,187	86.2	39	86.6	40	87.1	40	86.9	40	87.5	40	88.1	40	88.4	40	88.5	40
S12000039	West Dunbartonshire	159	93.3	587	93.0	585	92.5	582	92.0	578	91.5	576	91.4	575	91.4	575	91.2	574
S12000040	West Lothian	428	159.0	372	160.4	375	161.7	378	163.5	382	165.0	386	167.1	390	169.5	396	171.4	400
N92000002	NORTHERN IRELAND	13,588	1,688.8	124	1,697.5	125	1,704.9	125	1,714.0	126	1,727.7	127	1,743.1	128	1,761.7	130	1,779.2	131
N09000001	Antrim and Newtownabbey	572	128.8	225	129.5	226	130.4	228	131.1	229	132.4	231	133.2	233	134.8	236	136.1	238
N09000011	Ards and North Down	461	149.6	325	150.2	326	150.4	326	150.9	328	152.2	330	153.5	333	154.4	335	155.0	336
N09000002	Armagh City, Banbridge & Craigavon	1,337	176.0	132	177.4	133	179.0	134	180.8	135	183.9	138	187.2	140	190.5	143	193.6	145
N09000003	Belfast	132	328.7	2,481	328.5	2,479	327.2	2,470	326.3	2,463	325.5	2,457	326.0	2,461	327.4	2,471	330.1	2,491
N09000004	Causeway Coast and Glens	1,980	131.4	66	132.8	67	134.2	68	135.2	68	136.3	69	137.4	69	138.4	70	139.0	70
N09000005	Derry City and Strabane	1,238	143.8	116	144.3	116	144.6	117	145.0	117	145.4	117	145.9	118	146.7	118	147.5	119
N09000006	Fermanagh and Omagh	2,857	105.8	37	106.7	37	107.3	38	107.9	38	108.6	38	109.3	38	110.3	39	111.5	39
N09000007	Lisburn and Castlereagh	505	124.6	247	124.8	247	125.0	247	125.8	249	127.0	251	128.2	254	129.2	256	130.6	258
N09000008	Mid and East Antrim	1,046	127.5	122	128.3	123	129.2	123	129.9	124	131.0	125	132.0	126	133.3	127	134.2	128
N09000009	Mid Ulster	1,827	119.1	65	120.2	66	121.3	66	122.6	67	124.9	68	127.7	70	131.1	72	133.6	73
N09000010	Newry, Mourne and Down	1,633	153.7	94	155.0	95	156.4	96	158.5	97	160.5	98	162.7	100	165.6	101	168.0	103

MYE6: Median age of population for local authorities in the UK, mid-2001 to mid-2016

Code	Name	Mid-2001	Mid-2002	Mid-2003	Mid-2004	Mid-2005	Mid-2006	Mid-2007	Mid-2008	Mid-2009	Mid-2010	Mid-2011	Mid-2012	Mid-2013	Mid-2014	Mid-2015	Mid-2016
K02000001	UNITED KINGDOM	37.9	38.1	38.4	38.6	38.7	38.9	39.0	39.1	39.3	39.5	39.6	39.7	39.9	40.0	40.0	40.0
K03000001	GREAT BRITAIN	38.0	38.2	38.4	38.6	38.8	39.0	39.1	39.2	39.4	39.5	39.7	39.8	39.9	40.0	40.1	40.1
K04000001	ENGLAND AND WALES	37.9	38.1	38.3	38.5	38.7	38.8	39.0	39.1	39.2	39.4	39.5	39.6	39.8	39.9	39.9	39.9
E92000001	ENGLAND	37.8	38.1	38.3	38.4	38.6	38.7	38.9	39.0	39.1	39.3	39.4	39.5	39.7	39.7	39.8	39.8
E12000001	NORTH EAST	38.9	39.2	39.5	39.8	40.0	40.2	40.4	40.7	40.9	41.1	41.2	41.5	41.6	41.8	41.9	41.9
E06000047	County Durham	39.5	39.9	40.3	40.6	40.9	41.2	41.4	41.7	42.0	42.2	42.4	42.7	42.9	43.1	43.3	43.4
E06000005	Darlington	39.5	39.6	39.8	40.1	40.2	40.3	40.4	40.5	40.7	40.9	41.1	41.5	41.8	42.1	42.4	42.6
E06000001	Hartlepool	38.1	38.5	38.8	39.2	39.4	39.7	40.0	40.2	40.5	40.7	41.0	41.3	41.5	41.8	42.0	41.8
E06000002	Middlesbrough	35.9	36.2	36.6	36.7	36.8	36.9	37.0	37.1	37.4	37.3	37.1	37.0	36.8	36.7	36.5	36.3
E06000057	Northumberland	41.7	42.1	42.4	42.8	43.2	43.5	43.8	44.2	44.6	45.0	45.3	45.7	46.1	46.6	47.0	47.3
E06000003	Redcar and Cleveland	39.8	40.2	40.6	40.8	41.1	41.4	41.8	42.2	42.6	43.0	43.3	43.6	43.9	44.2	44.5	44.7
E06000004	Stockton-on-Tees	37.5	37.9	38.2	38.5	38.8	38.9	39.1	39.3	39.5	39.7	39.9	40.1	40.2	40.3	40.3	40.3
E11000007	Tyne and Wear (Met County)	38.4	38.6	38.8	39.0	39.2	39.3	39.4	39.6	39.7	39.8	40.0	40.1	40.1	40.1	40.0	39.9
E08000037	Gateshead	39.5	39.7	39.9	40.1	40.2	40.4	40.6	40.7	40.8	40.9	41.0	41.3	41.5	41.6	41.4	41.3
E08000021	Newcastle upon Tyne	36.2	36.1	36.0	35.7	35.4	35.1	34.8	34.7	34.5	34.1	33.8	33.5	33.3	33.1	32.9	32.9
E08000022	North Tyneside	40.1	40.3	40.5	40.7	40.9	41.1	41.2	41.3	41.5	41.7	41.9	42.2	42.4	42.7	43.1	43.2
E08000023	South Tyneside	39.4	39.8	40.2	40.6	40.9	41.3	41.5	41.8	42.1	42.4	42.7	43.0	43.1	43.4	43.6	43.6
E08000024	Sunderland	37.8	38.2	38.7	39.1	39.5	39.8	40.1	40.5	40.8	41.1	41.5	41.7	41.9	42.1	42.2	42.2
E12000002	NORTH WEST	38.1	38.4	38.6	38.8	38.9	39.1	39.3	39.5	39.7	39.9	40.0	40.2	40.4	40.5	40.5	40.4
E06000008	Blackburn with Darwen	34.1	34.3	34.6	34.8	34.9	35.0	35.1	35.2	35.3	35.4	35.5	35.6	35.6	35.8	35.9	36.0
E06000009	Blackpool	41.2	41.4	41.4	41.5	41.5	41.6	41.7	41.9	42.2	42.4	42.6	42.8	42.9	43.2	43.4	43.5
E06000049	Cheshire East	40.6	40.9	41.2	41.5	41.7	42.0	42.2	42.5	43.0	43.4	43.7	44.1	44.5	44.9	45.2	45.6
E06000050	Cheshire West and Chester	39.5	39.8	40.1	40.4	40.6	40.9	41.2	41.6	42.0	42.3	42.7	43.1	43.4	43.6	43.9	44.1
E06000006	Halton	37.2	37.6	37.8	38.0	38.3	38.5	38.7	38.9	39.1	39.4	39.8	40.1	40.3	40.5	40.7	40.8
E06000007	Warrington	37.9	38.3	38.7	39.0	39.3	39.6	39.7	39.9	40.1	40.4	40.6	40.8	41.1	41.3	41.5	41.7
E10000006	Cumbria	41.5	41.9	42.2	42.5	42.8	43.1	43.4	43.8	44.2	44.6	45.0	45.4	45.8	46.2	46.6	46.9
E07000026	Allerdale	41.8	42.2	42.4	42.8	43.2	43.6	43.8	44.2	44.6	45.0	45.3	45.8	46.1	46.5	46.8	47.2
E07000027	Barrow-in-Furness	39.4	39.9	40.3	40.6	41.0	41.3	41.5	41.8	42.1	42.6	42.9	43.4	43.7	44.0	44.3	44.6
E07000028	Carlisle	40.4	40.6	40.7	40.7	40.8	40.8	41.0	41.5	42.0	42.3	42.6	42.8	43.1	43.4	43.8	44.1
E07000029	Copeland	39.9	40.5	40.9	41.3	41.8	42.2	42.6	42.9	43.4	43.8	44.2	44.7	45.0	45.3	45.7	46.0
E07000030	Eden	42.7	43.1	43.5	43.9	44.2	44.6	45.0	45.4	45.9	46.3	46.8	47.3	47.7	48.3	48.9	49.4
E07000031	South Lakeland	44.3	44.7	45.1	45.4	45.7	46.2	46.4	46.9	47.2	47.7	48.2	48.6	49.0	49.5	49.8	50.2
E11000001	Greater Manchester (Met County)	36.7	36.8	36.9	37.0	37.1	37.1	37.1	37.2	37.3	37.3	37.3	37.3	37.3	37.3	37.1	37.0
E08000001	Bolton	37.1	37.3	37.5	37.7	37.9	38.1	38.2	38.3	38.4	38.6	38.8	38.8	38.9	39.0	39.0	38.8
E08000002	Bury	37.9	38.1	38.4	38.8	39.0	39.2	39.3	39.5	39.7	39.9	40.1	40.3	40.5	40.6	40.7	40.6
E08000003	Manchester	31.8	31.5	31.2	30.8	30.3	30.0	29.8	29.7	29.9	29.9	29.9	29.9	30.1	30.2	30.1	30.0
E08000004	Oldham	36.5	36.7	36.6	37.0	37.1	37.1	37.2	37.2	37.3	37.4	37.3	37.4	37.4	37.3	37.1	37.0
E08000005	Rochdale	36.6	36.9	37.0	37.3	37.4	37.5	37.6	37.7	37.9	38.0	38.1	38.3	38.4	38.4	38.3	38.2
E08000006	Salford	36.8	36.9	36.8	36.8	36.7	36.5	36.4	36.2	36.1	35.8	35.6	35.4	35.3	35.2	35.1	35.1
E08000007	Stockport	39.2	39.5	39.8	40.1	40.4	40.8	41.0	41.3	41.5	41.8	42.0	42.2	42.4	42.6	42.6	42.6

MYE6: Median age of population for local authorities in the UK, mid-2001 to mid-2016

Code	Name	Mid-2001	Mid-2002	Mid-2003	Mid-2004	Mid-2005	Mid-2006	Mid-2007	Mid-2008	Mid-2009	Mid-2010	Mid-2011	Mid-2012	Mid-2013	Mid-2014	Mid-2015	Mid-2016
E08000008	Tameside	37.4	37.7	38.0	38.3	38.7	38.9	39.1	39.3	39.5	39.7	40.0	40.2	40.4	40.6	40.6	40.5
E08000009	Trafford	38.5	38.7	38.8	39.0	39.2	39.2	39.3	39.5	39.6	39.8	40.0	40.2	40.4	40.4	40.5	40.6
E08000010	Wigan	37.9	38.2	38.5	38.8	39.1	39.4	39.6	39.8	40.1	40.4	40.7	41.1	41.4	41.7	41.9	42.1
E10000017	Lancashire	38.9	39.3	39.5	39.8	40.0	40.3	40.5	40.8	41.1	41.4	41.6	41.8	42.0	42.3	42.5	42.6
E07000117	Burnley	37.3	37.6	38.0	38.3	38.7	38.8	39.0	39.2	39.4	39.6	39.9	39.9	39.9	40.0	40.0	40.0
E07000118	Chorley	39.1	39.4	39.7	39.9	40.2	40.5	40.8	40.9	41.3	41.7	41.9	42.0	42.2	42.6	42.8	43.1
E07000119	Fylde	44.2	44.5	44.8	45.1	45.4	45.7	45.9	46.3	46.6	46.9	47.2	47.6	48.0	48.4	48.9	49.3
E07000120	Hyndburn	36.9	37.3	37.4	37.7	37.9	38.1	38.3	38.5	38.8	39.0	39.3	39.6	39.8	39.8	39.9	40.0
E07000121	Lancaster	38.1	38.5	38.7	38.9	39.0	39.3	39.7	40.2	40.4	40.4	40.4	40.2	40.2	40.2	40.2	40.1
E07000122	Pendle	37.5	37.8	38.1	38.4	38.5	38.6	38.7	38.8	38.9	39.0	39.1	39.2	39.3	39.5	39.5	39.5
E07000123	Preston	35.3	35.4	35.2	35.0	34.8	34.7	34.8	35.2	35.5	35.5	35.3	35.2	35.2	35.3	35.2	35.3
E07000124	Ribble Valley	41.3	41.5	41.9	42.2	42.7	43.1	43.4	43.9	44.4	44.7	45.0	45.4	45.8	46.3	46.7	47.2
E07000125	Rossendale	37.9	38.4	38.8	39.2	39.4	39.7	40.0	40.3	40.5	40.8	41.0	41.3	41.6	41.8	42.1	42.3
E07000126	South Ribble	39.4	39.5	39.9	40.2	40.6	40.8	41.1	41.3	41.5	41.8	42.1	42.5	42.8	43.2	43.6	43.8
E07000127	West Lancashire	39.6	40.0	40.2	40.6	40.9	41.3	41.6	41.9	42.3	42.7	43.1	43.3	43.5	43.7	44.0	44.3
E07000128	Wyre	43.6	44.0	44.3	44.6	44.8	45.2	45.6	46.1	46.4	46.8	47.2	47.5	47.9	48.2	48.5	48.8
E11000002	Merseyside (Met County)	38.3	38.6	38.8	39.1	39.2	39.5	39.7	39.9	40.1	40.3	40.5	40.7	40.8	40.8	40.7	40.6
E08000011	Knowsley	36.5	37.0	37.4	37.8	38.1	38.4	38.7	39.0	39.5	39.8	40.2	40.4	40.5	40.6	40.4	40.2
E08000012	Liverpool	35.9	35.9	35.9	35.7	35.6	35.6	35.7	35.8	35.8	35.7	35.5	35.2	35.2	35.2	35.0	34.9
E08000014	Sefton	40.8	41.2	41.6	41.9	42.4	42.8	43.1	43.5	43.9	44.2	44.5	44.9	45.2	45.4	45.7	45.9
E08000013	St. Helens	38.7	39.0	39.4	39.7	40.1	40.4	40.6	40.9	41.2	41.5	41.9	42.2	42.4	42.6	42.9	43.0
E08000015	Wirral	40.3	40.6	40.8	41.1	41.4	41.6	41.9	42.1	42.3	42.6	42.9	43.1	43.3	43.6	43.8	44.0
E12000003	**YORKSHIRE AND THE HUMBER**	38.0	38.3	38.5	38.6	38.7	38.9	39.0	39.2	39.4	39.5	39.7	39.8	40.0	40.1	40.1	40.1
E06000011	East Riding of Yorkshire	42.2	42.5	42.8	43.2	43.5	43.9	44.3	44.7	45.1	45.5	45.9	46.2	46.6	47.0	47.5	48.0
E06000010	Kingston upon Hull, City of	35.5	35.7	35.8	35.7	35.6	35.7	35.8	35.7	36.0	36.1	36.2	36.1	36.1	36.0	35.9	35.7
E06000012	North East Lincolnshire	38.3	38.7	39.0	39.4	39.7	40.0	40.2	40.4	40.7	40.9	41.1	41.3	41.6	41.9	42.0	42.2
E06000013	North Lincolnshire	40.1	40.4	40.7	40.8	41.1	41.3	41.5	41.7	41.9	42.2	42.4	42.7	43.0	43.3	43.5	43.8
E06000014	York	38.2	38.3	38.4	38.2	38.2	38.4	38.6	38.8	38.9	38.9	38.8	38.6	38.4	38.3	38.0	37.9
E10000023	North Yorkshire	41.4	41.8	42.1	42.5	42.8	43.1	43.4	43.7	44.1	44.5	44.8	45.2	45.6	46.2	46.6	47.0
E07000163	Craven	43.5	44.0	44.2	44.4	44.6	45.0	45.4	45.9	46.5	46.9	47.2	47.7	47.9	48.5	49.0	49.3
E07000164	Hambleton	42.0	42.4	42.8	43.3	43.7	43.9	44.2	44.6	45.2	45.6	46.0	46.5	47.0	47.5	48.1	48.4
E07000165	Harrogate	40.3	40.7	41.1	41.5	41.8	42.1	42.4	42.8	43.1	43.4	43.7	44.1	44.5	45.1	45.6	46.1
E07000166	Richmondshire	37.5	37.8	38.1	38.3	38.4	38.6	38.8	39.2	39.3	39.6	39.8	39.9	40.4	41.8	42.5	42.1
E07000167	Ryedale	44.1	44.4	44.7	45.0	45.3	45.7	45.9	46.3	46.7	47.2	47.6	48.0	48.4	48.7	49.1	49.3
E07000168	Scarborough	44.0	44.2	44.5	44.7	44.9	45.2	45.4	45.8	46.2	46.5	47.0	47.3	47.6	48.1	48.5	48.9
E07000169	Selby	39.5	39.9	40.2	40.6	41.0	41.3	41.6	41.7	42.1	42.5	42.9	43.3	43.5	43.9	44.2	44.4
E11000003	South Yorkshire (Met County)	38.1	38.3	38.5	38.6	38.7	38.8	39.0	39.1	39.2	39.3	39.4	39.5	39.5	39.5	39.4	39.2
E08000016	Barnsley	38.8	39.2	39.5	39.8	40.1	40.3	40.5	40.8	41.1	41.4	41.7	41.9	42.1	42.3	42.4	42.4
E08000017	Doncaster	38.8	39.0	39.3	39.5	39.7	39.9	40.0	40.1	40.2	40.4	40.6	40.8	41.0	41.2	41.3	41.3
E08000018	Rotherham	38.6	38.9	39.2	39.5	39.8	40.0	40.3	40.5	40.8	41.1	41.4	41.7	41.9	42.1	42.2	42.2
E08000019	Sheffield	37.0	37.1	37.2	37.0	36.9	36.9	37.0	37.0	37.0	36.8	36.5	36.2	36.1	36.0	35.8	35.7

MYE6: Median age of population for local authorities in the UK, mid-2001 to mid-2016

Code	Name	Mid-2001	Mid-2002	Mid-2003	Mid-2004	Mid-2005	Mid-2006	Mid-2007	Mid-2008	Mid-2009	Mid-2010	Mid-2011	Mid-2012	Mid-2013	Mid-2014	Mid-2015	Mid-2016
E11000006	West Yorkshire (Met County)	36.6	36.8	36.9	37.0	36.9	37.1	37.1	37.3	37.4	37.5	37.6	37.6	37.7	37.7	37.7	37.6
E08000032	Bradford	35.2	35.2	35.2	35.2	35.1	35.1	35.0	35.0	35.0	35.0	35.0	35.1	35.2	35.4	35.6	35.8
E08000033	Calderdale	38.5	38.7	39.0	39.2	39.4	39.6	39.8	40.0	40.2	40.5	40.8	41.1	41.4	41.7	41.9	41.9
E08000034	Kirklees	36.9	37.1	37.3	37.5	37.6	37.8	37.9	38.1	38.4	38.6	38.7	38.9	39.0	39.1	39.1	39.2
E08000035	Leeds	36.1	36.1	36.1	36.0	35.7	35.8	35.9	35.9	36.0	36.0	36.0	35.8	35.8	35.8	35.6	35.5
E08000036	Wakefield	38.3	38.7	39.0	39.3	39.7	40.0	40.3	40.5	40.8	41.1	41.4	41.7	41.9	42.1	42.2	42.1
E12000004	EAST MIDLANDS	38.5	38.8	39.0	39.2	39.5	39.7	39.9	40.1	40.3	40.5	40.7	41.0	41.2	41.3	41.4	41.4
E06000015	Derby	36.1	36.3	36.6	36.6	36.7	36.8	36.8	36.9	36.9	36.7	36.7	36.6	36.7	36.7	36.6	36.6
E06000016	Leicester	32.9	33.0	32.9	32.6	32.3	32.1	31.9	31.9	32.0	31.9	32.0	32.0	32.1	32.1	31.9	31.8
E06000018	Nottingham	32.7	32.5	32.2	31.8	31.6	31.5	31.5	31.4	31.3	31.2	31.1	30.8	30.8	30.6	30.3	30.0
E06000017	Rutland	40.3	40.4	40.7	41.4	41.8	42.1	42.3	42.6	43.2	43.5	43.9	44.9	44.9	45.1	45.7	46.1
E10000007	Derbyshire	40.1	40.4	40.7	41.0	41.3	41.6	41.9	42.2	42.6	42.9	43.3	43.7	44.0	44.3	44.7	45.0
E07000032	Amber Valley	40.2	40.4	40.7	41.0	41.3	41.7	42.1	42.4	42.8	43.1	43.5	43.9	44.3	44.6	45.1	45.4
E07000033	Bolsover	39.4	39.7	39.9	40.3	40.5	40.7	41.0	41.4	41.7	42.0	42.3	42.6	42.8	43.1	43.3	43.6
E07000034	Chesterfield	40.0	40.3	40.4	40.7	41.0	41.3	41.6	41.9	42.2	42.4	42.6	42.9	43.2	43.5	43.8	44.1
E07000035	Derbyshire Dales	43.7	44.1	44.6	44.8	45.1	45.5	45.8	46.1	46.6	47.0	47.5	47.9	48.4	48.8	49.4	49.8
E07000036	Erewash	38.5	38.8	39.1	39.5	39.9	40.3	40.7	41.0	41.3	41.7	42.0	42.4	42.6	42.9	43.1	43.4
E07000037	High Peak	39.6	40.0	40.4	40.7	41.0	41.3	41.6	42.0	42.3	42.7	43.1	43.6	44.0	44.5	44.8	45.2
E07000038	North East Derbyshire	42.2	42.6	42.9	43.2	43.5	43.8	44.1	44.4	44.7	45.1	45.5	45.9	46.2	46.6	46.9	47.1
E07000039	South Derbyshire	38.4	38.6	38.8	39.0	39.2	39.4	39.5	39.8	40.1	40.4	40.8	41.2	41.5	41.8	42.1	42.2
E10000018	Leicestershire	39.2	39.5	39.8	40.1	40.4	40.7	41.0	41.2	41.6	41.9	42.2	42.4	42.6	42.9	43.1	43.2
E07000129	Blaby	39.0	39.2	39.6	40.0	40.4	40.8	41.0	41.2	41.6	42.0	42.2	42.6	42.7	42.9	43.2	43.3
E07000130	Charnwood	37.3	37.8	38.0	38.2	38.4	38.6	38.8	38.9	39.1	39.3	39.5	39.4	39.5	39.3	39.1	38.7
E07000131	Harborough	40.3	40.4	40.7	41.1	41.6	41.9	42.2	42.6	43.0	43.4	43.8	44.2	44.5	45.0	45.2	45.6
E07000132	Hinckley and Bosworth	40.3	40.7	41.0	41.2	41.6	41.9	42.1	42.5	42.8	43.1	43.4	43.7	44.0	44.3	44.6	44.8
E07000133	Melton	40.2	40.6	41.0	41.4	41.8	42.1	42.4	42.9	43.3	43.6	43.9	44.3	44.8	45.2	45.7	46.1
E07000134	North West Leicestershire	39.7	39.9	40.1	40.3	40.5	40.8	41.0	41.3	41.7	42.1	42.5	42.8	43.0	43.3	43.5	43.7
E07000135	Oadby and Wigston	39.3	39.6	39.8	39.9	40.3	40.5	40.8	41.2	41.8	42.0	42.3	42.2	42.4	42.9	43.1	43.3
E10000019	Lincolnshire	41.5	41.9	42.2	42.5	42.7	42.9	43.2	43.4	43.7	43.9	44.2	44.5	44.7	44.9	45.1	45.3
E07000136	Boston	42.2	42.5	42.8	42.9	43.1	42.8	42.7	42.5	42.3	42.2	42.4	42.6	42.4	42.4	42.3	42.1
E07000137	East Lindsey	45.5	46.1	46.6	47.0	47.4	47.6	48.0	48.4	48.7	48.9	49.3	49.7	50.0	50.3	50.8	51.2
E07000138	Lincoln	35.6	35.8	35.6	35.1	35.0	34.8	34.7	34.9	34.9	34.7	34.5	34.1	34.1	34.1	34.0	33.9
E07000139	North Kesteven	41.1	41.5	41.8	42.2	42.6	42.9	43.2	43.5	43.7	44.1	44.4	44.8	45.1	45.2	45.5	45.8
E07000140	South Holland	44.2	44.3	44.4	44.4	44.4	44.4	44.4	44.4	44.6	44.8	45.1	45.5	45.7	45.7	45.9	45.9
E07000141	South Kesteven	39.9	40.4	41.0	41.4	41.8	42.1	42.3	42.6	43.0	43.4	43.7	44.1	44.4	44.7	45.1	45.3
E07000142	West Lindsey	42.4	42.8	43.0	43.3	43.7	44.0	44.3	44.6	45.0	45.4	45.8	46.2	46.5	46.8	47.0	47.2
E10000021	Northamptonshire	37.6	37.9	38.2	38.4	38.6	38.8	38.9	39.2	39.4	39.7	39.9	40.2	40.4	40.6	40.8	40.8
E07000150	Corby	37.0	37.4	37.7	37.9	38.0	38.0	37.9	37.9	37.9	37.8	37.4	37.3	37.3	37.3	37.2	37.2
E07000151	Daventry	38.9	39.2	39.4	39.9	40.2	40.6	41.0	41.6	42.1	42.8	43.2	43.8	44.2	44.7	45.0	45.3
E07000152	East Northamptonshire	38.5	38.9	39.0	39.4	39.7	40.0	40.2	40.7	41.1	41.7	42.1	42.5	43.0	43.5	43.7	44.1
E07000153	Kettering	38.2	38.4	38.6	38.8	39.1	39.2	39.2	39.4	39.8	40.0	40.2	40.5	40.7	40.9	41.1	41.2

Code	Name	Mid-2001	Mid-2002	Mid-2003	Mid-2004	Mid-2005	Mid-2006	Mid-2007	Mid-2008	Mid-2009	Mid-2010	Mid-2011	Mid-2012	Mid-2013	Mid-2014	Mid-2015	Mid-2016
E07000154	Northampton	35.7	35.9	36.1	36.3	36.3	36.2	36.2	36.2	36.2	36.3	36.2	36.3	36.4	36.6	36.6	36.7
E07000155	South Northamptonshire	39.6	39.7	40.0	40.3	40.5	40.8	41.2	41.8	42.3	42.9	43.4	43.8	44.1	44.5	44.7	45.1
E07000156	Wellingborough	38.0	38.3	38.6	38.9	39.2	39.4	39.5	39.7	40.1	40.4	40.6	40.9	41.3	41.5	41.8	41.8
E10000024	Nottinghamshire	39.6	39.9	40.1	40.4	40.7	41.1	41.3	41.6	41.9	42.2	42.5	42.8	43.0	43.2	43.4	43.6
E07000170	Ashfield	38.5	38.8	39.1	39.3	39.6	39.9	40.1	40.4	40.7	41.0	41.2	41.5	41.7	42.0	42.1	42.2
E07000171	Bassetlaw	39.8	40.1	40.5	40.8	41.3	41.7	42.0	42.3	42.7	43.0	43.4	43.8	44.2	44.5	44.8	45.2
E07000172	Broxtowe	39.5	39.8	40.2	40.4	40.7	41.0	41.3	41.7	42.0	42.2	42.4	42.5	42.7	42.9	43.0	43.2
E07000173	Gedling	40.3	40.5	40.8	41.0	41.3	41.7	41.9	42.1	42.3	42.6	42.9	43.1	43.2	43.4	43.6	43.7
E07000174	Mansfield	38.8	39.1	39.3	39.7	39.9	40.1	40.4	40.5	40.8	41.1	41.3	41.5	41.7	41.9	42.0	41.9
E07000175	Newark and Sherwood	40.6	40.9	41.1	41.3	41.6	41.9	42.2	42.4	42.8	43.1	43.5	43.8	44.1	44.3	44.6	44.8
E07000176	Rushcliffe	39.7	39.9	40.2	40.5	40.8	41.2	41.5	41.9	42.3	42.4	42.8	43.3	43.3	43.6	43.7	43.9
E12000005	**WEST MIDLANDS**	37.9	38.2	38.4	38.6	38.7	38.8	39.0	39.1	39.3	39.5	39.6	39.7	39.8	39.8	39.8	39.7
E06000019	Herefordshire, County of	42.2	42.6	42.9	43.3	43.7	43.8	43.9	44.1	44.4	44.7	45.1	45.4	45.6	45.8	46.1	46.4
E06000051	Shropshire	41.2	41.6	41.9	42.3	42.6	42.9	43.2	43.5	43.8	44.1	44.5	44.9	45.4	45.8	46.3	46.7
E06000021	Stoke-on-Trent	37.4	37.7	37.9	37.9	38.1	38.0	38.0	38.0	38.2	38.2	38.2	38.2	38.2	38.2	38.1	37.9
E06000020	Telford and Wrekin	36.1	36.5	36.9	37.2	37.4	37.6	37.8	38.1	38.4	38.6	38.7	38.9	39.1	39.3	39.3	39.3
E10000028	Staffordshire	39.6	40.0	40.3	40.6	40.9	41.2	41.4	41.8	42.1	42.4	42.7	43.1	43.4	43.7	44.1	44.3
E07000192	Cannock Chase	37.1	37.4	37.8	38.2	38.5	38.8	39.2	39.5	39.9	40.3	40.7	41.1	41.5	41.8	42.2	42.5
E07000193	East Staffordshire	38.6	38.8	39.0	39.3	39.6	39.8	40.0	40.2	40.4	40.6	40.8	41.1	41.4	41.6	41.8	41.8
E07000194	Lichfield	41.1	41.5	41.7	41.9	42.2	42.5	42.6	43.0	43.4	43.7	44.1	44.6	45.0	45.4	45.6	45.9
E07000195	Newcastle-under-Lyme	39.4	39.7	39.9	40.0	40.3	40.5	40.7	41.1	41.4	41.7	41.8	42.0	42.0	42.2	42.1	41.9
E07000196	South Staffordshire	41.4	41.8	42.3	42.8	43.2	43.6	44.0	44.3	44.8	45.2	45.5	46.0	46.0	46.4	46.8	47.2
E07000197	Stafford	40.9	41.1	41.3	41.6	41.8	42.0	42.2	42.4	42.8	43.0	43.3	43.6	43.9	44.3	44.7	44.8
E07000198	Staffordshire Moorlands	42.0	42.4	42.7	43.1	43.4	43.7	44.0	44.5	44.9	45.2	45.6	46.1	46.4	46.8	47.2	47.5
E07000199	Tamworth	35.8	36.2	36.6	37.0	37.3	37.6	37.9	38.2	38.5	38.9	39.3	39.7	40.1	40.5	40.7	40.9
E10000031	Warwickshire	39.7	39.8	40.0	40.2	40.4	40.6	40.8	41.0	41.3	41.7	42.0	42.3	42.6	42.9	43.1	43.2
E07000218	North Warwickshire	39.7	40.1	40.5	40.9	41.3	41.7	42.1	42.5	42.9	43.3	43.7	44.1	44.5	44.9	45.2	45.5
E07000219	Nuneaton and Bedworth	38.1	38.4	38.6	39.0	39.2	39.4	39.6	39.8	40.1	40.4	40.6	40.9	41.1	41.4	41.5	41.5
E07000220	Rugby	39.1	39.3	39.6	39.8	40.0	40.0	40.1	40.3	40.5	40.6	40.8	41.0	41.2	41.4	41.4	41.5
E07000221	Stratford-on-Avon	42.8	43.2	43.5	43.8	44.1	44.2	44.4	44.8	45.2	45.8	46.2	46.8	47.2	47.5	47.8	48.0
E07000222	Warwick	38.7	38.5	38.3	38.2	38.2	38.3	38.4	38.6	38.8	39.1	39.5	39.7	39.9	40.0	40.1	40.1
E11000005	West Midlands (Met County)	36.1	36.2	36.3	36.4	36.4	36.4	36.4	36.4	36.5	36.4	36.2	36.1	36.0	35.9	35.8	35.7
E08000025	Birmingham	33.8	33.8	33.7	33.6	33.3	33.3	33.2	33.0	33.0	32.9	32.9	32.8	32.8	32.9	32.8	32.6
E08000026	Coventry	35.1	35.4	35.6	35.8	35.9	35.8	35.8	35.6	35.5	35.2	34.7	34.2	33.9	33.6	33.0	32.6
E08000027	Dudley	39.3	39.5	39.7	39.9	40.1	40.3	40.5	40.6	40.9	41.2	41.4	41.7	41.9	42.1	42.2	42.3
E08000028	Sandwell	36.8	36.8	36.9	37.0	37.1	37.1	37.0	36.9	36.8	36.7	36.6	36.5	36.4	36.4	36.3	36.4
E08000029	Solihull	40.1	40.4	40.6	40.8	41.1	41.5	41.7	41.9	42.3	42.6	42.8	43.1	43.2	43.3	43.5	43.6
E08000030	Walsall	37.8	38.0	38.2	38.3	38.4	38.5	38.6	38.7	38.8	38.9	39.0	39.0	39.0	39.0	39.0	38.5
E08000031	Wolverhampton	37.0	37.1	37.2	37.4	37.5	37.5	37.6	37.7	37.9	38.0	38.0	38.1	38.1	38.1	37.9	37.7
E10000034	Worcestershire	40.1	40.4	40.8	41.1	41.4	41.7	41.9	42.2	42.6	43.0	43.3	43.6	43.9	44.2	44.4	44.7
E07000234	Bromsgrove	41.6	41.7	41.9	42.2	42.5	42.7	42.9	43.3	43.7	44.2	44.6	44.8	45.1	45.2	45.4	45.5

MYE6: Median age of population for local authorities in the UK, mid-2001 to mid-2016

Code	Name	Mid-2001	Mid-2002	Mid-2003	Mid-2004	Mid-2005	Mid-2006	Mid-2007	Mid-2008	Mid-2009	Mid-2010	Mid-2011	Mid-2012	Mid-2013	Mid-2014	Mid-2015	Mid-2016
E07000235	Malvern Hills	44.6	44.8	45.1	45.3	45.7	45.9	46.2	46.5	47.0	47.4	47.8	48.2	48.6	49.0	49.5	49.9
E07000236	Redditch	36.6	37.0	37.3	37.6	37.7	37.8	38.0	38.1	38.4	38.7	38.8	39.1	39.3	39.6	39.8	39.8
E07000237	Worcester	36.3	36.6	36.9	37.1	37.3	37.4	37.5	37.7	37.9	38.0	38.0	38.0	37.9	38.0	38.0	38.0
E07000238	Wychavon	41.8	42.2	42.6	43.0	43.4	43.8	44.2	44.6	45.0	45.5	45.9	46.3	46.6	46.9	47.2	47.6
E07000239	Wyre Forest	40.8	41.1	41.5	41.9	42.1	42.5	42.8	43.2	43.6	44.0	44.4	44.9	45.1	45.4	45.7	46.0
E12000006	**EAST**	38.8	39.0	39.2	39.5	39.7	39.9	40.1	40.3	40.5	40.6	40.8	41.0	41.2	41.3	41.4	41.5
E06000055	Bedford	37.1	37.3	37.6	37.8	38.2	38.5	38.7	38.9	39.1	39.1	39.2	39.5	39.6	39.8	39.9	40.0
E06000056	Central Bedfordshire	38.0	38.3	38.6	39.0	39.3	39.6	39.9	40.2	40.6	40.8	41.0	41.1	41.2	41.3	41.3	41.3
E06000032	Luton	33.4	33.7	33.8	34.0	33.9	33.7	33.4	33.1	33.1	32.8	32.5	32.6	32.9	33.0	33.1	33.4
E06000031	Peterborough	35.7	36.0	36.1	36.2	36.1	36.1	36.0	36.0	35.9	35.8	35.8	35.8	35.9	35.9	36.0	36.1
E06000033	Southend-on-Sea	39.4	39.5	39.6	39.8	39.9	40.0	40.0	40.1	40.1	40.3	40.3	40.6	40.8	41.0	41.3	41.4
E06000034	Thurrock	35.6	35.8	36.0	36.2	36.3	36.4	36.4	36.4	36.6	36.7	36.7	36.8	36.9	36.9	36.8	36.9
E10000003	Cambridgeshire	37.7	37.9	38.0	38.3	38.4	38.7	39.0	39.1	39.4	39.5	39.6	39.9	40.2	40.4	40.5	40.7
E07000008	Cambridge	31.4	31.4	31.2	31.0	30.7	30.9	31.2	31.3	31.7	31.6	31.6	31.8	31.8	31.8	31.5	31.4
E07000009	East Cambridgeshire	39.5	39.7	39.1	40.2	40.3	40.4	40.5	40.7	40.8	40.9	41.0	41.3	41.7	41.9	42.2	42.5
E07000010	Fenland	40.9	41.3	41.6	41.9	42.1	42.3	42.4	42.6	42.8	43.2	43.4	43.8	44.0	44.3	44.4	44.6
E07000011	Huntingdonshire	37.9	38.3	38.6	38.7	39.3	39.7	40.1	40.3	40.7	41.0	41.2	41.6	41.9	42.3	42.6	42.9
E07000012	South Cambridgeshire	39.4	39.5	39.6	39.9	40.2	40.4	40.5	40.7	40.9	41.0	41.1	41.5	42.0	42.2	42.4	42.5
E10000012	Essex	39.4	39.7	39.9	40.2	40.4	40.7	40.9	41.2	41.5	41.8	42.0	42.3	42.5	42.6	42.7	42.8
E07000066	Basildon	37.1	37.4	37.7	37.9	38.1	38.3	38.5	38.7	39.1	39.4	39.5	39.6	39.6	39.6	39.6	39.5
E07000067	Braintree	38.4	38.7	39.0	39.2	39.5	39.7	40.0	40.3	40.6	41.0	41.2	41.6	42.0	42.4	42.7	43.0
E07000068	Brentwood	41.2	41.3	41.6	41.6	41.8	41.9	42.1	42.3	42.6	42.8	43.1	43.3	43.4	43.2	43.2	43.3
E07000069	Castle Point	41.4	41.8	42.1	42.4	42.8	43.2	43.6	44.0	44.4	44.8	45.3	45.7	46.0	46.3	46.6	46.7
E07000070	Chelmsford	38.3	38.4	38.5	38.5	38.8	39.1	39.5	39.9	40.2	40.5	40.8	41.0	41.3	41.5	41.6	41.6
E07000071	Colchester	36.9	37.4	37.6	37.8	37.8	37.9	38.0	38.2	38.5	38.5	38.5	38.5	38.6	38.5	38.2	38.1
E07000072	Epping Forest	39.8	39.9	40.2	40.5	40.8	41.0	41.3	41.5	41.8	42.1	42.4	42.4	42.6	42.6	42.6	42.7
E07000073	Harlow	36.0	36.4	36.8	37.1	37.3	37.5	37.5	37.6	37.7	37.8	37.9	37.8	37.9	37.5	37.4	37.4
E07000074	Maldon	40.5	41.1	41.6	42.0	42.5	42.9	43.3	43.8	44.4	45.0	45.6	46.2	46.7	47.1	47.6	48.0
E07000075	Rochford	40.7	41.0	41.3	41.6	42.0	42.2	42.5	42.8	43.3	43.7	44.2	44.5	44.9	45.1	45.5	45.8
E07000076	Tendring	46.9	47.1	47.2	47.2	47.2	47.4	47.5	47.8	48.0	48.3	48.6	48.9	49.2	49.4	49.8	50.0
E07000077	Uttlesford	40.4	40.7	41.0	41.3	41.7	41.8	41.8	42.0	42.2	42.4	42.6	42.9	43.2	43.3	43.6	43.8
E10000015	Hertfordshire	37.8	38.0	38.3	38.5	38.7	38.9	39.0	39.0	39.2	39.3	39.4	39.6	39.7	39.7	39.7	39.8
E07000095	Broxbourne	37.5	37.8	38.0	38.3	38.5	38.7	38.8	39.0	39.3	39.6	39.8	39.9	40.0	40.1	40.1	40.1
E07000096	Dacorum	38.4	38.7	38.9	39.2	39.5	39.7	39.8	39.9	40.0	40.0	40.1	40.2	40.3	40.4	40.5	40.5
E07000242	East Hertfordshire	37.7	38.0	38.4	38.8	39.2	39.5	39.8	40.0	40.4	40.7	40.9	41.2	41.4	41.7	41.9	42.1
E07000098	Hertsmere	38.6	38.9	39.1	39.3	39.5	39.6	39.6	39.6	39.7	39.8	39.9	40.1	40.2	40.2	40.3	40.4
E07000099	North Hertfordshire	38.6	38.9	39.2	39.4	39.8	40.1	40.2	40.4	40.6	40.8	40.9	41.2	41.4	41.5	41.6	41.7
E10000240	St Albans	38.1	38.3	38.5	38.7	39.0	39.0	39.2	39.2	39.3	39.5	39.6	39.8	39.9	40.0	40.1	40.3
E07000243	Stevenage	35.8	36.1	36.4	36.8	37.1	37.3	37.5	37.6	37.8	37.9	37.9	38.0	38.1	38.2	38.1	37.9
E07000102	Three Rivers	39.5	39.6	39.7	40.0	40.2	40.4	40.5	40.6	40.7	41.0	41.1	41.2	41.3	41.4	41.4	41.5
E07000103	Watford	35.1	35.3	35.4	35.5	35.4	35.6	35.8	35.5	35.6	35.5	35.3	35.5	35.4	35.5	35.8	36.1

MYE6: Median age of population for local authorities in the UK, mid-2001 to mid-2016

Code	Name	Mid-2016	Mid-2015	Mid-2014	Mid-2013	Mid-2012	Mid-2011	Mid-2010	Mid-2009	Mid-2008	Mid-2007	Mid-2006	Mid-2005	Mid-2004	Mid-2003	Mid-2002	Mid-2001
E07000241	Welwyn Hatfield	35.4	35.8	36.0	36.3	36.4	36.4	36.6	36.8	36.6	36.6	36.9	37.4	37.8	37.9	38.0	38.1
E10000020	Norfolk	45.2	45.0	44.8	44.5	44.3	44.1	43.9	43.7	43.5	43.3	43.1	42.9	42.7	42.5	42.3	42.1
E07000143	Breckland	45.8	45.5	45.1	44.8	44.5	44.1	44.0	43.7	43.3	43.0	42.8	42.6	42.5	42.1	41.8	41.4
E07000144	Broadland	47.6	47.3	47.1	46.8	46.4	46.0	45.5	45.2	44.8	44.4	44.1	43.8	43.5	43.1	42.8	42.5
E07000145	Great Yarmouth	45.0	44.7	44.5	44.2	43.9	43.6	43.4	43.2	43.0	43.0	42.8	42.6	42.5	42.4	42.1	42.0
E07000146	King's Lynn and West Norfolk	46.6	46.3	46.1	45.9	45.6	45.2	45.1	44.8	44.6	44.4	44.2	44.1	43.9	43.7	43.5	43.3
E07000147	North Norfolk	53.0	52.7	52.4	52.0	51.7	51.3	51.3	50.9	50.6	50.2	49.8	49.5	49.2	48.8	48.5	48.1
E07000148	Norwich	33.5	33.7	33.8	33.8	34.0	34.2	34.4	34.6	34.7	34.8	34.8	35.0	35.1	35.3	35.3	35.4
E07000149	South Norfolk	46.1	45.8	45.7	45.5	45.5	45.1	45.0	44.8	44.7	44.6	44.5	44.2	43.9	43.6	43.4	43.3
E10000029	Suffolk	44.5	44.2	43.9	43.6	43.3	42.9	42.6	42.4	42.1	41.8	41.5	41.1	41.0	40.8	40.6	40.3
E07000200	Babergh	47.6	47.3	46.9	46.4	46.0	45.4	45.0	44.5	44.0	43.6	43.2	43.0	42.6	42.5	42.3	42.1
E07000201	Forest Heath	36.6	35.8	36.1	37.3	37.0	37.1	37.4	37.3	37.2	37.0	36.7	36.3	36.3	36.1	35.9	35.6
E07000202	Ipswich	37.3	37.2	37.2	37.0	36.9	36.8	36.9	37.0	37.0	37.0	36.8	36.6	36.8	36.9	36.9	36.7
E07000203	Mid Suffolk	46.9	46.4	45.9	45.5	45.1	44.7	44.4	43.9	43.5	43.0	42.7	42.5	42.1	41.9	41.5	41.1
E07000204	St Edmundsbury	43.6	43.3	43.0	42.5	42.1	41.7	41.5	41.3	41.0	40.8	40.6	40.3	40.0	39.9	39.6	39.3
E07000205	Suffolk Coastal	49.0	48.6	48.2	47.8	47.4	46.7	46.3	45.9	45.4	45.1	44.8	44.5	44.4	44.1	43.8	43.2
E07000206	Waveney	47.3	47.0	46.8	46.4	46.0	45.7	45.3	45.0	44.6	44.3	44.0	43.6	43.4	43.2	42.9	42.7
E12000007	**LONDON**	34.8	34.6	34.4	34.2	34.0	33.8	33.9	34.0	34.0	34.1	34.2	34.2	34.2	34.2	34.1	34.0
E09000007	Camden	33.8	33.6	33.5	33.4	33.2	33.2	33.5	33.5	33.2	33.0	32.9	32.7	32.7	32.8	32.6	32.4
E09000001	City of London	45.3	46.2	46.7	45.7	43.2	40.0	40.4	40.1	40.1	39.1	39.3	39.3	39.0	38.8	38.3	37.8
E09000012	Hackney	32.4	32.1	31.8	31.5	31.2	30.9	30.8	30.7	30.7	30.8	31.0	31.2	31.3	31.4	31.5	31.6
E09000013	Hammersmith and Fulham	34.4	33.9	33.7	33.3	32.9	32.6	32.6	32.5	32.4	32.5	32.5	32.5	32.4	32.4	32.3	32.3
E09000014	Haringey	34.5	34.2	33.9	33.7	33.3	33.0	32.8	32.6	32.4	32.6	32.7	32.7	32.6	32.6	32.5	32.4
E09000019	Islington	32.0	32.0	32.1	32.2	32.1	32.0	32.1	32.2	32.3	32.4	32.6	32.7	32.8	32.8	32.8	32.7
E09000020	Kensington and Chelsea	38.5	37.8	37.4	37.0	36.7	36.2	36.1	36.0	35.8	35.7	35.4	35.3	35.5	35.5	35.4	35.5
E09000022	Lambeth	32.7	32.5	32.4	32.2	32.1	32.0	32.0	32.0	32.0	32.0	32.1	32.1	32.1	32.0	31.9	31.6
E09000023	Lewisham	34.5	34.3	34.1	34.0	33.8	33.6	33.6	33.5	33.5	33.7	33.8	33.8	33.8	33.8	33.5	33.3
E09000025	Newham	31.1	30.8	30.5	30.1	29.7	29.4	29.3	29.3	29.2	29.3	29.7	29.9	29.9	29.9	29.9	30.0
E09000028	Southwark	32.9	32.7	32.6	32.5	32.4	32.3	32.3	32.3	32.2	32.3	32.5	32.7	32.8	32.9	32.8	32.6
E09000030	Tower Hamlets	30.7	30.4	30.1	29.8	29.5	29.3	29.2	29.2	29.2	29.2	29.3	29.3	29.3	29.2	29.1	29.1
E09000032	Wandsworth	33.4	33.2	33.0	32.8	32.6	32.4	32.5	32.4	32.3	32.2	32.2	32.2	32.1	32.0	32.0	32.0
E09000033	Westminster	35.7	35.4	35.4	35.1	35.1	34.5	34.6	34.5	34.1	33.9	33.6	33.4	33.6	33.7	33.7	34.0
E09000002	Barking and Dagenham	32.0	32.0	32.0	32.0	32.0	32.0	32.3	32.7	33.0	33.5	33.9	34.2	34.3	34.4	34.4	34.3
E09000003	Barnet	36.4	36.2	35.9	35.7	35.5	35.4	35.5	35.6	35.6	35.5	35.7	35.7	35.7	35.6	35.5	35.4
E09000004	Bexley	38.6	38.8	38.9	39.1	39.2	39.3	39.3	39.2	39.1	39.0	38.9	38.7	38.5	38.4	38.2	38.0
E09000005	Brent	34.6	34.4	34.1	33.7	33.7	33.0	33.1	33.1	33.1	33.4	33.6	33.8	33.9	33.9	33.4	33.2
E09000006	Bromley	40.5	40.4	40.4	40.6	40.6	40.6	40.4	40.2	40.0	39.9	39.9	39.7	39.5	39.2	38.9	38.7
E09000008	Croydon	36.7	36.5	36.2	36.0	35.9	35.8	35.9	36.0	36.0	36.1	36.2	36.2	36.1	36.0	35.8	35.6
E09000009	Ealing	35.8	35.4	35.1	34.7	34.3	34.0	34.0	33.9	33.8	33.9	33.9	33.9	33.9	34.0	33.6	33.7
E09000010	Enfield	35.5	35.3	35.3	35.1	34.9	34.8	35.0	35.2	35.4	35.6	35.8	35.9	35.9	35.8	35.7	35.7
E09000011	Greenwich	34.3	34.1	33.9	33.7	33.4	33.3	33.3	33.4	33.3	33.4	33.5	33.6	33.7	33.8	33.9	33.9

MYE6: Median age of population for local authorities in the UK, mid-2001 to mid-2016

Code	Name	Mid-2001	Mid-2002	Mid-2003	Mid-2004	Mid-2005	Mid-2006	Mid-2007	Mid-2008	Mid-2009	Mid-2010	Mid-2011	Mid-2012	Mid-2013	Mid-2014	Mid-2015	Mid-2016
E09000015	Harrow	36.5	36.5	36.7	36.6	36.4	36.4	36.4	36.4	36.4	36.3	36.3	36.5	36.7	37.0	37.1	37.4
E09000016	Havering	39.8	39.9	40.1	40.3	40.4	40.6	40.7	40.7	40.8	40.9	40.9	41.0	40.8	40.4	40.0	39.7
E09000017	Hillingdon	35.6	35.7	35.8	35.9	35.9	35.8	35.8	35.6	35.4	35.3	35.0	34.9	35.0	35.1	35.2	35.4
E09000018	Hounslow	33.6	33.8	34.1	34.1	34.0	33.9	33.8	33.6	33.7	33.6	33.7	33.9	34.2	34.5	34.9	35.3
E09000021	Kingston upon Thames	35.3	35.4	35.5	35.4	35.5	35.5	35.5	35.6	35.8	35.9	36.0	36.0	36.1	36.2	36.2	36.4
E09000024	Merton	34.6	34.8	35.0	35.1	35.0	34.9	34.8	34.8	34.9	34.9	34.9	35.1	35.4	35.6	35.9	36.2
E09000026	Redbridge	35.6	35.6	35.5	35.5	35.4	35.2	34.8	34.5	34.4	34.2	34.0	34.1	34.3	34.4	34.7	34.9
E09000027	Richmond upon Thames	37.1	37.2	37.2	37.3	37.3	37.5	37.7	37.9	38.2	38.3	38.4	38.7	38.9	39.2	39.6	39.9
E09000029	Sutton	36.4	36.8	37.2	37.4	37.7	37.8	37.8	37.9	38.1	38.3	38.4	38.5	38.6	38.7	38.7	38.8
E09000031	Waltham Forest	33.2	33.4	33.5	33.6	33.7	33.7	33.5	33.2	33.1	33.0	33.0	33.2	33.5	33.8	34.0	34.2
E12000008	SOUTH EAST	38.6	38.9	39.1	39.3	39.5	39.7	39.9	40.0	40.3	40.4	40.6	40.8	41.0	41.2	41.3	41.3
E06000036	Bracknell Forest	35.2	35.6	35.9	36.2	36.5	36.8	37.0	37.3	37.6	37.8	37.9	38.2	38.3	38.4	38.4	38.6
E06000043	Brighton and Hove	36.2	36.3	36.3	36.3	36.3	36.2	36.1	36.0	36.1	36.1	36.1	35.9	35.9	35.8	35.8	35.6
E06000046	Isle of Wight	44.7	44.8	44.9	45.0	45.1	45.2	45.4	45.7	46.1	46.4	46.7	47.1	47.6	48.1	48.5	49.1
E06000035	Medway	36.0	36.3	36.5	36.8	37.1	37.2	37.3	37.4	37.6	37.7	37.7	37.7	37.8	37.8	37.8	37.8
E06000042	Milton Keynes	34.6	34.8	35.0	35.3	35.4	35.6	35.6	35.7	35.7	35.8	35.8	36.0	36.2	36.5	36.7	36.9
E06000044	Portsmouth	35.1	35.3	35.2	34.8	34.6	34.7	35.0	35.0	34.8	34.4	34.1	33.9	34.1	34.1	34.0	33.8
E06000038	Reading	32.9	32.9	32.8	32.8	32.7	32.7	32.7	32.6	32.9	33.0	33.2	33.4	33.5	33.7	33.9	34.1
E06000039	Slough	33.0	33.2	33.2	33.2	33.0	32.9	33.0	33.0	32.4	33.0	32.3	32.6	33.0	33.4	33.7	34.0
E06000045	Southampton	33.3	33.3	33.1	33.0	32.9	32.9	33.0	33.0	33.1	33.0	32.8	32.7	32.8	32.8	32.6	32.3
E06000037	West Berkshire	37.9	38.3	38.6	38.9	39.1	39.4	39.5	39.8	40.2	40.5	40.9	41.3	41.6	42.0	42.2	42.5
E06000040	Windsor and Maidenhead	38.7	38.9	39.0	39.1	39.3	39.4	39.5	39.7	40.0	40.1	40.4	40.7	41.0	41.2	41.4	41.6
E06000041	Wokingham	37.4	37.8	38.3	38.7	39.0	39.2	39.4	39.6	39.9	40.3	40.7	40.9	41.1	41.3	41.4	41.5
E10000002	Buckinghamshire	38.6	38.9	39.2	39.4	39.7	39.9	40.1	40.4	40.7	41.0	41.2	41.4	41.6	41.8	41.8	41.9
E07000004	Aylesbury Vale	37.3	37.7	38.1	38.6	39.0	39.2	39.5	39.8	40.2	40.4	40.5	40.7	40.8	40.8	40.6	40.5
E07000005	Chiltern	41.6	41.9	41.9	41.9	42.3	42.4	42.6	43.0	43.4	43.7	44.1	44.4	44.6	44.7	44.7	44.9
E07000006	South Bucks	41.8	41.9	42.1	42.2	42.2	42.3	42.4	42.6	42.9	43.3	43.6	43.9	44.1	44.4	44.4	44.6
E07000007	Wycombe	37.3	37.5	37.7	37.9	38.1	38.3	38.5	38.7	39.0	39.2	39.4	39.6	39.9	40.1	40.3	40.6
E10000011	East Sussex	43.7	43.8	43.9	44.0	44.1	44.3	44.5	44.8	45.1	45.4	45.6	45.9	46.3	46.6	46.9	47.2
E07000061	Eastbourne	42.8	42.8	42.7	42.5	42.3	42.4	42.4	42.7	42.9	43.2	43.4	43.7	44.0	44.2	44.5	44.9
E07000062	Hastings	39.2	39.4	39.4	39.7	39.9	40.1	40.2	40.3	40.6	40.9	41.2	41.5	41.8	42.0	42.3	42.4
E07000063	Lewes	44.0	44.1	44.2	44.4	44.7	44.9	45.1	45.4	45.6	45.7	45.9	46.1	46.3	46.7	47.0	47.2
E07000064	Rother	49.2	49.3	49.3	49.3	49.3	49.4	49.6	49.7	50.0	50.2	50.5	50.7	51.1	51.5	51.7	52.1
E07000065	Wealden	43.9	44.2	44.3	44.5	44.8	45.0	45.2	45.6	46.0	46.4	46.6	47.0	47.3	47.6	47.9	48.2
E10000014	Hampshire	39.4	39.7	40.0	40.4	40.7	41.1	41.3	41.6	41.9	42.2	42.4	42.8	43.0	43.3	43.6	43.9
E07000084	Basingstoke and Deane	37.2	37.5	37.7	38.0	38.2	38.6	38.8	39.1	39.3	39.4	39.6	39.9	40.1	40.3	40.5	40.7
E07000085	East Hampshire	40.3	40.7	41.1	41.5	42.0	42.4	42.8	43.1	43.5	43.9	44.3	44.8	45.1	45.6	46.0	46.4
E07000086	Eastleigh	38.4	38.8	39.1	39.5	39.8	40.1	40.2	40.5	40.7	40.9	41.0	41.3	41.4	41.5	41.8	42.1
E07000087	Fareham	40.8	41.1	41.5	41.9	42.5	42.9	43.2	43.5	43.8	44.1	44.4	44.7	44.9	45.1	45.5	45.7
E07000088	Gosport	37.3	37.8	38.2	38.6	38.9	39.1	39.2	39.5	39.9	40.1	40.4	40.7	41.1	41.4	41.6	41.7
E07000089	Hart	38.4	38.7	38.9	39.2	39.5	39.7	40.0	40.3	40.7	41.0	41.4	41.7	42.0	42.3	42.6	43.0

MYE6: Median age of population for local authorities in the UK, mid-2001 to mid-2016

Code	Name	Mid-2016	Mid-2015	Mid-2014	Mid-2013	Mid-2012	Mid-2011	Mid-2010	Mid-2009	Mid-2008	Mid-2007	Mid-2006	Mid-2005	Mid-2004	Mid-2003	Mid-2002	Mid-2001
E07000090	Havant	45.5	45.3	45.0	44.7	44.4	44.1	43.9	43.6	43.3	43.0	42.7	42.4	42.2	41.8	41.6	41.2
E07000091	New Forest	49.7	49.2	48.8	48.4	48.1	47.6	47.3	46.9	46.6	46.3	46.0	45.7	45.5	45.1	44.8	44.6
E07000092	Rushmoor	37.5	37.6	37.2	36.9	36.5	36.1	36.0	35.9	35.6	35.5	35.3	35.3	35.1	34.8	34.6	34.2
E07000093	Test Valley	44.5	44.4	44.3	44.0	43.8	43.4	43.1	42.6	42.1	41.7	41.3	40.9	40.4	40.1	39.7	39.3
E07000094	Winchester	42.9	42.8	42.7	42.5	42.3	42.2	42.0	41.8	41.6	41.5	41.3	41.1	40.8	40.6	40.5	40.2
E10000016	Kent	42.1	42.1	41.9	41.7	41.5	41.3	41.1	41.0	40.8	40.6	40.4	40.2	40.0	39.9	39.7	39.4
E07000105	Ashford	41.9	41.8	41.6	41.3	41.2	40.9	40.6	40.4	40.1	39.9	39.7	39.5	39.4	39.3	39.0	38.9
E07000106	Canterbury	37.8	38.4	38.9	39.0	39.2	39.5	39.8	39.9	39.5	39.3	39.1	39.1	39.0	39.2	39.3	39.3
E07000107	Dartford	37.5	37.5	37.6	37.6	37.6	37.7	37.6	37.5	37.4	37.5	37.4	37.2	37.2	37.0	36.8	36.5
E07000108	Dover	46.0	45.7	45.3	44.9	44.6	44.2	43.8	43.5	43.1	42.7	42.5	42.1	41.9	41.6	41.3	41.0
E07000109	Gravesham	39.3	39.2	39.2	39.2	39.2	39.1	39.0	39.0	38.9	38.9	38.9	38.7	38.7	38.6	38.4	38.0
E07000110	Maidstone	41.6	41.6	41.5	41.5	41.3	41.1	40.9	40.8	40.5	40.4	40.3	40.1	39.9	39.6	39.5	39.3
E07000111	Sevenoaks	44.0	43.9	43.7	43.6	43.5	43.3	43.0	42.8	42.5	42.2	42.0	41.8	41.7	41.5	41.4	41.1
E07000112	Shepway	46.2	45.9	45.5	44.9	44.4	43.9	43.6	43.4	43.1	42.8	42.6	42.3	42.2	42.0	41.9	41.6
E07000113	Swale	41.5	41.6	41.5	41.3	41.1	40.8	40.6	40.4	40.1	39.9	39.9	39.5	39.1	38.7	38.3	38.0
E07000114	Thanet	44.4	44.1	43.8	43.7	43.5	43.3	43.1	43.0	42.9	42.8	42.7	42.5	42.4	42.2	42.1	42.0
E07000115	Tonbridge and Malling	42.3	42.2	42.1	41.8	41.6	41.3	41.0	40.9	40.6	40.4	40.2	40.0	39.7	39.4	39.1	38.8
E07000116	Tunbridge Wells	42.3	42.2	41.7	41.4	41.0	40.6	40.4	40.2	40.1	40.1	40.0	39.9	39.6	39.5	39.4	39.2
E10000025	Oxfordshire	39.5	39.5	39.3	39.2	39.1	38.8	38.8	38.6	38.4	38.1	37.9	37.7	37.5	37.4	37.2	36.9
E07000177	Chenwell	40.8	40.7	40.5	40.2	39.9	39.5	39.3	39.1	38.8	38.6	38.4	38.1	37.8	37.5	37.2	36.8
E07000178	Oxford	30.2	30.3	30.4	30.4	30.3	30.2	30.3	30.4	30.0	30.0	30.0	29.9	30.2	30.7	30.9	31.0
E07000179	South Oxfordshire	43.8	43.6	43.3	43.0	42.7	42.4	42.1	41.7	41.3	41.0	40.7	40.3	40.0	39.7	39.3	39.0
E07000180	Vale of White Horse	42.8	42.8	42.7	42.4	42.1	41.9	41.8	41.6	41.2	40.9	40.7	40.4	40.1	39.8	39.5	39.1
E07000181	West Oxfordshire	43.8	43.4	43.1	42.7	42.5	42.3	42.0	41.8	41.5	41.2	41.0	40.8	40.4	40.0	39.8	39.4
E10000030	Surrey	41.7	41.6	41.6	41.4	41.2	41.0	40.9	40.8	40.6	40.4	40.3	40.2	40.0	39.7	39.5	39.3
E07000207	Elmbridge	42.0	41.7	41.5	41.4	41.2	41.0	40.8	40.7	40.4	40.2	40.1	40.0	39.8	39.6	39.5	39.4
E07000208	Epsom and Ewell	41.2	41.2	41.2	41.1	41.1	40.9	40.8	40.8	40.5	40.4	40.5	40.5	40.3	40.2	40.2	40.1
E07000209	Guildford	37.6	37.8	38.3	38.4	38.4	38.5	38.7	38.7	38.6	38.6	38.6	38.6	38.4	38.1	37.9	37.5
E07000210	Mole Valley	46.3	46.0	45.6	45.3	45.1	44.7	44.4	44.1	43.8	43.5	43.4	43.1	42.9	42.7	42.7	42.4
E07000211	Reigate and Banstead	41.2	41.1	40.9	40.9	40.7	40.5	40.4	40.3	40.2	40.1	40.1	39.9	39.6	39.5	39.3	39.0
E07000212	Runnymede	38.6	39.1	39.2	39.3	39.4	39.6	39.5	39.5	39.4	39.3	39.4	39.3	39.0	38.6	38.4	37.9
E07000213	Spelthorne	41.6	41.5	41.5	41.4	41.3	41.1	41.1	40.9	40.7	40.5	40.4	40.3	40.0	39.7	39.4	39.1
E07000214	Surrey Heath	43.3	42.9	42.6	42.4	42.0	41.6	41.3	41.0	40.7	40.3	40.1	39.8	39.5	39.3	39.0	38.7
E07000215	Tandridge	44.0	43.9	43.7	43.5	43.4	43.1	42.9	42.6	42.3	42.1	42.0	41.8	41.5	41.2	41.1	40.7
E07000216	Waverley	44.2	44.0	43.8	43.5	43.2	43.0	42.8	42.5	42.3	42.0	41.8	41.6	41.4	41.2	41.1	40.9
E07000217	Woking	40.1	39.8	39.5	39.1	38.9	38.6	38.5	38.5	38.2	38.2	38.3	38.3	38.2	38.0	37.8	37.5
E10000032	West Sussex	44.7	44.4	44.3	44.0	43.8	43.5	43.3	43.0	42.8	42.6	42.4	42.2	42.0	41.8	41.6	41.4
E07000223	Adur	44.9	44.8	44.7	44.5	44.4	44.3	44.0	43.8	43.6	43.4	43.2	43.1	42.8	42.6	42.5	42.6
E07000224	Arun	48.8	48.5	48.2	47.9	47.6	47.4	47.1	46.8	46.7	46.4	46.2	46.1	46.2	46.1	46.0	45.9
E07000225	Chichester	48.2	48.0	47.9	47.3	47.1	46.8	46.5	46.2	46.0	45.7	45.6	45.4	45.2	45.0	44.8	44.7
E07000226	Crawley	36.5	36.3	36.1	36.0	35.9	35.8	35.9	36.0	36.0	36.2	36.2	36.3	36.2	36.1	35.9	35.5
E07000227	Horsham	45.7	45.6	45.4	45.1	44.7	44.3	43.8	43.5	43.0	42.6	42.2	41.8	41.4	41.0	40.8	40.4

MYE6: Median age of population for local authorities in the UK, mid-2001 to mid-2016

Code	Name	Mid-2001	Mid-2002	Mid-2003	Mid-2004	Mid-2005	Mid-2006	Mid-2007	Mid-2008	Mid-2009	Mid-2010	Mid-2011	Mid-2012	Mid-2013	Mid-2014	Mid-2015	Mid-2016
E07000228	Mid Sussex	40.4	40.5	40.7	40.9	41.2	41.4	41.5	41.7	41.9	42.1	42.3	42.6	42.8	43.0	43.2	43.3
E07000229	Worthing	41.8	41.8	41.8	41.7	41.8	42.0	42.1	42.2	42.4	42.7	42.8	43.3	43.5	43.9	44.1	44.4
E12000009	**SOUTH WEST**	40.5	40.8	41.0	41.2	41.3	41.5	41.7	42.0	42.3	42.5	42.7	42.9	43.1	43.3	43.5	43.6
E06000022	Bath and North East Somerset	39.4	39.4	39.5	39.5	39.9	39.9	39.9	40.0	40.4	40.5	40.6	40.5	40.3	40.2	39.6	39.0
E06000028	Bournemouth	39.5	39.3	39.3	39.3	39.1	39.2	38.8	38.8	38.8	38.4	38.2	38.1	38.1	38.3	38.3	38.3
E06000023	Bristol, City of	34.9	35.0	34.9	34.6	34.3	34.3	34.2	34.0	34.0	33.9	33.8	33.6	33.5	33.3	33.1	32.9
E06000052	Cornwall	43.4	43.6	43.8	43.9	44.1	44.4	44.4	44.7	45.0	45.2	45.4	45.6	45.9	46.1	46.4	46.6
E06000053	Isles of Scilly	43.5	43.9	43.9	42.7	44.3	43.6	43.9	44.2	45.0	46.0	46.1	46.3	45.8	46.7	46.5	47.2
E06000024	North Somerset	42.3	42.5	42.5	42.7	42.8	43.0	43.0	43.3	43.6	43.9	44.3	44.6	44.8	45.1	45.3	45.5
E06000026	Plymouth	37.5	37.8	38.0	38.1	38.0	38.0	38.0	38.2	38.4	38.4	38.3	38.3	38.2	38.1	38.1	38.0
E06000029	Poole	41.4	41.7	41.8	42.0	42.1	42.2	42.3	42.4	42.6	42.8	42.9	43.3	43.6	43.8	44.0	44.1
E06000025	South Gloucestershire	37.9	38.3	38.6	38.9	39.2	39.4	39.7	40.0	40.3	40.6	40.8	41.1	41.2	41.3	41.3	41.1
E06000030	Swindon	36.5	36.6	36.8	37.1	37.3	37.4	37.4	37.5	37.8	38.0	38.3	38.6	38.8	39.1	39.3	39.5
E06000027	Torbay	44.1	44.3	44.4	44.4	44.5	44.8	45.0	45.3	45.6	45.9	46.3	46.7	47.0	47.2	47.5	47.9
E06000054	Wiltshire	39.2	39.4	39.7	40.1	40.4	40.7	41.0	41.3	41.6	41.9	42.2	42.6	43.0	43.3	43.6	44.0
E10000008	Devon	43.2	43.5	43.7	43.9	44.0	44.3	44.5	44.8	45.2	45.5	45.8	46.0	46.3	46.5	46.6	46.8
E07000040	East Devon	48.1	48.3	48.4	48.5	48.5	48.6	48.7	48.9	49.2	49.4	49.6	49.7	50.0	50.2	50.2	50.5
E07000041	Exeter	36.0	36.3	36.4	36.5	36.0	36.1	36.1	36.2	36.3	36.1	35.7	35.2	34.8	34.6	34.2	34.0
E07000042	Mid Devon	41.9	42.2	42.4	42.6	42.9	43.1	43.2	43.5	43.9	44.2	44.5	44.8	45.2	45.4	45.7	46.1
E07000043	North Devon	43.3	43.6	43.6	43.8	43.9	44.1	44.3	44.6	44.9	45.2	45.5	45.8	46.2	46.5	46.9	47.1
E07000044	South Hams	44.7	45.1	45.5	45.9	46.3	46.6	46.8	47.2	47.7	48.2	48.6	49.0	49.3	49.8	50.0	50.5
E07000045	Teignbridge	44.0	44.3	44.6	44.8	45.0	45.4	45.7	46.1	46.4	46.8	47.1	47.6	47.9	48.0	48.3	48.6
E07000046	Torridge	44.3	44.7	45.1	45.4	45.7	45.9	46.2	46.5	47.0	47.2	47.6	47.8	48.2	48.6	49.0	49.4
E07000047	West Devon	44.6	44.5	45.1	45.4	45.6	45.8	46.1	46.3	46.7	47.1	47.6	48.2	48.8	49.2	49.7	50.1
E10000009	Dorset	45.1	45.3	45.5	45.8	46.0	46.2	46.5	46.8	47.2	47.5	47.8	48.3	48.6	49.1	49.4	49.8
E07000048	Christchurch	49.6	49.6	49.5	49.3	49.3	49.3	49.4	49.4	49.4	49.4	49.6	49.8	49.8	50.0	50.3	50.5
E07000049	East Dorset	47.6	47.9	48.0	48.2	48.3	48.6	48.8	49.1	49.4	49.7	50.1	50.5	50.8	51.2	51.4	51.7
E07000050	North Dorset	41.4	41.8	42.1	42.4	42.6	42.7	43.1	43.5	44.0	44.5	44.7	45.2	45.5	46.2	46.6	47.0
E07000051	Purbeck	44.6	45.0	45.4	45.7	45.8	46.1	46.3	46.5	46.9	47.2	47.6	47.8	48.2	48.6	48.7	49.1
E07000052	West Dorset	46.2	46.5	46.6	47.0	47.2	47.5	47.8	48.2	48.6	48.9	49.3	49.7	50.1	50.6	51.1	51.5
E07000053	Weymouth and Portland	41.9	42.0	42.2	42.6	42.9	43.1	43.4	43.8	44.1	44.4	44.8	45.3	45.8	46.3	46.8	47.4
E10000013	Gloucestershire	39.9	40.1	40.4	40.6	40.9	41.1	41.4	41.7	42.0	42.3	42.6	42.9	43.2	43.5	43.7	44.0
E07000078	Cheltenham	37.8	38.0	38.2	38.3	38.3	38.3	38.3	38.4	38.5	38.4	38.5	38.8	39.2	39.4	39.6	39.7
E07000079	Cotswold	42.9	43.3	43.5	43.8	44.1	44.4	44.7	45.2	45.7	46.2	46.5	47.0	47.3	47.6	48.0	48.4
E07000080	Forest of Dean	41.2	41.6	41.8	42.2	42.6	43.0	43.4	43.8	44.3	44.9	45.4	45.8	46.3	46.7	47.1	47.5
E07000081	Gloucester	36.8	37.1	37.3	37.5	37.6	37.7	37.7	37.7	38.0	38.1	38.2	38.3	38.4	38.5	38.5	38.5
E07000082	Stroud	41.3	41.6	41.8	42.1	42.4	42.7	43.0	43.3	43.7	44.1	44.4	44.9	45.2	45.4	45.6	45.8
E07000083	Tewkesbury	41.2	41.4	41.7	42.1	42.4	42.7	43.1	43.4	43.6	43.8	44.1	44.7	44.7	44.8	44.9	45.0
E10000027	Somerset	41.6	41.9	42.2	42.5	42.7	43.0	43.3	43.7	44.0	44.3	44.7	45.0	45.3	45.7	46.0	46.3
E07000187	Mendip	40.3	40.6	41.0	41.3	41.7	42.0	42.4	42.7	43.2	43.6	44.1	44.5	44.9	45.3	45.6	45.9
E07000188	Sedgemoor	41.8	42.1	42.4	42.7	43.0	43.2	43.4	43.7	44.0	44.3	44.6	44.9	45.1	45.3	45.6	45.9

MYE6: Median age of population for local authorities in the UK, mid-2001 to mid-2016

Code	Name	Mid-2001	Mid-2002	Mid-2003	Mid-2004	Mid-2005	Mid-2006	Mid-2007	Mid-2008	Mid-2009	Mid-2010	Mid-2011	Mid-2012	Mid-2013	Mid-2014	Mid-2015	Mid-2016
E07000189	South Somerset	41.6	41.9	42.2	42.5	42.8	43.2	43.5	43.8	44.1	44.5	44.8	45.1	45.5	45.9	46.2	46.6
E07000190	Taunton Deane	40.7	40.8	41.1	41.2	41.4	41.7	42.0	42.3	42.5	42.8	43.1	43.4	43.7	44.1	44.4	44.6
E07000191	West Somerset	48.8	49.2	49.6	49.9	50.4	50.7	50.9	51.1	51.1	51.3	51.8	52.2	52.7	53.3	53.8	54.5
W92000004	WALES	39.4	39.6	39.9	40.1	40.3	40.5	40.7	40.9	41.1	41.3	41.5	41.7	41.9	42.1	42.3	42.4
W06000001	Isle of Anglesey	42.2	42.7	43.1	43.4	43.6	43.9	44.2	44.5	44.8	45.2	45.5	45.8	46.0	46.3	46.7	47.2
W06000002	Gwynedd	40.6	40.9	41.2	41.3	41.6	41.9	42.2	42.5	42.6	42.6	42.7	42.8	43.1	43.3	43.2	43.2
W06000003	Conwy	44.0	44.3	44.6	44.8	45.1	45.3	45.5	45.8	46.1	46.5	46.9	47.3	47.5	47.9	48.3	48.7
W06000004	Denbighshire	41.8	42.0	42.4	42.7	43.0	43.3	43.5	43.7	43.9	44.2	44.4	44.8	45.0	45.3	45.6	45.9
W06000005	Flintshire	38.6	39.0	39.4	39.8	40.2	40.5	40.7	41.0	41.4	41.7	42.0	42.4	42.7	43.0	43.3	43.6
W06000006	Wrexham	38.7	39.0	39.2	39.5	39.7	39.8	40.0	40.1	40.2	40.4	40.5	40.9	41.2	41.4	41.7	41.9
W06000023	Powys	43.1	43.5	43.8	44.1	44.4	44.7	45.1	45.5	45.8	46.3	46.7	47.2	47.7	48.2	48.6	49.1
W06000008	Ceredigion	40.9	41.2	41.5	41.7	42.0	42.3	42.6	43.0	43.2	43.1	42.9	42.7	43.0	43.6	44.2	45.0
W06000009	Pembrokeshire	42.1	42.5	42.9	43.3	43.6	43.9	44.1	44.3	44.6	45.0	45.3	45.6	45.9	46.3	46.7	47.2
W06000010	Carmarthenshire	42.1	42.3	42.5	42.8	43.0	43.2	43.3	43.6	43.8	44.1	44.3	44.5	44.8	45.2	45.4	45.7
W06000011	Swansea	39.7	39.8	39.8	39.7	39.8	39.8	39.8	39.8	39.9	39.9	40.0	40.1	40.2	40.3	40.2	39.9
W06000012	Neath Port Talbot	40.7	40.9	41.0	41.2	41.4	41.7	41.8	42.0	42.2	42.4	42.5	42.8	43.0	43.2	43.4	43.4
W06000013	Bridgend	39.2	39.4	39.6	39.9	40.1	40.3	40.5	40.8	41.1	41.5	41.7	42.0	42.3	42.6	42.8	42.9
W06000014	Vale of Glamorgan	39.7	40.0	40.3	40.5	40.8	41.1	41.2	41.4	41.6	41.9	42.2	42.6	42.8	43.1	43.4	43.6
W06000015	Cardiff	34.5	34.5	34.5	34.3	34.2	34.2	34.0	33.9	33.9	33.8	33.8	33.6	33.6	33.7	33.7	33.6
W06000016	Rhondda Cynon Taf	38.1	38.4	38.6	38.6	38.9	39.1	39.3	39.5	39.9	40.1	40.4	40.5	40.7	40.8	40.8	40.7
W06000024	Merthyr Tydfil	38.3	38.6	39.0	39.3	39.5	39.7	39.8	39.8	40.0	40.3	40.5	40.8	40.8	40.9	40.8	40.7
W06000018	Caerphilly	37.8	38.0	38.3	38.6	38.9	39.1	39.4	39.6	39.9	40.2	40.4	40.8	41.0	41.2	41.3	41.5
W06000019	Blaenau Gwent	38.7	39.1	39.5	39.8	40.1	40.3	40.5	40.7	40.9	41.2	41.5	41.8	42.1	42.3	42.6	42.8
W06000020	Torfaen	39.1	39.5	39.8	40.1	40.4	40.7	40.8	41.0	41.1	41.4	41.7	41.9	42.1	42.3	42.5	42.6
W06000021	Monmouthshire	41.9	42.1	42.4	42.7	43.1	43.5	43.8	44.2	44.7	45.1	45.6	46.1	46.6	47.0	47.5	47.9
W06000022	Newport	37.7	37.9	38.1	38.4	38.5	38.7	38.8	38.8	38.9	39.0	39.0	39.0	39.1	39.1	39.1	39.0
S92000003	SCOTLAND	38.7	39.1	39.4	39.7	40.0	40.3	40.5	40.7	40.9	41.1	41.3	41.5	41.7	41.9	42.0	41.9
S12000033	Aberdeen City	36.9	37.2	37.5	37.9	38.0	38.0	37.8	37.7	37.4	37.1	36.8	36.6	36.4	36.2	36.1	36.3
S12000034	Aberdeenshire	39.3	39.7	40.1	40.4	40.8	41.1	41.3	41.6	41.9	42.0	42.2	42.4	42.5	42.6	42.8	43.0
S12000041	Angus	41.4	41.7	42.2	42.4	42.7	42.9	43.2	43.5	43.9	44.2	44.5	44.9	45.2	45.5	45.8	46.1
S12000035	Argyll and Bute	41.9	42.6	43.0	43.6	44.0	44.3	44.7	45.3	45.7	46.3	46.5	47.4	47.3	47.9	48.3	48.5
S12000036	City of Edinburgh	36.4	36.6	36.9	37.0	37.0	37.0	36.9	37.0	36.9	36.8	36.6	36.5	36.6	36.6	36.5	36.3
S12000005	Clackmannanshire	38.6	39.0	39.5	39.7	40.0	40.3	40.4	40.6	41.0	41.6	42.1	42.7	43.0	43.4	43.9	44.2
S12000006	Dumfries and Galloway	42.5	43.0	43.5	43.9	44.3	44.6	45.0	45.3	45.7	46.1	46.4	46.9	47.3	47.7	48.1	48.5
S12000042	Dundee City	38.4	38.8	38.8	39.1	39.0	39.1	39.1	38.9	38.7	38.5	38.1	37.7	37.5	37.5	37.3	37.2
S12000008	East Ayrshire	39.2	39.6	39.9	40.2	40.5	40.9	41.2	41.5	41.8	42.2	42.5	42.9	43.2	43.5	43.8	44.1
S12000045	East Dunbartonshire	40.1	40.8	41.3	41.8	42.3	42.8	43.3	43.8	44.2	44.6	45.0	45.3	45.6	45.8	45.9	46.0
S12000010	East Lothian	40.0	40.5	40.0	41.2	41.6	41.9	42.0	42.0	42.3	42.6	42.9	43.1	43.4	43.7	43.9	44.2
S12000011	East Renfrewshire	39.7	40.1	40.6	40.9	41.4	41.8	42.1	42.5	42.9	43.2	43.4	43.7	43.8	43.7	43.8	43.7
S12000014	Falkirk	38.6	38.9	39.1	39.4	39.5	39.8	40.1	40.4	40.7	41.0	41.3	41.6	42.0	42.4	42.6	42.8

MYE6: Median age of population for local authorities in the UK, mid-2001 to mid-2016

Code	Name	Mid-2001	Mid-2002	Mid-2003	Mid-2004	Mid-2005	Mid-2006	Mid-2007	Mid-2008	Mid-2009	Mid-2010	Mid-2011	Mid-2012	Mid-2013	Mid-2014	Mid-2015	Mid-2016
S12000015	Fife	39.1	39.5	39.9	40.2	40.4	40.7	41.0	41.4	41.6	42.0	42.2	42.5	42.7	43.1	43.4	43.4
S12000046	Glasgow City	36.2	36.3	36.4	36.6	36.7	36.8	36.7	36.7	36.5	36.4	36.2	36.1	36.0	36.0	35.8	35.7
S12000017	Highland	40.9	41.4	41.8	42.1	42.4	42.6	42.9	43.2	43.5	43.8	44.1	44.5	44.9	45.3	45.4	45.7
S12000018	Inverclyde	39.5	39.9	40.3	40.7	41.0	41.5	41.9	42.3	42.7	43.1	43.6	44.0	44.3	44.7	45.0	45.4
S12000019	Midlothian	39.0	39.5	39.9	40.3	40.7	41.1	41.3	41.3	41.7	42.0	42.1	42.3	42.5	42.5	42.3	42.2
S12000020	Moray	39.0	39.4	39.7	40.2	40.6	41.0	41.4	41.7	42.1	42.4	42.8	43.4	43.5	43.9	44.1	44.3
S12000013	Na h-Eileanan Siar	42.9	43.3	43.5	43.7	44.0	44.3	44.6	45.0	45.4	45.8	46.1	46.5	46.8	47.4	47.8	48.2
S12000021	North Ayrshire	39.5	40.0	40.4	40.8	41.3	41.7	42.1	42.3	42.7	43.2	43.6	44.1	44.5	45.0	45.3	45.6
S12000044	North Lanarkshire	37.1	37.5	37.8	38.1	38.4	38.7	38.9	39.1	39.4	39.7	40.0	40.3	40.6	40.8	41.1	41.2
S12000023	Orkney Islands	41.1	41.6	42.1	42.3	42.8	43.2	43.6	44.0	44.3	44.7	45.1	45.4	45.9	46.4	46.8	47.1
S12000024	Perth and Kinross	41.7	42.2	42.6	43.0	43.3	43.5	43.7	43.9	44.1	44.4	44.7	45.0	45.3	45.6	45.9	46.1
S12000038	Renfrewshire	39.0	39.4	39.7	40.1	40.4	40.7	41.0	41.2	41.6	41.8	42.1	42.5	42.8	43.1	43.3	43.2
S12000026	Scottish Borders	42.1	42.5	42.9	43.3	43.6	44.0	44.3	44.6	45.0	45.6	46.1	46.5	47.0	47.4	47.8	48.1
S12000027	Shetland Islands	38.2	38.6	39.1	39.4	39.7	40.3	40.6	40.9	41.2	41.2	41.4	42.0	42.2	42.6	42.8	43.1
S12000028	South Ayrshire	42.2	42.7	43.1	43.5	43.8	44.3	44.6	44.9	45.3	45.6	45.9	46.3	46.7	47.1	47.5	47.9
S12000029	South Lanarkshire	38.8	39.2	39.6	39.9	40.3	40.6	40.8	41.2	41.6	41.9	42.3	42.7	43.0	43.4	43.6	43.8
S12000030	Stirling	38.8	39.1	39.2	39.8	40.0	40.2	40.4	40.8	41.2	41.3	41.4	41.6	41.9	42.2	42.0	41.9
S12000039	West Dunbartonshire	38.4	38.8	39.1	39.5	40.0	40.3	40.6	40.9	41.2	41.6	42.0	42.2	42.5	42.8	42.9	43.0
S12000040	West Lothian	36.3	36.7	37.1	37.5	37.8	38.1	38.4	38.7	38.9	39.2	39.6	39.9	40.3	40.5	40.6	40.7
N92000002	**NORTHERN IRELAND**	34.7	35.0	35.4	35.7	36.0	36.2	36.4	36.6	36.8	37.1	37.4	37.6	37.8	38.0	38.1	38.3
N09000001	Antrim and Newtownabbey	35.3	35.6	35.9	36.2	36.4	36.7	36.9	37.0	37.1	37.4	37.7	38.0	38.2	38.5	38.7	38.9
N09000011	Ards and North Down	38.4	38.8	39.2	39.6	39.9	40.2	40.5	40.7	41.0	41.4	41.7	42.1	42.5	42.9	43.1	43.4
N09000002	Armagh City, Banbridge & Craigavon	34.4	34.8	35.2	35.5	35.7	35.8	36.0	36.1	36.2	36.4	36.6	36.7	37.0	37.1	37.2	37.3
N09000003	Belfast	34.3	34.3	34.4	34.5	34.7	34.8	34.8	34.8	34.8	34.9	35.1	35.2	35.2	35.3	35.4	35.5
N09000004	Causeway Coast and Glens	34.9	35.2	35.6	36.0	36.4	36.8	37.2	37.6	38.0	38.4	38.8	39.3	39.7	40.0	40.3	40.6
N09000005	Derry City and Strabane	31.5	32.0	32.4	32.9	33.4	33.9	34.2	34.6	35.0	35.3	35.7	35.9	36.2	36.5	36.8	37.2
N09000006	Fermanagh and Omagh	34.1	34.6	35.0	35.5	35.8	36.1	36.3	36.5	36.8	37.1	37.4	37.7	38.1	38.4	38.6	38.9
N09000007	Lisburn and Castlereagh	36.4	36.8	37.3	37.7	38.0	38.4	38.8	39.0	39.1	39.3	39.6	39.9	40.2	40.2	40.3	40.3
N09000008	Mid and East Antrim	36.7	37.1	37.5	37.9	38.2	38.6	38.9	39.3	39.6	40.1	40.4	40.9	41.2	41.5	41.7	41.9
N09000009	Mid Ulster	32.6	32.9	33.3	33.6	33.8	33.9	33.9	34.0	34.2	34.4	34.6	34.8	35.0	35.2	35.5	35.8
N09000010	Newry, Mourne and Down	33.3	33.7	34.1	34.4	34.7	35.0	35.1	35.2	35.5	35.8	36.1	36.3	36.5	36.8	37.0	37.2

Section 3 Vital Statistics

A. Live births by mothers' usual area of residence, 2016

Information, Terms and conditions

Table 1: Summary: Live births (numbers, rates and percentages): administrative area of usual residence, United Kingdom and constituent countries, 2016.

Table 2: Live births (numbers and rates): age and administrative area of usual residence of mother, England and Wales, 2016.

B. Mortality Statistics: Deaths Registered by Area of Usual Residence, 2016 Registrations

Information, Terms and conditions

Table 1a: Deaths (numbers and rates) by area of usual residence (administrative areas), 2016 registrations, United Kingdom and constituent countries.

Table 1b: Deaths (numbers and rates) by area of usual residence (regions/health areas), 2016 registrations, United Kingdom and constituent countries.

C. Estimates of the very old (including centenarians), 2002 to 2016

Statistical Bulletin: Estimates of the Very Old (including Centenarians): 2002 to 2016

Tables 1 -3: Mid-2002 to mid-2016 population estimates of the very old (including centenarians) by single year of age and by age groups:

Table 1: for the UK.

Table 2: for England.

Table 3: for Wales.

A. Live births by mothers' usual area of residence, 2016

Information on births by mothers' usual area of residence statistics

Things you need to know
- Birth statistics represent births which occurred in England and Wales in the calendar year, but include a very small number of late registrations from the previous year.
- Figures are compiled from information supplied when births are registered as part of civil registration, a legal
- Figures published here represent the area of usual residence of the mother for births which occurred in England and
- Births to women whose usual residence is outside England and Wales are included in total figures for England and Wales, but excluded from any sub-division of England and Wales by area of usual residence.

Quality and Methodology
The Birth Statistics Quality and Methodology Information document contains important information on:
- the strengths and limitations of the data
- the quality of the output: including the accuracy of the data, how it compares with related data
- uses and users
- how the output was created

Our User guide to birth statistics provides information on data quality, legislation and procedures relating to birth

The ONS guidance on protecting confidentiality in birth and death statistics (currently under revision) is available on our website.

The annual births dataset
The total number of births recorded in these tables for 2016 includes:
- births occurring in 2016 which were registered by 25 February 2017
- 229 births occurring in 2015 which were registered between 26 February 2016 and 25 February 2017 - births registered too late to be included in the 2015 annual births dataset

Birth rates and fertility rates
Information on how birth rates and fertility rates have been calculated is contained in our User guide to birth statistics

Population estimates used to calculate rates
The most up to date population estimates at the time of this release have been used to calculate rates.
Population estimates for England and Wales

Age of mother
Where age of mother is missing on the birth registration, we try to obtain the age from the birth notification. In recent years 0.1% of births have age of mother missing following birth notification matching. These records have age of mother imputed. More information on the imputation method, and the level of imputation in recent years is available in our User

Births within marriage or civil partnership
A birth within marriage or civil partnership is that of a child born to parents who were lawfully married or in a civil partnership either:
- at the date of the child's birth
- when the child was conceived, even if they later divorced or were granted a civil partnership dissolution or the father or second parent died before the child's birth

Births outside marriage and civil partnership
Births occurring outside marriage and civil partnership may be registered either jointly or solely. A joint registration records details of both parents, and requires them both to be present. A sole registration records only the mother's details. In a few cases a joint registration is made in the absence of the father or second parent if an affiliation order or statutory declaration is provided. Information from the birth registration is used to determine whether the parents jointly registering a birth outside marriage and civil partnership were usually resident at the same address at the time of registration. Births with both parents at the same address are identified by a single entry for the informant's usual address, while different addresses are identified by two entries.

Maternities
A maternity is a pregnancy resulting in the birth of one or more children, including stillbirths. It therefore represents the number for women giving birth - including stillbirths, rather than the number of babies born.

Stillbirth
A stillbirth is a baby born after 24 or more weeks completed gestation and which did not, at any time, breathe or show signs of life.

Symbols and conventions
In ONS birth statistics the symbols used are:
0 denotes nil
z denotes not applicable
: denotes not available
u denotes low reliability

Rates are not calculated where there are fewer than 3 births in a cell, denoted by (:u); rates based on such low numbers are susceptible to inaccurate interpretation.

Rates in tables calculated from between 3 and 19 births are denoted by (u) as a warning to the user that their reliability as a measure may be affected by the small number of events.

It is our practice not to calculate age-standardised rates, such as the total fertility rate (TFR), where there are fewer than 10 births in total across all ages. Rates based on such low numbers are susceptible to inaccurate interpretation.

Further guidance on the use of symbols in tables is available.

Further Information and Enquiries
Special extracts and tabulations of births data for England and Wales are available to order for a charge (subject to legal frameworks, disclosure control, resources and the ONS charging policy, where appropriate).
Enquiries should be made to Vital Statistics Outputs Branch (vsob@ons.gsi.gov.uk or telephone: +44 (0)1329 444110). User requested data will be published onto our website.

Access to microdata and disclosive data, that is, data which have the potential to identify an individual record, requires the approval of the ONS Microdata Release Procedure (MRP) before the data can be provided.

Feedback
We welcome feedback from users, please contact Vital Statistics Outputs Branch
email: vsob@ons.gsi.gov.uk
telephone: +44 (0)1329 444110

Terms and conditions

A National Statistics publication

National Statistics are produced to high professional standards set out in the Code of Practice for Official Statistics. They are produced free from any political interference.

The United Kingdom Statistics Authority has designated these statistics as National Statistics, in accordance with the Statistics and Registration Service Act 2007 and signifying compliance with the Code of Practice for Official Statistics.

Designation can be broadly interpreted to mean that the statistics:

• meet identified user needs

• are well explained and readily accessible

• are produced according to sound methods

• are managed impartially and objectively in the public interest

Once statistics have been designated as National Statistics it is a statutory requirement that the Code of Practice shall continue to be observed.

About us

We are the executive office of the UK Statistics Authority, a non-ministerial department which reports directly to Parliament and the UK government's single largest statistical producer. We compile information about the UK's society and economy, and provides the evidence-base for policy and decision-making, the allocation of resources, and public accountability.

Copyright and reproduction

© Crown copyright 2017

You may re-use this document/publication (not including logos) free of charge in any format or medium, under the terms of the Open Government Licence. Users should include a source accreditation to ONS - Source: Office for National Statistics (www.ons.gov.uk)

To view this licence visit http://www.nationalarchives.gov.uk/doc/open-government-licence/;

or write to the Information Policy Team, The National Archives, Kew, Richmond, Surrey, TW9 4DU; or email: psi@nationalarchives.gsi.gov.uk.

Where we have identified any third party copyright information you will need to obtain permission from the copyright holders concerned.

This document/publication is also available on our website at www.ons.gov.uk

Table 1   Summary: Live births (numbers, rates and percentages): administrative area of usual residence of mother, United Kingdom and constituent countries, 2016

England and Wales: regions (within England), unitary authorities, counties, districts, London Boroughs, local health boards (within Wales)
Scotland: council areas, Northern Ireland: 11 new Administrative Areas

Area of usual residence		Population — Numbers (thousands)			Live Births — Numbers[1] — All			Within marriage or civil partnership	Outside marriage or civil partnership — Total	Joint regis-trations same address	Joint regis-trations different address	Sole regis-trations	Rates[2] — Crude Birth Rate (CBR): all births per 1,000 population of all ages	General Fertility Rate (GFR): all live births per 1,000 women aged 15 to 44	Total Fertility Rate (TFR)[3]	Percentages — Percentage of live births outside marriage or civil partnership	Percentage of live births under 2.5kg	Maternities — Numbers Total	Maternity Rate[4]
		Total	Female	Females aged 15 to 44	Total	Male	Female												
K02000001	UNITED KINGDOM	65,648.0	33,270.4	12,566.0	774,835	397,707	377,128	404,890	369,945	247,222	83,083	39,640	11.8	61.7	1.79	47.7	:	765,931	61.0
K04000001, J99000001	ENGLAND, WALES AND ELSEWHERE[5]	58,381.2	29,546.3	11,167.2	696,271	357,046	339,225	364,521	331,750	223,711	71,917	36,122	11.9	62.3	1.81	47.6	7.0	688,262	61.6
E92000001	ENGLAND	55,268.1	27,967.1	10,607.6	663,157	340,159	322,998	350,979	312,178	210,483	67,546	34,149	12.0	62.5	1.81	47.1	7.0	655,467	61.8
E12000001	NORTH EAST	2,636.8	1,342.5	487.5	28,574	14,675	13,899	11,484	17,090	10,451	4,764	1,875	10.8	58.6	1.72	59.8	7.1	28,214	57.9
E06000047	County Durham	522.1	265.4	93.9	5,304	2,749	2,555	1,993	3,311	2,127	853	331	10.2	56.5	1.67	62.4	7.8	5,233	55.7
E06000005	Darlington	105.6	54.3	19.0	1,154	594	560	480	674	431	177	66	10.9	60.6	1.83	58.4	10.2	1,144	60.1
E06000001	Hartlepool	92.8	47.5	16.9	1,051	539	512	286	765	448	230	87	11.3	62.2	1.81	72.8	8.3	1,038	61.4
E06000002	Middlesbrough	140.4	71.1	27.6	1,908	981	927	722	1,186	617	404	165	13.6	69.0	1.98	62.2	8.9	1,888	68.3
E06000057	Northumberland	316.0	161.8	49.4	2,820	1,383	1,437	1,238	1,582	1,075	347	160	8.9	57.1	1.74	56.1	4.8	2,780	56.3
E06000003	Redcar and Cleveland	135.4	69.6	23.1	1,433	741	692	415	1,018	647	269	102	10.6	61.9	1.84	71.0	6.7	1,412	61.0
E06000004	Stockton-on-Tees	195.7	99.6	36.4	2,298	1,205	1,093	945	1,353	825	368	160	11.7	63.2	1.85	58.9	7.7	2,273	62.5
E11000007	Tyne and Wear (Met County)	1,128.8	573.1	221.2	12,606	6,483	6,123	5,405	7,201	4,281	2,116	804	11.2	57.0	1.66	57.1	6.5	12,446	56.3
E08000037	Gateshead	201.6	102.4	37.8	2,286	1,183	1,103	1,000	1,286	769	384	133	11.3	60.5	1.75	56.3	7.1	2,252	59.6
E08000021	Newcastle upon Tyne	296.5	146.2	67.8	3,393	1,724	1,669	1,702	1,691	979	521	191	11.4	50.0	1.56	49.8	5.6	3,351	49.4
E08000022	North Tyneside	203.3	105.0	36.9	2,254	1,165	1,089	1,050	1,204	765	319	120	11.1	61.0	1.80	53.4	5.8	2,221	60.2
E08000023	South Tyneside	149.4	77.0	26.7	1,687	851	836	597	1,090	616	335	139	11.3	63.1	1.85	64.6	6.7	1,671	62.5
E08000024	Sunderland	278.0	142.5	52.0	2,986	1,560	1,426	1,056	1,930	1,152	557	221	10.7	57.4	1.67	64.6	7.4	2,951	56.8
E12000002	NORTH WEST	7,219.6	3,658.7	1,358.0	86,069	44,292	41,777	39,571	46,498	30,430	10,826	5,242	11.9	63.4	1.85	54.0	7.1	85,193	62.7
E06000008	Blackburn with Darwen	147.0	73.6	28.5	2,156	1,071	1,085	1,141	1,015	672	213	130	14.7	75.7	2.25	47.1	11.9	2,138	75.1
E06000009	Blackpool	139.2	70.4	24.1	1,700	867	833	479	1,221	809	244	168	12.2	70.6	2.09	71.8	7.2	1,684	69.9
E06000049	Cheshire East	376.7	192.1	61.5	3,822	1,933	1,889	1,958	1,864	1,451	267	146	10.1	62.2	1.93	48.8	6.7	3,789	61.7
E06000050	Cheshire West and Chester	335.7	172.0	59.2	3,565	1,834	1,731	1,758	1,807	1,303	361	143	10.6	60.3	1.83	50.7	6.8	3,523	59.6
E06000006	Halton	126.9	64.9	23.6	1,503	774	729	500	1,003	634	270	99	11.8	63.6	1.90	66.7	6.1	1,489	63.0
E06000007	Warrington	208.8	105.1	37.8	2,297	1,178	1,119	1,099	1,198	912	199	87	11.0	60.8	1.80	52.2	6.6	2,262	59.9
E10000006	Cumbria	497.9	252.3	78.5	4,758	2,445	2,313	2,083	2,675	2,005	428	242	9.6	60.6	1.86	56.2	6.5	4,710	60.0
E07000026	Allerdale	97.0	49.1	15.0	902	474	428	381	521	397	88	36	9.3	60.3	1.87	57.8	5.1	897	60.0
E07000027	Barrow-in-Furness	67.3	34.1	11.4	780	388	392	265	515	363	96	56	11.6	68.4	2.06	66.0	8.3	771	67.6
E07000028	Carlisle	108.4	55.5	19.2	1,170	611	559	510	660	482	108	70	10.8	61.1	1.82	56.4	6.1	1,162	60.7
E07000029	Copeland	69.3	34.4	11.1	703	355	348	277	426	298	86	42	10.1	63.3	1.92	60.6	7.0	692	62.3
E07000030	Eden	52.6	26.6	7.5	409	204	205	205	204	170	22	12	7.8	54.3	1.72	49.9	5.6	404	53.7
E07000031	South Lakeland	103.3	52.6	14.4	794	413	381	445	349	295	28	26	7.7	55.3	1.77	44.0	7.2	784	54.6

Table 1 Summary: Live births (numbers, rates and percentages): administrative area of usual residence of mother, United Kingdom and constituent countries, 2016

England and Wales: regions (within England), unitary authorities, counties, districts, London Boroughs, local health boards (within Wales)
Scotland: council areas, Northern Ireland: 11 new Administrative Areas

Area code	Area of usual residence	Population Numbers (thousands) Total	Female	Females aged 15 to 44	Live Births Numbers All Total	Male	Female	Within marriage or civil partnership	Outside marriage or civil partnership Total	Joint regis-trations same address	Joint regis-trations different address	Sole regis-trations	Crude Birth Rate (CBR) per 1,000 population of all ages	General Fertility Rate (GFR): all live births per 1,000 women aged 15 to 44	Total Fertility Rate (TFR)[3]	Percentage of live births outside marriage or civil partnership	Percentage of live births under 2.5kg	Maternities Numbers Total	Maternity Rate[4]
E11000001	**Greater Manchester (Met County)**	**2,782.1**	**1,400.3**	**561.3**	**36,889**	**18,920**	**17,969**	**18,338**	**18,551**	**11,609**	**4,761**	**2,181**	**13.3**	**65.7**	**1.87**	**50.3**	**6.5**	**36,543**	**65.1**
E08000001	Bolton	283.1	142.6	53.0	3,816	2,000	1,816	1,950	1,866	1,231	449	186	13.5	72.0	2.12	48.9	6.6	3,787	71.5
E08000002	Bury	188.7	96.2	34.7	2,362	1,233	1,129	1,268	1,094	745	243	106	12.5	68.1	2.00	46.3	6.1	2,330	67.2
E08000003	Manchester	541.3	266.6	139.2	7,946	4,004	3,942	4,288	3,658	1,954	1,130	574	14.7	57.1	1.64	46.0	6.8	7,877	56.6
E08000004	Oldham	232.7	118.0	44.4	3,327	1,694	1,633	1,739	1,588	968	431	189	14.3	75.0	2.18	47.7	8.3	3,295	74.3
E08000005	Rochdale	216.2	109.7	41.6	3,072	1,595	1,477	1,443	1,629	936	480	213	14.2	73.9	2.16	53.0	6.8	3,041	73.1
E08000006	Salford	248.7	123.4	52.9	3,695	1,934	1,761	1,678	2,017	1,173	604	240	14.9	69.8	1.93	54.6	6.7	3,670	69.4
E08000007	Stockport	290.6	148.3	52.0	3,424	1,729	1,695	1,799	1,625	1,100	370	155	11.8	65.8	1.93	47.5	5.2	3,384	65.1
E08000008	Tameside	223.2	113.6	41.9	2,876	1,501	1,375	1,129	1,747	1,201	375	171	12.9	68.7	1.99	60.7	6.2	2,858	68.3
E08000009	Trafford	234.7	119.8	43.3	2,813	1,377	1,436	1,700	1,113	767	232	114	12.0	64.9	1.91	39.6	5.6	2,779	64.1
E08000010	Wigan	323.1	162.2	58.4	3,558	1,853	1,705	1,344	2,214	1,534	447	233	11.0	60.9	1.79	62.2	6.6	3,522	60.3
E10000017	**Lancashire**	**1,198.8**	**607.0**	**213.8**	**13,183**	**6,839**	**6,344**	**6,160**	**7,023**	**5,025**	**1,272**	**726**	**11.0**	**61.7**	**1.85**	**53.3**	**7.6**	**13,035**	**61.0**
E07000117	Burnley	87.5	44.3	16.0	1,207	645	562	477	730	498	150	82	13.8	75.3	2.19	60.5	10.5	1,196	74.7
E07000118	Chorley	114.4	57.0	19.9	1,226	643	583	610	616	478	90	48	10.7	61.5	1.83	50.2	5.6	1,204	60.4
E07000119	Fylde	78.0	39.8	11.0	629	324	305	310	319	240	40	39	8.1	57.3	1.79	50.7	6.7	620	56.5
E07000120	Hyndburn	80.5	40.7	14.9	1,057	533	524	441	616	424	119	73	13.1	71.2	2.09	58.3	9.7	1,047	70.5
E07000121	Lancaster	143.5	72.8	28.5	1,456	725	731	669	787	534	171	82	10.1	51.1	1.62	54.1	7.5	1,439	50.5
E07000122	Pendle	90.6	45.8	16.6	1,214	625	589	717	497	342	87	68	13.4	73.2	2.12	40.9	8.4	1,200	72.4
E07000123	Preston	141.8	70.0	29.6	1,893	998	895	914	979	669	211	99	13.3	64.0	1.90	51.7	8.6	1,878	63.5
E07000124	Ribble Valley	58.8	29.9	9.0	482	257	225	245	237	203	21	13	8.2	53.5	1.75	49.2	4.8	475	52.7
E07000125	Rossendale	69.9	35.4	12.5	818	437	381	367	451	315	88	48	11.7	65.4	1.97	55.1	8.6	810	64.7
E07000126	South Ribble	110.1	56.3	19.1	1,241	597	644	576	665	496	116	53	11.3	64.8	1.95	53.6	5.5	1,231	64.3
E07000127	West Lancashire	113.4	58.2	20.2	1,000	541	459	427	573	436	88	49	8.8	49.5	1.65	57.3	5.5	988	48.9
E07000128	Wyre	110.3	56.5	16.5	960	514	446	407	553	390	91	72	8.7	58.3	1.79	57.6	7.3	947	57.6
E11000002	**Merseyside (Met County)**	**1,406.4**	**720.9**	**269.8**	**16,196**	**8,431**	**7,765**	**6,055**	**10,141**	**6,010**	**2,811**	**1,320**	**11.5**	**60.0**	**1.75**	**62.6**	**7.9**	**16,020**	**59.4**
E08000011	Knowsley	147.9	77.5	28.5	1,933	1,010	923	516	1,417	739	504	174	13.1	67.8	1.94	73.3	8.4	1,914	67.1
E08000012	Liverpool	484.6	244.4	109.5	6,030	3,104	2,926	2,253	3,777	2,131	1,069	577	12.4	55.0	1.60	62.6	8.8	5,955	54.4
E08000014	Sefton	274.3	142.2	45.0	2,805	1,467	1,338	1,107	1,698	1,117	402	179	10.2	62.3	1.88	60.5	6.3	2,784	61.9
E08000013	St. Helens	178.5	90.8	31.9	1,994	1,027	967	753	1,241	791	304	146	11.2	62.5	1.83	62.2	6.6	1,976	61.9
E08000015	Wirral	321.2	166.0	54.8	3,434	1,823	1,611	1,426	2,008	1,232	532	244	10.7	62.6	1.88	58.5	8.2	3,391	61.8
E12000003	**YORKSHIRE AND THE HUMBER**	**5,425.7**	**2,747.5**	**1,027.7**	**63,823**	**32,943**	**30,880**	**29,961**	**33,862**	**23,115**	**7,186**	**3,561**	**11.8**	**62.1**	**1.82**	**53.1**	**7.6**	**63,215**	**61.5**
E06000011	**East Riding of Yorkshire**	**337.7**	**172.0**	**51.0**	**2,869**	**1,527**	**1,342**	**1,311**	**1,558**	**1,221**	**223**	**114**	**8.5**	**56.3**	**1.84**	**54.3**	**6.1**	**2,834**	**55.6**
E06000010	**Kingston upon Hull, City of**	**260.2**	**129.4**	**54.0**	**3,550**	**1,871**	**1,679**	**1,156**	**2,394**	**1,568**	**574**	**252**	**13.6**	**65.7**	**1.80**	**67.4**	**8.0**	**3,534**	**65.4**
E06000012	**North East Lincolnshire**	**159.1**	**81.0**	**27.9**	**1,861**	**969**	**892**	**595**	**1,266**	**851**	**266**	**149**	**11.7**	**66.6**	**1.95**	**68.0**	**8.3**	**1,829**	**65.5**
E06000013	**North Lincolnshire**	**170.8**	**86.2**	**29.0**	**1,773**	**893**	**880**	**717**	**1,056**	**779**	**190**	**87**	**10.4**	**61.2**	**1.82**	**59.6**	**8.8**	**1,758**	**60.7**
E06000014	**York**	**208.4**	**106.2**	**45.0**	**1,936**	**1,008**	**928**	**1,047**	**889**	**680**	**136**	**73**	**9.3**	**43.0**	**1.37**	**45.9**	**6.0**	**1,920**	**42.6**

Table 1 Summary: Live births (numbers, rates and percentages): administrative area of usual residence of mother, United Kingdom and constituent countries, 2016

England and Wales: regions (within England), unitary authorities, counties, districts, London Boroughs, local health boards (within Wales)
Scotland: council areas, Northern Ireland: 11 new Administrative Areas

Area of usual residence		Population (thousands)			Live Births — Numbers[1] — All			Within marriage or civil partnership	Outside marriage or civil partnership				Rates[2] CBR (all births per 1,000 population of all ages)	GFR (all live births per 1,000 women aged 15 to 44)	TFR[3]	% of live births outside marriage or civil partnership	% of live births under 2.5kg	Maternities Numbers Total	Maternity Rate[4]
		Total	Female	Females aged 15 to 44	Total	Male	Female		Total	Joint regis-trations same address	Joint regis-trations different address	Sole regis-trations							
E10000023	**North Yorkshire**	**604.9**	**306.9**	**91.1**	**5,712**	**2,966**	**2,746**	**3,076**	**2,636**	**2,018**	**388**	**230**	**9.4**	**62.7**	**1.96**	**46.1**	**6.3**	**5,619**	**61.7**
E07000163	Craven	56.3	29.0	8.1	432	230	202	234	198	169	21	8	7.7	53.7	1.74	45.8	5.3	424	52.7
E07000164	Hambleton	90.5	46.1	13.1	803	416	387	464	339	256	55	28	8.9	61.3	1.93	42.2	4.5	786	60.0
E07000165	Harrogate	156.3	80.1	23.8	1,475	756	719	903	572	430	87	55	9.4	62.1	1.98	38.8	6.2	1,447	60.9
E07000166	Richmondshire	53.7	24.7	7.8	555	281	274	354	201	160	24	17	10.3	71.4	2.14	36.2	6.1	548	70.5
E07000167	Ryedale	53.5	27.3	7.7	439	244	195	233	206	161	25	20	8.2	56.9	1.80	46.9	7.5	435	56.3
E07000168	Scarborough	107.8	55.4	16.0	1,034	541	493	384	650	467	113	70	9.6	64.7	1.97	62.9	6.3	1,024	64.1
E07000169	Selby	86.7	44.2	14.7	974	498	476	504	470	375	63	32	11.2	66.1	2.00	48.3	7.8	955	64.8
E11000003	**South Yorkshire (Met County)**	**1,385.0**	**698.7**	**269.3**	**16,003**	**8,226**	**7,777**	**6,683**	**9,320**	**6,340**	**2,022**	**958**	**11.6**	**59.4**	**1.72**	**58.2**	**7.6**	**15,859**	**58.9**
E08000016	Barnsley	241.2	122.1	43.4	2,832	1,463	1,369	926	1,906	1,351	373	182	11.7	65.3	1.92	67.3	7.6	2,802	64.6
E08000017	Doncaster	306.4	154.4	54.6	3,535	1,839	1,696	1,283	2,252	1,573	462	217	11.5	64.7	1.89	63.7	8.2	3,501	64.1
E08000018	Rotherham	261.9	133.0	47.0	3,104	1,618	1,486	1,223	1,881	1,264	435	182	11.9	66.1	1.96	60.6	7.5	3,083	65.6
E08000019	Sheffield	575.4	289.2	124.4	6,532	3,306	3,226	3,251	3,281	2,152	752	377	11.4	52.5	1.58	50.2	7.4	6,473	52.0
E11000006	**West Yorkshire (Met County)**	**2,299.7**	**1,167.0**	**460.3**	**30,119**	**15,483**	**14,636**	**15,376**	**14,743**	**9,658**	**3,387**	**1,698**	**13.1**	**65.4**	**1.91**	**48.9**	**8.0**	**29,862**	**64.9**
E08000032	Bradford	534.3	270.7	105.4	7,930	4,090	3,840	4,646	3,284	2,071	755	458	14.8	75.2	2.21	41.4	8.5	7,875	74.7
E08000033	Calderdale	209.8	106.7	37.8	2,470	1,252	1,218	1,149	1,321	922	269	130	11.8	65.4	1.97	53.5	8.6	2,451	64.9
E08000034	Kirklees	437.0	220.6	83.3	5,408	2,792	2,616	2,815	2,593	1,693	615	285	12.4	64.9	1.92	47.9	8.5	5,361	64.3
E08000035	Leeds	781.7	397.9	172.2	10,250	5,272	4,978	5,169	5,081	3,173	1,302	606	13.1	59.5	1.78	49.6	7.3	10,162	59.0
E08000036	Wakefield	336.8	171.2	61.6	4,061	2,077	1,984	1,597	2,464	1,799	446	219	12.1	65.9	1.93	60.7	7.6	4,013	65.1
E12000004	**EAST MIDLANDS**	**4,724.4**	**2,389.4**	**874.6**	**53,299**	**27,267**	**26,032**	**25,656**	**27,643**	**19,542**	**5,249**	**2,852**	**11.3**	**60.9**	**1.82**	**51.9**	**6.9**	**52,712**	**60.3**
E06000015	**Derby**	**256.2**	**129.0**	**51.1**	**3,294**	**1,659**	**1,635**	**1,645**	**1,649**	**1,037**	**373**	**239**	**12.9**	**64.5**	**1.86**	**50.1**	**8.4**	**3,279**	**64.2**
E06000016	**Leicester**	**348.3**	**174.4**	**80.3**	**5,150**	**2,639**	**2,511**	**3,063**	**2,087**	**1,201**	**561**	**325**	**14.8**	**64.1**	**1.86**	**40.5**	**9.1**	**5,099**	**63.5**
E06000018	**Nottingham**	**325.3**	**160.8**	**80.4**	**4,297**	**2,177**	**2,120**	**1,857**	**2,440**	**1,271**	**743**	**426**	**13.2**	**53.5**	**1.68**	**56.8**	**8.4**	**4,242**	**52.8**
E06000017	**Rutland**	**38.6**	**18.9**	**5.6**	**336**	**158**	**178**	**221**	**115**	**99**	**8**	**8**	**8.7**	**59.8**	**2.01**	**34.2**	**7.1**	**329**	**58.5**
E10000007	**Derbyshire**	**785.8**	**399.6**	**133.9**	**7,820**	**3,996**	**3,824**	**3,500**	**4,320**	**3,297**	**662**	**361**	**10.0**	**58.4**	**1.78**	**55.2**	**6.9**	**7,759**	**58.0**
E07000032	Amber Valley	124.6	63.4	21.3	1,223	658	565	532	691	521	111	59	9.8	57.5	1.76	56.5	7.6	1,215	57.1
E07000033	Bolsover	78.1	39.5	13.7	815	406	409	314	501	381	78	42	10.4	59.4	1.77	61.5	7.5	817	59.5
E07000034	Chesterfield	104.4	53.2	18.5	1,069	536	533	431	638	474	101	63	10.2	57.8	1.73	59.7	6.2	1,062	57.4
E07000035	Derbyshire Dales	71.3	36.2	9.8	516	255	261	276	240	199	26	15	7.2	52.5	1.76	46.5	5.2	512	52.1
E07000036	Erewash	114.9	58.6	20.6	1,216	618	598	545	671	490	114	67	10.6	58.9	1.73	55.2	6.4	1,207	58.5
E07000037	High Peak	91.7	46.5	15.5	890	470	420	396	494	397	73	24	9.7	57.6	1.78	55.5	5.6	885	57.2
E07000038	North East Derbyshire	100.4	51.4	16.0	961	497	464	457	504	397	68	39	9.6	59.9	1.85	52.4	6.0	947	59.0
E07000039	South Derbyshire	100.3	50.7	18.4	1,130	556	574	549	581	438	91	52	11.3	61.5	1.86	51.4	9.4	1,114	60.6

Table 1 Summary: Live births (numbers, rates and percentages): administrative area of usual residence of mother, United Kingdom and constituent countries, 2016

England and Wales: regions (within England), unitary authorities, counties, districts, London Boroughs, local health boards (within Wales)
Scotland: council areas, Northern Ireland: 11 new Administrative Areas

Code	Area of usual residence	Population Numbers (thousands) Total	Female	Females aged 15 to 44	Live Births All Total	Male	Female	Within marriage or civil partnership	Outside marriage or civil partnership Total	Joint regis-trations same address	Joint regis-trations different address	Sole regis-trations	Crude Birth Rate (CBR)	General Fertility Rate (GFR)	Total Fertility Rate (TFR)[3]	% of live births outside marriage or civil partnership	% of live births under 2.5kg	Maternities Numbers Total	Maternity Rate[4]
E10000018	**Leicestershire**	**683.0**	**344.7**	**121.5**	**7,117**	**3,697**	**3,420**	**3,765**	**3,352**	**2,566**	**503**	**283**	**10.4**	**58.6**	**1.77**	**47.1**	**6.0**	**7,027**	**57.8**
E07000129	Blaby	97.7	49.8	17.3	1,106	576	530	590	516	394	80	42	11.3	63.8	1.88	46.7	3.9	1,092	63.0
E07000130	Charnwood	179.4	88.8	35.5	1,922	1,016	906	1,064	858	628	144	86	10.7	54.1	1.64	44.6	5.9	1,902	53.5
E07000131	Harborough	90.4	45.6	14.4	803	404	399	470	333	267	41	25	8.9	55.8	1.78	41.5	5.2	791	55.0
E07000132	Hinckley and Bosworth	110.1	55.9	18.8	1,176	624	552	590	586	466	80	40	10.7	62.5	1.87	49.8	7.2	1,163	61.8
E07000133	Melton	50.9	26.0	8.2	512	253	259	250	262	199	36	27	10.1	62.3	1.93	51.2	5.9	501	60.9
E07000134	North West Leicestershire	98.6	49.8	17.3	1,012	511	501	468	544	425	80	39	10.3	58.3	1.77	53.8	6.2	1,002	57.8
E07000135	Oadby and Wigston	55.8	28.9	9.9	586	313	273	333	253	187	42	24	10.5	59.1	1.87	43.2	8.0	576	58.1
E10000019	**Lincolnshire**	**743.4**	**379.8**	**125.3**	**7,485**	**3,866**	**3,619**	**3,262**	**4,223**	**3,150**	**709**	**364**	**10.1**	**59.7**	**1.81**	**56.4**	**5.9**	**7,407**	**59.1**
E07000136	Boston	67.6	34.2	11.9	797	408	389	302	495	357	91	47	11.8	67.1	1.97	62.1	5.9	790	66.5
E07000137	East Lindsey	138.4	71.0	19.0	1,173	591	582	439	734	545	120	69	8.5	61.6	1.93	62.6	7.2	1,167	61.3
E07000138	Lincoln	97.8	49.5	23.0	1,176	635	541	446	730	519	150	61	12.0	51.2	1.56	62.1	5.5	1,169	50.9
E07000139	North Kesteven	113.3	57.9	18.4	1,110	564	546	605	505	402	71	32	9.8	60.4	1.85	45.5	4.2	1,097	59.7
E07000140	South Holland	92.4	47.0	15.2	963	518	445	411	552	439	74	39	10.4	63.4	1.93	57.3	5.0	952	62.7
E07000141	South Kesteven	140.2	72.4	23.2	1,368	702	666	661	707	529	119	59	9.8	59.0	1.85	51.7	6.4	1,350	58.3
E07000142	West Lindsey	93.7	47.9	14.7	898	448	450	398	500	359	84	57	9.6	61.3	1.92	55.7	6.7	882	60.2
E10000021	**Northamptonshire**	**733.1**	**370.9**	**134.9**	**9,113**	**4,652**	**4,461**	**4,434**	**4,679**	**3,477**	**798**	**404**	**12.4**	**67.5**	**2.03**	**51.3**	**6.9**	**8,997**	**66.7**
E07000150	Corby	68.2	34.6	13.5	1,004	515	489	397	607	424	128	55	14.7	74.4	2.15	60.5	7.1	992	73.5
E07000151	Daventry	81.3	40.7	13.0	819	433	386	469	350	284	45	21	10.1	63.2	2.00	42.7	6.5	809	62.4
E07000152	East Northamptonshire	91.0	46.0	15.5	997	524	473	485	512	394	69	49	11.0	64.4	2.05	51.4	8.7	978	63.2
E07000153	Kettering	99.0	50.3	18.0	1,250	613	637	555	695	554	91	50	12.6	69.5	2.13	55.6	6.6	1,235	68.7
E07000154	Northampton	225.5	113.7	46.5	3,278	1,659	1,619	1,606	1,672	1,175	336	161	14.5	70.5	2.02	51.0	7.2	3,233	69.5
E07000155	South Northamptonshire	90.0	45.7	14.6	806	394	412	501	305	261	31	13	9.0	55.1	1.76	37.8	5.3	799	54.6
E07000156	Wellingborough	78.2	39.9	13.9	959	514	445	421	538	385	98	55	12.3	69.1	2.13	56.1	5.5	951	68.5
E10000024	**Nottinghamshire**	**810.7**	**411.4**	**141.6**	**8,687**	**4,423**	**4,264**	**3,909**	**4,778**	**3,444**	**892**	**442**	**10.7**	**61.3**	**1.84**	**55.0**	**6.2**	**8,573**	**60.5**
E07000170	Ashfield	124.5	63.4	22.8	1,442	739	703	548	894	607	185	102	11.6	63.2	1.87	62.0	6.4	1,428	62.6
E07000171	Bassetlaw	114.8	57.8	18.8	1,274	633	641	482	792	574	153	65	11.1	67.9	2.12	62.2	5.9	1,265	67.4
E07000172	Broxtowe	112.7	56.8	20.3	1,195	617	578	650	545	395	101	49	10.6	59.0	1.72	45.6	6.0	1,170	57.8
E07000173	Gedling	116.5	59.8	20.7	1,269	661	608	601	668	494	133	41	10.9	61.4	1.82	52.6	6.3	1,252	60.6
E07000174	Mansfield	107.4	54.6	19.5	1,281	627	654	451	830	596	136	98	11.9	65.5	1.90	64.8	6.9	1,266	64.8
E07000175	Newark and Sherwood	119.6	60.6	19.8	1,187	607	580	497	690	501	131	58	9.9	59.9	1.84	58.1	6.4	1,171	59.1
E07000176	Rushcliffe	115.2	58.4	19.8	1,039	539	500	680	359	277	53	29	9.0	52.5	1.60	34.6	5.7	1,021	51.6
E12000005	**WEST MIDLANDS**	**5,800.7**	**2,928.1**	**1,092.1**	**71,041**	**36,396**	**34,645**	**35,752**	**35,289**	**22,916**	**8,242**	**4,131**	**12.2**	**65.0**	**1.91**	**49.7**	**8.3**	**70,280**	**64.4**
E06000019	Herefordshire, County of	189.3	95.6	29.8	1,767	915	852	880	887	665	136	86	9.3	59.3	1.79	50.2	6.3	1,743	58.5
E06000051	Shropshire	313.4	157.8	48.6	2,947	1,505	1,442	1,441	1,506	1,171	228	107	9.4	60.6	1.89	51.1	6.0	2,914	59.9
E06000021	Stoke-on-Trent	253.2	126.8	48.7	3,499	1,809	1,690	1,425	2,074	1,396	437	241	13.8	71.8	2.04	59.3	9.2	3,462	71.0

Table 1   Summary: Live births (numbers, rates and percentages): administrative area of usual residence of mother, United Kingdom and constituent countries, 2016

England and Wales: regions (within England), unitary authorities, counties, districts, London Boroughs, local health boards (within Wales)
Scotland: council areas, Northern Ireland: 11 new Administrative Areas

Area of usual residence		Population Numbers (thousands)			Live Births Numbers — All			Within marriage or civil partner-ship	Outside marriage or civil partnership Total	Joint regis-trations same address	Joint regis-trations different address	Sole regis-trations	Rates — Crude Birth Rate (CBR): all births per 1,000 population of all ages	General Fertility Rate (GFR): all live births per 1,000 women aged 15 to 44	Total Fertility Rate (TFR)[3]	Percentages — Percentage of live births outside marriage or civil partner-ship	Percentage of live births under 2.5kg	Maternities Numbers Total	Mater-nity Rate[4]
		Total	Female	Females aged 15 to 44	Total	Male	Female												
E06000020	Telford and Wrekin	173.0	87.1	32.3	2,079	1,093	986	852	1,227	855	241	131	12.0	64.3	1.93	59.0	7.2	2,060	63.7
E10000028	Staffordshire	867.1	435.7	149.0	8,691	4,507	4,184	4,097	4,594	3,443	742	409	10.0	58.9	1.78	52.9	7.3	8,592	58.2
E07000192	Cannock Chase	98.5	49.7	17.9	1,052	564	488	415	637	471	105	61	10.7	58.6	1.74	60.6	7.2	1,046	58.3
E07000193	East Staffordshire	116.7	58.3	20.3	1,455	774	681	761	694	517	107	70	12.5	71.8	2.14	47.7	7.1	1,447	71.4
E07000194	Lichfield	103.1	51.9	16.5	976	494	482	534	442	354	56	32	9.5	59.3	1.83	45.3	6.6	966	58.7
E07000195	Newcastle-under-Lyme	128.5	64.5	24.2	1,194	615	579	463	731	537	137	57	9.3	49.4	1.48	61.2	9.1	1,172	48.4
E07000196	South Staffordshire	111.2	55.8	17.1	965	496	469	490	475	356	82	37	8.7	56.4	1.78	49.2	7.2	951	55.5
E07000197	Stafford	134.2	66.6	22.0	1,280	653	627	686	594	442	102	50	9.5	58.1	1.76	46.4	7.2	1,264	57.4
E07000198	Staffordshire Moorlands	98.1	49.7	15.1	847	420	427	370	477	377	56	44	8.6	56.1	1.77	56.3	6.5	837	55.4
E07000199	Tamworth	77.0	39.1	14.5	922	491	431	378	544	389	97	58	12.0	63.6	1.89	59.0	7.5	909	62.7
E10000031	Warwickshire	556.8	281.6	97.6	5,951	3,068	2,883	3,181	2,770	1,985	535	250	10.7	61.0	1.83	46.5	6.9	5,879	60.2
E07000218	North Warwickshire	63.2	32.0	10.5	614	324	290	270	344	245	77	22	9.7	58.5	1.78	56.0	5.2	609	58.0
E07000220	Nuneaton and Bedworth	127.0	64.7	23.2	1,575	846	729	690	885	606	199	80	12.4	67.9	2.01	56.2	7.6	1,563	67.4
E07000220	Rugby	103.8	52.2	18.5	1,224	619	605	673	551	410	90	51	11.8	66.2	2.01	45.0	8.7	1,203	65.1
E07000221	Stratford-on-Avon	122.3	62.8	18.3	1,097	526	571	629	468	348	73	47	9.0	60.0	1.92	42.7	6.9	1,084	59.3
E07000222	Warwick	140.4	70.0	27.2	1,441	753	688	919	522	376	96	50	10.3	53.0	1.63	36.2	5.3	1,420	52.2
E11000005	West Midlands (Met County)	2,864.9	1,447.4	588.7	40,037	20,454	19,583	20,836	19,201	11,194	5,359	2,648	14.0	68.0	1.96	48.0	9.1	39,646	67.3
E08000025	Birmingham	1,124.6	568.2	249.7	17,404	8,996	8,408	10,085	7,319	3,968	2,173	1,178	15.5	69.7	2.04	42.1	9.4	17,252	69.1
E08000026	Coventry	352.9	174.5	79.0	4,531	2,324	2,207	2,325	2,206	1,346	573	287	12.8	57.3	1.65	48.7	8.4	4,487	56.8
E08000027	Dudley	317.6	161.7	56.8	3,816	1,977	1,839	1,786	2,030	1,343	462	225	12.0	67.2	1.98	53.2	8.0	3,772	66.4
E08000028	Sandwell	322.7	162.8	64.1	4,735	2,416	2,319	2,295	2,440	1,394	741	305	14.7	73.9	2.12	51.5	10.0	4,665	72.8
E08000029	Solihull	211.8	108.8	36.3	2,315	1,149	1,166	1,209	1,106	684	322	100	10.9	63.7	1.95	47.8	7.0	2,284	62.8
E08000030	Walsall	278.7	141.8	52.8	3,760	1,849	1,911	1,624	2,136	1,282	572	282	13.5	71.2	2.06	56.8	10.8	3,742	70.8
E08000031	Wolverhampton	256.6	129.6	49.9	3,476	1,743	1,733	1,512	1,964	1,177	516	271	13.5	69.7	2.01	56.5	8.3	3,444	69.0
E10000034	Worcestershire	583.1	296.0	98.7	6,070	3,045	3,025	3,040	3,030	2,207	564	259	10.4	61.5	1.86	49.9	7.8	5,984	60.6
E07000234	Bromsgrove	96.8	49.1	15.6	940	460	480	558	382	263	87	32	9.7	60.1	1.85	40.6	6.7	921	58.9
E07000235	Malvern Hills	76.1	39.0	10.9	566	282	284	255	311	232	56	23	7.4	52.1	1.71	54.9	7.4	555	51.1
E07000236	Redditch	85.0	42.8	16.0	1,065	531	534	525	540	376	116	48	12.5	66.4	1.95	50.7	8.5	1,059	66.0
E07000237	Worcester	102.3	51.7	21.3	1,200	599	601	577	623	450	109	64	11.7	56.4	1.67	51.9	9.0	1,185	55.7
E07000238	Wychavon	122.9	62.8	18.8	1,188	604	584	640	548	435	73	40	9.7	63.2	1.97	46.1	6.6	1,166	62.0
E07000239	Wyre Forest	99.9	50.6	16.1	1,111	569	542	485	626	451	123	52	11.1	69.1	2.10	56.3	8.4	1,098	68.3
E12000006	EAST	6,130.5	3,108.9	1,118.1	72,250	37,020	35,230	39,062	33,188	24,400	5,743	3,045	11.8	64.6	1.91	45.9	6.6	71,331	63.8
E06000055	Bedford	168.8	85.3	31.8	2,209	1,160	1,049	1,292	917	633	195	89	13.1	69.6	2.07	41.5	7.3	2,182	68.7
E06000056	Central Bedfordshire	278.9	140.9	51.7	3,309	1,648	1,661	1,834	1,475	1,144	217	114	11.9	64.0	1.86	44.6	5.1	3,281	63.5
E06000032	Luton	216.8	107.0	46.1	3,608	1,869	1,739	2,388	1,220	715	305	200	16.6	78.2	2.18	33.8	8.6	3,558	77.1

Table 1   Summary: Live births (numbers, rates and percentages): administrative area of usual residence of mother, United Kingdom and constituent countries, 2016

England and Wales: regions (within England), unitary authorities, counties, districts, London Boroughs, local health boards (within Wales)
Scotland: council areas, Northern Ireland: 11 new Administrative Areas

	Area of usual residence	Population (thousands)			Live Births														Maternities	
					Numbers[1]								Rates[2]			Percentages			Numbers	Rate
				Females aged 15 to 44	All			Within marriage or civil partnership	Outside marriage or civil partnership				Crude Birth Rate (CBR): all births per 1,000 population of all ages	General Fertility Rate (GFR): all live births per 1,000 women aged 15 to 44	Total Fertility Rate (TFR)[3]	Percentage of live births outside marriage or civil partnership	Percentage of live births under 2.5kg		Maternity Rate[4]
		Total	Female		Total	Male	Female		Total	Joint registrations same address	Joint registrations different address	Sole registrations						Total	
E06000031	**Peterborough**	**197.1**	**98.3**	**39.2**	**3,076**	**1,533**	**1,543**	**1,528**	**1,548**	**1,060**	**286**	**202**	**15.6**	**78.4**	**2.26**	**50.3**	**7.0**	**3,046**	**77.7**
E06000033	**Southend-on-Sea**	**179.8**	**91.8**	**33.4**	**2,260**	**1,144**	**1,116**	**976**	**1,284**	**878**	**271**	**135**	**12.6**	**67.7**	**2.04**	**56.8**	**7.4**	**2,227**	**66.7**
E06000034	**Thurrock**	**167.0**	**84.7**	**34.4**	**2,498**	**1,300**	**1,198**	**1,187**	**1,311**	**881**	**290**	**140**	**15.0**	**72.7**	**2.12**	**52.5**	**7.2**	**2,465**	**71.7**
E10000003	**Cambridgeshire**	**651.9**	**325.5**	**123.0**	**7,232**	**3,700**	**3,532**	**4,211**	**3,021**	**2,376**	**405**	**240**	**11.1**	**58.8**	**1.75**	**41.8**	**6.6**	**7,141**	**58.0**
E07000008	Cambridge	131.8	63.2	32.5	1,413	693	720	917	496	341	110	45	10.7	43.5	1.45	35.1	6.8	1,394	42.9
E07000009	East Cambridgeshire	87.8	44.6	15.5	979	495	484	585	394	331	31	32	11.1	63.3	1.92	40.2	5.8	966	62.5
E07000010	Fenland	100.2	50.6	16.9	1,130	583	547	402	728	571	96	61	11.3	66.7	1.99	64.4	6.7	1,118	66.0
E07000011	Huntingdonshire	175.7	87.9	30.8	1,973	1,041	932	1,116	857	688	112	57	11.2	64.1	1.90	43.4	6.5	1,957	63.6
E07000012	South Cambridgeshire	156.5	79.1	27.4	1,737	888	849	1,191	546	445	56	45	11.1	63.4	1.88	31.4	6.8	1,706	62.3
E10000012	**Essex**	**1,455.3**	**743.7**	**258.4**	**16,536**	**8,567**	**7,969**	**8,505**	**8,031**	**6,012**	**1,334**	**685**	**11.4**	**64.0**	**1.91**	**48.6**	**5.8**	**16,330**	**63.2**
E07000066	Basildon	183.4	94.3	35.3	2,487	1,268	1,219	1,145	1,342	964	258	120	13.6	70.4	2.05	54.0	7.0	2,455	69.5
E07000067	Braintree	151.0	76.8	26.4	1,715	918	797	869	846	675	112	59	11.4	65.0	1.97	49.3	6.9	1,692	64.1
E07000068	Brentwood	76.4	39.3	13.6	848	393	455	503	345	257	67	21	11.1	62.5	1.86	40.7	5.4	835	61.5
E07000069	Castle Point	89.7	46.1	14.5	860	444	416	405	455	324	83	48	9.6	59.5	1.85	52.9	6.5	846	58.5
E07000070	Chelmsford	174.1	88.0	32.0	2,039	1,059	980	1,172	867	658	140	69	11.7	63.7	1.86	42.5	5.4	2,011	62.8
E07000071	Colchester	186.6	94.0	37.4	2,204	1,152	1,052	1,154	1,050	762	189	99	11.8	58.9	1.72	47.6	6.5	2,181	58.3
E07000072	Epping Forest	130.3	67.3	23.8	1,592	812	780	881	711	548	114	49	12.2	66.8	1.96	44.7	4.1	1,577	66.2
E07000073	Harlow	86.0	44.2	17.1	1,303	693	610	626	677	475	128	74	15.2	76.2	2.15	52.0	4.6	1,274	74.5
E07000074	Maldon	63.4	32.2	9.6	531	298	233	273	258	204	40	14	8.4	55.2	1.80	48.6	3.8	529	54.9
E07000075	Rochford	85.7	43.7	14.1	751	405	346	433	318	265	36	17	8.8	53.3	1.70	42.3	4.1	745	52.9
E07000076	Tendring	142.6	74.0	20.2	1,284	649	635	446	838	613	136	89	9.0	63.6	1.99	65.3	6.2	1,275	63.1
E07000077	Uttlesford	86.2	43.8	14.4	922	476	446	598	324	267	31	26	10.7	63.9	1.99	35.1	5.4	910	63.1
E10000015	**Hertfordshire**	**1,176.7**	**600.1**	**227.7**	**14,601**	**7,429**	**7,172**	**9,009**	**5,592**	**4,018**	**1,073**	**501**	**12.4**	**64.1**	**1.86**	**38.3**	**6.0**	**14,400**	**63.2**
E07000095	Broxbourne	96.8	50.0	18.4	1,245	612	633	668	577	409	127	41	12.9	67.6	1.96	46.3	6.3	1,224	66.4
E07000096	Dacorum	152.7	77.5	28.9	1,868	912	956	1,096	772	584	127	61	12.2	64.7	1.86	41.3	6.7	1,852	64.2
E07000242	East Hertfordshire	146.3	74.6	26.9	1,659	849	810	1,024	635	512	76	47	11.3	61.7	1.86	38.3	3.9	1,623	60.4
E07000098	Hertsmere	103.5	53.7	19.4	1,301	667	634	893	408	247	110	51	12.6	67.0	1.95	31.4	6.2	1,288	66.3
E07000099	North Hertfordshire	132.7	67.6	24.4	1,512	799	713	891	621	459	103	59	11.4	61.8	1.82	41.1	4.8	1,496	61.2
E07000240	St Albans	146.3	74.7	27.5	1,824	923	901	1,332	492	354	91	47	12.5	66.4	1.91	27.0	6.0	1,787	65.1
E07000243	Stevenage	87.1	44.2	17.2	1,223	660	563	597	626	453	127	46	14.0	70.9	2.00	51.2	6.4	1,204	69.8
E07000102	Three Rivers	92.5	47.5	17.0	1,069	536	533	690	379	266	81	32	11.6	63.0	1.88	35.5	6.5	1,056	62.2
E07000103	Watford	96.8	48.8	21.0	1,500	723	777	999	501	346	97	58	15.5	71.3	1.94	33.4	7.8	1,485	70.6
E07000241	Welwyn Hatfield	122.0	61.6	27.0	1,400	748	652	819	581	388	134	59	11.5	51.9	1.61	41.5	5.8	1,385	51.4
E10000020	**Norfolk**	**892.9**	**454.2**	**150.6**	**9,057**	**4,645**	**4,412**	**4,153**	**4,904**	**3,729**	**775**	**400**	**10.1**	**60.2**	**1.79**	**54.1**	**7.4**	**8,928**	**59.3**
E07000143	Breckland	137.0	69.0	21.8	1,434	726	708	678	756	608	93	55	10.5	65.7	1.97	52.7	7.5	1,404	64.3
E07000144	Broadland	127.5	65.3	19.9	1,103	567	536	605	498	401	66	31	8.7	55.6	1.75	45.1	6.0	1,085	54.7
E07000145	Great Yarmouth	99.2	50.2	16.2	1,086	547	539	343	743	553	123	67	11.0	67.2	1.99	68.4	7.8	1,071	66.3

Table 1 Summary: Live births (numbers, rates and percentages): administrative area of usual residence of mother, United Kingdom and constituent countries, 2016

England and Wales: regions (within England), unitary authorities, counties, districts, London Boroughs, local health boards (within Wales)
Scotland: council areas, Northern Ireland: 11 new Administrative Areas

Area of usual residence		Population Numbers (thousands)			Live Births Numbers[1]				Outside marriage or civil partnership				Rates[2]			Percentages		Maternities	
		Total	Female	Females aged 15 to 44	All Total	Male	Female	Within marriage or civil partnership	Total	Joint regis-trations same address	Joint regis-trations different address	Sole regis-trations	Crude Birth Rate (CBR): all births per 1,000 population of all ages	General Fertility Rate (GFR): all live births per 1,000 women aged 15 to 44	Total Fertility Rate (TFR)[3]	Percent-age of live births outside marriage or civil partner-ship	Percent-age of live births under 2.5kg	Numbers Total	Mater-nity Rate[4]
E07000146	King's Lynn and West Norfolk	151.6	77.3	23.5	1,580	818	762	722	858	631	149	78	10.4	67.2	2.03	54.3	7.5	1,553	66.1
E07000147	North Norfolk	103.8	53.3	13.5	789	415	374	331	458	373	58	27	7.6	58.5	1.81	58.0	8.2	781	57.9
E07000148	Norwich	141.0	71.0	34.2	1,728	879	849	721	1,007	706	200	101	12.3	50.5	1.46	58.3	8.1	1,715	50.1
E07000149	South Norfolk	132.8	68.1	21.5	1,337	693	644	753	584	457	86	41	10.1	62.1	1.95	43.7	6.7	1,319	61.2
E10000029	Suffolk	745.3	377.5	121.8	7,864	4,025	3,839	3,979	3,885	2,954	592	339	10.6	64.6	1.95	49.4	7.2	7,773	63.8
E07000200	Babergh	89.5	45.9	13.3	739	364	375	386	353	277	43	33	8.3	55.7	1.79	47.8	6.5	731	55.1
E07000201	Forest Heath	64.4	31.9	12.2	1,016	513	503	649	367	298	38	31	15.8	83.3	2.31	36.1	8.0	999	81.9
E07000202	Ipswich	135.9	68.0	26.9	1,985	1,006	979	883	1,102	758	239	105	14.6	73.8	2.11	55.5	7.8	1,965	73.1
E07000203	Mid Suffolk	100.0	50.6	15.4	823	417	406	453	370	310	35	25	8.2	53.4	1.67	45.0	7.8	806	52.3
E07000204	St Edmundsbury	112.9	56.4	18.5	1,135	574	561	662	473	387	53	33	10.0	61.5	1.84	41.7	5.7	1,128	61.1
E07000205	Suffolk Coastal	126.0	64.7	17.6	1,005	553	452	544	461	360	62	39	8.0	57.0	1.93	45.9	5.8	990	56.2
E07000206	Waveney	116.5	60.1	18.0	1,161	598	563	402	759	564	122	73	10.0	64.5	1.96	65.4	8.4	1,154	64.2
E12000007	LONDON	8,787.9	4,408.6	2,026.4	128,803	65,997	62,806	81,792	47,011	26,683	13,257	7,071	14.7	63.6	1.72	36.5	7.2	127,168	62.8
E13000001	Inner London	3,529.3	1,749.7	908.8	50,096	25,671	24,425	30,941	19,155	10,196	5,946	3,013	14.2	55.1	1.47	38.2	7.5	49,475	54.4
E09000007	Camden	246.2	122.2	61.3	2,732	1,417	1,315	1,854	878	451	276	151	11.1	44.6	1.26	32.1	8.1	2,695	44.0
E09000001	City of London	9.4	4.2	2.0	54	27	27	33	21	11	6	4	5.7	27.5	0.75	38.9	7.4	53	27.0
E09000012	Hackney	273.5	137.2	74.5	4,447	2,249	2,198	2,682	1,765	880	581	304	16.3	59.7	1.64	39.7	7.9	4,390	59.0
E09000013	Hammersmith and Fulham	179.7	90.9	44.9	2,509	1,296	1,213	1,703	806	431	234	141	14.0	55.9	1.49	32.1	6.6	2,478	55.2
E09000014	Haringey	278.5	138.0	67.0	4,114	2,144	1,970	2,357	1,757	1,002	513	242	14.8	61.4	1.68	42.7	7.4	4,057	60.6
E09000019	Islington	232.9	115.7	65.3	2,945	1,518	1,427	1,701	1,244	658	418	168	12.6	45.1	1.30	42.2	6.1	2,909	44.6
E09000020	Kensington and Chelsea	156.7	78.3	33.9	1,729	875	854	1,260	469	250	148	71	11.0	51.1	1.33	27.1	6.6	1,700	50.2
E09000022	Lambeth	327.9	163.0	88.9	4,209	2,113	2,096	2,258	1,951	967	649	335	12.8	47.4	1.31	46.4	7.1	4,156	46.8
E09000023	Lewisham	301.9	152.8	74.1	4,721	2,476	2,245	2,431	2,290	1,108	793	389	15.6	63.7	1.72	48.5	6.8	4,662	62.9
E09000025	Newham	341.0	161.7	80.8	6,027	3,015	3,012	3,916	2,111	1,161	597	353	17.7	74.6	1.99	35.0	9.7	5,983	74.0
E09000028	Southwark	313.2	157.2	82.9	4,503	2,340	2,163	2,378	2,125	1,048	714	363	14.4	54.3	1.47	47.2	6.7	4,435	53.5
E09000030	Tower Hamlets	304.9	145.8	85.8	4,592	2,314	2,278	2,995	1,597	932	477	188	15.1	53.5	1.39	34.8	8.7	4,555	53.1
E09000032	Wandsworth	316.1	164.1	89.8	4,860	2,539	2,321	3,443	1,417	868	346	203	15.4	54.1	1.40	29.2	6.2	4,787	53.3
E09000033	Westminster	247.6	118.7	57.9	2,654	1,348	1,306	1,930	724	429	194	101	10.7	45.9	1.20	27.3	7.6	2,615	45.2
E13000002	Outer London	5,258.5	2,658.9	1,117.6	78,707	40,326	38,381	50,851	27,856	16,487	7,311	4,058	15.0	70.4	1.96	35.4	6.9	77,693	69.5
E09000002	Barking and Dagenham	206.5	105.0	45.9	3,973	2,015	1,958	2,089	1,884	991	564	329	19.2	86.5	2.47	47.4	7.5	3,933	85.6
E09000003	Barnet	386.1	195.2	81.8	5,301	2,726	2,575	3,834	1,467	884	364	219	13.7	64.8	1.78	27.7	7.3	5,230	63.9
E09000004	Bexley	244.8	126.6	48.8	3,091	1,646	1,445	1,660	1,431	909	381	141	12.6	63.4	1.83	46.3	5.4	3,065	62.9
E09000005	Brent	328.3	161.2	71.5	5,146	2,685	2,461	3,720	1,426	759	413	254	15.7	71.9	1.98	27.7	8.0	5,096	71.2
E09000006	Bromley	326.9	169.8	63.4	4,326	2,186	2,140	2,630	1,696	1,071	420	205	13.2	68.3	1.94	39.2	5.7	4,266	67.3
E09000008	Croydon	382.3	196.6	79.9	5,894	3,075	2,819	3,252	2,642	1,452	719	471	15.4	73.7	2.10	44.8	7.3	5,823	72.9
E09000009	Ealing	343.2	170.5	73.5	5,250	2,644	2,606	3,769	1,481	885	394	202	15.3	71.4	1.97	28.2	7.3	5,160	70.2
E09000010	Enfield	331.4	169.6	70.5	5,000	2,557	2,443	2,857	2,143	1,030	745	368	15.1	70.9	2.01	42.9	7.6	4,918	69.7

119

Table 1   Summary: Live births (numbers, rates and percentages): administrative area of usual residence of mother, United Kingdom and constituent countries, 2016

England and Wales: regions (within England), unitary authorities, counties, districts, London Boroughs, local health boards (within Wales)
Scotland: council areas, Northern Ireland: 11 new Administrative Areas

Area of usual residence		Population (thousands) Total	Female	Females aged 15 to 44	Live Births All Total	Male	Female	Within marriage or civil partnership	Outside marriage or civil partnership Total	Joint regs same address	Joint regs different address	Sole registrations	Crude Birth Rate (CBR)	General Fertility Rate (GFR)	Total Fertility Rate (TFR)[3]	% of live births outside marriage or civil partnership	% of live births under 2.5kg	Maternities Numbers Total	Maternity Rate[4]
E09000011	Greenwich	279.8	139.1	64.3	4,621	2,311	2,310	2,552	2,069	1,111	631	327	16.5	71.9	1.97	44.8	7.1	4,572	71.1
E09000015	Harrow	248.8	124.6	49.6	3,606	1,822	1,784	2,907	699	408	175	116	14.5	72.7	2.03	19.4	8.3	3,551	71.5
E09000016	Havering	252.8	131.3	49.2	3,423	1,764	1,659	1,831	1,592	1,081	325	186	13.5	69.6	1.98	46.5	5.3	3,386	68.8
E09000017	Hillingdon	302.5	150.6	64.8	4,508	2,352	2,156	3,053	1,455	824	392	239	14.9	69.6	1.95	32.3	5.6	4,449	68.7
E09000018	Hounslow	271.1	133.4	59.5	4,351	2,252	2,099	2,928	1,423	866	360	197	16.0	73.1	1.99	32.7	7.0	4,307	72.4
E09000021	Kingston upon Thames	176.1	89.3	40.1	2,204	1,111	1,093	1,549	655	428	161	66	12.5	54.9	1.55	29.7	6.3	2,172	54.1
E09000024	Merton	205.0	104.2	46.0	3,246	1,692	1,554	2,312	934	577	236	121	15.8	70.5	1.86	28.8	6.7	3,200	69.5
E09000026	Redbridge	299.2	149.9	65.0	4,782	2,460	2,322	3,480	1,302	847	277	178	16.0	73.6	2.04	27.2	7.3	4,729	72.7
E09000027	Richmond upon Thames	195.8	100.7	39.4	2,544	1,269	1,275	1,847	697	530	96	71	13.0	64.6	1.72	27.4	5.8	2,494	63.3
E09000029	Sutton	202.2	103.6	41.3	2,741	1,375	1,366	1,660	1,081	709	256	116	13.6	66.4	1.88	39.4	7.7	2,709	65.7
E09000031	Waltham Forest	275.8	137.6	63.1	4,700	2,384	2,316	2,921	1,779	1,125	402	252	17.0	74.5	2.02	37.9	7.6	4,633	73.5
E12000008	SOUTH EAST	9,026.3	4,579.1	1,659.9	101,982	52,135	49,847	58,031	43,951	32,069	7,911	3,971	11.3	61.4	1.84	43.1	6.0	100,742	60.7
E06000036	Bracknell Forest	119.4	60.1	23.8	1,397	729	668	829	568	430	98	40	11.7	58.7	1.71	40.7	4.7	1,387	58.3
E06000043	Brighton and Hove	289.2	143.8	68.5	2,850	1,449	1,401	1,453	1,397	1,025	238	134	9.9	41.6	1.30	49.0	6.7	2,804	40.9
E06000046	Isle of Wight	139.8	71.5	20.5	1,142	604	538	427	715	531	120	64	8.2	55.8	1.74	62.6	6.3	1,133	55.4
E06000035	Medway	278.5	140.3	55.3	3,657	1,835	1,822	1,645	2,012	1,393	424	195	13.1	66.2	1.91	55.0	3.8	3,606	65.2
E06000042	Milton Keynes	264.5	133.5	53.5	3,649	1,837	1,812	1,981	1,668	1,112	376	180	13.8	68.2	1.98	45.7	6.9	3,607	67.4
E06000044	Portsmouth	214.8	105.3	46.7	2,592	1,313	1,279	1,199	1,393	924	318	151	12.1	55.5	1.61	53.7	7.8	2,566	54.9
E06000038	Reading	162.7	80.6	37.6	2,494	1,244	1,250	1,484	1,010	638	237	135	15.3	66.4	1.87	40.5	6.0	2,468	65.7
E06000039	Slough	147.2	73.1	32.3	2,628	1,329	1,299	1,807	821	546	147	128	17.9	81.4	2.29	31.2	9.7	2,594	80.3
E06000045	Southampton	254.3	124.4	60.0	3,194	1,608	1,586	1,603	1,591	1,079	338	174	12.6	53.2	1.56	49.8	6.5	3,180	53.0
E06000037	West Berkshire	156.8	79.2	27.3	1,764	913	851	1,054	710	525	121	64	11.2	64.7	2.04	40.2	5.0	1,736	63.6
E06000040	Windsor and Maidenhead	148.8	74.9	26.5	1,757	887	870	1,235	522	414	66	42	11.8	66.2	1.94	29.7	7.3	1,721	64.8
E06000041	Wokingham	161.9	82.2	29.0	1,809	929	880	1,270	539	414	88	37	11.2	62.3	1.93	29.8	4.3	1,786	61.5
E10000002	Buckinghamshire	534.7	272.4	95.4	6,102	3,072	3,030	3,985	2,117	1,591	346	180	11.4	63.9	1.92	34.7	7.5	6,012	63.0
E07000004	Aylesbury Vale	193.1	97.6	35.8	2,280	1,154	1,126	1,378	902	687	140	75	11.8	63.8	1.87	39.6	7.4	2,251	62.9
E07000005	Chiltern	95.1	49.0	15.0	902	470	432	644	258	212	31	15	9.5	60.0	1.94	28.6	5.2	887	59.0
E07000006	South Bucks	69.6	36.0	11.6	754	374	380	518	236	178	38	20	10.8	65.0	1.92	31.3	7.7	742	64.0
E07000007	Wycombe	176.9	89.8	33.1	2,166	1,074	1,092	1,445	721	514	137	70	12.2	65.5	1.95	33.3	8.4	2,132	64.5
E10000011	East Sussex	547.8	282.8	85.3	5,219	2,680	2,539	2,489	2,730	2,000	468	262	9.5	61.2	1.91	52.3	5.9	5,165	60.6
E07000061	Eastbourne	103.1	53.1	17.4	1,048	520	528	506	542	397	93	52	10.2	60.4	1.83	51.7	6.2	1,045	60.2
E07000062	Hastings	92.2	47.3	16.6	1,115	566	549	391	724	473	163	88	12.1	67.2	1.99	64.9	6.5	1,109	66.8
E07000063	Lewes	101.4	52.1	15.6	898	480	418	470	428	329	66	33	8.9	57.5	1.82	47.7	6.3	891	57.1
E07000064	Rother	93.6	48.6	12.2	751	391	360	331	420	297	81	42	8.0	61.3	1.98	55.9	6.0	738	60.3
E07000066	Wealden	157.6	61.7	23.4	1,407	723	684	791	616	504	65	47	8.9	60.0	1.94	43.8	5.0	1,382	58.9

Table 1   Summary: Live births (numbers, rates and percentages): administrative area of usual residence of mother, United Kingdom and constituent countries, 2016

England and Wales: regions (within England), unitary authorities, counties, districts, London Boroughs, local health boards (within Wales)
Scotland: council areas, Northern Ireland: 11 new Administrative Areas

Area of usual residence	Population Numbers (thousands) Total	Female	Females aged 15 to 44	Live Births All Total	Male	Female	Within marriage or civil partnership	Outside marriage or civil partnership Total	Joint regis-trations same address	Joint regis-trations different address	Sole regis-trations	Crude Birth Rate (CBR): all births per 1,000 population of all ages	General Fertility Rate (GFR): all live births per 1,000 women aged 15 to 44	Total Fertility Rate (TFR)[3]	Percentage of live births outside marriage or civil partnership	Percentage of live births under 2.5kg	Maternities Numbers Total	Maternity Rate[4]
E10000014 Hampshire	**1,360.4**	**694.3**	**233.3**	**14,379**	**7,392**	**6,987**	**8,367**	**6,012**	**4,465**	**1,064**	**483**	**10.6**	**61.6**	**1.89**	**41.8**	**6.3**	**14,211**	**60.9**
E07000084 Basingstoke and Deane	174.6	88.1	32.5	2,186	1,130	1,056	1,283	903	662	155	86	12.5	67.3	1.99	41.3	6.6	2,159	66.4
E07000085 East Hampshire	118.0	61.0	18.6	1,027	512	515	650	377	293	61	23	8.7	55.2	1.82	36.7	4.6	1,020	54.8
E07000086 Eastleigh	129.6	66.1	23.7	1,445	730	715	809	636	492	98	46	11.1	61.1	1.80	44.0	5.3	1,435	60.6
E07000087 Fareham	115.4	58.8	18.7	1,049	540	509	636	413	316	68	29	9.1	56.0	1.74	39.4	6.5	1,037	55.4
E07000088 Gosport	85.4	42.9	15.2	924	449	475	392	532	367	105	60	10.8	60.8	1.81	57.6	7.6	915	60.2
E07000089 Hart	94.3	47.4	15.8	950	503	447	668	282	221	46	15	10.1	60.3	1.92	29.7	4.1	940	59.6
E07000090 Havant	123.6	63.8	20.4	1,330	702	628	591	739	508	163	68	10.8	65.3	1.96	55.6	8.8	1,310	64.4
E07000091 New Forest	179.2	93.0	26.0	1,483	777	706	798	685	509	126	50	8.3	57.0	1.79	46.2	6.6	1,459	56.1
E07000092 Rushmoor	96.3	47.7	19.8	1,410	704	706	882	528	384	103	41	14.6	71.2	2.05	37.4	6.6	1,398	70.6
E07000093 Test Valley	122.0	62.6	20.4	1,386	727	659	847	539	412	89	38	11.4	68.0	2.12	38.9	5.9	1,371	67.2
E07000094 Winchester	122.0	62.8	22.3	1,189	618	571	811	378	301	50	27	9.7	53.3	1.79	31.8	5.9	1,167	52.3
E10000016 Kent	**1,541.9**	**785.3**	**277.8**	**17,374**	**8,985**	**8,389**	**8,448**	**8,926**	**6,461**	**1,612**	**853**	**11.3**	**62.5**	**1.90**	**51.4**	**4.5**	**17,179**	**61.8**
E07000105 Ashford	126.2	64.8	22.8	1,565	831	734	748	817	614	142	61	12.4	68.7	2.10	52.2	4.5	1,550	68.1
E07000106 Canterbury	162.4	82.8	33.9	1,382	762	620	681	701	492	132	77	8.5	40.8	1.42	50.7	4.7	1,360	40.2
E07000107 Dartford	105.5	53.6	21.8	1,514	798	716	828	686	477	162	47	14.3	69.4	1.94	45.3	5.8	1,492	68.3
E07000108 Dover	114.2	58.0	18.3	1,173	587	586	448	725	521	143	61	10.3	64.2	1.99	61.8	5.0	1,155	63.2
E07000109 Gravesham	106.8	54.1	20.3	1,417	710	707	674	743	502	163	78	13.3	69.7	2.05	52.4	4.8	1,411	69.4
E07000110 Maidstone	166.4	84.1	30.2	2,035	1,030	1,005	1,076	959	710	148	101	12.2	67.4	1.99	47.1	3.1	2,014	66.7
E07000111 Sevenoaks	119.1	61.4	19.9	1,246	631	615	736	510	382	84	44	10.5	62.7	1.97	40.9	4.7	1,236	62.2
E07000112 Shepway	111.2	56.3	17.7	1,054	531	523	463	591	441	81	69	9.5	59.5	1.83	56.1	5.0	1,042	58.8
E07000113 Swale	145.0	73.3	25.9	1,813	956	857	728	1,085	756	224	105	12.5	70.0	2.11	59.8	3.0	1,787	69.0
E07000114 Thanet	140.7	72.6	23.6	1,553	848	705	534	1,019	713	185	121	11.0	65.9	2.00	65.6	4.7	1,543	65.5
E07000115 Tonbridge and Malling	127.3	65.0	23.0	1,431	715	716	818	613	464	101	48	11.2	62.2	1.95	42.8	4.1	1,413	61.5
E07000116 Tunbridge Wells	117.1	59.3	20.5	1,191	586	605	714	477	389	47	41	10.2	58.0	1.80	40.1	5.2	1,176	57.3
E10000025 Oxfordshire	**683.2**	**342.6**	**131.5**	**7,757**	**3,983**	**3,774**	**4,841**	**2,916**	**2,198**	**496**	**222**	**11.4**	**59.0**	**1.76**	**37.6**	**4.7**	**7,683**	**58.4**
E07000177 Cherwell	146.3	73.8	26.9	1,836	926	910	1,074	762	586	122	54	12.5	68.2	2.03	41.5	5.3	1,813	67.3
E07000178 Oxford	161.3	79.1	41.6	1,811	948	863	1,144	667	442	157	68	11.2	43.5	1.43	36.8	4.8	1,804	43.3
E07000179 South Oxfordshire	138.1	70.1	22.7	1,540	800	740	982	558	456	68	34	11.1	67.7	2.10	36.2	4.2	1,522	66.9
E07000180 Vale of White Horse	128.7	64.5	22.0	1,436	730	706	948	488	374	84	30	11.2	65.2	1.96	34.0	4.0	1,422	64.6
E07000181 West Oxfordshire	108.7	55.0	18.2	1,134	579	555	693	441	340	65	36	10.4	62.4	1.89	38.9	5.1	1,122	61.7
E10000030 Surrey	**1,176.5**	**599.0**	**213.9**	**13,423**	**6,798**	**6,625**	**8,963**	**4,460**	**3,412**	**715**	**333**	**11.4**	**62.8**	**1.90**	**33.2**	**6.3**	**13,231**	**61.9**
E07000207 Elmbridge	132.8	68.8	22.4	1,646	857	789	1,195	451	344	78	29	12.4	73.4	2.23	27.4	6.7	1,622	72.3
E07000208 Epsom and Ewell	79.6	40.9	15.1	950	490	460	646	304	241	40	23	11.9	63.0	1.91	32.0	6.1	942	62.5
E07000209 Guildford	148.0	73.8	30.6	1,533	760	773	1,053	480	368	80	32	10.4	50.1	1.59	31.3	5.1	1,512	49.4
E07000210 Mole Valley	86.2	44.1	13.3	770	391	379	508	262	207	33	22	8.9	57.9	1.85	34.0	6.2	756	56.8
E07000211 Reigate and Banstead	145.6	74.4	26.9	1,796	883	913	1,165	631	496	99	36	12.3	66.8	1.93	35.1	7.7	1,755	65.3
E07000212 Runnymede	86.9	44.5	18.9	954	464	490	596	358	260	64	34	11.0	50.4	1.64	37.5	5.7	941	49.8

Table 1 Summary: Live births (numbers, rates and percentages): administrative area of usual residence of mother, United Kingdom and constituent countries, 2016

England and Wales: regions (within England), unitary authorities, counties, districts, London Boroughs, local health boards (within Wales)
Scotland: council areas, Northern Ireland: 11 new Administrative Areas

Area code	Area of usual residence	Pop. Total	Pop. Female	Females aged 15 to 44	All Total	All Male	All Female	Within marriage or civil partnership	Outside Total	Joint same address	Joint diff. address	Sole	CBR	GFR	TFR[3]	% outside marriage/civil partnership	% under 2.5kg	Maternities Total	Maternity Rate[4]
E07000213	Spelthorne	98.9	50.1	18.2	1,346	687	659	811	535	384	113	38	13.6	74.0	2.14	39.7	7.9	1,330	73.1
E07000214	Surrey Heath	88.4	44.6	15.1	884	455	429	567	317	238	46	33	10.0	58.5	1.83	35.9	6.3	875	57.9
E07000215	Tandridge	86.7	44.4	14.8	956	496	460	598	358	280	52	26	11.0	64.5	1.96	37.4	6.0	947	63.9
E07000216	Waverley	123.8	63.3	20.1	1,251	621	630	871	380	303	50	27	10.1	62.2	2.00	30.4	5.2	1,228	61.0
E07000217	Woking	99.7	50.1	18.4	1,337	694	643	953	384	291	60	33	13.4	72.6	2.14	28.7	5.3	1,323	71.8
E10000032	**West Sussex**	**843.8**	**433.8**	**141.7**	**8,795**	**4,548**	**4,247**	**4,951**	**3,844**	**2,911**	**639**	**294**	**10.4**	**62.1**	**1.88**	**43.7**	**7.1**	**8,673**	**61.2**
E07000223	Adur	63.5	32.6	10.6	671	349	322	347	324	259	51	14	10.6	63.4	1.92	48.3	6.0	660	62.4
E07000224	Arun	157.0	81.8	23.6	1,552	793	759	712	840	622	152	66	9.9	65.8	2.00	54.1	8.2	1,527	64.7
E07000225	Chichester	118.2	61.3	17.9	955	479	476	570	385	291	63	31	8.1	53.4	1.72	40.3	5.9	949	53.1
E07000226	Crawley	111.4	55.7	23.2	1,584	816	768	916	668	470	133	65	14.2	68.3	1.93	42.2	8.6	1,564	67.4
E07000227	Horsham	138.0	70.9	22.3	1,324	687	637	803	521	412	73	36	9.6	59.5	1.89	39.4	6.7	1,305	58.6
E07000228	Mid Sussex	147.1	75.2	25.3	1,610	836	774	1,050	560	451	73	36	10.9	63.7	1.92	34.8	6.4	1,573	62.2
E07000229	Worthing	108.6	56.3	18.9	1,099	588	511	553	546	406	94	46	10.1	58.2	1.74	49.7	6.5	1,095	58.0
E12000009	**SOUTH WEST**	**5,516.0**	**2,804.4**	**963.2**	**57,316**	**29,434**	**27,882**	**29,670**	**27,646**	**20,877**	**4,368**	**2,401**	**10.4**	**59.5**	**1.79**	**48.2**	**6.1**	**56,612**	**58.8**
E06000022	Bath and North East Somerset	187.8	95.1	38.2	1,799	915	884	970	829	612	141	76	9.6	47.1	1.63	46.1	5.6	1,787	46.7
E06000028	Bournemouth	197.7	98.0	41.6	2,180	1,085	1,095	1,148	1,032	767	165	100	11.0	52.4	1.54	47.3	6.1	2,155	51.8
E06000023	Bristol, City of	454.2	226.8	108.4	6,400	3,322	3,078	3,459	2,941	2,053	584	304	14.1	59.0	1.72	46.0	5.6	6,323	58.3
E06000052, E06000053	Cornwall and Isles of Scilly[6]	556.0	286.1	89.0	5,312	2,719	2,593	2,404	2,908	2,271	414	223	9.6	59.7	1.87	54.7	6.5	5,256	59.1
E06000024	North Somerset	211.7	108.6	34.5	2,188	1,138	1,050	1,180	1,008	768	141	99	10.3	63.4	1.94	46.1	5.5	2,149	62.3
E06000026	Plymouth	264.2	132.7	52.5	2,912	1,512	1,400	1,316	1,596	1,122	309	165	11.0	55.4	1.62	54.8	7.8	2,870	54.6
E06000029	Poole	151.5	77.0	26.1	1,593	827	766	841	752	559	118	75	10.5	61.1	1.81	47.2	6.8	1,573	60.3
E06000025	South Gloucestershire	277.6	139.8	51.3	3,090	1,543	1,547	1,744	1,346	1,056	195	95	11.1	60.2	1.77	43.6	4.3	3,058	59.6
E06000030	Swindon	217.9	109.3	42.0	2,848	1,456	1,392	1,565	1,283	941	240	102	13.1	67.8	2.01	45.0	5.4	2,807	66.8
E06000027	Torbay	133.9	69.0	20.3	1,314	665	649	507	807	543	184	80	9.8	64.8	1.97	61.4	6.6	1,297	64.0
E06000054	Wiltshire	488.4	247.2	80.0	5,119	2,649	2,470	2,975	2,144	1,660	290	194	10.5	64.0	2.03	41.9	5.5	5,067	63.3
E10000008	**Devon**	**779.8**	**399.5**	**125.2**	**6,964**	**3,530**	**3,434**	**3,574**	**3,390**	**2,658**	**454**	**278**	**8.9**	**55.6**	**1.71**	**48.7**	**6.2**	**6,878**	**55.0**
E07000040	East Devon	139.9	72.3	19.1	1,139	562	577	589	550	428	83	39	8.1	59.7	1.89	48.3	6.4	1,122	58.8
E07000041	Exeter	129.8	65.5	30.9	1,292	667	625	701	591	426	99	66	10.0	41.8	1.34	45.7	7.0	1,274	41.2
E07000042	Mid Devon	79.8	40.8	12.6	737	361	376	381	356	292	37	27	9.2	58.4	1.81	48.3	4.7	730	57.8
E07000043	North Devon	94.6	48.3	14.4	946	479	467	481	465	372	57	36	10.0	65.6	2.01	49.2	4.7	937	64.9
E07000044	South Hams	84.3	43.6	11.4	599	288	311	316	283	224	38	21	7.1	52.6	1.69	47.2	6.5	592	52.0
E07000045	Teignbridge	129.9	67.0	19.4	1,155	591	564	581	574	461	73	40	8.9	59.6	1.83	49.7	6.1	1,143	59.0
E07000046	Torridge	67.0	34.2	9.7	632	334	298	292	340	266	40	34	9.4	65.3	2.04	53.8	6.0	627	64.8
E07000047	West Devon	54.0	27.0	7.7	434	218	216	233	231	189	27	15	8.5	60.6	1.96	49.8	8.8	453	59.2

Table 1   Summary: Live births (numbers, rates and percentages): administrative area of usual residence of mother, United Kingdom and constituent countries, 2016

England and Wales: regions (within England), unitary authorities, counties, districts, London Boroughs, local health boards (within Wales)
Scotland: council areas, Northern Ireland: 11 new Administrative Areas

Area of usual residence		Population (thousands) Numbers			Live Births Numbers All			Within marriage or civil partnership	Outside marriage or civil partnership Total	Joint regis-trations same address	Joint regis-trations different address	Sole regis-trations	Rates CBR	GFR	TFR	% live births outside marriage or civil partnership	% live births under 2.5kg	Maternities Numbers Total	Maternity Rate
		Total	Female	Females aged 15 to 44	Total	Male	Female												
E10000009	**Dorset**	**422.7**	**216.4**	**59.2**	**3,388**	**1,757**	**1,631**	**1,786**	**1,602**	**1,257**	**209**	**136**	**8.0**	**57.2**	**1.82**	**47.3**	**6.3**	**3,337**	**56.4**
E07000048	Christchurch	49.5	25.6	6.8	360	191	169	194	166	125	23	18	7.3	52.8	1.67	46.1	5.3	353	51.7
E07000049	East Dorset	89.1	46.2	11.8	644	352	292	394	250	202	31	17	7.2	54.4	1.75	38.8	5.3	630	53.2
E07000050	North Dorset	71.1	35.6	10.5	631	323	308	346	285	235	33	17	8.9	60.3	1.93	45.2	6.8	626	59.8
E07000051	Purbeck	46.3	23.4	6.5	346	181	165	185	161	132	16	13	7.5	53.1	1.67	46.5	7.5	342	52.5
E07000052	West Dorset	101.4	52.6	13.6	763	395	368	418	345	273	46	26	7.5	56.3	1.82	45.2	6.7	752	55.5
E07000053	Weymouth and Portland	65.4	33.1	10.0	644	315	329	249	395	290	60	45	9.9	64.4	2.00	61.3	6.5	634	63.4
E10000013	**Gloucestershire**	**623.1**	**317.9**	**108.1**	**6,739**	**3,517**	**3,222**	**3,606**	**3,133**	**2,325**	**540**	**268**	**10.8**	**62.4**	**1.88**	**46.5**	**6.4**	**6,642**	**61.5**
E07000078	Cheltenham	117.5	60.1	23.8	1,328	691	637	774	554	421	98	35	11.3	55.7	1.65	41.7	8.1	1,302	54.6
E07000079	Cotswold	85.8	44.3	12.7	730	385	345	440	290	230	29	31	8.5	57.3	1.88	39.7	4.4	715	56.1
E07000080	Forest of Dean	85.4	43.4	13.2	844	426	418	387	457	362	68	27	9.9	63.8	2.06	54.1	6.4	833	63.0
E07000081	Gloucester	128.5	65.1	25.0	1,768	944	824	840	928	595	218	115	13.8	70.9	2.03	52.5	6.7	1,754	70.3
E07000082	Stroud	117.4	59.7	18.7	1,094	554	540	608	486	391	63	32	9.3	58.5	1.84	44.4	6.0	1,075	57.5
E07000083	Tewkesbury	88.6	45.2	14.6	975	517	458	557	418	326	64	28	11.0	66.6	1.97	42.9	5.7	963	65.8
E10000027	**Somerset**	**549.4**	**281.1**	**86.8**	**5,470**	**2,799**	**2,671**	**2,595**	**2,875**	**2,285**	**384**	**206**	**10.0**	**63.0**	**1.95**	**52.6**	**6.4**	**5,413**	**62.3**
E07000187	Mendip	112.5	57.8	18.1	1,080	551	529	540	540	440	73	27	9.6	59.7	1.91	50.0	5.5	1,071	59.2
E07000188	Sedgemoor	121.4	61.8	19.4	1,298	673	625	529	769	590	112	67	10.7	66.8	2.05	59.2	6.7	1,283	66.0
E07000189	South Somerset	165.6	84.3	25.6	1,651	849	802	802	849	697	97	55	10.0	64.4	1.99	51.4	6.7	1,633	63.7
E07000190	Taunton Deane	115.5	59.4	19.4	1,206	610	596	625	581	443	94	44	10.4	62.1	1.87	48.2	6.8	1,192	61.4
E07000191	West Somerset	34.3	17.8	4.3	235	116	119	99	136	115	8	13	6.9	55.2	1.71	57.9	4.7	234	55.0
W92000004	**WALES**	**3,113.2**	**1,579.1**	**559.6**	**32,936**	**16,806**	**16,130**	**13,420**	**19,516**	**13,189**	**4,363**	**1,964**	**10.6**	**58.9**	**1.74**	**59.3**	**6.9**	**32,573**	**58.2**
W06000001	Isle of Anglesey	69.7	35.4	10.6	716	364	352	258	458	332	88	38	10.3	67.6	2.04	64.0	9.1	708	66.8
W06000002	Gwynedd	123.6	62.4	21.9	1,156	591	565	444	712	515	123	74	9.4	52.7	1.65	61.6	6.3	1,149	52.4
W06000003	Conwy	116.5	59.8	17.1	1,050	531	519	387	663	478	106	79	9.0	61.3	1.88	63.1	6.8	1,042	60.8
W06000004	Denbighshire	94.8	48.1	15.0	1,012	541	471	355	657	465	123	69	10.7	67.6	2.09	64.9	9.9	996	66.5
W06000005	Flintshire	154.4	78.3	26.5	1,587	811	776	706	881	639	152	90	10.3	60.0	1.80	55.5	7.2	1,568	59.3
W06000006	Wrexham	136.7	68.4	24.1	1,491	798	693	578	913	648	187	78	10.9	61.8	1.81	61.2	8.9	1,479	61.4
W06000023	Powys	132.2	66.8	18.9	1,179	612	567	511	668	549	76	43	8.9	62.5	1.99	56.7	5.5	1,168	61.9
W06000008	Ceredigion	74.1	37.0	12.7	612	314	298	251	361	292	36	33	8.3	48.2	1.65	59.0	5.7	605	47.7
W06000009	Pembrokeshire	124.0	63.1	19.1	1,133	557	576	431	702	501	131	70	9.1	59.2	1.81	62.0	7.2	1,128	59.0
W06000010	Carmarthenshire	185.6	94.8	30.4	1,878	970	908	777	1,101	838	186	77	10.1	61.8	1.86	58.6	6.0	1,856	61.1
W06000011	Swansea	244.5	122.2	46.1	2,475	1,249	1,226	1,041	1,434	926	373	135	10.1	53.7	1.60	57.9	6.6	2,450	53.1
W06000012	Neath Port Talbot	141.6	72.0	24.9	1,519	764	755	551	968	654	235	79	10.7	61.1	1.82	63.7	7.6	1,499	60.3
W06000013	Bridgend	143.2	72.2	24.9	1,501	772	729	578	923	619	211	93	10.5	60.2	1.82	61.5	7.0	1,479	59.3
W06000014	Vale of Glamorgan	128.5	66.0	21.8	1,321	647	674	565	756	470	198	88	10.3	60.5	1.88	57.2	5.3	1,307	59.9
W06000015	Cardiff	361.5	183.3	84.0	4,418	2,237	2,181	2,316	2,102	1,195	625	282	12.2	52.6	1.59	47.6	6.0	4,369	52.0
W06000016	Rhondda Cynon Taff	238.3	121.4	45.2	2,782	1,408	1,374	922	1,860	1,185	488	187	11.7	61.6	1.78	66.9	8.4	2,744	60.7

Table 1   Summary: Live births (numbers, rates and percentages): administrative area of usual residence of mother, United Kingdom and constituent countries, 2016

England and Wales: regions (within England), unitary authorities, counties, districts, London Boroughs, local health boards (within Wales)
Scotland: council areas, Northern Ireland: 11 new Administrative Areas

Area of usual residence		Population (thousands) Numbers (thousands)			Live Births — Numbers[1] — All			Within marriage or civil partner-ship	Outside marriage or civil partnership				Rates[2]			Percentages		Maternities	
		Total	Female	Females aged 15 to 44	Total	Male	Female		Total	Joint regis-trations same address	Joint regis-trations different address	Sole regis-trations	Crude Birth Rate (CBR): all births per 1,000 population of all ages	General Fertility Rate (GFR): all live births per 1,000 women aged 15 to 44	Total Fertility Rate (TFR)[3]	Percent-age of live births outside marriage or civil partner-ship	Percent-age of live births under 2.5kg	Numbers Total	Mater-nity Rate[4]
W06000024	Merthyr Tydfil	59.8	30.4	11.3	715	331	384	209	506	283	167	56	12.0	63.5	1.82	70.8	6.9	719	63.9
W06000018	Caerphilly	180.5	92.1	33.6	2,017	1,036	981	751	1,266	868	283	115	11.2	60.0	1.76	62.8	5.3	1,988	59.1
W06000019	Blaenau Gwent	69.6	35.3	12.8	726	346	380	235	491	331	123	37	10.4	56.9	1.63	67.6	7.0	712	55.8
W06000020	Torfaen	92.1	47.2	16.7	1,005	520	485	360	645	434	130	81	10.9	60.2	1.76	64.2	8.1	988	59.2
W06000021	Monmouthshire	92.8	47.1	13.8	740	417	323	368	372	296	53	23	8.0	53.8	1.74	50.3	4.9	735	53.4
W06000022	Newport	149.1	75.8	28.4	1,903	990	913	826	1,077	671	269	137	12.8	67.1	1.94	56.6	7.3	1,884	66.4
W11000023	Betsi Cadwaladr University	695.8	352.4	115.2	7,012	3,636	3,376	2,728	4,284	3,077	779	428	10.1	60.9	1.83	61.1	7.9	6,942	60.3
W11000024	Powys Teaching	132.2	66.8	18.9	1,179	612	567	511	668	549	76	43	8.9	62.5	1.99	56.7	5.5	1,168	61.9
W11000025	Hywel Dda	383.7	194.8	62.2	3,623	1,841	1,782	1,459	2,164	1,631	353	180	9.4	58.3	1.77	59.7	6.3	3,589	57.7
W11000026	Abertawe Bro Morgannwg University	529.3	266.4	95.9	5,495	2,785	2,710	2,170	3,325	2,199	819	307	10.4	57.3	1.70	60.5	7.0	5,428	56.6
W11000027	Cwm Taf	298.1	151.9	56.4	3,497	1,739	1,758	1,131	2,366	1,468	655	243	11.7	62.0	1.79	67.7	8.1	3,463	61.4
W11000028	Aneurin Bevan	584.1	297.5	105.2	6,391	3,309	3,082	2,540	3,851	2,600	858	393	10.9	60.7	1.79	60.3	6.4	6,307	59.9
W11000029	Cardiff and Vale University	489.9	249.3	105.8	5,739	2,884	2,855	2,881	2,858	1,665	823	370	11.7	54.2	1.63	49.8	5.9	5,676	53.7
J99000001	Usual residence outside England and Wales where birth occurred in England and Wales[5]	:	:	:	178	81	97	122	56	39	8	9	:	:	:	31.5	23.0	222	:
S92000003	SCOTLAND	5,404.7	2,777.2	1,035.1	54,488	28,236	26,252	26,761	27,727	19,394	6,012	2,321	10.1	52.6	1.52	50.9	:	53,898	52.1
S12000033	Aberdeen City	229.8	115.7	53.0	2,521	1,285	1,236	1,398	1,123	866	171	86	11.0	47.6	1.32	44.5	:	2,497	47.1
S12000034	Aberdeenshire	262.2	131.8	45.6	2,811	1,475	1,336	1,712	1,099	925	99	75	10.7	61.6	1.87	39.1	:	2,780	61.0
S12000041	Angus	116.5	59.8	19.2	1,025	540	485	480	545	421	71	53	8.8	53.5	1.65	53.2	:	1,020	53.2
S12000035	Argyll and Bute	87.1	43.8	12.5	699	356	343	321	378	296	58	24	8.0	55.9	1.77	54.1	:	689	55.1
S12000036	City of Edinburgh[7]	507.2	260.4	122.2	5,300	2,716	2,584	3,243	2,057	1,580	290	187	10.5	43.4	1.22	38.8	:	5,233	42.8
S12000005	Clackmannanshire	51.4	26.2	8.9	505	268	237	187	318	211	77	30	9.8	56.4	1.74	63.0	:	505	56.4
S12000006	Dumfries and Galloway	149.5	77.0	23.0	1,318	655	663	535	783	599	112	72	8.8	57.3	1.74	59.4	:	1,311	57.0
S12000042	Dundee City	148.3	76.8	32.5	1,576	842	734	604	972	593	268	111	10.6	48.5	1.37	61.7	:	1,560	48.0
S12000008	East Ayrshire	122.2	62.9	21.7	1,275	669	606	494	781	548	160	73	10.4	58.9	1.77	61.3	:	1,255	57.9
S12000045	East Dunbartonshire	107.5	55.5	17.1	951	490	461	611	340	235	82	23	8.8	55.6	1.79	35.8	:	935	54.6
S12000010	East Lothian	104.1	54.3	18.4	1,041	555	486	535	506	371	101	34	10.0	56.5	1.74	48.6	:	1,034	56.1
S12000011	East Renfrewshire	93.8	49.2	15.9	861	442	419	620	241	160	67	14	9.2	54.3	1.77	28.0	:	849	53.6
S12000014	Falkirk	159.4	81.4	29.3	1,565	832	733	732	833	605	161	67	9.8	53.3	1.61	53.2	:	1,554	53.0
S12000015	Fife	370.3	190.8	67.6	3,739	1,930	1,809	1,674	2,065	1,469	416	180	10.1	55.3	1.66	55.2	:	3,705	54.8
S12000046	Glasgow City	615.1	316.0	144.3	6,833	3,505	3,328	3,262	3,571	2,107	1,095	369	11.1	47.4	1.31	52.3	:	6,790	47.1
S12000017	Highland	234.8	119.9	38.8	2,150	1,129	1,021	1,005	1,145	894	179	72	9.2	55.5	1.69	53.3	:	2,135	55.1
S12000018	Inverclyde	79.2	41.3	13.8	706	376	330	287	419	246	148	25	8.9	51.3	1.55	59.3	:	695	50.5
S12000019	Midlothian	88.6	46.0	16.3	1,088	563	525	517	571	400	120	51	12.3	66.8	1.99	52.5	:	1,074	65.9
S12000020	Moray	96.1	48.4	16.3	939	498	441	467	472	364	71	37	9.8	57.5	1.75	50.3	:	923	56.5

Table 1　Summary: Live births (numbers, rates and percentages): administrative area of usual residence of mother, United Kingdom and constituent countries, 2016

England and Wales: regions (within England), unitary authorities, counties, districts, London Boroughs, local health boards (within Wales)
Scotland: council areas, Northern Ireland: 11 new Administrative Areas

Area of usual residence		Population — Numbers (thousands)			Live Births — Numbers[1]				Outside marriage or civil partnership				Rates[2]			Percentages		Maternities	
		Total	Female	Females aged 15 to 44	All Total	All Male	All Female	Within marriage or civil partnership	Total	Joint regis-trations same address	Joint regis-trations different address	Sole regis-trations	Crude Birth Rate (CBR): all births per 1,000 population of all ages	General Fertility Rate (GFR): all live births per 1,000 women aged 15 to 44	Total Fertility Rate (TFR)[3]	Percentage of live births outside marriage or civil partner-ship	Percentage of live births under 2.5kg	Numbers Total	Mater-nity Rate[4]
S12000013	Na h-Eileanan Siar[7]	26.9	13.6	4.1	238	126	112	144	94	81	10	3	8.8	58.6	1.82	39.5	:	236	58.1
S12000021	North Ayrshire	135.9	71.2	23.3	1,244	651	593	448	796	503	218	75	9.2	53.3	1.64	64.0	:	1,230	52.7
S12000044	North Lanarkshire	339.4	175.1	64.8	3,511	1,824	1,687	1,458	2,053	1,328	563	162	10.3	54.2	1.62	58.5	:	3,471	53.6
S12000023	Orkney Islands	21.9	11.0	3.5	178	89	89	97	81	70	8	3	8.1	51.1	1.53	45.5	:	177	50.8
S12000024	Perth and Kinross	150.7	76.7	24.7	1,325	673	652	650	675	541	86	48	8.8	53.5	1.62	50.9	:	1,314	53.1
S12000038	Renfrewshire	175.9	91.2	32.4	1,773	929	844	837	936	610	257	69	10.1	54.7	1.62	52.8	:	1,745	53.9
S12000026	Scottish Borders	114.5	59.0	17.5	1,005	522	483	495	510	395	69	46	8.8	57.4	1.83	50.7	:	987	56.4
S12000027	Shetland Islands	23.2	11.4	4.0	266	141	125	155	111	96	12	3	11.5	66.9	2.02	41.7	:	263	66.2
S12000028	South Ayrshire	112.5	58.8	18.0	976	502	474	412	564	398	126	40	8.7	54.1	1.67	57.8	:	967	53.6
S12000029	South Lanarkshire	317.1	164.1	57.1	3,315	1,740	1,575	1,655	1,660	1,097	437	126	10.5	58.1	1.74	50.1	:	3,260	57.1
S12000030	Stirling	93.8	48.7	18.7	807	404	403	432	375	266	85	24	8.6	43.1	1.38	46.5	:	800	42.8
S12000039	West Dunbartonshire	89.9	47.1	16.6	958	487	471	354	604	361	190	53	10.7	57.8	1.68	63.0	:	946	57.1
S12000040	West Lothian	180.1	91.9	34.2	1,989	1,022	967	940	1,049	758	205	86	11.0	58.2	1.75	52.7	:	1,958	57.3
N92000002	NORTHERN IRELAND	1,862.1	946.9	363.7	24,076	12,425	11,651	13,608	10,468	4,117	5,154	1,197	12.9	66.2	1.95	43.5	:	23,771	65.4
N09000001	Antrim and Newtownabbey	141.0	72.5	27.7	1,759	889	870	999	760	358	337	65	12.5	63.4	1.90	43.2	:	1,736	62.6
N09000011	Ards and North Down	159.6	82.2	27.9	1,650	847	803	997	653	348	233	72	10.3	59.1	1.78	39.6	:	1,631	58.4
N09000002	Armagh City, Banbridge & Craigavon	210.3	105.9	40.7	2,943	1,476	1,467	1,767	1,176	592	487	97	14.0	72.3	2.11	40.0	:	2,894	71.1
N09000003	Belfast	339.6	175.1	74.3	4,593	2,418	2,175	1,948	2,645	759	1,522	364	13.5	61.8	1.77	57.6	:	4,531	60.9
N09000004	Causeway Coast and Glens	143.5	72.4	26.7	1,655	874	781	874	781	308	372	101	11.5	62.1	1.92	47.2	:	1,639	61.5
N09000005	Derry City and Strabane	150.1	76.4	30.2	2,001	1,051	950	884	1,117	230	684	203	13.3	66.3	1.99	55.8	:	1,970	65.3
N09000006	Fermanagh and Omagh	115.8	57.8	21.5	1,513	749	764	1,054	459	210	210	39	13.1	70.3	2.09	30.3	:	1,489	69.2
N09000007	Lisburn and Castlereagh	141.2	72.0	26.2	1,745	914	831	1,139	606	313	252	41	12.4	66.6	1.96	34.7	:	1,723	65.7
N09000008	Mid and East Antrim	137.8	70.3	25.1	1,571	816	755	916	655	281	310	64	11.4	62.7	1.89	41.7	:	1,559	62.2
N09000009	Mid Ulster	145.4	72.4	29.1	2,147	1,085	1,062	1,479	668	328	271	69	14.8	73.7	2.15	31.1	:	2,128	73.1
N09000010	Newry, Mourne and Down	177.8	89.7	34.2	2,499	1,306	1,193	1,551	948	390	476	82	14.1	73.0	2.15	37.9	:	2,471	72.2

1 The Human Fertilisation and Embryology Act (HFEA) 2008 contained provisions enabling two females in a same sex couple to register a birth from 1 September 2009 onwards. Due to the small numbers, births registered to a same sex couple in a marriage or civil partnership (1,011 in 2016) are included with marital births while births registered to a same sex couple outside a marriage or civil partnership (393 in 2016) are included with births outside marriage. Births registered under HFEA are reported only for England and Wales and no sub division thereof.

2 All rates have been calculated using the mid-2016 population estimates.

3 The Total Fertility Rate (TFR) is the average number of live children that a group of women would bear if they experienced the age-specific fertility rates of the calendar year in question throughout their childbearing lifespan.

The national TFRs have been calculated using the number of live births by single year of age.

The sub-national TFRs have been calculated using the number of live births by five year age groups.

4 Maternities per 1,000 women aged 15 to 44. A maternity is a pregnancy resulting in the birth of one or more children, including stillbirths.

5 A birth to a mother whose usual residence is outside England and Wales is included in total figures for "England, Wales and elsewhere " but are excluded from any sub-divisions of England and Wales. The England and Wales and elsewhere figures correspond to figures published at the national level for England and Wales not based on area of usual residence.

6 To preserve confidentiality, counts for Isles of Scilly have been combined with Cornwall.

7 The alphabetical order of the council areas has changed due to adoption of the preferred forms of reference to the Edinburgh and Western Isles council areas. Previous versions of this table used the forms 'Edinburgh, City of' and 'Eilean Siar'.

Source: Office for National Statistics (ONS), National Records of Scotland, Northern Ireland Statistics and Research Agency

Released: 20 November 2017

Table 2 Live births (numbers and rates): age and administrative area of usual residence of mother, England and Wales, 2016
England and Wales: regions, counties, unitary authorities, local authority districts, local health boards (within Wales)

Rates per 1,000 women in age group[1,2]

Area of usual residence of mother		Numbers — Age of mother at birth									Rates per 1,000 — Age of mother at birth								
Code	Area	All ages	Under 18	Under 20	20 to 24	25 to 29	30 to 34	35 to 39	40 to 44	45 and over	All ages	Under 18	Under 20	20 to 24	25 to 29	30 to 34	35 to 39	40 to 44	45 and over
K04000001, J99000001	ENGLAND, WALES AND ELSEWHERE[3]	696,271	5,417	22,465	102,607	196,132	220,129	125,205	27,447	2,286	62.3	5.7	13.7	55.8	98.8	112.0	66.9	14.7	1.1
E92000001	ENGLAND	663,157	5,025	20,963	96,519	185,960	210,731	120,330	26,447	2,207	62.5	5.6	13.5	55.6	98.5	112.4	67.5	14.9	1.1
E12000001	NORTH EAST	28,574	425	1,481	5,451	8,676	8,234	3,946	741	45	58.6	10.2	20.0	60.6	101.4	99.6	51.5	9.4	0.5
E06000047	County Durham	5,304	87	281	1,098	1,689	1,433	668	128	7	56.5	10.9	19.2	60.8	107.5	92.4	45.8	8.3	0.4 u
E06000005	Darlington	1,154	10	67	226	360	312	157	32	0	60.6	5.5 u	22.9	82.5	109.2	94.4	48.4	9.1	: u
E06000001	Hartlepool	1,051	26	81	245	370	254	78	22	1	62.2	15.6	30.1	86.5	121.7	85.4	29.3	8.2	: u
E06000002	Middlesbrough	1,908	27	105	420	596	519	216	48	4	69.0	10.9	23.9	73.7	119.5	112.0	54.0	12.2	0.9 u
E06000057	Northumberland	2,820	39	154	486	826	819	439	90	6	57.1	7.8	19.3	68.8	102.2	96.3	51.7	9.7	0.5 u
E06000003	Redcar and Cleveland	1,433	30	81	342	458	347	172	32	1	61.9	13.6	22.0	92.4	111.4	85.9	46.9	8.1	: u
E06000004	Stockton-on-Tees	2,298	40	126	429	684	673	315	67	4	63.2	12.3	23.4	74.6	108.9	99.9	51.8	11.0	0.6 u
E11000007	Tyne and Wear (Met County)	12,606	166	586	2,205	3,693	3,877	1,901	322	22	57.0	9.7	18.1	50.0	92.3	104.9	56.2	9.5	0.6
E08000037	Gateshead	2,286	27	105	424	629	705	351	68	4	60.5	8.6	18.8	72.7	92.1	99.2	55.7	11.1	0.6 u
E08000021	Newcastle upon Tyne	3,393	40	145	533	956	1,106	528	115	10	50.0	9.5	14.5	27.4	77.0	113.1	63.9	14.6	1.2 u
E08000022	North Tyneside	2,254	26	86	323	635	736	420	51	3	61.0	8.3	16.8	64.8	101.9	106.9	61.7	7.4	0.4 u
E08000023	South Tyneside	1,687	22	86	318	512	503	230	37	1	63.1	9.1	21.2	76.0	106.3	105.6	52.3	8.2	: u
E08000024	Sunderland	2,986	51	164	607	961	827	372	51	4	57.4	12.0	21.7	62.8	98.8	98.4	46.1	5.9	0.4 u
E12000002	NORTH WEST	86,069	781	3,217	14,122	25,994	26,173	13,618	2,731	214	63.4	6.6	15.7	60.4	106.8	111.7	62.8	12.2	0.8
E06000008	Blackburn with Darwen	2,156	25	94	375	779	560	296	51	1	75.7	8.6	20.1	88.7	160.5	107.0	62.9	10.7	: u
E06000009	Blackpool	1,700	34	122	442	510	400	193	30	3	70.6	14.4	31.1	108.7	119.0	98.8	52.9	7.3	0.6 u
E06000049	Cheshire East	3,822	27	118	505	958	1,298	761	169	13	62.2	4.3	11.8	57.8	104.6	126.3	70.5	13.5	0.9 u
E06000050	Cheshire West and Chester	3,565	23	111	518	1,015	1,152	614	139	16	60.3	4.3	12.0	51.9	105.3	119.0	63.0	12.8	1.3 u
E06000006	Halton	1,503	26	90	328	473	370	199	41	2	63.6	11.7	25.2	90.6	113.4	90.1	51.1	9.6	: u
E06000007	Warrington	2,297	18	79	331	654	720	408	96	9	60.8	5.1 u	14.0	62.7	100.4	107.5	61.2	13.7	1.1 u
E10000006	Cumbria	4,758	49	203	803	1,518	1,372	733	122	7	60.6	6.3	15.9	67.1	119.2	104.7	56.6	8.2	0.4 u
E07000026	Allerdale	902	8	42	160	275	251	147	26	1	60.3	5.1 u	16.6	72.5	116.2	101.7	57.7	9.2	: u
E07000027	Barrow-in-Furness	780	15	45	162	271	197	93	10	2	68.4	13.1 u	24.2	90.1	135.0	102.4	54.2	4.8 u	: u
E07000028	Carlisle	1,170	13	55	194	375	361	168	16	1	61.1	7.8 u	19.1	56.4	118.4	109.5	55.4	4.8 u	: u
E07000029	Copeland	703	5	33	143	227	183	101	14	2	63.3	4.9 u	19.1	91.2	114.7	96.5	55.6	6.6 u	: u
E07000030	Eden	409	2	7	58	132	134	59	19	0	54.3	: u	5.3 u	55.6	114.0	109.7	46.1	12.6 u	: u
E07000031	South Lakeland	794	6	21	86	238	246	165	37	1	55.3	3.9 u	8.4	45.0	116.0	107.0	64.4	12.1	: u
E11000001	Greater Manchester (Met County)	36,889	280	1,270	5,927	11,033	11,389	5,939	1,236	95	65.7	6.0	15.9	61.2	104.1	112.7	65.9	14.1	1.0
E08000001	Bolton	3,816	33	143	683	1,224	1,087	545	124	10	72.0	6.6	17.5	83.5	127.4	117.2	63.4	13.5	1.0 u
E08000002	Bury	2,362	15	74	360	658	769	408	86	7	68.1	4.7 u	14.4	76.1	105.8	120.8	67.4	13.9	1.0 u
E08000003	Manchester	7,946	54	244	1,202	2,315	2,448	1,386	320	31	57.1	6.8	13.9	34.8	77.3	101.7	75.8	21.5	2.1
E08000004	Oldham	3,327	31	123	639	1,129	923	433	76	4	75.0	7.0	17.2	93.8	139.8	115.1	59.4	10.8	0.5 u
E08000005	Rochdale	3,072	24	136	526	966	904	447	86	7	73.9	6.2	21.2	84.5	126.8	122.4	63.6	12.4	0.9 u
E08000006	Salford	3,695	31	151	668	1,071	1,141	535	117	12	69.8	7.9	22.5	71.7	97.5	109.6	66.3	15.8	1.5 u
E08000007	Stockport	3,424	21	91	402	891	1,207	686	138	9	65.8	4.3	11.7	57.4	100.7	129.5	72.2	14.5	0.8 u
E08000008	Tameside	2,876	27	118	533	943	801	403	73	5	68.7	7.2	19.5	84.9	119.7	103.6	59.0	10.3	0.6 u
E08000009	Trafford	2,813	9	46	231	642	1,084	676	129	5	64.9	2.2 u	7.2	45.9	99.6	136.0	77.2	14.7	0.6 u
E08000010	Wigan	3,558	35	141	600	1,104	1,023	420	81	5	60.9	6.7	16.9	77.3	114.9	97.7	43.2	8.3	0.4 u
E10000017	Lancashire	13,183	146	521	2,256	4,112	3,953	1,982	328	31	61.7	7.4	15.1	59.2	113.8	112.9	59.2	9.0	0.7
E07000117	Burnley	1,207	20	58	277	378	319	135	36	4	75.3	14.3	24.9	112.6	126.7	109.4	49.9	13.7	1.3

Table 2   Live births (numbers and rates): age and administrative area of usual residence of mother, England and Wales, 2016
England and Wales: regions, counties, unitary authorities, local authority districts, local health boards (within Wales)

Area of usual residence of mother		All ages	Under 18	Under 20	20 to 24	25 to 29	30 to 34	35 to 39	40 to 44	45 and over	All ages	Under 18	Under 20	20 to 24	25 to 29	30 to 34	35 to 39	40 to 44	45 and over
		Numbers									Rates per 1,000 women in age group[1,2]								
E07000118	Chorley	1,226	17	49	195	329	405	207	40	1	61.5	9.6 u	17.1	69.7	95.8	113.1	60.4	10.4	: u
E07000119	Fylde	629	5	22	87	187	211	111	10	1	57.3	4.2 u	11.9	63.1	107.0	112.4	58.6	4.5 u	: u
E07000120	Hyndburn	1,057	13	65	209	364	250	145	23	1	71.2	9.3 u	28.3	90.8	133.6	95.0	60.6	9.2	: u
E07000121	Lancaster	1,456	16	52	249	450	452	214	34	5	51.1	6.8 u	10.4	34.2	102.7	110.0	56.6	8.7	1.1 u
E07000122	Pendle	1,214	8	41	211	408	360	167	23	4	73.2	5.1 u	16.7	89.6	133.7	113.5	59.9	8.3	1.3 u
E07000123	Preston	1,893	20	74	342	615	558	249	50	5	64.0	8.8	16.3	48.9	117.4	124.0	59.8	12.1	1.1 u
E07000124	Ribble Valley	482	1	5	48	140	181	92	15	1	53.5	: u	2.9 u	41.7	102.1	133.0	62.0	7.8 u	: u
E07000125	Rossendale	818	12	35	145	258	243	118	18	1	65.4	10.1 u	18.7	85.3	117.6	110.3	54.8	7.5 u	: u
E07000126	South Ribble	1,241	6	36	181	392	397	209	24	2	64.8	3.3 u	12.3	68.8	115.0	122.6	64.8	6.5	: u
E07000127	West Lancashire	1,000	14	36	148	295	303	184	32	2	49.5	7.7 u	9.3	33.2	100.3	110.4	66.4	9.3	: u
E07000128	Wyre	960	14	48	164	296	274	151	23	4	58.3	8.3 u	17.8	62.5	111.1	102.6	55.9	7.4	1.0 u
E11000002	**Merseyside (Met County)**	**16,196**	**153**	**609**	**2,637**	**4,942**	**4,959**	**2,493**	**519**	**37**	**60.0**	**6.8**	**14.9**	**51.7**	**98.8**	**109.9**	**61.2**	**12.4**	**0.8**
E08000011	Knowsley	1,933	15	75	350	652	574	232	46	4	67.8	5.8 u	16.8	74.1	119.8	114.1	52.9	10.3	0.7 u
E08000012	Liverpool	6,030	45	197	993	1,828	1,866	953	178	15	55.0	6.4	12.5	37.2	86.5	105.5	64.6	13.2	1.0 u
E08000014	Sefton	2,805	23	106	378	843	888	476	111	3	62.3	5.1	14.5	55.8	105.9	119.6	65.8	13.4	0.3 u
E08000013	St. Helens	1,994	33	94	367	621	585	268	57	2	62.5	11.5	20.0	74.3	104.7	104.4	53.2	10.0	0.3
E08000015	Wirral	3,434	37	137	549	998	1,046	564	127	13	62.6	6.7	15.8	70.1	104.6	111.7	60.4	12.6	1.1 u
E12000003	**YORKSHIRE AND THE HUMBER**	**63,823**	**683**	**2,697**	**11,706**	**19,626**	**18,507**	**9,242**	**1,923**	**122**	**62.1**	**7.7**	**17.1**	**62.1**	**109.1**	**106.6**	**57.4**	**11.5**	**0.6**
E06000011	**East Riding of Yorkshire**	**2,869**	**21**	**94**	**522**	**886**	**859**	**418**	**82**	**8**	**56.3**	**3.8**	**10.4**	**75.1**	**117.5**	**108.9**	**47.0**	**7.7**	**0.6 u**
E06000010	**Kingston upon Hull, City of**	**3,550**	**54**	**200**	**862**	**1,203**	**845**	**363**	**71**	**6**	**65.7**	**14.5**	**28.5**	**78.4**	**107.0**	**88.9**	**47.9**	**9.2**	**0.7 u**
E06000012	**North East Lincolnshire**	**1,861**	**31**	**124**	**452**	**661**	**392**	**199**	**30**	**3**	**66.6**	**12.0**	**28.8**	**105.7**	**123.3**	**78.8**	**45.6**	**6.5**	**0.5 u**
E06000013	**North Lincolnshire**	**1,773**	**12**	**60**	**383**	**598**	**488**	**206**	**33**	**5**	**61.2**	**4.3 u**	**13.2**	**90.7**	**116.5**	**93.1**	**43.9**	**6.4**	**0.8 u**
E06000014	**York**	**1,936**	**16**	**56**	**237**	**539**	**638**	**388**	**72**	**6**	**43.0**	**5.5 u**	**7.8**	**20.4**	**71.4**	**98.6**	**63.1**	**11.8**	**0.9 u**
E10000023	**North Yorkshire**	**5,712**	**36**	**179**	**865**	**1,670**	**1,819**	**959**	**198**	**22**	**62.7**	**3.7**	**11.6**	**70.2**	**114.1**	**122.3**	**62.2**	**10.7**	**1.0**
E07000163	Craven	432	4	13	57	120	141	79	20	2	53.7	4.2 u	8.9 u	52.2	99.2	117.8	57.4	11.7	: u
E07000164	Hambleton	803	3	18	129	242	240	148	24	2	61.3	2.0 u	8.0 u	71.3	114.1	114.8	68.1	9.1	: u
E07000165	Harrogate	1,475	4	27	153	358	542	323	67	5	62.1	1.5 u	6.5	55.1	106.5	141.0	73.7	12.8	0.8 u
E07000166	Richmondshire	555	5	19	107	190	173	49	15	2	71.4	6.4 u	15.5 u	100.4	139.0	122.6	38.6	10.5 u	: u
E07000167	Ryedale	439	2	11	62	152	130	64	20	0	56.9	: u	7.7 u	55.4	123.0	108.6	52.6	13.1	: u
E07000168	Scarborough	1,034	10	57	214	318	271	140	27	7	64.7	6.3 u	22.1	83.4	114.1	105.9	56.5	9.0	1.9 u
E07000169	Selby	974	8	34	143	290	322	156	25	4	66.1	5.5 u	15.1	75.3	113.6	125.0	61.7	8.6	1.1 u
E11000003	**South Yorkshire (Met County)**	**16,003**	**218**	**778**	**3,265**	**4,995**	**4,374**	**2,127**	**443**	**21**	**59.4**	**9.9**	**19.2**	**61.8**	**101.7**	**97.5**	**52.7**	**10.7**	**0.4**
E08000016	Barnsley	2,832	51	173	671	925	670	325	66	2	65.3	13.4	26.8	97.5	118.2	85.8	46.5	8.9	: u
E08000017	Doncaster	3,535	57	194	819	1,147	927	361	87	0	64.7	11.5	23.9	98.4	111.6	92.5	41.3	9.5	: u
E08000018	Rotherham	3,104	45	154	662	990	817	394	84	3	66.1	9.8	21.0	93.9	116.7	98.6	51.9	10.2	0.3 u
E08000019	Sheffield	6,532	65	257	1,113	1,933	1,960	1,047	206	16	52.5	7.4	13.7	36.4	85.7	104.6	61.4	12.3	0.8 u
E11000006	**West Yorkshire (Met County)**	**30,119**	**295**	**1,206**	**5,120**	**9,074**	**9,092**	**4,582**	**994**	**51**	**65.4**	**7.5**	**17.2**	**60.1**	**114.4**	**113.9**	**62.3**	**13.7**	**0.6**
E08000032	Bradford	7,930	84	297	1,383	2,527	2,370	1,099	248	6	75.2	7.8	17.1	86.3	138.7	123.1	62.0	14.8	0.3 u
E08000033	Calderdale	2,470	26	117	464	728	730	353	75	3	65.4	7.1	19.9	84.7	112.2	112.4	54.0	10.9	0.4 u
E08000034	Kirklees	5,408	47	212	924	1,726	1,546	796	197	7	64.9	6.0	16.1	67.2	120.9	109.0	57.3	14.0	0.4 u
E08000035	Leeds	10,250	93	386	1,493	2,794	3,336	1,842	368	31	59.5	7.9	15.6	36.6	96.8	117.2	72.5	15.4	1.2
E08000036	Wakefield	4,061	45	194	856	1,299	1,110	492	106	4	65.9	8.2	21.9	93.7	113.3	97.4	49.5	9.8	0.3 u
E12000004	**EAST MIDLANDS**	**53,299**	**471**	**1,960**	**9,100**	**15,960**	**16,106**	**8,197**	**1,847**	**129**	**60.9**	**6.1**	**14.3**	**58.6**	**107.6**	**110.7**	**58.5**	**12.4**	**0.8**
E06000015	**Derby**	**3,294**	**42**	**148**	**574**	**965**	**1,034**	**471**	**93**	**9**	**64.5**	**9.9**	**19.3**	**64.2**	**102.1**	**116.2**	**57.0**	**11.9**	**1.0 u**
E06000016	**Leicester**	**5,150**	**60**	**201**	**857**	**1,628**	**1,496**	**758**	**192**	**18**	**64.1**	**10.4**	**17.3**	**45.2**	**106.4**	**114.7**	**67.8**	**18.9**	**1.8 u**

Table 2 Live births (numbers and rates): age and administrative area of usual residence of mother, England and Wales, 2016

England and Wales: regions, counties, unitary authorities, local authority districts, local health boards (within Wales)

Numbers

Area of usual residence of mother		All ages	Under 18	Under 20	20 to 24	25 to 29	30 to 34	35 to 39	40 to 44	45 and over
E06000018	Nottingham	4,297	51	178	830	1,373	1,194	548	160	14
E06000017	Rutland	336	1	7	44	93	103	67	19	3
E10000007	Derbyshire	7,820	62	268	1,383	2,281	2,368	1,235	266	19
E07000032	Amber Valley	1,223	11	48	227	349	356	196	42	5
E07000033	Bolsover	815	10	38	159	265	232	104	17	0
E07000034	Chesterfield	1,069	5	38	225	335	291	140	40	0
E07000035	Derbyshire Dales	516	0	5	73	130	174	106	26	2
E07000036	Erewash	1,216	10	44	191	371	377	192	37	4
E07000037	High Peak	890	9	25	153	246	269	157	37	3
E07000038	North East Derbyshire	961	7	30	174	251	325	150	27	4
E07000039	South Derbyshire	1,130	10	40	181	334	344	190	40	1
E10000018	Leicestershire	7,117	42	182	1,012	2,060	2,337	1,244	266	16
E07000129	Blaby	1,106	6	22	131	332	410	168	42	1
E07000130	Charnwood	1,922	12	47	281	539	627	354	67	7
E07000131	Harborough	803	2	21	91	200	266	183	39	3
E07000132	Hinckley and Bosworth	1,176	5	27	187	353	381	184	42	2
E07000133	Melton	512	3	11	62	159	159	95	26	0
E07000134	North West Leicestershire	1,012	7	35	162	309	314	158	33	1
E07000135	Oadby and Wigston	586	7	19	98	168	180	102	17	2
E10000019	Lincolnshire	7,485	66	332	1,476	2,361	2,096	981	220	19
E07000136	Boston	797	10	37	172	265	194	107	16	6
E07000137	East Lindsey	1,173	22	78	279	389	269	133	22	3
E07000138	Lincoln	1,176	10	51	245	372	331	145	30	2
E07000139	North Kesteven	1,110	1	37	161	347	355	171	39	0
E07000140	South Holland	963	9	38	200	329	265	97	34	0
E07000141	South Kesteven	1,368	5	48	237	391	423	209	58	2
E07000142	West Lindsey	898	9	43	182	268	259	119	21	6
E10000021	Northamptonshire	9,113	73	322	1,437	2,653	2,893	1,453	337	18
E07000150	Corby	1,004	11	41	181	346	297	110	25	4
E07000151	Daventry	819	5	18	114	229	257	169	30	2
E07000152	East Northamptonshire	997	5	27	164	278	318	169	36	5
E07000153	Kettering	1,250	13	59	251	336	364	203	37	0
E07000154	Northampton	3,278	25	117	483	996	1,077	475	126	4
E07000155	South Northamptonshire	806	4	13	76	202	285	178	50	2
E07000156	Wellingborough	959	10	47	168	266	295	149	33	1
E10000024	Nottinghamshire	8,687	74	322	1,487	2,546	2,585	1,440	294	13
E07000170	Ashfield	1,442	12	63	310	452	397	186	33	1
E07000171	Bassetlaw	1,274	11	48	277	414	335	157	41	2
E07000172	Broxtowe	1,195	7	26	153	332	390	245	47	2
E07000173	Gedling	1,269	8	37	165	352	428	238	48	1
E07000174	Mansfield	1,281	13	69	267	433	320	161	29	2
E07000175	Newark and Sherwood	1,187	16	62	240	372	311	168	32	2
E07000176	Rushcliffe	1,039	7	17	75	191	404	285	64	3
E12000005	**WEST MIDLANDS**	71,041	605	2,726	12,112	21,634	21,165	10,887	2,344	173
E06000019	Herefordshire, County of	1,767	9	56	301	562	504	280	58	6
E06000051	Shropshire	2,947	15	84	499	872	906	472	109	5

Rates per 1,000 women in age group[1,2]

Area of usual residence of mother		All ages	Under 18	Under 20	20 to 24	25 to 29	30 to 34	35 to 39	40 to 44	45 and over
E06000018	Nottingham	53.5	10.8	13.8	33.3	98.8	110.2	59.4	18.5	1.5 u
E06000017	Rutland	59.8	: u	5.8 u	55.3	120.8	129.2	70.5	17.3 u	2.2 u
E10000007	Derbyshire	58.4	4.7	12.8	68.1	102.5	106.0	54.8	10.5	0.6 u
E07000032	Amber Valley	57.5	5.4 u	14.4	70.7	101.1	100.2	54.1	10.2	1.0 u
E07000033	Bolsover	59.4	7.7 u	18.0	73.9	111.7	93.6	49.2	6.8 u	: u
E07000034	Chesterfield	57.8	3.0 u	13.9	75.1	102.4	98.0	44.7	11.8	: u
E07000035	Derbyshire Dales	52.5	: u	2.7 u	52.3	96.9	120.2	66.4	12.1	: u
E07000036	Erewash	58.9	5.5 u	14.9	60.9	99.1	105.0	55.8	9.8	0.9 u
E07000037	High Peak	57.6	5.5 u	9.7	60.5	103.4	108.4	60.4	12.8	0.8 u
E07000038	North East Derbyshire	59.9	4.4 u	11.5	70.7	97.6	123.4	56.0	8.7	1.0 u
E07000039	South Derbyshire	61.5	5.5 u	14.2	74.8	106.9	108.1	56.7	11.5	: u
E10000018	Leicestershire	58.6	3.7	9.4	50.0	104.7	115.3	62.2	12.1	0.6 u
E07000129	Blaby	63.8	3.5 u	8.2	57.3	112.4	128.4	57.6	12.7	: u
E07000130	Charnwood	54.1	4.4 u	8.5	35.0	93.6	109.5	68.0	12.7	1.1 u
E07000131	Harborough	55.8	: u	8.4	50.4	94.7	119.9	69.7	12.4	0.8 u
E07000132	Hinckley and Bosworth	62.5	2.7 u	9.6	73.0	108.2	115.5	55.6	11.8	: u
E07000133	Melton	62.3	3.5 u	8.0 u	53.2	122.5	119.1	66.6	16.0	: u
E07000134	North West Leicestershire	58.3	4.2 u	13.4	60.8	108.2	107.2	54.3	9.8	: u
E07000135	Oadby and Wigston	59.1	7.7 u	10.0 u	57.1	117.2	114.4	63.8	10.1 u	: u
E10000019	Lincolnshire	59.7	5.4	15.9	71.3	114.6	100.3	48.6	10.0	0.7 u
E07000136	Boston	67.1	9.2 u	21.5	107.1	116.0	85.2	53.0	8.1 u	2.6 u
E07000137	East Lindsey	61.6	10.3	22.8	102.2	120.5	90.4	44.0	6.0	0.6 u
E07000138	Lincoln	51.2	7.4 u	13.4	37.0	101.6	98.4	49.2	11.6	: u
E07000139	North Kesteven	60.4	: u	12.0	65.1	117.6	109.9	54.9	11.1	: u
E07000140	South Holland	63.4	6.0 u	15.8	95.0	125.3	99.5	38.7	11.8	: u
E07000141	South Kesteven	59.0	1.9 u	12.3	79.7	107.9	107.2	50.6	12.6	0.5 u
E07000142	West Lindsey	61.3	5.6 u	16.8	83.0	120.3	106.1	48.3	7.6	1.7 u
E10000021	Northamptonshire	67.5	5.8	15.8	75.7	120.3	118.3	61.4	13.3	0.7 u
E07000150	Corby	74.4	9.1 u	21.3	100.1	144.5	102.0	47.8	11.6	1.7 u
E07000151	Daventry	63.2	3.8 u	8.4 u	65.6	114.8	124.9	74.5	10.8	: u
E07000152	East Northamptonshire	64.4	2.9 u	10.0	83.7	118.0	123.7	61.6	11.4	1.4 u
E07000153	Kettering	69.5	7.8 u	22.2	104.1	109.9	114.6	64.2	10.5	: u
E07000154	Northampton	70.5	6.9	18.2	63.2	125.5	120.7	60.3	16.4	0.5 u
E07000155	South Northamptonshire	55.1	2.6 u	5.4 u	45.2	97.8	126.4	62.0	14.9	: u
E07000156	Wellingborough	69.1	7.3 u	21.5	97.1	117.9	115.1	60.9	12.2	: u
E10000024	Nottinghamshire	61.3	5.7	15.0	69.3	104.8	107.8	59.6	11.2	0.4 u
E07000170	Ashfield	63.2	5.9 u	18.8	89.9	104.7	102.2	49.4	8.1	: u
E07000171	Bassetlaw	67.9	5.7 u	15.3	96.8	137.8	111.8	50.0	11.3	: u
E07000172	Broxtowe	59.0	4.2 u	8.8	50.5	87.6	109.4	73.5	13.1	: u
E07000173	Gedling	61.4	4.3 u	12.0	56.2	102.1	118.0	63.8	12.5	: u
E07000174	Mansfield	65.5	8.1 u	25.0	86.6	121.2	89.4	49.4	8.8	: u
E07000175	Newark and Sherwood	59.9	8.2 u	19.6	76.3	113.0	98.5	51.3	8.5	: u
E07000176	Rushcliffe	52.5	3.6 u	5.5 u	25.4	66.3	127.4	78.0	15.9	0.7 u
E12000005	**WEST MIDLANDS**	65.0	6.1	16.1	63.9	111.6	114.6	62.1	13.1	0.8
E06000019	Herefordshire, County of	59.3	3.0 u	11.4	72.2	109.2	99.4	54.5	10.8	0.9 u
E06000051	Shropshire	60.6	2.8 u	9.8	70.9	111.6	116.3	58.0	11.8	0.4 u

Table 2 Live births (numbers and rates): age and administrative area of usual residence of mother, England and Wales, 2016

England and Wales: regions, counties, unitary authorities, local authority districts, local health boards (within Wales)

Area of usual residence of mother		All ages	Under 18	Under 20	20 to 24	25 to 29	30 to 34	35 to 39	40 to 44	45 and over	All ages	Under 18	Under 20	20 to 24	25 to 29	30 to 34	35 to 39	40 to 44	45 and over
		Numbers									**Rates per 1,000 women in age group[1,2]**								
E06000021	**Stoke-on-Trent**	**3,499**	**32**	**164**	**746**	**1,134**	**954**	**419**	**80**	**2**	**71.8**	**7.9**	**23.4**	**84.2**	**124.1**	**109.2**	**56.6**	**10.5**	**: u**
E06000020	**Telford and Wrekin**	**2,079**	**31**	**102**	**474**	**610**	**546**	**280**	**61**	**6**	**64.3**	**10.1**	**19.1**	**88.8**	**116.1**	**96.8**	**52.4**	**11.3**	**0.9 u**
E10000028	**Staffordshire**	**8,691**	**63**	**331**	**1,473**	**2,640**	**2,588**	**1,358**	**277**	**24**	**58.9**	**4.5**	**14.2**	**63.2**	**106.2**	**105.5**	**56.1**	**10.1**	**0.7**
E07000192	Cannock Chase	1,052	8	49	212	332	285	140	29	5	58.6	5.0 u	18.2	77.7	104.4	88.5	48.6	9.0	1.3 u
E07000193	East Staffordshire	1,455	10	52	241	488	401	218	51	4	71.8	5.1 u	16.5	81.7	138.4	111.9	63.8	14.0	0.9 u
E07000194	Lichfield	976	2	19	131	261	323	191	47	4	59.3	: u	7.3 u	57.7	101.6	120.2	63.8	14.1	1.0 u
E07000195	Newcastle-under-Lyme	1,194	13	66	231	363	338	160	34	2	49.4	6.8 u	16.9	46.2	87.5	89.7	45.4	8.8	: u
E07000196	South Staffordshire	965	5	31	142	266	334	160	30	2	56.4	2.7 u	10.5	54.0	95.6	127.6	58.4	8.8	: u
E07000197	Stafford	1,280	7	39	192	351	419	235	39	5	58.1	3.3 u	11.6	56.6	96.0	114.9	62.4	9.3	1.0 u
E07000198	Staffordshire Moorlands	847	6	28	149	279	243	116	30	2	56.1	3.7 u	11.1	66.2	115.1	104.3	46.3	9.8	: u
E07000199	Tamworth	922	12	47	175	300	245	138	17	0	63.6	8.9 u	21.7	83.3	117.2	91.4	57.9	6.5 u	: u
E10000031	**Warwickshire**	**5,951**	**36**	**188**	**878**	**1,658**	**1,905**	**1,076**	**226**	**20**	**61.0**	**4.0**	**12.5**	**58.7**	**101.5**	**116.0**	**64.6**	**12.4**	**1.0**
E07000218	North Warwickshire	614	8	23	99	177	197	106	12	0	58.5	7.8 u	13.9	67.2	98.4	110.3	60.6	5.9 u	: u
E07000219	Nuneaton and Bedworth	1,575	11	80	329	522	404	193	43	4	67.9	5.1 u	22.8	97.3	125.6	94.6	49.7	10.8	0.9 u
E07000220	Rugby	1,224	7	33	165	355	408	202	55	6	66.2	3.6 u	11.1	75.6	121.2	116.5	59.2	15.7	1.6 u
E07000221	Stratford-on-Avon	1,097	4	23	148	258	370	230	64	4	60.0	2.0 u	7.4	62.6	94.2	130.3	72.9	15.8	0.8 u
E07000222	Warwick	1,441	6	29	137	346	526	345	52	6	53.0	3.1 u	7.6	24.6	73.3	130.6	77.4	11.3	1.2 u
E11000005	**West Midlands (Met County)**	**40,037**	**384**	**1,606**	**6,796**	**12,438**	**11,851**	**5,959**	**1,288**	**99**	**68.0**	**7.6**	**17.9**	**61.2**	**114.1**	**118.4**	**65.1**	**14.8**	**1.0**
E08000025	Birmingham	17,404	149	591	2,725	5,466	5,289	2,655	628	50	69.7	7.0	15.0	52.1	119.1	130.6	70.3	18.5	1.4
E08000026	Coventry	4,531	34	170	739	1,385	1,386	699	137	15	57.3	6.3	15.4	40.4	86.1	109.2	64.7	13.5	1.4
E08000027	Dudley	3,816	30	155	723	1,149	1,128	565	93	3	67.2	5.7	17.8	82.6	114.2	112.0	59.8	9.5	0.3 u
E08000028	Sandwell	4,735	59	213	832	1,507	1,364	676	136	7	73.9	10.5	23.2	86.1	128.9	116.5	62.5	13.3	0.6 u
E08000029	Solihull	2,315	12	72	313	634	770	427	92	7	63.7	3.1 u	12.0	59.3	107.1	129.4	67.1	13.5	0.9 u
E08000030	Walsall	3,760	58	235	786	1,198	1,000	438	96	7	71.2	11.5	28.2	92.5	120.5	106.8	52.7	11.4	0.7 u
E08000031	Wolverhampton	3,476	42	170	678	1,099	914	499	106	10	69.7	9.8	23.2	82.6	116.7	102.0	61.9	13.4	1.1 u
E10000034	**Worcestershire**	**6,070**	**35**	**195**	**945**	**1,720**	**1,911**	**1,043**	**245**	**11**	**61.5**	**3.7**	**12.5**	**63.0**	**105.1**	**116.1**	**62.2**	**13.2**	**0.5 u**
E07000234	Bromsgrove	940	2	25	94	226	356	204	34	1	60.1	: u	10.4	42.0	90.7	144.2	72.7	10.5	: u
E07000235	Malvern Hills	566	2	16	91	153	179	100	24	3	52.1	: u	7.7 u	58.3	94.7	114.5	53.7	10.9	1.1 u
E07000236	Redditch	1,065	5	28	201	316	330	156	33	1	66.4	3.6 u	12.3	95.1	110.8	106.6	53.7	11.8	: u
E07000237	Worcester	1,200	15	47	194	360	342	197	58	2	56.4	9.3 u	14.8	45.6	96.5	98.1	61.1	17.1	0.5 u
E07000238	Wychavon	1,188	9	36	173	319	380	215	62	3	63.2	4.5 u	11.4	68.2	109.1	122.4	65.9	16.2	0.9 u
E07000239	Wyre Forest	1,111	2	43	192	346	324	171	34	1	69.1	: u	17.3	83.4	125.9	118.2	63.4	11.0	0.6 u
E12000006	**EAST**	**72,250**	**520**	**2,091**	**9,980**	**20,326**	**23,458**	**13,307**	**2,870**	**218**	**64.6**	**5.1**	**12.5**	**59.6**	**107.4**	**119.4**	**67.6**	**14.3**	**1.0**
E06000055	**Bedford**	**2,209**	**12**	**50**	**277**	**655**	**710**	**428**	**87**	**2**	**69.6**	**4.1 u**	**10.4**	**63.0**	**131.0**	**122.6**	**70.8**	**15.2**	**: u**
E06000056	**Central Bedfordshire**	**3,309**	**21**	**78**	**375**	**971**	**1,104**	**623**	**146**	**12**	**64.0**	**4.6**	**11.1**	**56.0**	**108.5**	**116.4**	**63.5**	**15.1**	**1.1 u**
E06000032	**Luton**	**3,608**	**27**	**93**	**519**	**1,167**	**1,151**	**545**	**125**	**8**	**78.2**	**6.8**	**14.2**	**71.8**	**134.7**	**125.5**	**69.7**	**18.7**	**1.2 u**
E06000031	**Peterborough**	**3,076**	**32**	**113**	**581**	**959**	**879**	**441**	**100**	**3**	**78.4**	**9.6**	**21.2**	**109.4**	**132.6**	**110.8**	**62.3**	**15.8**	**0.5 u**
E06000033	**Southend-on-Sea**	**2,260**	**29**	**106**	**354**	**604**	**687**	**417**	**86**	**6**	**67.7**	**9.7**	**21.7**	**75.9**	**111.9**	**115.1**	**68.2**	**13.5**	**0.9 u**
E06000034	**Thurrock**	**2,498**	**11**	**63**	**358**	**783**	**821**	**381**	**83**	**9**	**72.7**	**3.8 u**	**13.2**	**77.8**	**133.8**	**124.6**	**59.4**	**13.5**	**1.5 u**
E10000003	**Cambridgeshire**	**7,232**	**44**	**191**	**909**	**1,828**	**2,429**	**1,521**	**327**	**27**	**58.8**	**4.2**	**10.4**	**43.3**	**90.5**	**117.4**	**71.3**	**15.2**	**1.2**
E07000008	Cambridge	1,413	12	30	131	290	498	368	87	9	43.5	7.1 u	6.4	13.8	52.9	106.1	84.5	23.1	2.6
E07000009	East Cambridgeshire	979	3	24	99	302	342	165	40	7	63.3	2.1 u	10.9	57.6	128.1	120.0	52.8	12.5	2.1 u
E07000010	Fenland	1,130	13	63	282	338	289	133	22	3	66.7	7.9 u	23.6	106.1	112.4	96.2	50.3	7.5	0.8 u
E07000011	Huntingdonshire	1,973	7	40	256	550	678	378	69	2	64.1	2.4 u	8.8	64.7	102.3	126.0	66.6	11.9	: u

Table 2 Live births (numbers and rates): age and administrative area of usual residence of mother, England and Wales, 2016

England and Wales: regions, counties, unitary authorities, local authority districts, local health boards (within Wales)

Area of usual residence of mother		Numbers — Age of mother at birth									Rates per 1,000 women in age group[1,2] — Age of mother at birth								
		All ages	Under 18	Under 20	20 to 24	25 to 29	30 to 34	35 to 39	40 to 44	45 and over	All ages	Under 18	Under 20	20 to 24	25 to 29	30 to 34	35 to 39	40 to 44	45 and over
E07000012	South Cambridgeshire	1,737	9	34	141	348	622	477	109	6	63.4	3.3 u	8.1	44.7	87.3	130.7	85.9	19.0	1.0 u
E10000012	**Essex**	**16,536**	**113**	**469**	**2,218**	**4,799**	**5,400**	**3,003**	**594**	**53**	**64.0**	**4.6**	**11.9**	**57.3**	**109.2**	**123.9**	**66.7**	**12.4**	**1.0**
E07000066	Basildon	2,487	13	87	372	739	794	414	80	1	70.4	4.1 u	17.0	73.9	117.9	122.5	66.3	13.0	: u
E07000067	Braintree	1,715	18	51	246	535	526	287	66	4	65.0	7.2 u	12.7	70.3	120.8	115.1	61.0	12.8	0.7 u
E07000068	Brentwood	848	4	16	68	200	332	193	36	3	62.5	2.9 u	7.5 u	36.0	90.7	145.4	77.4	14.0	1.0 u
E07000069	Castle Point	860	6	25	119	262	286	143	21	4	59.5	3.8 u	10.1	51.2	110.4	126.5	62.1	7.7	1.2 u
E07000070	Chelmsford	2,039	9	47	202	575	698	423	87	7	63.7	3.1 u	10.4	43.3	105.1	124.8	73.0	14.6	1.1 u
E07000071	Colchester	2,204	10	61	364	647	680	371	70	11	58.9	3.4 u	11.4	52.1	93.0	111.4	61.9	11.7	1.7 u
E07000072	Epping Forest	1,592	9	29	153	407	590	343	65	5	66.8	4.2 u	8.6	45.0	98.8	145.5	77.8	14.5	1.0 u
E07000073	Harlow	1,303	12	37	171	431	403	209	44	8	76.2	8.5 u	16.2	72.4	137.5	116.8	69.3	15.4	2.7 u
E07000074	Maldon	531	3	14	84	149	169	101	13	1	55.2	2.8 u	8.3 u	61.9	100.8	122.4	60.8	6.3 u	: u
E07000075	Rochford	751	8	19	70	227	269	129	35	2	53.3	5.4 u	7.9 u	32.4	105.3	128.2	53.5	12.3	: u
E07000076	Tendring	1,284	18	68	286	433	307	152	36	2	63.6	8.1 u	18.8	88.4	132.6	101.7	46.8	9.4	: u
E07000077	Uttlesford	922	3	15	83	194	346	238	41	5	63.9	1.9 u	6.2 u	47.1	93.7	151.1	85.9	13.2	1.4 u
E10000015	**Hertfordshire**	**14,601**	**81**	**292**	**1,390**	**3,386**	**5,214**	**3,438**	**813**	**68**	**64.1**	**4.0**	**9.0**	**43.6**	**90.3**	**127.9**	**81.0**	**19.1**	**1.5**
E07000095	Broxbourne	1,245	5	26	134	353	426	241	59	6	67.6	3.1 u	9.6	53.1	111.4	127.1	71.3	17.9	1.6 u
E07000096	Dacorum	1,868	13	41	166	425	670	439	115	12	64.7	4.8 u	9.8	44.9	87.2	126.7	80.7	21.4	2.1 u
E07000242	East Hertfordshire	1,659	7	23	127	370	622	405	104	8	61.7	2.5 u	5.5	37.5	89.8	139.3	79.3	18.5	1.3 u
E07000098	Hertsmere	1,301	5	18	118	285	513	293	65	9	67.0	2.8 u	6.4 u	45.1	89.0	146.9	82.7	17.3	2.3 u
E07000099	North Hertfordshire	1,512	12	32	162	341	504	383	88	9	61.8	5.3 u	9.3	54.9	88.8	112.1	80.6	17.8	2.1 u
E07000240	St Albans	1,824	6	26	93	292	703	562	136	12	66.4	2.2 u	6.5	31.5	72.1	150.0	98.2	22.6	2.1 u
E07000243	Stevenage	1,223	15	44	183	350	400	194	49	3	70.9	10.8 u	19.7	74.4	106.0	117.1	64.3	17.4	0.9 u
E07000102	Three Rivers	1,069	3	20	109	224	385	259	69	3	63.0	1.8 u	7.7	52.6	82.8	134.1	76.5	20.7	0.8 u
E07000103	Watford	1,500	5	29	137	378	533	353	66	4	71.3	3.2 u	11.8	52.9	99.0	119.2	85.0	18.6	1.2 u
E07000241	Welwyn Hatfield	1,400	10	33	161	368	458	309	62	9	51.9	5.2 u	8.3	24.3	83.1	108.6	78.1	16.5	2.4 u
E10000020	**Norfolk**	**9,057**	**71**	**355**	**1,669**	**2,732**	**2,692**	**1,342**	**248**	**19**	**60.2**	**5.2**	**14.9**	**64.9**	**105.8**	**105.3**	**56.4**	**9.6**	**0.6 u**
E07000143	Breckland	1,434	12	52	263	459	412	210	35	3	65.7	5.7 u	14.8	80.5	123.5	107.5	59.0	8.8	0.6 u
E07000144	Broadland	1,103	6	28	141	310	377	212	31	4	55.6	2.8 u	8.2	53.9	104.3	115.2	60.3	7.6	0.8 u
E07000145	Great Yarmouth	1,086	14	66	271	343	268	111	26	1	67.2	8.4 u	24.3	103.4	120.7	94.0	45.8	9.6	: u
E07000146	King's Lynn and West Norfolk	1,580	16	78	323	514	410	215	40	0	67.2	7.1 u	20.6	100.7	124.6	95.5	56.0	9.4	: u
E07000147	North Norfolk	789	7	37	162	239	218	116	15	0	58.5	4.9 u	15.9	76.3	108.5	101.1	53.7	6.0 u	: u
E07000148	Norwich	1,728	9	63	328	481	537	253	60	6	50.5	5.3 u	13.9	35.7	73.1	96.4	56.5	15.5	1.5 u
E07000149	South Norfolk	1,337	7	31	181	386	470	225	41	3	62.1	2.9 u	8.5	67.3	114.2	131.3	58.7	9.3	0.6 u
E10000029	**Suffolk**	**7,864**	**79**	**281**	**1,330**	**2,442**	**2,371**	**1,168**	**261**	**11**	**64.6**	**6.5**	**14.3**	**77.2**	**117.6**	**113.3**	**56.2**	**11.6**	**0.4 u**
E07000200	Babergh	739	5	25	101	216	247	120	28	2	55.7	3.2 u	10.5	56.1	107.1	120.3	53.3	10.1	: u
E07000201	Forest Heath	1,016	3	16	181	360	308	130	21	0	83.3	3.3 u	8.2	110.2	156.0	114.2	61.0	11.3	: u
E07000202	Ipswich	1,985	33	109	387	613	573	240	60	3	73.8	15.7	29.7	94.0	116.0	116.1	52.7	13.9	0.7 u
E07000203	Mid Suffolk	823	6	21	100	242	254	164	41	1	53.4	3.4 u	7.8	48.4	99.3	105.0	59.8	13.4	: u
E07000204	St Edmundsbury	1,135	8	35	172	344	365	173	45	1	61.5	4.4 u	12.2	66.5	108.8	111.0	56.2	12.9	: u
E07000205	Suffolk Coastal	1,005	7	22	147	297	318	180	38	3	57.0	3.1 u	6.2	64.4	122.7	122.8	58.0	10.3	0.6 u
E07000206	Waveney	1,161	17	53	242	370	306	161	28	1	64.5	9.5 u	17.7	88.8	118.1	104.3	55.1	8.5	: u
E12000007	**LONDON**	**128,803**	**521**	**2,300**	**12,794**	**30,437**	**44,944**	**30,191**	**7,345**	**792**	**63.6**	**3.8**	**10.1**	**45.0**	**73.0**	**107.3**	**82.1**	**23.6**	**2.7**
E13000001	**Inner London**	**50,096**	**173**	**820**	**4,750**	**10,669**	**17,537**	**12,721**	**3,251**	**348**	**55.1**	**3.5**	**9.7**	**35.3**	**49.7**	**88.3**	**82.4**	**26.7**	**3.2**
E09000007	Camden	2,732	7	38	178	489	983	790	226	26	44.0	2.1 u	6.0	16.5	35.5	83.5	80.9	25.7	3.6
E09000001	City of London	54	0	0	4	11	18	14	7	0	27.5	: u	: u	10.8 u	22.0 u	45.2 u	44.9 u	27.5 u	: u
E09000012	Hackney	4,447	19	90	617	987	1,365	1,077	287	24	59.7	4.7 u	13.5	70.0	53.9	74.8	83.4	30.1	3.0

Table 2　Live births (numbers and rates): age and administrative area of usual residence of mother, England and Wales, 2016

England and Wales: regions, counties, unitary authorities, local authority districts, local health boards (within Wales)

Area code	Area of usual residence of mother	Numbers									Rates per 1,000 women in age group[1,2]								
		All ages	Under 18	Under 20	20 to 24	25 to 29	30 to 34	35 to 39	40 to 44	45 and over	All ages	Under 18	Under 20	20 to 24	25 to 29	30 to 34	35 to 39	40 to 44	45 and over
E09000013	Hammersmith and Fulham	2,509	6	32	147	411	952	751	190	26	55.9	2.6 u	8.5	22.7	39.8	99.3	95.7	27.5	4.1
E09000014	Haringey	4,114	22	85	495	946	1,287	1,006	266	29	61.4	4.9	11.5	55.2	69.6	91.0	80.0	25.8	3.0
E09000019	Islington	2,945	12	43	243	565	1,066	807	188	33	45.1	4.2 u	7.5	18.3	34.1	79.0	89.3	26.2	5.0
E09000020	Kensington and Chelsea	1,729	3	12	79	265	659	522	166	26	51.1	1.5 u	3.8 u	18.1	42.0	94.1	75.8	27.3	4.7
E09000022	Lambeth	4,209	22	81	358	792	1,450	1,189	300	39	47.4	5.3	11.5	29.5	31.3	74.9	82.5	28.2	3.9
E09000023	Lewisham	4,721	19	114	466	958	1,628	1,219	308	28	63.7	4.2 u	15.2	45.4	64.2	103.2	86.9	26.5	2.7
E09000025	Newham	6,027	22	117	833	1,891	1,986	961	216	23	74.6	3.7	11.6	62.7	108.8	118.6	73.1	21.2	2.3
E09000028	Southwark	4,503	16	75	443	930	1,570	1,159	300	26	54.3	3.8 u	10.2	33.9	44.9	89.7	85.2	28.1	2.6
E09000030	Tower Hamlets	4,592	6	63	448	1,285	1,643	922	211	20	53.5	1.4 u	8.0	32.3	57.4	86.6	67.4	23.5	2.9
E09000032	Wandsworth	4,860	18	50	269	658	1,925	1,571	361	26	54.1	5.0 u	8.1	24.9	28.7	85.2	100.8	30.7	2.6
E09000033	Westminster	2,654	1	20	170	481	1,005	733	225	20	45.9	: u	3.7	20.9	40.5	76.7	69.6	25.5	2.6
E13000002	**Outer London**	**78,707**	**348**	**1,480**	**8,044**	**19,768**	**27,407**	**17,470**	**4,094**	**444**	**70.4**	**4.0**	**10.4**	**53.7**	**97.8**	**124.5**	**81.8**	**21.6**	**2.4**
E09000002	Barking and Dagenham	3,973	30	103	582	1,206	1,253	669	142	18	86.5	7.8	16.3	93.7	148.0	137.5	78.4	18.7	2.5 u
E09000003	Barnet	5,301	8	60	484	1,257	1,891	1,273	302	34	64.8	1.3 u	6.0	43.0	83.2	116.5	83.3	21.7	2.5
E09000004	Bexley	3,091	13	56	309	907	1,089	600	115	15	63.4	3.0 u	7.9	41.6	103.2	127.9	69.0	14.1	1.6 u
E09000005	Brent	5,146	22	109	622	1,405	1,681	1,035	261	33	71.9	4.1	12.3	63.9	100.8	112.7	81.4	22.9	3.1
E09000006	Bromley	4,326	20	75	315	911	1,603	1,177	221	24	68.3	3.6	8.9	41.3	86.7	140.9	89.7	18.0	1.9
E09000008	Croydon	5,894	29	135	736	1,595	1,943	1,153	301	31	73.7	4.1	12.2	73.8	111.1	123.2	75.7	22.2	2.2
E09000009	Ealing	5,250	16	80	461	1,287	1,812	1,222	345	43	71.4	2.9 u	9.0	50.7	94.4	123.9	85.9	26.5	3.6
E09000010	Enfield	5,000	36	131	617	1,341	1,606	988	284	33	70.9	6.1	13.6	63.7	103.0	115.9	77.6	24.4	2.7
E09000011	Greenwich	4,621	42	135	504	1,112	1,555	1,021	253	41	71.9	9.6	18.1	55.7	89.8	119.1	82.6	25.3	4.3
E09000015	Harrow	3,606	15	65	384	972	1,327	716	126	16	72.7	3.7 u	9.9	57.9	111.0	136.2	75.1	15.0	1.9 u
E09000016	Havering	3,423	20	88	381	978	1,209	629	130	8	69.6	4.6	12.5	52.2	106.8	134.2	72.4	16.3	0.9 u
E09000017	Hillingdon	4,508	20	73	451	1,229	1,645	914	174	22	69.6	3.9	8.4	44.5	106.1	133.8	77.0	17.1	2.2
E09000018	Hounslow	4,351	19	81	430	1,118	1,494	964	239	25	73.1	4.6 u	11.8	55.3	101.2	118.7	82.9	24.9	2.8
E09000021	Kingston upon Thames	2,204	4	28	161	387	811	638	165	14	54.9	1.5 u	5.8	23.3	55.3	111.5	87.6	24.2	2.3 u
E09000024	Merton	3,246	8	45	242	645	1,205	909	186	14	70.5	2.7 u	9.4	47.5	77.0	121.7	91.0	23.7	1.9 u
E09000026	Redbridge	4,782	13	58	498	1,317	1,741	959	193	16	73.6	2.4 u	6.6	57.9	111.9	135.0	77.1	18.4	1.6 u
E09000027	Richmond upon Thames	2,544	3	18	107	282	933	926	252	26	64.6	1.0 u	3.8 u	24.9	51.1	126.8	105.9	28.9	3.3
E09000029	Sutton	2,741	10	49	255	623	1,022	619	161	12	66.4	3.0 u	9.1	53.2	92.2	126.0	73.3	20.7	1.5 u
E09000031	Waltham Forest	4,700	20	91	505	1,196	1,587	1,058	244	19	74.5	4.6	12.8	62.0	97.7	117.1	87.5	24.5	2.0 u
E12000008	**SOUTH EAST**	**101,982**	**652**	**2,797**	**12,847**	**26,970**	**33,891**	**20,711**	**4,421**	**345**	**61.4**	**4.3**	**10.9**	**48.9**	**100.6**	**121.2**	**70.9**	**14.7**	**1.0**
E06000036	Bracknell Forest	1,397	3	20	124	370	506	319	51	7	58.7	1.3 u	5.7	43.4	99.2	115.1	65.5	11.5	1.5 u
E06000043	Brighton and Hove	2,850	17	65	269	582	980	728	208	18	41.6	4.3 u	7.2	16.4	45.5	95.1	72.7	20.8	1.8 u
E06000046	Isle of Wight	1,142	16	65	245	343	263	175	49	2	55.8	7.0 u	17.7	79.4	103.8	80.6	54.2	12.5	: u
E06000035	Medway	3,657	47	153	646	1,200	1,003	563	84	8	66.2	9.7	18.7	68.4	117.9	106.3	61.1	9.5	0.8 u
E06000042	Milton Keynes	3,649	22	101	424	1,013	1,231	721	152	7	68.2	4.7	14.2	69.4	114.9	114.9	66.0	15.5	0.7 u
E06000044	Portsmouth	2,592	18	101	398	851	796	366	76	4	55.5	5.8 u	15.3	35.9	99.9	101.4	57.7	12.1	0.6 u
E06000038	Reading	2,494	21	64	289	686	873	474	104	4	66.4	8.6	13.3	39.9	99.7	127.0	72.8	19.9	0.8 u
E06000039	Slough	2,628	10	49	304	767	929	476	96	7	81.4	3.8 u	11.8	81.7	142.8	132.2	70.0	18.4	1.5 u
E06000045	Southampton	3,194	30	106	575	957	949	514	85	8	53.2	8.6	12.7	35.8	86.8	99.4	62.7	12.5	1.2 u
E06000037	West Berkshire	1,764	6	45	207	438	608	371	89	6	64.7	1.9 u	9.6	62.5	111.0	134.3	73.4	15.5	1.0 u
E06000040	Windsor and Maidenhead	1,757	3	26	144	344	642	469	122	10	66.2	1.1 u	6.5	48.2	86.8	132.6	89.0	22.3	1.7 u
E06000041	Wokingham	1,809	6	25	143	435	673	438	84	11	62.3	2.1 u	5.5	40.5	114.1	138.3	72.4	13.5	1.7 u
E10000002	**Buckinghamshire**	**6,102**	**23**	**116**	**592**	**1,394**	**2,161**	**1,523**	**298**	**18**	**63.9**	**2.4**	**7.8**	**46.0**	**91.9**	**135.7**	**84.6**	**16.1**	**0.9 u**
E07000004	Aylesbury Vale	2,280	8	44	263	572	792	515	90	4	63.8	2.4 u	8.4	56.9	93.8	125.4	76.4	13.3	0.5 u
E07000005	Chiltern	902	3	15	62	176	310	282	53	4	60.0	1.6 u	5.5 u	33.5	87.2	149.5	94.7	15.6	1.0 u
E07000006	South Bucks	754	3	13	55	136	287	221	41	1	65.0	2.5 u	7.1 u	35.6	76.2	146.9	100.1	18.0	: u

Table 2   Live births (numbers and rates): age and administrative area of usual residence of mother, England and Wales, 2016
England and Wales: regions, counties, unitary authorities, local authority districts, local health boards (within Wales)

Area code	Area of usual residence of mother	Numbers — All ages	Under 18	Under 20	20 to 24	25 to 29	30 to 34	35 to 39	40 to 44	45 and over	Rates — All ages	Under 18	Under 20	20 to 24	25 to 29	30 to 34	35 to 39	40 to 44	45 and over
		Numbers									**Rates per 1,000 women in age group[1,2]**								
E07000007	Wycombe	2,166	9	44	212	510	772	505	114	9	65.5	2.8 u	8.5	43.7	96.8	138.3	83.2	18.6	1.3 u
E10000011	**East Sussex**	**5,219**	**42**	**186**	**839**	**1,479**	**1,568**	**916**	**206**	**25**	**61.2**	**4.7**	**12.6**	**68.2**	**110.1**	**114.3**	**63.0**	**12.5**	**1.3**
E07000061	Eastbourne	1,048	9	44	178	282	338	166	39	1	60.4	5.6 u	15.7	66.3	106.3	111.5	54.2	12.5	u
E07000062	Hastings	1,115	14	67	236	341	256	180	33	2	67.2	8.8 u	24.9	90.0	112.7	90.3	68.4	11.8	u
E07000063	Lewes	898	3	16	113	243	295	182	44	5	57.5	1.8 u	6.0 u	54.8	101.5	120.3	65.6	13.6	1.3 u
E07000064	Rother	751	10	32	128	220	201	127	40	3	61.3	7.0 u	13.7	72.2	117.3	113.0	62.5	16.4	1.0 u
E07000065	Wealden	1,407	6	27	184	393	478	261	50	14	60.0	2.3 u	6.3	58.4	112.7	132.0	64.7	10.2	2.3 u
E10000014	**Hampshire**	**14,379**	**92**	**374**	**1,844**	**4,011**	**4,828**	**2,697**	**587**	**38**	**61.6**	**4.0**	**10.0**	**55.4**	**107.6**	**125.5**	**65.6**	**12.8**	**0.7**
E07000084	Basingstoke and Deane	2,186	9	58	272	595	752	426	77	6	67.3	3.1 u	12.4	67.3	111.5	123.7	69.3	12.4	0.9 u
E07000085	East Hampshire	1,027	3	21	118	252	344	233	58	1	55.2	1.4 u	6.1	46.9	96.0	132.1	68.9	14.4	u
E07000086	Eastleigh	1,445	8	29	180	412	508	267	43	6	61.1	3.8 u	8.6	58.1	98.2	124.1	60.3	9.6	1.3 u
E07000087	Fareham	1,049	9	23	106	306	368	198	46	2	56.0	4.6 u	7.4	39.5	104.8	119.9	63.7	12.0	u
E07000088	Gosport	924	10	35	170	309	257	128	24	1	60.8	6.6 u	14.8	73.3	118.5	93.3	52.8	8.8	u
E07000089	Hart	950	2	10	77	202	377	217	66	1	60.3	:	4.0 u	44.5	93.9	154.2	69.0	17.5	u
E07000090	Havant	1,330	15	53	234	429	393	181	40	0	65.3	7.1 u	15.2	71.6	119.9	116.7	57.8	11.4	0
E07000091	New Forest	1,483	9	41	205	419	470	272	71	5	57.0	3.3 u	9.5	55.1	102.3	115.4	61.9	13.1	0.8 u
E07000092	Rushmoor	1,410	8	37	188	430	463	243	45	4	71.2	5.0 u	14.2	70.0	118.6	125.9	67.7	12.5	1.1 u
E07000093	Test Valley	1,386	12	39	191	407	464	231	50	4	68.0	5.8 u	12.1	70.1	124.2	141.1	63.7	11.8	0.8 u
E07000094	Winchester	1,189	7	28	103	250	432	301	67	8	53.3	3.4 u	6.8	23.0	86.7	142.4	80.7	16.4	1.9 u
E10000016	**Kent**	**17,374**	**161**	**667**	**2,812**	**5,027**	**5,271**	**2,961**	**590**	**46**	**62.5**	**6.0**	**14.7**	**63.2**	**111.4**	**113.8**	**63.3**	**11.9**	**0.8**
E07000105	Ashford	1,565	11	63	277	455	477	230	59	4	68.7	4.7 u	16.7	88.0	120.3	121.4	58.4	14.1	0.8 u
E07000106	Canterbury	1,382	12	48	218	421	387	256	46	6	40.8	4.8 u	7.7	21.1	86.8	93.0	64.2	10.6	1.2 u
E07000107	Dartford	1,514	15	43	180	474	518	242	50	7	69.4	8.6 u	15.1	64.5	112.6	119.1	61.1	13.6	1.8 u
E07000108	Dover	1,173	19	66	242	364	307	162	31	7	64.2	9.6 u	20.8	87.1	126.3	100.6	53.8	9.2	u
E07000109	Gravesham	1,417	11	45	257	430	425	218	38	4	69.7	5.9 u	14.8	85.7	117.4	118.7	62.5	10.7	1.0 u
E07000110	Maidstone	2,035	14	68	277	603	661	349	72	5	67.4	5.0 u	15.3	65.9	117.0	119.8	65.1	13.0	0.8 u
E07000111	Sevenoaks	1,246	3	22	148	272	432	309	60	3	62.7	1.4 u	6.7	56.9	93.8	141.3	79.6	14.4	0.6 u
E07000112	Shepway	1,054	8	51	199	311	296	169	28	0	59.5	4.5 u	17.4	76.7	102.9	103.7	56.8	8.4	u
E07000113	Swale	1,813	28	100	370	548	495	255	42	3	70.0	10.8	23.7	97.0	127.3	106.8	57.9	9.3	0.6 u
E07000114	Thanet	1,553	24	95	352	499	379	186	38	4	65.9	10.2	24.3	94.4	129.9	93.3	47.7	9.2	0.8 u
E07000115	Tonbridge and Malling	1,431	6	36	173	376	486	293	65	2	62.2	2.4 u	9.2	55.9	109.9	131.0	70.3	13.9	u
E07000116	Tunbridge Wells	1,191	10	30	119	274	408	292	61	7	58.0	4.0 u	8.0	50.0	88.8	118.9	78.4	14.6	1.5 u
E10000025	**Oxfordshire**	**7,757**	**35**	**191**	**864**	**1,864**	**2,775**	**1,700**	**333**	**30**	**59.0**	**3.1**	**9.5**	**36.5**	**89.0**	**121.6**	**78.2**	**14.9**	**1.2**
E07000177	Cherwell	1,836	6	41	226	472	647	382	65	3	68.2	2.3 u	10.1	69.5	112.8	123.8	76.1	12.5	0.5 u
E07000178	Oxford	1,811	10	52	186	409	642	420	96	6	43.5	4.6 u	8.9	14.4	59.0	96.4	83.4	22.5	1.4 u
E07000179	South Oxfordshire	1,540	8	36	170	331	559	358	73	13	67.7	3.3 u	9.6	63.8	99.4	144.4	84.7	14.9	2.3 u
E07000180	Vale of White Horse	1,436	4	23	163	361	549	280	57	3	65.2	1.9 u	6.6	61.1	100.9	141.1	67.8	13.3	0.6 u
E07000181	West Oxfordshire	1,134	7	39	119	291	378	260	42	5	62.4	3.8 u	13.6	54.2	100.1	119.1	77.9	11.4	1.2 u
E10000030	**Surrey**	**13,423**	**52**	**228**	**1,062**	**2,869**	**4,892**	**3,483**	**823**	**66**	**62.8**	**2.6**	**6.9**	**34.3**	**90.4**	**142.6**	**85.1**	**19.3**	**1.5**
E07000207	Elmbridge	1,646	5	25	78	251	614	545	124	9	73.4	2.1 u	7.1	34.7	102.3	171.3	106.0	22.6	1.6 u
E07000208	Epsom and Ewell	950	3	6	74	184	364	259	56	7	63.0	2.0 u	2.5 u	34.0	85.4	150.6	87.9	18.9	2.3 u
E07000209	Guildford	1,533	4	21	129	342	557	386	91	7	50.1	1.8 u	4.6	18.9	62.8	127.9	83.5	18.8	1.4 u
E07000210	Mole Valley	770	3	14	57	155	263	220	54	7	57.9	1.9 u	5.8 u	35.0	85.6	139.2	84.6	18.3	2.0 u
E07000211	Reigate and Banstead	1,796	3	28	136	399	675	452	98	8	66.8	1.2 u	7.3	42.9	95.8	139.3	81.3	18.4	1.5 u
E07000212	Runnymede	954	8	32	81	220	334	214	68	5	50.4	6.3 u	11.0	18.4	67.0	128.6	78.8	22.6	1.7 u
E07000213	Spelthorne	1,346	4	17	131	382	457	279	76	4	74.0	2.6 u	7.1 u	55.0	130.0	136.3	75.3	22.4	1.0 u
E07000214	Surrey Heath	884	4	16	86	215	332	187	46	2	58.5	2.5 u	6.5 u	44.4	96.6	138.9	65.7	14.2	u

Table 2 Live births (numbers and rates): age and administrative area of usual residence of mother, England and Wales, 2016
England and Wales: regions, counties, unitary authorities, local authority districts, local health boards (within Wales)

Area of usual residence of mother		Numbers									Rates per 1,000 women in age group[1,2]								
		All ages	Under 18	Under 20	20 to 24	25 to 29	30 to 34	35 to 39	40 to 44	45 and over	All ages	Under 18	Under 20	20 to 24	25 to 29	30 to 34	35 to 39	40 to 44	45 and over
E07000215	Tandridge	956	9	25	82	194	340	253	58	4	64.5	5.5 u	10.0	45.2	87.9	139.7	88.4	19.3	1.2 u
E07000216	Waverley	1,251	2	19	91	231	450	360	93	7	62.2	:	5.1 u	37.4	99.4	146.6	89.7	20.3	1.5 u
E07000217	Woking	1,337	7	25	117	296	506	328	59	6	72.6	4.3 u	10.0	58.9	108.1	150.1	83.3	15.1	1.6 u
E10000032	**West Sussex**	**8,795**	**48**	**215**	**1,066**	**2,340**	**2,943**	**1,817**	**384**	**30**	**62.1**	**3.6**	**9.9**	**55.9**	**106.1**	**121.2**	**68.4**	**13.7**	**1.0**
E07000223	Adur	671	5	14	70	171	227	154	34	1	63.4	5.4 u	9.3 u	52.5	107.2	125.0	73.6	15.2	:
E07000224	Arun	1,552	7	42	265	502	466	228	45	4	65.8	3.3 u	11.6	75.0	128.4	118.5	55.4	10.1	0.7 u
E07000225	Chichester	955	4	20	125	243	302	225	36	4	53.4	2.4 u	6.4	40.5	96.5	115.3	74.6	10.3	1.0 u
E07000226	Crawley	1,584	15	47	217	475	525	264	51	5	68.3	8.2 u	16.4	74.9	112.8	109.7	57.9	13.1	1.3 u
E07000227	Horsham	1,324	10	30	125	319	467	307	72	4	59.5	3.9 u	7.6	42.6	102.5	135.6	72.7	15.6	0.7 u
E07000228	Mid Sussex	1,610	3	27	131	354	598	395	97	8	63.7	1.2 u	7.0	45.1	95.3	138.7	79.1	17.7	1.4 u
E07000229	Worthing	1,099	4	35	133	276	358	244	49	4	58.2	2.4 u	12.9	55.5	92.0	106.1	68.6	12.8	1.0 u
E12000009	**SOUTH WEST**	**57,316**	**367**	**1,694**	**8,407**	**16,337**	**18,253**	**10,231**	**2,225**	**169**	**59.5**	**4.2**	**11.0**	**51.1**	**100.9**	**114.7**	**65.3**	**13.3**	**0.9**
E06000022	Bath and North East Somerset	1,799	7	38	218	442	664	346	88	3	47.1	2.4 u	5.7	21.2	75.2	137.8	69.3	15.7	0.5 u
E06000028	Bournemouth	2,180	14	66	268	591	730	406	113	6	52.4	5.7 u	11.8	28.6	87.4	99.1	60.4	19.4	1.0 u
E06000023	Bristol, City of	6,400	33	149	704	1,542	2,268	1,418	293	26	59.0	5.1	11.2	28.7	66.6	120.5	92.7	22.0	2.0
E06000052, E06000053	Cornwall and Isles of Scilly[4]	5,312	42	190	946	1,558	1,554	863	188	13	59.7	4.7	12.5	64.5	117.1	109.9	58.3	11.2	0.6 u
E06000024	North Somerset	2,188	14	58	314	571	680	471	85	9	63.4	4.0 u	10.6	67.0	107.4	115.0	74.5	12.5	1.1 u
E06000026	Plymouth	2,912	21	130	535	969	810	390	73	5	55.4	5.3	16.5	45.1	108.1	92.2	52.0	9.7	0.6 u
E06000029	Poole	1,593	8	39	211	433	517	326	56	11	61.1	3.2 u	9.5	56.7	102.1	109.8	69.8	12.1	2.1 u
E06000025	South Gloucestershire	3,090	9	47	356	941	1,098	541	99	8	60.2	2.0 u	6.1	43.8	107.4	124.5	60.4	11.1	0.8 u
E06000030	Swindon	2,848	18	88	446	854	878	484	89	9	67.8	4.8 u	14.5	82.7	116.9	110.9	63.8	11.5	1.1 u
E06000027	Torbay	1,314	11	60	258	417	346	194	37	2	64.8	5.4 u	18.0	83.6	121.6	103.9	57.3	10.0	: u
E06000054	Wiltshire	5,119	38	138	806	1,470	1,600	882	212	11	64.0	4.3	10.0	78.7	119.2	120.1	63.6	12.9	0.6 u
E10000008	**Devon**	**6,964**	**52**	**209**	**984**	**1,975**	**2,272**	**1,219**	**284**	**21**	**55.6**	**4.4**	**10.0**	**45.6**	**96.5**	**115.0**	**60.5**	**12.7**	**0.8**
E07000040	East Devon	1,139	15	47	150	295	394	206	46	1	59.7	7.2 u	14.0	60.5	100.4	128.7	62.1	11.7	:
E07000041	Exeter	1,292	10	34	165	322	486	230	47	8	41.8	5.9 u	7.3	18.3	59.3	107.4	60.7	13.4	2.1 u
E07000042	Mid Devon	737	4	19	103	233	234	123	23	2	58.4	2.9 u	8.7 u	60.3	113.7	111.3	56.8	9.6	:
E07000043	North Devon	946	3	28	151	281	300	142	41	3	65.6	2.0 u	11.7	74.6	117.3	125.7	57.6	14.9	0.9 u
E07000044	South Hams	599	4	11	69	158	200	126	34	1	52.6	2.9 u	5.2 u	49.4	99.8	107.1	61.0	14.4	:
E07000045	Teignbridge	1,155	9	36	162	346	350	222	38	1	59.6	4.6 u	11.5	61.4	107.6	109.1	66.8	9.9	:
E07000046	Torridge	632	5	25	115	209	167	85	29	2	65.3	4.8 u	15.4	83.4	128.1	114.5	51.1	15.1	:
E07000047	West Devon	464	2	9	69	131	141	85	26	3	60.6	: u	6.4 u	75.6	106.3	123.9	62.5	16.2	1.5 u
E10000009	**Dorset**	**3,388**	**25**	**111**	**541**	**961**	**1,015**	**609**	**143**	**8**	**57.2**	**3.6**	**10.3**	**67.1**	**103.8**	**108.7**	**61.2**	**12.1**	**0.5 u**
E07000048	Christchurch	360	0	11	58	87	104	80	19	1	52.8	:	9.2 u	62.6	81.8	99.9	66.0	13.7 u	:
E07000049	East Dorset	644	6	11	83	174	208	139	27	2	54.4	4.4 u	5.3 u	47.6	97.3	117.8	69.4	11.0	:
E07000050	North Dorset	631	5	19	107	199	181	100	23	2	60.3	4.0 u	9.8 u	80.5	121.6	103.7	57.5	11.1	:
E07000051	Purbeck	346	2	14	49	107	110	46	20	0	53.1	:	12.1 u	54.6	105.9	104.0	42.1	15.4	:
E07000052	West Dorset	763	6	22	110	218	229	149	33	2	56.3	3.5 u	8.3	62.6	103.1	110.8	67.0	12.0	:
E07000053	Weymouth and Portland	644	6	34	134	176	183	95	21	1	64.4	5.4 u	18.9	95.4	107.1	110.2	56.7	11.5	:
E10000013	**Gloucestershire**	**6,739**	**37**	**177**	**864**	**1,960**	**2,244**	**1,208**	**269**	**17**	**62.4**	**3.5**	**10.1**	**52.2**	**108.3**	**124.3**	**66.8**	**13.6**	**0.7 u**
E07000078	Cheltenham	1,328	3	26	141	324	482	285	68	2	55.7	1.5 u	6.8	32.8	77.0	117.3	76.1	18.6	:
E07000079	Cotswold	730	1	11	77	184	250	165	39	4	57.3	: u	4.9 u	38.4	106.2	135.8	74.7	14.3	1.2 u
E07000080	Forest of Dean	844	7	30	133	274	249	128	28	2	63.8	4.7 u	11.7	63.5	136.5	125.4	63.4	10.9	:
E07000081	Gloucester	1,768	17	70	286	559	558	243	47	5	70.9	7.8 u	18.7	75.5	120.4	119.8	58.9	11.8	1.1 u
E07000082	Stroud	1,094	6	21	113	313	375	216	53	3	58.5	3.0 u	6.8	45.2	107.4	129.2	65.9	13.3	0.6 u
E07000083	Tewkesbury	975	3	19	114	306	330	171	34	1	66.6	2.1 u	8.8 u	61.2	118.1	129.1	63.5	12.2	: u

Table 2 Live births (numbers and rates); age and administrative area of usual residence of mother, England and Wales, 2016
England and Wales: regions, counties, unitary authorities, local authority districts, local health boards (within Wales)

Area of usual residence of mother		Numbers — Age of mother at birth									Rates per 1,000 women in age group[1,2] — Age of mother at birth								
		All ages	Under 18	Under 20	20 to 24	25 to 29	30 to 34	35 to 39	40 to 44	45 and over	All ages	Under 18	Under 20	20 to 24	25 to 29	30 to 34	35 to 39	40 to 44	45 and over
E10000027	Somerset	5,470	38	194	956	1,653	1,577	874	196	20	63.0	4.1	12.9	78.2	112.7	112.7	60.6	11.9	1.0
E07000187	Mendip	1,080	10	38	160	305	320	212	41	4	59.7	4.7 u	11.1	68.0	106.2	114.4	68.9	11.5	0.9 u
E07000188	Sedgemoor	1,298	12	64	278	395	330	183	43	5	66.8	5.8 u	19.1	95.9	119.4	105.1	57.7	12.1	1.1 u
E07000189	South Somerset	1,651	9	52	287	531	475	238	62	6	64.4	3.3 u	11.9	79.5	120.1	116.5	56.7	12.6	1.0 u
E07000190	Taunton Deane	1,206	5	35	177	367	380	199	44	4	62.1	2.5 u	11.2	67.6	107.1	115.1	60.2	12.1	0.9 u
E07000191	West Somerset	235	2	5	54	55	72	42	6	1	55.2	: u	6.6 u	72.7	85.0	106.2	63.3	7.9 u	: u
W92000004	WALES	32,936	392	1,500	6,066	10,125	9,347	4,834	986	78	58.9	7.7	17.0	59.8	103.1	102.2	54.9	10.7	0.7
W06000001	Isle of Anglesey	716	5	34	138	236	188	101	14	5	67.6	4.7 u	19.7	89.4	125.8	104.9	57.9	7.3 u	2.1
W06000002	Gwynedd	1,156	13	47	221	389	282	182	31	4	52.7	7.0 u	12.2	42.7	105.1	96.1	62.8	9.2	1.0
W06000003	Conwy	1,050	15	41	203	312	293	166	30	5	61.3	7.9 u	13.9	79.2	107.7	105.8	59.2	9.5	1.2 u
W06000004	Denbighshire	1,012	16	65	205	300	264	145	33	0	67.6	10.2 u	26.0	88.8	113.3	119.0	59.8	11.5	: u
W06000005	Flintshire	1,587	27	60	286	469	489	232	48	3	60.0	10.5	14.7	74.5	98.0	110.2	52.3	9.8	0.5 u
W06000006	Wrexham	1,491	16	71	258	454	437	217	50	4	61.8	7.4 u	20.1	73.0	103.1	99.4	54.7	11.7	0.8 u
W06000023	Powys	1,179	8	45	207	346	361	172	45	3	62.5	3.6 u	13.0	74.0	112.2	128.6	56.8	12.2	0.6 u
W06000008	Ceredigion	612	3	24	127	185	166	84	25	1	48.2	2.8 u	10.4	32.9	106.8	112.1	53.2	14.3	:
W06000009	Pembrokeshire	1,133	9	52	244	385	293	112	44	3	59.2	4.3 u	15.8	80.5	114.7	100.4	36.4	12.8	0.7 u
W06000010	Carmarthenshire	1,878	13	72	351	623	510	262	53	7	61.8	4.3 u	14.9	71.7	118.6	104.4	50.9	9.9	1.1 u
W06000011	Swansea	2,475	28	109	434	770	678	399	80	5	53.7	7.5	15.3	45.2	95.1	94.7	58.6	10.9	0.6 u
W06000012	Neath Port Talbot	1,519	18	69	286	490	425	212	36	1	61.1	7.9 u	17.9	77.0	115.8	94.5	50.6	8.2	: u
W06000013	Bridgend	1,501	20	80	278	497	387	224	32	3	60.2	8.3	20.5	79.3	112.8	91.5	52.1	7.0	0.6 u
W06000014	The Vale of Glamorgan	1,321	15	64	208	352	389	260	44	4	60.5	6.6 u	17.6	64.6	103.6	112.6	66.0	10.6	0.8 u
W06000015	Cardiff	4,418	55	165	655	1,137	1,458	821	169	13	52.6	10.3	13.7	30.2	75.0	110.3	71.0	16.5	1.2 u
W06000016	Rhondda, Cynon, Taff	2,782	52	166	573	927	738	309	65	4	61.6	12.8	24.2	74.8	109.2	95.5	43.6	8.8	0.5 u
W06000024	Merthyr Tydfil	715	14	58	156	217	208	64	12	0	63.5	13.9 u	33.9	86.3	105.1	95.1	37.0	6.8 u	: u
W06000018	Caerphilly	2,017	22	103	385	669	550	247	56	7	60.0	7.2	20.4	73.5	113.8	90.8	43.0	9.9	1.0 u
W06000019	Blaenau Gwent	726	11	31	172	258	175	70	19	0	56.9	9.3 u	15.7	78.3	104.4	81.2	35.7	9.5 u	: u
W06000020	Torfaen	1,005	10	52	225	311	255	133	29	0	60.2	6.4 u	19.5	83.5	99.9	88.4	49.7	10.9	: u
W06000021	Monmouthshire	740	2	18	100	178	261	150	32	1	53.8	: u	7.1 u	49.8	87.7	127.8	63.2	11.6	: u
W06000022	Newport	1,903	20	74	354	620	540	272	39	4	67.1	7.7	17.0	78.0	121.1	103.4	58.5	8.7	0.7
W11000023	Betsi Cadwaladr University	7,012	92	318	1,311	2,160	1,953	1,043	206	21	60.9	8.3	17.1	69.1	106.3	105.3	57.1	10.1	0.8
W11000024	Powys Teaching	1,179	8	45	207	346	361	172	45	3	62.5	3.6 u	13.0	74.0	112.2	128.6	56.8	12.2	0.6 u
W11000025	Hywel Dda	3,623	25	148	722	1,193	969	458	122	11	58.3	4.0	14.2	61.3	115.3	104.4	46.7	11.6	0.9 u
W11000026	Abertawe Bro Morgannwg University	5,495	66	258	998	1,757	1,490	835	148	9	57.3	7.8	17.4	59.3	105.0	93.8	54.6	9.1	0.5 u
W11000027	Cwm Taf	3,497	66	224	729	1,144	946	373	77	4	62.0	13.0	26.1	77.0	108.4	95.4	42.3	8.5	0.4 u
W11000028	Aneurin Bevan	6,391	65	278	1,236	2,036	1,781	872	175	13	60.7	6.5	16.7	74.1	109.4	97.0	50.1	9.9	0.6 u
W11000029	Cardiff and Vale University	5,739	70	229	863	1,489	1,847	1,081	213	17	54.2	9.2	14.6	34.7	80.2	110.8	69.8	14.8	1.1 u
J99000001	Usual residence outside England and Wales	178	0	2	22	47	51	41	14	1	z	z	z	z	z	z	z	z	z

1 The rates for women of all ages, under 18, under 20 and 45 and over have been calculated using mid-2016 population estimates for the female population aged 15 to 44, 15 to 17, 15 to 19 and 45 to 49 respectively.

2 Rates are not calculated where there are fewer than 3 births, denoted by (:u), rates based on such low numbers are susceptible to inaccurate interpretation. Rates which are based on between 3 and 19 births are displayed in tables but are denoted by (u) as a warning to the user that their reliability as a measure may be affected by the small number of births.

3 A birth to a mother whose usual residence is outside England and Wales is included in total figures for "England, Wales and elsewhere" but are excluded from any sub-divisions of England and Wales. The England and Wales and elsewhere figures correspond to figures published at the national level for England and Wales not based on area of usual residence.

4 To preserve confidentiality, counts for Isles of Scilly have been combined with Cornwall.

Source: Office for National Statistics (ONS)

Released: 20 November 2017

B. Mortality Statistics: Deaths Registered by Area of Usual Residence, 2016 Registrations

Information

Introduction
• The figures presented in tables represent deaths registered in England and Wales, Scotland and Northern Ireland in 2016.
• Deaths registered in England and Wales where the area of usual residence of the deceased is outside England and Wales are included in total figures for 'England and Wales', but excluded from any sub-division of England and Wales.
• The deaths of those whose usual residence is outside Scotland and Northern Ireland are included in total figures for Scotland and Northern Ireland and also in any sub-division of Scotland and Northern Ireland based on where the death occurred.

Things you need to know
• Death statistics are compiled from information supplied when deaths are certified and registered as part of civil registration, a legal requirement.
• Figures represent the number of deaths registered in the calendar year
• Figures represent deaths which occurred in England and Wales, Scotland and Northern Ireland. These include the deaths of individuals whose usual residence was outside these countries

Quality and Methodology
The Mortality Statistics Quality and Methodology Information document contains important information on:
• the strengths and limitations of the data
• the quality of the output: including the accuracy of the data, how it compares with related data
• uses and users
• how the output was created

Our User guide to mortality statistics provides information on data quality, legislation and procedures relating to deaths.

The ONS policy on protecting confidentiality in birth and death statistics (currently under revision) is available on the ONS website.

Mortality rates
Information on how the mortality rates have been calculated is contained in our User guide to mortality statistics

Infant mortality definitions
Infant deaths (under 1 year) at various ages are defined as:
Perinatal – Stillbirths and early neonatal deaths (under 7 days)
Neonatal – deaths under 28 days

Population estimates used to calculate mortality rates
The most up to date population estimates at the time of this release have been used to calculate mortality rates.
Population estimates for England and Wales

Symbols and conventions
In ONS mortality outputs symbols used are:
: denotes not available
u low reliability

Further guidance on the use of symbols in tables is available.

Rates are not calculated where there are fewer than 3 deaths in a cell, denoted by (u). It is ONS practice not to calculate rates where there are fewer than 3 deaths in a cell, as rates based on such low numbers are susceptible to inaccurate interpretation. Rates which are based on between 3 and 19 deaths are displayed in tables but are denoted by (u) as a warning to the user that their reliability as a measure may be affected by the small number of events.

Further Information and Enquiries

Special extracts and tabulations of mortality data for England and Wales are available to order for a charge (subject to legal frameworks, disclosure control, resources and the ONS charging policy, where appropriate). Enquiries should be made to:

Vital Statistics Outputs Branch (vsob@ons.gsi.gov.uk or telephone: +44 (0)1329 444110).

User requested data will be published onto our website.

Access to microdata and disclosive data, that is, data which have the potential to identify an individual record, requires the approval of the ONS Microdata Release Procedure (MRP) before the data can be provided.

Feedback

We welcome feedback from users, please contact Vital Statistics Outputs Branch

Email: vsob@ons.gsi.gov.uk

Telephone: +44 (0)1329 444110

Terms and conditions

A National Statistics publication

National Statistics are produced to high professional standards set out in the Code of Practice for Official Statistics. They are produced free from any political interference.

The United Kingdom Statistics Authority has designated these statistics as National Statistics, in accordance with the Statistics and Registration Service Act 2007 and signifying compliance with the Code of Practice for Official Statistics.

Designation can be broadly interpreted to mean that the statistics:
• meet identified user needs;
• are well explained and readily accessible;
• are produced according to sound methods, and
• are managed impartially and objectively in the public interest.

Once statistics have been designated as National Statistics it is a statutory requirement that the Code of Practice shall continue to be observed.

About us

We are the executive office of the UK Statistics Authority, a non-ministerial department which reports directly to Parliament and the UK government's single largest statistical producer. We compile information about the UK's society and economy, and provide the evidence-base for policy and decision-making, the allocation of resources, and public accountability.

Copyright and reproduction

This document/publication is also available on our website at www.ons.gov.uk

Table 1a: Deaths (numbers and rates) by area of usual residence (administrative areas), 2016 registrations, United Kingdom and constituent countries
England and Wales: regions, unitary authorities/counties/districts
Scotland: council areas, Northern Ireland: local government districts

United Kingdom and constituent countries

Area codes	Area of usual residence	Populations Number (thousands) All ages			Deaths (numbers) All ages			Infant (under 1 year)	Neonatal (under 4 weeks)	Perinatal (stillbirths and deaths under 1 week)	Crude death rate (deaths per 1,000 population)	Age-standardised mortality rate[1]			Infant mortality rate (per 1,000 live births)	Neonatal mortality rate (per 1,000 live births)	Perinatal mortality rate (per 1,000 births and stillbirths)
		Persons	Males	Females	Persons	Males	Females					Persons	Males	Females			
K02000001	UNITED KINGDOM	65,648.1	32,377.7	33,270.4	597,206	293,001	304,205	3,004	2,136	5,125	9.1	982.5	1,145.9	852.5	3.9	2.8	6.6
	ELSEWHERE[3]	58,381.2	28,835.0	29,546.3	525,048	257,811	267,237	2,711	1,929	4,648	9.0	966.9	1,128.4	838.2	3.9	2.8	6.6
E92000001	ENGLAND	55,268.1	27,300.9	27,967.1	490,791	240,721	250,070	2,587	1,855	4,373	8.9	959.8	1,119.5	832.7	3.9	2.8	6.6
E12000001	NORTH EAST	2,636.8	1,294.4	1,342.5	27,836	13,624	14,212	99	71	157	10.6	1,098.9	1,272.6	963.2	3.5	2.5	5.5
E06000047	County Durham	522.1	256.7	265.4	5,672	2,776	2,896	29	21	31	10.9	1,118.5	1,280.5	993.0	5.5	4.0	5.8
E06000005	Darlington	105.6	51.4	54.3	1,076	526	550	5	4	9	10.2	1,002.7	1,158.6	877.7	4.3 u	3.5 u	7.8 u
E06000001	Hartlepool	92.8	45.3	47.5	990	505	485	3	2	5	10.7	1,112.8	1,352.2	932.8	2.9 u	u	4.7 u
E06000002	Middlesbrough	140.4	69.3	71.1	1,466	726	740	10	3	8	10.4	1,285.4	1,505.7	1,123.3	5.2 u	1.6 u	4.2 u
E06000057	Northumberland	316.0	154.2	161.8	3,653	1,770	1,883	7	6	13	11.6	1,012.4	1,140.9	898.7	2.5 u	2.1 u	4.6 u
E06000003	Redcar and Cleveland	135.4	65.8	69.6	1,547	770	777	7	4	9	11.4	1,074.8	1,251.5	933.4	4.9 u	2.8 u	6.3 u
E06000004	Stockton-on-Tees	195.7	96.1	99.6	1,924	942	982	7	6	20	9.8	1,108.2	1,283.8	980.9	3.0 u	2.6 u	8.6
E11000007	Tyne and Wear (Met County)	1,128.8	555.7	573.1	11,508	5,609	5,899	31	25	62	10.2	1,111.9	1,302.4	966.3	2.5	2.0	4.9
E08000037	Gateshead	201.6	99.2	102.4	2,230	1,110	1,120	9	8	18	11.1	1,136.1	1,322.2	993.0	3.9 u	3.5 u	7.8 u
E08000021	Newcastle upon Tyne	296.5	150.3	146.2	2,504	1,235	1,269	7	5	16	8.4	1,098.2	1,271.4	960.7	2.1 u	1.5 u	4.7 u
E08000022	North Tyneside	203.3	98.3	105.0	2,130	1,047	1,083	4	4	10	10.5	1,043.8	1,272.9	872.2	1.8 u	1.8 u	4.4 u
E08000023	South Tyneside	149.4	72.4	77.0	1,705	807	898	6	5	10	11.4	1,123.2	1,320.6	980.9	3.6 u	3.0 u	5.9 u
E08000024	Sunderland	278.0	135.5	142.5	2,939	1,410	1,529	5	3	8	10.6	1,163.7	1,343.4	1,027.4	1.7 u	1.0 u	2.7 u
E12000002	NORTH WEST	7,219.6	3,560.9	3,658.7	71,315	34,858	36,457	419	284	580	9.9	1,069.4	1,233.1	937.6	4.9	3.3	6.7
E06000008	Blackburn with Darwen	147.0	73.4	73.6	1,349	687	662	7	4	18	9.2	1,284.2	1,504.4	1,105.7	3.2 u	1.9 u	8.3 u
E06000009	Blackpool	139.2	68.8	70.4	1,862	957	905	8	6	13	13.4	1,287.8	1,568.5	1,065.2	4.7 u	3.5 u	7.6 u
E06000049	Cheshire East	376.7	184.6	192.1	3,961	1,942	2,019	12	9	24	10.5	924.2	1,079.7	794.7	3.1 u	2.4 u	6.2
E06000050	Cheshire West and Chester	335.7	163.7	172.0	3,520	1,730	1,790	12	7	11	10.5	998.7	1,172.8	868.0	3.4 u	2.0 u	3.1 u
E06000006	Halton	126.9	62.0	64.9	1,252	619	633	6	3	7	9.9	1,186.8	1,315.0	1,071.4	4.0 u	2.0 u	4.6 u
E06000007	Warrington	208.8	103.7	105.1	1,916	903	1,013	11	9	10	9.2	1,036.9	1,148.6	946.2	4.8 u	3.9 u	4.3 u
E10000006	Cumbria	497.9	245.6	252.3	5,635	2,735	2,900	22	13	22	11.3	972.7	1,121.0	855.2	4.6	2.7 u	4.6
E07000026	Allerdale	97.0	47.8	49.1	1,121	553	568	5	3	4	11.6	999.9	1,157.0	869.5	5.5 u	3.3 u	4.4 u
E07000027	Barrow-in-Furness	67.3	33.2	34.1	795	391	404	1	1	2	11.8	1,164.2	1,355.2	1,022.7	u	u	u
E07000028	Carlisle	108.4	53.0	55.5	1,186	578	608	9	5	8	10.9	1,021.6	1,188.5	895.1	7.7 u	4.3 u	6.8 u
E07000029	Copeland	69.3	34.9	34.4	759	386	373	5	2	4	11.0	1,049.0	1,226.9	903.6	7.1 u	u	5.7 u
E07000030	Eden	52.6	26.1	26.6	554	268	286	2	2	1	10.5	820.1	951.3	716.8	u	u	u
E07000031	South Lakeland	103.3	50.7	52.6	1,220	559	661	0	0	3	11.8	836.1	933.7	761.1	u	u	3.8 u
E11000001	Greater Manchester (Met County)	2,782.1	1,381.8	1,400.3	24,438	11,992	12,446	199	142	278	8.8	1,101.0	1,260.0	969.1	5.4	3.8	7.5
E08000001	Bolton	283.1	140.5	142.6	2,595	1,290	1,305	13	7	31	9.2	1,095.7	1,244.2	962.7	3.4 u	1.8 u	8.1
E08000002	Bury	188.7	92.5	96.2	1,817	882	935	12	11	16	9.6	1,089.7	1,244.8	965.5	5.1 u	4.7 u	6.7 u
E08000003	Manchester	541.3	274.7	266.6	3,581	1,792	1,789	61	50	77	6.6	1,284.4	1,513.1	1,113.6	7.7	6.3	9.6
E08000004	Oldham	232.7	114.8	118.0	2,127	1,044	1,083	24	17	28	9.1	1,150.9	1,314.9	1,005.3	7.2	5.1 u	8.4
E08000005	Rochdale	216.2	106.5	109.7	2,049	998	1,051	11	6	17	9.5	1,154.9	1,304.1	1,024.7	3.6 u	2.0 u	5.5 u
E08000006	Salford	248.7	125.3	123.4	2,194	1,089	1,105	21	14	33	8.8	1,154.8	1,330.8	1,009.4	5.7	3.8 u	8.9
E08000007	Stockport	290.6	142.3	148.3	2,696	1,304	1,392	22	14	22	9.3	912.0	1,051.6	804.8	6.4	4.1 u	6.4

Table 1a: Deaths (numbers and rates) by area of usual residence (administrative areas), 2016 registrations, United Kingdom and constituent countries
England and Wales: regions, unitary authorities/counties/districts
Scotland: council areas, Northern Ireland: local government districts

Area codes	Area of usual residence	Pop Persons	Pop Males	Pop Females	Deaths Persons	Deaths Males	Deaths Females	Infant (under 1 year)	Neonatal (under 4 weeks)	Perinatal (stillbirths & deaths under 1 week)	Crude death rate (per 1,000 pop)	ASMR Persons	ASMR Males	ASMR Females	Infant mortality rate (per 1,000 live births)	Neonatal mortality rate (per 1,000 live births)	Perinatal mortality rate (per 1,000 births and stillbirths)
E08000008	Tameside	223.2	109.6	113.6	2,202	1,069	1,133	12	8	17	9.9	1,162.7	1,327.5	1,027.3	4.2 u	2.8 u	5.9 u
E08000009	Trafford	234.7	114.9	119.8	1,983	970	1,013	10	8	15	8.5	909.4	1,075.6	780.9	3.6 u	2.8 u	5.3 u
E08000010	Wigan	323.1	160.8	162.2	3,194	1,554	1,640	13	7	22	9.9	1,144.1	1,261.1	1,037.0	3.7 u	2.0 u	6.2
E10000017	**Lancashire**	**1,198.8**	**591.8**	**607.0**	**12,333**	**5,956**	**6,377**	**65**	**36**	**82**	**10.3**	**1,025.5**	**1,177.0**	**904.4**	**4.9**	**2.7**	**6.2**
E07000117	Burnley	87.5	43.2	44.3	865	450	415	4	3	14	9.9	1,084.5	1,365.7	873.9	3.3 u	2.5 u	11.5 u
E07000118	Chorley	114.4	57.3	57.0	1,087	532	555	5	2	2	9.5	1,053.0	1,200.8	925.7	4.1 u	u	u
E07000119	Fylde	78.0	38.2	39.8	1,055	471	584	2	2	2	13.5	993.5	1,093.9	906.1	u	u	u
E07000120	Hyndburn	80.5	39.8	40.7	845	423	422	9	5	7	10.5	1,180.3	1,390.6	1,026.6	8.5 u	4.7 u	6.6 u
E07000121	Lancaster	143.5	70.7	72.8	1,530	761	769	6	1	6	10.7	1,078.5	1,309.7	913.5	4.1 u	u	4.1 u
E07000122	Pendle	90.6	44.8	45.8	835	394	441	5	2	6	9.2	1,025.3	1,121.3	937.2	4.1 u	u	4.9 u
E07000123	Preston	141.8	71.8	70.0	1,177	554	623	9	4	13	8.3	1,083.8	1,190.6	1,001.2	4.8 u	2.1 u	6.8 u
E07000124	Ribble Valley	58.8	28.9	29.9	611	265	346	2	2	2	10.4	892.6	926.1	851.4	u	u	u
E07000125	Rossendale	69.9	34.4	35.4	621	287	334	3	3	6	8.9	1,011.5	1,096.4	934.5	3.7 u	3.7 u	7.3 u
E07000126	South Ribble	110.1	53.8	56.3	1,021	510	511	5	3	8	9.3	914.8	1,075.7	791.5	4.0 u	2.4 u	6.4 u
E07000127	West Lancashire	113.4	55.2	58.2	1,210	593	617	7	4	7	10.7	1,183.5	1,183.5	899.3	7.0 u	4.0 u	7.0 u
E07000128	Wyre	110.3	53.8	56.5	1,476	716	760	8	5	9	13.4	998.6	1,161.4	867.0	8.3 u	5.2 u	9.3 u
E11000002	**Merseyside (Met County)**	**1,406.4**	**685.6**	**720.9**	**15,049**	**7,337**	**7,712**	**77**	**55**	**115**	**10.7**	**1,120.8**	**1,307.0**	**976.5**	**4.8**	**3.4**	**7.1**
E08000011	Knowsley	147.9	70.5	77.5	1,601	780	821	5	3	12	10.8	1,230.0	1,458.8	1,075.3	2.6 u	1.6 u	6.2 u
E08000012	Liverpool	484.6	240.2	244.4	4,477	2,226	2,251	39	28	47	9.2	1,209.3	1,380.7	1,062.1	6.5	4.6	7.8
E08000014	Sefton	274.3	132.0	142.2	3,286	1,576	1,710	10	6	17	12.0	1,011.0	1,204.4	868.3	3.6 u	2.1 u	6.0 u
E08000013	St. Helens	178.5	87.7	90.8	1,967	948	1,019	4	3	9	11.0	1,153.8	1,284.1	1,040.9	2.0 u	1.5 u	4.5 u
E08000015	Wirral	321.2	155.2	166.0	3,718	1,807	1,911	19	15	30	11.6	1,070.4	1,271.3	923.3	5.5 u	4.4 u	8.7
E12000003	**YORKSHIRE AND THE HUMBER**	**5,425.7**	**2,678.3**	**2,747.5**	**51,513**	**25,319**	**26,194**	**234**	**152**	**433**	**9.5**	**1,029.6**	**1,209.3**	**891.1**	**3.7**	**2.4**	**6.8**
E06000011	**East Riding of Yorkshire**	**337.7**	**165.7**	**172.0**	**3,831**	**1,881**	**1,950**	**6**	**6**	**16**	**11.3**	**950.5**	**1,109.8**	**825.5**	**2.1 u**	**2.1 u**	**5.6 u**
E06000010	**Kingston upon Hull, City of**	**260.2**	**130.8**	**129.4**	**2,487**	**1,268**	**1,219**	**11**	**6**	**28**	**9.6**	**1,255.3**	**1,466.6**	**1,075.1**	**3.1 u**	**1.7 u**	**7.8**
E06000012	**North East Lincolnshire**	**159.1**	**78.1**	**81.0**	**1,761**	**910**	**851**	**7**	**6**	**7**	**11.1**	**1,093.3**	**1,357.6**	**892.6**	**3.8 u**	**3.2 u**	**3.8 u**
E06000013	**North Lincolnshire**	**170.8**	**84.6**	**86.2**	**1,766**	**889**	**877**	**7**	**6**	**13**	**10.3**	**1,022.2**	**1,228.8**	**865.4**	**3.9 u**	**3.4 u**	**7.3 u**
E06000014	**York**	**208.4**	**102.2**	**106.2**	**1,810**	**856**	**954**	**8**	**3**	**7**	**8.7**	**912.9**	**1,056.2**	**802.3**	**4.1 u**	**1.5 u**	**3.6 u**
E10000023	**North Yorkshire**	**604.9**	**298.0**	**306.9**	**6,438**	**3,147**	**3,291**	**8**	**5**	**23**	**10.6**	**895.1**	**1,070.0**	**767.0**	**1.4 u**	**0.9 u**	**4.0**
E07000163	Craven	56.3	27.3	29.0	678	314	364	0	0	0	12.0	884.6	1,066.9	776.3	u	u	u
E07000164	Hambleton	90.5	44.5	46.1	921	473	448	0	0	1	10.2	829.8	1,026.0	686.7	u	u	u
E07000165	Harrogate	156.3	76.2	80.1	1,625	758	867	6	3	8	10.4	853.1	1,007.7	744.0	4.1 u	2.0 u	5.4 u
E07000166	Richmondshire	53.7	29.0	24.7	461	246	215	0	0	2	8.6	907.4	1,113.7	740.5	u	u	u
E07000167	Ryedale	53.5	26.2	27.3	593	309	284	1	0	2	11.1	866.3	1,088.8	706.0	u	u	u
E07000168	Scarborough	107.8	52.4	55.4	1,354	663	691	1	1	5	12.6	983.1	1,151.0	846.0	u	u	4.8 u
E07000169	Selby	86.7	42.5	44.2	806	384	422	1	1	5	9.3	971.5	1,102.3	872.4	u	u	5.1 u
E11000003	**South Yorkshire (Met County)**	**1,385.0**	**686.2**	**698.7**	**13,177**	**6,417**	**6,760**	**58**	**36**	**104**	**9.5**	**1,053.7**	**1,211.3**	**928.4**	**3.6**	**2.2**	**6.5**
E08000016	Barnsley	241.2	119.1	122.1	2,317	1,133	1,184	5	2	16	9.6	1,021.4	1,175.4	907.4	1.8 u	u	5.6 u
E08000017	Doncaster	306.4	152.0	154.4	3,205	1,565	1,640	16	8	17	10.5	1,120.4	1,291.9	985.0	4.5 u	2.3 u	4.8 u
E08000018	Rotherham	261.9	128.9	133.0	2,744	1,357	1,387	5	3	22	10.6	1,106.0	1,202.6	1,067.6	1.6 u	1.0 u	7.0
E08000019	Sheffield	575.4	286.2	289.2	4,911	2,362	2,549	32	23	49	8.5	1,003.0	1,141.5	888.3	4.9	3.5	7.5

1

Table 1a: Deaths (numbers and rates) by area of usual residence (administrative areas), 2016 registrations, United Kingdom and constituent countries
England and Wales: regions, unitary authorities/counties/districts
Scotland: council areas, Northern Ireland: local government districts

United Kingdom and constituent countries

Area codes	Area of usual residence	Populations (Number thousands) All ages			Deaths (numbers) All ages			Infant (under 1 year)	Neonatal (under 4 weeks)	Perinatal (stillbirths and deaths under 1 week)	Crude death rate (deaths per 1,000 population)	Age-standardised mortality rate[1]			Rates — Infant mortality rate (per 1,000 live births)	Neonatal mortality rate (per 1,000 live births)	Perinatal mortality rate (per 1,000 births and stillbirths)
		Persons	Males	Females	Persons	Males	Females					Persons	Males	Females			
E11000006	**West Yorkshire (Met County)**	**2,299.7**	**1,132.7**	**1,167.0**	**20,243**	**9,951**	**10,292**	**129**	**84**	**235**	**8.8**	**1,063.4**	**1,255.0**	**918.7**	**4.3**	**2.8**	**7.8**
E08000032	Bradford	534.3	263.6	270.7	4,571	2,254	2,317	39	29	78	8.6	1,114.2	1,302.8	964.4	4.9	3.7	9.8
E08000033	Calderdale	209.8	103.1	106.7	1,952	946	1,006	11	6	19	9.3	1,029.4	1,230.1	886.1	4.5 u	2.4 u	7.6 u
E08000034	Kirklees	437.0	216.5	220.6	3,827	1,898	1,929	16	11	38	8.8	1,034.7	1,227.5	885.1	3.0 u	2.0 u	7.0
E08000035	Leeds	781.7	383.8	397.9	6,592	3,244	3,348	49	26	75	8.4	1,062.0	1,264.4	912.8	4.8	2.5	7.3
E08000036	Wakefield	336.8	165.7	171.2	3,301	1,609	1,692	14	12	25	9.8	1,060.6	1,229.7	935.5	3.4 u	3.0 u	6.1
E12000004	**EAST MIDLANDS**	**4,724.4**	**2,335.0**	**2,389.4**	**44,027**	**21,720**	**22,307**	**215**	**163**	**375**	**9.3**	**979.8**	**1,143.3**	**851.2**	**4.0**	**3.1**	**7.0**
E06000015	**Derby**	**256.2**	**127.3**	**129.0**	**2,281**	**1,114**	**1,167**	**19**	**14**	**33**	**8.9**	**1,014.3**	**1,199.2**	**872.3**	**5.8 u**	**4.3 u**	**10.0**
E06000016	**Leicester**	**348.3**	**174.0**	**174.4**	**2,532**	**1,268**	**1,264**	**34**	**27**	**58**	**7.3**	**1,105.7**	**1,321.7**	**943.5**	**6.6**	**5.2**	**11.2**
E06000018	**Nottingham**	**325.3**	**164.5**	**160.8**	**2,343**	**1,157**	**1,186**	**15**	**11**	**27**	**7.2**	**1,134.0**	**1,330.5**	**983.2**	**3.5 u**	**2.6 u**	**6.3**
E06000017	**Rutland**	**38.6**	**19.7**	**18.9**	**339**	**175**	**164**	**0**	**0**	**1**	**8.8**	**705.9**	**883.3**	**583.8**	**u**	**u**	**u**
E10000007	**Derbyshire**	**785.8**	**386.2**	**399.6**	**8,123**	**4,004**	**4,119**	**25**	**17**	**57**	**10.3**	**997.6**	**1,172.9**	**859.9**	**3.2**	**2.2 u**	**7.3**
E07000032	Amber Valley	124.6	61.2	63.4	1,250	606	644	6	4	8	10.0	948.7	1,092.2	831.7	4.9 u	3.3 u	6.5 u
E07000033	Bolsover	78.1	38.6	39.5	827	390	437	2	2	10	10.6	1,101.9	1,295.5	974.6	u	u	12.1 u
E07000034	Chesterfield	104.4	51.2	53.2	1,167	583	584	2	2	9	11.2	1,062.4	1,287.4	888.3	u	u	8.4 u
E07000035	Derbyshire Dales	71.3	35.1	36.2	814	393	421	3	1	3	11.4	898.2	1,072.2	778.9	5.8 u	u	5.8 u
E07000036	Erewash	114.9	56.3	58.6	1,174	581	593	3	3	13	10.2	998.0	1,195.6	852.2	2.5 u	2.5 u	10.6 u
E07000037	High Peak	91.7	45.2	46.5	898	444	454	5	2	5	9.8	998.8	1,170.5	858.5	3.4 u	u	5.6 u
E07000038	North East Derbyshire	100.4	49.1	51.4	1,135	570	565	2	1	2	11.3	994.0	1,130.1	872.2	u	u	u
E07000039	South Derbyshire	100.3	49.6	50.7	858	437	421	4	2	7	8.6	1,032.8	1,218.7	878.7	3.5 u	u	6.2 u
E10000018	**Leicestershire**	**683.0**	**338.2**	**344.7**	**6,112**	**3,011**	**3,101**	**26**	**20**	**44**	**8.9**	**891.9**	**1,055.6**	**769.1**	**3.7**	**2.8**	**6.2**
E07000129	Blaby	97.7	47.9	49.8	887	464	423	0	0	5	9.1	910.5	1,168.1	733.5	u	u	4.5 u
E07000130	Charnwood	179.4	90.6	88.8	1,529	776	753	8	6	12	8.5	934.4	1,131.0	785.7	4.2 u	3.1 u	6.2 u
E07000131	Harborough	90.4	44.8	45.6	783	391	392	1	0	4	8.7	812.9	963.9	689.0	2.6 u	u	5.0 u
E07000132	Hinckley and Bosworth	110.1	54.2	55.9	964	468	496	3	2	5	8.8	855.9	984.9	751.7	u	u	4.2 u
E07000133	Melton	50.9	24.9	26.0	470	225	245	4	3	3	9.2	869.1	968.4	783.8	u	u	3.6 u
E07000134	North West Leicestershire	98.6	48.9	49.8	896	420	476	8	7	12	9.1	953.1	1,106.1	866.3	7.8 u	5.9 u	5.8 u
E07000135	Oadby and Wigston	55.8	27.0	28.9	583	267	316	2	2	3	10.4	883.1	1,003.4	792.5	7.9 u	6.9 u	11.8 u
E10000019	**Lincolnshire**	**743.4**	**363.6**	**379.8**	**8,078**	**4,064**	**4,014**	**25**	**19**	**44**	**10.9**	**972.8**	**1,135.6**	**838.7**	**3.3**	**2.5 u**	**5.9**
E07000136	Boston	67.6	33.4	34.2	756	388	368	5	5	7	11.2	1,064.8	1,293.4	881.7	6.3 u	6.3 u	8.8 u
E07000137	East Lindsey	138.4	67.5	71.0	1,953	996	957	4	3	10	14.1	1,067.7	1,249.3	920.2	3.4 u	2.6 u	8.5 u
E07000138	Lincoln	97.8	48.3	49.5	871	428	443	4	3	6	8.9	1,100.0	1,320.5	941.7	3.4 u	2.6 u	5.1 u
E07000139	North Kesteven	113.3	55.4	57.9	1,079	541	538	1	1	4	9.5	846.9	966.7	740.2	u	u	3.6 u
E07000140	South Holland	92.4	45.4	47.0	1,033	507	526	4	3	6	11.2	930.4	1,043.6	828.1	4.2 u	3.1 u	6.2 u
E07000141	South Kesteven	140.2	67.8	72.4	1,436	698	738	2	2	7	10.2	934.7	1,086.3	817.3	u	u	5.1 u
E07000142	West Lindsey	93.7	45.8	47.9	950	506	444	5	2	4	10.1	914.8	1,097.7	759.6	5.6 u	u	4.4 u
E10000021	**Northamptonshire**	**733.1**	**362.2**	**370.9**	**6,209**	**3,036**	**3,173**	**36**	**30**	**67**	**8.5**	**970.7**	**1,111.9**	**857.7**	**4.0**	**3.3**	**7.3**
E07000150	Corby	68.2	33.5	34.6	570	304	266	2	2	6	8.4	1,191.7	1,507.9	973.0	u	u	5.9 u
E07000151	Daventry	81.3	40.6	40.7	689	311	378	5	5	6	8.5	893.2	917.7	861.5	6.1 u	6.1 u	7.3 u
E07000152	East Northamptonshire	91.0	45.0	46.0	835	397	438	3	3	9	9.2	932.4	1,050.6	847.6	3.0 u	3.0 u	9.0 u
E07000153	Kettering	99.0	48.7	50.3	873	414	459	6	4	9	8.8	956.3	1,112.9	835.4	4.8 u	3.2 u	7.2 u

Table 1a: Deaths (numbers and rates) by area of usual residence (administrative areas), 2016 registrations, United Kingdom and constituent countries
England and Wales: regions, unitary authorities/counties/districts
Scotland: council areas, Northern Ireland: local government districts

Area codes	Area of usual residence	Populations (thousands) All ages			Deaths (numbers) All ages			Infant (under 1 year)	Neonatal (under 4 weeks)	Perinatal (stillbirths and deaths under 1 week)	Crude death rate (deaths per 1,000 population)	Age-standardised mortality rate[1]			Infant mortality rate (per 1,000 live births)	Neonatal mortality rate (per 1,000 live births)	Perinatal mortality rate (per 1,000 births and stillbirths)
		Persons	Males	Females	Persons	Males	Females					Persons	Males	Females			
E07000154	Northampton	225.5	111.8	113.7	1,754	866	888	15	11	21	7.8	1,013.6	1,165.9	886.9	4.6 u	3.4 u	6.4
E07000155	South Northamptonshire	90.0	44.3	45.7	730	372	358	1	1	5	8.1	828.9	987.4	713.2	u	u	6.2 u
E07000156	Wellingborough	78.2	38.3	39.9	758	372	386	4	4	11	9.7	1,041.2	1,195.2	913.6	4.2 u	4.2 u	11.4 u
E10000024	**Nottinghamshire**	**810.7**	**399.3**	**411.4**	**8,010**	**3,891**	**4,119**	**35**	**25**	**44**	**9.9**	**986.1**	**1,131.5**	**872.4**	**4.0**	**2.9**	**5.0**
E07000170	Ashfield	124.5	61.1	63.4	1,227	635	592	8	7	11	9.9	1,105.4	1,315.6	930.5	5.5 u	4.9 u	7.6 u
E07000171	Bassetlaw	114.8	57.0	57.8	1,202	587	615	5	5	11	10.5	1,024.3	1,147.0	919.8	3.9 u	3.9 u	8.6 u
E07000172	Broxtowe	112.7	55.9	56.8	1,080	505	575	5	4	3	9.6	933.6	1,012.7	864.9	3.3 u	3.3 u	2.5 u
E07000173	Gedling	116.5	56.7	59.8	1,081	490	591	5	3	3	9.3	923.9	1,007.0	858.6	3.9 u	2.4 u	2.4 u
E07000174	Mansfield	107.4	52.8	54.6	1,151	553	598	8	3	9	10.7	1,135.7	1,315.7	1,011.5	6.2 u	2.3 u	7.0 u
E07000175	Newark and Sherwood	119.6	59.0	60.6	1,225	629	596	2	1	3	10.2	981.2	1,210.7	821.1	u	u	2.5 u
E07000176	Rushcliffe	115.2	56.8	58.4	1,044	492	552	3	2	4	9.1	831.9	954.4	734.2	2.9 u	u	3.8 u
E12000005	**WEST MIDLANDS**	**5,800.7**	**2,872.6**	**2,928.1**	**53,814**	**26,839**	**26,975**	**440**	**325**	**586**	**9.3**	**989.3**	**1,171.7**	**844.9**	**6.2**	**4.6**	**8.2**
E06000019	**Herefordshire, County of**	**189.3**	**93.7**	**95.6**	**2,104**	**1,026**	**1,078**	**10**	**8**	**13**	**11.1**	**937.2**	**1,085.8**	**812.3**	**5.7 u**	**4.5 u**	**7.3 u**
E06000051	**Shropshire**	**313.4**	**155.5**	**157.8**	**3,482**	**1,687**	**1,795**	**9**	**6**	**18**	**11.1**	**939.8**	**1,102.9**	**818.5**	**3.1 u**	**2.0 u**	**6.1 u**
E06000021	**Stoke-on-Trent**	**253.2**	**126.4**	**126.8**	**2,504**	**1,298**	**1,206**	**25**	**20**	**37**	**9.9**	**1,189.3**	**1,449.5**	**985.1**	**7.1**	**5.7**	**10.5**
E06000020	**Telford and Wrekin**	**173.0**	**85.9**	**87.1**	**1,454**	**734**	**720**	**5**	**4**	**14**	**8.4**	**1,058.0**	**1,231.1**	**917.1**	**2.4 u**	**1.9 u**	**6.7 u**
E10000028	**Staffordshire**	**867.1**	**431.5**	**435.7**	**8,519**	**4,190**	**4,329**	**47**	**36**	**53**	**9.8**	**960.1**	**1,110.6**	**839.7**	**5.4**	**4.1**	**6.1**
E07000192	Cannock Chase	98.5	48.8	49.7	895	451	444	5	2	5	9.1	995.1	1,169.3	852.2	4.8 u	u	4.7 u
E07000193	East Staffordshire	116.7	58.4	58.3	1,087	528	559	12	9	18	9.3	994.4	1,165.1	870.1	8.2 u	6.2 u	12.3 u
E07000194	Lichfield	103.1	51.2	51.9	1,056	502	554	4	4	6	10.2	939.6	1,040.2	850.0	4.1 u	4.1 u	6.1 u
E07000195	Newcastle-under-Lyme	128.5	63.9	64.5	1,309	627	682	8	6	5	10.2	1,030.6	1,169.4	924.6	6.7 u	5.0 u	4.2 u
E07000196	South Staffordshire	111.2	55.4	55.8	1,139	568	571	0	0	3	10.2	885.0	1,085.0	756.4	u	u	3.1 u
E07000197	Stafford	134.2	67.6	66.6	1,268	624	644	6	5	8	9.5	893.0	998.1	791.6	4.7 u	3.9 u	6.2 u
E07000198	Staffordshire Moorlands	98.1	48.4	49.7	1,126	572	554	4	3	2	11.5	997.6	1,169.3	844.4	4.7 u	3.5 u	3.5 u
E07000199	Tamworth	77.0	37.8	39.1	639	318	321	8	7	6	8.3	980.9	1,154.7	852.2	8.7 u	7.6 u	6.5 u
E10000031	**Warwickshire**	**556.8**	**275.1**	**281.6**	**5,441**	**2,629**	**2,812**	**25**	**24**	**43**	**9.8**	**934.7**	**1,079.0**	**815.6**	**4.2**	**4.0**	**7.2**
E07000218	North Warwickshire	63.2	31.2	32.0	742	363	379	0	0	2	11.7	1,133.0	1,320.3	974.9	u	u	u
E07000219	Nuneaton and Bedworth	127.0	62.3	64.7	1,176	575	601	8	7	15	9.3	1,018.9	1,193.7	889.2	5.1 u	4.4 u	9.5 u
E07000220	Rugby	103.8	51.6	52.2	980	501	479	7	7	8	9.4	941.6	1,137.5	795.5	5.7 u	5.7 u	6.5 u
E07000221	Stratford-on-Avon	122.3	59.5	62.8	1,358	627	731	3	3	8	11.1	856.4	952.7	759.7	2.7 u	2.7 u	7.3 u
E07000222	Warwick	140.4	70.4	70.0	1,185	563	622	7	7	10	8.4	856.7	978.2	759.8	4.9 u	4.9 u	6.9 u
E11000005	**West Midlands (Met County)**	**2,864.9**	**1,417.5**	**1,447.4**	**24,451**	**12,344**	**12,107**	**289**	**206**	**371**	**8.5**	**1,026.4**	**1,228.6**	**866.1**	**7.2**	**5.1**	**9.2**
E08000025	Birmingham	1,124.6	556.3	568.2	8,426	4,267	4,159	146	105	196	7.5	1,035.3	1,230.1	876.1	8.4	6.0	11.2
E08000026	Coventry	352.9	178.4	174.5	2,712	1,370	1,342	29	18	36	7.7	1,016.3	1,208.4	852.9	6.4	4.0 u	7.9
E08000027	Dudley	317.6	155.9	161.7	3,119	1,588	1,531	20	14	26	9.8	980.9	1,183.5	823.4	5.2	3.7 u	6.8
E08000028	Sandwell	322.7	159.9	162.8	2,913	1,467	1,446	38	31	42	9.0	1,115.3	1,346.4	941.6	8.0	6.5	8.8
E08000029	Solihull	211.8	103.0	108.8	2,034	1,039	995	13	7	17	9.6	866.8	1,090.6	708.0	5.6 u	3.0 u	7.3 u
E08000030	Walsall	278.7	136.9	141.8	2,666	1,334	1,332	22	19	36	9.6	1,048.9	1,251.8	891.5	5.9	5.1 u	9.5
E08000031	Wolverhampton	256.6	127.0	129.6	2,581	1,279	1,302	21	12	18	10.1	1,109.8	1,298.7	956.9	6.0	3.5 u	5.2 u

Table 1a: Deaths (numbers and rates) by area of usual residence (administrative areas), 2016 registrations, United Kingdom and constituent countries
England and Wales: regions, unitary authorities/counties/districts
Scotland: council areas, Northern Ireland: local government districts

United Kingdom and constituent countries

Area codes	Area of usual residence	Populations Number (thousands) All ages Persons	Males	Females	Deaths All ages Persons	Males	Females	Infant (under 1 year)	Neonatal (under 4 weeks)	Perinatal (stillbirths and deaths under 1 week)	Crude death rate (deaths per 1,000 population)	Age-standardised mortality rate[1] Persons	Males	Females	Rates Infant mortality rate (per 1,000 live births)	Neonatal mortality rate (per 1,000 live births)	Perinatal mortality rate (per 1,000 births and stillbirths)
E10000034	**Worcestershire**	**583.1**	**287.0**	**296.0**	**5,859**	**2,931**	**2,928**	**30**	**21**	**37**	**10.0**	**906.4**	**1,098.6**	**764.1**	**4.9**	**3.5**	**6.1**
E07000234	Bromsgrove	96.8	47.7	49.1	1,061	507	554	6	4	4	11.0	918.3	1,103.7	795.7	6.4 u	4.3 u	4.2 u
E07000235	Malvern Hills	76.1	37.1	39.0	1,003	471	532	1	0	2	13.2	919.8	1,047.1	820.1	u	u	u
E07000236	Redditch	85.0	42.2	42.8	702	360	342	5	3	10	8.3	998.4	1,217.0	846.8	4.7 u	2.8 u	9.3 u
E07000237	Worcester	102.3	50.6	51.7	804	402	402	6	6	11	7.9	907.4	1,123.8	746.1	5.0 u	5.0 u	9.1 u
E07000238	Wychavon	122.9	60.1	62.8	1,186	627	559	5	4	4	9.6	795.9	1,011.8	640.8	4.2 u	3.4 u	3.4 u
E07000239	Wyre Forest	99.9	49.3	50.6	1,103	564	539	7	4	6	11.0	953.4	1,138.2	806.6	6.3 u	3.6 u	5.4 u
E12000006	**EAST**	**6,130.5**	**3,021.7**	**3,108.9**	**56,134**	**27,396**	**28,738**	**230**	**164**	**434**	**9.2**	**912.4**	**1,059.2**	**795.3**	**3.2**	**2.3**	**6.0**
E06000055	**Bedford**	**168.8**	**83.4**	**85.3**	**1,432**	**686**	**746**	**7**	**5**	**15**	**8.5**	**920.0**	**1,044.2**	**817.9**	**3.2 u**	**2.3 u**	**6.8 u**
E06000056	**Central Bedfordshire**	**278.9**	**138.1**	**140.9**	**2,068**	**1,070**	**998**	**8**	**6**	**22**	**7.4**	**871.0**	**1,017.4**	**746.4**	**2.4 u**	**1.8 u**	**6.6**
E06000032	**Luton**	**216.8**	**109.8**	**107.0**	**1,514**	**790**	**724**	**22**	**16**	**24**	**7.0**	**1,041.0**	**1,225.4**	**881.3**	**6.1**	**4.4 u**	**6.6**
E06000031	**Peterborough**	**197.1**	**98.8**	**98.3**	**1,591**	**808**	**783**	**15**	**13**	**25**	**8.1**	**1,044.9**	**1,241.4**	**892.2**	**4.9 u**	**4.2 u**	**8.1**
E06000033	**Southend-on-Sea**	**179.8**	**88.0**	**91.8**	**1,927**	**915**	**1,012**	**7**	**4**	**11**	**10.7**	**1,020.8**	**1,207.5**	**885.7**	**3.1 u**	**1.8 u**	**4.9 u**
E06000034	**Thurrock**	**167.0**	**82.4**	**84.7**	**1,250**	**590**	**660**	**6**	**4**	**14**	**7.5**	**1,065.0**	**1,179.6**	**964.9**	**2.4 u**	**1.6 u**	**5.6 u**
E10000003	**Cambridgeshire**	**651.9**	**326.5**	**325.5**	**5,275**	**2,577**	**2,698**	**25**	**21**	**46**	**8.1**	**857.9**	**990.9**	**755.2**	**3.5**	**2.9**	**6.3**
E07000008	Cambridge	131.8	68.6	63.2	844	399	445	5	5	9	6.4	890.0	1,026.9	776.5	3.5 u	3.5 u	6.3 u
E07000009	East Cambridgeshire	87.8	43.2	44.6	721	365	356	2	2	5	8.2	829.1	1,019.5	704.6	u	u	5.1 u
E07000010	Fenland	100.2	49.5	50.6	1,130	572	558	5	3	7	11.3	1,003.7	1,197.7	861.4	4.4 u	2.7 u	6.2 u
E07000011	Huntingdonshire	175.7	87.7	87.9	1,419	668	751	4	3	11	8.1	857.1	939.5	784.1	2.0 u	1.5 u	5.5 u
E07000012	South Cambridgeshire	156.5	77.4	79.1	1,161	573	588	9	8	14	7.4	757.3	878.8	664.1	5.2 u	4.6 u	8.0 u
E10000012	**Essex**	**1,455.3**	**711.7**	**743.7**	**14,275**	**6,837**	**7,438**	**45**	**28**	**97**	**9.8**	**945.2**	**1,079.0**	**835.3**	**2.7**	**1.7**	**5.8**
E07000066	Basildon	183.4	89.1	94.3	1,589	732	857	3	1	13	8.7	981.3	1,082.3	897.8	1.2 u	u	5.2 u
E07000067	Braintree	151.0	74.2	76.8	1,418	650	768	5	2	10	9.4	945.9	1,024.5	857.9	2.9 u	u	5.8 u
E07000068	Brentwood	76.4	37.1	39.3	755	354	401	0	0	5	9.9	863.4	1,002.8	760.4	u	u	5.9 u
E07000069	Castle Point	89.7	43.7	46.1	1,043	493	550	4	2	6	11.6	999.4	1,099.1	915.9	4.7 u	u	6.9 u
E07000070	Chelmsford	174.1	86.0	88.0	1,463	705	758	9	6	10	8.4	863.9	964.7	770.5	4.4 u	2.9 u	4.9 u
E07000071	Colchester	186.6	92.6	94.0	1,609	791	818	10	5	18	8.6	993.9	1,166.4	860.4	4.5 u	2.3 u	8.1 u
E07000072	Epping Forest	130.3	63.0	67.3	1,245	583	662	3	2	8	9.6	908.9	1,032.2	808.0	1.9 u	u	5.0 u
E07000073	Harlow	86.0	41.8	44.2	738	377	361	3	2	4	8.6	1,000.0	1,282.3	811.0	2.3 u	u	3.1 u
E07000074	Maldon	63.4	31.2	32.2	659	331	328	0	0	5	10.4	926.9	1,089.4	798.0	u	u	9.3 u
E07000075	Rochford	85.7	41.9	43.7	836	412	424	1	1	5	9.8	862.0	1,024.1	748.0	u	u	6.6 u
E07000076	Tendring	142.6	68.6	74.0	2,180	1,069	1,111	5	5	6	15.3	1,064.8	1,241.6	911.4	3.9 u	3.9 u	4.7 u
E07000077	Uttlesford	86.2	42.4	43.8	740	340	400	2	2	7	8.6	840.4	942.0	769.0	u	u	7.6 u
E10000015	**Hertfordshire**	**1,176.7**	**576.6**	**600.1**	**9,331**	**4,448**	**4,883**	**41**	**29**	**75**	**7.9**	**862.4**	**1,002.2**	**755.8**	**2.8**	**2.0**	**5.1**
E07000095	Broxbourne	96.8	46.8	50.0	746	363	383	2	1	7	7.7	824.7	965.3	713.7	u	u	5.6 u
E07000096	Dacorum	152.7	75.2	77.5	1,238	599	639	3	2	10	8.1	864.7	1,022.4	747.4	1.6 u	u	5.3 u
E07000242	East Hertfordshire	146.3	71.7	74.6	1,043	510	533	3	2	3	7.1	781.4	904.7	675.8	1.8 u	u	1.8 u
E07000098	Hertsmere	103.5	49.8	53.7	867	396	471	3	3	5	8.4	836.5	946.7	749.7	2.3 u	2.3 u	3.8 u
E07000099	North Hertfordshire	132.7	65.1	67.6	1,209	540	669	4	3	11	9.1	901.8	981.0	833.8	2.6 u	2.0 u	7.2 u
E07000240	St Albans	146.3	71.6	74.7	1,047	520	527	5	2	3	7.2	776.0	922.0	673.7	2.7 u	u	1.6 u
E07000243	Stevenage	87.1	42.9	44.2	748	381	367	2	1	4	8.6	1,034.5	1,291.1	854.0	u	u	3.3 u
E07000102	Three Rivers	92.5	45.1	47.5	774	352	422	4	4	7	8.4	841.5	945.5	765.1	3.7 u	3.7 u	6.5 u

Table 1a: Deaths (numbers and rates) by area of usual residence (administrative areas), 2016 registrations, United Kingdom and constituent countries
England and Wales: regions, unitary authorities/counties/districts
Scotland: council areas, Northern Ireland: local government districts

Area codes	Area of usual residence	Populations Number (thousands) All ages			Deaths (numbers) All ages			Deaths Infant (under 1 year)	Deaths Neonatal (under 4 weeks)	Deaths Perinatal (stillbirths and deaths under 1 week)	Crude death rate (deaths per 1,000 population)	Age-standardised mortality rate[1]			Rates Infant mortality rate (per 1,000 live births)	Rates Neonatal mortality rate (per 1,000 live births)	Rates Perinatal mortality rate (per 1,000 births and stillbirths)
		Persons	Males	Females	Persons	Males	Females					Persons	Males	Females			
E07000103	Watford	96.8	48.0	48.8	697	328	369	9	6	15	7.2	989.2	1,142.4	858.4	6.0 u	4.0 u	9.9 u
E07000241	Welwyn Hatfield	122.0	60.4	61.6	962	459	503	6	5	10	7.9	892.5	1,071.6	769.7	4.3 u	3.6 u	7.1 u
E10000020	**Norfolk**	**892.9**	**438.7**	**454.2**	**9,903**	**4,983**	**4,920**	**29**	**19**	**51**	**11.1**	**923.4**	**1,099.8**	**781.9**	**3.2**	**2.1 u**	**5.6**
E07000143	Breckland	137.0	68.0	69.0	1,585	831	754	5	5	8	11.6	946.2	1,167.0	783.0	3.5 u	3.5 u	5.6 u
E07000144	Broadland	127.5	62.2	65.3	1,508	747	761	0	0	3	11.8	920.7	1,103.7	769.4	u	u	2.7 u
E07000145	Great Yarmouth	99.2	49.0	50.2	1,174	592	582	2	0	4	11.8	1,026.7	1,216.0	874.0	u	u	3.7 u
E07000146	King's Lynn and West Norfolk	151.6	74.3	77.3	1,751	870	881	7	3	12	11.6	930.2	1,083.3	809.0	4.4 u	1.9 u	7.6 u
E07000147	North Norfolk	103.8	50.5	53.3	1,435	710	725	2	2	4	13.8	873.8	1,039.8	734.7	u	u	5.1 u
E07000148	Norwich	141.0	70.0	71.0	1,103	564	539	6	4	13	7.8	960.5	1,156.8	794.2	3.5 u	2.3 u	7.5 u
E07000149	South Norfolk	132.8	64.7	68.1	1,347	669	678	7	5	7	10.1	849.7	984.5	743.6	5.2 u	3.7 u	5.2 u
E10000029	**Suffolk**	**745.3**	**367.7**	**377.5**	**7,568**	**3,692**	**3,876**	**25**	**19**	**54**	**10.2**	**869.5**	**1,008.9**	**757.3**	**3.2**	**2.4 u**	**6.8**
E07000200	Babergh	89.5	43.6	45.9	1,008	493	515	2	2	6	11.3	880.0	1,005.1	760.7			8.1 u
E07000201	Forest Heath	64.4	32.5	31.9	532	271	261	4	4	6	8.3	891.9	1,024.4	766.8	3.9 u	3.9 u	5.9 u
E07000202	Ipswich	135.9	67.9	68.0	1,137	565	572	4	4	10	8.4	938.9	1,103.1	807.1	2.0 u	2.0 u	5.0 u
E07000203	Mid Suffolk	100.0	49.4	50.6	938	452	486	1	0	3	9.4	810.9	906.0	723.0			3.6 u
E07000204	St Edmundsbury	112.9	56.6	56.4	1,087	521	566	1	1	11	9.6	858.4	990.9	755.3			9.6 u
E07000205	Suffolk Coastal	126.0	61.3	64.7	1,407	654	753	2	1	3	11.2	797.6	909.0	720.7			3.0 u
E07000206	Waveney	116.5	56.4	60.1	1,459	736	723	11	7	15	12.5	938.2	1,140.2	790.1	9.5 u	6.0 u	12.8 u
E12000007	**LONDON**	**8,787.9**	**4,379.3**	**4,408.6**	**48,607**	**24,511**	**24,096**	**419**	**294**	**865**	**5.5**	**858.8**	**1,013.3**	**734.6**	**3.3**	**2.3**	**6.7**
E13000001	**INNER LONDON**	**3,529.3**	**1,779.7**	**1,749.7**	**15,280**	**8,031**	**7,249**	**155**	**110**	**339**	**4.3**	**854.5**	**1,007.7**	**724.4**	**3.1**	**2.2**	**6.7**
E09000007	Camden	246.2	124.0	122.2	1,098	602	496	5	5	13	4.5	689.9	868.3	544.2	1.8 u	1.8 u	4.7 u
E09000001	City of London	9.4	5.2	4.2	41	27	14	1	0	0	4.4	557.1	797.9	361.6 u	u	u	u
E09000012	Hackney	273.5	136.3	137.2	1,095	588	507	20	18	39	4.0	948.9	1,110.0	809.3	4.5	4.0 u	8.7
E09000013	Hammersmith and Fulham	179.7	88.8	90.9	861	449	412	8	7	14	4.8	856.3	1,023.6	716.7	3.2 u	2.8 u	5.6 u
E09000014	Haringey	278.5	140.5	138.0	1,163	620	543	9	5	25	4.2	829.6	1,007.9	691.1	2.2 u	1.2 u	6.0
E09000019	Islington	232.9	117.2	115.7	1,001	521	480	4	2	13	4.3	888.3	1,009.4	781.3	1.4 u	u	4.4 u
E09000020	Kensington and Chelsea	156.7	78.4	78.3	807	419	388	3	0	7	5.1	667.4	765.8	568.5	1.7 u	u	4.0 u
E09000022	Lambeth	327.9	164.9	163.0	1,440	763	677	18	10	33	4.4	958.9	1,135.5	806.5	4.3 u	2.4 u	7.8
E09000023	Lewisham	301.9	149.1	152.8	1,467	731	736	12	10	30	4.9	905.5	1,072.2	785.0	2.5 u	2.1 u	6.3
E09000025	Newham	341.0	179.3	161.7	1,263	681	582	16	8	46	3.7	903.3	1,060.0	770.7	2.7 u	1.3 u	7.6
E09000028	Southwark	313.2	156.0	157.2	1,354	728	626	10	9	29	4.3	921.8	1,114.1	763.1	2.2 u	2.0 u	6.4
E09000030	Tower Hamlets	304.9	159.1	145.8	1,059	570	489	24	17	45	3.5	978.2	1,152.0	832.1	5.2	3.7 u	9.7
E09000032	Wandsworth	316.1	152.0	164.1	1,508	743	765	14	12	27	4.8	929.1	1,095.7	794.9	2.9 u	2.5 u	5.5
E09000033	Westminster	247.6	129.0	118.7	1,123	589	534	11	7	18	4.5	710.7	813.6	618.8	4.1 u	2.6 u	6.7 u
E13000002	**OUTER LONDON**	**5,258.5**	**2,599.6**	**2,658.9**	**33,327**	**16,480**	**16,847**	**264**	**184**	**526**	**6.3**	**858.5**	**1,014.0**	**737.5**	**3.4**	**2.3**	**6.7**
E09000002	Barking and Dagenham	206.5	101.4	105.0	1,191	611	580	16	11	29	5.8	1,005.9	1,255.4	823.2	4.0 u	2.8 u	7.3
E09000003	Barnet	386.1	190.8	195.2	2,430	1,195	1,235	9	6	33	6.3	787.3	940.7	669.8	1.7 u	1.1 u	6.2
E09000004	Bexley	244.8	118.2	126.6	2,005	968	1,037	9	3	18	8.2	897.2	1,095.4	765.5	2.9 u	1.0 u	5.8 u
E09000005	Brent	328.3	167.1	161.2	1,702	912	790	16	9	44	5.2	824.9	1,001.7	682.3	3.1 u	1.7 u	8.5
E09000006	Bromley	326.9	157.0	169.8	2,655	1,279	1,376	14	10	22	8.1	842.2	1,014.0	716.7	3.2 u	2.3 u	5.1
E09000008	Croydon	382.3	185.7	196.6	2,424	1,203	1,221	18	9	31	6.3	880.1	1,029.7	762.0	3.1 u	1.5 u	5.2
E09000009	Ealing	343.2	172.7	170.5	1,950	1,031	919	10	10	32	5.7	852.6	1,014.8	719.9	1.9 u	1.9 u	6.1

United Kingdom and constituent countries

Table 1a: Deaths (numbers and rates) by area of usual residence (administrative areas), 2016 registrations, United Kingdom and constituent countries
England and Wales: regions, unitary authorities/counties/districts
Scotland: council areas, Northern Ireland: local government districts

Area codes	Area of usual residence	Populations Number (thousands) All ages Persons	Males	Females	Deaths (numbers) All ages Persons	Males	Females	Infant (under 1 year)	Neonatal (under 4 weeks)	Perinatal (stillbirths and deaths under 1 week)	Crude death rate (deaths per 1,000 population)	Age-standardised mortality rate[1] Persons	Males	Females	Infant mortality rate (per 1,000 live births)	Neonatal mortality rate (per 1,000 live births)	Perinatal mortality rate (per 1,000 births and stillbirths)
E09000010	Enfield	331.4	161.8	169.6	2,017	1,040	977	19	11	35	6.1	861.4	1,079.0	697.9	3.8 u	2.2 u	7.0
E09000011	Greenwich	279.8	140.7	139.1	1,616	764	852	26	21	42	5.8	996.5	1,102.4	908.1	5.6	4.5	9.0
E09000015	Harrow	248.8	124.1	124.6	1,468	713	755	26	21	31	5.9	706.4	784.9	641.9	7.2	5.8	8.6
E09000016	Havering	252.8	121.5	131.3	2,387	1,136	1,251	9	8	26	9.4	942.9	1,146.7	796.6	2.6 u	2.3 u	7.6
E09000017	Hillingdon	302.5	151.8	150.6	1,833	908	925	5	4	28	6.1	848.9	970.4	747.6	1.1 u	0.9 u	6.2
E09000018	Hounslow	271.1	137.7	133.4	1,517	780	737	22	14	38	5.6	907.2	1,058.4	773.8	5.1	3.2 u	8.7
E09000021	Kingston upon Thames	176.1	86.8	89.3	1,067	513	554	15	14	20	6.1	802.9	935.4	693.3	6.8 u	6.4 u	9.0
E09000024	Merton	205.0	100.8	104.2	1,206	575	631	13	10	23	5.9	861.5	981.1	766.6	4.0 u	3.1 u	7.1
E09000026	Redbridge	299.2	149.3	149.9	1,738	830	908	10	8	21	5.8	845.7	955.7	757.6	2.1 u	1.7 u	4.4
E09000027	Richmond upon Thames	195.8	95.2	100.7	1,176	583	593	2	1	9	6.0	728.0	904.9	603.1	u	u	3.5 u
E09000029	Sutton	202.2	98.6	103.6	1,527	714	813	13	7	16	7.6	918.7	1,038.0	816.8	4.7 u	2.6 u	5.8 u
E09000031	Waltham Forest	275.8	138.3	137.6	1,418	725	693	12	7	28	5.1	872.1	1,040.7	742.3	2.6 u	1.5 u	5.9
E12000008	**SOUTH EAST**	**9,026.3**	**4,447.2**	**4,579.1**	**80,429**	**38,818**	**41,611**	**351**	**272**	**645**	**8.9**	**889.3**	**1,034.0**	**773.7**	**3.4**	**2.7**	**6.3**
E06000036	**Bracknell Forest**	**119.4**	**59.3**	**60.1**	**718**	**342**	**376**	**0**	**0**	**4**	**6.0**	**822.9**	**893.4**	**750.5**	**u**	**u**	**2.9 u**
E06000043	**Brighton and Hove**	**289.2**	**145.5**	**143.8**	**2,137**	**1,022**	**1,115**	**11**	**8**	**20**	**7.4**	**974.8**	**1,104.6**	**862.7**	**3.9 u**	**2.8 u**	**7.0**
E06000046	**Isle of Wight**	**139.8**	**68.3**	**71.5**	**1,760**	**846**	**914**	**4**	**3**	**4**	**12.6**	**928.6**	**1,077.2**	**803.8**	**3.5 u**	**2.6 u**	**3.5 u**
E06000035	**Medway**	**278.5**	**138.3**	**140.3**	**2,144**	**1,110**	**1,034**	**14**	**11**	**21**	**7.7**	**1,000.4**	**1,221.3**	**833.7**	**3.8 u**	**3.0 u**	**5.7**
E06000042	**Milton Keynes**	**264.5**	**130.9**	**133.5**	**1,761**	**867**	**894**	**19**	**14**	**23**	**6.7**	**990.8**	**1,156.8**	**863.6**	**5.2 u**	**3.8 u**	**6.3**
E06000044	**Portsmouth**	**214.8**	**109.5**	**105.3**	**1,746**	**878**	**868**	**7**	**6**	**15**	**8.1**	**1,070.1**	**1,289.0**	**891.1**	**2.7 u**	**2.3 u**	**5.8 u**
E06000038	**Reading**	**162.7**	**82.1**	**80.6**	**1,107**	**580**	**527**	**6**	**4**	**22**	**6.8**	**1,004.6**	**1,205.5**	**837.0**	**2.4 u**	**1.6 u**	**8.8**
E06000039	**Slough**	**147.2**	**74.1**	**73.1**	**859**	**452**	**407**	**16**	**14**	**28**	**5.8**	**1,057.5**	**1,272.0**	**887.4**	**6.1 u**	**5.3 u**	**10.6**
E06000045	**Southampton**	**254.3**	**129.9**	**124.4**	**1,924**	**962**	**962**	**16**	**14**	**32**	**7.6**	**1,063.6**	**1,268.6**	**897.0**	**5.0 u**	**4.4 u**	**10.0**
E06000037	**West Berkshire**	**156.8**	**77.6**	**79.2**	**1,231**	**616**	**615**	**9**	**8**	**11**	**7.8**	**869.1**	**998.6**	**757.4**	**5.1 u**	**4.5 u**	**6.2 u**
E06000040	**Windsor and Maidenhead**	**148.8**	**73.9**	**74.9**	**1,224**	**559**	**665**	**12**	**11**	**15**	**8.2**	**823.5**	**915.4**	**747.2**	**6.8 u**	**6.3 u**	**8.5 u**
E06000041	**Wokingham**	**161.9**	**79.7**	**82.2**	**1,194**	**591**	**603**	**5**	**4**	**11**	**7.4**	**828.1**	**993.4**	**705.2**	**2.8 u**	**2.2 u**	**6.1 u**
E10000002	**Buckinghamshire**	**534.7**	**262.4**	**272.4**	**4,069**	**1,938**	**2,131**	**24**	**19**	**41**	**7.6**	**784.6**	**909.9**	**690.4**	**3.9**	**3.1 u**	**6.7**
E07000004	Aylesbury Vale	193.1	95.5	97.6	1,392	652	740	6	2	9	7.2	852.9	980.8	762.0	2.6 u	u	3.9 u
E07000005	Chiltern	95.1	46.1	49.0	759	369	390	3	3	3	8.0	690.6	831.7	587.8	3.3 u	3.3 u	3.3 u
E07000006	South Bucks	69.6	33.6	36.0	695	302	393	5	4	8	10.0	849.1	934.6	782.2	6.6 u	5.3 u	10.6 u
E07000007	Wycombe	176.9	87.1	89.8	1,223	615	608	10	10	21	6.9	749.6	887.5	642.8	4.6 u	4.6 u	9.6
E10000011	**East Sussex**	**547.8**	**265.0**	**282.8**	**6,445**	**3,045**	**3,400**	**13**	**8**	**27**	**11.8**	**877.4**	**1,029.2**	**756.0**	**2.5 u**	**1.5 u**	**5.2**
E07000061	Eastbourne	103.1	49.9	53.1	1,284	589	695	2	0	8	12.5	903.8	1,041.5	787.8	u	u	7.6 u
E07000062	Hastings	92.2	45.0	47.3	1,040	522	518	5	4	10	11.3	1,113.1	1,337.2	924.1	4.5 u	3.6 u	8.9 u
E07000063	Lewes	101.4	49.3	52.1	1,121	535	586	1	1	4	11.1	807.9	977.0	683.5	u	u	4.4 u
E07000064	Rother	93.6	44.9	48.6	1,271	581	690	1	0	1	13.6	827.2	936.2	738.4	u	u	u
E07000065	Wealden	157.6	75.9	81.7	1,729	818	911	4	3	4	11.0	833.6	980.1	725.1	2.8 u	2.1 u	2.8 u
E10000014	**Hampshire**	**1,360.4**	**666.1**	**694.3**	**12,663**	**6,068**	**6,595**	**53**	**48**	**92**	**9.3**	**852.2**	**979.3**	**751.0**	**3.7**	**3.3**	**6.4**
E07000084	Basingstoke and Deane	174.6	86.5	88.1	1,319	667	652	9	8	15	7.6	900.2	1,042.9	784.0	4.1 u	3.7 u	6.8 u
E07000085	East Hampshire	118.0	56.9	61.0	1,203	561	642	4	3	8	10.2	872.2	984.0	774.8	3.9 u	2.9 u	7.8 u
E07000086	Eastleigh	129.6	63.5	66.1	1,030	474	556	5	5	14	7.9	805.5	873.5	742.8	3.5 u	3.5 u	9.6 u
E07000087	Fareham	115.4	56.6	58.8	1,263	616	647	5	5	7	10.9	935.9	1,094.4	815.4	4.8 u	4.8 u	6.7 u
E07000088	Gosport	85.4	42.5	42.9	815	391	424	3	2	5	9.5	958.3	1,081.4	849.2	3.2 u	u	5.4 u

Table 1a: Deaths (numbers and rates) by area of usual residence (administrative areas), 2016 registrations, United Kingdom and constituent countries
England and Wales: regions, unitary authorities/counties/districts
Scotland: council areas, Northern Ireland: local government districts

Area codes	Area of usual residence	Populations Number (thousands) All ages Persons	Males	Females	Deaths (numbers) All ages Persons	Males	Females	Infant (under 1 year)	Neonatal (under 4 weeks)	Perinatal (stillbirths and deaths under 1 week)	Crude death rate (deaths per 1,000 population)	Age-standardised mortality rate[1] Persons	Males	Females	Infant mortality rate (per 1,000 live births)	Neonatal mortality rate (per 1,000 live births)	Perinatal mortality rate (per 1,000 births and stillbirths)
E07000089	Hart	94.3	46.8	47.4	704	340	364	1	1	3	7.5	767.6	879.8	683.8	u	u	3.2 u
E07000090	Havant	123.6	59.9	63.8	1,367	667	700	7	6	10	11.1	920.6	1,059.7	809.8	5.3 u	4.5 u	7.5 u
E07000091	New Forest	179.2	86.3	93.0	2,120	1,010	1,110	6	6	9	11.8	761.8	896.3	656.1	4.0 u	4.0 u	6.1 u
E07000092	Rushmoor	96.3	48.6	47.7	703	339	364	5	5	8	7.3	1,010.1	1,197.1	882.0	3.5 u	3.5 u	5.7 u
E07000093	Test Valley	122.0	59.4	62.6	1,104	560	544	5	4	9	9.0	850.3	1,047.2	704.6	3.6 u	2.9 u	6.5 u
E07000094	Winchester	122.0	59.1	62.8	1,035	443	592	3	3	4	8.5	757.3	810.5	716.3	2.5 u	2.5 u	3.4 u
E10000016	**Kent**	**1,541.9**	**756.6**	**785.3**	**14,744**	**7,126**	**7,618**	**71**	**47**	**125**	**9.6**	**943.8**	**1,099.1**	**823.0**	**4.1**	**2.7**	**7.2**
E07000105	Ashford	126.2	61.3	64.8	1,077	518	559	8	7	15	8.5	891.4	1,036.5	782.7	5.1 u	4.5 u	9.5 u
E07000106	Canterbury	162.4	79.6	82.8	1,601	759	842	10	9	13	9.9	937.3	1,098.6	814.9	7.2 u	6.5 u	9.4 u
E07000107	Dartford	105.5	51.9	53.6	913	434	479	9	6	10	8.7	1,072.6	1,219.7	953.0	5.9 u	4.0 u	6.6 u
E07000108	Dover	114.2	56.2	58.0	1,296	629	667	3	2	8	11.3	999.7	1,129.9	874.1	2.6 u	u	6.8 u
E07000109	Gravesham	106.8	52.7	54.1	866	444	422	6	3	14	8.1	934.0	1,106.8	794.4	4.2 u	2.1 u	9.8 u
E07000110	Maidstone	166.4	82.2	84.1	1,519	718	801	5	3	10	9.1	958.7	1,125.2	837.8	2.5 u	1.5 u	4.9 u
E07000111	Sevenoaks	119.1	57.8	61.4	1,002	495	507	2	0	11	8.4	774.8	938.9	656.5	u	u	8.8 u
E07000112	Shepway	111.2	54.9	56.3	1,259	603	656	3	3	9	11.3	929.1	1,068.0	826.3	2.8 u	2.8 u	8.5 u
E07000113	Swale	145.0	71.8	73.3	1,322	634	688	8	4	8	9.1	1,002.4	1,104.6	905.1	4.4 u	2.2 u	4.4 u
E07000114	Thanet	140.7	68.1	72.6	1,798	873	925	8	5	13	12.8	1,097.1	1,309.9	937.9	5.2 u	3.2 u	8.3 u
E07000115	Tonbridge and Malling	127.3	62.3	65.0	1,025	521	504	5	4	6	8.1	866.0	1,044.8	739.4	3.5 u	2.8 u	4.2 u
E07000116	Tunbridge Wells	117.1	57.8	59.3	1,066	498	568	4	1	8	9.1	873.0	1,011.8	768.1	3.4 u	u	6.7 u
E10000025	**Oxfordshire**	**683.2**	**340.6**	**342.6**	**5,435**	**2,638**	**2,797**	**18**	**16**	**42**	**8.0**	**849.2**	**980.4**	**738.8**	**2.3 u**	**2.1 u**	**5.4**
E07000177	Cherwell	146.3	72.5	73.8	1,237	588	649	5	4	9	8.5	933.5	1,036.7	840.7	2.7 u	2.2 u	4.9 u
E07000178	Oxford	161.3	82.2	79.1	907	442	465	5	4	14	5.6	861.1	997.4	743.1	2.8 u	2.2 u	7.7 u
E07000179	South Oxfordshire	138.1	68.0	70.1	1,226	606	620	3	3	8	8.9	831.6	990.4	706.2	1.9 u	1.9 u	5.2 u
E07000180	Vale of White Horse	128.7	64.3	64.5	1,033	517	516	3	3	6	8.0	764.2	915.9	642.0	2.1 u	2.1 u	4.2 u
E07000181	West Oxfordshire	108.7	53.6	55.0	1,032	485	547	2	2	5	9.5	866.1	961.6	779.8	u	u	4.4 u
E10000030	**Surrey**	**1,176.5**	**577.5**	**599.0**	**10,234**	**4,913**	**5,321**	**34**	**26**	**68**	**8.7**	**842.7**	**981.3**	**733.8**	**2.5**	**1.9**	**5.0**
E07000207	Elmbridge	132.8	64.0	68.8	1,078	533	545	8	7	14	8.1	774.2	944.2	645.1	4.9 u	4.3 u	8.5 u
E07000208	Epsom and Ewell	79.6	38.7	40.9	619	305	314	3	3	3	7.8	817.0	966.1	701.0	3.2 u	3.2 u	3.2 u
E07000209	Guildford	148.0	74.2	73.8	1,101	523	578	5	5	5	7.4	831.1	948.7	734.0	3.3 u	2.0 u	3.3 u
E07000210	Mole Valley	86.2	42.1	44.1	881	457	424	0	0	5	10.2	819.3	1,024.8	660.7	u	u	6.5 u
E07000211	Reigate and Banstead	145.6	71.2	74.4	1,323	626	697	1	1	6	9.1	896.6	1,070.3	774.0	u	u	3.3 u
E07000212	Runnymede	86.9	42.4	44.5	736	357	379	2	2	3	8.5	886.4	1,038.8	775.8	u	u	3.1 u
E07000213	Spelthorne	98.9	48.8	50.1	868	405	463	5	4	11	8.8	877.8	966.7	797.4	3.7 u	3.0 u	8.1 u
E07000214	Surrey Heath	88.4	43.8	44.6	768	355	413	1	1	3	8.7	858.7	973.7	782.7	u	u	3.4 u
E07000215	Tandridge	86.7	42.2	44.4	819	400	419	0	0	3	9.5	858.1	988.2	742.3	u	u	3.1 u
E07000216	Waverley	123.8	60.5	63.3	1,189	566	623	3	3	7	9.6	787.5	951.3	665.5	2.4 u	2.4 u	5.6 u
E07000217	Woking	99.7	49.6	50.1	852	386	466	6	6	8	8.5	913.7	942.4	880.2	4.5 u	2.2 u	6.0 u
E10000032	**West Sussex**	**843.8**	**410.0**	**433.8**	**9,034**	**4,265**	**4,769**	**19**	**11**	**44**	**10.7**	**880.1**	**1,026.1**	**764.3**	**2.2 u**	**1.3 u**	**5.0**
E07000223	Adur	63.5	30.9	32.6	666	305	361	0	0	3	10.5	860.8	955.5	778.5	u	u	4.5 u
E07000224	Arun	157.0	75.2	81.8	2,219	1,048	1,171	7	3	8	14.1	957.9	1,113.2	836.4	4.5 u	1.9 u	5.1 u
E07000225	Chichester	118.2	56.9	61.3	1,415	703	712	0	0	5	12.0	842.6	1,034.0	681.9	u	u	5.2 u
E07000226	Crawley	111.4	55.7	55.7	759	346	413	3	3	7	6.8	900.1	964.1	847.9	1.9 u	1.9 u	4.4 u
E07000227	Horsham	138.0	67.1	70.9	1,262	581	681	1	1	8	9.1	787.8	891.3	712.1	u	u	6.0 u

Table 1a: Deaths (numbers and rates) by area of usual residence (administrative areas), 2016 registrations, United Kingdom and constituent countries
England and Wales: regions, unitary authorities/counties/districts
Scotland: council areas, Northern Ireland: local government districts

United Kingdom and constituent countries

Area codes	Area of usual residence	Populations (Number thousands) Persons	Males	Females	Deaths All ages Persons	Males	Females	Infant (under 1 year)	Neonatal (under 4 weeks)	Perinatal (stillbirths and deaths under 1 week)	Crude death rate (deaths per 1,000 population)	Age-standardised mortality rate[1] Persons	Males	Females	Infant mortality rate (per 1,000 live births)	Neonatal mortality rate (per 1,000 live births)	Perinatal mortality rate (per 1,000 births and stillbirths)
E07000228	Mid Sussex	147.1	71.9	75.2	1,343	653	690	5	1	3	9.1	833.8	997.0	694.5	3.1 u	u	1.9 u
E07000229	Worthing	108.6	52.3	56.3	1,370	629	741	3	3	10	12.6	971.6	1,162.1	839.3	2.7 u	2.7	9.0 u
E12000009	SOUTH WEST	5,516.0	2,711.6	2,804.4	57,116	27,636	29,480	180	130	298	10.4	926.7	1,081.6	803.1	3.1	2.3	5.2
E06000022	Bath and North East Somerset	187.8	92.6	95.1	1,719	866	853	4	1	6	9.2	909.2	1,110.6	750.3	2.2 u	u	3.3 u
E06000028	Bournemouth	197.7	99.6	98.0	2,006	975	1,031	9	7	13	10.1	990.7	1,164.3	842.5	4.1 u	3.2 u	5.9 u
E06000023	Bristol, City of	454.2	227.4	226.8	3,379	1,646	1,733	24	17	33	7.4	1,016.2	1,189.5	876.6	3.8	2.7 u	5.1
E06000052, E06000053	Cornwall and Isles of Scilly[4]	556.0	269.8	286.1	6,306	3,066	3,240	18	15	33	11.3	961.0	1,117.2	833.9	3.4 u	2.8 u	6.2
E06000024	North Somerset	211.7	103.1	108.6	2,431	1,160	1,271	4	2	7	11.5	946.6	1,107.8	816.1	1.8 u	u	3.2 u
E06000026	Plymouth	264.2	131.5	132.7	2,474	1,173	1,301	2	2	13	9.4	1,026.4	1,137.7	928.2	u	u	4.4 u
E06000029	Poole	151.5	74.5	77.0	1,652	751	901	3	1	7	10.9	919.5	1,020.8	828.4	1.9 u	u	4.4 u
E06000025	South Gloucestershire	277.6	137.9	139.8	2,222	1,111	1,111	10	8	17	8.0	846.1	998.6	726.2	3.2 u	2.6 u	5.5 u
E06000030	Swindon	217.9	108.7	109.3	1,700	863	837	8	8	12	7.8	960.0	1,135.5	821.8	2.8 u	2.8 u	4.2 u
E06000027	Torbay	133.9	64.9	69.0	1,854	892	962	4	4	6	13.8	1,045.8	1,215.9	907.6	3.0 u	3.0 u	4.6 u
E06000054	Wiltshire	488.4	241.2	247.2	4,613	2,182	2,431	11	8	31	9.4	880.5	1,009.4	782.6	2.1 u	1.6 u	6.0
E10000008	Devon	779.8	380.3	399.5	8,965	4,274	4,691	28	21	38	11.5	900.6	1,053.6	783.5	4.0	3.0	5.4
E07000040	East Devon	139.9	67.6	72.3	1,932	902	1,030	3	3	5	13.8	854.2	976.4	764.9	2.6 u	2.6 u	4.4 u
E07000041	Exeter	129.8	64.3	65.5	1,108	540	568	5	4	10	8.5	967.2	1,229.8	788.1	3.9 u	3.1 u	7.7 u
E07000042	Mid Devon	79.8	39.0	40.8	814	405	409	1	1	4	10.2	875.4	1,026.9	749.4	u	u	5.4 u
E07000043	North Devon	94.6	46.3	48.3	1,150	564	586	1	1	3	12.2	968.7	1,142.4	840.6	u	u	3.2 u
E07000044	South Hams	84.3	40.7	43.6	940	439	501	4	3	6	11.1	833.7	909.7	763.7	6.7 u	5.0 u	10.0 u
E07000045	Teignbridge	129.9	62.9	67.0	1,568	740	828	4	2	5	12.1	898.4	1,082.1	763.1	3.5 u	u	4.3 u
E07000046	Torridge	67.0	32.8	34.2	795	377	418	4	3	3	11.9	946.2	1,047.1	855.2	6.3 u	4.7 u	4.7 u
E07000047	West Devon	54.6	26.6	27.9	658	307	351	6	4	2	12.1	911.8	1,050.4	810.7	12.9 u	8.6 u	
E10000009	Dorset	422.7	206.3	216.4	5,310	2,574	2,736	15	10	16	12.6	861.8	1,001.3	744.2	4.4 u	3.0 u	4.7 u
E07000048	Christchurch	49.5	23.8	25.6	682	326	356	0	0	0	13.8	809.7	958.9	704.0			
E07000049	East Dorset	89.1	42.9	46.2	1,157	567	590	1	1	0	13.0	789.0	917.7	685.3			
E07000050	North Dorset	71.1	35.5	35.6	752	351	401	2	2	5	10.6	828.4	946.1	736.7			7.9 u
E07000051	Purbeck	46.3	22.9	23.4	512	260	252	2	1	2	11.0	822.1	956.6	703.1			
E07000052	West Dorset	101.4	48.8	52.6	1,402	693	709	8	6	6	13.8	906.0	1,083.6	751.2	10.5 u		7.8 u
E07000053	Weymouth and Portland	65.4	32.3	33.1	805	377	428	2	1	3	12.3	1,018.5	1,104.0	922.2			4.6 u
E10000013	Gloucestershire	623.1	305.3	317.9	6,441	3,154	3,287	22	14	38	10.3	964.5	1,141.6	823.6	3.3	2.1 u	5.6
E07000078	Cheltenham	117.5	57.4	60.1	1,194	565	629	4	3	5	10.2	972.6	1,136.2	831.6	3.0 u	2.3 u	3.8 u
E07000079	Cotswold	85.8	41.5	44.3	908	423	485	2	0	3	10.6	820.0	923.9	734.2			4.1 u
E07000080	Forest of Dean	85.4	42.0	43.4	971	456	515	1	1	5	11.4	995.8	1,132.9	892.4			5.9 u
E07000081	Gloucester	128.5	63.4	65.1	1,151	608	543	5	4	17	9.0	1,041.9	1,292.9	839.1	2.8 u	2.3 u	9.5 u
E07000082	Stroud	117.4	57.7	59.7	1,305	655	650	8	5	5	11.1	1,040.8	1,298.8	862.0	7.3 u	4.6 u	4.6 u
E07000083	Tewkesbury	88.6	43.4	45.2	912	447	465	2	1	3	10.3	908.6	1,076.7	779.4			3.1 u
E10000027	Somerset	549.4	268.3	281.1	6,044	2,949	3,095	18	12	28	11.0	892.8	1,060.7	766.8	3.3 u	2.2 u	5.1
E07000187	Mendip	112.5	54.8	57.8	1,122	545	577	1	0	3	10.0	863.3	1,026.3	741.9			2.8 u

Rates

Table 1a: Deaths (numbers and rates) by area of usual residence (administrative areas), 2016 registrations, United Kingdom and constituent countries
England and Wales: regions, unitary authorities/counties/districts
Scotland: council areas, Northern Ireland: local government districts

Area codes	Area of usual residence	Populations Number (thousands) All ages Persons	Males	Females	Deaths (numbers) All ages Persons	Males	Females	Infant (under 1 year)	Neonatal (under 4 weeks)	Perinatal (stillbirths and deaths under 1 week)	Crude death rate (deaths per 1,000 population)	Age-standardised mortality rate[1] Persons	Males	Females	Infant mortality rate (per 1,000 live births)	Neonatal mortality rate (per 1,000 live births)	Perinatal mortality rate (per 1,000 births and stillbirths)
E07000188	Sedgemoor	121.4	59.6	61.8	1,225	615	610	4	3	7	10.1	872.4	1,055.1	736.6	3.1 u	2.3 u	5.4 u
E07000189	South Somerset	165.6	81.3	84.3	1,851	927	924	6	4	11	11.2	890.8	1,075.3	748.2	3.6 u	2.4 u	6.6 u
E07000190	Taunton Deane	115.5	56.1	59.4	1,336	642	694	7	5	5	11.6	949.5	1,122.1	819.6	5.8 u	4.1 u	4.1 u
E07000191	West Somerset	34.3	16.5	17.8	510	220	290	0	0	2	14.9	888.7	962.9	841.3	u	u	u
W92000004	**WALES**	**3,113.2**	**1,534.0**	**1,579.1**	**33,066**	**16,382**	**16,684**	**101**	**66**	**217**	**10.6**	**1,045.7**	**1,227.3**	**898.8**	**3.1**	**2.0**	**6.6**
W06000001	Isle of Anglesey	69.7	34.3	35.4	821	402	419	7	5	7	11.8	974.0	1,131.6	841.8	9.8 u	7.0 u	9.7 u
W06000002	Gwynedd	123.6	61.3	62.4	1,318	654	664	8	8	11	10.7	937.8	1,122.3	778.1	6.9 u	6.9 u	9.5 u
W06000003	Conwy	116.5	56.7	59.8	1,470	733	737	1	1	3	12.6	906.0	1,084.2	757.3	u	u	2.9 u
W06000004	Denbighshire	94.8	46.7	48.1	1,258	640	618	2	2	3	13.3	1,199.6	1,367.1	1,029.6	u	u	3.0 u
W06000005	Flintshire	154.4	76.1	78.3	1,514	757	757	9	9	16	9.8	1,012.4	1,154.2	894.8	5.7	5.7	10.0 u
W06000006	Wrexham	136.7	68.3	68.4	1,425	660	765	4	1	11	10.4	1,114.0	1,187.8	1,038.5	2.7 u	u	7.3 u
W06000023	Powys	132.2	65.4	66.8	1,561	799	762	4	1	5	11.8	903.2	1,098.2	745.5	3.4 u	u	4.2 u
W06000008	Ceredigion	74.1	37.2	37.0	780	385	395	1	1	4	10.5	891.6	1,023.9	761.0	u	u	6.5 u
W06000009	Pembrokeshire	124.0	60.9	63.1	1,435	721	714	0	0	10	11.6	941.2	1,096.6	800.9	u	u	8.7 u
W06000010	Carmarthenshire	185.6	90.8	94.8	2,266	1,143	1,123	3	1	11	12.2	1,083.3	1,287.5	921.6	1.6 u	u	5.8 u
W06000011	Swansea	244.5	122.3	122.2	2,685	1,319	1,366	10	8	15	11.0	1,107.9	1,294.7	955.7	4.0 u	3.2 u	6.0 u
W06000012	Neath Port Talbot	141.6	69.6	72.0	1,690	825	865	4	1	11	11.9	1,185.7	1,433.8	1,027.6	2.6 u	u	7.2 u
W06000013	Bridgend	143.2	70.9	72.2	1,543	765	778	3	3	11	10.8	1,122.3	1,327.2	974.6	2.0 u	2.0 u	7.3 u
W06000014	Vale of Glamorgan	128.5	62.5	66.0	1,301	653	648	5	2	11	10.1	978.4	1,228.8	802.6	3.8 u	u	8.3 u
W06000015	Cardiff	361.5	178.1	183.3	2,821	1,398	1,423	11	5	34	7.8	1,025.4	1,246.4	852.2	2.5 u	1.1 u	7.6
W06000016	Rhondda Cynon Taf	238.3	116.9	121.4	2,487	1,209	1,278	7	6	14	10.4	1,143.3	1,311.0	1,005.7	2.5 u	2.2 u	5.0 u
W06000024	Merthyr Tydfil	59.8	29.4	30.4	637	311	326	1	1	7	10.7	1,187.3	1,356.4	1,055.2	u	u	9.7 u
W06000018	Caerphilly	180.5	88.4	92.1	1,797	890	907	1	1	7	10.0	1,117.8	1,282.0	986.0	u	u	3.5 u
W06000019	Blaenau Gwent	69.6	34.3	35.3	817	418	399	5	4	6	11.7	1,234.8	1,532.3	1,036.1	6.9 u	5.5 u	8.2 u
W06000020	Torfaen	92.1	44.8	47.2	986	489	497	3	1	3	10.7	1,060.5	1,245.3	907.7	3.0 u	u	3.0 u
W06000021	Monmouthshire	92.8	45.8	47.1	982	489	493	3	1	5	10.6	872.6	1,035.2	746.7	4.1 u	u	6.7 u
W06000022	Newport	149.1	73.3	75.8	1,472	722	750	9	5	12	9.9	1,118.7	1,316.1	968.4	4.7 u	2.6 u	6.3 u
J99000001	**Outside England and Wales**	:	:	:	**1,191**	**708**	**483**	**23**	**8**	**58**	:	:	:	:	:	:	:
S92000003	**SCOTLAND[5]**	**5,404.7**	**2,627.5**	**2,777.2**	**56,728**	**27,760**	**28,968**	**181**	**121**	**326**	**10.5**	**1,136.4**	**1,326.5**	**988.5**	**3.3**	**2.2**	**6.0**
	Council areas																
S12000033	Aberdeen City	229.8	114.1	115.7	2,129	1,024	1,105	8	5	16	9.3	1,150.5	1,321.6	1,003.6	3.2 u	2.0 u	6.3 u
S12000034	Aberdeenshire	262.2	130.4	131.8	2,360	1,170	1,190	7	6	16	9.0	1,026.2	1,173.8	903.5	2.5 u	2.1 u	5.7 u
S12000041	Angus	116.5	56.8	59.8	1,433	693	740	5	4	5	12.3	1,095.3	1,277.9	960.2	4.9 u	3.9 u	4.9 u
S12000035	Argyll and Bute	87.1	43.3	43.8	1,110	560	550	1	1	2	12.7	1,100.5	1,338.9	908.7	u	u	u
S12000036	City of Edinburgh	507.2	246.8	260.4	4,361	2,092	2,269	20	17	23	8.6	1,057.9	1,244.3	912.7	3.8	3.2 u	4.3
S12000005	Clackmannanshire	51.4	25.2	26.2	546	263	283	1	0	5	10.6	1,201.8	1,329.1	1,091.4	u	u	9.8 u
S12000006	Dumfries and Galloway	149.5	72.5	77.0	1,858	971	887	6	3	13	12.4	1,055.3	1,282.9	875.5	4.6 u	2.3 u	9.8 u
S12000042	Dundee City	148.3	71.4	76.8	1,691	822	869	12	11	19	11.4	1,246.4	1,468.7	1,080.8	7.6 u	7.0 u	12.0 u
S12000008	East Ayrshire	122.2	59.3	62.9	1,453	709	744	2	2	5	11.9	1,263.8	1,445.3	1,125.8	u	u	3.9 u
S12000045	East Dunbartonshire	107.5	52.0	55.5	1,114	514	600	2	0	3	10.4	943.3	1,054.4	858.8	u	u	3.1 u
S12000010	East Lothian	104.1	49.8	54.3	1,001	476	525	4	3	9	9.6	989.3	1,117.2	881.5	3.8 u	2.9 u	8.6 u
S12000011	East Renfrewshire	93.8	44.6	49.2	883	397	486	1	1	5	9.4	906.5	1,054.9	803.4	u	u	5.8 u
S12000014	Falkirk	159.4	78.0	81.4	1,734	844	890	8	5	15	10.9	1,223.4	1,380.0	1,087.6	5.1 u	3.2 u	9.5 u

Table 1a: Deaths (numbers and rates) by area of usual residence (administrative areas), 2016 registrations, United Kingdom and constituent countries
England and Wales: regions, unitary authorities/counties/districts
Scotland: council areas, Northern Ireland: local government districts

Area codes	Area of usual residence	Populations Number (thousands) All ages			Deaths (numbers) All ages			Infant (under 1 year)	Neonatal (under 4 weeks)	Perinatal (stillbirths and deaths under 1 week)	Crude death rate (deaths per 1,000 population)	Age-standardised mortality rate[1]			Rates Infant mortality rate (per 1,000 live births)	Neonatal mortality rate (per 1,000 live births)	Perinatal mortality rate (per 1,000 births and stillbirths)
		Persons	Males	Females	Persons	Males	Females					Persons	Males	Females			
S12000015	Fife	370.3	179.6	190.8	4,091	1,967	2,124	24	17	34	11.0	1,143.9	1,301.2	1,019.9	6.4	4.5 u	9.0
S12000046	Glasgow City	615.1	299.0	316.0	6,321	3,142	3,179	29	15	60	10.3	1,389.1	1,696.9	1,162.7	4.2	2.2 u	8.7
S12000017	Highland	234.8	114.8	119.9	2,397	1,260	1,137	3	2	9	10.2	994.2	1,226.6	812.7	1.4 u	u	u
S12000018	Inverclyde	79.2	37.8	41.3	1,006	491	515	1	1	0	12.7	1,235.9	1,520.9	1,032.9	u	u	4.2 u
S12000019	Midlothian	88.6	42.6	46.0	848	425	423	2	1	4	9.6	1,079.0	1,256.7	939.7	u	u	u
S12000020	Moray	96.1	47.7	48.4	979	494	485	1	1	1	10.2	1,008.8	1,197.0	863.6	u	u	3.7 u
S12000013	Na h-Eileanan Siar	26.9	13.3	13.6	359	183	176	0	0	1	13.3	1,093.0	1,396.3	899.9	u	u	u
S12000021	North Ayrshire	135.9	64.7	71.2	1,593	800	793	8	3	6	11.7	1,148.7	1,381.0	976.3	6.4 u	2.4 u	4.8 u
S12000044	North Lanarkshire	339.4	164.2	175.1	3,568	1,791	1,777	4	1	21	10.5	1,300.6	1,522.2	1,127.5	1.1 u	u	5.9
S12000023	Orkney Islands	21.9	10.9	11.0	223	100	123	0	0	0	10.2	948.5	979.8	921.8	u	u	u
S12000024	Perth and Kinross	150.7	74.0	76.7	1,617	750	867	8	5	7	10.7	945.6	1,045.6	859.8	6.0 u	3.8 u	5.3 u
S12000038	Renfrewshire	175.9	84.7	91.2	2,070	1,015	1,055	2	0	4	11.8	1,264.8	1,481.1	1,104.5	u	u	2.3 u
S12000026	Scottish Borders	114.5	55.5	59.0	1,277	635	642	2	1	2	11.1	990.1	1,174.5	853.9	u	u	u
S12000027	Shetland Islands	23.2	11.8	11.4	232	122	110	0	0	0	10.0	1,124.5	1,464.0	918.1	u	u	u
S12000028	South Ayrshire	112.5	53.7	58.8	1,445	683	762	3	3	6	12.8	1,098.1	1,257.2	983.6	3.1 u	3.1 u	6.1 u
S12000029	South Lanarkshire	317.1	153.0	164.1	3,529	1,697	1,832	9	7	14	11.1	1,196.7	1,380.5	1,050.9	2.7 u	2.1 u	4.2 u
S12000030	Stirling	93.8	45.1	48.7	899	436	463	0	0	7	9.6	1,046.3	1,219.6	909.8	u	u	8.6 u
S12000039	West Dunbartonshire	89.9	42.7	47.1	1,050	493	557	1	1	5	11.7	1,300.9	1,520.0	1,147.3	u	u	5.2 u
S12000040	West Lothian	180.1	88.3	91.9	1,551	741	810	7	5	9	8.6	1,135.0	1,233.3	1,053.3	3.5 u	2.5 u	4.5 u
N92000002	NORTHERN IRELAND[6]	1,862.1	915.2	946.9	15,430	7,430	8,000	112	86	151	8.3	1015.9	1177.6	892.9	4.6	3.5	6.2
	Local Government District																
N09000001	Antrim and Newtownabbey	141.0	68.5	72.5	1,183	535	648	5	3	10	8.4	1,031.9	1,159.4	953.0	2.8 u	1.7 u	5.7 u
N09000011	Ards and North Down	159.6	77.3	82.2	1,550	700	850	2	2	8	9.7	985.7	1,114.1	897.7	u	u	4.8 u
N09000002	Craigavon	210.3	104.3	105.9	1,503	736	767	18	15	17	7.1	942.3	1,062.4	834.8	6.1 u	5.1 u	5.7 u
N09000003	Belfast	339.6	164.4	175.1	3,112	1,485	1,627	19	16	31	9.2	1,139.3	1,358.1	975.2	4.1 u	3.5 u	6.7
N09000005	Causeway Coast and Glens	143.5	71.2	72.4	1,128	580	548	9	5	13	7.9	918.4	1,136.1	765.3	5.4 u	3.0 u	7.8 u
N09000005	Derry City and Strabane	150.1	73.7	76.4	1,143	570	573	11	9	17	7.6	1,079.8	1,231.9	966.2	5.2 u	4.3 u	8.1 u
N09000006	Fermanagh and Omagh	115.8	58.0	57.8	951	481	470	5	4	7	8.2	1,006.4	1,176.7	868.1	3.3 u	2.6 u	4.6 u
N09000007	Lisburn and Castlereagh	141.2	69.2	72.0	1,167	550	617	11	8	14	8.3	955.3	1,126.3	842.7	6.3 u	4.6 u	8.0 u
N09000008	Mid and East Antrim	137.8	67.5	70.3	1,280	615	665	9	5	9	9.3	1,006.0	1,195.0	866.8	5.7 u	3.2 u	5.7 u
N09000009	Mid Ulster	145.4	73.0	72.4	1,059	512	547	10	8	13	7.3	1,024.5	1,195.0	910.3	4.7 u	3.7 u	6.0 u
N09000010	Newry, Mourne and Down	177.8	88.1	89.7	1,354	666	688	13	11	12	7.6	988.1	1,099.5	871.6	5.1 u	4.4 u	4.7 u

Note: Infant, neonatal and perinatal mortality rates for local areas can fluctuate quite substantially between years due to the small number of deaths recorded at these ages.

1 The age-standardised mortality rates for 2016 are standardised to the 2013 European Standard Population, expressed per 100,000 population. Age-standardised rates are used to allow comparison between populations which may contain different proportions of people of different ages. ASMRs are based on mid-2016 population estimates. For more information on these rates please see our User guide to mortality statistics.

2 K04000001 is England and Wales; J99000001 is Elsewhere (outside England and Wales).

3 The deaths of those whose usual residence is outside England and Wales are included in total figures for England and Wales, but excluded from any sub-division of England and Wales.

4 The Isles of Scilly were recoded on 1 April 2009. They are separately administered by an Isles of Scilly council and do not form part of Cornwall but, for the purposes of the representation of statistical data, they have been combined with Cornwall.

5 The deaths of those whose usual residence is outside Scotland are included in total figures for Scotland, and are also included in any sub-division of Scotland based on where the death occurred.

6 The deaths of those whose usual residence is outside Northern Ireland are included in total figures for Northern Ireland, and are also included in any sub-division of Northern Ireland based on where the death occurred.

Source: Office for National Statistics, National Records Scotland, Northern Ireland Statistics and Research Agency

Released: 27 November 2017

United Kingdom
and constituent countries

Table 1b: Deaths (numbers and rates) by area of usual residence (regions/health areas), 2016 registrations, United Kingdom and constituent countries
England: Regions, Wales: Local Health Boards
Scotland: NHS Board Areas, Northern Ireland: Health and Social Care Trusts

Area codes	Area of usual residence	Populations (thousands) Number, All ages			Deaths (numbers) All ages			Infant (under 1 year)	Neonatal (under 4 weeks)	Perinatal (stillbirths and deaths under 1 week)	Crude death rate (deaths per 1,000 population)	Rates, Age-standardised mortality rate[1]			Infant mortality rate (per 1,000 live births)	Neonatal mortality rate (per 1,000 live births)	Perinatal mortality rate (per 1,000 live births and stillbirths)
		Persons	Males	Females	Persons	Males	Females					Persons	Males	Females			
K02000001	UNITED KINGDOM	65,648.1	32,377.7	33,270.4	597,206	293,001	304,205	3,004	2,136	5,125	9.1	982.5	1,145.9	852.5	3.9	2.8	6.6
K04000001, J99000001[2]	ENGLAND, WALES AND ELSEWHERE[3]	58,381.2	28,835.0	29,546.3	525,048	257,811	267,237	2,711	1,929	4,648	9.0	966.9	1,128.4	838.2	3.9	2.8	6.6
E92000001	ENGLAND	55,268.1	27,300.9	27,967.1	490,791	240,721	250,070	2,587	1,855	4,373	8.9	959.8	1,119.5	832.7	3.9	2.8	6.6
	Regions																
E12000001	North East	2,636.8	1,294.4	1,342.5	27,836	13,624	14,212	99	71	157	10.6	1,098.9	1,272.6	963.2	3.5	2.5	5.5
E12000002	North West	7,219.6	3,560.9	3,658.7	71,315	34,858	36,457	419	284	580	9.9	1,069.4	1,233.1	937.6	4.9	3.3	6.7
E12000003	Yorkshire and The Humber	5,425.7	2,678.3	2,747.5	51,513	25,319	26,194	234	152	433	9.5	1,029.6	1,209.3	891.1	3.7	2.4	6.8
E12000004	East Midlands	4,724.4	2,335.0	2,389.4	44,027	21,720	22,307	215	163	375	9.3	979.8	1,143.3	851.2	4.0	3.1	7.0
E12000005	West Midlands	5,800.7	2,872.6	2,928.1	53,814	26,839	26,975	440	325	586	9.3	989.3	1,171.7	844.9	6.2	4.6	8.2
E12000006	East	6,130.5	3,021.7	3,108.9	56,134	27,396	28,738	230	164	434	9.2	912.4	1,059.2	795.3	3.2	2.3	6.0
E12000007	London	8,787.9	4,379.3	4,408.6	48,607	24,511	24,096	419	294	865	5.5	858.8	1,013.3	734.6	3.3	2.3	6.7
E12000008	South East	9,026.3	4,447.2	4,579.1	80,429	38,818	41,611	351	272	645	8.9	889.3	1,034.0	773.7	3.4	2.7	6.3
E12000009	South West	5,516.0	2,711.6	2,804.4	57,116	27,636	29,480	180	130	298	10.4	926.7	1,081.6	803.1	3.1	2.3	5.2
W92000004	WALES	3,113.2	1,534.0	1,579.1	33,066	16,382	16,684	101	66	217	10.6	1,045.7	1,227.3	898.8	3.1	2.0	6.6
	Local Health Boards																
W11000023	Betsi Cadwaladr University Health Board	695.8	343.4	352.4	7,806	3,846	3,960	31	26	51	11.2	1,009.8	1,161.8	876.2	4.4	3.7	7.2
W11000024	Powys Teaching Health Board	132.2	65.4	66.8	1,561	799	762	4	1	5	11.8	903.2	1,098.2	745.5	3.4 u	u	4.2 u
W11000025	Hywel Dda University Health Board	383.7	188.9	194.8	4,481	2,249	2,232	4	2	25	11.7	996.9	1,168.6	849.1	1.1 u	u	6.9
W11000026	Abertawe Bro Morgannwg University Health Board	529.3	262.9	266.4	5,918	2,909	3,009	17	12	37	11.2	1,131.6	1,335.1	979.2	3.1 u	2.2 u	6.7
W11000027	Cwm Taf University Health Board	298.1	146.3	151.9	3,124	1,520	1,604	8	7	21	10.5	1,152.0	1,320.3	1,015.7	2.3 u	2.0 u	6.0
W11000028	Aneurin Bevan University Health Board	584.1	286.6	297.5	6,054	3,008	3,046	21	11	33	10.4	1,073.5	1,261.4	927.3	3.3	1.7 u	5.1
W11000029	Cardiff and Vale University Health Board	489.9	240.6	249.3	4,122	2,051	2,071	16	7	45	8.4	1,007.5	1,235.1	834.6	2.8 u	1.2 u	7.8
J99000001	Outside England and Wales	..	..	..	1,191	708	483	23	8	58	..	..	..	..	..	..	..
S92000003	SCOTLAND[4]	5,404.7	2,627.5	2,777.2	56,728	27,760	28,968	181	121	326	10.5	1,136.4	1,326.5	988.5	3.3	2.2	6.0
	Health Boards																
S08000015	Ayrshire and Arran	370.6	177.6	193.0	4,491	2,192	2,299	13	8	17	12.1	1,163.7	1,356.0	1,020.9	3.7 u	2.3 u	4.9 u
S08000016	Borders	114.5	55.5	59.0	1,277	635	642	2	1	2	11.1	990.1	1,174.5	853.9	u	u	u
S08000017	Dumfries and Galloway	149.5	72.5	77.0	1,858	971	887	6	3	13	12.4	1,055.3	1,282.9	875.5	4.6 u	2.3 u	9.8 u
S08000018	Fife	370.3	179.6	190.8	4,091	1,967	2,124	24	17	34	11.0	1,143.9	1,301.2	1,019.9	6.4	4.5 u	9.0
S08000019	Forth Valley	304.5	148.3	156.2	3,179	1,543	1,636	9	5	27	10.4	1,164.7	1,321.9	1,032.1	3.1 u	1.7 u	9.3
S08000020	Grampian	588.1	292.1	296.0	5,468	2,688	2,780	16	12	33	9.3	1,065.9	1,228.7	931.6	2.6 u	1.9 u	5.2
S08000021	Greater Glasgow and Clyde	1,161.4	560.9	600.4	12,444	6,052	6,392	36	18	77	10.7	1,248.7	1,490.7	1,069.2	3.0	1.5 u	6.3
S08000022	Highland	321.9	158.2	163.7	3,507	1,820	1,687	4	3	11	10.9	1,025.1	1,257.4	842.5	1.4 u	1.1 u	3.8 u
S08000023	Lanarkshire	656.5	317.2	339.3	7,097	3,488	3,609	13	8	35	10.8	1,246.9	1,449.3	1,087.4	1.9 u	1.2 u	5.1
S08000024	Lothian	880.0	427.4	452.6	7,761	3,734	4,027	33	26	45	8.8	1,066.1	1,225.6	939.0	3.5	2.8	4.8
S08000025	Orkney	21.9	10.9	11.0	223	100	123	0	0	0	10.2	948.5	979.8	921.8	u	u	u
S08000026	Shetland	23.2	11.8	11.4	232	122	110	0	0	0	10.0	1,124.5	1,464.0	918.1	u	u	u
S08000027	Tayside	415.5	202.2	213.3	4,741	2,265	2,476	25	20	31	11.4	1,084.4	1,246.0	959.0	6.4	5.1	7.9
S08000028	Western Isles	26.9	13.3	13.6	359	183	176	0	0	1	13.3	1,093.0	1,396.3	899.9	u	u	u

Table 1b: Deaths (numbers and rates) by area of usual residence (regions/health areas), 2016 registrations, United Kingdom and constituent countries
England: Regions, Wales: Local Health Boards
Scotland: NHS Board Areas, Northern Ireland: Health and Social Care Trusts

United Kingdom and constituent countries

Area codes	Area of usual residence	Populations Number (thousands) All ages			Deaths (numbers) All ages			Infant (under 1 year)	Neonatal (under 4 weeks)	Perinatal (stillbirths and deaths under 1 week)	Crude death rate (deaths per 1,000 population)	Rates Age-standardised mortality rate[1]			Infant mortality rate (per 1,000 live births)	Neonatal mortality rate (per 1,000 live births)	Perinatal mortality rate (per 1,000 live births and stillbirths)
		Persons	Males	Females	Persons	Males	Females					Persons	Males	Females			
N92000002	NORTHERN IRELAND[5] Health and Social Care Board	1,862.1	915.2	946.9	15,430	7,430	8,000	112	86	151	8.3	1,015.9	1,177.6	892.9	4.6	3.5	6.2
ZT001	Belfast	354.7	172.0	182.7	3,331	1,595	1,736	19	16	31	9.4	1,120.3	1,350.6	953.2	4.1 u	3.4 u	6.6
ZT002	Northern	473.1	232.3	240.8	3,968	1,909	2,059	25	15	33	8.4	988.1	1,166.7	865.4	4.4	2.6 u	5.7
ZT003	Southern	377.2	187.8	189.4	2,708	1,326	1,382	28	22	31	7.2	984.9	1,111.4	871.0	5.0	4.0	5.6
ZT004	South Eastern	356.7	173.9	182.7	3,094	1,429	1,665	21	18	29	8.7	973.5	1,093.5	881.2	5.0	4.3 u	6.8
ZT005	Western	300.4	149.1	151.3	2,329	1,171	1,158	19	15	27	7.8	1,033.9	1,193.3	908.9	4.7 u	3.7 u	6.6

1 The age-standardised mortality rates for 2016 are standardised to the 2013 European Standard Population, expressed per 100,000 population. Age-standardised rates are used to allow comparison between populations which may contain different proportions of people of different ages. ASMRs are based on mid-2016 population estimates. For more information on these rates please see our User guide to mortality statistics.

2 K04000001 is England and Wales; J99000001 is Elsewhere (outside England and Wales).

3 The deaths of those whose usual residence is outside England and Wales are included in total figures for England and Wales, but excluded from any sub-division of England and Wales.

4 The deaths of those whose usual residence is outside Scotland are included in total figures for Scotland, and are also included in any sub-division of Scotland based on where the death occurred.

5 The deaths of those whose usual residence is outside Northern Ireland are included in total figures for Northern Ireland, and are also included in any sub-division of Northern Ireland based on where the death occurred.

Source: Office for National Statistics, National Records Scotland, Northern Ireland Statistics and Research Agency

Released: 27 November 2017

Office for
National Statistics

Statistical bulletin

Estimates of the Very Old (including Centenarians): 2002 to 2016

People in the oldest age groups in the UK (90 to 104 and 105 and over) by sex and age, and comparisons of the oldest populations in the 4 constituent countries of the UK.

Contact:
Ngaire Coombs
pop.info@ons.gsi.gov.uk
+44 (0)1329 444661

Release date:
27 September 2017

Next release:
September 2018

Table of contents

1 . Main points

- The population aged 90 and over has grown more rapidly than most younger ages in recent years but it remains a small part of the total UK population

- Historical birth patterns which resulted in rapid ageing and growth of the population aged 90 and over in recent years have now largely played out, and ageing and growth have returned to a longer-term average

- The proportion of men in the population aged 90 and over continues to rise

- An estimated 14,910 people were aged 100 and over (centenarians) in the UK in 2016, or 2 for every 10,000 people; this is a rise from 14,520 in 2015

2 . Statistician's comment

"The population aged 90 and over grew rapidly in recent years, but this was largely driven by people who were born during the post World War 1 baby boom reaching age 90 and progressing through the oldest ages, causing both population growth and ageing within this age group. As these people have now largely progressed through the oldest population, growth and ageing of the 90 and over population have slowed. Despite the growth in this population, people aged 90 and over still make up less than 1% of the total UK population"

Ngaire Coombs, Demographic Analysis Unit, Office for National Statistics

3 . Things you need to know about this release

These are annual mid-year estimates by sex and single year of age for people aged 90 to 104 and for the 105 and over age group. Figures for 2002 to 2015 update the figures previously published in September 2016 for England, Wales and for the UK. Corresponding estimates for Scotland and for Northern Ireland for 2002 to 2016 are also published today by National Records of Scotland (NRS) and the Northern Ireland Statistics and Research Agency (NISRA) respectively.

To provide users with a consistent set of estimates by single year of age up to age 105 and over, the Estimates of the very old (including centenarians) series is constrained to the age 90 and over totals in the mid-year population estimates.

4 . More people are aged 90 and over than ever, but they are still a small proportion of the population

There were 571,245 people aged 90 and over living in the UK in 2016. This was the highest estimate ever. Figure 1 shows the population has been rising continuously for the last few decades, with the only exception in 2008. The dip in the population aged 90 and over in 2008 reflects low birth numbers 90 years previously, during World War 1, followed by higher numbers of births immediately after the war (see Figure 4 for more details).

Figure 1: People aged 90 and over

UK, 1986 to 2016

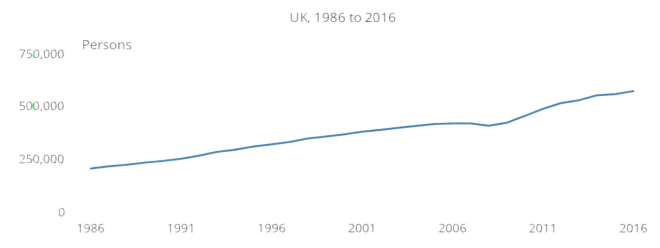

Figure 1: People aged 90 and over

UK, 1986 to 2016

Source: Office for National Statistics, National Records of Scotland, Northern Ireland Statistics and Research Agency

Still, the population aged 90 and over is a very small part of the population. Figure 2 shows the number of people in the UK for every year of age, in 2016. The shaded tail on the right-hand side represent ages 90 and over. Together they make up less than 1 in 100 of the total population.

Figure 2: UK population age structure in 2016

UK

However, the population aged 90 and over has been growing more quickly than most younger ages.

Figure 3 overlays the previous figure with population growth at different ages between 2002 and 2016.[1] In general, older ages have grown faster than younger ages resulting in an older overall population age structure.

Figure 3: UK population age structure in 2016, and percentage change between 2002 and 2016

UK

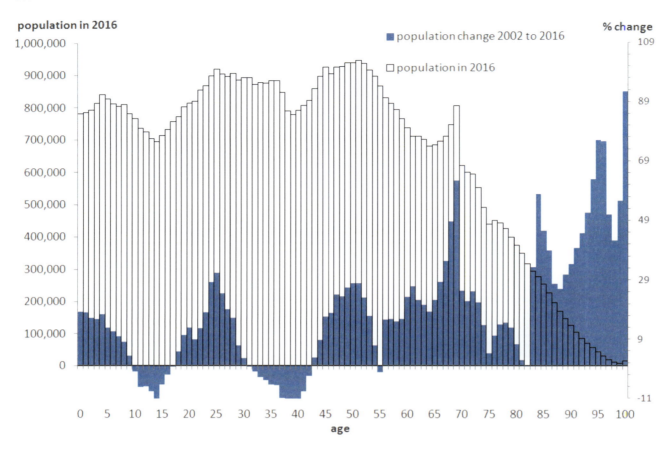

The main driver of population ageing in recent decades has been improving mortality at all ages, but particularly at older ages. Improvements in survival to older ages are due to a combination of factors such as improved medical treatments, housing and living standards, nutrition, and changes in the population's smoking habits. However, improvements in life expectancy in the UK have slowed in recent years (for more information see the National life tables, UK: 2014 to 2016 statistical bulletin).

Notes for: More people are aged 90 and over than ever, but they are still a small proportion of the population

1. Care should be taken when interpreting percentage changes in small populations.

5 . Centenarians are increasing fastest, but their numbers are still relatively small

Figure 4: Population age structure at all ages, and at ages 90 and over

UK, 2016

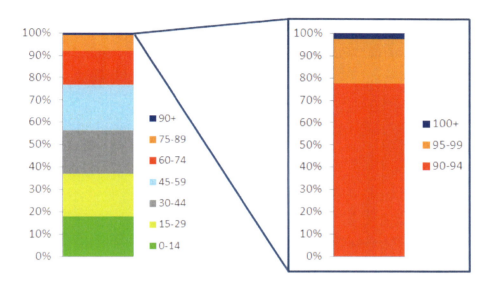

Figure 4 shows that, in 2016, almost four in five of the population aged 90 and over living in the UK (77.6%) were aged under 95; while 19.8% were aged between 95 and 99 and 2.6% were centenarians (those aged 100 and over).

Centenarians make up a very small proportion of the total UK population (0.02% in 2016), but their numbers have grown rapidly. Figure 3 shows centenarian numbers increased at a faster rate than any other age group over the period 2002 to 2016 with numbers almost doubling from 7,750 to 14,910 over the period. In fact, over the past 30 years numbers have more than quadrupled from 3,642 centenarians in 1986.

Most centenarians are women with five female centenarians for every male centenarian in 2016.

6 . The oldest old are getting older

Figure 5 shows the proportions of the 90 and over population by single year of age over the period 2002 to 2016. Proportions decrease with age; in other words, in every year there are higher proportions of 90-year-olds than 91-year-olds, and higher proportions of 91-year-olds than 92-year-olds and so on.

The youngest ages, 90 to 92, make up over half of the 90 and over population over the entire period. But we also see that in 2016 compared with 2002, these younger ages make up a little less of the 90 and over population, and the older ages a little more. In other words, the population aged 90 and over has become older.

The distinctive wave-like pattern reflects birth patterns around World War 1 (1914 to 1918). There were unusually few people born during the war and relatively more people born immediately afterwards. People born during 1914, the first year of the war, who survived to age 90 entered the population aged 90 and over in 2004. The smaller number of wartime births decreased the proportion of those aged 90 in the population (between 2004 and 2008), and then the post-war increase in births boosted the proportion aged 90, before it again decreased. The same pattern can be observed in the other ages in turn.

As a result, the structure of the 90 and over population firstly became older, then younger, and then older again in quick succession. As the population moved from being younger to older again, rapid ageing occurred.

A detailed analysis can be found in the report The impact of the First World War on the 90 and over population of the UK.

So although the 90 and over population is gradually becoming older over time, recent structural changes and rapid ageing were largely due to historical birth patterns. These effects have now largely played out and the ageing of the 90 and over population has slowed.

Figure 5: People aged 90 to 99 as a percentage of all people aged 90 and over

UK, 2002 to 2016

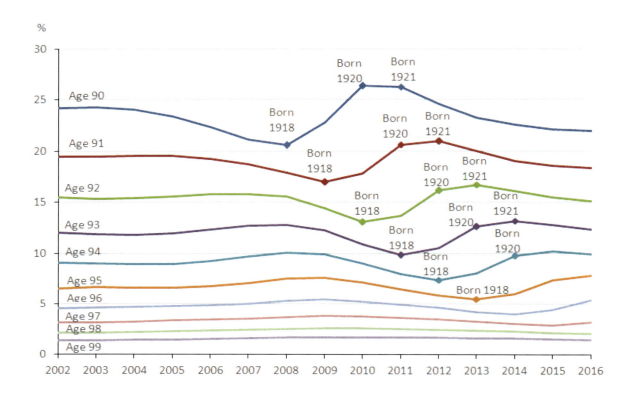

7 . Growth of the 90 and over population

The population aged 90 and over may not grow as quickly as it has in the recent past. Figure 6 illustrates this point. While it looks similar to Figure 5, Figure 6 shows estimates of the oldest population by single age years rather than proportions.

At every age the number of people decline as the World War 1 birth years enter the population, and then grow strongly as those born in the large post-war boom enter the population, before growth stabilises.

So while the total population aged 90 and over grew rapidly over recent years, much of this growth seems to derive from the post World War 1 peak birth years. This effect has now largely played out.

In summary, both the population structure and the speed of population growth of those aged 90 and over may be returning to a longer-time average.

Figure 6: Number of people aged 90 to 99

UK, 2002 to 2016

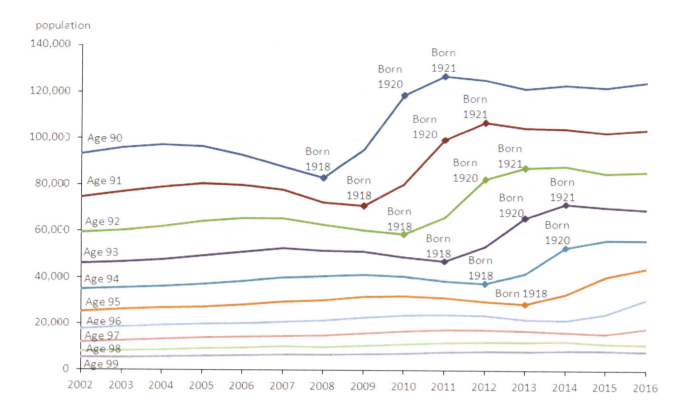

8 . History may repeat itself

The World War 1 birth patterns described in the previous section are also apparent in the population pyramid shown in Figure 7. The large pyramid on the left displays the population structure from age 60 in both 2002 and 2016, and the inset pyramid on the right zooms in on ages 90 and over.

There is a tapering at ages 83 and 84 in 2002, reflecting low birth numbers at the end of World War 1, followed by relatively large groups of people aged 80 and 81 born in the post World War 1 baby boom. After the post-war peak in births the number of people born each year reduced to below World War 1 levels. This is illustrated in another article, Trends in births and deaths over the last century. These birth patterns, however, are not apparent in the population pyramid. This could possibly be explained by medical and public health advances following World War 1 resulting in a larger proportion of people born in these smaller birth years surviving to older ages.

Looking further ahead, the population pyramid also shows the population that will feed into the oldest old in the future. There was also an increase in births after World War 2; people aged around 70 years old in 2016. When these people enter the 90 and over population in 20 years time they will have a similar effect as people born immediately after World War 1.

Figure 7: Population pyramid, ages 60 and over

UK, 2002 and 2016

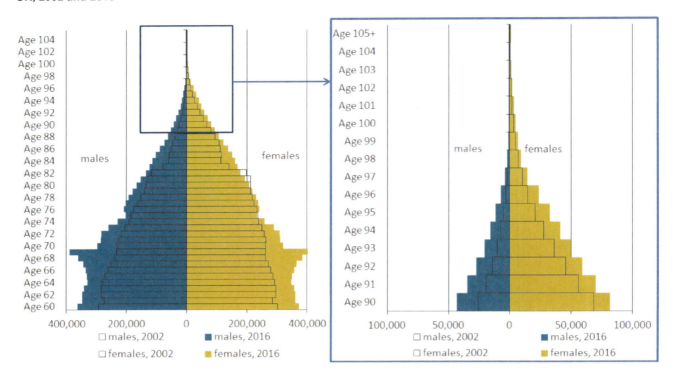

9 . More women than men aged 90 and over, but growth is faster for men

Figure 7 also shows population growth and ageing by sex. The inlay shows that at all ages 90 and over there are more women than men, reflecting women's higher life expectancy, and this is increasingly so at higher ages. However, relative to their smaller population, the number of men has grown faster than the number of women at all ages. For example, for every 100 men aged 90 in 2002 there were 73 more in 2016, compared with an additional 20 women for every 100 women aged 90 in 2002.

While women outnumber men at all 90 and over ages, the difference has narrowed. Figure 8 shows the number of women for every man by age group over the period 2002 to 2016. For all age groups the ratio of women to men has decreased and the decrease is more marked with age. In 2002 there were three women aged 90 to 94 for every man of that age, five women aged 95 to 99 and eight women aged 100 to 104. By 2016 these figures had fallen to two, three and five respectively. At age 105 and over, while there were still eight women for every man, this was three fewer than in 2002. Still, in every age group there are at least twice as many women as men.

Figure 8: Number of women per man, selected age groups
UK, 2002 to 2016

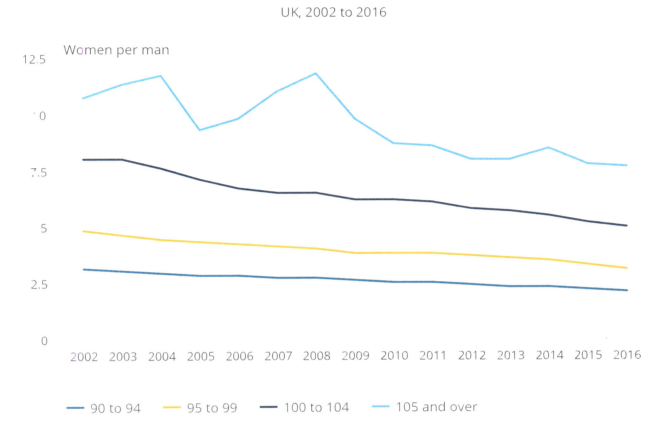

Figure 8: Number of women per man, selected age groups

UK, 2002 to 2016

Source: Office for National Statistics, National Records of Scotland, Northern Ireland Statistics and Research Agency

10 . All UK countries are ageing, but some faster than others

In 2016, Wales had the highest proportion of those aged 90 and over in the population at 951 per 100,000, followed by England at 883, Scotland at 760, and Northern Ireland with the lowest at 684 (Figure 9).

The proportion of the population aged 90 and over increased in every UK country between 1986 and 2016, but there were differences in the speed of increase. Northern Ireland had the slowest growth and Wales had the fastest. As a result, there are now far bigger differences between UK countries in the proportion of the oldest population. In 1986, the gap between the UK country with the most people aged 90 and over and the country with the fewest was only 77 per 100,000 (365 in England compared with 288 in Northern Ireland). By 2016 this gap had increased to 267 per 100,000 (951 in Wales compared with 684 in Northern Ireland).

11 . Links to related statistics

More information on the topic of the UK population is available:

- Population Estimates for UK, England and Wales, Scotland and Northern Ireland, Mid-2015

- Overview of population statistics

- National life tables

Figure 9: Number of people aged 90 and over per 100,000 population, by country
UK countries, 1986 to 2016

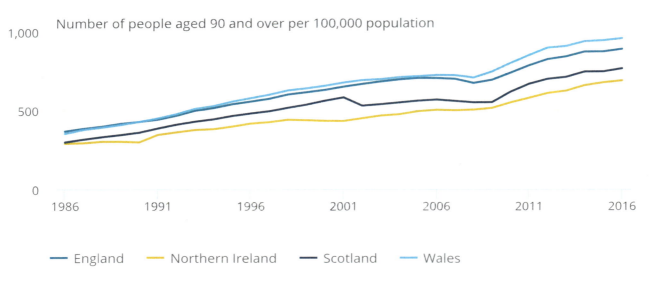

Figure 9: Number of people aged 90 and over per 100,000 population, by country

UK countries, 1986 to 2016

Source: Office for National Statistics, National Records of Scotland, Northern Ireland Statistics and Research Agency

12 . Quality and methodology

In 2011 the estimates were assessed by the UK Statistics Authority and have since been published as National Statistics. The estimates were re-assessed in 2016 and their National Statistics status was retained.

Estimates for the UK, England and for Wales are produced by Office for National Statistics (ONS) while estimates for Scotland and Northern Ireland are produced by the National Records of Scotland (NRS) and the Northern Ireland Statistics and Research Agency (NISRA) respectively. Although the estimates for each country are produced using a comparable methodology, a comparison paper has been published to explain any differences.

The Population estimates of the very old (including centenarians) Quality and Methodology Information report contains important information on:

- the strengths and limitations of the data and how it compares with related data

- uses and users of the data

- how the output was created

- the quality of the output including the accuracy of the data

We have published a review of the methodology for producing Estimates of the very old.

Mid-2002 to mid-2016 population estimates of the very old (including centenarians) (provisional)[1].
United Kingdom

Rounded to the nearest ten

Mid-year population	90 & over	90-99	100 & over	Age (years) 90	91	92	93	94	95	96	97	98	99	100	101	102	103	104	105 & over
Persons																			
2002	384,980	377,220	7,750	93,260	74,870	59,620	46,350	34,890	25,240	17,650	12,020	8,060	5,270	3,300	1,990	1,160	620	330	350
2003	395,090	387,020	8,070	95,860	76,940	60,510	46,950	35,700	26,260	18,470	12,560	8,330	5,440	3,440	2,070	1,190	660	340	370
2004	404,510	396,080	8,430	97,280	79,140	62,180	47,760	36,160	26,860	19,240	13,140	8,680	5,630	3,580	2,170	1,230	700	380	380
2005	413,600	404,750	8,860	96,700	80,850	64,360	49,490	37,080	27,380	19,870	13,920	9,190	5,900	3,710	2,290	1,320	730	390	410
2006	416,370	407,040	9,330	92,960	80,130	65,670	51,160	38,440	28,130	20,240	14,330	9,730	6,260	3,920	2,370	1,410	780	430	430
2007	416,700	406,710	9,980	87,890	77,940	65,840	52,810	40,230	29,500	20,980	14,690	10,150	6,710	4,190	2,530	1,480	840	460	480
2008	406,020	395,640	10,380	83,440	72,600	63,050	51,990	40,800	30,360	21,570	14,930	10,110	6,780	4,370	2,640	1,540	850	470	510
2009	420,510	409,440	11,080	95,580	71,280	60,760	51,620	41,660	31,790	23,080	15,940	10,700	7,020	4,590	2,850	1,680	940	490	540
2010	452,680	441,070	11,610	119,230	80,710	59,020	49,260	40,880	32,170	23,920	17,010	11,420	7,440	4,720	2,950	1,790	1,030	560	580
2011	485,890	473,720	12,170	127,460	100,100	66,520	47,660	38,770	31,510	24,180	17,480	12,130	7,910	4,990	3,010	1,830	1,070	610	660
2012	513,450	500,640	12,810	126,050	107,590	82,900	53,920	37,870	30,070	23,770	17,680	12,450	8,350	5,280	3,220	1,860	1,100	620	720
2013	527,240	513,910	13,330	122,390	105,390	88,090	66,430	42,230	28,970	22,330	17,180	12,440	8,470	5,490	3,380	1,990	1,110	640	720
2014	550,820	536,570	14,250	123,950	104,860	88,620	72,490	53,590	33,120	22,100	16,590	12,480	8,780	5,800	3,640	2,160	1,230	660	770
2015	556,270	541,740	14,520	123,050	103,370	85,880	71,080	56,820	40,840	24,580	15,950	11,660	8,510	5,810	3,700	2,230	1,280	710	790
2016	571,250	556,340	14,910	125,280	104,560	86,250	70,230	56,840	44,420	30,980	18,140	11,460	8,200	5,770	3,780	2,320	1,390	770	870
Males																			
2002	88,360	87,520	840	25,080	19,010	14,130	10,280	7,210	4,840	3,140	1,970	1,180	690	390	230	120	50	30	30
2003	92,470	91,590	880	26,170	19,910	14,720	10,590	7,560	5,170	3,330	2,110	1,290	750	420	220	120	70	30	30
2004	96,830	95,880	960	27,010	20,860	15,480	11,150	7,830	5,440	3,610	2,270	1,400	840	470	240	120	70	40	30
2005	100,980	99,900	1,080	27,500	21,620	16,300	11,820	8,300	5,660	3,820	2,490	1,500	890	520	280	140	70	40	40
2006	102,810	101,630	1,180	26,740	21,840	16,790	12,380	8,760	5,990	3,970	2,580	1,610	970	560	310	160	80	40	40
2007	104,220	102,900	1,310	25,660	21,590	17,230	12,920	9,330	6,440	4,280	2,710	1,730	1,040	610	340	180	90	50	40
2008	102,510	101,150	1,360	24,640	20,330	16,760	13,040	9,580	6,710	4,460	2,850	1,960	1,060	620	360	190	100	50	40
2009	109,980	108,490	1,490	29,240	20,640	16,660	13,390	10,190	7,210	4,890	3,150	1,960	1,160	690	390	220	110	50	50
2010	120,360	118,770	1,590	36,770	23,650	16,290	12,840	10,030	7,380	5,080	3,360	2,110	1,280	720	400	230	130	60	60
2011	130,130	128,440	1,690	39,510	29,300	18,410	12,400	9,390	7,240	5,190	3,440	2,210	1,350	780	420	220	130	70	70
2012	141,160	139,310	1,860	39,930	32,430	23,520	14,410	9,480	7,000	5,220	3,590	2,310	1,430	860	470	240	130	70	80
2013	148,140	146,170	1,970	39,620	32,440	25,720	18,170	10,870	6,940	4,960	3,600	2,370	1,490	890	510	280	140	70	80
2014	157,790	155,640	2,160	41,130	32,930	26,340	20,370	14,100	8,180	5,040	3,500	2,470	1,590	960	560	310	170	80	80
2015	163,520	161,220	2,300	42,000	33,470	26,190	20,490	15,430	10,360	5,820	3,500	2,350	1,610	1,010	590	340	180	100	90
2016	171,710	169,280	2,430	43,410	34,740	27,200	20,790	15,830	11,650	7,560	4,120	2,400	1,590	1,030	620	360	200	110	100

Mid-2002 to mid-2016 population estimates of the very old (including centenarians) (provisional)[1].
United Kingdom

Rounded to the nearest ten

Mid-year population	90 & over	90-99	100 & over	Age (years)															
				90	91	92	93	94	95	96	97	98	99	100	101	102	103	104	105 & over
Females																			
2002	296,620	289,700	6,910	68,170	55,860	45,490	36,080	27,680	20,400	14,520	10,050	6,880	4,580	2,910	1,760	1,040	570	310	320
2003	302,620	295,430	7,190	69,690	57,040	45,790	36,360	28,140	21,090	15,130	10,450	7,030	4,690	3,030	1,850	1,070	600	310	340
2004	307,670	300,200	7,470	70,280	58,280	46,700	36,610	28,330	21,420	15,630	10,880	7,290	4,790	3,110	1,930	1,110	630	340	350
2005	312,630	304,850	7,780	69,210	59,230	48,070	37,660	28,780	21,730	16,050	11,430	7,690	5,010	3,190	2,010	1,190	660	360	370
2006	313,560	305,410	8,150	66,220	58,290	48,880	38,780	29,680	22,140	16,270	11,750	8,110	5,300	3,360	2,060	1,250	700	390	390
2007	312,480	303,810	8,670	62,230	56,350	48,600	39,890	30,910	23,060	16,700	11,970	8,440	5,670	3,580	2,190	1,300	750	410	440
2008	303,510	294,490	9,020	58,810	52,270	46,290	38,950	31,230	23,650	17,120	12,080	8,380	5,710	3,740	2,290	1,350	750	420	470
2009	310,540	300,950	9,580	66,340	50,640	44,100	38,230	31,470	24,590	18,190	12,800	8,740	5,860	3,900	2,470	1,460	830	440	490
2010	332,320	322,300	10,020	82,460	57,070	42,730	36,420	30,840	24,800	18,840	13,650	9,320	6,170	3,990	2,550	1,560	900	500	520
2011	355,760	345,280	10,480	87,950	70,810	48,110	35,260	29,380	24,270	18,990	14,040	9,920	6,560	4,210	2,590	1,610	940	540	600
2012	372,290	361,340	10,950	86,120	75,160	59,380	39,520	28,390	23,080	18,550	14,090	10,140	6,920	4,420	2,750	1,620	970	550	640
2013	379,100	367,740	11,360	82,760	72,950	62,370	48,260	31,370	22,030	17,380	13,590	10,070	6,980	4,600	2,870	1,710	970	560	640
2014	393,030	380,940	12,090	82,830	71,930	62,280	52,120	39,490	24,940	17,060	13,090	10,000	7,200	4,840	3,090	1,850	1,060	580	680
2015	392,750	380,530	12,220	81,040	69,900	59,690	50,600	41,390	30,480	18,760	12,450	9,310	6,910	4,800	3,100	1,890	1,100	620	700
2016	399,540	387,060	12,480	81,870	69,810	59,050	49,440	41,010	32,770	23,420	14,020	9,060	6,610	4,740	3,160	1,960	1,190	660	770

Source: Office for National Statistics

Notes:

1. The method used to produce the estimates updates the back years so figures for previous years are revised each time estimates are produced for the latest year. This is why the figures are labelled as provisional.

2. **Please note these figures are estimates.** Although they are rounded to the nearest ten people, they cannot be guaranteed to be precise even to that level of detail.

3. Figures may not add due to rounding.

4. The 90 & over totals are also rounded to the nearest 10 in the table for consistency. However, please note that unrounded 90 & over totals are published unrounded in the Mid Year Estimates

164

Mid-2002 to mid-2016 population estimates of the very old (including centenarians) (provisional)[1].

England

Mid-year population	90 & over	90-99	100 & over	Age (years) 90	91	92	93	94	95	96	97	98	99	100	101	102	103	104	105 & over
Persons																			
2002	330,570	323,860	6,710	80,070	64,360	51,170	39,720	29,840	21,650	15,140	10,360	6,990	4,560	2,850	1,730	1,010	530	290	310
2003	339,620	332,610	7,000	82,340	66,180	52,060	40,330	30,600	22,490	15,880	10,820	7,190	4,710	2,980	1,790	1,050	580	290	320
2004	347,710	340,380	7,330	83,370	68,070	53,560	41,090	31,060	23,020	16,510	11,330	7,500	4,870	3,100	1,890	1,080	610	320	330
2005	355,450	347,730	7,730	82,710	69,300	55,440	42,710	31,960	23,570	17,060	11,920	7,940	5,100	3,240	2,000	1,150	640	350	350
2006	357,180	349,030	8,140	79,370	68,450	56,220	44,060	33,180	24,250	17,410	12,310	8,370	5,430	3,400	2,080	1,230	690	370	380
2007	357,580	348,850	8,720	75,050	66,670	56,330	45,250	34,730	25,520	18,110	12,690	8,740	5,780	3,650	2,200	1,300	750	410	420
2008	347,350	338,360	8,990	70,840	61,910	53,900	44,510	34,960	26,170	18,640	12,860	8,750	5,830	3,750	2,300	1,340	740	420	450
2009	360,120	350,560	9,560	81,980	60,590	51,810	44,200	35,700	27,300	19,880	13,790	9,230	6,090	3,950	2,450	1,450	810	430	470
2010	386,270	376,200	10,070	100,890	69,180	50,110	41,970	35,020	27,550	20,560	14,630	9,880	6,430	4,110	2,540	1,530	890	480	510
2011	414,410	403,890	10,530	108,800	84,600	57,020	40,440	33,100	26,970	20,690	15,030	10,410	6,840	4,290	2,630	1,580	930	530	580
2012	438,080	426,990	11,090	107,250	91,960	70,140	46,320	32,190	25,700	20,350	15,170	10,720	7,190	4,570	2,770	1,630	950	540	630
2013	450,410	438,880	11,530	104,280	89,800	75,500	56,330	36,380	24,700	19,140	14,750	10,710	7,300	4,730	2,920	1,710	980	550	640
2014	470,410	458,110	12,300	105,360	89,470	75,650	62,260	45,440	28,600	18,850	14,250	10,710	7,540	4,990	3,140	1,860	1,060	580	660
2015	474,970	462,410	12,560	104,290	88,010	73,420	60,810	48,890	34,730	21,260	13,640	10,040	7,320	5,010	3,190	1,930	1,120	610	700
2016	487,850	474,920	12,930	106,040	88,860	73,700	60,210	48,770	38,300	26,450	15,690	9,830	7,070	4,990	3,270	2,020	1,210	670	770
Males																			
2002	76,620	75,870	740	21,760	16,520	12,260	8,890	6,210	4,180	2,720	1,720	1,030	600	340	200	100	50	30	20
2003	80,150	79,390	770	22,610	17,290	12,790	9,210	6,540	4,450	2,880	1,840	1,140	660	360	190	110	60	30	30
2004	83,980	83,140	840	23,390	18,040	13,470	9,680	6,800	4,720	3,110	1,960	1,230	740	410	210	110	60	30	30
2005	87,540	86,580	960	23,740	18,710	14,120	10,330	7,230	4,940	3,330	2,110	1,280	790	470	240	120	60	30	30
2006	88,920	87,860	1,060	23,060	18,810	14,490	10,700	7,660	5,220	3,460	2,250	1,380	820	500	280	140	70	30	30
2007	90,150	89,010	1,140	22,100	18,650	14,890	11,170	8,070	5,640	3,720	2,380	1,490	890	520	300	160	80	40	40
2008	88,470	87,310	1,160	21,070	17,510	14,490	11,300	8,280	5,820	3,910	2,480	1,520	930	530	300	160	80	40	40
2009	94,980	93,690	1,290	25,220	17,640	14,320	11,620	8,860	6,280	4,250	2,780	1,710	1,020	600	330	180	90	40	40
2010	103,510	102,110	1,400	31,420	20,360	13,900	11,010	8,690	6,410	4,420	2,930	1,860	1,110	640	360	190	100	50	50
2011	111,800	110,320	1,490	33,930	24,990	15,860	10,550	8,110	6,260	4,500	3,000	1,920	1,190	680	370	200	110	60	60
2012	121,250	119,610	1,640	34,180	27,880	20,070	12,430	8,080	6,060	4,520	3,130	2,010	1,250	750	420	220	120	70	70
2013	127,320	125,560	1,750	33,920	27,810	22,170	15,540	9,400	5,940	4,290	3,100	2,090	1,300	780	460	240	130	70	70
2014	135,570	133,640	1,930	35,100	28,250	22,660	17,610	12,070	7,090	4,320	3,030	2,130	1,390	850	500	280	150	70	80
2015	140,350	138,300	2,050	35,740	28,600	22,530	17,650	13,380	8,900	5,060	3,000	2,040	1,400	890	520	300	170	80	90
2016	147,380	145,220	2,160	36,940	29,700	23,330	17,920	13,650	10,110	6,530	3,580	2,070	1,390	910	550	320	180	100	100

Mid-2002 to mid-2016 population estimates of the very old (including centenarians) (provisional)[1].
England

Rounded to the nearest ten

Mid-year population	90 & over	90-99	100 & over	Age (years)															
				90	91	92	93	94	95	96	97	98	99	100	101	102	103	104	105 & over
Females																			
2002	253,960	247,980	5,970	58,320	47,840	38,910	30,840	23,630	17,480	12,420	8,640	5,960	3,970	2,510	1,540	900	480	260	290
2003	259,460	253,230	6,240	59,740	48,890	39,270	31,120	24,070	18,050	13,000	8,980	6,060	4,060	2,620	1,590	940	520	270	300
2004	263,730	257,240	6,490	59,980	50,030	40,090	31,410	24,260	18,310	13,410	9,370	6,270	4,120	2,700	1,680	970	550	290	300
2005	267,920	261,150	6,770	58,970	50,590	41,330	32,380	24,740	18,630	13,740	9,810	6,660	4,310	2,770	1,760	1,030	580	320	320
2006	268,260	261,180	7,090	56,310	49,640	41,730	33,360	25,520	19,020	13,960	10,050	6,990	4,600	2,900	1,800	1,090	620	340	340
2007	267,430	259,840	7,590	52,940	48,020	41,440	34,070	26,650	19,880	14,390	10,310	7,250	4,900	3,130	1,900	1,140	670	370	380
2008	258,880	251,050	7,830	49,780	44,400	39,410	33,210	26,680	20,350	14,730	10,380	7,230	4,900	3,210	2,000	1,170	660	370	410
2009	265,140	256,870	8,270	56,760	42,950	37,480	32,580	26,840	21,020	15,630	11,020	7,520	5,060	3,340	2,120	1,270	720	390	430
2010	282,760	274,090	8,670	69,470	48,820	36,210	30,950	26,330	21,140	16,140	11,700	8,020	5,320	3,460	2,190	1,340	790	430	460
2011	302,610	293,570	9,040	74,870	59,610	41,160	29,880	24,990	20,710	16,180	12,030	8,490	5,660	3,610	2,260	1,370	810	470	520
2012	316,830	307,380	9,450	73,070	64,080	50,070	33,890	24,110	19,650	15,830	12,040	8,710	5,940	3,820	2,350	1,420	840	480	560
2013	323,100	313,320	9,780	70,360	61,980	53,320	40,790	26,980	18,760	14,850	11,640	8,630	6,010	3,950	2,470	1,470	850	480	560
2014	334,840	324,470	10,370	70,260	61,220	52,990	44,650	33,370	21,510	14,530	11,210	8,580	6,140	4,150	2,640	1,580	910	510	590
2015	334,620	324,110	10,510	68,550	59,410	50,890	43,160	35,510	25,830	16,190	10,640	8,000	5,930	4,120	2,670	1,630	950	530	610
2016	340,470	329,700	10,770	69,090	59,160	50,360	42,300	35,120	28,200	19,920	12,110	7,760	5,680	4,080	2,710	1,700	1,030	580	670

Source: Office for National Statistics

Notes:

1. The method used to produce the estimates updates the back years so figures for previous years are revised each time estimates are produced for the latest year. This is why the figures are labelled as provisional.

2. **Please note these figures are estimates.** Although they are rounded to the nearest ten people, they cannot be guaranteed to be precise even to that level of detail.

3. Figures may not add due to rounding.

4. The 90 & over totals are also rounded to the nearest 10 in the table for consistency. However, please note that unrounded 90 & over totals are published unrounded in the Mid Year Estimates

166

Mid-2002 to mid-2016 population estimates of the very old (including centenarians) (provisional)[1].
Wales

Mid-year population	90 & over	90-99	100 & over	90	91	92	93	94	95	96	97	98	99	100	101	102	103	104	105 & over
Persons																			
2002	20,130	19,730	400	4,840	3,910	3,120	2,440	1,830	1,320	940	650	430	270	170	100	60	30	20	20
2003	20,430	20,020	410	4,920	3,960	3,130	2,430	1,870	1,380	960	650	440	290	180	100	60	30	20	20
2004	20,910	20,470	440	5,010	4,060	3,180	2,470	1,900	1,410	1,000	680	460	300	200	110	60	30	20	20
2005	21,160	20,710	460	4,960	4,130	3,280	2,510	1,900	1,420	1,030	710	470	300	190	120	70	40	20	20
2006	21,490	21,030	470	4,890	4,130	3,380	2,620	1,950	1,450	1,060	730	490	320	190	120	80	40	20	20
2007	21,620	21,120	490	4,730	4,050	3,370	2,710	2,050	1,500	1,080	770	520	340	210	120	70	50	20	20
2008	21,300	20,770	530	4,570	3,880	3,260	2,670	2,100	1,540	1,100	770	530	350	230	130	70	50	30	20
2009	22,550	21,970	580	5,290	3,960	3,290	2,710	2,160	1,640	1,180	830	560	370	240	150	90	40	30	30
2010	24,260	23,650	610	6,320	4,470	3,280	2,660	2,140	1,670	1,240	880	600	390	250	160	100	50	30	40
2011	25,880	25,240	640	6,760	5,270	3,660	2,630	2,080	1,640	1,250	910	630	420	260	160	100	60	30	40
2012	27,420	26,730	690	6,700	5,730	4,390	2,970	2,090	1,610	1,240	910	650	450	290	170	100	60	30	40
2013	27,800	27,080	720	6,350	5,560	4,660	3,480	2,310	1,590	1,180	880	640	440	300	180	110	60	40	40
2014	28,830	28,050	780	6,380	5,420	4,640	3,820	2,810	1,810	1,200	880	640	450	310	200	120	70	40	50
2015	29,060	28,270	790	6,430	5,300	4,420	3,730	2,990	2,130	1,340	870	620	440	310	200	120	70	40	50
2016	29,600	28,820	780	6,560	5,410	4,370	3,590	2,950	2,300	1,610	990	620	430	300	200	120	70	40	50
Males																			
2002	4,510	4,470	40	1,300	970	710	520	370	250	160	100	60	40	20	10	10	0	0	0
2003	4,710	4,670	50	1,340	1,030	760	540	370	260	170	110	70	40	20	10	10	0	0	0
2004	4,950	4,900	50	1,380	1,070	800	580	400	270	180	120	70	40	30	10	10	0	0	0
2005	5,060	5,000	50	1,380	1,080	820	600	420	290	180	120	80	40	20	20	10	0	0	0
2006	5,240	5,180	60	1,400	1,110	850	630	440	310	200	120	80	50	30	10	10	0	0	0
2007	5,330	5,270	60	1,380	1,110	860	650	470	330	220	130	80	50	30	10	10	10	0	0
2008	5,210	5,140	70	1,350	1,060	830	640	470	330	220	140	80	50	30	20	10	10	0	0
2009	5,860	5,780	80	1,620	1,160	900	690	510	360	240	150	100	60	30	20	10	10	0	0
2010	6,320	6,250	80	1,920	1,300	910	690	500	360	250	170	110	60	30	20	10	10	0	0
2011	6,600	6,520	70	2,020	1,480	980	670	480	340	240	160	110	70	40	20	10	10	0	0
2012	7,180	7,100	80	2,060	1,640	1,180	760	510	350	240	170	110	80	40	20	10	10	0	0
2013	7,480	7,390	90	2,030	1,650	1,280	890	570	370	260	170	110	70	40	20	10	0	0	10
2014	7,970	7,880	90	2,100	1,690	1,330	1,010	690	430	270	180	120	70	40	30	10	10	0	10
2015	8,290	8,190	100	2,150	1,700	1,340	1,040	770	510	300	190	130	70	40	30	10	10	0	10
2016	8,750	8,650	100	2,260	1,760	1,360	1,070	810	580	380	220	130	80	50	30	10	10	0	0

Age (years)

Mid-2002 to mid-2016 population estimates of the very old (including centenarians) (provisional)[1].
Wales

Rounded to the nearest ten, except where number is 5 or fewer

Mid-year population	90 & over	90-99	100 & over	Age (years)															
				90	91	92	93	94	95	96	97	98	99	100	101	102	103	104	105 & over
Females																			
2002	**15,620**	**15,260**	**350**	3,540	2,940	2,400	1,920	1,470	1,080	780	540	360	240	150	90	50	30	20	20
2003	**15,720**	**15,350**	**360**	3,580	2,930	2,370	1,890	1,490	1,120	790	540	380	250	160	90	50	30	20	20
2004	**15,960**	**15,570**	**390**	3,630	2,990	2,380	1,900	1,490	1,140	830	560	390	270	170	100	60	30	20	20
2005	**16,100**	**15,700**	**400**	3,580	3,050	2,460	1,910	1,480	1,140	850	590	390	260	170	110	70	30	20	20
2006	**16,250**	**15,840**	**410**	3,490	3,030	2,540	1,990	1,510	1,140	860	610	410	270	160	100	70	40	20	20
2007	**16,280**	**15,850**	**430**	3,350	2,940	2,510	2,070	1,590	1,170	870	630	440	290	180	110	70	40	20	20
2008	**16,090**	**15,630**	**460**	3,230	2,820	2,430	2,040	1,630	1,210	880	640	450	310	200	120	60	40	20	20
2009	**16,690**	**16,190**	**510**	3,670	2,800	2,390	2,020	1,650	1,280	940	670	470	320	210	130	70	40	20	30
2010	**17,940**	**17,400**	**540**	4,400	3,170	2,370	1,970	1,640	1,310	990	720	490	330	220	140	80	40	20	30
2011	**19,280**	**18,720**	**570**	4,740	3,800	2,690	1,960	1,600	1,300	1,020	750	520	350	230	140	90	50	20	40
2012	**20,240**	**19,640**	**610**	4,640	4,090	3,210	2,210	1,580	1,260	990	750	540	370	240	150	90	60	30	30
2013	**20,320**	**19,690**	**630**	4,320	3,910	3,370	2,590	1,750	1,220	930	700	530	380	250	160	100	60	30	30
2014	**20,850**	**20,170**	**690**	4,280	3,730	3,310	2,810	2,120	1,380	930	690	520	380	270	180	110	60	40	40
2015	**20,780**	**20,080**	**700**	4,280	3,600	3,090	2,700	2,220	1,620	1,040	680	500	370	270	180	110	60	30	50
2016	**20,860**	**20,180**	**680**	4,300	3,650	3,000	2,530	2,140	1,720	1,230	770	490	350	250	170	110	60	40	40

Source: Office for National Statistics

Notes:

1. The method used to produce the estimates updates the back years so figures for previous years are revised each time estimates are produced for the latest year. This is why the figures are labelled as provisional.
2. **Please note these figures are estimates.** Although they are rounded to the nearest ten people, they cannot be guaranteed to be precise even to that level of detail.
3. Figures may not add due to rounding.
4. The 90 & over totals are also rounded to the nearest 10 in the table for consistency. However, please note that unrounded 90 & over totals are published unrounded in the Mid Year Estimates

168

Notes

These estimates of the very old (including centenarians) are produced using the Kannisto-Thatcher (KT) method[1] and more specifically using a survivor ratio based approach which provides age-specific estimates of the population for those aged 90 and over, using data from death registrations.
The population estimates for the very old by single year of age and sex are constrained to the ONS 90+ mid-year population estimates for England and Wales. Population estimates for those aged up to 89 are produced using the cohort component method2.

For more details of the methodology used to create the estimates see:
Calculating population estimates of the very old

1. Thatcher R, et al, (2002) 'The survivor ratio method for estimating numbers at high ages'
www.demographic-research.org/volumes/vol6/1/
2. Population Estimates Methodology

https://www.ons.gov.uk/peoplepopulationandcommunity/populationandmigration/populationestimates/method ologies/nationalandlocalauthoritylevelpopulationestimates

Terms and conditions

National Statistics

National Statistics are produced to high professional standards set out in the Code of Practice for Official Statistics. They are produced free from any political interference. In 2011 'Estimates of the Very Old (including Centenarians)' were assessed by the UK Statistics Authority and have since been published as National Statistics. The estimates were re-assessed in 2015 and their National Statistics status is subject to confirmation once all the requirements in the assessment report have been met.

Designation can be broadly interpreted to mean that the statistics:
• meet identified user needs;
• are well explained and readily accessible;
• are produced according to sound methods, and
• are managed impartially and objectively in the public interest.

Once statistics have been designated as National Statistics it is a statutory requirement that the Code of Practice shall continue to be observed.

Copyright and reproduction

You may re-use this information (not including logos) free of charge in any format or medium, under the terms of the Open Government Licence. Users should include a source accreditation to ONS -
Source: Office for National Statistics (www.ons.gov.uk)

© Crown copyright 2017

To view this licence, go to: www.nationalarchives.gov.uk/doc/open-government-licence/
or write to the Information Policy Team,
The National Archives, Kew, London TW9 4DU   email: psi@nationalarchives.gsi.gov.uk.

Data supplier:
Demographic Analysis Unit
Population Statistics Division
Office for National Statistics
Segensworth Road
FAREHAM
PO15 5RR

email: pop.info@ons.gsi.gov.uk   tel: +44 (0)1329 444661

Section 4 Provisional Long Term International Migration (LTIM) estimates Year Ending Dec 2017

Table 1: LTIM estimates by citizenship

Table 2: LTIM estimates by main reason for migration

Table 3: IPS estimates by citizenship and by main reason for migration

Table 4: IPS outflow estimates by citizenship and, for former immigrants, previous main reason for immigration

Chart 1 TS: Times series chart of LTIM estimates by selected citizenship group

Chart 1 Net: Composition of net long-term international migration by citizenship group, YE Mar 17 - YE Dec 2017

Chart 2a: Times series chart of LTIM estimates by main reason for migration groups by selected flow direction

Chart 2b: Times series chart of LTIM estimates by selected main reason for migration group

Chart 3: Times series chart of IPS estimates by all citizenship groups and all main reasons for migration

NOTES

Correction

YE June 2017 data
Data for YE June 2017 published in November 2017 and February 2018 contained a minor error. This was due to a small error in the weights given to some shifts, which was identified during a review of the International Passenger Survey data.

YE September 2017 data
Data for YE September 2017 published in February 2018 contained an error. This was due to an error in the way data collected on paper questionnaires were merged and processed with data collected on tablets. This was identified during a review of the unpublished October to December 2017 International Passenger Survey data, where an error was identified in the processing system which also affected the July to September 2017 data.

The July 2018 spreadsheet contains the corrected data.

A full review of the assurance process can be found in part 2 of the Report on the quality and complexity of migration statistics

We apologise for any inconvenience.

Former student emigration statistics labelled as experimental statistics

Recently, a range of concerns about the robustness of the former student emigration estimate were raised with the Office for Statistics Regulation (OSR).
As a result, OSR carried out a review on 'The quality of long-term student migration statistics' which was published on 27 July 2017.
The main focus of their report was the 'student migration gap' – the difference between the estimate of the number of migrants entering the UK for formal study (student immigration) and the estimate of the number of former students leaving the UK (former student emigration).

The estimate of former student emigration is the only source of information about when a student leaves the UK. As a result, OSR were *"concerned that the former student emigration estimate does not bear the weight that is put on it in public debate. This estimate should add clarity on the pattern of student migration in the UK. Instead, it creates doubts by not providing a complete and coherent picture of former student emigration, as these figures alone do not provide information on all the different outcomes for international students"*.

OSR noted that *"... it is standard practice for new figures to be labelled as experimental while they bed in and it is unfortunate that this was not followed in this case when the new breakdown of emigration figures by previous reason for immigration was first introduced"*. This judgement applies only to the student migration component of ONS's migration statistics; it is not a judgement about the quality of the overall estimates of immigration and emigration derived from the IPS.

As a result, from 24 August 2017, we have labelled the former student emigration estimate as "experimental statistics" in all publications. Once we are satisfied that we have a sufficient understanding of former student outcomes, including the extent to which the IPS accurately captures student departures, we will request the OSR to reassess our former student emigration estimate. All other statistics in this spreadsheet retain their status as National Statistics.

Our latest understanding of student migration can be found in 'What's happening with international student migration?'.

Revisions

Net migration figures for the United Kingdom for calendar years 2001 to 2011 and for mid years 2001-2002 to 2010-2011 have been revised in light of the results of the 2011 Census. These revisions are shown below and in the body of **Table 1**. The original net migration estimates are shown to the right of **Table 1**.

A review of the quality of Long-Term International Migration (LTIM) estimates from 2001 to 2011 has been published alongside the revised net migration series on our website. Please see the downloadable document "Quality of Long-Term International Migration estimates from 2001 to 2011 - Full Report" on our website:
    International Migration Methodology Downloads

Users should continue to use the published 1, 2, 3 and 4-series tables to analyse detailed breakdowns of inflows and outflows of long-term international migrants by a range of variables, but, in doing so, should bear in mind that the headline net migration estimates have been revised. Please see the downloadable document "Guidance note for net international migration revisions" on our website:
    International Migration Methodology Downloads

Revised Net Long-Term International Migration time series, calendar years 2001-2011, mid years 2001-2002 to 2010-2011			United Kingdom *Thousands*
Year	Revised net migration estimate	Original net migration estimate	Difference between original and revised net migration estimates
Balance			
YE Dec 01	+ 179	+ 171	+ 8
YE Jun 02	+ 174	+ 148	+ 26
YE Dec 02	+ 172	+ 153	+ 19
YE Jun 03	+ 172	+ 148	+ 24
YE Dec 03	+ 185	+ 148	+ 37
YE Jun 04	+ 194	+ 174	+ 20
YE Dec 04	+ 268	+ 245	+ 23
YE Jun 05	+ 320	+ 260	+ 60
YE Dec 05	+ 267	+ 206	+ 61
YE Jun 06	+ 234	+ 177	+ 57
YE Dec 06	+ 265	+ 198	+ 67
YE Jun 07	+ 287	+ 208	+ 79
YE Dec 07	+ 273	+ 233	+ 40
YE Jun 08	+ 267	+ 196	+ 71
YE Dec 08	+ 229	+ 163	+ 66
YE Jun 09	+ 205	+ 166	+ 39
YE Dec 09	+ 229	+ 198	+ 31
YE Jun 10	+ 244	+ 235	+ 9
YE Dec 10	+ 256	+ 252	+ 4
YE Jun 11	+ 263	+ 247	+ 16
YE Dec 11	+ 205	+ 215	- 10

Definition of a migrant

The UN recommendation for defining a long-term international migrant is used. That is, a migrant is someone who changes his or her country of usual residence for a period of at least a year, so that the country of destination effectively becomes the country of usual residence. This definition does not necessarily coincide with those used by other organisations.

Data sources

The following sources of data are used to compile the National Statistics estimates of long-term international migration into and out of the UK:

The International Passenger Survey (IPS) is the prime source of long-term international migration data, providing estimates of both inflows and outflows, but it does not cover all migration types. The IPS is a continuous voluntary survey conducted at all principal air and sea routes and the Channel Tunnel. It is a sample survey and the resultant figures are grossed up by weighting factors dependent on route and time of year. The figures produced are therefore estimates, not exact counts.

The Labour Force Survey (LFS), which provides a geographical distribution of long-term immigrants for the calibration of IPS inflow data.

The Home Office, which provides data on asylum seekers and their dependants and, from January 2013, on enforced removals of migrants who have never claimed asylum and, from October 2015, on people resettled in the UK under the various resettlement schemes.

The Irish Central Statistics Office, which provides estimates of migration of all citizenships between the UK and Republic of Ireland from 1991 to 2007.

The Northern Ireland Statistics and Research Agency (NISRA) which provides data for estimating long-term international migration to and from Northern Ireland for 2008 onwards.

Combining data from these sources, with some adjustments for people whose intentions changed with respect to their length of stay, produces the most inclusive estimate and is referred to as Long-Term International Migration (LTIM). This information is used in **Table 1** and **Table 2** of this spreadsheet.

LTIM = IPS flows + Irish flows + adjustments for asylum seekers and enforced removals + adjustments for people who change their intentions (switchers).

Some detailed analyses, because of the characteristics of the other data sources, are only possible when based upon IPS data alone. **Table 3** and **Table 4** in this spreadsheet are only able to use IPS data.

Migration between the UK and the Republic of Ireland is included in IPS estimates for 2008 onwards but excluded for previous years.

Data comparability

The LTIM estimates in **Table 1** are directly comparable with the new citizenship grouping estimates in our published 2-series (LTIM) tables.

The LTIM estimates in **Table 2** are directly comparable with the estimates in our published 2-series (LTIM) tables.

The IPS estimates in **Table 3** and **Table 4** are directly comparable with the new citizenship groupings estimates in our published 3-series (IPS) tables.

For comparable LTIM data back to 1991 and IPS data back to 1975, look at the data section on our website which also contains estimates broken down by other migrant characteristics:
All data related to international migration

Provisional data

The 2017 data used to compile the LTIM and IPS estimates in this report are provisional. Estimates in all tables for year ending March 2017, year ending June 2017 and year ending September 2017are therefore provisional. Final estimates will be published on 29 November 2018.

Migration flows

Estimates of flows of migrants into the UK ("Immigration estimates") are identified in these tables as "Inflow". Inflow estimates are held in Excel as positive numbers formatted to appear unsigned in black (immigrants add to the population of the UK).

Estimates of flows of migrants out of the UK ("Emigration estimates") are identified in these tables as "Outflow". Outflow estimates are held in Excel as negative numbers formatted to appear unsigned but in red (emigrants reduce the population of the UK).

Estimates of the numbers of migrants entering minus the numbers of migrants leaving the UK ("Net migration estimates") are identified in these tables as "Balance". Balance estimates are held in Excel as numbers and are formatted to appear as signed numbers in black. A positive number indicates that the inflow exceeds the outflow and that the net flow has increased the population of the UK. A negative number indicates that the outflow exceeds the inflow and that the net flow has decreased the population of the UK. Because of the way inflow and outflow estimates are stored in Excel, the balance estimates are the mathematical sum (before rounding) of the corresponding inflow and outflow

Citizenship

In response to the Consultation on Country Groupings in International Migration Statistics conducted in January 2014 to March 2014, the Migration Statistics Unit has changed the way countries are grouped in its outputs.

The new citizenship groupings are based around British / Non-British and EU / Non-EU with the non-EU citizenships grouped geographically. Estimates by citizenship are based upon membership of the relevant groupings in effect at the time of migration.

British citizenship includes citizens of British Overseas territories.

Non-EU citizens are grouped geographically in two main groups, Asia and Rest of the World. Asia is subdivided into Middle East and Central Asia, East Asia, South Asia and South East Asia. Rest of the World is subdivided into Sub-Saharan Africa, North Africa, North America (USA and Canada), Central and South America, and Oceania. Stateless migrants are shown separately.

For a full definition of all the new citizenship groupings, please see 'Citizenship / Nationality groupings' in:
International Migration - Table of Contents

Main reason for migration

The IPS asks migrants to identify their main reason for migration.
"No reason stated" includes non-responses and the non-specific response "Emigrating / Immigrating".

Table 3 shows separate estimates for the reason "Going home to live". However, "Going home to live" is only recorded when no other reason relating to work, study or accompany/join is provided. It should be noted that people migrating for these reasons may also be going home to live. For example, if a student was leaving the UK to go back home but also had a job in their home country, then they would be coded as emigrating from the UK for work related reasons even if they stated that going home was their primary motive.

It is only possible to produce estimates for the reason "Going home to live" based on IPS data alone. **Table 2** includes "Going home to live" in "No reason stated".

Please note that "main reason for migration" always refers to the reason for the current migration. For a former immigrant leaving the UK this is their main reason for leaving and may well be different to their previous main reason for immigrating into the UK. Because former immigrants' reasons for immigration and emigration can vary in this way, care should be taken if comparing inflow and outflow by "main reason for migration". Furthermore, the inflow and outflow estimates cover the same period (rolling year) and thus do not consider the same cohort of people. To avoid potential confusion about the contribution that particular groups of migrants make to total net migration figures, the previously published 'balance' figures by reason have been removed

Since January 2012, the IPS has also asked former immigrants about their previous main reason for immigrating. Please see "Previous Main Reason for Immigration" below. This information is presented in **Table 4**.

Previous main reason for immigration

Since January 2012 the IPS has asked 'Former Immigrants' about their previous main reason for immigration. The following 3-series tables give further cross tabulations of this variable:

    3.21 IPS Previous Main Reason for Immigration by Main Reason for Emigration
    3.22 IPS Previous Main Reason for Immigration by Usual Occupation Prior to Emigration
    3.23 IPS Previous Main Reason for Immigration by Year of Arrival in UK

A 'Former Immigrant' is defined as a person who previously entered the UK as a long-term international immigrant who then leaves the UK as a long-term international emigrant (please see the UN recommended definition of a long-term international migrant above).

A 'New Emigrant' is defined as a person who has never lived outside the UK long enough to establish usual residence elsewhere, who leaves the UK for the first time as a long-term international emigrant (please see UN definition of a long-term international migrant above).

The concept of previous main reason for immigration does not apply to 'New Emigrants'. However, an estimate of 'New Emigrants' is included in **Table 4** in order to complete the total picture of migration outflow.

It is possible that an emigrant born outside the UK has never established residence anywhere outside the UK, for instance if they entered the UK as a baby. Such a migrant is regarded as a new emigrant if when asked their year of arrival in the UK they state that they have never established residence outside the UK. Emigrants born outside the UK who do not respond to the question are assumed to be previous

It is possible that an emigrant born in the UK has previously established residence outside the UK. Such a migrant is regarded as a former immigrant if when asked their year of arrival in the UK they give the year of their latest immigration. Emigrants born in the UK who do not respond to this question are assumed to be new emigrants.

UK born former immigrants were not asked their previous main reason for immigration until 1 April 2013. Numbers of UK born former immigrants who were not asked their previous main reason for migration are shown separately in **Table 4** for year ending December 2013 and

The IPS does not collect equivalent information for immigrants who are former emigrants.

LTIM estimates are not possible for previous main reason for immigration.

For further information on Previous Main Reason for Immigration and how to interpret **Table 4** please see the downloadable document "International Migration - How to interpret Table 4" on our website:

    International Migration Methodology Downloads

Reliability of LTIM estimates

This publication uses the 95% confidence interval of the IPS component of an LTIM estimate to indicate the reliability of the LTIM estimates in **Table 1** and **Table 2**.

The confidence interval of the IPS component of an LTIM estimate gives a good indication of the reliability of the LTIM estimate. The IPS component of an LTIM estimate typically exceeds 90% of the overall LTIM estimate. The Northern Ireland and Asylum Seeker components of an LTIM estimate are based on administrative data and are not subject to sampling error. The methodology used to calculate the Migrant Switcher and Visitor Switcher components of an LTIM estimate do not currently enable us to adjust the confidence interval of the IPS component to obtain an overall confidence interval for the LTIM estimate, but these components are small compared to the overall LTIM

95% confidence intervals give a readily understood range in which the true value is likely to lie - there is a 95% probability that the true figure lies in the range: estimate +/- confidence interval. Users are advised to be cautious when making inferences from estimates with relatively large confidence intervals. For inflow and outflow estimates where the lower confidence limit is below zero users should assume the estimate is

Reliability of IPS estimates

This publication uses 95% confidence intervals to indicate the reliability of the IPS estimates in **Table 3** and **Table 4**. 95% confidence intervals give a readily understood range in which the true value is likely to lie - there is a 95% probability that the true figure lies in the range: estimate +/- confidence interval. Users are advised to be cautious when making inferences from estimates with relatively large confidence intervals. For inflow and outflow estimates where the lower confidence limit is below zero users should assume the estimate is above zero.

In the past, we have used standard error expressed as a percentage to indicate the reliability of IPS inflow and outflow estimates. Confidence intervals and standard errors are mathematically related:

    Standard error % = 95% confidence interval / (0.0196 x estimate)

Statistically significant changes

The latest estimates have been compared with the corresponding estimates for the period one year earlier. A tick box in the control panel at the top of each table enables the user to select whether or not those estimates which are statistically significantly different from the previous year are highlighted. If selected, the relevant estimates are highlighted by setting their background colour to salmon pink if statistically significantly higher and pale blue if statistically significantly lower.

The determination of whether a change is statistically significant or not is based on analysis of the unrounded data. A change is considered statistically significant if the change exceeds the 95% confidence interval for the difference between the two estimates.

The 95% confidence interval for the difference between the IPS components of the two LTIM estimates is used to test for statistically significant change in the LTIM estimates in **Table 1** and **Table 2**.

Outflow estimates are held in Excel as negative numbers formatted to appear unsigned but in red (see Migration Flows above). A change in outflow is regarded as an increase if the absolute value of the estimate increases.

Users are advised to be cautious when making inferences from any changes that are not identified as statistically significant. It is possible for such changes to be caused purely by the variability inherent to sample surveys, rather than because of any changes in real migration levels.

Rounding

All estimates in this spreadsheet are individually rounded to the nearest thousand. Totals may not add exactly due to this rounding.

All confidence intervals in this spreadsheet are also rounded to the nearest thousand. In particular, please note that a confidence interval which rounds to zero does not imply certainty, only that the confidence interval is less than 500.

When calculating the upper and lower confidence interval limits for a given estimate, please take into account that both the estimate and the confidence interval have been rounded to the nearest thousand.

Special values

The following special values are used for estimates and their associated confidence intervals:

z   Not applicable
   This value is used where estimates for the particular migrant characteristics are not applicable in a given year.
   For example, from 2014 onwards, UK born former immigrants were asked their previous reason for migration, so after 2013 the estimates in Table 4 for those not asked are set to "z".

:   Not available
   This value is used where estimates for the particular migrant characteristics are not available in a given year.
   For example, calibrated IPS estimates of migration are only available for calendar years and mid years up to YE Dec 2009, so before 2009 estimates for years ending in Q1 and Q3 are set to ":".

.   No contact.
   This value is used where the IPS has had no contact with any migrant having the particular characteristics in a given year.
   For example, if no EU8 citizen emigrating from the UK for a work related reason was interviewed by the IPS in a given year the estimate for that combination of citizenship and reason for migration is set to ".".
   Please note: The IPS is a sample survey. Where no contact has occurred no estimate is possible, but this does not imply that the actual number is zero (although it is probably low).

0~ Rounds to zero.
   Please see notes on Rounding above.

Using the time series charts (Chart 1 TS, Chart 2a, Chart 2b and Chart 3)

The tables in this spreadsheet have accompanying charts intended to help the user observe trends in the data over time.

The charts in this spreadsheet enable the user to select the exact data required. To select the data, click on the up/down arrows in the yellow box at the top of each chart. The chart title will alter to reflect the information selected.

When comparing different selections of data, please be aware that the charts adjust their vertical scales to suit the data displayed. The vertical scale is displayed to the left of the chart.

Some combinations of citizenship and reason for migration that can be selected in **Chart 3** involve very small groups for which estimates can be unreliable. Please refer to **Table 3** for full details of the confidence intervals surrounding the estimates. Users are advised to be cautious when making inferences from estimates with large confidence intervals.

Please note:

Further time series charts for the principal migrant characteristics are now available in the relevant 2-Series tables:
All data related to international migration

Further time series charts for combinations of the principal migrant characteristics are now available in all relevant 3-Series tables:
All data related to international migration

We also publish an interactive tool which allows users to see a visual representation of international migration over time, compared with other key figures and key events. The migration timeline is available at:
Long-Term International Migration Timeline

Using the net migration chart (Chart 1 Net)

Table 1 in this spreadsheet has an accompanying chart intended to help the user observe the changing composition of net migration over time.

The chart enables the user to select the data by year. To select the year, click on the up/down arrows in the yellow box at the top of the chart. The chart titles will alter to reflect the year selected.

Please note:

Further net migration charts for the principal migrant characteristics are now available in the relevant 2-Series tables.
All data related to international migration

A National Statistics publication

National Statistics are produced to high professional standards set out in the Code of Practice for Official Statistics. They are produced free from any political interference:
UK Statistics Authority Code of Practice

The United Kingdom Statistics Authority has designated these statistics as National Statistics, in accordance with the Statistics and Registration Service Act 2007 and signifying compliance with the Code of Practice for Official Statistics.

Designation can be broadly interpreted to mean that the statistics:
meet identified user needs
are well explained and readily accessible
are produced according to sound methods
are managed impartially and objectively in the public interest

Once statistics have been designated as National Statistics it is a statutory requirement that the Code of Practice shall continue to be

Copyright and reproduction

Further information

For further information about long-term international migration, please email migstatsunit@ons.gsi.gov.uk

Data supplier:
Migration Statistics Unit
Population Statistics Division
Room 2300
Office for National Statistics
Segensworth Road
FAREHAM
PO15 5RR

Table 1 Long-Term International Migration - Rolling annual data for the United Kingdom, year ending December 2017

United Kingdom
thousands

Citizenship																			
	All citizenships (2011 Census Revisions [1])		British (Including Overseas Territories)		Non-British		European Union [2]		European Union EU15		European Union EU8		European Union EU2		European Union Other		Non-European Union [3] All[3]		Other Europe[3]
Year	Est	+/-CI	Est	+/-CI	Est	+/-CI	Est	+/-CI	Est	+/-CI	Est	+/-CI	Est	+/-CI	Est	+/-CI	Est	+/-CI	Est	+/-CI
Inflow																				
YE Mar 08																				
YE Jun 08	571	38	81	15	490	35	184	27	69	16	106	21	8	5	1	1	306	23	12	5
YE Sep 08																				
YE Dec 08	590	39	85	16	505	36	198	28	90	19	89	19	15	9	3	3	307	22	12	5
YE Mar 09																				
YE Jun 09	563	37	88	15	475	34	183	27	82	17	84	20	14	8	4	3	292	20	11	4
YE Sep 09																				
YE Dec 09	567	30	96	14	471	26	167	19	82	13	68	13	13	5	4	4	303	18	10	4
YE Mar 10	587	30	97	15	490	26	172	19	81	13	73	13	15	5	3	3	318	18	10	4
YE Jun 10	582	30	96	14	487	26	176	20	86	13	72	13	15	5	3	3	311	17	10	4
YE Sep 10	600	32	92	15	508	28	182	22	83	15	86	16	10	3	4	4	326	18	10	4
YE Dec 10	591	31	93	15	498	27	176	21	76	13	86	16	10	3	4	4	322	17	10	4
YE Mar 11	578	30	92	14	486	27	169	20	78	13	82	15	8	3	4	4	317	17	10	3
YE Jun 11	589	30	88	13	501	27	175	20	79	12	86	15	7	2	4	3	327	18	9	3
YE Sep 11	581	29	81	13	500	26	166	18	83	12	75	13	11	4	1	1	334	19	10	3
YE Dec 11	566	28	78	12	488	25	174	18	82	11	77	12	13	4	1	1	314	18	10	3
YE Mar 12	536	28	74	11	463	26	166	18	82	11	71	13	12	4	1	1	296	18	10	3
YE Jun 12	517	26	77	12	440	24	158	16	79	11	63	11	10	3	2	2	282	17	13	4
YE Sep 12	497	26	79	11	418	24	149	16	85	12	59	11	11	4	2	2	269	17	13	4
YE Dec 12	498	27	80	12	418	25	158	18	92	12	60	13	11	4	2	2	260	17	14	4
YE Mar 13	493	27	76	12	417	25	170	18	96	13	63	13	13	4	2	2	246	17	14	4
YE Jun 13	502	29	77	12	425	26	183	21	107	14	66	14	20	7	3	3	242	16	15	5
YE Sep 13	530	30	79	12	450	27	208	21	104	13	73	13	25	9	3	3	242	17	16	5
YE Dec 13	526	29	77	12	449	27	201	20	112	14	70	12	25	10	3	3	248	17	15	5
YE Mar 14	552	31	79	11	473	28	213	22	113	15	68	12	30	12	3	3	260	18	16	5
YE Jun 14	574	31	83	12	491	28	223	22	124	16	73	13	34	9	3	3	268	18	16	4
YE Sep 14	615	35	81	15	534	32	246	24	129	17	76	14	40	10	5	5	289	21	15	4
YE Dec 14	632	36	81	14	551	34	264	25	128	16	80	15	49	10	5	5	287	22	15	6
YE Mar 15	644	35	85	13	560	32	270	25	134	17	81	15	57	11	4	4	290	21	15	6
YE Jun 15	639	34	85	14	553	31	265	24	131	15	73	13	54	11	4	4	288	20	13	5
YE Sep 15	619	32	88	13	531	29	256	22	130	15	68	12	55	14	2	2	275	19	15	4
YE Dec 15	631	33	84	12	548	30	269	24	128	16	73	12	65	14	2	2	279	19	15	5
YE Mar 16	638	33	83	13	555	31	267	24	138	17	68	12	69	15	3	3	288	19	15	5
YE Jun 16	652	34	77	12	575	32	284	26	133	17	73	13	70	15	3	2	291	19	16	5
YE Sep 16	598	34	72	13	526	32	267	26	132	17	57	13	74	14	3	3	259	19	17	5
YE Dec 16	589	34	74	14	515	31	249	24	131	17	48	10	67	13	3	3	265	20	16	5
YE Mar 17p	585	35	74	16	511	31	245	23	116	16	50	10	59	12	4	4	266	21	16	5
YE Jun 17p4	557	35	76	16	481	31	223	23	122	18	46	10	56	12	4	4	258	20	17	5
YE Sep 17p4	626	38	76	16	550	35	245	26	118	18	52	11	62	13	9	8	305	23	16	7
YE Dec 17p	630	39	80	16	551	36	240	27	118	18	52	12	60	14	11	9	311	23	16	7
Latest year change	+ 41		+ 6		+ 36		- 9		- 14		+ 4		- 7		+ 8		+ 46		0	
Percentage	7%		8%		7%		-4%		-11%		8%		-10%		267%		17%		0%	

179

Table 1 Long-Term International Migration - Rolling annual data for the United Kingdom, year ending December 2017

Citizenship

United Kingdom
thousands

Year	All citizenships 2011 Census Revisions[1] Est.	+/-CI	British (Including Overseas Territories) Est.	+/-CI	Non-British Est.	+/-CI	European Union[2] Est.	+/-CI	EU15 Est.	+/-CI	EU8 Est.	+/-CI	EU2 Est.	+/-CI	EU Other Est.	+/-CI	Non-EU All[3] Est.	+/-CI	Other Europe[3] Est.	+/-CI
Outflow																				
YE Mar 08	..	..	..	..	..	..	..	..	..	..	..	..	..	..	..	..	..	..	..	..
YE Jun 08	375	38	169	23	206	31	96	29	41	14	43	16	10	19	2	3	110	10	..	4
YE Sep 08	..	..	..	..	..	..	..	..	..	..	..	..	..	..	..	..	..	..	..	..
YE Dec 08	427	41	173	22	255	34	134	32	54	15	69	21	12	19	0~	1	120	12	..	5
YE Mar 09	..	..	..	..	..	..	..	..	..	..	..	..	..	..	..	..	..	..	..	..
YE Jun 09	397	28	158	15	239	23	121	21	55	11	62	17	4	3	1	1	118	11	..	4
YE Sep 09	..	..	..	..	..	..	..	..	..	..	..	..	..	..	..	..	..	..	..	..
YE Dec 09	368	22	140	11	228	18	109	16	53	11	52	12	3	1	1	1	119	9	5	2
YE Mar 10	365	23	131	11	233	20	115	18	58	13	52	12	4	2	2	2	119	9	6	2
YE Jun 10	347	21	128	10	219	18	104	16	53	13	46	10	3	2	1	1	115	8	6	2
YE Sep 10	345	20	136	11	209	17	101	16	61	13	36	7	3	2	1	1	108	8	6	2
YE Dec 10	339	20	136	11	203	16	99	14	58	12	37	8	2	2	1	1	104	8	6	2
YE Mar 11	336	18	141	11	194	15	92	13	52	9	37	8	2	1	1	1	102	7	5	2
YE Jun 11	342	19	143	11	199	16	95	13	51	9	40	9	3	2	1	1	104	9	8	5
YE Sep 11	339	20	142	11	197	16	91	13	46	9	39	9	5	3	1	1	106	10	8	6
YE Dec 11	351	22	149	13	202	17	92	14	49	10	37	9	5	3	1	1	110	10	8	6
YE Mar 12	352	22	150	13	202	17	90	14	49	10	36	9	4	3	1	1	112	10	8	6
YE Jun 12	349	22	153	16	196	16	86	13	49	10	32	8	3	2	1	1	110	9	6	2
YE Sep 12	343	22	150	16	192	15	84	13	49	10	31	7	3	2	2	2	108	8	5	2
YE Dec 12	321	20	143	14	179	14	75	11	41	8	30	8	3	2	1	1	103	8	5	2
YE Mar 13	318	20	141	14	177	14	75	12	42	8	29	8	3	2	1	1	102	8	4	2
YE Jun 13	320	19	140	12	180	15	77	12	44	9	30	8	3	2	1	1	103	8	6	3
YE Sep 13	320	19	137	12	182	15	78	13	47	10	26	7	4	2	2	2	104	8	6	3
YE Dec 13	317	19	134	12	183	15	78	12	47	10	26	7	3	2	2	2	105	9	7	3
YE Mar 14	316	20	129	11	187	17	83	14	49	12	27	7	4	2	2	2	104	8	7	3
YE Jun 14	320	22	131	13	189	18	85	15	49	12	29	8	5	4	2	2	105	9	7	3
YE Sep 14	323	23	135	13	188	19	87	15	47	12	34	9	5	3	1	1	101	11	7	3
YE Dec 14	319	22	137	13	182	18	89	15	51	12	32	9	5	3	1	1	93	10	6	3
YE Mar 15	308	21	133	13	176	17	86	13	49	9	30	8	5	3	1	1	90	10	6	3
YE Jun 15	303	20	131	12	172	16	85	12	49	9	29	7	6	3	1	1	86	10	5	2
YE Sep 15	297	19	128	12	169	15	85	12	51	9	27	7	6	5	2	2	84	8	4	2
YE Dec 15	299	20	124	13	175	16	86	13	50	10	27	7	7	5	2	2	90	9	4	2
YE Mar 16	311	21	126	13	184	16	89	13	52	10	28	7	8	5	2	2	95	9	4	2
YE Jun 16	316	21	127	12	190	17	95	14	54	10	31	8	9	5	2	1	95	9	4	2
YE Sep 16	325	22	128	13	197	18	102	15	52	10	38	9	10	5	2	2	95	11	3	2
YE Dec 16	340	23	134	13	206	19	116	16	59	11	43	10	13	6	2	2	90	10	3	2
YE Mar 17p	341	23	133	13	208	19	121	16	58	10	45	10	16	7	2	1	87	10	3	2
YE Jun 17p4	331	23	125	12	207	19	118	16	61	11	39	9	16	7	2	2	89	10	5	2
YE Sep 17p4	352	25	127	13	226	21	137	19	73	14	43	10	19	7	1	1	89	10	7	3
YE Dec 17p	349	26	126	13	223	22	139	20	71	15	46	11	19	7	3	2	84	10	6	3
Latest year change	+ 9		- 8		+ 17		+ 23		+ 12		+ 3		+ 6		+ 1		- 6		+ 3	
Percentage	3%		-6%		8%		20%		20%		7%		46%		50%		-7%		100%	

180

Table 1 Long-Term International Migration - Rolling annual data for the United Kingdom, year ending December 2017

United Kingdom
thousands

Citizenship / Year	All citizenships (2011 Census Revisions[1]) Est	+/-CI	British (Including Overseas Territories) Est	+/-CI	Non-British Est	+/-CI	European Union[2] Est	+/-CI	EU15 Est	+/-CI	EU8 Est	+/-CI	EU2 Est	+/-CI	EU Other Est	+/-CI	Non-EU All[3] Est	+/-CI	Other Europe[3] Est	+/-CI
Balance																				
YE Mar 08	:	:	:	:	:	:	:	:	:	:	:	:	:	:	:	:	:	:	:	:
YE Jun 08	+ 267	:	- 87	27	+ 284	46	+ 88	39	28	21	63	26	2	20	1	3	+ 196	25	4	6
YE Sep 08	:	:	:	:	:	:	:	:	:	:	:	:	:	:	:	:	:	:	:	:
YE Dec 08	+ 229	:	- 87	28	+ 250	50	+ 63	43	37	24	20	28	4	21	3	3	+ 187	25	1	7
YE Mar 09	:	:	:	:	:	:	:	:	:	:	:	:	:	:	:	:	:	:	:	:
YE Jun 09	+ 205	:	- 70	22	+ 236	41	+ 62	34	27	20	22	26	11	8	3	3	+ 174	23	2	6
YE Sep 09	:	:	:	:	:	:	:	:	:	:	:	:	:	:	:	:	:	:	:	:
YE Dec 09	+ 229	:	- 44	18	+ 242	32	+ 58	25	29	17	16	18	11	5	2	3	+ 184	20	5	4
YE Mar 10	:	:	- 34	18	+ 257	33	+ 58	26	23	18	21	17	11	6	2	3	+ 199	20	3	4
YE Jun 10	+ 244	:	- 33	18	+ 268	32	+ 72	26	33	18	26	17	11	5	2	3	+ 196	19	4	5
YE Sep 10	:	:	- 44	18	+ 299	33	+ 81	27	22	20	50	17	7	4	3	4	+ 218	19	5	4
YE Dec 10	+ 256	:	- 43	18	+ 294	32	+ 77	25	18	17	49	18	7	4	3	4	+ 217	19	5	4
YE Mar 11	:	:	- 50	17	+ 292	30	+ 77	24	24	16	44	17	7	3	3	4	+ 215	19	5	4
YE Jun 11	+ 263	:	- 55	17	+ 302	32	+ 79	24	26	16	46	17	4	3	3	4	+ 222	20	2	6
YE Sep 11	:	:	- 60	17	+ 303	30	+ 75	22	32	15	36	16	7	5	0~	1	+ 228	21	2	7
YE Dec 11	+ 205	:	- 70	18	+ 286	31	+ 82	23	34	16	40	15	8	5	0~	2	+ 204	20	2	6
YE Mar 12	+ 184	35	- 77	18	+ 260	31	+ 76	23	33	15	35	16	9	5	0~	2	+ 185	21	4	4
YE Jun 12	+ 167	34	- 76	19	+ 244	28	+ 72	21	32	15	31	14	9	4	0~	2	+ 172	19	8	4
YE Sep 12	+ 154	34	- 72	19	+ 226	28	+ 65	21	30	15	28	14	8	3	0~	2	+ 160	19	9	5
YE Dec 12	+ 177	34	- 63	19	+ 239	28	+ 82	21	44	14	30	15	8	4	1	2	+ 157	19	9	5
YE Mar 13	+ 175	34	- 65	18	+ 240	28	+ 95	22	50	15	34	15	10	5	1	2	+ 145	18	9	5
YE Jun 13	+ 182	34	- 63	17	+ 245	30	+ 106	24	53	16	36	16	17	8	1	2	+ 139	18	9	6
YE Sep 13	+ 210	36	- 58	17	+ 268	31	+ 130	25	60	17	48	15	22	10	1	3	+ 138	19	9	5
YE Dec 13	+ 209	35	- 57	17	+ 266	31	+ 123	24	58	16	44	14	21	10	1	3	+ 142	19	8	5
YE Mar 14	+ 236	37	- 50	16	+ 286	33	+ 130	26	62	19	40	14	26	12	1	3	+ 156	20	9	5
YE Jun 14	+ 254	38	- 48	17	+ 302	33	+ 138	27	64	19	44	15	29	10	4	3	+ 164	20	8	5
YE Sep 14	+ 292	42	- 54	20	+ 346	37	+ 158	28	77	20	42	17	35	10	4	4	+ 188	24	9	5
YE Dec 14	+ 313	43	- 55	19	+ 368	38	+ 174	29	79	21	48	18	44	11	4	4	+ 194	25	9	7
YE Mar 15	+ 336	41	- 48	18	+ 384	36	+ 184	28	79	19	51	17	51	11	3	3	+ 200	23	9	7
YE Jun 15	+ 336	39	- 46	18	+ 382	35	+ 180	27	84	19	44	15	49	12	3	3	+ 202	22	10	5
YE Sep 15	+ 322	37	- 40	18	+ 362	33	+ 171	26	80	18	41	14	48	12	1	2	+ 192	20	9	5
YE Dec 15	+ 332	38	- 40	18	+ 372	34	+ 184	27	80	18	46	14	58	15	1	2	+ 189	20	11	5
YE Mar 16	+ 327	39	- 43	19	+ 371	35	+ 178	28	76	18	39	14	61	15	1	2	+ 193	21	12	6
YE Jun 16	+ 336	40	- 49	18	+ 386	36	+ 189	30	84	20	42	15	62	16	2	2	+ 196	21	13	5
YE Sep 16	+ 273	41	- 56	18	+ 330	37	+ 165	30	81	20	19	16	64	15	1	3	+ 165	21	13	5
YE Dec 16	+ 249	41	- 60	19	+ 308	37	+ 133	29	73	20	5	14	54	14	1	3	+ 175	23	13	5
YE Mar 17p	+ 243	42	- 59	20	+ 302	37	+ 123	28	73	20	5	14	43	14	3	4	+ 179	23	12	5
YE Jun 17p4	+ 226	41	- 49	20	+ 275	36	+ 105	28	56	19	7	14	40	14	2	4	+ 170	23	12	6
YE Sep 17p4	+ 274	46	- 50	20	+ 324	41	+ 108	32	49	23	8	15	42	15	8	8	+ 216	25	9	8
YE Dec 17p	+ 282	47	- 46	20	+ 328	42	+ 101	33	46	23	6	16	40	16	8	9	+ 227	25	10	7

Source: Office for National Statistics (ONS), Home Office, Central Statistics Office (CSO) Ireland, Northern Ireland Statistics and Research Agency (NISRA).
Totals may not sum due to rounding.

Table 1 Long-Term International Migration - Rolling annual data for the United Kingdom, year ending December 2017

United Kingdom
thousands

Citizenship	Asia										Non-European Union[3]				Rest of the World								Stateless		All citizenships	
	All		Middle East and Central		East Asia		South Asia		South East Asia		All		Sub-Saharan Africa		North Africa		North America		Central and South		Oceania				Original Estimates[1]	
Year	Est	+/-CI	Est	+/-CI	Est	+/-CI	Est	+/-CI	Est	+/-CI	Est	+/-CI	Est	+/-CI	Est	+/-CI	Est	+/-CI	Est	+/-CI	Est	+/-CI	Est	+/-CI	Est	+/-CI
Inflow																										
YE Mar 08	…	…	…	…	…	…	…	…	…	…	…	…	…	…	…	…	…	…	…	…	…	…	…	…	…	…
YE Jun 08	182	18	22	3	39	9	94	13	28	9	111	13	45	8	6	5	22	5	11	4	27	5	0~	0~	…	…
YE Sep 08	…	…	…	…	…	…	…	…	…	…	…	…	…	…	…	…	…	…	…	…	…	…	…	…	…	…
YE Dec 08	177	16	28	6	35	8	83	9	31	8	118	15	48	9	8	4	26	7	14	6	23	5	0~	0~	…	…
YE Mar 09	…	…	…	…	…	…	…	…	…	…	…	…	…	…	…	…	…	…	…	…	…	…	…	…	…	…
YE Jun 09	176	15	27	6	34	7	89	10	26	6	104	13	46	9	7	4	21	6	11	5	19	5	0~	0~	…	…
YE Sep 09	…	…	…	…	…	…	…	…	…	…	…	…	…	…	…	…	…	…	…	…	…	…	…	…	…	…
YE Dec 09	202	14	24	4	39	6	110	10	29	5	90	10	39	7	3	3	23	6	8	3	17	4	0~	0~	…	…
YE Mar 10	219	14	23	4	40	6	123	10	33	6	88	10	33	6	3	3	24	6	9	4	19	4	0~	0~	…	…
YE Jun 10	215	13	22	4	40	6	121	9	32	6	86	10	30	5	3	2	24	6	10	4	18	4	0~	0~	…	…
YE Sep 10	229	14	21	4	43	6	130	10	34	6	87	10	30	5	7	5	20	5	11	4	19	4	0~	0~	…	…
YE Dec 10	221	13	20	4	43	6	126	9	32	6	90	10	29	5	7	5	21	5	10	4	22	5	0~	0~	…	…
YE Mar 11	220	14	20	4	43	7	127	10	29	6	87	10	26	4	8	5	22	5	9	3	22	5	1	0~	…	…
YE Jun 11	233	14	20	4	41	6	143	11	28	6	84	10	26	5	9	5	19	5	8	4	21	5	1	0~	…	…
YE Sep 11	243	16	21	4	55	9	145	11	23	5	81	9	24	4	5	2	24	6	6	3	21	4	1	0~	…	…
YE Dec 11	226	15	22	4	56	9	129	10	20	4	76	9	25	5	4	1	23	6	6	2	18	4	0~	0~	…	…
YE Mar 12	207	14	22	5	57	8	107	10	21	4	79	11	25	5	4	1	23	8	6	2	21	5	0~	0~	…	…
YE Jun 12	191	14	19	5	56	8	91	9	21	4	81	9	25	5	3	1	26	6	6	2	22	5	0~	0~	…	…
YE Sep 12	173	13	17	4	57	8	74	8	22	5	83	11	27	6	5	3	23	6	7	3	21	6	0~	0~	…	…
YE Dec 12	165	13	16	3	55	8	71	8	22	5	81	11	24	5	6	4	23	6	7	3	21	5	0~	0~	…	…
YE Mar 13	156	12	16	3	53	7	66	8	21	5	76	11	23	5	6	4	24	6	7	3	15	4	0~	0~	…	…
YE Jun 13	155	12	18	3	57	8	60	7	21	5	71	10	22	5	7	4	22	6	7	3	14	4	0~	0~	…	…
YE Sep 13	156	13	20	4	63	10	56	7	19	5	70	9	18	4	12	6	18	4	6	3	15	3	0~	0~	…	…
YE Dec 13	156	14	20	4	64	11	53	6	20	5	77	10	20	4	14	7	19	5	8	3	15	3	0~	0~	…	…
YE Mar 14	161	13	26	4	66	10	54	6	20	5	84	11	22	4	15	7	18	4	11	5	17	4	0~	0~	…	…
YE Jun 14	164	13	26	3	64	10	59	7	21	5	89	11	24	4	15	7	21	5	11	5	19	4	0~	0~	…	…
YE Sep 14	168	17	29	5	51	10	67	11	23	6	105	13	23	4	12	5	31	7	18	7	21	4	0~	0~	…	…
YE Dec 14	168	17	31	5	53	10	67	12	23	6	104	13	25	5	9	3	31	8	17	7	22	4	0~	0~	…	…
YE Mar 15	172	15	28	5	53	10	68	9	23	5	102	12	27	5	8	2	30	8	14	6	23	5	0~	0~	…	…
YE Jun 15	172	15	29	6	56	9	64	10	21	5	101	12	25	5	8	3	31	8	15	5	21	5	0~	0~	…	…
YE Sep 15	165	14	31	5	61	9	53	8	23	5	97	12	30	6	7	1	28	7	11	5	21	5	0~	0~	…	…
YE Dec 15	168	14	32	4	62	9	55	8	23	5	95	11	28	5	8	1	25	6	12	6	22	6	1	0~	…	…
YE Mar 16	177	14	33	5	63	10	59	8	23	5	94	11	27	5	9	2	25	5	12	5	21	6	1	0~	…	…
YE Jun 16	179	14	32	4	61	10	61	7	25	6	94	11	28	5	8	2	23	5	15	7	18	4	1	0~	…	…
YE Sep 16	159	14	29	4	53	10	58	7	16	4	83	11	24	6	6	2	21	5	15	7	17	4	1	0~	…	…
YE Dec 16	163	16	33	5	56	12	58	8	17	4	85	12	25	8	7	2	21	5	15	7	17	4	1	0~	…	…
YE Mar 17p	161	16	32	5	58	12	54	8	17	4	89	13	28	8	6	2	25	7	11	5	19	5	1	0~	…	…
YE Jun 17p4	156	15	29	5	57	12	56	8	14	4	86	12	26	7	6	2	24	7	11	5	18	5	0~	0~	…	…
YE Sep 17p4	194	18	29	6	74	12	69	10	22	6	95	14	32	8	7	2	24	7	8	3	24	7	0~	0~	…	…
YE Dec 17p	198	17	26	4	75	11	74	10	23	6	96	14	30	7	7	4	25	7	7	3	27	9	0~	0~	…	…
Latest year change	+ 35		- 7		+ 19		+ 16		+ 6		+ 11		+ 5		0		+ 4		- 8		+ 10		- 1			
Percentage	21%		-21%		34%		28%		35%		13%		20%		0%		19%		-53%		59%		-100%			

Table 1 Long-Term International Migration - Rolling annual data for the United Kingdom, year ending December 2017

United Kingdom
thousands

Citizenship	Non-European Union[3]																					Stateless		All citizenships Original Estimates[1]	
	Asia										Non-European Union[3]				Rest of the World						Oceania					
	All		Middle East and Central		East Asia		South Asia		South East Asia		All		Sub-Saharan Africa		North Africa		North America		Central and South							
Year	Est	+/-CI	Est	+/-CI	Est	+/-CI	Est	+/-CI	Est	+/-CI	Est	+/-CI	Est	+/-CI	Est	+/-CI	Est	+/-CI	Est	+/-CI	Est	+/-CI	Est	+/-CI	Est	+/-CI
Outflow																										
YE Mar 08																							0~			
YE Jun 08	45	7	5	1	16	4	19	5	6	2	56	7	14	3	2	2	11	3	7	3	24	4	0~			
YE Sep 08																							0~			
YE Dec 08	47	7	5	1	16	4	20	5	6	1	62	8	14	5	2	2	13	4	7	3	25	4	0~			
YE Mar 09																							0~			
YE Jun 09	49	7	5	1	17	4	22	5	6	2	59	7	15	4	1	1	12	3	6	3	25	4	0~			
YE Sep 09																							0~			
YE Dec 09	55	5	6	1	19	3	23	3	7	2	59	7	13	3	1	1	16	4	4	2	26	4	0~			
YE Mar 10	57	6	7	1	22	4	23	3	6	2	55	6	12	3	2	1	14	4	5	2	23	4	0~			
YE Jun 10	55	5	7	1	19	4	22	3	6	2	54	6	11	2	2	1	14	4	5	2	21	4	0~			
YE Sep 10	55	5	7	2	20	4	21	3	6	2	47	5	12	3	1	1	11	3	5	2	18	3	0~			
YE Dec 10	53	5	7	2	19	4	21	3	6	2	46	5	12	3	1	1	12	3	5	2	16	3	0~			
YE Mar 11	51	5	6	2	16	3	22	3	7	2	46	5	11	2	2	2	13	3	5	2	16	3	0~			
YE Jun 11	52	5	7	2	15	3	24	3	6	2	44	5	10	2	2	1	12	3	4	2	16	3	0~			
YE Sep 11	53	5	6	2	17	3	24	4	7	2	45	6	9	3	1	1	13	3	4	2	17	3	0~			
YE Dec 11	61	6	6	2	17	3	29	4	9	2	41	6	9	3	1	1	12	3	3	2	16	3	0~			
YE Mar 12	63	6	5	1	19	3	30	4	9	3	41	6	9	3	1	1	11	3	3	1	16	3	0~			
YE Jun 12	65	6	5	1	20	4	29	4	9	3	40	6	9	3	1	1	12	3	3	1	15	3	0~			
YE Sep 12	69	7	6	2	22	4	30	4	11	3	35	5	9	3	1	1	10	3	3	1	12	3	0~			
YE Dec 12	63	6	5	2	21	4	26	4	11	3	36	5	8	2	1	1	11	3	4	2	12	3	0~			
YE Mar 13	63	6	6	2	22	4	26	4	9	2	34	5	7	2	1	1	10	2	4	2	11	3	0~			
YE Jun 13	62	5	6	2	21	4	27	4	8	2	34	5	7	2	1	1	10	2	5	2	12	3	0~			
YE Sep 13	59	6	4	1	19	3	27	4	8	2	39	6	7	2	2	2	12	4	5	2	14	3	0~			
YE Dec 13	59	6	5	2	21	4	26	4	8	2	39	6	8	2	2	2	13	4	4	2	13	3	0~			
YE Mar 14	59	6	5	2	22	4	24	3	8	2	39	6	8	2	2	2	13	4	3	2	12	3	0~			
YE Jun 14	59	6	5	2	23	4	23	3	9	3	38	6	9	2	2	2	13	4	3	2	12	3	0~			
YE Sep 14	62	9	6	2	28	8	20	3	8	3	32	5	7	2	2	2	9	3	2	1	12	3	0~			
YE Dec 14	59	9	5	2	27	8	21	3	7	3	27	4	6	2	1	1	9	3	1	1	10	3	0~			
YE Mar 15	56	9	5	2	25	8	20	3	6	2	27	5	4	2	2	2	9	3	1	1	11	3	0~			
YE Jun 15	55	9	5	2	24	7	20	3	7	3	27	4	5	2	1	1	9	3	1	1	10	3	0~			
YE Sep 15	51	6	5	2	21	4	19	3	7	2	28	5	6	2	1	1	10	3	4	2	7	2	0~			
YE Dec 15	53	6	5	2	20	4	20	4	9	3	33	5	7	2	1	1	10	3	5	2	9	3	0~			
YE Mar 16	57	7	6	4	20	4	21	4	9	3	34	5	7	2	2	2	12	3	5	2	8	3	0~			
YE Jun 16	55	7	6	4	21	4	20	4	9	3	35	5	6	2	2	2	11	3	5	2	11	3	0~			
YE Sep 16	52	7	6	4	18	4	20	4	8	3	39	7	6	3	2	2	16	5	4	2	11	3	0~			
YE Dec 16	51	7	7	2	18	4	18	4	8	3	36	7	5	3	2	2	16	5	4	2	9	3	0~			
YE Mar 17 p	49	6	7	2	18	4	17	4	7	3	34	7	4	3	2	2	15	5	4	2	9	3	0~			
YE Jun 17 p[4]	49	7	7	4	18	4	16	4	8	3	35	8	4	3	3	2	15	5	4	2	9	3	0~			
YE Sep 17 p[4]	52	7	9	4	21	4	15	3	7	3	30	6	5	3	2	1	10	4	4	2	9	3	0~			
YE Dec 17 p	47	7	9	4	21	4	12	3	6	3	30	7	5	3	2	1	10	5	3	3	9	3	0~			
Latest year change	- 4		+ 2		+ 3		- 6		- 2		- 6		0		0		- 6		0		0		0			
Percentage	-8%		29%		17%		-33%		-25%		-17%		0%		0%		-38%		0%		0%		N/A			

183

Table 1 Long-Term International Migration - Rolling annual data for the United Kingdom, year ending December 2017

United Kingdom
thousands

Citizenship

Year	Asia: All Est	+/-CI	Asia: Middle East and Central Est	+/-CI	Asia: East Asia Est	+/-CI	Asia: South Asia Est	+/-CI	Asia: South East Asia Est	+/-CI	Non-European Union[3]: All Est	+/-CI	Sub-Saharan Africa Est	+/-CI	Rest of the World: North Africa Est	+/-CI	North America Est	+/-CI	Central and South Est	+/-CI	Oceania Est	+/-CI	Stateless Est	+/-CI	All citizenships Original Estimates[1] Est	+/-CI
Balance																										
YE Mar 08	..	..	..	..	..	..	..	..	..	..	..	..	..	..	..	..	..	..	..	..	..	..	..	..	..	..
YE Jun 08	+137	19+	17	3+	23	10+	75	14+	22	9	55	14+	32	8+	4	5+	11	6+	4	4	7	4	0~	0~	+196	54
YE Sep 08	..	..	..	..	..	..	..	..	..	..	..	..	..	..	..	..	..	..	..	..	..	..	0~	0~	..	..
YE Dec 08	+130	17+	23	6+	18	9+	63	11+	26	8	56	17+	33	10+	5	4+	13	8+	7	7-	2	2	0~	0~	+163	57
YE Mar 09	..	..	..	..	..	..	..	..	..	..	..	..	..	..	..	..	..	..	..	..	..	..	0~	0~	..	..
YE Jun 09	+127	16+	22	6+	17	8+	68	11+	20	7	45	15+	31	10+	5	4+	9	7+	6	6	6	6	0~	0~	+166	47
YE Sep 09	..	..	..	..	..	..	..	..	..	..	..	..	..	..	..	..	..	..	..	..	..	..	0~	0~	..	..
YE Dec 09	+147	15+	18	4+	20	7+	87	11+	23	6	31	12+	26	7+	2	3+	8	7+	4	3-	8	8	0~	0~	+198	37
YE Mar 10	+162	15+	16	4+	19	8+	100	11+	27	6	34	12+	21	6+	2	3+	10	7+	5	4-	4	4	0~	0~	+222	37
YE Jun 10	+160	14+	15	4+	21	7+	99	10+	26	6	32	11+	19	6+	2	3+	10	7+	5	4-	4	4	0~	0~	+235	37
YE Sep 10	+174	15+	14	5+	23	7+	109	10+	28	7	39	11+	18	6+	5	5+	9	5+	6	4+	1	1	0~	0~	+255	38
YE Dec 10	+168	14+	12	4+	24	7+	106	10+	25	6	45	11+	17	5+	6	5+	10	6+	5	5+	7	5	0~	0~	+252	37
YE Mar 11	+168	15+	14	4+	28	7+	105	10+	22	6	41	11+	15	5+	7	5+	10	6+	5	4+	5	5	0~	0~	+242	35
YE Jun 11	+181	15+	13	5+	26	7+	119	11+	22	6	40	12+	16	5+	7	5+	8	6+	4	4+	5	5	0~	0~	+247	36
YE Sep 11	+190	16+	14	4+	40	10+	120	11+	15	5	36	11+	15	5+	4	2+	11	7+	2	3+	3	3	0~	0~	+242	35
YE Dec 11	+165	16+	16	5+	39	9+	99	11+	12	5	36	11+	16	6+	3	1+	12	7+	3	3+	2	2	0~	0~	+215	35
YE Mar 12	+144	16+	17	5+	38	9+	77	11+	12	5	38	12+	17	5+	2	1+	11	9+	2	3+	5	5	0~	0~		
YE Jun 12	+126	15+	18	5+	37	9+	61	10+	10	5	42	11+	15	6+	2	2+	14	7+	3	3+	8	8	0~	0~		
YE Sep 12	+104	14+	13	4+	35	9+	45	9+	11	6	48	12+	18	6+	3	3+	13	6+	4	4+	9	9	0~	0~		
YE Dec 12	+103	14+	12	4+	35	8+	45	9+	11	6	45	12+	16	6+	4	4+	13	7+	2	3+	9	9	0~	0~		
YE Mar 13	+94	13+	11	4+	31	8+	40	8+	13	6	41	11+	15	5+	5	4+	14	6+	2	3+	4	4	0~	0~		
YE Jun 13	+92	13+	11	3+	35	8+	33	8+	11	5	37	11+	12	4+	6	4+	12	6+	1	2+	2	2	0~	0~		
YE Sep 13	+97	14+	14	4+	44	11+	29	7+	11	5	31	11+	13	4+	7	6+	6	6+	5	3+	1	1	0~	0~		
YE Dec 13	+97	15+	14	4+	43	11+	27	7+	12	5	38	11+	13	4+	7	7+	6	6+	7	4+	2	2	0~	0~		
YE Mar 14	+102	15+	15	4+	44	11+	30	7+	12	5	45	12+	15	4+	7	7+	6	6+	8	5+	5	5	0~	0~		
YE Jun 14	+104	16+	15	4+	41	11+	36	7+	12	6	51	12+	15	5+	7	7+	8	6+	16	7+	7	7	0~	0~		
YE Sep 14	+106	19+	20	5+	24	13+	47	11+	15	6	73	13+	16	5+	5	5+	21	8+	16	7+	9	9	0~	0~		
YE Dec 14	+109	19+	21	5+	26	13+	47	12+	15	6	76	14+	19	5+	3	3+	23	8+	15	6+	11	11	0~	0~		
YE Mar 15	+116	18+	24	6+	29	11+	48	9+	16	6	75	13+	22	6+	3	3+	22	8+	13	6+	12	12	0~	0~		
YE Jun 15	+117	17+	26	6+	32	10+	44	10+	15	5	74	13+	20	6+	3	3+	18	7+	14	6+	14	14	0~	0~		
YE Sep 15	+114	15+	23	5+	40	10+	34	8+	16	6	68	13+	24	6+	2	2+	14	6+	6	5+	13	13	1	0~		
YE Dec 15	+115	15+	24	5+	42	10+	35	9+	14	6	61	13+	22	6+	2	2+	13	6+	7	6+	13	13	1	0~		
YE Mar 16	+120	16+	25	6+	43	10+	38	9+	16	6	60	13+	20	6+	2	2+	12	6+	7	5+	12	12	1	0~		
YE Jun 16	+124	16+	27	6+	40	11+	41	9+	8	5	59	12+	23	6+	3	3+	12	6+	7	6+	7	7	1	0~		
YE Sep 16	+106	16+	26	6+	34	11+	38	9+	9	5	44	13+	17	6+	3	3+	5	7+	11	7+	8	8	0~	0~		
YE Dec 16	+112	17+	26	6+	38	12+	40	9+	9	5	49	14+	21	8+	5	3+	5	7+	11	7+	8	5+	0~	0~		
YE Mar 17p	+111	17+	26	6+	39	12+	36	9+	10	5	55	15+	24	8+	4	3+	10	9+	7	5+	10	6	0~	0~		
YE Jun 17p4	+107	17+	22	5+	40	12+	40	9+	9	5	51	14+	22	8+	4	3+	9	9+	6	5+	10	6	0~	0~		
YE Sep 17p4	+142	19+	20	7+	53	13+	54	10+	15	6	65	15+	27	9+	4	3+	14	8+	4	4+	15	7	0~	0~		
YE Dec 17p	+151	18+	17	6+	54	12+	62	10+	17	6	66	16+	26	7+	5	4+	14	9+	3	4+	18	10	0~	0~		

Source: Office for National Statistics (ONS), Home Office, Central Statistics Office (CSO) Ireland, Northern Ireland Statistics and Research Agency (NISRA).
Totals may not sum due to rounding.

Table 1 Long-Term International Migration - Rolling annual data for the United Kingdom, year ending December 2017

Citizenship

".." - Not available, "0~" - Rounds to zero. Please see the Notes worksheet for more information.

YE = Year Ending

p = Year includes provisional estimates for 2017

Long-Term International Migration estimates by citizenship are only available for mid years and calendar years up to YE Dec 2009. For old country grouping data back to 1991 and new country grouping data back to 2004, please see 2-series tables 2.01a and 2.10 in the data section on the ONS website:

All data related to international migration

2 European Union estimates are for the EU15 (Austria, Belgium, Denmark, Finland, France, Germany, Greece, Republic of Ireland, Italy, Luxembourg, Netherlands, Portugal, Spain and Sweden) up to 2003, the EU25 (the EU15 and the EU8 groupings plus Malta and Cyprus) from 2004 to 2006, the EU27 (the EU25 plus Bulgaria and Romania) from 2007 and the EU28 (the EU27 plus Croatia) from July 2013. Estimates are also shown separately for the EU15, the EU8 (Czech Republic, Estonia, Hungary, Latvia, Lithuania, Poland, Slovakia and Slovenia), the EU2 (Bulgaria and Romania) and EU Other (Malta, Cyprus and Croatia). British citizens are excluded from all citizenship groupings and are shown separately.

3 Excludes British and other European Union citizens as defined in footnote 2.

4. Please see the correction notice on the Contents and Notes page for information relating to YE Jun 17[p] and YE Sep 17[p]

This table uses 95% confidence intervals (CI) to indicate the robustness of each estimate. Please see the Notes worksheet for more information.

Statistically Significant Increase   Statistically Significant Decrease

The latest estimates (year ending December 2017) have been compared with the corresponding estimates for the period one year earlier. Where changes have been found to be statistically significant, the relevant pair of estimates have been highlighted by setting their background colour. Please see the Notes worksheet for more information.

Latest year change (change from year ending December 2016 to year ending December 2017):

These indications of change are intended only as an aid to identifying trends.
Users are advised that the estimates that have been compared are rounded estimates that have a degree of uncertainty as indicated by their associated confidence intervals.
Users are advised to be cautious when making inferences from any changes that are not identified as statistically significant. It is possible for such changes to be caused purely by the variability inherent to sample surveys, rather than because of any changes in real migration levels.
Please see the Notes worksheet for more information on "Reliability of LTIM estimates" and "Statistically significant changes".

Table 2 Long-Term International Migration - Rolling annual data for the United Kingdom, year ending December 2017

United Kingdom
thousands

Main reason for migration

Year	All reasons		Work Related						Accompany / Join		Formal study		Other		No reason stated1	
			All		Definite job		Looking for work									
	Estimate	+/-CI	Estimate	+/-CI	Estimate	+/-CI	Estimate	+/-CI	Estimate	+/-CI	Estimate	+/-CI	Estimate	+/-CI	Estimate	+/-CI
Inflow																
YE Mar 08	:	:	:	:	:	:	:	:	:	:	:	:	:	:	:	:
YE Jun 08	:	:	:	:	:	:	:	:	:	:	:	:	:	:	:	:
YE Sep 08	:	:	:	:	:	:	:	:	:	:	:	:	:	:	:	:
YE Dec 08	590	39	220	25	145	21	75	14	88	15	175	15	64	11	44	13
YE Mar 09	:	:	:	:	:	:	:	:	:	:	:	:	:	:	:	:
YE Jun 09	:	:	:	:	:	:	:	:	:	:	:	:	:	:	:	:
YE Sep 09	:	:	:	:	:	:	:	:	:	:	:	:	:	:	:	:
YE Dec 09	567	30	193	20	129	17	64	9	76	12	211	12	50	5	36	9
YE Mar 10	587	30	194	19	131	17	63	9	78	11	235	11	44	5	36	10
YE Jun 10	582	30	196	20	130	17	66	9	73	10	235	10	42	5	35	10
YE Sep 10	600	32	204	21	129	18	76	11	76	11	245	11	42	5	33	10
YE Dec 10	591	31	203	20	122	16	81	12	80	11	238	11	40	4	29	10
YE Mar 11	578	30	194	19	116	16	79	12	81	12	232	12	39	4	32	9
YE Jun 11	589	30	194	20	117	15	76	12	85	12	239	12	40	5	30	8
YE Sep 11	581	29	183	17	113	13	70	11	80	11	246	11	38	4	34	10
YE Dec 11	566	28	184	17	115	13	69	11	74	11	232	11	41	4	35	10
YE Mar 12	536	28	177	16	114	13	64	10	71	12	213	12	43	5	32	11
YE Jun 12	517	26	173	15	108	12	65	9	68	9	197	9	43	5	35	11
YE Sep 12	497	26	175	16	109	12	66	11	63	9	187	9	43	5	29	8
YE Dec 12	498	27	180	17	113	13	67	11	62	9	180	9	43	6	32	10
YE Mar 13	493	27	190	18	116	13	74	13	59	9	176	9	40	5	28	10
YE Jun 13	502	29	202	20	125	15	77	14	60	9	175	9	41	6	25	9
YE Sep 13	530	30	217	20	138	17	80	11	66	9	175	9	45	6	26	10
YE Dec 13	526	29	214	20	132	16	83	11	71	10	177	10	43	5	20	8
YE Mar 14	552	31	225	21	137	18	88	12	80	11	176	11	47	6	24	7
YE Jun 14	574	31	241	21	145	16	96	13	82	11	175	11	49	7	26	8
YE Sep 14	615	35	265	25	163	21	101	13	88	12	190	12	49	7	23	9
YE Dec 14	632	36	278	26	175	22	104	14	89	12	191	12	48	7	26	8
YE Mar 15	644	35	292	24	184	20	108	14	84	11	192	11	50	7	27	8
YE Jun 15	639	34	294	25	187	21	107	13	80	11	193	11	48	6	24	7
YE Sep 15	619	32	289	23	169	18	120	15	77	10	175	10	50	7	29	8
YE Dec 15	631	33	308	25	178	19	130	17	74	9	168	9	53	6	29	8
YE Mar 16	638	33	303	25	177	19	126	16	80	10	166	10	58	6	30	10
YE Jun 16	652	34	312	25	182	19	130	17	80	11	164	11	64	7	34	11
YE Sep 16	598	34	293	26	190	20	103	16	74	10	134	10	62	5	35	11
YE Dec 16	589	34	275	24	180	19	94	14	85	12	137	12	60	5	32	11
YE Mar 17p	585	35	272	24	186	20	86	13	80	12	139	12	63	11	30	9
YE Jun 17p2	557	35	252	24	181	21	72	11	78	12	138	12	63	11	26	8
YE Sep 17p2	626	38	267	25	189	22	77	12	85	14	189	14	60	11	26	7
YE Dec 17p	630	39	269	26	193	23	76	13	79	14	191	14	59	11	33	9
Latest year change	+ 41		- 6		+ 13		- 18		- 6		+ 54		- 1		+ 1	
Percentage	7%		-2%		7%		-19%		-7%		39%		-2%		3%	

186

Table 2 Long-Term International Migration - Rolling annual data for the United Kingdom, year ending December 2017

Main reason for migration

United Kingdom
thousands

Year	All reasons		Work Related All		Definite job		Looking for work		Accompany / Join		Formal study		Other		No reason stated1	
	Estimate	+/-CI	Estimate	+/-CI	Estimate	+/-CI	Estimate	+/-CI	Estimate	+/-CI	Estimate	+/-CI	Estimate	+/-CI	Estimate	+/-CI
Outflow																
YE Mar 08	:	:	:	:	:	:	:	:	:	:	:	:	:	:	:	:
YE Jun 08	:	:	:	:	:	:	:	:	:	:	:	:	:	:	:	:
YE Sep 08	:	:	:	:	:	:	:	:	:	:	:	:	:	:	:	:
YE Dec 08	427	41	219	26	136	20	82	16	57	12	23	8	41	5	88	28
YE Mar 09	:	:	:	:	:	:	:	:	:	:	:	:	:	:	:	:
YE Jun 09	:	:	:	:	:	:	:	:	:	:	:	:	:	:	:	:
YE Sep 09	:	:	:	:	:	:	:	:	:	:	:	:	:	:	:	:
YE Dec 09	368	22	211	17	119	13	92	11	46	7	23	4	42	4	46	9
YE Mar 10	365	23	210	18	119	13	92	11	43	7	27	7	40	4	44	9
YE Jun 10	347	21	198	16	113	12	85	10	42	7	25	7	38	4	45	9
YE Sep 10	345	20	192	15	116	13	77	8	40	6	30	8	39	4	44	8
YE Dec 10	339	20	189	13	114	11	75	8	39	6	29	9	35	3	46	9
YE Mar 11	336	18	182	12	108	9	74	8	38	6	26	6	37	4	52	10
YE Jun 11	342	19	190	14	114	11	76	8	37	6	26	6	37	4	52	10
YE Sep 11	339	20	191	14	115	12	75	8	35	5	21	5	39	5	54	11
YE Dec 11	351	22	201	15	123	12	78	9	33	5	19	5	41	7	57	12
YE Mar 12	352	22	206	16	127	13	79	9	33	5	19	5	42	7	53	12
YE Jun 12	349	22	199	14	124	11	75	9	33	5	21	5	46	11	50	11
YE Sep 12	343	22	198	14	127	12	71	8	35	6	20	4	43	10	46	11
YE Dec 12	321	20	182	13	115	10	67	7	36	6	21	5	40	9	43	10
YE Mar 13	318	20	184	13	115	11	69	7	35	6	19	4	40	9	40	9
YE Jun 13	320	19	187	14	116	11	71	7	33	6	18	4	36	4	46	11
YE Sep 13	320	19	186	14	113	12	73	7	30	5	22	5	35	4	46	10
YE Dec 13	317	19	187	14	111	11	75	8	29	5	23	5	36	4	43	10
YE Mar 14	316	20	182	15	107	10	76	11	29	5	24	5	34	4	46	11
YE Jun 14	320	22	180	16	107	12	73	11	30	5	23	5	37	7	50	11
YE Sep 14	323	23	180	16	105	11	75	12	29	5	22	5	38	7	53	13
YE Dec 14	319	22	178	16	110	11	68	11	28	5	24	6	38	7	51	12
YE Mar 15	308	21	167	14	105	11	61	8	28	5	25	6	37	7	51	11
YE Jun 15	303	20	171	13	103	10	67	9	28	6	24	6	34	6	47	11
YE Sep 15	297	19	167	14	103	11	64	8	26	6	28	6	33	6	42	8
YE Dec 15	299	20	166	14	99	11	66	9	27	6	26	6	31	6	50	11
YE Mar 16	311	21	170	14	101	11	69	9	25	5	24	5	35	6	57	12
YE Jun 16	316	21	168	14	104	12	64	8	23	4	27	6	36	6	62	12
YE Sep 16	325	22	167	14	105	12	62	8	25	5	23	5	34	5	76	14
YE Dec 16	340	23	179	15	116	13	62	8	26	6	24	6	33	5	78	15
YE Mar 17p	341	23	180	15	121	13	59	8	28	6	25	6	33	6	74	14
YE Jun 17p2	331	23	177	15	118	13	59	8	28	6	23	5	31	5	72	14
YE Sep 17p2	352	25	192	16	127	14	65	9	26	6	21	5	36	5	77	16
YE Dec 17p	349	26	188	18	129	15	59	9	23	5	19	5	42	4	77	15
Latest year change	+ 9		+ 9		+ 13		- 3		- 3		- 5		+ 9		- 1	
Percentage	3%		5%		11%		-5%		-12%		-21%		27%		-1%	

187

Table 2 Long-Term International Migration - Rolling annual data for the United Kingdom, year ending December

Source: Office for National Statistics (ONS), Home Office, Central Statistics Office (CSO) Ireland, Northern Ireland Statistics and Research Agency (NISRA).

Totals may not sum due to rounding.

"," - Not available, "0~" - Rounds to zero. Please see the Notes worksheet for more information.

YE = Year Ending
p = Year includes provisional estimates for 2017

Long-Term International Migration estimates by reason for migration are only available for calendar years up to YE Dec 2009. For data back to 1991, please see 2-series table 2.04 in the data section on the ONS website:
All data related to international migration

1 "No reason stated" includes non-responses and the non-specific responses "Emigrating / Immigrating" and "Returning home to live".
2. Please see the correction notice on the Contents and Notes page for information relating to YE Jun 17p and YE Sep 17p

Care should be taken when comparing inflow and outflow by main reason for migration. Returning migrants are asked their reason for returning, not their original reason for migrating. A former immigrant's main reason for leaving the UK may well differ from their previous main reason for immigrating into the UK. Because of this, no balance estimates are displayed. Please see the Notes worksheet for more information.

This table uses 95% confidence intervals (CI) to indicate the robustness of each estimate. Please see the Notes worksheet for more information.

Statistically Significant Increase   Statistically Significant Decrease
The latest estimates (year ending December 2017) have been compared with the corresponding estimates for the period one year earlier. Where changes have been found to be statistically significant, the relevant pair of estimates have been highlighted by setting their background colour. Please see the Notes worksheet for more information.

Latest year change (change from year ending December 2016 to year ending December 2017):

These indications of change are intended only as an aid to identifying trends.
Users are advised that the estimates that have been compared are rounded estimates that have a degree of uncertainty as indicated by their associated confidence intervals. Users are advised to be cautious when making inferences from any changes that are not identified as statistically significant. It is possible for such changes to be caused purely by the variability inherent to sample surveys, rather than because of any changes in real migration levels.
Please see the Notes worksheet for more information on "Reliability of LTIM estimates" and "Statistically significant changes".

Table 3 International Passenger Survey (IPS) estimates of long-term international migration - Rolling annual data for the United Kingdom, year ending December 2017

Abbreviation: Est. (Estimate)
Citizenship by main reason for migration

United Kingdom
thousands

Main reason for migration	All citizenships Est.	+/-CI	British (Including Overseas Territories) Est.	+/-CI	Non-British Est.	+/-CI	European Union[1] Est.	+/-CI	European Union EU15 Est.	+/-CI	European Union EU8 Est.	+/-CI	European Union EU2 Est.	+/-CI	European Union Other Est.	+/-CI	Non-European Union[2] All Est.	+/-CI	Other Europe[3] Est.	+/-CI	Asia All Est.	+/-CI
Inflow																						
All reasons																						
YE Mar 08	:	:	:	:	:	:	:	:	:	:	:	:	:	:	:	:	:	:	:	:	:	:
YE Jun 08	521	38	78	15	443	35	163	27	58	16	95	21	9	5	1	1	280	23	11	5	169	18
YE Sep 08	:	:							:	:			:	:			:	:			:	:
YE Dec 08	538	39	82	16	456	36	178	28	83	19	76	19	17	9	3	3	278	22	10	5	163	16
YE Mar 09	:												:	:			:	:			:	
YE Jun 09	518	37	89	15	429	34	165	27	76	17	71	20	14	8	4	3	264	20	10	4	165	15
YE Sep 09	:												:	:			:	:			:	:
YE Dec 09	528	30	98	14	430	26	150	19	76	13	57	13	13	5	4	3	280	18	9	4	193	14
YE Mar 10	553	30	98	15	455	26	157	19	75	13	64	13	15	5	3	3	298	18	9	4	212	14
YE Jun 10	548	30	96	14	452	26	159	20	79	13	62	13	14	5	3	3	293	17	9	4	208	13
YE Sep 10	566	32	92	15	475	28	165	22	76	15	76	16	9	3	4	3	310	18	9	4	222	14
YE Dec 10	553	31	93	15	460	27	156	21	68	13	76	16	9	3	4	3	304	17	9	4	212	13
YE Mar 11	540	30	91	14	449	27	149	20	67	13	71	15	7	3	4	4	300	17	9	3	211	14
YE Jun 11	553	30	87	13	466	27	157	20	70	13	77	15	6	2	4	3	309	18	8	3	224	14
YE Sep 11	546	29	81	13	465	26	148	18	71	12	66	13	10	4	1	1	317	19	9	3	233	16
YE Dec 11	531	28	78	12	453	25	158	18	76	12	69	12	12	4	1	1	295	18	9	3	216	15
YE Mar 12	506	28	74	11	431	26	152	18	75	12	65	13	11	4	1	1	279	18	9	3	197	14
YE Jun 12	483	26	77	12	406	24	144	16	76	11	56	11	11	3	1	1	263	17	8	3	179	14
YE Sep 12	460	26	78	11	382	24	137	16	72	11	54	11	9	3	2	2	245	17	11	4	158	13
YE Dec 12	462	27	79	12	383	25	147	18	80	12	56	13	9	4	2	2	236	17	12	4	150	13
YE Mar 13	454	27	76	12	379	25	157	18	86	12	57	13	12	4	2	2	222	17	12	4	140	12
YE Jun 13	463	29	77	12	387	26	171	21	90	13	61	14	18	7	2	2	216	16	13	5	138	12
YE Sep 13	490	30	82	12	408	27	194	21	102	14	65	13	24	9	3	3	214	17	13	5	139	13
YE Dec 13	485	29	80	12	405	27	186	20	99	13	61	12	23	10	3	3	219	17	12	5	139	14
YE Mar 14	510	31	81	11	429	28	197	22	106	14	60	12	28	12	3	3	232	18	13	5	144	13
YE Jun 14	530	31	86	12	445	28	205	22	106	15	64	13	31	9	3	3	240	18	12	4	148	13
YE Sep 14	569	35	82	15	487	32	224	24	114	16	68	14	37	10	5	3	263	21	12	4	158	17
YE Dec 14	583	36	80	14	504	34	240	25	118	17	72	15	46	10	5	3	264	22	14	6	159	17
YE Mar 15	586	35	83	13	504	32	245	25	117	16	72	15	52	11	4	3	258	21	14	6	157	15
YE Jun 15	581	34	84	14	496	31	242	24	123	17	64	13	50	11	4	3	254	20	13	5	155	15
YE Sep 15	558	32	87	13	471	29	232	22	119	15	60	12	51	11	2	2	239	19	11	4	146	14
YE Dec 15	565	33	83	12	482	30	244	24	117	15	64	12	61	14	2	2	238	19	12	5	146	14
YE Mar 16	567	33	82	13	485	31	243	24	116	16	60	12	65	14	2	2	242	19	13	5	150	14
YE Jun 16	582	34	76	12	506	32	264	26	127	17	66	13	68	15	3	2	242	19	14	5	149	14
YE Sep 16	531	34	70	13	461	32	249	26	123	17	55	13	68	14	3	3	211	19	14	5	126	14
YE Dec 16	527	34	73	14	454	31	231	24	123	17	44	10	61	13	3	3	223	20	13	5	134	16
YE Mar 17[p]	526	35	73	16	453	31	228	23	123	17	47	10	54	12	4	4	225	21	12	5	132	16
YE Jun 17[p7]	499	35	75	16	424	31	206	23	108	16	44	10	51	12	4	4	218	20	13	5	128	15
YE Sep 17[p7]	578	38	75	16	503	35	232	26	117	18	49	11	57	13	10	8	270	23	13	7	171	18
YE Dec 17[p]	586	39	79	16	506	36	230	27	113	18	50	12	57	14	11	9	276	23	13	7	176	17
Work related[4]																						
YE Mar 08	:	:	:	:	:	:	:	:	:	:	:	:	:	:			:	:	:	:	:	:
YE Jun 08	232	27	39	9	192	26	118	24	42	14	69	18	7	4	.	.	74	10	5	4	31	6
YE Sep 08	:	:					:	:					:	:			:	:			:	:
YE Dec 08	207	25	42	10	165	23	99	21	36	11	48	15	14	8	1	1	66	10	5	4	28	6
YE Mar 09	:	:					:	:					:	:			:	:			:	:
YE Jun 09	188	24	40	9	148	22	89	20	33	9	45	16	11	8	1	1	59	8	4	3	29	5
YE Sep 09	:	:					:	:					:	:			:	:			:	:
YE Dec 09	187	20	45	9	142	18	88	16	38	10	43	12	7	4	.	.	54	8	3	2	28	5
YE Mar 10	188	19	44	8	143	17	93	16	35	10	50	12	8	4	.	.	51	7	3	2	26	5
YE Jun 10	188	20	46	8	142	18	94	16	39	10	47	12	8	3	.	.	48	7	3	2	24	4
YE Sep 10	196	21	46	9	150	19	102	18	40	12	57	13	5	3	.	.	49	6	2	1	25	4
YE Dec 10	193	20	49	10	144	18	91	16	32	9	54	14	5	3	.	.	52	7	2	2	24	4
YE Mar 11	182	19	47	10	135	17	84	15	32	9	47	12	4	2	.	.	51	7	2	2	25	4
YE Jun 11	183	20	44	9	140	17	90	16	34	10	53	12	3	1	.	.	50	7	2	1	26	5
YE Sep 11	173	17	38	8	135	15	84	14	35	9	45	10	5	2	.	.	51	7	2	1	25	5
YE Dec 11	176	17	36	7	140	15	93	14	40	9	47	10	5	2	0~	1	47	7	2	1	26	5
YE Mar 12	170	16	32	6	138	15	90	14	41	9	44	10	5	2	0~	1	48	7	2	1	25	5
YE Jun 12	165	15	33	6	132	14	83	12	41	8	37	9	5	2	0~	1	48	7	2	1	24	5
YE Sep 12	168	16	34	6	134	15	89	13	42	8	41	10	5	2	0~	1	45	7	2	1	21	4
YE Dec 12	175	17	35	6	139	16	95	14	49	9	40	11	6	3	.	.	44	7	1	1	19	4
YE Mar 13	183	18	36	7	147	16	103	15	53	9	43	11	7	3	.	.	44	7	1	1	19	4
YE Jun 13	196	20	36	7	160	19	118	18	59	10	46	13	13	7	.	.	42	7	2	2	19	4
YE Sep 13	210	20	39	7	171	19	128	18	65	11	46	11	17	9	0~	1	42	7	3	2	18	4
YE Dec 13	206	20	37	7	169	19	125	17	62	10	46	11	16	9	0~	1	44	7	3	2	20	4
YE Mar 14	218	21	36	7	182	20	134	19	67	11	44	11	22	11	1	2	48	6	4	2	22	4
YE Jun 14	232	21	39	7	193	20	138	18	66	12	46	12	24	8	1	1	55	7	4	2	26	5
YE Sep 14	255	25	46	11	209	22	143	19	70	13	46	11	27	8	1	1	66	11	4	2	34	9
YE Dec 14	267	26	44	11	222	23	155	20	71	14	48	12	35	8	1	1	67	12	3	3	35	9
YE Mar 15	274	24	47	11	227	22	162	20	69	13	51	12	42	9	0~	0~	65	9	3	3	31	5
YE Jun 15	280	25	50	11	230	22	162	20	74	13	46	10	42	10	0~	0~	67	10	3	3	33	7
YE Sep 15	275	23	43	9	232	21	164	19	73	11	46	10	44	11	1	1	68	10	3	2	31	7
YE Dec 15	294	25	44	9	250	23	177	21	75	12	49	10	52	14	1	1	73	11	5	3	34	7
YE Mar 16	290	25	41	8	249	23	178	21	79	13	46	11	51	13	1	1	72	10	5	3	34	7
YE Jun 16	299	25	35	7	264	24	190	22	85	13	51	12	52	13	2	1	74	10	5	3	35	6
YE Sep 16	283	26	35	8	247	24	180	23	84	14	45	13	50	12	1	1	68	9	4	3	33	6
YE Dec 16	263	24	36	8	227	22	161	20	81	14	36	10	44	11	0~	1	66	9	5	3	31	6
YE Mar 17[p]	262	24	34	8	228	23	157	20	81	14	36	9	40	11	0~	1	71	11	6	4	30	6
YE Jun 17[p7]	242	24	37	9	205	22	141	20	71	13	31	9	39	11	.	.	64	10	6	4	26	5
YE Sep 17[p7]	258	25	34	8	224	24	143	20	69	13	28	9	47	13	.	.	80	13	8	6	37	7
YE Dec 17[p]	264	26	36	9	228	25	141	21	65	14	29	9	47	13	.	.	87	13	7	6	43	8

Table 3 International Passenger Survey (IPS) estimates of long-term international migration - Rolling annual data for the United Kingdom, year ending December 2017

Abbreviation: Est. (Estimate)

United Kingdom
thousands

Citizenship by main reason for migration

Main reason for migration	All citizenships Est	+/-CI	British (Including Overseas Territories) Est	+/-CI	Non-British Est	+/-CI	European Union[1] Est	+/-CI	European Union EU15 Est	+/-CI	European Union EU8 Est	+/-CI	European Union EU2 Est	+/-CI	European Union Other Est	+/-CI	Non-European Union[2] All Est	+/-CI	Other Europe[3] Est	+/-CI	Asia All Est	+/-CI
Definite job																						
YE Mar 08	:	:	:	:	:	:	:	:	:	:	:	:	:	:	:	:	:	:	:	:	:	:
YE Jun 08	161	24	22	7	139	22	89	21	33	13	49	15	7	4	.	.	50	8	3	4	24	5
YE Sep 08	:	:	:	:	:	:	:	:	:	:	:	:	:	:	.	.	:	:	:	:	:	:
YE Dec 08	137	21	23	8	113	19	70	18	25	10	35	13	9	6	0~	1	43	8	3	4	23	5
YE Mar 09	:	:	:	:	:	:	:	:	:	:	:	:	:	:	.	.	:	:	:	:	:	:
YE Jun 09	122	21	19	6	103	20	59	18	20	8	34	16	5	4	0~	1	43	7	3	3	24	5
YE Sep 09	:	:	:	:	:	:	:	:	:	:	:	:	:	:	.	.	41	7	3	2	22	5
YE Dec 09	124	17	25	7	100	16	59	14	26	9	29	11	4	3	.	.	38	7	2	2	20	4
YE Mar 10	125	17	25	6	101	15	63	14	26	9	32	10	5	3	.	.	35	6	2	2	19	4
YE Jun 10	123	17	23	6	100	16	66	15	29	10	32	11	4	2	.	.	35	5	2	1	20	4
YE Sep 10	123	18	20	6	103	17	68	16	30	11	35	11	3	2	.	.	35	5	2	1	18	4
YE Dec 10	114	16	23	7	91	15	57	13	23	8	30	11	3	2	.	.	36	6	2	1	20	4
YE Mar 11	108	16	21	7	87	14	51	13	22	8	26	10	2	2	.	.	36	6	1	1	21	5
YE Jun 11	110	15	20	6	90	14	54	12	22	8	30	9	1	1	.	.	37	6	1	1	21	5
YE Sep 11	106	13	18	6	88	12	51	10	22	6	27	8	2	1	.	.	37	6	1	1	22	5
YE Dec 11	110	13	18	5	92	12	56	10	25	7	28	8	3	2	.	.	36	6	1	1	21	5
YE Mar 12	109	13	16	4	94	12	58	11	27	7	28	8	2	1	.	.	36	6	1	1	20	4
YE Jun 12	104	12	18	5	86	11	50	10	26	7	21	7	3	2	.	.	32	5	1	1	19	4
YE Sep 12	104	12	20	5	84	11	51	10	28	7	21	7	2	1	.	.	31	5	1	1	16	4
YE Dec 12	108	13	21	5	87	12	56	10	31	7	22	7	2	1	.	.	32	6	1	1	17	4
YE Mar 13	110	13	21	5	89	11	57	10	33	8	21	6	3	2	.	.	31	6	2	1	17	4
YE Jun 13	120	15	21	6	99	14	67	13	38	9	22	7	7	6	0~	1	32	5	2	1	16	3
YE Sep 13	135	17	23	6	112	16	80	15	41	9	27	9	11	7	0~	1	33	5	2	2	19	4
YE Dec 13	128	16	20	5	109	16	76	15	39	9	25	9	11	8	0~	1	37	6	3	2	21	4
YE Mar 14	135	18	20	5	115	17	79	16	42	9	23	8	12	10	1	2	43	6	4	2	23	4
YE Jun 14	142	16	21	5	122	16	79	14	43	10	24	9	11	5	1	1	52	10	4	2	31	9
YE Sep 14	160	21	26	10	134	18	82	15	46	11	24	9	11	4	1	1	55	11	3	3	32	9
YE Dec 14	171	22	23	10	148	19	92	16	49	12	28	9	14	5	1	1	52	8	3	3	28	5
YE Mar 15	174	20	23	9	151	18	99	16	49	11	28	9	22	7	0~	0~	54	9	3	2	30	6
YE Jun 15	179	21	23	9	156	19	102	17	51	12	26	9	25	9	0~	0~	50	8	2	1	28	7
YE Sep 15	162	18	16	6	145	17	95	15	45	9	21	7	28	9	1	1	51	9	2	1	30	7
YE Dec 15	171	19	20	6	151	17	100	15	46	9	23	7	31	10	1	1	51	8	1	1	31	7
YE Mar 16	170	19	18	5	152	18	102	16	48	10	22	7	30	10	1	1	51	7	1	1	31	6
YE Jun 16	176	19	17	5	159	18	108	17	51	10	25	8	31	10	2	1	49	8	2	2	29	5
YE Sep 16	182	20	19	6	162	19	113	17	59	12	23	7	30	10	1	1	48	7	3	2	28	5
YE Dec 16	172	19	19	6	153	18	105	16	58	12	20	6	27	9	0~	1	52	9	4	3	26	5
YE Mar 17[p]	179	20	17	6	162	19	110	17	61	13	21	7	27	9	0~	1	48	9	5	4	24	5
YE Jun 17[p7]	174	21	19	7	154	20	106	17	59	12	21	7	27	10	.	.	59	11	6	6	33	7
YE Sep 17[p7]	185	22	18	6	167	21	107	18	53	12	18	7	36	12	.	.	66	11	5	5	38	7
YE Dec 17[p]	189	23	19	7	170	22	104	19	51	12	19	7	35	12	.	.	66	11	5	5	38	7
Looking for work																						
YE Mar 08	:	:	:	:	:	:	:	:	:	:	:	:	:	:	:	:	:	:	:	:	:	:
YE Jun 08	71	13	17	5	53	12	29	11	9	5	20	10	:	:	:	:	24	5	0~	0~	7	3
YE Sep 08	:	:	:	:	:	:	:	:	:	:	:	:	:	:	:	:	:	:	:	:	:	:
YE Dec 08	70	14	19	6	52	13	29	11	11	5	13	8	5	6	0~	0~	22	6	0~	0~	5	3
YE Mar 09	:	:	:	:	:	:	:	:	:	:	:	:	:	:	:	:	:	:	:	:	:	:
YE Jun 09	66	12	21	7	45	9	30	9	13	4	11	4	6	6	0~	0~	15	3	0~	0~	5	2
YE Sep 09	:	:	:	:	:	:	:	:	:	:	:	:	:	:	:	:	:	:	:	:	:	:
YE Dec 09	63	9	20	6	43	7	29	7	12	4	14	5	3	3	.	.	13	3	1	1	6	2
YE Mar 10	62	9	19	5	43	8	30	7	9	3	18	6	3	2	.	.	13	3	1	1	6	2
YE Jun 10	65	9	23	5	42	8	29	7	9	3	15	5	4	3	.	.	14	3	1	1	5	2
YE Sep 10	73	11	26	7	47	9	33	8	10	4	22	7	2	2	.	.	14	3	0~	1	5	2
YE Dec 10	78	12	26	7	52	10	35	9	8	3	24	9	2	2	.	.	18	4	1	1	6	2
YE Mar 11	75	12	27	7	48	10	33	9	10	4	21	8	2	2	.	.	15	4	1	1	5	2
YE Jun 11	73	12	23	6	50	10	36	10	12	5	22	8	1	1	.	.	14	4	1	1	5	2
YE Sep 11	66	11	20	5	47	10	33	9	13	6	17	7	3	2	.	.	14	3	0~	0~	5	2
YE Dec 11	66	11	18	5	47	10	37	9	15	6	19	7	3	2	0~	1	10	3	0~	0~	4	1
YE Mar 12	60	10	16	4	44	9	32	8	14	6	16	6	2	2	0~	1	12	3	0~	0~	4	2
YE Jun 12	61	9	16	4	45	8	33	7	14	5	16	6	2	2	0~	1	12	3	0~	0~	4	2
YE Sep 12	65	11	14	4	51	10	38	9	14	4	20	8	3	1	0~	1	13	5	0~	1	3	1
YE Dec 12	67	11	15	4	52	11	39	10	17	5	18	8	4	2	.	.	13	5	0~	0~	3	2
YE Mar 13	73	13	15	4	58	12	47	11	20	5	23	9	4	2	.	.	12	5	0~	0~	2	1
YE Jun 13	77	14	16	4	61	13	51	12	21	5	24	11	6	4	.	.	11	5	0~	0~	1	1
YE Sep 13	75	11	16	4	59	10	48	9	23	5	19	6	6	4	.	.	10	4	0~	1	2	1
YE Dec 13	77	11	17	5	60	10	50	9	24	5	21	7	5	4	.	.	11	4	0~	1	1	1
YE Mar 14	83	12	17	4	66	11	55	10	25	6	21	6	10	5	.	.	11	3	0~	1	2	2
YE Jun 14	89	13	18	5	71	12	59	11	23	6	22	7	13	6	.	.	12	4	0~	1	3	2
YE Sep 14	95	13	20	5	75	12	61	11	24	7	21	7	16	7	.	.	13	4	.	.	3	2
YE Dec 14	96	14	22	6	75	12	63	12	22	6	20	7	20	7	.	.	12	4	.	.	3	2
YE Mar 15	100	14	24	6	76	12	63	11	20	6	23	7	20	7	.	.	13	4	.	.	3	2
YE Jun 15	100	13	26	7	74	11	61	10	24	6	20	7	17	6	.	.	13	4	0~	0~	3	2
YE Sep 15	113	15	26	7	87	13	69	11	28	7	24	7	16	6	.	.	18	6	2	2	3	2
YE Dec 15	123	17	24	6	99	15	77	14	29	7	27	8	21	9	.	.	22	7	3	3	4	2
YE Mar 16	120	16	23	6	97	15	76	14	31	7	24	8	21	8	.	.	21	6	3	3	3	2
YE Jun 16	123	17	17	5	105	16	82	15	34	8	27	9	21	8	.	.	24	7	4	3	4	3
YE Sep 16	101	16	16	5	85	16	67	15	26	7	22	11	19	7	.	.	18	5	2	2	4	3
YE Dec 16	91	14	17	5	74	13	55	12	23	7	16	7	16	6	.	.	18	6	2	2	4	3
YE Mar 17[p]	83	13	16	6	66	12	47	10	19	6	15	6	13	6	.	.	19	6	2	2	4	3
YE Jun 17[p7]	68	11	18	6	50	10	34	9	12	4	10	5	12	6	.	.	16	5	1	1	3	2
YE Sep 17[p7]	73	12	16	5	57	11	36	8	16	6	9	4	11	5	.	.	21	7	2	3	5	3
YE Dec 17[p]	75	13	18	5	57	12	37	10	15	6	10	4	13	6	.	.	20	7	2	2	5	3

Table 3 International Passenger Survey (IPS) estimates of long-term international migration - Rolling annual data for the United Kingdom, year ending December 2017

Abbreviation: Est. (Estimate)
Citizenship by main reason for migration

United Kingdom
thousands

Main reason for migration	All citizenships		British (Including Overseas Territories)		Non-British		European Union[1]		European Union EU15		European Union EU8		European Union EU2		European Union Other		Non-European Union[2] All		Other Europe[3]		Asia All	
	Est.	+/-CI	Est.	+/-CI	Est.	+/-CI	Est.	+/-CI	Est.	+/-CI	Est.	+/-CI	Est.	+/-CI	Est.	+/-CI	Est.	+/-CI	Est.	+/-CI	Est.	+/-CI
Accompany/Join																						
YE Mar 08	:	:	:	:	:	:	:	:	:	:	:	:	:	:			:	:	:	:	:	:
YE Jun 08	81	12	8	4	73	11	9	5	2	2	6	5	0~	0~	.	.	64	10	3	2	43	8
YE Sep 08	:	:	:	:	:	:	:	:	:	:	:	:	:	:			:	:	:	:	:	:
YE Dec 08	87	15	7	4	80	14	19	10	10	8	8	6	0~	1	.	.	61	10	2	2	37	6
YE Mar 09	:	:	:	:	:	:	:	:	:	:	:	:	:	:			:	:	:	:	:	:
YE Jun 09	87	15	11	5	76	14	19	10	11	7	8	7	1	1	.	.	57	10	2	2	35	6
YE Sep 09	:	:	:	:	:	:	:	:	:	:	:	:	:	:			:	:	:	:	:	:
YE Dec 09	76	12	16	7	60	9	9	4	3	3	5	3	0~	1	.	.	52	8	1	1	32	6
YE Mar 10	76	11	14	6	62	9	9	4	3	3	5	3	1	1	.	.	53	8	1	1	33	6
YE Jun 10	71	10	13	6	59	8	8	4	3	2	4	3	0~	1	.	.	51	8	2	2	30	5
YE Sep 10	74	11	14	6	60	9	6	3	3	2	3	2	.	.	.	.	55	9	3	3	32	5
YE Dec 10	78	11	14	6	63	9	7	4	3	2	4	3	0~	0~	.	.	56	8	3	3	34	5
YE Mar 11	79	12	15	7	64	10	7	4	2	2	4	3	0~	0~	.	.	57	9	3	3	35	6
YE Jun 11	85	12	16	7	69	10	9	5	3	2	6	4	0~	0~	.	.	60	9	2	2	39	6
YE Sep 11	81	11	15	6	66	9	11	5	5	3	6	4	0~	0~	.	.	55	8	1	1	37	6
YE Dec 11	75	11	13	6	61	9	10	4	5	3	5	3	0~	0~	.	.	52	8	1	1	35	6
YE Mar 12	74	12	13	5	60	10	9	4	5	3	4	2	0~	0~	.	.	51	10	1	1	34	6
YE Jun 12	68	9	12	5	56	8	9	3	5	3	3	2	0~	0~	.	.	47	7	1	1	32	6
YE Sep 12	61	9	11	4	50	8	9	4	6	3	3	2	.	.	0~	0~	41	6	1	1	28	5
YE Dec 12	61	9	10	4	51	8	12	5	8	4	3	2	.	.	0~	0~	39	7	1	1	27	5
YE Mar 13	59	9	9	4	49	8	12	5	8	4	4	2	.	.	0~	0~	37	6	1	1	25	5
YE Jun 13	59	9	10	4	49	8	14	5	7	4	6	3	0~	1	0~	0~	35	6	1	1	24	5
YE Sep 13	64	9	10	4	55	8	16	4	7	3	8	3	1	1	.	.	39	7	1	1	26	5
YE Dec 13	69	10	11	4	58	9	15	4	6	3	7	3	1	1	.	.	44	8	1	1	26	5
YE Mar 14	77	11	11	4	66	11	16	5	7	3	8	4	1	1	.	.	50	9	1	1	27	5
YE Jun 14	80	11	12	4	68	10	16	5	7	3	8	4	1	1	.	.	52	9	1	1	28	5
YE Sep 14	85	12	10	4	75	12	22	7	10	4	9	6	2	1	1	1	54	9	2	2	31	5
YE Dec 14	86	12	11	4	75	12	25	8	11	4	11	6	3	1	1	1	50	8	2	2	31	5
YE Mar 15	81	11	10	4	71	10	25	8	12	5	9	5	3	1	1	1	47	7	2	1	32	6
YE Jun 15	77	11	9	4	68	10	24	7	12	5	8	5	3	1	1	1	45	7	2	1	32	6
YE Sep 15	74	10	12	4	62	9	19	6	10	4	6	3	4	2	.	.	43	7	0~	1	30	6
YE Dec 15	71	9	10	4	61	8	18	5	8	4	5	2	5	2	.	.	43	7	2	2	29	5
YE Mar 16	78	10	10	3	68	10	21	7	6	3	5	3	9	5	.	.	47	7	3	2	30	6
YE Jun 16	78	11	8	3	70	10	24	7	9	4	5	3	10	5	.	.	46	7	3	2	29	6
YE Sep 16	72	10	5	2	67	10	22	7	8	4	5	3	9	5	.	.	45	7	4	2	29	6
YE Dec 16	83	12	6	3	77	12	25	8	12	5	3	2	10	5	.	.	53	9	3	2	33	7
YE Mar 17P	78	12	7	4	71	11	22	6	12	5	3	2	6	3	.	.	49	9	1	1	32	8
YE Jun 17P	77	12	7	4	70	11	20	7	10	5	4	3	6	3	.	.	49	9	2	1	32	8
YE Sep 17P	86	14	10	5	76	13	26	8	13	6	8	5	6	3	.	.	50	10	3	2	30	8
YE Dec 17F	80	14	10	6	70	13	22	8	9	5	8	5	5	3	.	.	48	10	3	2	28	6
Formal study																						
YE Mar 08	:	:	:	:	:	:	:	:	:	:	:	:	:	:	:	:	:	:	:	:	:	:
YE Jun 08	141	18	10	6	131	17	25	9	11	6	12	7	1	2	1	1	106	14	3	3	78	12
YE Sep 08	:	:	:	:	:	:	:	:	:	:	:	:	:	:	:	:	:	:	:	:	:	:
YE Dec 08	172	21	6	3	166	21	40	13	28	11	7	6	2	2	2	3	126	16	3	2	91	13
YE Mar 09	:	:	:	:	:	:	:	:	:	:	:	:	:	:	:	:	:	:	:	:	:	:
YE Jun 09	169	19	7	3	161	19	35	12	24	11	6	5	2	2	3	3	126	15	4	2	94	12
YE Sep 09	:	:	:	:	:	:	:	:	:	:	:	:	:	:	:	:	:	:	:	:	:	:
YE Dec 09	209	16	11	4	197	16	42	9	28	7	5	3	5	3	3	3	155	13	4	3	127	11
YE Mar 10	234	17	11	4	223	16	44	9	30	7	6	3	6	4	3	3	179	14	4	3	146	12
YE Jun 10	234	16	10	4	223	16	45	9	31	7	5	3	6	4	3	3	178	13	3	3	148	11
YE Sep 10	243	18	8	4	235	17	45	11	29	8	10	6	2	1	4	3	190	13	4	2	159	12
YE Dec 10	234	17	8	3	227	17	45	11	28	8	11	6	2	1	4	3	181	13	4	2	151	11
YE Mar 11	227	17	7	3	220	16	44	11	28	8	11	6	2	1	4	4	175	13	4	2	147	11
YE Jun 11	235	17	7	3	228	17	45	11	28	8	11	6	2	1	4	3	183	13	4	2	155	12
YE Sep 11	241	17	5	2	236	17	40	8	27	7	8	4	5	3	1	1	196	15	5	2	166	13
YE Dec 11	226	16	5	2	222	16	41	8	27	6	8	4	5	3	1	1	180	14	5	2	150	13
YE Mar 12	208	15	5	2	203	15	39	8	26	6	7	3	5	3	1	1	163	13	5	2	134	12
YE Jun 12	193	15	5	2	187	15	39	8	27	7	7	3	5	2	1	1	148	13	5	2	118	11
YE Sep 12	181	15	8	3	173	15	31	7	20	6	6	4	3	2	1	2	143	13	8	3	104	11
YE Dec 12	175	16	8	3	167	15	28	7	17	5	6	4	3	2	2	2	139	13	9	4	100	11
YE Mar 13	170	15	8	3	161	15	29	7	18	6	5	3	4	3	1	2	132	13	9	4	93	10
YE Jun 13	169	15	9	3	160	14	28	7	17	5	5	3	4	3	1	2	132	13	9	4	93	10
YE Sep 13	170	17	8	3	162	16	39	9	24	7	5	2	7	4	2	3	123	14	9	4	91	12
YE Dec 13	171	17	9	4	162	16	40	9	27	7	5	2	5	3	2	3	122	13	7	4	90	12
YE Mar 14	171	16	10	4	161	16	38	9	26	8	5	2	5	3	2	3	123	13	7	3	91	12
YE Jun 14	169	16	9	4	160	16	39	10	27	8	6	3	4	3	2	3	120	13	7	3	89	11
YE Sep 14	184	19	6	3	178	19	46	11	31	8	8	6	4	2	3	3	132	15	7	3	90	13
YE Dec 14	187	20	5	3	182	20	48	11	32	8	8	6	4	2	3	3	134	17	9	5	89	13
YE Mar 15	186	20	6	3	181	20	46	10	32	8	8	6	3	2	3	3	134	17	8	5	90	13
YE Jun 15	184	19	7	3	178	19	47	10	34	9	6	5	3	2	3	3	131	16	7	4	87	12
YE Sep 15	165	17	10	4	156	16	38	9	28	7	7	4	2	2	1	1	118	14	6	4	82	11
YE Dec 15	157	16	9	4	148	15	36	8	25	6	6	4	4	3	1	1	112	13	5	3	80	10
YE Mar 16	156	16	8	4	148	15	34	8	23	6	7	4	4	3	1	1	113	13	5	3	81	11
YE Jun 16	155	16	9	4	147	16	34	8	22	6	7	4	4	3	1	1	113	14	6	3	81	11
YE Sep 16	127	16	6	3	121	16	33	9	22	7	3	2	6	3	2	3	87	13	4	3	59	11
YE Dec 16	132	18	7	5	125	17	32	8	21	7	3	2	5	3	2	3	92	15	4	3	64	12
YE Mar 17P	135	18	7	5	127	17	34	9	21	7	4	3	5	3	4	4	94	15	4	3	65	12
YE Jun 17P7	133	17	7	5	126	17	33	8	20	6	4	3	5	3	4	4	93	14	3	2	66	12
YE Sep 17P7	189	22	7	5	182	21	52	14	31	10	8	4	4	2	10	8	130	16	2	2	100	14
YE Dec 17P	189	21	5	3	184	20	56	14	34	11	8	3	3	2	11	9	128	14	3	2	98	13

Table 3 International Passenger Survey (IPS) estimates of long-term international migration - Rolling annual data for the United Kingdom, year ending December 2017

Abbreviation: Est. (Estimate)

Citizenship by main reason for migration

United Kingdom
thousands

Main reason for migration	All citizenships Est.	+/-CI	British (Including Overseas Territories) Est.	+/-CI	Non-British Est.	+/-CI	European Union[1] Est.	+/-CI	European Union EU15 Est.	+/-CI	European Union EU8 Est.	+/-CI	European Union EU2 Est.	+/-CI	European Union Other Est.	+/-CI	Non-European Union[2] All Est.	+/-CI	Other Europe[3] Est.	+/-CI	Asia All Est.	+/-CI
Going home to live[5]																						
YE Mar 08	:	:	:	:	:	:	:	:	:	:	.	.	.	.	.	.	:	:	:	:	:	:
YE Jun 08	10	6	9	6	1	2	1	2	1	2	.	.	.	.	.	.	0~	0~	.	.	.	.
YE Sep 08	:	:	:	:	:	:	:	:	:	:	.	.	.	.	.	.	:	:	:	:	:	:
YE Dec 08	20	9	17	9	3	3	1	1	1	1	.	.	.	.	.	.	2	3	.	.	2	3
YE Mar 09	:	:	:	:	:	:	:	:	:	:	.	.	.	.	.	.	:	:	:	:	:	:
YE Jun 09	24	9	22	8	2	2	0~	1	0~	1	.	.	.	.	.	.	2	2	.	.	2	2
YE Sep 09	:	:	:	:	:	:	:	:	:	:	.	.	.	.	.	.	:	:	:	:	:	:
YE Dec 09	21	7	19	7	1	1	1	1	0~	0~	1	1	.	.	.	.	0~	1	.	.	0~	1
YE Mar 10	24	9	22	9	1	1	1	1	0~	0~	1	1	.	.	.	.	0~	1	.	.	0~	1
YE Jun 10	24	9	22	9	1	1	1	1	0~	0~	1	1	.	.	.	.	0~	1	.	.	0~	1
YE Sep 10	21	9	21	9	0~	0~	0~	0~	0~	0~	.	.	.	.	.	.	.	.	.	.	.	.
YE Dec 10	19	8	19	8	.	.	.	.	.	.	.	.	.	.	.	.	.	.	.	.	.	.
YE Mar 11	19	6	18	6	1	1	.	.	.	.	.	.	.	.	.	.	1	1	.	.	.	.
YE Jun 11	17	6	16	6	1	1	.	.	.	.	.	.	.	.	.	.	1	1	.	.	0~	0~
YE Sep 11	20	7	18	7	1	2	.	.	.	.	.	.	.	.	.	.	1	2	.	.	0~	0~
YE Dec 11	21	8	20	7	2	2	.	.	.	.	.	.	.	.	.	.	2	2	.	.	0~	0~
YE Mar 12	23	9	20	7	3	5	2	5	.	.	2	5	.	.	.	.	0~	1	.	.	0~	0~
YE Jun 12	26	9	22	8	4	4	2	3	0~	1	2	3	.	.	.	.	2	3	.	.	.	.
YE Sep 12	23	8	21	7	3	3	1	2	0~	1	1	2	.	.	.	.	1	2	.	.	.	.
YE Dec 12	24	8	21	8	4	3	2	2	1	1	1	2	.	.	.	.	2	2	0~	1	0~	1
YE Mar 13	21	8	17	7	3	3	2	2	2	2	.	.	.	.	.	.	2	2	0~	1	0~	0~
YE Jun 13	18	8	16	7	3	3	2	2	2	2	.	.	.	.	.	.	1	1	0~	1	0~	0~
YE Sep 13	22	8	20	8	2	2	1	2	1	2	.	.	.	.	.	.	1	1	0~	0~	0~	0~
YE Dec 13	19	8	18	7	2	2	1	1	1	1	.	.	.	.	.	.	1	1	.	.	.	.
YE Mar 14	18	7	17	7	1	1	0~	1	0~	1	.	.	.	.	.	.	1	1	.	.	.	.
YE Jun 14	20	7	20	7	1	1	0~	0~	0~	0~	.	.	.	.	.	.	1	1	.	.	.	.
YE Sep 14	16	8	14	8	1	1	0~	0~	0~	0~	.	.	.	.	.	.	1	1	.	.	.	.
YE Dec 14	16	6	14	6	1	1	0~	0~	0~	0~	.	.	.	.	.	.	1	1	.	.	.	.
YE Mar 15	18	6	16	6	1	1	0~	1	0~	0~	0~	0~	.	.	.	.	1	1	.	.	0~	0~
YE Jun 15	16	6	15	6	1	1	0~	1	0~	0~	0~	0~	.	.	.	.	1	1	.	.	0~	0~
YE Sep 15	21	8	19	7	2	2	2	2	1	2	0~	0~	.	.	.	.	0~	0~	.	.	0~	0~
YE Dec 15	17	6	15	6	2	2	1	2	1	2	0~	0~	.	.	.	.	0~	0~	.	.	0~	0~
YE Mar 16	19	8	18	8	1	3	1	3	1	3	.	.	.	.	.	.	.	.	.	.	.	.
YE Jun 16	18	8	16	8	2	3	2	3	2	3	.	.	.	.	.	.	.	.	.	.	.	.
YE Sep 16	18	9	18	9	0~	1	0~	1	0~	1	.	.	.	.	.	.	.	.	.	.	.	.
YE Dec 16	19	9	19	9	0~	1	0~	1	0~	1	.	.	.	.	.	.	.	.	.	.	.	.
YE Mar 17[p]	16	7	16	7	0~	0~	0~	0~	0~	0~	.	.	.	.	.	.	.	.	.	.	.	.
YE Jun 17[p7]	15	6	15	6	0~	1	0~	1	0~	1	.	.	.	.	.	.	.	.	.	.	.	.
YE Sep 17[p7]	16	6	15	6	1	1	0~	0~	0~	0~	.	.	.	.	.	.	0~	0~	.	.	.	.
YE Dec 17[p]	17	6	17	6	0~	0~	0~	0~	0~	0~	.	.	.	.	.	.	0~	0~	.	.	.	.
Other																						
YE Mar 08	:	:	:	:	:	:	:	:	:	:	.	.	.	.	:	:	:	:	:	:	:	:
YE Jun 08	32	8	5	5	27	7	1	1	0~	1	.	.	.	.	0~	1	26	7	0~	1	7	5
YE Sep 08	:	:	:	:	:	:	:	:	:	:	.	.	.	.	:	:	:	:	:	:	:	:
YE Dec 08	34	11	8	8	26	7	6	6	4	5	2	3	0~	1	.	.	20	5	.	.	5	2
YE Mar 09	:	:	:	:	:	:	:	:	:	:	:	:	.	.	:	:	:	:	.	.	:	:
YE Jun 09	28	9	5	6	23	7	6	5	3	4	2	3	.	.	0~	1	17	4	0~	0~	4	2
YE Sep 09	:	:	:	:	:	:	:	:	:	:	:	:	:	:	:	:	:	:	:	:	:	:
YE Dec 09	22	5	3	2	19	5	3	2	2	2	1	1	0~	0~	0~	0~	16	5	0~	0~	5	2
YE Mar 10	20	5	3	2	17	4	4	3	3	2	2	1	0~	0~	0~	0~	13	4	0~	0~	5	2
YE Jun 10	21	5	3	2	17	4	4	2	2	2	2	1	0~	0~	.	.	13	4	0~	0~	5	2
YE Sep 10	21	5	3	2	18	4	4	2	1	1	2	2	1	1	.	.	13	3	0~	0~	4	2
YE Dec 10	19	4	3	2	16	4	5	2	1	1	3	2	1	1	.	.	11	3	.	.	2	1
YE Mar 11	18	4	2	2	16	4	4	2	1	1	2	2	1	1	.	.	12	3	0~	0~	2	1
YE Jun 11	19	5	3	2	15	4	5	2	2	2	2	2	1	1	.	.	11	3	0~	0~	2	1
YE Sep 11	16	4	2	2	13	4	3	2	1	1	2	2	0~	0~	0~	0~	10	3	0~	0~	2	1
YE Dec 11	18	4	3	2	14	4	4	2	2	1	2	2	0~	0~	0~	0~	10	3	0~	0~	2	1
YE Mar 12	19	5	3	2	16	5	3	2	1	1	2	2	0~	0~	0~	0~	13	4	0~	0~	2	1
YE Jun 12	19	5	3	2	17	5	3	2	1	1	2	2	0~	0~	0~	0~	13	4	0~	0~	2	1
YE Sep 12	19	5	4	3	15	5	3	2	1	1	1	1	0~	0~	.	.	12	4	0~	0~	3	2
YE Dec 12	18	6	4	3	14	5	5	4	2	3	2	2	.	.	.	.	10	3	.	.	2	1
YE Mar 13	13	5	3	3	10	4	5	4	2	3	2	3	.	.	.	.	5	2	.	.	2	1
YE Jun 13	13	6	4	3	9	5	4	4	2	3	2	2	.	.	.	.	5	2	1	2	2	1
YE Sep 13	17	6	3	2	14	6	6	5	3	4	3	3	.	.	.	.	7	3	1	2	3	2
YE Dec 13	16	5	4	2	12	5	4	3	2	2	2	2	.	.	.	.	8	3	1	2	2	2
YE Mar 14	20	6	5	2	15	6	5	4	3	4	2	2	.	.	.	.	10	4	1	2	4	3
YE Jun 14	22	7	4	2	18	7	8	6	3	3	3	3	2	4	.	.	10	4	0~	0~	4	3
YE Sep 14	20	7	3	2	17	7	8	6	1	1	3	3	4	5	.	.	9	3	0~	0~	2	1
YE Dec 14	19	7	3	2	16	7	8	6	1	1	2	3	4	5	.	.	9	3	0~	0~	2	1
YE Mar 15	19	7	3	2	16	6	8	6	2	2	3	4	3	4	.	.	9	3	0~	1	2	1
YE Jun 15	17	6	3	2	14	6	5	4	2	2	1	3	2	3	.	.	9	3	0~	1	1	1
YE Sep 15	17	7	3	2	14	7	6	6	6	6	.	.	.	.	.	.	8	3	0~	1	2	1
YE Dec 15	16	6	4	3	12	6	5	5	5	5	.	.	.	.	.	.	8	3	0~	1	2	1
YE Mar 16	16	6	4	3	12	5	4	4	3	4	.	.	0~	0~	.	.	8	3	0~	1	3	2
YE Jun 16	17	7	5	4	12	5	5	5	4	5	1	1	1	1	.	.	7	3	0~	1	3	2
YE Sep 16	16	5	4	3	12	4	4	2	3	2	1	1	1	1	.	.	8	3	2	2	2	2
YE Dec 16	17	5	3	2	14	5	6	3	4	3	1	1	1	1	.	.	8	4	2	2	3	2
YE Mar 17[p]	21	11	7	10	14	5	6	3	4	3	1	1	0~	1	.	.	8	4	1	2	2	1
YE Jun 17[p7]	22	11	7	9	15	5	6	3	4	3	1	2	0~	0~	.	.	9	4	1	2	2	1
YE Sep 17[p7]	21	11	8	10	13	5	6	4	4	3	2	2	0~	1	.	.	7	3	.	.	2	1
YE Dec 17[p]	21	11	8	10	13	5	5	3	3	2	2	2	0~	1	.	.	8	4	.	.	3	2

Table 3 International Passenger Survey (IPS) estimates of long-term international migration - Rolling annual data for the United Kingdom, year ending December 2017

Abbreviation: Est. 'Estimate)
Citizenship by main reason for migration

United Kingdom
thousands

Main reason for migration	All citizenships		British (Including Overseas Territories)		Non-British		European Union[1]		European Union EU15		European Union EU8		European Union EU2		European Union Other		Non-European Union[2] All		Other Europe[3]		Asia All	
	Est.	+/-CI	Est.	+/-CI	Est.	+/-CI	Est.	+/-CI	Est.	+/-CI	Est.	+/-CI	Est.	+/-CI	Est.	+/-CI	Est.	+/-CI	Est.	+/-CI	Est.	+/-CI
No reason stated[6]																						
YE Mar 08	:	:	:	:	:	:	:	:	:	:	:	:					:	:			:	:
YE Jun 08	25	12	6	6	19	10	9	6	1	1	8	6	.	.	.	.	10	8	.	.	10	8
YE Sep 08	:	:	:	:	:	:	:	:	:	:	:	:					:	:			:	:
YE Dec 08	19	9	2	3	17	9	15	8	4	4	10	7	0~	1			3	3			1	1
YE Mar 09	:	:	:	:	:	:	:	:	:	:	:	:					:	:			:	:
YE Jun 09	22	10	4	3	18	9	14	8	4	4	10	8	0~	1			4	3			1	1
YE Sep 09	:	:	:	:	:	:	:	:	:	:	:	:					:	:			:	:
YE Dec 09	14	6	4	3	10	5	8	5	4	3	4	4	0~	0~			3	2	0~	0~	1	1
YE Mar 10	12	4	4	3	8	3	6	3	4	3	1	1	0~	0~			2	1	0~	0~	1	1
YE Jun 10	11	5	2	2	9	5	7	4	4	2	3	4	0~	0~			2	1	0~	0~	1	1
YE Sep 10	12	6	1	1	11	6	8	5	3	3	4	5	0~	1			4	2	0~	0~	2	1
YE Dec 10	11	6	1	1	10	5	7	5	3	3	3	4	0~	1			3	2	0~	0~	2	1
YE Mar 11	15	7	1	1	13	7	10	6	3	3	6	5	0~	1			4	2	0~	0~	2	1
YE Jun 11	15	6	1	1	13	6	9	5	3	3	5	4	1	2			4	2	0~	0~	2	1
YE Sep 11	15	6	2	2	14	6	10	6	3	3	6	5	1	1			4	2	1	2	2	2
YE Dec 11	16	6	2	2	14	6	10	6	2	2	7	5	1	1			5	3	1	1	2	2
YE Mar 12	13	6	1	1	12	6	8	6	1	1	6	5	1	1			4	2	1	1	2	1
YE Jun 12	13	6	1	1	11	6	7	6	1	1	5	5	1	1			4	2	1	1	2	2
YE Sep 12	7	3	1	1	6	3	4	3	2	2	2	1	1	1			2	2	0~	0~	1	1
YE Dec 12	9	6	1	1	8	6	6	6	3	3	3	5	0~	0~			2	1	0~	0~	1	1
YE Mar 13	8	6	1	1	7	6	6	5	3	2	3	5	0~	0~			1	1	0~	0~	1	1
YE Jun 13	7	5	2	2	5	5	5	5	3	3	2	4	.	.			0~	1	0~	0~	0~	1
YE Sep 13	6	5	2	2	4	5	4	5	1	1	2	5	.	.			1	1			0~	1
YE Dec 13	3	2	1	1	2	1	2	1	1	1	0~	0~	0~	0~			0~	1	0~	0~	0~	0~
YE Mar 14	6	3	2	2	4	2	4	2	2	2	1	1	0~	0~			1	1	0~	0~	0~	0~
YE Jun 14	7	3	2	2	6	3	4	2	3	2	1	1	0~	0~			2	2	0~	0~	2	2
YE Sep 14	9	4	2	2	7	4	6	3	2	1	3	3	1	1			2	2	0~	0~	1	2
YE Dec 14	8	4	2	2	6	4	5	3	2	1	2	3	1	1			2	2			1	2
YE Mar 15	7	4	1	1	7	4	4	3	1	1	3	3	1	1			3	2			2	2
YE Jun 15	7	4	1	1	5	4	4	3	0~	1	3	3	1	1			2	1			1	1
YE Sep 15	7	3	1	1	5	3	3	2	1	1	1	2	0~	1			3	2			1	1
YE Dec 15	11	5	1	1	10	5	7	4	3	3	3	2	1	1			3	2			2	1
YE Mar 16	9	4	2	2	7	4	5	3	2	3	2	2	1	1			2	2			1	1
YE Jun 16	14	7	2	2	12	6	9	6	5	5	2	2	2	3			2	2			1	1
YE Sep 16	15	7	2	2	14	7	10	6	6	5	2	2	3	3			4	3			3	3
YE Dec 16	12	6	1	1	11	6	8	6	5	5	1	1	2	3			3	2			2	2
YE Mar 17[p]	13	6	1	1	12	6	9	5	5	4	2	2	2	3			3	2			2	2
YE Jun 17[p,7]	10	4	1	1	8	4	6	4	2	2	3	3	1	1			2	2			2	2
YE Sep 17[p]	9	4	2	2	7	4	4	3	0~	1	3	3	1	1			3	3	0~	0~	1	1
YE Dec 17[p]	15	7	3	3	12	6	6	4	1	2	3	3	1	1			6	5	0~	0~	3	4
Outflow																						
All reasons																						
YE Mar 08	:	:	:	:	:	:	:	:	:	:	:	:	:	:	:	:	:	:	:	:	:	:
YE Jun 08	357	38	162	23	196	31	95	29	40	14	43	16	10	19	2	3	101	10	7	4	41	7
YE Sep 08	:	:	:	:	:	:	:	:	:	:	:	:	:	:	:	:	:	:	:	:	:	:
YE Dec 08	409	41	166	22	243	34	133	32	54	15	67	21	12	19	0~	1	110	12	9	5	41	7
YE Mar 09	:	:	:	:	:	:	:	:	:	:	:	:	:	:	:	:	:	:	:	:	:	:
YE Jun 09	370	28	146	15	224	23	116	21	54	11	57	17	3	3	1	1	109	11	8	4	43	7
YE Sep 09	:	:	:	:	:	:	:	:	:	:	:	:	:	:	:	:	:	:	:	:	:	:
YE Dec 09	337	22	127	11	211	18	102	16	52	11	47	12	2	1	1	1	109	9	4	2	48	5
YE Mar 10	335	23	119	11	216	20	107	18	57	13	46	12	3	2	1	1	109	9	6	2	51	6
YE Jun 10	316	21	115	10	201	18	96	16	52	13	40	10	3	2	1	1	105	8	5	2	48	5
YE Sep 10	312	20	122	11	189	17	91	16	59	13	29	7	2	2	1	1	98	8	5	2	49	5
YE Dec 10	310	20	125	11	185	16	91	14	57	12	31	8	2	2	1	1	94	8	5	2	46	5
YE Mar 11	307	18	130	11	177	15	84	13	50	9	32	8	1	1	1	1	93	7	5	2	45	5
YE Jun 11	315	19	131	11	183	16	89	13	50	9	35	9	3	2	1	1	95	9	7	5	46	5
YE Sep 11	318	20	134	11	184	16	86	13	45	9	35	9	4	3	1	1	98	10	8	6	48	5
YE Dec 11	332	22	142	13	190	17	87	14	48	10	33	9	4	3	1	1	103	10	7	6	56	6
YE Mar 12	333	22	144	13	189	17	85	14	48	10	31	9	3	2	1	1	104	10	7	6	58	6
YE Jun 12	331	22	148	16	184	16	81	13	48	10	28	8	3	2	2	1	103	9	5	2	59	6
YE Sep 12	322	22	143	16	179	15	78	13	47	10	27	7	2	2	2	1	101	8	5	2	64	7
YE Dec 12	298	20	134	14	165	14	69	11	39	8	26	8	3	2	1	1	96	8	4	2	58	6
YE Mar 13	295	20	133	14	162	14	69	12	40	8	25	8	3	2	1	1	93	8	4	2	57	6
YE Jun 13	297	19	131	12	166	15	71	12	42	9	26	8	2	2	1	1	94	8	5	3	53	5
YE Sep 13	296	19	128	12	168	15	72	13	45	10	22	7	3	2	2	1	96	8	6	3	53	5
YE Dec 13	295	19	125	12	170	15	73	12	45	10	23	7	3	2	2	1	97	9	6	3	54	6
YE Mar 14	294	20	121	11	174	17	77	14	48	12	24	7	3	2	2	2	97	8	6	3	54	6
YE Jun 14	299	22	122	13	177	18	79	15	47	12	26	8	4	4	2	1	98	9	6	3	55	6
YE Sep 14	302	23	125	13	176	18	82	15	46	12	31	9	4	3	1	1	95	11	6	3	58	9
YE Dec 14	297	22	127	13	171	18	83	15	49	12	29	9	4	3	1	1	87	10	6	3	55	9
YE Mar 15	284	21	122	13	162	17	79	13	47	9	27	8	4	3	1	1	83	10	6	3	52	9
YE Jun 15	279	20	120	12	159	16	79	12	47	9	26	7	4	3	1	1	80	10	4	2	51	9
YE Sep 15	275	19	118	12	157	15	79	12	48	9	24	7	5	5	1	1	78	8	3	2	48	6
YE Dec 15	279	20	114	13	165	16	79	13	48	10	24	7	6	5	1	1	85	9	3	2	50	6
YE Mar 16	287	21	116	13	171	16	83	13	50	10	26	7	7	5	1	1	88	9	4	2	52	7
YE Jun 16	293	21	116	12	177	17	88	14	52	10	28	8	7	5	1	1	88	9	4	2	51	7
YE Sep 16	300	22	116	13	184	18	96	15	50	10	36	9	9	5	2	2	88	11	3	2	48	7
YE Dec 16	316	23	121	13	195	19	111	16	57	11	40	10	12	6	2	1	84	10	3	2	47	7
YE Mar 17[p]	316	23	119	13	197	19	116	16	56	10	43	10	15	7	2	1	81	10	4	2	46	6
YE Jun 17[p,7]	306	23	109	12	197	19	113	16	59	11	38	9	15	7	2	2	84	10	4	2	49	7
YE Sep 17[p,7]	329	25	110	13	219	21	134	19	72	14	43	10	18	7	1	1	85	10	6	3	45	7
YE Dec 17[p]	321	26	106	13	214	22	135	20	70	15	45	11	18	7	3	2	80	10	6	3	45	7

Table 3 International Passenger Survey (IPS) estimates of long-term international migration - Rolling annual data for the United Kingdom, year ending December 2017

Abbreviation: Est. (Estimate)
Citizenship by main reason for migration

United Kingdom
thousands

Main reason for migration	All citizenships Est.	+/-CI	British (Including Overseas Territories) Est.	+/-CI	Non-British Est.	+/-CI	European Union[1] Est.	+/-CI	European Union EU15 Est.	+/-CI	European Union EU8 Est.	+/-CI	European Union EU2 Est.	+/-CI	European Union Other Est.	+/-CI	Non-European Union[2] All Est.	+/-CI	Other Europe[3] Est.	+/-CI	Asia All Est.	+/-CI
Work related[4]																						
YE Mar 08	:	:	:	:	:	:	:	:	:	:	:	:	:	:	:	:	:	:	:	:	:	:
YE Jun 08	195	23	87	18	107	14	39	12	18	8	19	9			2	3	69	7	2	1	30	5
YE Sep 08	:	:	:	:	:	:	:	:	:	:	:	:	:	:	:	:	:	:	:	:	:	:
YE Dec 08	217	26	91	18	127	19	53	17	23	8	29	15	0~	1	0~	1	74	9	5	4	29	5
YE Mar 09	:	:	:	:	:	:	:	:	:	:	:	:	:	:	:	:	:	:	:	:	:	:
YE Jun 09	209	21	75	11	134	18	60	16	29	8	30	14	1	1	1	1	74	8	4	3	31	5
YE Sep 09	:	:	:	:	:	:	:	:	:	:	:	:	:	:	:	:	:	:	:	:	:	:
YE Dec 09	203	17	64	9	139	15	60	13	35	10	23	8	1	1	1	1	79	7	2	1	36	4
YE Mar 10	203	18	60	8	144	16	66	14	38	11	24	8	2	2	1	1	78	7	3	1	38	5
YE Jun 10	190	16	59	7	131	14	55	13	33	10	19	7	2	2	1	1	76	7	3	1	36	4
YE Sep 10	182	15	61	8	121	13	52	12	34	10	15	5	2	2	1	1	69	6	3	1	37	4
YE Dec 10	181	13	67	8	114	11	46	9	28	6	15	6	2	2	1	1	68	6	4	2	35	4
YE Mar 11	173	12	69	7	105	9	37	7	23	5	13	5	1	1	1	1	68	6	4	2	35	4
YE Jun 11	181	14	70	8	110	11	41	8	25	6	15	6	1	1	0~	1	69	8	6	5	36	4
YE Sep 11	185	14	73	8	112	12	40	8	23	5	16	6	1	1	1	1	72	8	7	6	37	5
YE Dec 11	196	15	78	9	117	12	41	9	25	7	14	6	1	1	1	1	76	9	6	5	45	5
YE Mar 12	202	16	81	10	121	13	44	9	28	7	15	6	1	1	1	1	77	9	6	5	45	5
YE Jun 12	196	14	82	9	114	11	41	8	26	6	13	5	0~	1	1	1	73	7	4	2	45	5
YE Sep 12	193	14	79	9	114	11	39	8	27	7	10	4	0~	0~	2	1	74	7	4	2	48	6
YE Dec 12	175	13	72	8	103	10	33	7	23	6	9	3	1	1	1	1	70	7	3	2	42	5
YE Mar 13	177	13	74	9	104	10	34	8	23	6	9	4	0~	1	1	1	70	7	3	2	42	5
YE Jun 13	181	14	75	9	106	10	35	8	23	6	10	4	0~	1	1	1	72	7	3	1	43	5
YE Sep 13	180	14	75	9	104	11	34	8	23	7	9	4	1	1	1	1	70	7	2	1	40	5
YE Dec 13	181	14	74	9	107	11	37	8	24	7	11	4	0~	1	1	1	70	7	3	1	40	5
YE Mar 14	176	15	68	8	108	13	39	11	26	10	11	4	1	1	1	1	69	7	2	1	41	5
YE Jun 14	174	16	68	9	107	13	40	11	25	10	11	5	3	3	1	1	67	7	3	2	39	5
YE Sep 14	174	16	67	9	107	13	45	12	27	10	15	6	3	3	1	1	62	7	3	2	39	5
YE Dec 14	171	16	67	8	104	13	46	12	29	10	13	6	3	3	1	1	58	6	3	2	38	5
YE Mar 15	159	14	65	8	94	11	40	9	25	6	12	5	3	3	1	1	54	6	3	2	34	5
YE Jun 15	163	13	64	8	99	11	43	9	28	7	12	5	1	2	1	1	57	6	3	2	36	5
YE Sep 15	160	14	61	8	99	11	43	9	30	7	10	5	2	4	1	1	56	6	3	2	35	5
YE Dec 15	159	14	57	8	102	11	42	9	28	7	11	5	2	4	1	1	60	7	3	2	36	5
YE Mar 16	163	14	58	9	105	11	44	9	29	7	12	5	3	4	1	1	61	7	3	2	37	5
YE Jun 16	161	14	60	9	101	11	42	9	26	6	12	5	3	4	1	1	59	7	2	1	37	5
YE Sep 16	159	14	57	9	102	11	41	8	24	6	13	5	4	4	1	1	61	8	1	1	34	5
YE Dec 16	171	15	65	9	106	12	48	9	26	6	16	5	6	5	0~	0~	58	8	1	1	34	5
YE Mar 17[p]	173	15	64	9	109	12	53	9	30	6	17	5	6	5	0~	0~	56	8	1	1	33	5
YE Jun 17[p7]	169	15	56	8	112	13	54	9	32	7	15	5	6	5	0~	1	58	8	3	2	32	5
YE Sep 17[p7]	184	16	60	9	124	14	60	10	36	8	18	6	6	4	1	1	64	9	4	3	39	6
YE Dec 17[p]	178	18	54	9	124	15	65	13	38	9	18	7	6	4	2	2	59	9	4	3	34	6
Definite job																						
YE Mar 08	:	:	:	:	:	:	:	:	:	:	:	:	:	:	:	:	:	:	:	:	:	:
YE Jun 08	124	20	71	17	54	9	18	8	8	4	9	6			1	3	36	6	2	1	18	4
YE Sep 08	:	:	:	:	:	:	:	:	:	:	:	:	:	:	:	:	:	:	:	:	:	:
YE Dec 08	134	20	72	18	62	10	26	9	15	6	11	6	0~	1	0~	1	36	5	2	2	14	3
YE Mar 09	:	:	:	:	:	:	:	:	:	:	:	:	:	:	:	:	:	:	:	:	:	:
YE Jun 09	120	14	52	10	68	11	32	9	21	7	10	6	1	1	0~	1	36	5	1	1	16	3
YE Sep 09	:	:	:	:	:	:	:	:	:	:	:	:	:	:	:	:	:	:	:	:	:	:
YE Dec 09	113	13	42	7	71	12	32	10	22	9	8	4	1	1	1	1	39	5	1	1	19	3
YE Mar 10	113	13	38	5	75	12	36	11	24	10	9	4	2	2	1	1	40	5	2	1	20	3
YE Jun 10	107	12	40	6	67	11	29	10	20	9	7	3	2	2	1	1	38	5	2	1	18	3
YE Sep 10	108	13	44	6	64	11	32	10	23	9	7	3	1	2	0~	0~	32	4	2	1	16	3
YE Dec 10	108	11	49	7	58	8	26	7	19	5	6	3	1	2	0~	0~	32	4	3	1	15	3
YE Mar 11	102	9	52	7	50	7	21	5	15	3	6	3	1	1	0~	0~	29	4	3	2	13	3
YE Jun 11	108	11	53	7	55	7	24	6	17	5	7	4	1	1	0~	0~	30	7	5	5	14	3
YE Sep 11	111	12	55	7	56	9	21	5	15	5	5	3	0~	0~	0~	0~	35	7	6	5	16	3
YE Dec 11	120	12	59	8	60	9	24	6	17	5	6	3	0~	0~	1	1	36	7	5	5	20	4
YE Mar 12	124	13	62	9	62	9	25	6	17	5	6	3	0~	1	1	1	37	7	5	5	20	4
YE Jun 12	122	11	63	9	59	7	24	5	17	4	6	3	0~	0~	1	1	36	7	5	2	20	3
YE Sep 12	123	12	64	9	59	8	24	6	18	5	6	3	0~	0~	1	1	35	5	5	2	20	3
YE Dec 12	110	10	57	7	53	7	21	5	15	5	5	2	0~	0~	0~	0~	32	5	2	1	17	3
YE Mar 13	110	11	55	8	55	8	23	6	17	6	5	2	0~	0~	0~	0~	32	5	1	1	17	3
YE Jun 13	111	11	56	8	55	8	23	7	17	6	6	3			0~	1	32	5	1	1	17	3
YE Sep 13	108	12	54	8	54	9	24	7	18	7	6	3			0~	1	30	5	1	1	16	3
YE Dec 13	107	11	53	8	54	9	24	7	17	6	7	3			0~	1	29	5	1	1	16	3
YE Mar 14	101	10	50	7	51	8	23	6	15	4	7	3			1	1	28	5	1	1	16	3
YE Jun 14	102	12	51	7	51	8	24	7	15	6	7	4	1	3	1	1	27	5	1	1	15	3
YE Sep 14	100	11	50	7	50	8	25	7	13	4	9	5	2	3	1	1	25	4	2	1	15	3
YE Dec 14	104	11	51	8	53	8	27	7	16	4	8	5	3	3	1	1	25	4	1	1	16	3
YE Mar 15	100	11	49	8	50	8	26	7	16	5	7	4	3	3	0~	0~	24	4	1	1	14	3
YE Jun 15	98	10	47	7	51	7	23	6	15	4	7	4	1	2	0~	0~	28	5	2	1	16	3
YE Sep 15	97	11	46	7	51	8	25	6	18	5	7	4	0~	1	0~	0~	27	5	2	2	16	3
YE Dec 15	94	11	43	7	51	8	23	6	15	5	7	4	0~	1	1	1	27	5	2	2	15	3
YE Mar 16	95	11	44	8	51	8	25	7	15	5	9	4	1	1	0~	1	27	5	2	2	15	3
YE Jun 16	98	12	46	8	52	8	26	7	16	5	9	5	1	1	0~	1	26	4	1	1	16	4
YE Sep 16	99	12	45	8	54	9	24	7	13	4	9	4	3	3	0~	1	29	6	1	1	16	4
YE Dec 16	110	13	52	8	57	10	28	7	15	4	10	4	4	4			29	6	1	1	17	4
YE Mar 17[p]	115	13	53	8	62	10	32	8	18	5	10	5	4	4			30	6	1	1	17	4
YE Jun 17[p7]	111	13	47	7	64	10	33	8	20	5	8	4	5	4	0~	1	31	6	1	1	13	3
YE Sep 17[p7]	120	14	48	8	72	11	37	8	22	6	11	6	4	3	0~	1	34	7	3	2	20	5
YE Dec 17[p]	120	15	44	8	76	13	43	11	25	8	12	6	6	4	1	1	33	8	2	2	17	5

Table 3 International Passenger Survey (IPS) estimates of long-term international migration - Rolling annual data for the United Kingdom, year ending December 2017

Abbreviation: Est. (Estimate)
Citizenship by main reason for migration

United Kingdom
thousands

Main reason for migration	All citizenships		British (Including Overseas Territories)		Non-British		European Union[1]		European Union EU15		European Union EU8		European Union EU2		European Union Other		Non-European Union[2] All		Other Europe[3]		Asia All	
	Est.	+/-CI	Est.	+/-CI	Est.	+/-CI	Est.	+/-CI	Est.	+/-CI	Est.	+/-CI	Est.	+/-CI	Est.	+/-CI	Est.	+/-CI	Est.	+/-CI	Est.	+/-CI
Looking for work																						
YE Mar 08	:	:	:	:	:	:	:	:	:	:	:	:	:	:	:	:	:	:	:	:	:	:
YE Jun 08	70	12	17	6	54	11	21	10	10	7	10	7			0~	1	33	4	1	1	12	3
YE Sep 08	:	:	:	:	:	:	:	:	:	:	:	:					:	:	:	:	:	:
YE Dec 08	84	16	19	4	65	16	27	14	8	6	19	13					38	7	3	3	14	4
YE Mar 09	:	:	:	:	:	:	:	:	:	:	:	:					:	:	:	:	:	:
YE Jun 09	88	15	23	6	66	14	28	13	8	3	19	12	0~	1	0~	0~	38	6	3	3	15	4
YE Sep 09	:	:	:	:	:	:	:	:	:	:	:	:					:	:	:	:	:	:
YE Dec 09	90	11	22	5	68	10	28	8	13	5	14	7	0~	1	0~	0~	40	5	1	1	17	3
YE Mar 10	91	11	22	6	68	10	30	8	13	5	16	7	0~	1	0~	0~	38	5	1	1	18	3
YE Jun 10	83	10	19	5	64	9	26	8	13	4	12	6	0~	0~	0~	0~	38	5	1	1	18	3
YE Sep 10	74	8	17	4	57	7	20	5	11	4	9	4	0~	0~	0~	0~	37	5	1	1	21	3
YE Dec 10	73	8	18	4	56	7	20	5	10	3	10	4	0~	0~	0~	0~	36	4	1	1	20	3
YE Mar 11	72	8	17	4	55	7	16	5	9	3	7	4			0~	0~	38	5	1	1	22	3
YE Jun 11	73	8	17	4	56	7	17	5	8	3	8	5	0~	1	0~	0~	39	5	2	1	22	3
YE Sep 11	74	8	18	4	55	8	18	6	7	2	10	5	0~	1	1	1	37	5	1	1	21	3
YE Dec 11	76	9	19	4	57	8	17	6	9	4	8	4	0~	1	0~	0~	40	5	1	1	25	4
YE Mar 12	78	9	19	4	59	8	20	7	10	5	8	5	0~	1	0~	0~	39	5	1	1	24	4
YE Jun 12	74	9	19	4	54	8	17	6	10	5	7	4	0~	0~	0~	0~	37	5	1	1	24	4
YE Sep 12	70	8	15	3	55	7	15	5	10	5	5	3			1	1	40	5	2	1	27	4
YE Dec 12	65	7	15	3	49	6	12	4	7	3	4	2	0~	1	1	1	37	5	2	1	25	4
YE Mar 13	67	7	18	4	49	6	11	4	6	3	4	3	0~	1	1	1	38	5	2	1	25	4
YE Jun 13	70	7	18	4	51	6	11	4	5	2	5	3	0~	1	1	1	40	5	2	1	26	4
YE Sep 13	72	7	22	4	50	6	10	4	5	2	3	3	1	1	0~	1	40	5	2	1	25	4
YE Dec 13	74	8	21	5	53	6	13	4	7	3	5	3	0~	1	0~	1	41	5	2	1	24	4
YE Mar 14	75	11	18	4	57	10	16	9	11	8	4	3	1	1	0~	0~	41	5	2	1	25	4
YE Jun 14	73	11	17	4	56	10	16	9	10	8	5	3	1	1	0~	0~	40	5	2	1	25	4
YE Sep 14	74	12	17	4	57	11	20	9	14	9	6	4	0~	0~	0~	0~	37	5	1	1	25	4
YE Dec 14	67	11	16	4	51	11	19	9	13	9	5	4	0~	0~	1	1	32	5	1	1	23	4
YE Mar 15	60	8	16	4	44	7	14	5	9	4	5	3			1	1	29	5	1	1	20	4
YE Jun 15	66	9	17	4	49	8	20	6	14	5	5	4	0~	0~	1	1	29	5	1	1	20	4
YE Sep 15	63	8	15	4	48	8	19	6	12	4	4	3	2	3	1	1	29	5	1	1	19	4
YE Dec 15	65	9	13	3	52	8	19	6	13	4	4	3	2	3	0~	1	33	5	1	1	21	4
YE Mar 16	67	9	14	4	53	8	19	6	14	5	3	2	2	4	0~	1	34	5	0~	0~	22	4
YE Jun 16	63	8	14	4	49	8	16	6	10	4	3	2	3	4	0~	0~	33	5	0~	1	21	4
YE Sep 16	60	8	12	4	48	7	16	5	11	4	4	2	1	1	0~	0~	31	5	0~	1	18	4
YE Dec 16	61	8	13	4	48	7	19	5	11	4	6	3	2	2	0~	0~	29	5	0~	0~	18	4
YE Mar 17[p]	58	8	11	3	47	7	21	5	12	4	7	3	2	2	0~	0~	26	5	0~	0~	17	4
YE Jun 17[p7]	58	8	10	3	48	7	21	5	12	4	7	3	2	2			28	5	1	1	17	4
YE Sep 17[p7]	64	9	12	4	52	8	23	6	14	5	7	3	2	2	0~	1	29	5	2	1	19	4
YE Dec 17[p]	58	9	10	3	48	8	22	6	13	5	7	4	1	1	1	2	27	5	2	1	17	4
Accompany/Join																						
YE Mar 08	:	:	:	:	:	:	:	:	:	:	:	:	:	:	:	:	:	:	:	:	:	:
YE Jun 08	46	9	34	9	12	3	4	2	2	1	2	2					8	2	0~	0~	4	2
YE Sep 08	:	:	:	:	:	:	:	:	:	:	:	:					:	:	:	:	:	:
YE Dec 08	58	12	36	10	22	6	8	4	5	4	2	2					14	4	1	1	6	3
YE Mar 09	:	:	:	:	:	:	:	:	:	:	:	:					:	:	:	:	:	:
YE Jun 09	51	9	31	7	20	6	7	4	5	4	2	1					13	4	1	1	4	3
YE Sep 09	:	:	:	:	:	:	:	:	:	:	:	:					:	:	:	:	:	:
YE Dec 09	43	7	28	5	16	5	6	4	2	1	4	4					9	2			3	1
YE Mar 10	41	7	25	5	16	5	6	4	2	1	4	4					10	2	0~	1	4	1
YE Jun 10	40	7	24	5	16	5	6	4	2	1	4	4					10	2	0~	1	3	1
YE Sep 10	37	6	24	5	14	3	5	2	4	2	1	1					9	2	1	1	3	1
YE Dec 10	37	6	22	4	15	4	7	3	6	3	1	2					8	2	1	1	3	1
YE Mar 11	36	6	22	4	14	4	6	3	5	3	1	2					7	2	0~	0~	3	1
YE Jun 11	35	6	22	4	13	4	6	3	5	3	1	2					7	2	0~	0~	3	1
YE Sep 11	32	5	21	4	11	3	4	3	3	2	1	2					7	2	0~	0~	3	1
YE Dec 11	31	5	22	4	9	2	2	1	2	1	1	1					7	2	1	1	2	1
YE Mar 12	30	5	22	5	9	2	2	1	2	1	1	1					7	2	1	1	2	1
YE Jun 12	31	5	21	5	10	3	3	2	2	1	1	1					7	2	0~	1	3	1
YE Sep 12	33	6	21	5	11	3	5	3	3	2	2	1	1	2			6	2	0~	0~	2	1
YE Dec 12	33	6	22	5	11	3	5	3	3	2	2	1	1	2			6	2	0~	0~	2	1
YE Mar 13	32	6	20	4	12	3	5	3	3	2	2	1	1	2			7	2	0~	0~	3	1
YE Jun 13	31	6	19	4	12	4	6	3	4	2	1	1	1	2			6	2	0~	0~	3	1
YE Sep 13	28	5	16	4	12	4	4	3	3	3	0~	1	0~	0~			8	2	1	1	4	1
YE Dec 13	27	5	15	3	13	4	4	3	3	3	1	1	0~	0~			9	2	1	1	4	2
YE Mar 14	27	5	14	3	13	4	5	3	3	3	1	1	0~	0~			8	2	1	1	3	1
YE Jun 14	28	5	15	3	13	3	5	3	3	2	2	1					8	2	1	1	4	2
YE Sep 14	28	5	16	3	12	4	5	3	2	1	3	3	0~	0~			6	2	0~	1	3	1
YE Dec 14	26	5	17	3	9	3	5	3	2	1	3	3	0~	0~			4	2	0~	1	2	1
YE Mar 15	26	5	16	4	10	4	6	4	3	2	3	3	0~	0~			4	2	0~	1	2	1
YE Jun 15	26	6	17	5	9	4	6	4	3	3	3	3	0~	0~			3	2	0~	0~	2	1
YE Sep 15	24	6	16	5	8	3	4	3	3	3	1	1					4	2			3	1
YE Dec 15	25	6	15	5	10	4	5	3	3	3	1	1					6	2			3	2
YE Mar 16	22	5	14	5	9	3	3	2	2	2	1	1	0~	0~			6	2			4	2
YE Jun 16	21	4	14	3	8	2	2	2	2	1	0~	1	0~	0~			6	2			3	1
YE Sep 16	23	5	14	4	9	4	2	2	2	2	0~	0~	0~	0~			7	3			3	2
YE Dec 16	24	6	14	4	10	4	4	2	3	2	0~	0~	0~	0~			7	3			4	2
YE Mar 17[p]	27	6	16	5	10	4	4	2	3	2	0~	0~					8	3			4	2
YE Jun 17[p7]	26	6	15	4	11	4	4	3	3	2	1	1					7	4	0~	0~	4	2
YE Sep 17[p7]	25	6	17	5	8	3	4	3	3	3	1	2					4	2	0~	0~	2	1
YE Dec 17[p]	21	5	15	4	6	3	3	2	2	2	1	1					3	2	0~	0~	2	1

Table 3 International Passenger Survey (IPS) estimates of long-term international migration - Rolling annual data for the United Kingdom, year ending December 2017

Abbreviation: Est. (Estimate)

United Kingdom
thousands

Citizenship by main reason for migration

Main reason for migration	All citizenships		British (Including Overseas Territories)		Non-British		European Union[1]		European Union EU15		European Union EU8		European Union EU2		European Union Other		Non-European Union[2] All		Other Europe[3]		Asia All	
	Est.	+/-CI	Est.	+/-CI	Est.	+/-CI	Est.	+/-CI	Est.	+/-CI	Est.	+/-CI	Est.	+/-CI	Est.	+/-CI	Est.	+/-CI	Est.	+/-CI	Est.	+/-CI
Formal study																						
YE Mar 08	:	:	:	:	:	:	:	:	:	:	:	:	:	:	:	:	:	:	:	:	:	:
YE Jun 08	15	5	4	2	11	4	3	3	0~	1	3	3			0~	0~	7	3	1	2	2	1
YE Sep 08	:	:	:	:	:	:	:	:	:	:	:	:	:	:	:	:	:	:	:	:	:	:
YE Dec 08	21	8	3	1	18	7	13	7	3	3	9	6					5	3	1	1	2	2
YE Mar 09	:	:	:	:	:	:	:	:	:	:	:	:	:	:	:	:	:	:	:	:	:	:
YE Jun 09	23	8	4	2	19	7	14	7	4	3	9	6	0~	0~	0~	0~	5	3	1	1	2	2
YE Sep 09	:	:	:	:	:	:	:	:	:	:	:	:	:	:	:	:	6	2	0~	0~	2	1
YE Dec 09	19	4	7	3	13	3	7	3	3	2	3	2	0~	0~	0~	0~	6	2	0~	0~	2	1
YE Mar 10	23	7	7	3	16	7	9	6	6	6	3	1	0~	0~	0~	0~	6	2	0~	0~	2	1
YE Jun 10	21	7	7	3	14	7	8	6	6	6	2	1	.	.	.	.	6	2	0~	0~	2	1
YE Sep 10	26	8	8	3	18	8	12	8	9	7	2	2	0~	0~	0~	0~	6	2	0~	0~	2	1
YE Dec 10	26	9	8	3	19	8	13	8	9	7	3	2	0~	0~	0~	0~	6	2	.	.	2	1
YE Mar 11	23	6	7	3	16	5	10	5	6	4	3	3	0~	0~	0~	0~	6	2	.	.	2	1
YE Jun 11	23	6	6	3	17	5	10	5	7	4	3	2	0~	0~	0~	0~	7	3	0~	1	3	2
YE Sep 11	19	5	5	2	13	4	6	3	4	3	2	2	0~	0~	0~	0~	6	3	0~	1	3	2
YE Dec 11	17	5	6	2	11	4	5	3	4	2	1	1	0~	0~	0~	0~	7	3	0~	1	4	2
YE Mar 12	17	5	6	2	11	4	4	3	4	2	0~	0~	0~	0~	0~	0~	7	3	1	1	4	2
YE Jun 12	20	5	6	2	14	5	7	4	6	3	1	2	0~	0~	0~	0~	5	2	1	1	3	1
YE Sep 12	18	4	6	2	12	4	6	3	5	3	2	2	0~	0~	.	.	5	2	1	1	3	1
YE Dec 12	18	5	6	2	12	4	7	4	5	3	2	2	0~	0~	.	.	4	1	1	1	3	1
YE Mar 13	17	4	6	2	11	4	7	3	5	3	2	2	0~	0~	.	.	4	2	1	1	3	1
YE Jun 13	16	4	6	2	10	3	6	3	5	3	1	1	0~	0~	.	.	4	2	1	1	3	1
YE Sep 13	20	5	6	3	13	4	8	4	6	3	1	1	1	2	1	1	5	2	1	1	3	1
YE Dec 13	21	5	6	3	15	5	8	4	5	3	2	2	1	2	1	1	7	2	1	1	4	1
YE Mar 14	22	5	7	3	15	5	8	4	5	3	1	2	1	2	1	1	7	2	1	1	4	2
YE Jun 14	21	5	7	3	14	4	7	4	4	3	1	2	1	2	1	1	6	2	1	1	3	2
YE Sep 14	19	5	8	3	11	4	6	3	4	3	1	2	0~	1	.	.	6	2	1	1	4	2
YE Dec 14	21	6	8	3	13	5	7	4	5	3	2	3	0~	0~	.	.	6	2	1	1	4	2
YE Mar 15	22	6	8	3	14	5	8	4	6	3	2	3	0~	0~	0~	0~	6	2	1	1	4	2
YE Jun 15	20	5	7	3	13	4	7	4	4	3	2	3	0~	0~	0~	0~	6	2	0~	0~	4	2
YE Sep 15	25	6	9	3	16	5	8	5	5	3	3	4	0~	1	0~	0~	8	3	0~	1	5	3
YE Dec 15	22	6	8	3	14	5	6	3	4	2	2	2	0~	1	0~	0~	9	3	0~	1	4	3
YE Mar 16	20	5	8	3	13	5	5	3	3	2	2	2	0~	1	.	.	8	3	0~	1	4	3
YE Jun 16	23	6	8	3	15	5	7	4	5	3	2	3	0~	1	.	.	8	3	0~	1	4	3
YE Sep 16	19	5	7	3	11	4	5	3	4	3	1	1	1	1	0~	1	6	3	0~	0~	3	3
YE Dec 16	20	6	7	3	13	5	7	4	6	3	1	1	1	1	0~	1	5	3	0~	0~	3	3
YE Mar 17[p]	21	6	7	3	13	5	8	4	6	4	1	1	1	1	0~	1	6	3	0~	0~	4	3
YE Jun 17[p7]	18	5	7	3	11	4	5	3	5	3	.	.	1	1			5	3	0~	0~	4	3
YE Sep 17[p7]	16	5	4	2	12	5	8	4	6	3	2	2	0~	1			4	2	0~	0~	3	2
YE Dec 17[p]	14	4	4	2	10	4	5	3	3	2	2	2	.	.			4	2	0~	0~	3	2
Going home to live[5]																						
YE Mar 08	:	:	:	:	:	:	:	:	:	:	:	:	:	:	:	:	:	:	:	:	:	:
YE Jun 08	47	25	1	1	46	25	38	25	11	11	17	12	10	19	.	.	8	4	1	1	1	1
YE Sep 08	:	:	:	:	:	:	:	:	:	:	:	:	:	:	:	:	:	:	:	:	:	:
YE Dec 08	62	26	1	1	61	26	50	26	15	11	24	13	12	19	.	.	10	5	1	1	3	3
YE Mar 09	:	:	:	:	:	:	:	:	:	:	:	:	:	:	:	:	:	:	:	:	:	:
YE Jun 09	40	11	2	1	38	11	29	10	11	6	16	8	2	3	0~	0~	9	4	1	1	4	3
YE Sep 09	:	:	:	:	:	:	:	:	:	:	:	:	:	:	:	:	:	:	:	:	:	:
YE Dec 09	29	7	1	1	28	7	19	6	6	3	12	6	1	1	0~	0~	9	3	1	1	4	3
YE Mar 10	29	7	1	1	28	7	19	6	7	3	11	6	1	1	0~	0~	9	3	1	1	5	3
YE Jun 10	29	7	1	1	28	7	19	6	7	4	11	5	1	1	0~	0~	9	3	1	1	5	3
YE Sep 10	28	7	2	1	27	7	18	6	8	4	9	5	1	1	0~	0~	9	3	1	1	5	3
YE Dec 10	31	8	1	1	30	8	22	7	10	5	11	5	0~	0~	0~	0~	8	3	1	1	5	3
YE Mar 11	35	9	2	1	33	9	26	8	11	6	14	6	0~	0~	0~	0~	7	3	1	1	3	1
YE Jun 11	36	9	2	1	35	9	27	8	11	5	15	6	1	2	0~	0~	7	3	0~	1	3	1
YE Sep 11	39	9	2	2	37	9	30	9	13	6	16	6	2	2	.	.	7	2	0~	0~	3	1
YE Dec 11	42	11	4	5	38	10	30	9	13	6	15	7	2	2	.	.	8	3	0~	0~	3	2
YE Mar 12	39	10	4	5	35	9	26	9	11	6	13	6	2	2	.	.	9	3	0~	0~	4	2
YE Jun 12	34	10	4	5	30	8	20	8	10	5	9	5	1	1	.	.	10	3	0~	0~	6	2
YE Sep 12	31	10	5	6	25	8	16	7	7	4	9	5	1	1	.	.	9	3	.	.	6	3
YE Dec 12	26	8	3	4	23	7	14	6	4	3	9	5	1	1	.	.	9	3	.	.	7	3
YE Mar 13	24	8	3	4	21	7	14	6	5	3	8	5	1	1	.	.	7	3	.	.	5	2
YE Jun 13	28	9	3	4	25	8	18	7	6	4	11	6	1	1	.	.	7	3	1	2	4	2
YE Sep 13	28	8	2	1	27	8	20	8	9	5	10	6	1	1	0~	0~	7	3	1	2	3	2
YE Dec 13	27	8	2	1	25	8	19	7	9	5	8	5	1	1	0~	0~	7	3	1	2	3	2
YE Mar 14	29	9	1	1	27	9	20	8	10	6	9	5	1	1	0~	0~	8	3	2	2	3	2
YE Jun 14	33	9	0~	0~	33	9	22	9	10	6	10	6	1	1	0~	0~	11	4	1	2	6	3
YE Sep 14	35	11	0~	1	34	11	19	8	9	5	10	6	0~	0~	0~	0~	15	8	1	2	10	7
YE Dec 14	33	10	0~	1	32	10	18	7	9	5	9	5	0~	0~	0~	0~	14	8	1	2	10	7
YE Mar 15	33	10	0~	1	33	10	19	7	10	5	8	5	1	1	0~	0~	14	8	1	2	10	7
YE Jun 15	28	9	0~	1	28	9	18	6	9	5	7	3	3	2	0~	0~	10	7	0~	0~	7	7
YE Sep 15	25	7	0~	0~	25	7	18	6	7	4	8	3	3	3	0~	1	7	3	0~	1	4	2
YE Dec 15	30	8	0~	1	29	8	22	8	9	6	9	5	3	3	0~	1	8	3	0~	1	4	2
YE Mar 16	35	9	0~	1	34	9	24	8	12	6	10	5	3	3	0~	1	10	5	1	1	6	4
YE Jun 16	39	10	1	1	38	10	28	9	13	6	12	6	2	2	0~	1	10	5	1	1	6	4
YE Sep 16	48	12	1	2	47	11	37	11	15	7	19	8	3	3	1	1	9	4	1	1	5	4
YE Dec 16	53	13	1	2	52	13	43	12	17	7	20	8	4	4	1	1	9	5	1	1	5	4
YE Mar 17[p]	52	12	2	2	51	12	44	12	13	7	22	8	8	5	1	1	7	3	1	1	3	2
YE Jun 17[p7]	51	12	2	2	49	12	42	11	14	7	19	7	8	5	1	1	7	3	1	1	4	2
YE Sep 17[p7]	59	14	1	1	58	14	50	14	21	10	18	7	11	6	0~	0~	8	4	1	1	4	2
YE Dec 17[p]	58	14	1	1	57	14	48	13	19	10	20	8	9	6	.	.	9	4	1	1	4	3

Table 3 International Passenger Survey (IPS) estimates of long-term international migration - Rolling annual data for the United Kingdom, year ending December 2017

Abbreviation: Est. (Estimate)
Citizenship by main reason for migration

Main reason for migration	All citizenships		British (Including Overseas Territories)		Non-British		European Union[1]		European Union EU15		European Union EU8		European Union EU2		European Union Other		Non-European Union[2] All		Other Europe[3]		Asia All	
	Est.	+/-CI	Est.	+/-CI	Est.	+/-CI	Est.	+/-CI	Est.	+/-CI	Est.	+/-CI	Est.	+/-CI	Est.	+/-CI	Est.	+/-CI	Est.	+/-CI	Est.	+/-CI
Other																						
YE Mar 08	:	:	:	:	:	:	:	:	:	:	:	:					:	:	:	:	:	:
YE Jun 08	33	9	21	7	12	6	5	4	4	4	1	2					7	4	0~	1	4	3
YE Sep 08	:	:	:	:	:	:	:	:	:	:	:	:					:	:	:	:	:	:
YE Dec 08	26	5	18	5	8	3	3	2	2	2	1	1			0~	0~	4	2	0~	1	1	1
YE Mar 09	:	:	:	:	:	:	:	:	:	:	:	:					:	:	:	:	:	:
YE Jun 09	29	6	20	5	9	3	4	2	2	2	1	1	0~	1	0~	0~	5	2	0~	0~	1	1
YE Sep 09	:	:	:	:	:	:	:	:	:	:	:	:					:	:	:	:	:	:
YE Dec 09	26	4	17	3	9	3	4	2	2	1	1	1	0~	1			5	2	0~	0~	1	1
YE Mar 10	24	4	17	3	7	2	3	2	2	1	1	1	0~	0~			4	2	0~	0~	1	1
YE Jun 10	22	4	16	3	6	2	2	1	1	1	1	1	0~	0~			3	1			1	1
YE Sep 10	23	4	18	3	5	2	1	1	1	1	1	1	0~	1			4	2			1	1
YE Dec 10	20	3	16	3	4	1	1	1	1	1	1	1	0~	0~			3	1			1	1
YE Mar 11	22	4	17	3	5	2	1	1	1	1	1	1	0~	0~			4	1			2	1
YE Jun 11	23	4	18	3	6	2	1	1	1	1	1	1	0~	0~			5	2			2	1
YE Sep 11	26	5	19	4	8	3	3	2	1	1	1	1	1	2			5	2	0~	1	2	1
YE Dec 11	30	7	19	4	10	5	6	5	3	4	2	2	1	2			5	2	0~	1	2	1
YE Mar 12	30	7	20	4	11	5	6	5	3	4	3	2	1	2			4	2	0~	1	2	1
YE Jun 12	35	11	24	9	11	5	6	5	3	4	3	2	1	2			4	2	0~	1	2	1
YE Sep 12	32	10	22	9	10	5	6	5	4	4	3	2					4	2			3	1
YE Dec 12	29	9	22	9	7	3	3	2	1	1	2	2					4	2	0~	0~	2	1
YE Mar 13	29	9	22	9	7	2	3	2	2	1	1	1					4	1	0~	0~	3	1
YE Jun 13	25	4	17	4	7	2	3	2	2	2	1	1					4	2	0~	1	3	1
YE Sep 13	23	4	18	4	6	2	2	2	2	2	0~	0~					3	1	0~	1	2	1
YE Dec 13	24	4	17	4	8	3	3	2	3	2	0~	0~					4	2	0~	1	3	1
YE Mar 14	23	4	16	3	7	3	4	2	3	2	1	1					3	2	0~	1	2	1
YE Jun 14	26	7	20	6	6	3	3	2	2	2	1	1	0~	0~			3	2			2	1
YE Sep 14	28	7	21	7	7	3	3	2	1	1	1	2	0~	0~			4	2	0~	0~	1	1
YE Dec 14	28	7	21	7	7	3	3	2	2	2	2	2	0~	0~			4	1	0~	0~	1	1
YE Mar 15	26	7	20	7	6	3	3	2	2	2	1	1	0~	0~			3	1	0~	0~	1	1
YE Jun 15	24	6	17	5	7	3	3	2	2	2	1	1					3	1	0~	0~	1	1
YE Sep 15	24	6	19	6	5	2	3	2	2	2	1	1					2	1			1	1
YE Dec 15	23	6	19	6	4	2	2	1	1	1	1	1					2	1			1	1
YE Mar 16	24	6	20	6	4	2	2	1	1	1	1	1					2	1			1	1
YE Jun 16	26	5	20	5	6	3	3	2	1	1	1	1	1	1			3	2	0~	0~	1	1
YE Sep 16	24	5	18	4	6	3	3	2	1	1	1	1	1	1			3	2	0~	0~	1	1
YE Dec 16	23	5	17	4	6	3	3	2	1	1	1	1	1	1			3	2	0~	1	1	1
YE Mar 17[p]	23	5	17	4	6	3	3	2	1	1	1	1	1	1			3	2	0~	1	1	1
YE Jun 17[E7]	19	5	14	4	5	2	2	2	1	1	1	1	0~	1			3	2	0~	0~	1	1
YE Sep 17[p7]	24	6	18	6	7	3	4	3	2	2	1	1	1	1	0~	1	3	2	0~	0~	2	1
YE Dec 17[p]	29	7	21	6	8	4	5	3	3	3	1	1	1	1	0~	1	3	2			1	1
No reason stated[6]																						
YE Mar 08	:	:	:	:	:	:	:	:	:	:	:	:					:	:	:	:	:	:
YE Jun 08	23	9	15	7	8	6	6	5	4	4	2	3			0~	1	3	3	2	3	0~	0~
YE Sep 08	:	:	:	:	:	:	:	:	:	:	:	:					:	:	:	:	:	:
YE Dec 08	25	9	17	7	8	5	6	5	5	4	1	2					2	2	1	2	1	0~
YE Mar 09	:	:	:	:	:	:	:	:	:	:	:	:					:	:	:	:	:	:
YE Jun 09	19	6	15	6	4	3	2	2	1	2	1	1					2	2	1	2	1	0~
YE Sep 09	:	:	:	:	:	:	:	:	:	:	:	:					:	:	:	:	:	:
YE Dec 09	17	5	10	3	7	4	5	4	2	2	3	4					1	1	0~	1	1	1
YE Mar 10	15	5	9	3	6	4	5	4	2	2	3	4					1	1	0~	1	1	1
YE Jun 10	15	5	8	3	7	4	6	4	3	2	3	4					1	1	0~	0~	0~	1
YE Sep 10	15	4	10	4	5	2	3	2	2	2	1	2			0~	0~	1	1			1	1
YE Dec 10	15	5	12	4	3	2	3	2	2	2	0~	0~			0~	0~	1	1			0~	0~
YE Mar 11	18	5	13	5	5	2	4	2	3	2	0~	0~	0~	0~	0~	0~	1	1			0~	0~
YE Jun 11	17	5	14	5	4	2	3	2	2	2	0~	0~	0~	0~	0~	0~	1	0~			0~	0~
YE Sep 11	17	6	13	5	4	2	3	2	2	2	0~	0~	0~	0~			1	1			0~	0~
YE Dec 11	16	6	13	5	4	2	3	2	2	2	1	1	0~	0~			1	1			0~	0~
YE Mar 12	15	5	12	5	3	2	2	2	1	1	0~	1	0~	0~			1	1			0~	0~
YE Jun 12	16	6	10	5	5	3	3	3	1	2	2	2	0~	0~			2	1			1	1
YE Sep 12	16	6	10	4	6	3	4	3	2	2	2	2	0~	0~			2	1			1	1
YE Dec 12	17	6	8	4	8	4	6	4	3	3	3	3	0~	0~			2	1			2	1
YE Mar 13	16	6	8	4	8	4	6	4	3	3	3	3	0~	0~			2	1			2	1
YE Jun 13	17	6	11	5	6	4	4	4	3	3	2	2			0~	0~	2	1			1	1
YE Sep 13	17	6	11	5	6	4	5	4	3	3	2	2			0~	0~	1	1			1	1
YE Dec 13	15	6	12	5	3	2	2	2	1	1	1	1			0~	0~	1	1			0~	0~
YE Mar 14	17	6	14	6	3	2	2	2	1	1	1	1			0~	0~	1	1			0~	0~
YE Jun 14	17	6	12	5	5	3	3	3	2	2	1	1					1	1	1	1	0~	0~
YE Sep 14	18	6	14	5	4	3	3	2	2	2	1	1	0~	0~			1	1	1	1	0~	1
YE Dec 14	18	6	13	5	5	3	3	2	2	2	1	1	0~	0~			2	1	1	1	1	1
YE Mar 15	17	5	12	4	5	3	3	2	2	2	1	1	0~	0~			2	1	1	1	1	1
YE Jun 15	18	5	14	5	3	2	2	1	1	1	1	1	0~	0~			1	1			1	1
YE Sep 15	16	5	13	5	3	2	2	2	2	1	1	1					1	1			1	1
YE Dec 15	20	7	15	6	5	3	3	3	3	3	0~	0~	0~	1			1	1			1	1
YE Mar 16	23	7	17	6	6	4	5	3	3	3	1	1	1	1			2	1			1	1
YE Jun 16	23	7	15	6	8	4	7	4	5	4	1	1	1	1			2	1			1	1
YE Sep 16	27	8	19	7	9	5	7	4	5	4	1	1	1	1			2	1			1	1
YE Dec 16	25	7	16	6	9	4	7	4	4	3	3	2	1	1			2	1			1	1
YE Mar 17[p]	21	7	14	5	7	4	6	4	3	3	2	2	0~	0~			2	1			1	1
YE Jun 17[p7]	22	7	14	6	8	4	6	4	3	3	3	2	0~	0~			2	1			1	1
YE Sep 17[p7]	20	6	11	4	9	5	8	5	4	3	4	3					1	1			0~	1
YE Dec 17[p]	21	7	12	5	9	4	8	4	5	4	3	2	1	1			1	1			0~	0~

Table 3 International Passenger Survey (IPS) estimates of long-term international migration - Rolling annual data for the United Kingdom, year ending December 2017

Abbreviation: Est. (Estimate)

Citizenship by main reason for migration

United Kingdom
thousands

	Non-European Union[2] (contd.) Asia (contd.) Middle East and Central Asia		East Asia		South Asia		South East Asia		Rest of the World All		Sub-Saharan Africa		North Africa		North America		Central and South America		Oceania		Stateless	
	Est.	+/-CI	Est.	+/-CI	Est.	+/-CI	Est.	+/-CI	Est.	+/-CI	Est.	+/-CI	Est.	+/-CI	Est.	+/-CI	Est.	+/-CI	Est.	+/-CI	Est.	+/-CI
Inflow																						
All reasons																						
YE Mar 08	:	:	:	:	:	:	:	:	:	:	:	:	:	:	:	:	:	:	:	:	:	:
YE Jun 08	14	3	36	9	92	13	28	9	100	13	37	8	6	5	20	5	10	4	27	5	0~	0~
YE Sep 08	:	:	:	:	:	:	:	:	:	:	:	:	:	:	:	:	:	:	:	:	:	:
YE Dec 08	18	6	32	8	80	9	32	8	105	15	38	9	7	4	24	7	13	6	23	5	0~	0~
YE Mar 09	:	:	:	:	:	:	:	:	:	:	:	:	:	:	:	:	:	:	:	:	:	:
YE Jun 09	19	6	32	7	86	10	27	6	90	13	35	9	6	4	20	6	10	5	18	5	0~	0~
YE Sep 09	:	:	:	:	:	:	:	:	:	:	:	:	:	:	:	:	:	:	:	:	:	:
YE Dec 09	17	4	38	6	110	10	29	5	77	10	29	7	2	3	23	6	7	3	17	4	0~	0~
YE Mar 10	17	4	39	6	123	10	33	6	78	10	25	6	2	3	24	6	8	4	18	4	0~	0~
YE Jun 10	16	4	39	6	121	9	32	6	76	10	24	5	2	2	24	6	9	4	17	4	0~	0~
YE Sep 10	16	4	42	6	130	10	34	6	78	10	24	5	6	5	20	5	10	4	19	4	0~	0~
YE Dec 10	15	4	42	6	124	9	31	6	82	10	23	5	6	5	22	5	9	4	22	5	0~	0~
YE Mar 11	16	4	42	7	125	10	28	6	80	10	21	4	6	5	23	5	8	3	21	5	0~	0~
YE Jun 11	15	4	40	6	140	11	28	6	77	10	22	5	7	5	21	5	7	4	21	5	0~	0~
YE Sep 11	15	4	54	9	142	11	22	5	74	9	20	4	3	2	26	6	5	3	20	4	0~	0~
YE Dec 11	16	4	55	9	125	10	20	4	71	9	22	5	2	1	25	6	5	2	18	4	0~	0~
YE Mar 12	16	5	56	8	104	10	20	4	74	11	21	5	1	1	26	8	5	2	21	5	0~	0~
YE Jun 12	17	5	55	8	87	9	20	4	75	9	21	5	1	1	26	6	5	2	22	5	.	.
YE Sep 12	13	4	56	8	68	8	21	5	77	11	22	6	3	3	24	6	6	3	21	6	.	.
YE Dec 12	11	3	54	8	64	8	21	5	75	11	19	5	4	4	25	6	6	3	21	5	.	.
YE Mar 13	10	3	51	7	59	8	20	5	70	11	19	5	5	4	25	6	6	3	15	4	.	.
YE Jun 13	10	3	55	8	53	7	20	5	64	10	17	5	6	4	22	6	6	3	13	4	.	.
YE Sep 13	11	3	61	10	48	7	19	5	61	9	13	4	10	6	18	4	6	3	14	3	.	.
YE Dec 13	13	4	61	11	44	6	20	5	68	10	15	4	12	7	18	5	8	5	15	3	.	.
YE Mar 14	14	4	64	10	46	6	20	5	75	11	16	4	13	7	18	4	10	5	17	4	.	.
YE Jun 14	14	3	61	10	52	7	21	5	80	11	18	4	13	7	20	5	10	5	19	4	.	.
YE Sep 14	20	5	52	10	64	11	22	6	93	13	16	4	9	5	30	7	17	7	21	4	.	.
YE Dec 14	20	5	53	10	65	12	21	5	91	13	18	5	6	3	30	8	15	7	21	4	.	.
YE Mar 15	22	5	53	10	60	9	21	5	88	12	19	5	4	2	29	8	13	6	22	4	.	.
YE Jun 15	23	6	54	9	59	10	19	5	86	12	18	5	4	3	29	8	14	6	21	4	.	.
YE Sep 15	18	5	58	9	48	8	22	5	82	12	22	6	3	1	27	7	9	5	21	5	.	.
YE Dec 15	16	4	59	9	51	8	21	5	80	11	21	5	3	1	24	6	10	6	22	6	.	.
YE Mar 16	15	5	60	10	53	8	22	5	79	11	19	5	4	2	24	6	11	5	21	6	.	.
YE Jun 16	14	4	59	10	53	7	23	6	79	11	20	5	4	2	23	5	11	5	22	6	.	.
YE Sep 16	12	4	50	10	49	7	15	4	71	11	17	6	3	2	20	5	13	7	18	4	.	.
YE Dec 16	15	5	53	12	49	8	16	4	76	12	21	8	4	2	20	5	14	7	17	4	.	.
YE Mar 17[p]	16	5	55	12	45	8	16	4	80	13	24	8	3	2	25	7	10	5	19	5	.	.
YE Jun 17[p7]	13	5	55	12	47	8	13	4	76	12	21	7	3	2	24	7	10	5	18	5	.	.
YE Sep 17[p7]	15	6	73	12	62	10	21	6	87	14	29	8	3	2	24	7	7	3	24	7	.	.
YE Dec 17[p]	12	4	74	11	68	10	22	6	87	14	25	7	4	4	24	7	6	3	28	9	.	.
Work related[4]																						
YE Mar 08	:	:	:	:	:	:	:	:	:	:	:	:	:	:	:	:	:	:	:	:	:	:
YE Jun 08	3	2	3	2	21	5	4	2	38	7	13	4	0~	1	9	4	3	2	13	3	.	.
YE Sep 08	:	:	:	:	:	:	:	:	:	:	:	:	:	:	:	:	:	:	:	:	:	:
YE Dec 08	3	1	3	2	18	5	5	2	34	7	11	5	1	2	8	3	3	3	10	3	.	.
YE Mar 09	:	:	:	:	:	:	:	:	:	:	:	:	:	:	:	:	:	:	:	:	:	:
YE Jun 09	2	1	6	3	18	4	3	2	26	6	9	4	1	2	6	2	2	2	8	3	.	.
YE Sep 09	:	:	:	:	:	:	:	:	:	:	:	:	:	:	:	:	:	:	:	:	:	:
YE Dec 09	4	2	6	2	16	4	2	1	22	6	6	3	0~	0~	7	4	1	1	8	3	0~	0~
YE Mar 10	3	2	6	2	15	4	2	1	21	5	3	2	0~	0~	7	3	1	1	10	3	0~	0~
YE Jun 10	3	2	4	2	14	3	2	1	21	5	3	2	0~	0~	8	3	1	1	9	3	0~	0~
YE Sep 10	3	2	3	1	17	4	2	1	22	4	4	2	1	1	6	2	1	1	10	3	.	.
YE Dec 10	3	1	2	1	17	4	2	1	26	5	5	2	1	1	8	3	1	1	12	3	.	.
YE Mar 11	3	2	2	1	18	4	2	1	25	5	5	2	1	1	7	3	0~	0~	12	4	.	.
YE Jun 11	4	2	2	1	18	4	2	1	23	5	4	2	1	1	6	3	.	.	12	4	.	.
YE Sep 11	3	2	3	1	17	4	2	1	23	5	3	2	1	1	7	3	0~	0~	12	3	.	.
YE Dec 11	3	2	3	1	17	4	2	2	19	4	3	2	1	1	6	2	0~	0~	10	3	.	.
YE Mar 12	3	2	4	2	16	4	2	1	21	4	3	2	0~	0~	6	2	0~	0~	11	3	.	.
YE Jun 12	2	2	4	2	15	4	3	2	23	4	3	2	0~	0~	7	2	0~	0~	12	3	.	.
YE Sep 12	1	1	4	2	13	3	3	2	22	6	3	2	0~	0~	7	3	0~	0~	11	4	.	.
YE Dec 12	1	1	4	2	11	3	3	2	24	6	3	2	0~	0~	8	3	1	1	12	4	.	.
YE Mar 13	1	1	3	1	12	4	2	2	24	6	2	2	0~	0~	11	4	1	1	10	4	.	.
YE Jun 13	1	1	4	2	10	3	3	2	21	6	2	2	0~	0~	10	4	1	1	8	4	.	.
YE Sep 13	2	1	3	1	10	3	2	1	22	5	2	1	1	2	8	4	1	1	10	3	.	.
YE Dec 13	2	1	5	2	11	3	2	1	21	5	3	2	1	2	7	3	1	2	9	3	.	.
YE Mar 14	2	1	5	2	13	3	2	1	21	4	3	2	1	2	5	2	1	1	10	3	.	.
YE Jun 14	2	1	4	2	17	4	3	2	26	5	4	2	2	2	7	3	1	1	12	3	.	.
YE Sep 14	3	2	7	2	22	8	2	1	28	6	2	1	2	2	10	4	1	1	13	3	.	.
YE Dec 14	4	2	6	2	23	9	2	1	29	6	3	2	2	2	9	4	0~	0~	15	4	.	.
YE Mar 15	4	2	7	3	18	4	2	1	31	6	3	2	1	2	10	4	1	1	15	4	.	.
YE Jun 15	4	3	8	3	19	5	1	1	31	7	3	2	2	2	11	4	1	1	14	4	.	.
YE Sep 15	4	2	7	3	17	5	3	2	33	7	4	2	1	1	11	4	1	2	16	5	.	.
YE Dec 15	3	2	7	3	20	6	3	2	34	7	3	2	1	1	11	4	2	2	17	5	.	.
YE Mar 16	3	2	7	3	21	6	3	2	32	7	2	2	2	1	10	4	2	1	17	5	.	.
YE Jun 16	3	2	6	3	20	4	5	3	35	7	4	2	1	1	8	3	3	3	19	6	.	.
YE Sep 16	3	2	6	3	21	5	4	2	30	6	3	2	1	1	8	3	3	3	15	4	.	.
YE Dec 16	3	2	6	3	18	4	4	3	31	6	5	3	1	1	8	3	4	3	14	4	.	.
YE Mar 17[p]	2	1	8	3	16	4	5	3	35	8	5	3	1	1	13	6	4	3	13	4	.	.
YE Jun 17[p7]	2	1	6	3	15	4	3	2	32	8	2	2	1	1	12	6	3	3	12	4	.	.
YE Sep 17[p7]	3	2	7	3	22	5	5	3	35	9	5	3	1	1	11	6	3	2	15	5	.	.
YE Dec 17[p]	3	2	9	3	26	6	6	3	36	9	5	3	2	3	11	6	2	2	16	6	.	.

Table 3 International Passenger Survey (IPS) estimates of long-term international migration - Rolling annual data for the United Kingdom, year ending December 2017

Abbreviation: Est. "Estimate"
Citizenship by main reason for migration

United Kingdom
thousands

	Non-European Union[2] (contd.)								Rest of the World												Stateless	
	Asia (contd.)								All													
	Middle East and Central Asia		East Asia		South Asia		South East Asia				Sub-Saharan Africa		North Africa		North America		Central and South America		Oceania			
	Est.	+/-CI	Est.	+/-CI	Est.	+/-CI	Est.	+/-CI	Est.	+/-CI	Est.	+/-CI	Est.	+/-CI	Est.	+/-CI	Est.	+/-CI	Est.	+/-CI	Est.	+/-CI
Definite job																						
YE Mar 08	:	:	:	:	:	:	:	:	:	:	:	:	:	:	:	:	:	:	:	:	.	.
YE Jun 08	2	1	3	2	16	4	3	1	21	5	6	3	0~	1	7	3	2	1	6	3	.	.
YE Sep 08	:	:	:	:	:	:	:	:	:	:	:	:	:	:	:	:	:	:	:	:	.	.
YE Dec 08	2	1	3	2	13	4	4	2	16	4	4	3	1	2	6	2	1	1	4	2	:	:
YE Mar 09	:	:	:	:	:	:	:	:	:	:	:	:	:	:	:	:	:	:	:	:	:	:
YE Jun 09	2	1	5	3	14	4	3	2	16	5	5	3	1	2	5	2	1	1	4	2	:	:
YE Sep 09	:	:	:	:	:	:	:	:	:	:	:	:	:	:	:	:	:	:	:	:	:	:
YE Dec 09	3	2	5	2	13	3	1	1	16	5	4	2	0~	0~	6	4	1	1	5	2	0~	0~
YE Mar 10	2	1	5	2	12	3	2	1	15	5	2	2	0~	0~	7	3	0~	0~	6	3	0~	0~
YE Jun 10	2	1	3	2	11	3	2	1	13	4	2	1	.	.	7	3	0~	0~	4	2	0~	0~
YE Sep 10	2	1	2	1	13	3	2	1	14	3	2	1	1	1	5	2	0~	0~	5	2	.	.
YE Dec 10	2	1	2	1	12	3	2	1	15	4	3	2	1	1	6	2	0~	0~	5	2	.	.
YE Mar 11	3	2	1	1	14	4	2	1	15	4	3	2	1	1	5	2	0~	0~	5	2	.	.
YE Jun 11	3	2	2	1	14	4	1	1	14	4	3	2	1	1	4	2	.	.	5	2	.	.
YE Sep 11	3	2	3	1	14	4	1	1	15	4	2	2	1	1	6	2	0~	0~	5	2	.	.
YE Dec 11	3	2	3	1	14	4	2	2	13	3	2	1	1	1	5	2	0~	0~	5	2	.	.
YE Mar 12	3	2	4	2	13	4	2	1	13	3	2	1	0~	0~	6	2	0~	0~	5	2	.	.
YE Jun 12	2	1	4	2	12	3	2	1	14	3	1	1	0~	0~	7	2	0~	0~	6	2	.	.
YE Sep 12	1	1	3	1	11	3	2	2	13	3	1	1	0~	0~	7	3	0~	0~	4	2	.	.
YE Dec 12	1	1	3	1	10	3	2	1	14	4	1	1	0~	0~	7	3	0~	1	5	2	.	.
YE Mar 13	1	1	3	1	11	4	2	1	14	4	1	1	0~	0~	9	3	0~	0~	4	1	.	.
YE Jun 13	1	1	4	2	10	3	2	2	12	3	1	1	0~	0~	8	3	0~	0~	3	1	.	.
YE Sep 13	2	1	3	1	9	3	2	1	13	4	1	1	1	2	6	2	0~	0~	5	2	.	.
YE Dec 13	2	1	4	2	10	3	2	1	12	3	1	1	1	2	5	2	0~	0~	5	2	.	.
YE Mar 14	2	1	5	2	11	3	2	1	13	3	2	1	1	2	4	2	0~	0~	5	2	.	.
YE Jun 14	2	1	4	1	15	3	3	1	16	4	2	1	1	2	6	3	0~	1	6	2	.	.
YE Sep 14	3	2	6	2	20	8	2	1	18	4	1	1	1	2	8	3	0~	1	7	2	.	.
YE Dec 14	4	2	5	2	21	9	2	1	20	5	2	1	2	2	8	3	0~	0~	9	3	.	.
YE Mar 15	4	2	5	2	17	4	2	1	21	5	2	1	1	2	8	3	0~	0~	9	3	.	.
YE Jun 15	4	3	7	3	18	5	1	1	22	5	2	1	2	2	9	4	0~	0~	9	3	.	.
YE Sep 15	3	2	6	3	16	5	3	2	20	5	3	2	0~	1	9	4	1	1	8	3	.	.
YE Dec 15	3	2	6	3	18	6	3	2	19	5	2	2	0~	1	9	3	1	1	7	2	.	.
YE Mar 16	3	2	6	3	19	6	3	2	18	4	2	2	1	1	8	3	1	1	6	2	.	.
YE Jun 16	3	2	5	2	19	4	4	3	19	5	3	2	1	1	6	2	3	3	7	3	.	.
YE Sep 16	2	1	4	2	19	4	3	2	19	5	2	1	0~	1	7	3	3	3	6	3	.	.
YE Dec 16	2	2	4	2	18	4	4	3	18	5	2	1	1	1	7	3	2	2	6	2	.	.
YE Mar 17[p]	1	1	5	2	16	4	4	3	22	7	2	1	1	1	11	6	3	2	6	2	.	.
YE Jun 17[p7]	1	1	5	2	15	4	3	2	19	7	1	1	1	1	11	6	2	2	5	2	.	.
YE Sep 17[p]	2	1	5	3	20	5	5	3	21	7	3	3	1	1	10	6	2	2	5	2	.	.
YE Dec 17[p]	3	2	6	3	24	6	6	3	22	7	4	3	0~	0~	10	5	2	2	6	2	.	.
Looking for work																						
YE Mar 08	:	:	:	:	:	:	:	:	:	:	:	:	.	.	:	:	:	:	:	:	.	.
YE Jun 08	0~	1	0~	0~	6	3	1	2	17	5	7	3	.	.	2	2	1	2	7	2	.	.
YE Sep 08	:	:	:	:	:	:	:	:	:	:	:	:	.	.	:	:	:	:	:	:	.	.
YE Dec 08	0~	0~	0~	0~	5	3	0~	0~	17	5	7	4	.	.	2	2	2	3	7	2	.	.
YE Mar 09	:	:	:	:	:	:	:	:	:	:	:	:	.	.	:	:	:	:	:	:	.	.
YE Jun 09	0~	0~	0~	1	4	1	0~	0~	10	3	5	2	.	.	1	1	1	1	4	2	.	.
YE Sep 09	:	:	:	:	:	:	:	:	:	:	:	:	.	.	:	:	:	:	:	:	.	.
YE Dec 09	1	1	1	1	3	2	0~	1	7	2	2	2	0~	0~	0~	0~	1	1	3	2	.	.
YE Mar 10	1	1	1	1	3	2	0~	0~	7	2	1	1	0~	0~	0~	0~	1	1	4	2	.	.
YE Jun 10	1	1	1	1	3	1	0~	0~	8	3	1	1	0~	0~	1	1	1	1	4	2	.	.
YE Sep 10	1	1	0~	1	4	2	0~	0~	8	3	1	1	.	.	1	1	1	1	5	2	.	.
YE Dec 10	0~	0~	1	1	5	2	0~	0~	11	4	2	1	.	.	2	2	1	1	7	3	.	.
YE Mar 11	0~	0~	0~	0~	4	2	.	.	10	3	2	1	.	.	2	2	0~	0~	6	3	.	.
YE Jun 11	0~	0~	0~	0~	4	2	0~	0~	9	3	1	1	.	.	1	1	.	.	6	3	.	.
YE Sep 11	0~	0~	0~	0~	4	1	0~	0~	9	3	1	1	.	.	1	1	.	.	7	2	.	.
YE Dec 11	0~	0~	0~	0~	3	1	0~	0~	6	2	1	1	.	.	0~	1	.	.	5	2	.	.
YE Mar 12	0~	0~	0~	1	3	1	1	1	8	3	2	1	.	.	1	1	.	.	6	2	.	.
YE Jun 12	0~	0~	0~	0~	3	1	1	1	8	3	2	2	.	.	1	1	.	.	6	2	.	.
YE Sep 12	0~	0~	1	1	1	1	1	1	10	5	2	2	.	.	1	1	.	.	7	4	.	.
YE Dec 12	.	.	1	1	1	1	1	1	10	4	2	2	.	.	1	1	0~	1	7	4	.	.
YE Mar 13	.	.	0~	0~	1	1	1	1	10	5	1	2	.	.	2	3	0~	1	6	4	.	.
YE Jun 13	.	.	0~	0~	1	1	0~	1	9	5	1	2	.	.	2	3	0~	1	5	3	.	.
YE Sep 13	.	.	0~	0~	1	1	0~	1	8	3	1	1	.	.	2	3	1	1	5	2	.	.
YE Dec 13	.	.	0~	0~	1	1	.	.	9	4	1	1	0~	0~	2	3	1	1	4	2	.	.
YE Mar 14	.	.	0~	0~	2	2	.	.	8	3	1	1	0~	0~	1	1	1	1	5	2	.	.
YE Jun 14	.	.	1	1	2	2	.	.	9	3	1	1	0~	0~	1	1	1	1	6	2	.	.
YE Sep 14	.	.	1	1	2	2	.	.	11	4	1	1	0~	1	2	2	1	1	6	2	.	.
YE Dec 14	0~	0~	1	1	2	2	0~	0~	9	3	1	1	.	.	2	2	.	.	6	2	.	.
YE Mar 15	0~	0~	1	1	1	1	0~	0~	10	4	1	2	.	.	2	2	1	1	6	2	.	.
YE Jun 15	0~	0~	2	1	1	1	0~	0~	10	4	1	2	0~	1	2	2	1	1	5	2	.	.
YE Sep 15	0~	1	1	1	1	1	0~	0~	13	5	1	2	1	1	2	2	1	1	8	4	.	.
YE Dec 15	0~	1	1	1	2	1	0~	1	15	6	1	2	1	1	2	2	1	1	10	5	.	.
YE Mar 16	0~	1	1	1	1	1	0~	0~	14	5	0~	1	1	1	2	2	0~	0~	11	5	.	.
YE Jun 16	0~	1	2	2	1	1	1	1	16	6	1	1	0~	1	2	2	0~	0~	13	5	.	.
YE Sep 16	0~	1	2	2	1	1	1	1	12	4	1	1	0~	0~	2	1	0~	1	9	3	.	.
YE Dec 16	1	1	2	2	0~	0~	1	1	13	4	3	2	.	.	1	1	1	2	8	3	.	.
YE Mar 17[p]	1	1	3	3	0~	0~	0~	1	13	5	3	2	.	.	2	2	1	2	8	3	.	.
YE Jun 17[p7]	1	1	1	1	0~	1	0~	0~	12	4	2	2	.	.	2	2	1	2	7	3	.	.
YE Sep 17[p7]	1	1	2	1	1	1	0~	0~	15	6	2	2	.	.	1	1	1	2	10	5	.	.
YE Dec 17[p]	.	.	3	2	2	2	0~	0~	14	6	1	1	2	3	1	1	.	.	11	5	.	.

Table 3 International Passenger Survey (IPS) estimates of long-term international migration - Rolling annual data for the United Kingdom, year ending December 2017

Abbreviation: Est. (Estimate)

Citizenship by main reason for migration

Column grouping: Non-European Union[2] (contd.) — Asia (contd.) [Middle East and Central Asia, East Asia, South Asia, South East Asia]; Rest of the World [All, Sub-Saharan Africa, North Africa, North America, Central and South America, Oceania]; Stateless

	Middle East and Central Asia Est	+/-CI	East Asia Est	+/-CI	South Asia Est	+/-CI	South East Asia Est	+/-CI	All Est	+/-CI	Sub-Saharan Africa Est	+/-CI	North Africa Est	+/-CI	North America Est	+/-CI	Central and South America Est	+/-CI	Oceania Est	+/-CI	Stateless Est	+/-CI
Accompany/Join																						
YE Mar 08	:	:	:	:	:	:	:	:	:	:	:	:	:	:	:	:	:	:	:	:	:	:
YE Jun 08	5	2	2	1	31	8	4	2	19	5	8	4	1	1	5	2	2	1	2	1	0~	0~
YE Sep 08	:	:	:	:	:	:	:	:	:	:	:	:	:	:	:	:	:	:	:	:	:	:
YE Dec 08	3	1	4	2	26	6	4	2	22	8	8	5	2	2	8	5	3	4	1	1	0~	0~
YE Mar 09	:	:	:	:	:	:	:	:	:	:	:	:	:	:	:	:	:	:	:	:	:	:
YE Jun 09	4	2	3	2	24	5	3	2	20	8	8	5	2	2	7	4	2	3	1	1	0~	0~
YE Sep 09	:	:	:	:	:	:	:	:	:	:	:	:	:	:	:	:	:	:	:	:	:	:
YE Dec 09	5	2	2	1	22	5	4	2	18	5	7	3	2	2	7	3	1	1	2	1	0~	0~
YE Mar 10	5	2	2	1	22	5	4	2	19	5	6	3	2	2	7	3	2	2	2	1	0~	0~
YE Jun 10	4	2	2	1	20	4	4	2	19	5	6	2	2	2	7	3	3	2	2	1	0~	0~
YE Sep 10	3	2	2	2	22	4	4	2	20	6	5	2	4	4	6	3	4	2	1	1	0~	0~
YE Dec 10	3	1	3	2	23	4	5	2	20	5	5	2	3	4	7	3	4	2	2	1	0~	0~
YE Mar 11	3	2	3	2	25	5	4	2	19	6	5	2	3	4	7	3	3	2	2	1	0~	0~
YE Jun 11	3	2	3	2	29	5	4	2	19	6	5	2	3	5	7	3	2	2	1	1	0~	0~
YE Sep 11	2	1	2	2	30	5	3	1	16	5	4	2	0~	0~	8	4	2	2	1	1	0~	0~
YE Dec 11	2	2	2	1	29	5	2	1	16	5	5	2	0~	0~	8	5	1	1	1	1	0~	0~
YE Mar 12	4	2	2	1	26	5	2	1	16	7	5	2	1	0~	9	7	0~	1	1	1	.	.
YE Jun 12	4	3	2	1	23	5	3	1	14	4	4	2	1	1	7	3	1	1	1	1	.	.
YE Sep 12	4	2	1	1	20	4	3	2	12	4	4	2	1	0~	6	3	1	1	1	0~	.	.
YE Dec 12	3	2	1	1	19	5	3	2	12	4	4	2	0~	0~	5	3	1	1	1	1	.	.
YE Mar 13	2	1	1	1	18	4	3	2	11	4	4	2	1	1	5	3	1	1	1	1	.	.
YE Jun 13	2	1	1	1	18	5	3	2	9	3	3	2	1	1	4	2	1	1	1	1	.	.
YE Sep 13	3	2	2	1	19	4	2	1	12	5	3	2	5	4	3	2	1	1	1	1	.	.
YE Dec 13	4	2	3	1	17	4	3	1	16	6	3	1	7	6	3	2	2	1	1	1	.	.
YE Mar 14	5	2	3	1	17	4	3	1	22	8	3	2	8	6	5	2	4	4	2	1	.	.
YE Jun 14	4	2	3	1	17	3	3	2	23	8	4	2	8	6	5	2	3	4	3	1	.	.
YE Sep 14	5	2	2	1	20	4	4	2	21	7	5	2	4	4	5	3	4	4	2	1	.	.
YE Dec 14	5	2	2	1	20	4	4	2	18	6	7	3	2	2	4	2	4	5	2	1	.	.
YE Mar 15	5	3	2	1	21	4	4	2	13	4	8	3	1	1	2	1	0~	1	2	1	.	.
YE Jun 15	7	3	3	2	19	4	4	2	11	3	6	3	1	1	2	1	2	1	1	1	.	.
YE Sep 15	7	3	2	1	18	4	3	2	12	4	6	3	1	1	3	2	2	1	1	1	.	.
YE Dec 15	5	3	2	2	18	4	3	2	12	4	5	2	1	1	4	2	2	2	1	1	.	.
YE Mar 16	5	3	2	1	20	4	3	2	13	4	4	2	1	1	4	2	3	2	2	1	.	.
YE Jun 16	4	2	2	1	20	5	3	2	14	4	5	2	1	1	4	2	2	2	1	1	.	.
YE Sep 16	3	2	2	1	20	5	3	2	13	4	5	3	1	1	4	2	2	2	1	1	.	.
YE Dec 16	5	3	2	1	23	6	3	2	17	5	8	4	1	1	4	2	3	2	1	1	.	.
YE Mar 17[p]	5	4	3	2	21	6	3	2	15	5	8	4	1	1	4	2	1	2	1	1	.	.
YE Jun 17[p7]	4	3	3	2	24	6	2	2	15	5	8	4	1	1	4	2	1	2	1	1	.	.
YE Sep 17[p7]	5	4	3	2	22	6	1	1	17	6	10	5	1	1	4	2	1	2	1	1	4	6
YE Dec 17[p]	2	1	3	2	24	6	0~	0~	16	8	7	4	0~	0~	4	3	1	1	.	.	.	.
Formal study																						
YE Mar 08	:	:	:	:	:	:	:	:	:	:	:	:	:	:	:	:	:	:	:	:	:	:
YE Jun 08	6	2	28	8	30	6	15	6	25	8	12	5	4	5	4	3	4	3	1	1	.	.
YE Sep 08	:	:	:	:	:	:	:	:	:	:	:	:	:	:	:	:	:	:	:	:	.	.
YE Dec 08	13	6	25	7	31	5	22	7	31	9	16	7	3	3	6	4	6	4	0~	0~	.	.
YE Mar 09	:	:	:	:	:	:	:	:	:	:	:	:	:	:	:	:	:	:	:	:	.	.
YE Jun 09	13	5	23	7	40	7	19	6	28	8	14	5	3	3	5	3	5	4	0~	0~	.	.
YE Sep 09	:	:	:	:	:	:	:	:	:	:	:	:	:	:	:	:	:	:	:	:	.	.
YE Dec 09	7	3	29	6	67	8	22	5	25	6	12	4	0~	1	6	3	4	2	2	2	.	.
YE Mar 10	8	3	30	6	82	8	26	5	29	7	15	5	0~	1	7	3	5	3	2	2	.	.
YE Jun 10	8	3	32	6	82	8	25	5	27	6	14	4	0~	1	7	3	4	2	2	2	.	.
YE Sep 10	9	3	37	6	87	8	27	6	27	6	14	4	1	2	6	2	5	2	1	1	.	.
YE Dec 10	9	3	37	6	81	7	24	6	27	6	13	4	3	3	6	3	4	2	1	1	.	.
YE Mar 11	9	3	37	6	80	7	22	6	24	5	10	3	2	2	6	2	5	3	1	1	.	.
YE Jun 11	8	3	35	6	91	8	21	6	24	6	11	3	2	2	6	2	5	3	1	1	.	.
YE Sep 11	9	3	48	9	91	8	17	5	25	6	10	3	1	2	10	4	3	2	1	1	.	.
YE Dec 11	9	3	50	9	76	8	15	4	25	5	10	3	0~	1	9	4	4	2	1	2	.	.
YE Mar 12	9	3	50	8	59	7	16	4	24	5	10	3	0~	0~	9	4	4	2	1	1	.	.
YE Jun 12	10	4	48	8	45	6	15	4	25	5	11	4	0~	0~	9	3	3	2	1	1	.	.
YE Sep 12	7	2	50	8	32	6	15	4	31	7	13	4	2	3	9	3	5	3	2	2	.	.
YE Dec 12	6	3	48	7	30	5	15	4	30	7	13	4	4	4	9	3	4	3	1	1	.	.
YE Mar 13	7	2	47	7	26	5	14	4	30	7	13	4	4	4	8	3	4	2	2	1	.	.
YE Jun 13	6	2	49	7	22	4	15	4	31	7	12	4	5	4	8	4	4	2	2	1	.	.
YE Sep 13	6	2	54	10	17	4	14	4	23	5	8	3	4	4	6	2	4	2	1	1	.	.
YE Dec 13	7	3	53	10	16	4	14	4	25	5	9	3	3	3	6	2	5	3	1	0~	.	.
YE Mar 14	7	2	54	10	15	4	15	4	25	5	10	3	4	3	6	2	5	2	1	0~	.	.
YE Jun 14	6	2	52	10	16	4	14	4	24	5	9	3	3	3	6	2	5	3	1	1	.	.
YE Sep 14	11	4	42	9	21	6	16	5	36	8	9	3	3	2	11	5	12	5	2	1	.	.
YE Dec 14	10	4	44	10	20	6	15	5	36	9	8	4	2	1	14	6	11	5	1	1	.	.
YE Mar 15	11	4	44	10	20	6	15	5	36	9	8	4	1	1	14	6	12	6	2	1	.	.
YE Jun 15	11	4	43	8	19	7	14	5	36	10	8	4	1	1	14	6	11	6	2	1	.	.
YE Sep 15	6	3	49	8	14	4	15	5	29	8	12	4	1	1	10	4	6	5	0~	0~	.	.
YE Dec 15	6	2	48	8	11	4	15	4	26	7	12	4	1	1	7	3	6	5	0~	0~	.	.
YE Mar 16	6	3	49	9	11	4	15	5	26	7	13	4	1	1	7	3	6	4	0~	0~	.	.
YE Jun 16	6	3	49	9	11	3	15	5	26	7	12	4	1	1	7	3	6	4	0~	0~	.	.
YE Sep 16	6	3	38	9	7	3	13	5	24	8	11	4	1	1	6	3	8	6	0~	0~	.	.
YE Dec 16	7	3	41	11	7	3	8	3	24	9	9	6	2	2	6	3	7	6	0~	1	.	.
YE Mar 17[p]	8	3	42	11	8	3	8	3	24	8	10	6	1	2	6	3	5	4	1	2	.	.
YE Jun 17[p7]	7	3	43	11	8	3	8	3	22	7	9	5	1	2	6	3	5	4	1	1	.	.
YE Sep 17[p7]	7	4	62	12	17	5	14	5	27	8	13	6	2	2	8	4	2	1	3	2	.	.
YE Dec 17[p]	6	3	60	10	17	5	15	5	27	7	12	5	1	1	9	4	2	2	2	2	.	.

Abbreviation: Est. (Estimate)
Citizenship by main reason for migration

United Kingdom
thousands

| | Non-European Union[2] (contd.) Asia (contd.) | | | | | | | | Rest of the World | | | | | | | | | | | | Stateless | |
| | Middle East and Central Asia | | East Asia | | South Asia | | South East Asia | | All | | Sub-Saharan Africa | | North Africa | | North America | | Central and South America | | Oceania | | | |
	Est.	+/-CI	Est.	+/-CI	Est.	+/-CI	Est.	+/-CI	Est.	+/-CI	Est.	+/-CI	Est.	+/-CI	Est.	+/-CI	Est.	+/-CI	Est.	+/-CI	Est.	+/-CI
Going home to live[5]																						
YE Mar 08	:	:	:	:	:	:			:	:	:	:	:	:	:	:	:	:	:	:	:	:
YE Jun 08	.	.	.	.	.	.	.	.	0~	0~	0~	0~	.	.	0~	0~	.	.	.	.	.	.
YE Sep 08	.	.	.	.	.	.	.	.	:	:	.	.	.	.	:	:	.	.	.	.	.	.
YE Dec 08	.	.	.	.	2	3	.	.	0~	1	.	.	.	.	0~	1	.	.	.	.	.	.
YE Mar 09	.	.	.	.	.	.	.	.	:	:	.	.	.	.	:	:	.	.	.	.	.	.
YE Jun 09	.	.	.	.	2	2	.	.	0~	0~	.	.	.	.	0~	0~	.	.	.	.	.	.
YE Sep 09	.	.	.	.	.	.	.	.	:	:	.	.	.	.	:	:	.	.	.	.	.	.
YE Dec 09	.	.	.	.	.	.	0~	1	.	.	.	.	.	.	.	.	.	.	.	.	.	.
YE Mar 10	.	.	.	.	.	.	0~	1	.	.	.	.	.	.	.	.	.	.	.	.	.	.
YE Jun 10	.	.	.	.	.	.	0~	1	.	.	.	.	.	.	.	.	.	.	.	.	.	.
YE Sep 10	.	.	.	.	.	.	.	.	.	.	.	.	.	.	.	.	.	.	.	.	.	.
YE Dec 10	.	.	.	.	.	.	.	.	.	.	.	.	.	.	.	.	.	.	.	.	.	.
YE Mar 11	.	.	.	.	.	.	.	.	1	1	1	1	.	.	.	.	.	.	.	.	.	.
YE Jun 11	.	.	.	.	0~	0~	.	.	1	1	1	1	.	.	.	.	.	.	.	.	.	.
YE Sep 11	.	.	.	.	0~	0~	.	.	1	2	1	2	.	.	.	.	.	.	0~	0~	.	.
YE Dec 11	.	.	.	.	0~	0~	.	.	2	2	1	2	.	.	0~	0~	.	.	0~	0~	.	.
YE Mar 12	.	.	.	.	0~	0~	.	.	0~	1	.	.	.	.	0~	0~	.	.	0~	0~	.	.
YE Jun 12	.	.	.	.	.	.	.	.	2	3	.	.	.	.	2	3	.	.	0~	0~	.	.
YE Sep 12	.	.	.	.	.	.	.	.	1	2	.	.	.	.	1	2	.	.	.	.	.	.
YE Dec 12	.	.	.	.	0~	1	.	.	1	2	.	.	.	.	1	2	.	.	.	.	.	.
YE Mar 13	.	.	.	.	0~	0~	.	.	1	2	.	.	.	.	1	2	.	.	.	.	.	.
YE Jun 13	.	.	.	.	0~	0~	.	.	0~	1	.	.	.	.	.	.	.	.	0~	1	.	.
YE Sep 13	.	.	.	.	0~	0~	.	.	0~	1	0~	0~	.	.	.	.	.	.	0~	1	.	.
YE Dec 13	.	.	.	.	.	.	.	.	1	1	0~	0~	.	.	.	.	.	.	0~	1	.	.
YE Mar 14	.	.	.	.	.	.	.	.	1	1	0~	0~	.	.	.	.	.	.	0~	1	.	.
YE Jun 14	.	.	.	.	.	.	.	.	1	1	0~	0~	.	.	.	.	.	.	1	1	.	.
YE Sep 14	.	.	.	.	.	.	.	.	1	1	.	.	.	.	.	.	.	.	1	1	.	.
YE Dec 14	.	.	.	.	.	.	.	.	1	1	.	.	.	.	.	.	.	.	1	1	.	.
YE Mar 15	.	.	.	.	0~	0~	.	.	1	1	.	.	.	.	.	.	.	.	1	1	.	.
YE Jun 15	.	.	.	.	0~	0~	.	.	0~	1	.	.	.	.	.	.	.	.	0~	1	.	.
YE Sep 15	.	.	.	.	0~	0~	.	.	.	.	.	.	.	.	.	.	.	.	.	.	.	.
YE Dec 15	.	.	.	.	0~	0~	.	.	.	.	.	.	.	.	.	.	.	.	.	.	.	.
YE Mar 16	.	.	.	.	.	.	.	.	.	.	.	.	.	.	.	.	.	.	.	.	.	.
YE Jun 16	.	.	.	.	.	.	.	.	.	.	.	.	.	.	.	.	.	.	.	.	.	.
YE Sep 16	.	.	.	.	.	.	.	.	.	.	.	.	.	.	.	.	.	.	.	.	.	.
YE Dec 16	.	.	.	.	.	.	.	.	.	.	.	.	.	.	.	.	.	.	.	.	.	.
YE Mar 17[p]	.	.	.	.	.	.	.	.	.	.	.	.	.	.	.	.	.	.	.	.	.	.
YE Jun 17[p7]	.	.	.	.	.	.	.	.	.	.	.	.	.	.	.	.	.	.	.	.	.	.
YE Sep 17[p7]	.	.	.	.	.	.	.	.	0~	0~	.	.	.	.	0~	0~	.	.	0~	0~	.	.
YE Dec 17[p]	.	.	.	.	.	.	.	.	0~	0~	.	.	.	.	0~	0~	.	.	0~	0~	.	.
Other																						
YE Mar 08	:	:	:	:	:	:	:	:	:	:	:	:	:	:	:	:	:	:	:	:	:	:
YE Jun 08	0~	0~	2	4	3	2	2	2	19	5	4	2	0~	0~	2	2	0~	0~	12	4	.	.
YE Sep 08	:	:	:	:	:	:	:	:	:	:	:	:	:	:	:	:	:	:	:	:	.	.
YE Dec 08	0~	0~	1	1	2	2	2	1	16	4	3	1	.	.	3	2	0~	0~	9	3	.	.
YE Mar 09	:	:	:	:	:	:	:	:	:	:	:	:	.	.	:	:	:	:	:	:	.	.
YE Jun 09	0~	0~	1	1	2	1	1	1	13	4	4	3	.	.	1	1	.	.	8	2	.	.
YE Sep 09	:	:	:	:	:	:	:	:	:	:	:	:	.	.	:	:	:	:	:	:	.	.
YE Dec 09	1	1	0~	0~	3	2	0~	0~	11	4	3	3	.	.	2	2	0~	1	5	2	.	.
YE Mar 10	1	1	0~	0~	3	2	0~	0~	8	3	0~	0~	.	.	2	2	0~	1	5	2	.	.
YE Jun 10	1	1	0~	0~	3	2	0~	0~	8	3	0~	0~	.	.	2	2	0~	1	5	2	.	.
YE Sep 10	1	1	1	1	2	1	0~	0~	9	3	1	1	.	.	1	2	0~	0~	7	2	.	.
YE Dec 10	0~	0~	1	1	1	1	0~	0~	9	3	1	1	.	.	0~	1	.	.	8	3	.	.
YE Mar 11	0~	0~	1	1	1	1	.	.	9	3	1	0~	.	.	2	2	.	.	7	3	.	.
YE Jun 11	.	.	0~	0~	1	1	.	.	9	3	1	1	.	.	2	2	.	.	7	3	.	.
YE Sep 11	0~	0~	0~	0~	1	1	.	.	8	3	1	1	.	.	1	1	0~	1	6	2	.	.
YE Dec 11	0~	0~	0~	0~	2	1	.	.	8	3	2	2	.	.	1	1	0~	1	4	2	.	.
YE Mar 12	0~	0~	0~	0~	2	1	.	.	11	4	2	2	.	.	1	1	0~	0~	7	3	.	.
YE Jun 12	0~	0~	0~	0~	2	1	0~	0~	11	4	2	2	.	.	1	1	0~	1	7	3	.	.
YE Sep 12	0~	0~	0~	0~	2	1	0~	0~	10	4	2	2	.	.	1	1	0~	0~	6	3	.	.
YE Dec 12	0~	0~	0~	0~	2	1	0~	0~	8	3	0~	0~	.	.	1	1	0~	0~	6	3	.	.
YE Mar 13	0~	0~	0~	0~	2	1	.	.	3	1	0~	0~	.	.	0~	1	0~	0~	3	1	.	.
YE Jun 13	0~	0~	0~	0~	1	1	0~	0~	3	1	0~	0~	.	.	1	1	0~	0~	2	1	.	.
YE Sep 13	0~	0~	1	2	1	1	1	1	4	2	0~	0~	.	.	1	1	.	.	3	1	.	.
YE Dec 13	0~	0~	1	2	1	1	0~	1	5	2	0~	0~	.	.	1	1	.	.	3	2	.	.
YE Mar 14	0~	1	1	2	2	1	1	1	5	2	0~	0~	.	.	1	1	0~	0~	4	2	.	.
YE Jun 14	1	1	1	2	1	1	1	1	6	3	0~	0~	0~	0~	2	2	0~	0~	3	1	.	.
YE Sep 14	0~	0~	0~	0~	1	1	0~	0~	6	3	0~	0~	0~	0~	3	3	0~	0~	2	1	.	.
YE Dec 14	1	1	0~	0~	1	1	0~	0~	6	3	0~	0~	0~	0~	3	3	0~	0~	3	1	.	.
YE Mar 15	1	1	0~	0~	1	1	0~	0~	7	3	0~	0~	0~	0~	3	2	.	.	3	1	.	.
YE Jun 15	1	1	0~	0~	0~	1	.	.	7	3	1	1	0~	0~	2	2	0~	0~	4	2	.	.
YE Sep 15	1	1	0~	0~	0~	0~	.	.	6	2	1	1	0~	0~	1	1	0~	0~	3	2	.	.
YE Dec 15	1	1	0~	0~	0~	0~	.	.	6	2	1	1	0~	0~	1	1	0~	0~	3	1	.	.
YE Mar 16	1	1	1	2	1	1	.	.	5	2	1	1	0~	0~	2	1	0~	0~	3	1	.	.
YE Jun 16	1	1	2	2	1	1	.	.	3	2	0~	0~	.	.	2	1	.	.	2	1	.	.
YE Sep 16	0~	0~	2	2	0~	0~	.	.	4	2	.	.	.	.	2	2	.	.	2	1	.	.
YE Dec 16	0~	0~	2	2	0~	1	0~	0~	4	2	.	.	.	.	2	2	.	.	2	1	.	.
YE Mar 17[p]	0~	0~	2	1	0~	0~	0~	0~	5	3	.	.	.	.	2	2	.	.	4	2	.	.
YE Jun 17[p7]	0~	0~	1	1	0~	0~	0~	0~	6	3	0~	1	.	.	1	2	0~	1	4	2	.	.
YE Sep 17[p7]	1	1	1	1	1	1	0~	0~	5	3	0~	1	.	.	0~	0~	1	1	3	2	.	.
YE Dec 17[p]	1	1	1	1	1	1	.	.	5	3	0~	1	.	.	.	.	1	1	3	2	.	.

Table 3 International Passenger Survey (IPS) estimates of long-term international migration - Rolling annual data for the United Kingdom, year ending December 2017

Abbreviation: Est. (Estimate)

Citizenship by main reason for migration

	Non-European Union[2] (contd.) Asia (contd.)						Rest of the World															Stateless	
	Middle East and Central Asia		East Asia		South Asia		South East Asia		All		Sub-Saharan Africa		North Africa		North America		Central and South America		Oceania			Stateless	
	Est.	+/-CI	Est.	+/-CI	Est.	+/-CI	Est.	+/-CI	Est.	+/-CI	Est.	+/-CI	Est.	+/-CI	Est.	+/-CI	Est.	+/-CI	Est.	+/-CI		Est.	+/-CI
No reason stated[6]																							
YE Mar 08	:	.	:	:	:	:	:	:	:	:	:								:			:	:
YE Jun 08					6	7	3	5	0~	0~	0~	0~											
YE Sep 08	:		:	:	:		:	:	:	:													
YE Dec 08	:				0~	0~	1	1	2	3									0~	1		1	3
YE Mar 09	:		:	:	:		:	:	:	:													
YE Jun 09					0~	1	1	1	3	3					1	1	1	1	2	3			
YE Sep 09	:		:	:	:	:	:	:	:	:									:				
YE Dec 09			0~	0~	1	1			1	1	0~	1			1	1			0~	1			
YE Mar 10			0~	0~	1	1			1	1	0~	1			0~	1							
YE Jun 10	.		0~	0~	1	1	.		1	1	0~	1			0~	0~							
YE Sep 10	0~	0~	0~	0~	2	1	0~	0~	1	1					1	1			0~	1			
YE Dec 10	0~	0~			1	1	0~	0~	1	1					1	1			0~	1			
YE Mar 11	1	1			1	1	0~	0~	2	2			0~	1	1	2			0~	1			
YE Jun 11	1	1	.		1	1	0~	0~	2	2	0~	0~	0~	1	1	2			0~	1			
YE Sep 11	1	1	0~	1	1	1			1	1	0~	0~	0~	1					0~	0~			
YE Dec 11	1	2	0~	1	1	1			1	1	0~	0~	0~	1					0~	1			
YE Mar 12	1	1	0~	1	1	1			1	1	1	1							0~	1			
YE Jun 12	0~	1	0~	1	2	1			1	1	1	1							1	1			
YE Sep 12	0~	1	0~	0~	1	1			1	1	0~	1							0~	1			
YE Dec 12	.		.		1	1			0~	1	0~	1							.				
YE Mar 13	.		.		1	1			0~	0~	0~	0~							.				
YE Jun 13	.		.		0~	1			.														
YE Sep 13	.		.		0~	1			0~	0~					0~	0~			.				
YE Dec 13					0~	0~			0~	0~					0~	0~			.				
YE Mar 14	.		.		0~	0~			0~	0~					0~	0~			0~	0~			
YE Jun 14	1	1	0~	0~	1	1			0~	0~					0~	0~			0~	0~			
YE Sep 14	1	1	0~	0~	1	1			0~	0~					.				0~	0~			
YE Dec 14	1	1	0~	0~	1	1			0~	0~					0~	0~			0~	0~			
YE Mar 15	1	2	1	1	1	1			0~	0~					0~	0~			0~	0~			
YE Jun 15	1	1	0~	0~	1	1			0~	0~					0~	0~			0~	0~			
YE Sep 15	0~	1	0~	0~	1	1			1	2	0~	0~			1	2			0~	0~			
YE Dec 15	0~	1	0~	0~	1	1			1	2	0~	0~			1	2			0~	0~			
YE Mar 16	.		0~	0~	1	1			1	2	0~	0~			1	2	0~	0~					
YE Jun 16	.		0~	0~	1	1	.		2	2	0~	1			1	2	0~	0~					
YE Sep 16	0~	1	1	2	1	1	0~	1	1	1	1	1			.		0~	0~					
YE Dec 16	0~	1	1	2	0~	0~	0~	1	1	1	0~	1			0~	0~	0~	0~	0~	0~			
YE Mar 17[p]	0~	1	1	2	0~	0~	0~	0~	1	1	1	1			0~	0~	.		0~	0~			
YE Jun 17[p7]	0~	1	1	2	0~	0~	0~	0~	0~	0~	0~	0~			0~	0~	.		0~	0~			
YE Sep 17[p7]	.		0~	1	0~	0~	0~	1	2	2	.				0~	0~	.		.			2	2
YE Dec 17[p]	1	1	2	4	0~	0~	0~	1	2	3	0~	1			0~	0~	.		.			2	3
Outflow																							
All reasons																							
YE Mar 08	:	:	:	:	:	:	:	:	:	:	:	:	:	:	:	:	:	:	:	:		:	:
YE Jun 08	2	1	15	4	18	5	6	2	54	7	12	3	1	2	10	3	6	3	26	4		0~	0~
YE Sep 08	:	:	:	:	:	:	:	:	:	:	:	:	:	:	:	:	:	:	:	:		:	:
YE Dec 08	2	1	15	4	19	5	5	1	60	8	12	5	2	2	12	4	7	3	26	4		0~	0~
YE Mar 09	:	:	:	:	:	:	:	:	:	:	:	:	:	:	:	:	:	:	:	:		:	:
YE Jun 09	2	1	15	4	20	5	6	2	57	7	14	4	1	1	12	3	5	3	26	4		0~	0~
YE Sep 09	:	:	:	:	:	:	:	:	:	:	:	:	:	:	:	:	:	:	:	:		:	:
YE Dec 09	3	1	18	3	21	3	6	2	57	7	11	3	1	1	15	4	4	2	26	4		0~	0~
YE Mar 10	4	1	20	4	21	3	6	2	52	6	10	3	1	1	14	4	4	2	23	4		0~	0~
YE Jun 10	4	1	18	4	20	3	6	2	52	6	10	2	1	1	14	4	5	2	22	4			
YE Sep 10	4	2	19	4	19	3	6	2	45	5	10	3	1	1	11	3	5	2	18	3			
YE Dec 10	5	2	17	4	18	3	6	2	43	5	10	3	1	1	11	3	4	2	16	3			
YE Mar 11	4	2	14	3	20	3	7	2	43	5	9	2	1	1	12	3	4	2	16	3			
YE Jun 11	4	2	14	3	22	3	6	2	41	5	9	2	1	1	11	3	4	2	16	3		0~	0~
YE Sep 11	4	2	14	3	22	4	7	2	43	6	8	3	1	1	13	3	4	2	17	3		0~	0~
YE Dec 11	4	2	17	3	27	4	8	2	39	6	7	3	1	1	11	3	3	2	16	3		0~	0~
YE Mar 12	3	1	18	3	27	4	9	3	39	6	8	3	1	1	11	3	3	1	16	3		0~	0~
YE Jun 12	3	1	19	4	27	4	11	3	38	6	8	3	1	1	12	3	3	1	15	3			
YE Sep 12	4	2	22	4	27	4	11	3	33	5	8	3	1	1	10	3	3	1	12	3			
YE Dec 12	4	2	20	4	24	4	10	3	34	5	7	2	1	1	10	3	4	2	12	3			
YE Mar 13	4	2	21	4	24	4	9	2	32	5	6	2	1	1	10	2	4	2	11	3			
YE Jun 13	4	2	20	4	24	4	8	2	32	5	6	2	1	1	9	2	4	2	12	3			
YE Sep 13	3	1	18	3	24	4	8	2	38	6	6	2	1	1	12	3	5	2	13	3			
YE Dec 13	4	2	20	4	22	4	7	2	38	6	7	2	2	1	13	4	4	2	13	3			
YE Mar 14	4	2	21	4	18	3	8	2	37	6	8	2	1	1	13	4	3	2	12	3			
YE Jun 14	4	2	22	4	20	3	9	3	37	6	8	2	1	1	12	4	3	2	12	3			
YE Sep 14	5	2	27	8	17	3	8	3	31	5	6	2	1	1	9	3	2	1	12	3			
YE Dec 14	4	2	26	8	18	3	7	3	26	4	5	2	1	1	8	3	1	1	11	3			
YE Mar 15	4	2	24	8	16	3	7	3	26	5	5	2	1	1	9	3	1	1	11	3			
YE Jun 15	4	2	24	7	17	3	6	2	25	4	4	2	1	1	9	3	1	1	10	3			
YE Sep 15	4	2	21	4	17	3	7	2	27	5	5	2	1	1	9	3	4	2	7	2			
YE Dec 15	4	2	20	4	18	4	8	3	32	5	6	2	1	1	10	3	5	2	9	3			
YE Mar 16	5	4	20	4	19	4	9	3	32	5	6	2	1	1	12	3	5	2	8	3			
YE Jun 16	4	4	21	4	18	4	8	3	33	5	5	2	2	1	11	3	5	2	11	3			
YE Sep 16	5	4	18	4	18	4	8	3	38	7	6	3	2	2	16	5	4	2	11	3			
YE Dec 16	6	4	17	4	16	4	8	3	34	7	4	3	2	2	16	5	3	2	9	3			
YE Mar 17[p]	6	2	18	4	16	4	7	3	33	7	3	3	2	2	15	5	4	2	9	3		0~	0~
YE Jun 17[p7]	6	4	17	4	15	4	8	3	34	8	3	3	2	2	15	5	4	2	9	3		0~	0~
YE Sep 17[p7]	9	4	21	4	13	4	7	3	29	6	4	3	2	1	10	4	3	2	9	3		0~	0~
YE Dec 17[p]	8	4	20	4	10	3	6	3	29	7	4	3	2	1	10	5	3	3	9	3		0~	0~

Table 3 International Passenger Survey (IPS) estimates of long-term international migration - Rolling annual data for the United Kingdom, year ending December 2017

Abbreviation: Est. (Estimate)
Citizenship by main reason for migration

United Kingdom
thousands

| | Non-European Union[2] (contd.) Asia (contd.) | | | | | | | | Rest of the World | | | | | | | | | | | | Stateless | |
| | Middle East and Central Asia | | East Asia | | South Asia | | South East Asia | | All | | Sub-Saharan Africa | | North Africa | | North America | | Central and South America | | Oceania | | | |
	Est.	+/-CI	Est.	+/-CI	Est.	+/-CI	Est.	+/-CI	Est.	+/-CI	Est.	+/-CI	Est.	+/-CI	Est.	+/-CI	Est.	+/-CI	Est.	+/-CI	Est.	+/-CI
Work related[4]																						
YE Mar 08	:	:	:	:	:	:	:	:	:	:	:	:	:	:	:	:	:	:	:	:	:	:
YE Jun 08	1	1	12	3	11	3	5	2	36	5	9	3	1	2	4	1	4	2	19	3	0~	0~
YE Sep 08	:	:	:	:	:	:	:	:	:	:	:	:	:	:	:	:	:	:	:	:	:	:
YE Dec 08	1	1	11	3	12	3	5	1	40	6	10	4	1	2	6	2	3	1	20	3	:	:
YE Mar 09	:	:	:	:	:	:	:	:	:	:	:	:	:	:	:	:	:	:	:	:	:	:
YE Jun 09	1	1	11	3	14	3	5	1	39	6	9	4	0~	0~	7	2	2	1	20	4	0~	0~
YE Sep 09	:	:	:	:	:	:	:	:	:	:	:	:	:	:	:	:	:	:	:	:	:	:
YE Dec 09	2	1	13	3	15	3	5	2	40	5	7	2	1	1	10	3	2	1	20	3	0~	0~
YE Mar 10	3	1	15	3	15	3	5	1	37	5	6	2	1	1	9	3	3	1	18	3	0~	0~
YE Jun 10	3	1	13	3	15	3	5	2	37	5	6	2	1	1	10	3	3	1	17	3		
YE Sep 10	3	1	13	3	16	3	4	1	30	4	7	2	1	1	6	2	3	1	13	3		
YE Dec 10	4	1	12	3	15	3	4	1	29	4	8	2	1	1	6	2	3	1	12	3		
YE Mar 11	3	1	10	2	17	3	5	1	28	4	6	2	1	1	6	2	3	2	12	3		
YE Jun 11	3	1	10	2	18	3	4	1	27	4	6	2	1	1	6	2	2	1	12	3	0~	0~
YE Sep 11	3	1	11	2	18	3	5	2	28	4	5	2	1	1	6	2	2	1	14	3	0~	0~
YE Dec 11	3	1	13	3	22	4	7	2	25	4	4	1	1	1	6	2	3	1	12	3	0~	0~
YE Mar 12	2	1	14	3	22	4	7	2	26	4	4	2	1	1	6	2	2	1	13	3	0~	0~
YE Jun 12	2	1	14	3	21	3	7	2	25	4	4	2	1	1	7	2	2	1	11	3		
YE Sep 12	3	2	17	3	22	3	6	2	23	4	5	2	1	1	6	2	2	1	9	2		
YE Dec 12	3	2	15	3	19	3	6	2	24	4	5	2	1	1	7	2	3	1	9	2		
YE Mar 13	3	2	15	3	19	3	5	2	25	4	5	2	1	1	7	2	3	1	9	2		
YE Jun 13	3	2	15	3	20	3	5	2	26	4	5	2	1	1	6	2	3	1	10	3		
YE Sep 13	2	1	13	3	19	3	6	2	28	5	4	2	1	1	8	4	4	2	11	3		
YE Dec 13	2	1	15	3	17	3	6	2	27	5	5	2	1	1	8	4	3	2	10	2		
YE Mar 14	3	1	16	3	16	3	6	2	26	5	5	2	1	1	7	3	2	2	9	2		
YE Jun 14	3	1	15	3	14	3	6	2	25	5	5	2	1	1	8	4	2	2	8	2		
YE Sep 14	4	2	17	4	13	3	5	2	20	4	4	1	1	1	5	2	2	1	8	2		
YE Dec 14	3	1	17	4	14	3	4	2	17	4	3	1	0~	0~	5	2	1	1	7	2		
YE Mar 15	3	1	15	3	13	3	3	2	16	4	2	1	0~	1	6	2	1	1	7	2		
YE Jun 15	3	1	16	4	14	3	3	2	17	4	3	2	0~	0~	6	2	1	1	7	2		
YE Sep 15	2	1	16	3	14	3	4	2	18	4	4	2	1	1	7	2	2	1	5	2		
YE Dec 15	2	1	15	3	14	3	6	2	21	4	5	2	1	1	7	2	2	2	6	2		
YE Mar 16	2	1	15	3	14	3	6	2	21	4	5	2	1	1	8	2	2	1	5	2		
YE Jun 16	2	1	16	3	13	3	6	2	20	4	4	1	1	1	6	2	3	1	6	2		
YE Sep 16	3	1	13	3	13	3	5	2	25	6	4	3	2	2	9	4	3	2	7	2		
YE Dec 16	4	2	14	3	12	3	5	2	22	6	3	3	2	2	9	4	3	2	6	2		
YE Mar 17[p]	4	2	14	3	11	3	4	2	21	6	3	3	2	2	8	4	3	2	6	3		
YE Jun 17[p7]	5	2	13	3	10	3	4	2	24	6	3	3	2	2	8	4	3	2	7	3		
YE Sep 17[p7]	7	4	17	4	9	3	6	2	21	5	4	3	1	1	6	2	3	2	7	3		
YE Dec 17[p]	6	3	16	4	8	2	4	2	21	6	3	3	1	1	7	4	2	2	7	3		
Definite job																						
YE Mar 08	:	:	:	:	:	:	:	:	:	:	:	:	:	:	:	:	:	:	:	:	:	:
YE Jun 08	0~	0~	4	2	9	3	4	2	16	3	5	2	:	:	3	1	2	1	7	2	0~	0~
YE Sep 08	:	:	:	:	:	:	:	:	:	:	:	:	:	:	:	:	:	:	:	:	:	:
YE Dec 08	0~	0~	3	1	8	2	3	1	19	5	6	4	0~	0~	4	2	2	1	7	2		
YE Mar 09	:	:	:	:	:	:	:	:	:	:	:	:	:	:	:	:	:	:	:	:		
YE Jun 09	0~	0~	3	1	9	2	3	1	20	5	6	3	0~	0~	5	2	2	1	7	2		
YE Sep 09	:	:	:	:	:	:	:	:	:	:	:	:	:	:	:	:	:	:	:	:		
YE Dec 09	1	1	6	2	10	2	3	1	19	3	4	1	1	1	6	2	1	1	7	2		
YE Mar 10	1	1	7	2	10	2	2	1	18	3	4	2	1	1	5	2	1	1	7	2		
YE Jun 10	2	1	6	2	9	2	2	1	18	3	3	2	1	1	5	2	1	1	7	2		
YE Sep 10	2	1	5	2	9	2	1	1	14	3	4	2	0~	1	3	1	1	1	6	2		
YE Dec 10	2	1	4	1	8	2	1	1	15	3	5	2	1	1	3	1	1	1	6	2		
YE Mar 11	1	1	3	1	7	2	1	1	14	3	3	1	1	1	3	1	2	1	6	2		
YE Jun 11	1	1	3	1	8	2	1	1	12	3	3	1	1	1	2	1	1	1	5	2		
YE Sep 11	1	1	4	2	9	2	2	1	13	3	2	1	1	1	3	1	2	1	6	2		
YE Dec 11	2	1	5	2	11	3	3	1	11	3	2	1	1	1	2	1	2	1	5	2		
YE Mar 12	1	1	5	2	11	3	3	1	12	3	2	1	1	1	2	1	1	1	5	2		
YE Jun 12	1	1	6	2	10	2	3	1	13	3	3	1	1	1	3	1	1	1	5	2		
YE Sep 12	1	1	5	2	10	2	4	1	12	3	3	2	1	1	3	1	1	1	4	1		
YE Dec 12	1	1	5	2	9	2	3	1	14	3	3	2	0~	1	3	1	2	1	5	2		
YE Mar 13	1	1	5	2	8	2	3	1	14	3	3	2	0~	0~	4	2	2	1	5	2		
YE Jun 13	1	1	5	2	9	2	3	1	13	3	3	2	0~	0~	3	1	2	1	5	2		
YE Sep 13	1	1	4	1	9	2	3	1	14	4	2	1	0~	0~	5	3	2	1	5	2		
YE Dec 13	1	1	5	2	7	2	2	1	13	4	3	1	0~	0~	4	3	1	1	4	2		
YE Mar 14	1	1	5	2	7	2	3	1	11	4	3	1	0~	0~	4	3	1	1	3	1		
YE Jun 14	2	1	4	2	6	2	3	1	11	4	3	1	0~	0~	4	3	1	1	3	1		
YE Sep 14	2	1	5	2	5	2	2	1	9	2	2	1	0~	0~	2	1	1	1	4	2		
YE Dec 14	2	1	5	2	6	2	2	1	8	2	1	1	0~	0~	3	1	1	1	4	2		
YE Mar 15	2	1	5	2	6	2	1	1	9	3	1	1	0~	0~	3	1	1	1	4	2		
YE Jun 15	2	1	5	2	8	2	1	1	10	3	2	1	0~	0~	4	2	1	1	3	2		
YE Sep 15	1	1	5	2	8	2	2	1	9	2	2	1	1	1	4	1	1	1	2	1		
YE Dec 15	0~	0~	4	2	8	2	3	1	10	3	3	1	1	1	3	1	1	1	2	1		
YE Mar 16	0~	0~	4	2	8	3	3	1	9	3	2	1	1	1	3	1	1	1	2	1		
YE Jun 16	1	1	5	2	7	3	3	1	9	3	2	1	1	1	3	1	1	1	3	1		
YE Sep 16	2	1	4	2	8	3	2	1	13	5	2	3	1	1	5	3	1	1	3	1		
YE Dec 16	3	2	4	2	8	3	2	1	12	5	2	3	1	1	5	3	1	1	3	2		
YE Mar 17[p]	3	2	4	2	8	2	1	1	12	5	2	3	0~	0~	5	3	1	1	4	2		
YE Jun 17[p7]	3	2	3	1	8	2	1	1	14	5	2	3	0~	1	6	3	2	2	4	2		
YE Sep 17[p7]	5	3	5	2	7	2	3	2	12	5	3	3	1	1	4	2	1	2	3	2		
YE Dec 17[p]	5	3	5	2	6	2	2	2	13	6	2	3	1	1	5	4	2	2	3	2		

Table 3 International Passenger Survey (IPS) estimates of long-term international migration - Rolling annual data for the United Kingdom, year ending December 2017

Abbreviation: Est. (Estimate)
Citizenship by main reason for migration

	Non-European Union² (contd.) Asia (contd.)								Rest of the World												Stateless	
	Middle East and Central Asia		East Asia		South Asia		South East Asia		All		Sub-Saharan Africa		North Africa		North America		Central and South America		Oceania		Stateless	
	Est.	+/-CI	Est.	+/-CI	Est.	+/-CI	Est.	+/-CI	Est.	+/-CI	Est.	+/-CI	Est.	+/-CI	Est.	+/-CI	Est.	+/-CI	Est.	+/-CI	Est.	+/-CI
Looking for work																						
YE Mar 08	:	:	:	:	:	:	:	:	:	:	:	:	:	:	:	:	:	:	:	:	:	:
YE Jun 08	1	1	8	2	3	1	1	1	20	4	4	2	1	2	1	1	2	1	11	2	0~	0~
YE Sep 08	:	:	:	:	:	:	:	:	:	:	:	:	:	:	:	:	:	:	:	:	:	:
YE Dec 08	1	1	8	3	4	3	2	1	21	4	4	2	1	2	2	1	1	1	13	3	:	:
YE Mar 09	:	:	:	:	:	:	:	:	:	:	:	:	:	:	:	:	:	:	:	:	:	:
YE Jun 09	1	1	7	3	5	3	2	1	19	4	3	2	0~	0~	2	1	0~	0~	13	3	0~	0~
YE Sep 09	:	:	:	:	:	:	:	:	:	:	:	:	:	:	:	:	:	:	:	:	:	:
YE Dec 09	1	1	8	2	5	2	3	1	21	4	3	1			4	3	1	1	12	3	0~	0~
YE Mar 10	2	1	8	2	6	2	2	1	19	4	3	1	0~	0~	4	3	2	1	11	2	0~	0~
YE Jun 10	1	1	8	2	6	2	3	1	19	4	3	1	0~	0~	4	3	2	1	10	2		
YE Sep 10	2	1	8	2	7	2	3	1	15	3	3	1	0~	0~	3	1	2	1	8	2		
YE Dec 10	2	1	8	2	8	2	3	1	14	3	3	1	0~	0~	3	1	1	1	6	2		
YE Mar 11	2	1	7	2	10	2	4	1	14	3	3	1	0~	0~	3	1	1	1	7	2		
YE Jun 11	2	1	7	2	10	2	3	1	15	3	3	1	0~	0~	3	2	1	1	7	2	0~	0~
YE Sep 11	2	1	6	2	9	2	4	1	15	3	3	1	0~	0~	4	2	1	1	8	2	0~	0~
YE Dec 11	2	1	8	2	11	3	4	2	14	3	2	1	0~	0~	4	2	1	1	7	2	0~	0~
YE Mar 12	1	1	9	2	11	2	4	2	14	3	2	1			3	2	1	1	7	2	0~	0~
YE Jun 12	1	1	8	2	11	2	4	2	12	3	2	1			3	2	1	1	6	2		
YE Sep 12	2	2	11	3	12	2	3	2	11	2	2	1	0~	0~	3	1	1	1	5	2		
YE Dec 12	2	2	10	3	10	2	3	2	11	2	2	1	0~	0~	3	1	2	1	4	1		
YE Mar 13	2	2	10	3	10	2	2	1	11	2	2	1	1	1	3	1	2	1	4	1		
YE Jun 13	2	2	11	3	11	2	3	1	13	3	2	1	1	1	3	1	2	1	5	2		
YE Sep 13	1	1	9	2	11	2	4	1	14	3	2	1	1	1	4	1	2	1	5	2		
YE Dec 13	1	1	10	2	10	2	3	1	14	3	2	1	1	1	3	1	2	1	6	2		
YE Mar 14	2	1	11	2	9	2	4	1	14	3	2	1	1	1	3	1	1	1	6	2		
YE Jun 14	2	1	11	2	9	2	3	1	14	3	3	1	1	1	4	2	1	1	5	2		
YE Sep 14	2	1	12	3	8	2	3	2	11	3	2	1	1	1	3	2	1	1	5	2		
YE Dec 14	1	1	11	3	8	2	2	1	9	3	2	1	0~	0~	2	2	0~	0~	4	2		
YE Mar 15	1	1	10	3	7	2	2	1	8	3	1	1	0~	0~	3	2	0~	0~	3	1		
YE Jun 15	1	1	11	3	6	2	2	1	8	2	1	1	0~	0~	3	2	0~	0~	4	2		
YE Sep 15	1	1	11	3	6	2	2	1	9	3	2	1			3	2	1	1	3	1		
YE Dec 15	1	1	11	3	6	2	3	1	11	3	2	1			4	2	1	1	4	2		
YE Mar 16	1	1	11	3	6	2	3	2	12	3	3	2	0~	0~	4	2	1	1	3	2		
YE Jun 16	1	1	11	3	6	2	3	2	11	3	2	1	0~	1	4	2	2	1	3	2		
YE Sep 16	1	1	9	3	5	2	3	2	13	4	2	1	1	2	5	2	2	1	4	2		
YE Dec 16	1	1	9	3	4	2	3	2	11	3	1	1	1	2	3	2	2	1	3	1		
YE Mar 17ᵖ	1	1	9	3	4	1	3	1	9	3	1	1	1	2	2	2	2	1	2	1		
YE Jun 17ᵖ⁷	1	1	10	3	3	1	3	1	10	3	1	1	1	2	3	2	2	1	3	1		
YE Sep 17ᵖ⁷	2	1	13	3	2	1	3	2	9	3	1	1	1	1	2	1	2	2	3	1		
YE Dec 17ᵖ	2	1	11	3	2	1	2	1	9	3	1	1	1	1	2	2	1	1	4	2		
Accompany/Join																						
YE Mar 08	:	:	:	:	:	:	:	:	:	:	:	:	:	:	:	:	:	:	:	:		
YE Jun 08	0~	0~	1	1	2	2	0~	0~	4	1	1	0~			2	1	0~	0~	1	0~		
YE Sep 08	:	:	:	:	:	:	:	:	:	:	:	:	:	:	:	:	:	:	:	:		
YE Dec 08	0~	0~	2	1	3	3	0~	0~	8	3	1	1	1	1	3	1	1	1	2	1		
YE Mar 09	:	:	:	:	:	:	:	:	:	:	:	:	:	:	:	:	:	:	:	:		
YE Jun 09	0~	0~	2	1	2	2	0~	0~	8	3	2	1	1	1	3	1	1	1	2	1		
YE Sep 09	:	:	:	:	:	:	:	:	:	:	:	:	:	:	:	:	:	:	:	:		
YE Dec 09			2	1	2	1	0~	0~	6	2	1	1			3	1	0~	0~	2	1		
YE Mar 10			2	1	2	1	0~	0~	6	2	1	1	0~	0~	3	1	0~	0~	2	1		
YE Jun 10			1	1	2	1	0~	0~	6	2	1	1	0~	0~	3	1	1	0~	2	1		
YE Sep 10			1	1	1	1	1	1	5	2	1	1	0~	0~	3	1	1	0~	1	1		
YE Dec 10	0~	0~	1	0~	1	1	1	1	5	2	1	1	0~	0~	3	1	0~	0~	1	1		
YE Mar 11	0~	0~	1	1	1	1	1	1	4	2	1	1	0~	0~	3	1	0~	0~	1	1		
YE Jun 11	0~	0~	1	1	1	1	1	1	4	1	0~	0~	0~	0~	2	1	0~	0~	1	1		
YE Sep 11	0~	0~	1	1	1	1	0~	0~	4	1	1	1	0~	0~	2	1	0~	0~	1	1		
YE Dec 11	0~	0~	1	1	1	1	1	1	4	1	1	1	0~	0~	2	1			1	1		
YE Mar 12	0~	0~	1	1	1	1	1	1	4	1	1	1	0~	0~	2	1			1	1		
YE Jun 12	0~	0~	1	1	1	1	1	1	4	1	1	1	0~	0~	2	1	0~	0~	1	1		
YE Sep 12	0~	0~	0~	1	1	1	1	1	4	1	0~	0~	0~	0~	2	1	0~	0~	1	1		
YE Dec 12	0~	0~	1	1	1	1	1	1	4	1	0~	0~			2	1	0~	0~	1	1		
YE Mar 13	0~	0~	1	1	1	1	1	1	3	1	0~	0~			1	1	0~	0~	1	1		
YE Jun 13	0~	0~	1	1	1	1	1	1	3	1	0~	0~			2	1	0~	0~	1	1		
YE Sep 13			1	1	2	1	1	1	4	1	1	1	0~	0~	2	1	0~	0~	1	1		
YE Dec 13	0~	0~	1	1	2	1	1	1	4	1	1	1	0~	0~	2	1	0~	0~	1	1		
YE Mar 14	0~	0~	1	1	2	1	1	1	4	2	1	1	0~	0~	2	1	0~	0~	1	1		
YE Jun 14	0~	0~	1	1	2	1	0~	0~	4	2	1	1	0~	1	2	1	0~	0~	1	1		
YE Sep 14	0~	0~	1	0~	2	1			3	1	1	1	0~	0~	2	1	0~	0~	1	0~		
YE Dec 14	0~	0~	1	1	1	1			2	1	1	1	0~	0~	1	1	0~	0~	0~	0~		
YE Mar 15	0~	0~	1	1	1	1			2	1	0~	0~	0~	1	1	1			0~	0~		
YE Jun 15	0~	0~	1	1	1	1	0~	0~	1	1	0~	0~	0~	0~	0~	1			0~	0~		
YE Sep 15	1	1	1	1	1	1	0~	1	1	1			0~	0~	1	1			0~	1		
YE Dec 15	1	1	1	1	1	1	0~	1	2	1	0~	0~	0~	0~	1	1			1	1		
YE Mar 16	1	1	1	1	1	1	0~	1	2	1	0~	0~			1	1			1	1		
YE Jun 16	1	1	1	1	1	1	0~	0~	3	1	0~	0~			2	1			1	1		
YE Sep 16	0~	1	0~	0~	1	1	1	1	4	3	0~	0~			3	3			1	1		
YE Dec 16	0~	0~	1	1	1	1	1	1	4	3					4	3			0~	0~		
YE Mar 17ᵖ	1	1	1	1	1	1	1	1	4	3			0~	0~	4	3			0~	0~		
YE Jun 17ᵖ⁷	1	1	1	1	1	1	1	1	3	3			0~	0~	3	3						
YE Sep 17ᵖ⁷	1	1	1	1	1	1			2	1	0~	0~	0~	0~	1	1						
YE Dec 17ᵖ	0~	1	0~	1	1	1			2	1	0~	0~	0~	0~	1	1	0~	0~	0~	1		

Table 3 International Passenger Survey (IPS) estimates of long-term international migration - Rolling annual data for the United Kingdom, year ending December 2017

Abbreviation: Est (Estimate)

Citizenship by main reason for migration

United Kingdom
thousands

Non-European Union[2] (contd.)

	Asia (contd.)								Rest of the World												Stateless	
	Middle East and Central Asia		East Asia		South Asia		South East Asia		All		Sub-Saharan Africa		North Africa		North America		Central and South America		Oceania			
	Est.	+/-CI	Est.	+/-CI	Est.	+/-CI	Est.	+/-CI	Est.	+/-CI	Est.	+/-CI	Est.	+/-CI	Est.	+/-CI	Est.	+/-CI	Est.	+/-CI	Est.	+/-CI
Formal study																						
YE Mar 08	:	:	:	:	:	:	:	:	:	:	:	:	:	:	:	:	:	:	:	:	:	:
YE Jun 08	0~	0~	1	1	0~	1	0~	0~	5	3	1	1	0~	1	1	1	2	2	1	0~	:	:
YE Sep 08	:	:	:	:	:	:	:	:	:	:	:	:	:	:	:	:	:	:	:	:	:	:
YE Dec 08	0~	0~	2	2	0~	0~	0~	0~	2	1	0~	0~			0~	0~	1	1	1	1	0~	0~
YE Mar 09	:	:	:	:	:	:	:	:	:	:	:	:	:	:	:	:	:	:	:	:	:	:
YE Jun 09	0~	0~	2	2	0~	0~	0~	1	2	1	1	1			0~	0~	0~	0~	1	0~		
YE Sep 09	:	:	:	:	:	:	:	:	:	:	:	:	:	:	:	:	:	:	:	:	:	:
YE Dec 09	0~	0~	1	1	1	1	1	1	4	2	1	1			1	1	0~	0~	1	1		
YE Mar 10	0~	0~	1	1	1	1	1	1	3	2	1	1			1	1	0~	0~	1	1		
YE Jun 10	0~	0~	2	1	0~	0~	0~	0~	3	1	0~	0~			1	1	0~	0~	1	1		
YE Sep 10	0~	0~	2	1	0~	0~			4	2	1	1			1	1	1	1	2	1		
YE Dec 10	0~	0~	2	1	0~	0~			4	2	1	1			1	1	1	1	1	1		
YE Mar 11	0~	0~	1	1	0~	0~			4	2	1	1			1	1	1	1	1	1		
YE Jun 11	0~	0~	1	1	0~	0~			4	2	1	1			1	1	1	1	1	1		
YE Sep 11	0~	0~	1	1	1	1			4	2	0~	0~			2	2	0~	1	1	1		
YE Dec 11	0~	0~	2	1	1	1			2	2	0~	0~			2	2	0~	0~	0~	0~		
YE Mar 12	0~	0~	2	1	2	1			3	2	0~	0~			1	2			1	1		
YE Jun 12			2	1	2	1	0~	0~	3	2	0~	0~			1	2			1	1		
YE Sep 12	0~	0~	1	1	1	1	1	1	1	1	0~	0~			0~	0~			1	1		
YE Dec 12	0~	0~	1	1	1	1	1	1	1	1	0~	0~			0~	0~			1	1		
YE Mar 13	0~	0~	1	1	1	1	1	1	1	1	0~	0~	0~	0~	0~	0~			0~	0~		
YE Jun 13	0~	0~	1	1	1	1	1	1	1	1			0~	0~	0~	0~	0~	1	0~	0~		
YE Sep 13	0~	0~	1	1	1	1	0~	0~	2	1	0~	0~	0~	0~	1	1	0~	1				
YE Dec 13	0~	0~	2	1	1	1	0~	0~	2	1	1	1	0~	0~	1	1	0~	1	0~	0~		
YE Mar 14	0~	0~	2	1	1	1	0~	0~	2	1	1	1			1	1	1	1	0~	0~		
YE Jun 14	0~	0~	2	1	1	1	0~	0~	2	1	1	1			1	1	0~	0~	0~	0~		
YE Sep 14	0~	0~	2	1	1	1	1	1	2	1	0~	0~			1	1	0~	0~	0~	0~		
YE Dec 14	1	1	2	1	1	1	1	1	2	1	0~	1			1	1	0~	0~	0~	0~		
YE Mar 15	0~	1	1	1	1	1	1	1	2	1	0~	1			1	1	0~	0~	0~	0~		
YE Jun 15	1	1	1	1	1	1	1	1	2	1	0~	1			1	1	0~	0~	0~	0~		
YE Sep 15	1	1	2	1	1	1	1	1	3	2	1	1			1	1	2	1	0~	0~		
YE Dec 15	1	1	2	1	2	2	1	1	3	2	1	1	0~	0~	0~	0~	2	1	0~	0~		
YE Mar 16	1	1	1	1	2	2	0~	1	3	2	1	1	0~	0~	0~	0~	2	1	0~	0~		
YE Jun 16	0~	0~	2	1	2	2	0~	1	4	2	1	1	0~	0~	1	1	2	1	0~	0~		
YE Sep 16			2	1	1	2	1	1	2	1	1	1	0~	0~	1	1	0~	0~	0~	0~		
YE Dec 16	0~	0~	1	1	1	2	1	1	2	1	0~	1			1	1	0~	0~	0~	1		
YE Mar 17[F]	0~	0~	2	1	1	2	1	1	2	1	0~	1			1	1	0~	0~	0~	1		
YE Jun 17[P7]	0~	0~	2	1	1	2	1	1	2	1			0~	0~	1	1	0~	0~	0~	1		
YE Sep 17[*7]	0~	0~	1	1	1	2	0~	1	2	1			0~	0~	1	1	0~	0~	0~	1		
YE Dec 17[3]	0~	0~	1	1	0~	0~	1	1	1	1			0~	0~	1	1			0~	0~		
Going home to live[5]																						
YE Mar 08	:	:	:	:	:	:	:	:	:	:	:	:	:	:	:	:	:	:	:	:		
YE Jun 08	0~	0~	0~	1	1	1			5	4	1	1			2	2			3	3		
YE Sep 08	:	:	:	:	:	:	:	:	:	:	:	:	:	:	:	:	:	:	:	:		
YE Dec 08			1	1	2	3			6	4	1	1			2	2	1	2	2	2		
YE Mar 09	:	:	:	:	:	:	:	:	:	:	:	:	:	:	:	:	:	:	:	:		
YE Jun 09	0~	1	1	1	3	3			4	3	1	1	0~	0~	0~	0~	1	2	1	0~		
YE Sep 09	:	:	:	:	:	:	:	:	:	:	:	:	:	:	:	:	:	:	:	:		
YE Dec 09	0~	1	1	1	2	1	0~	0~	4	2	1	1	0~	0~	0~	0~	0~	0~	2	1		
YE Mar 10	0~	1	2	2	2	1	0~	0~	3	2	1	1			0~	0~	0~	1	2	2		
YE Jun 10	0~	1	2	2	2	1	0~	0~	3	2	1	1					0~	1	1	1		
YE Sep 10	1	1	2	2	1	1	1	1	3	2	1	1			1	1	0~	1	1	1		
YE Dec 10	1	1	2	2	1	1	1	1	2	2	0~	0~			1	1	0~	0~	1	1		
YE Mar 11	0~	1	1	1	1	1	1	1	3	2	1	1			1	1	0~	0~	1	1		
YE Jun 11	0~	1	1	1	1	1	1	1	4	2	1	1			1	1	0~	0~	1	1		
YE Sep 11			1	1	1	1	1	1	4	2	1	1			1	1	0~	0~	1	1		
YE Dec 11	0~	0~	2	1	1	1	0~	1	5	2	2	2			1	1			2	1		
YE Mar 12	0~	0~	2	1	1	1	1	1	4	2	2	2			1	1	0~	0~	1	1		
YE Jun 12	0~	0~	2	2	1	1	2	2	4	2	2	2			1	1	0~	0~	1	1		
YE Sep 12	0~	0~	2	2	1	1	2	2	2	2	1	1			1	1	0~	0~	0~	1		
YE Dec 12	0~	0~	2	2	1	1	3	2	2	2	1	1			1	1	0~	1	1	1		
YE Mar 13	0~	0~	2	2	1	1	2	1	1	1	0~	0~			0~	1	0~	1	1	1		
YE Jun 13	0~	0~	2	2	1	1	1	1	2	1	0~	0~			0~	1	0~	1	1	1		
YE Sep 13	0~	0~	2	1	1	1	0~	0~	2	1	0~	1			1	1	0~	1	1	1		
YE Dec 13	1	1	2	1	1	1	0~	0~	2	1	0~	0~			1	1			1	1		
YE Mar 14	1	1	1	1	1	1	0~	0~	3	1	1	1			1	1			1	1		
YE Jun 14	1	1	2	2	2	1	1	2	3	2	1	1	0~	0~	1	1			2	1		
YE Sep 14	1	1	6	7	2	1	2	2	3	2	1	1	0~	0~	1	1			2	2		
YE Dec 14			6	7	2	1	2	2	3	2	1	1	0~	0~	1	1			1	2		
YE Mar 15	0~	0~	6	7	2	1	2	2	3	2	0~	0~	0~	1	0~	1			2	2		
YE Jun 15	0~	1	5	6	1	1	1	1	2	2	0~	0~	0~	0~	1	1			1	1		
YE Sep 15	0~	1	1	1	1	1	1	1	2	1	0~	0~	0~	0~	1	1			1	1		
YE Dec 15	0~	1	2	1	1	1	1	1	3	2	1	1	0~	0~	1	1	1	1	1	1		
YE Mar 16	2	3	2	1	1	1	1	1	3	2	1	1			1	1	1	1	1	1		
YE Jun 16	2	3	2	1	1	1	1	1	3	2	0~	1			1	1	1	1	1	1		
YE Sep 16	2	3	1	1	1	1	1	1	3	2	1	1			1	1	1	1	1	1		
YE Dec 16	2	3	1	1	1	1	1	1	4	2	0~	1			2	2			1	1		
YE Mar 17[P]	1	1	1	1	1	1	1	1	3	2	0~	1			2	2			1	1	0~	0~
YE Jun 17[P7]	1	1	1	1	1	1	1	2	3	2	0~	1			2	2			1	1	0~	0~
YE Sep 17[P7]	1	1	1	1	1	1	1	1	3	2	0~	1	0~	1	2	2			0~	0~	0~	0~
YE Dec 17[P]	1	2	2	1	1	1	1	1	3	2	0~	1	0~	1	1	1	1	1	0~	1	0~	0~

Table 3 International Passenger Survey (IPS) estimates of long-term international migration - Rolling annual data for the United Kingdom, year ending December 2017

Abbreviation: Est. (Estimate)

United Kingdom
thousands

Citizenship by main reason for migration

| | Non-European Union[2] (contd.) Asia (contd.) | | | | | | | | Rest of the World | | | | | | | | | | | | Stateless | |
| | Middle East and Central Asia | | East Asia | | South Asia | | South East Asia | | All | | Sub-Saharan Africa | | North Africa | | North America | | Central and South America | | Oceania | | | |
	Est.	+/-CI	Est.	+/-CI	Est.	+/-CI	Est.	+/-CI	Est.	+/-CI	Est.	+/-CI	Est.	+/-CI	Est.	+/-CI	Est.	+/-CI	Est.	+/-CI	Est.	+/-CI
Other																						
YE Mar 08	:	:	:	:	:	:	:	:	:	:	:	:			:	:	:	:	:	:		
YE Jun 08	0~	0~	1	1	3	3	0~	0~	3	2	1	1			1	2	0~	0~	1	1		
YE Sep 08	:	:	:	:	:	:	:	:	:	:	:	:			:	:	:	:	:	:		
YE Dec 08	0~	0~	0~	0~	0~	0~	0~	0~	3	2	1	1			0~	0~	1	1	2	1	0~	0~
YE Mar 09	:	:			:	:	:	:	:	:	:	:			:	:	:	:	:	:		
YE Jun 09	0~	0~			1	1	0~	0~	4	2	0~	0~			0~	1	1	1	3	2	0~	0~
YE Sep 09	:	:			:	:	:	:	:	:	:	:			:	:	:	:	:	:		
YE Dec 09					1	1	0~	0~	3	2	1	1			0~	1	0~	1	2	2		
YE Mar 10	0~	0~	0~	0~	1	1	0~	0~	3	1	1	1			0~	0~	0~	1	1	1		
YE Jun 10	0~	0~	0~	0~	1	0~	0~	0~	2	1	1	1			0~	0~	0~	1	1	1		
YE Sep 10	0~	0~	0~	0~	0~	0~	0~	0~	3	1	1	1			1	1	0~	1	1	1		
YE Dec 10	0~	0~	0~	0~	0~	0~	0~	0~	2	1	1	1			1	1			1	1		
YE Mar 11	0~	0~	0~	0~	1	1	0~	0~	2	1	0~	0~			1	1			1	1		
YE Jun 11	0~	0~	0~	0~	1	1	0~	0~	2	1	0~	0~			1	1	0~	1	1	1		
YE Sep 11	0~	0~	0~	0~	1	1	0~	0~	2	1	0~	0~			1	1	1	1	1	1		
YE Dec 11	0~	1	0~	0~	2	1	0~	0~	2	1	0~	0~			0~	1	1	1	1	1		
YE Mar 12	0~	0~	0~	0~	2	1	0~	0~	2	1	0~	1			0~	1	1	1	0~	0~		
YE Jun 12	0~	0~	0~	0~	2	1	0~	0~	2	1	1	1			1	1	0~	1	0~	0~		
YE Sep 12	0~	1	1	1	2	1	0~	0~	1	1	0~	0~			1	1			0~	0~		
YE Dec 12	0~	0~	1	1	2	1			2	1	1	1			1	1			0~	0~		
YE Mar 13	0~	0~	1	1	2	1			1	1	0~	0~			0~	0~	0~	0~	0~	0~		
YE Jun 13	0~	0~	1	1	1	1			1	1	0~	0~			1	1	0~	0~	0~	0~		
YE Sep 13	0~	0~	1	1	1	1			1	1	0~	0~			0~	0~	0~	0~	0~	0~		
YE Dec 13	0~	0~	2	1	1	1			2	1	0~	0~			1	1	0~	0~	0~	0~		
YE Mar 14			1	1	0~	1			1	1	0~	0~			1	1			0~	0~		
YE Jun 14			1	1	0~	0~			1	1	0~	0~			1	1			0~	0~		
YE Sep 14			1	1	0~	0~			3	2	1	1			1	1			1	1		
YE Dec 14			1	1	0~	1			2	1	1	1			0~	0~			1	1		
YE Mar 15			1	1	0~	0~			2	1	1	1			0~	0~			1	1		
YE Jun 15			0~	1	0~	0~			2	1	0~	0~			1	1			1	1		
YE Sep 15			0~	1	0~	0~	0~	0~	1	1					1	1			1	1		
YE Dec 15			0~	1	0~	0~	0~	0~	1	1					1	1			0~	0~		
YE Mar 16			0~	1	0~	0~	0~	0~	1	1					1	1			1	1		
YE Jun 16			1	1	0~	0~	0~	0~	2	2					1	1			1	1		
YE Sep 16			1	1	0~	0~			2	2					0~	1	0~	0~	1	1		
YE Dec 16			1	1	1	1	0~	0~	2	1					0~	0~	0~	0~	1	1		
YE Mar 17[p]			1	1	1	1	0~	0~	1	1					0~	0~	0~	0~	1	1		
YE Jun 17[p7]	0~	0~	0~	0~	1	1	0~	0~	1	1					0~	0~	0~	1	1	1		
YE Sep 17[p7]	0~	0~	0~	0~	1	1	0~	0~	1	1					0~	0~	0~	0~	1	1		
YE Dec 17[p]	0~	0~	0~	0~	1	1			1	1					0~	0~	0~	0~	1	1		
No reason stated[6]																						
YE Mar 08	:	:	:	:					:	:	:	:			:	:			:	:		
YE Jun 08	0~	0~	0~	0~					1	1	0~	0~			0~	1			0~	0~		
YE Sep 08	:	:	:	:					:	:					:	:			:	:		
YE Dec 08	0~	0~	0~	0~	0~	0~	0~	0~	1	1					0~	0~	0~	1	0~	0~		
YE Mar 09	:	:	:	:	:	:	:	:	:	:					:	:	:	:	:	:		
YE Jun 09			0~	0~	0~	0~	0~	0~	1	1					0~	0~	0~	1	0~	0~		
YE Sep 09	:	:	:	:	:	:	:	:	:	:					:	:	:	:	:	:		
YE Dec 09			0~	0~	0~	0~	0~	0~	0~	0~			0~	0~			0~	0~	0~	0~		
YE Mar 10			0~	0~	0~	0~	0~	0~	0~	0~			0~	0~			0~	0~	0~	0~		
YE Jun 10			0~	0~			0~	0~	1	1	0~	0~	0~	0~			0~	0~	0~	0~		
YE Sep 10	0~	0~	0~	0~	0~	0~	0~	1	0~	0~	0~	0~							0~	0~		
YE Dec 10	0~	0~	0~	0~	0~	0~	0~	0~	0~	0~	0~	0~							0~	0~		
YE Mar 11	0~	0~	0~	0~	0~	0~	0~	0~	0~	0~	0~	0~							0~	0~		
YE Jun 11	0~	0~	0~	0~	0~	0~	0~	0~	0~	0~	0~	0~							0~	0~		
YE Sep 11							0~	0~	1	1					1	1			0~	0~		
YE Dec 11							0~	0~	1	1	0~	0~			1	1			0~	0~		
YE Mar 12							0~	0~	1	1	0~	0~			1	1			0~	0~		
YE Jun 12					0~	0~	0~	0~	1	1	0~	1			1	1			0~	0~		
YE Sep 12	0~	0~	0~	0~	0~	0~	0~	1	1	1	0~	1			0~	0~			0~	0~		
YE Dec 12	0~	0~	0~	0~	1	1	0~	1	1	1	0~	1			0~	0~			0~	0~		
YE Mar 13	0~	0~	0~	1	1	1	0~	1	0~	1	0~	1							0~	0~		
YE Jun 13	0~	0~	0~	1	0~	0~	0~	1	0~	1									0~	0~		
YE Sep 13	0~	0~	0~	0~	0~	0~	0~	0~	1	1	0~	0~							0~	1		
YE Dec 13			0~	0~	0~	0~	0~	0~	1	1	0~	0~							0~	1		
YE Mar 14					0~	0~	0~	0~	1	1	0~	0~							0~	1		
YE Jun 14					0~	0~	0~	0~	1	1	0~	0~							0~	1		
YE Sep 14			0~	1					0~	0~									0~	0~		
YE Dec 14			0~	1	0~	0~			0~	1									0~	0~		
YE Mar 15			0~	1	0~	0~	0~	0~	0~	1	0~	0~							0~	0~		
YE Jun 15			0~	1	0~	0~	0~	0~	0~	1	0~	0~							0~	0~		
YE Sep 15			0~	0~	0~	0~	0~	0~	1	1	0~	0~			0~	1	0~	0~	0~	.		
YE Dec 15			0~	1			0~	0~	1	1					0~	1			0~	.		
YE Mar 16			0~	1	0~	0~			1	1					1	1	0~	0~	0~	0~		
YE Jun 16			0~	1	0~	0~			1	1					1	1	0~	0~	0~	0~		
YE Sep 16			0~	0~	0~	0~	1	1	1	1					0~	0~			0~	0~		
YE Dec 16			0~	0~	0~	0~	1	1	1	1	0~	0~			0~	0~			0~	0~		
YE Mar 17[p]			0~	1	0~	0~	1	1	1	1									1	1		
YE Jun 17[p7]			0~	1	0~	0~	1	1	1	1					0~	0~			1	1		
YE Sep 17[p7]			0~	0~	0~	0~			1	1					0~	1			0~	1		
YE Dec 17[p]			0~	0~			0~	0~	1	1					0~	1			1	1		

Table 3 International Passenger Survey (IPS) estimates of long-term international migration - Rolling annual data for the United Kingdom, year ending December 2017

Source: Office for National Statistics (ONS).

Totals may not sum due to rounding.

":" - Not available, "." - No contact, "0~" - Rounds to zero. Please see the Notes worksheet for more information.

YE = Year Ending
p = Year includes provisional estimates for 2017

Migration between the UK and the Republic of Ireland is included in IPS estimates for 2008 onwards but excluded for previous years. All estimates are calibrated.

Calibrated IPS estimates of migration are only available for calendar years and mid years up to YE Dec 2009. For data back to 1977, please see 3-series table 3.08 in the data section on the ONS website:

All data related to international migration

1 European Union estimates are for the EU15 (Austria, Belgium, Denmark, Finland, France, Germany, Greece, Republic of Ireland, Italy, Luxembourg, Netherlands, Portugal, Spain and Sweden) up to 2003, the EU25 (the EU15 and the EU8 groupings plus Malta and Cyprus) from 2004 to 2006, the EU27 (the EU25 plus Bulgaria and Romania) from 2007 and the EU28 (the EU27 plus Croatia) from July 2013. Estimates are also shown separately for the EU15, the EU8 (Czech Republic, Estonia, Hungary, Latvia, Lithuania, Poland, Slovakia and Slovenia), the EU2 (Bulgaria and Romania) and EU Other (Malta, Cyprus and Croatia). British citizens are excluded from all citizenship groupings and are shown separately.

2 Excludes British and other European Union citizens as defined in footnote 1.

3 From 2004 onwards, Other Europe excludes the eight central and eastern European member states that joined the EU in May 2004 (the EU8), Malta and Cyprus. From 2007 onwards, Other Europe excludes Bulgaria and Romania which joined the EU in January 2007. From July 2013 onwards, Other Europe excludes Croatia which joined the EU in July 2013.

4 "Work related" includes "Definite job" and "Looking for work"

5 "Going home to live" is recorded when no other reason relating to work, study or accompany/join is provided.

6 "No reason stated" includes non-responses and the non-specific response "Emigrating / Immigrating".

7. Please see the correction notice on the Contents and Notes page for information relating to YE Jun 17p and YE Sep 17p

Care should be taken when comparing inflow and outflow by main reason for migration. Returning migrants are asked their reason for returning, not their original reason for migrating. A former immigrant's main reason for leaving the UK may well differ from their previous main reason for immigrating into the UK. Because of this, no balance estimates are displayed. Please see the Notes worksheet for more information.

IPS estimates of former immigrants' previous main reason for immigrating are shown in Table 4. Please see the Notes worksheet for more information.

This table uses 95% confidence intervals (CI) to indicate the robustness of each estimate. Please see the Notes worksheet for more information.

Statistically Significant Increase   Statistically Significant Decrease

The latest estimates (year ending December 2017) have been compared with the corresponding estimates for the period one year earlier. Where changes have been found to be statistically significant, the relevant pair of estimates have been highlighted by setting their background colour. Please see the Notes worksheet for more information.

Table 4 International Passenger Survey (IPS) estimates of long-term international migration - Rolling annual data for the United Kingdom, year ending December 2017

Former immigrants - Formal Study are designated as Experimental Statistics. This follows a report from the Office for Statistics Regulation recommending this until ONS has a more complete and coherent picture of former student emigration

Our latest student update report 'What's happening with international student migration2' was published 24 August 2017

United Kingdom
thousands

Outflow of migrants by citizenship and, for former immigrants[1], previous main reason for immigration

Migration status and, for former immigrants[1], Previous main reason for immigration	All citizenships Estimate	+/-CI	British (Including Overseas Territories) Estimate	+/-CI	Non-British Estimate	+/-CI	European Union[2] Estimate	+/-CI	European Union EU15 Estimate	+/-CI	European Union EU8 Estimate	+/-CI	European Union EU2 Estimate	+/-CI	European Union Other Estimate	+/-CI	Non-European Union[3] All Estimate	+/-CI	Other Europe[4] Estimate	+/-CI	Asia All Estimate	+/-CI
Outflow																						
All emigrants																						
YE Dec 12	298	20	134	14	165	14	69	11	39	8	26	8	3	2	1	1	96	8	4	2	58	6
YE Mar 13	295	20	133	14	162	14	69	12	40	8	25	8	3	2	1	1	93	8	4	2	57	6
YE Jun 13	297	19	131	12	166	15	71	12	42	9	26	8	2	2	1	1	94	8	5	3	57	6
YE Sep 13	296	19	128	12	168	15	72	13	45	10	22	7	3	2	2	1	96	8	6	3	53	5
YE Dec 13	295	19	125	12	170	15	73	12	45	10	23	7	3	2	2	2	97	9	6	3	54	6
YE Mar 14	294	20	121	11	174	17	77	14	48	12	24	7	3	2	2	2	97	8	6	3	54	6
YE Jun 14	299	22	122	13	177	18	79	15	47	12	26	8	4	4	2	2	98	9	6	3	55	6
YE Sep 14	302	23	125	13	176	19	82	15	46	12	31	9	4	3	1	1	95	11	6	3	58	9
YE Dec 14	297	22	127	13	171	18	83	15	49	12	29	9	3	3	1	1	87	10	6	3	55	9
YE Mar 15	284	21	122	13	162	17	79	13	47	9	27	8	3	3	1	1	83	10	6	3	52	9
YE Jun 15	279	20	120	12	159	16	79	12	47	9	26	7	3	3	1	1	80	10	4	2	51	9
YE Sep 15	275	19	118	12	157	15	79	12	48	9	24	7	5	5	1	1	78	8	3	2	48	6
YE Dec 15	279	20	114	13	165	16	79	13	48	10	24	7	5	5	1	1	85	9	3	2	50	6
YE Mar 16	287	21	116	13	171	16	83	13	50	10	26	7	6	5	1	1	88	9	4	2	52	7
YE Jun 16	293	21	116	12	177	17	88	14	52	10	28	8	7	5	1	1	88	9	4	2	51	7
YE Sep 16	300	22	116	13	184	18	96	15	50	10	36	9	7	5	2	2	88	11	3	2	48	7
YE Dec 16	316	23	121	13	195	19	111	16	57	11	40	10	9	6	2	2	84	10	3	2	47	7
YE Mar 17 p	316	23	119	13	197	19	116	16	56	10	43	10	12	7	2	2	81	10	3	2	46	6
YE Jun 17 p9	306	23	109	12	197	19	113	16	59	11	38	9	15	7	2	2	84	10	4	2	46	7
YE Sep 17 p9	329	25	110	13	219	21	134	19	72	14	43	10	18	7	2	2	85	10	6	3	49	7
YE Dec 17 p	321	26	106	13	214	22	135	20	70	15	45	11	18	7	3	3	80	10	6	3	45	7
Former immigrants - All reasons																						
YE Dec 12	206	18	44	11	162	14	67	11	39	8	25	8	3	2	1	1	95	8	4	2	58	6
YE Mar 13	201	18	41	11	160	14	68	12	40	8	24	8	3	2	1	1	93	8	4	2	57	6
YE Jun 13	199	16	36	7	164	15	70	12	41	9	25	8	2	2	1	1	94	8	5	3	56	6
YE Sep 13	198	16	31	5	167	15	72	13	45	10	22	7	3	2	2	2	95	8	6	3	52	5
YE Dec 13	196	15	27	5	169	15	72	12	45	10	23	7	3	2	2	2	97	9	6	3	54	6
YE Mar 14	199	17	28	4	171	17	75	14	47	12	23	7	3	2	2	2	96	8	6	3	54	6
YE Jun 14	200	18	26	5	174	18	78	15	47	12	25	8	4	4	2	2	96	9	6	3	54	6
YE Sep 14	199	19	28	5	172	18	79	15	45	12	29	8	4	3	1	1	92	11	5	3	57	9
YE Dec 14	196	19	29	5	166	18	81	15	48	12	27	8	4	3	1	1	85	10	5	3	55	9
YE Mar 15	187	17	29	5	158	16	77	12	46	9	26	8	4	3	1	1	81	10	5	3	51	9
YE Jun 15	185	16	31	6	154	15	75	12	46	9	24	7	3	3	1	1	79	10	4	2	50	9
YE Sep 15	186	16	32	7	154	14	76	12	47	9	24	7	4	4	1	1	77	8	3	2	47	6
YE Dec 15	194	17	34	7	160	15	76	13	47	10	23	7	5	5	1	1	84	8	3	2	49	6
YE Mar 16	201	17	33	7	168	16	81	13	49	10	25	7	6	4	1	1	86	9	4	2	51	7
YE Jun 16	208	18	33	6	175	17	88	14	52	10	28	8	7	5	1	1	87	9	4	2	50	7
YE Sep 16	212	19	30	6	182	18	96	15	49	10	36	9	9	5	2	2	87	11	3	2	47	7
YE Dec 16	227	20	33	7	193	19	111	16	56	11	40	10	12	6	2	1	83	10	2	2	47	7
YE Mar 17 p	229	20	34	7	196	19	116	16	56	10	43	10	15	7	2	2	80	10	2	2	46	6
YE Jun 17 p9	230	20	30	7	194	19	111	16	57	10	38	9	15	7	2	2	82	10	4	2	45	7
YE Sep 17 p9	243	22	29	7	214	21	132	19	69	14	43	10	18	7	1	1	82	10	5	3	49	5
YE Dec 17 p	235	23	25	6	210	22	132	19	67	14	45	11	18	7	3	2	77	10	5	2	44	7

Table 4 International Passenger Survey (IPS) estimates of long-term international migration - Rolling annual data for the United Kingdom, year ending December 2017

Former immigrants - Formal Study are designated as Experimental Statistics. This follows a report from the Office for Statistics Regulation recommending this until ONS has a more complete and coherent picture of former student emigration

Our latest student update report 'What's happening with international student migration?' was published 24 August 2017

United Kingdom
thousands

Outflow of migrants by citizenship and, for former immigrants[1], previous main reason for immigration

Migration status and, for former immigrants[1], Previous main reason for immigration	All citizenships		British (Including Overseas Territories)		Non-British		European Union[2]		European Union EU15		European Union EU8		European Union EU2		European Union Other		Non-European Union[3] All		Other Europe[4]		Asia All	
	Estimate	+/-CI	Estimate	+/-CI	Estimate	+/-CI	Estimate	+/-CI	Estimate	+/-CI	Estimate	+/-CI	Estimate	+/-CI	Estimate	+/-CI	Estimate	+/-CI	Estimate	+/-CI	Estimate	+/-CI
Former immigrants - Work related[5]																						
YE Dec 12	68	9	4	2	64	9	38	8	22	6	15	5	1	1	0~	0~	26	4	2	1	12	3
YE Mar 13	64	9	4	2	61	9	36	8	21	6	13	5	1	1	0~	0~	25	4	1	1	11	3
YE Jun 13	67	9	5	2	62	9	37	8	20	6	16	5	1	1	.	.	25	4	1	1	10	2
YE Sep 13	72	10	8	2	63	9	36	8	19	5	15	5	2	1	.	.	27	5	1	1	9	2
YE Dec 13	72	10	9	2	63	9	38	8	20	5	17	6	1	1	.	.	25	5	1	1	9	2
YE Mar 14	77	10	11	3	65	10	40	9	21	6	18	6	1	1	1	1	25	5	1	1	10	3
YE Jun 14	81	12	11	3	70	11	44	10	23	7	18	6	3	3	1	1	25	5	2	2	11	3
YE Sep 14	84	13	12	4	72	11	47	10	22	7	22	7	3	3	1	1	25	8	2	2	13	7
YE Dec 14	87	13	13	4	73	13	48	10	24	7	20	7	3	3	1	1	25	8	3	3	14	7
YE Mar 15	85	13	14	4	71	13	48	10	26	7	19	7	3	3	.	.	24	8	3	3	12	7
YE Jun 15	85	12	14	4	71	12	46	9	26	7	17	6	3	2	.	.	25	8	2	1	13	7
YE Sep 15	80	11	13	3	67	10	46	10	27	7	16	5	3	4	.	.	21	4	2	1	10	3
YE Dec 15	84	12	13	3	70	12	46	10	26	7	17	6	4	4	.	.	24	5	2	2	10	4
YE Mar 16	84	12	10	3	74	12	50	10	26	7	19	6	5	5	.	.	25	5	2	2	11	4
YE Jun 16	86	12	8	3	78	12	52	11	26	7	20	7	6	6	.	.	25	5	2	2	11	4
YE Sep 16	93	13	4	2	88	13	62	12	27	7	28	8	6	6	.	.	27	5	2	2	12	4
YE Dec 16	103	14	4	2	99	14	74	13	32	8	33	9	6	4	0~	0~	25	5	1	1	12	3
YE Mar 17p	108	15	5	3	103	15	79	14	33	8	34	9	11	6	0~	0~	24	5	1	1	12	3
YE Jun 17p9	109	15	7	4	103	15	78	14	36	8	31	9	10	6	.	.	25	5	1	2	11	3
YE Sep 17p9	122	17	8	4	114	17	92	16	42	11	35	9	14	7	1	1	23	5	2	2	8	2
YE Dec 17p	124	19	7	4	117	18	94	17	45	13	35	9	14	6	1	1	23	6	2	2	7	2
Former immigrants - Definite job																						
YE Dec 12	53	8	3	1	50	8	30	7	17	5	12	4	1	1	0~	0~	20	4	1	1	9	2
YE Mar 13	53	8	3	1	50	8	30	7	18	6	11	4	1	1	0~	0~	20	4	1	1	9	2
YE Jun 13	55	9	4	2	51	8	31	8	17	6	13	5	1	1	.	.	20	4	1	1	9	2
YE Sep 13	58	9	7	2	51	9	30	7	17	5	12	5	1	1	.	.	21	5	1	1	8	2
YE Dec 13	56	9	7	2	49	8	30	7	17	5	12	5	0~	1	.	.	19	4	1	1	8	2
YE Mar 14	61	10	9	3	51	9	32	8	18	6	13	5	1	1	1	1	19	4	1	1	9	2
YE Jun 14	63	11	9	3	54	10	35	9	19	7	13	5	2	3	1	1	20	5	2	2	9	2
YE Sep 14	67	12	9	3	58	12	39	10	19	7	17	6	3	3	1	1	19	7	2	2	11	7
YE Dec 14	71	13	11	3	60	12	39	12	20	8	15	6	3	3	1	1	21	8	2	3	12	7
YE Mar 15	67	12	11	3	56	11	36	11	20	8	13	6	3	3	.	.	20	8	2	3	11	7
YE Jun 15	63	11	11	3	52	10	30	10	17	7	11	5	2	2	.	.	22	7	2	2	12	7
YE Sep 15	59	9	10	3	48	8	30	8	17	7	10	4	2	3	.	.	19	4	1	1	9	3
YE Dec 15	62	10	10	3	52	9	31	9	16	5	12	5	3	4	.	.	20	5	1	1	10	3
YE Mar 16	63	11	7	2	56	10	36	9	18	6	15	6	3	4	.	.	20	5	1	1	10	4
YE Jun 16	68	11	6	2	62	11	42	10	19	6	17	7	5	5	.	.	21	5	1	1	10	4
YE Sep 16	74	12	3	2	71	12	49	11	21	6	22	8	5	4	.	.	22	5	1	1	11	4
YE Dec 16	83	13	2	1	80	13	59	12	26	7	25	8	7	5	0~	0~	21	5	1	1	11	3
YE Mar 17p	86	14	3	2	82	13	61	13	26	7	27	9	8	6	0~	0~	21	5	1	1	11	3
YE Jun 17p9	88	14	5	3	83	13	61	12	29	8	24	8	7	5	.	.	23	5	1	1	10	3
YE Sep 17p9	94	15	5	3	89	15	68	14	34	11	26	8	8	5	1	1	21	5	2	2	7	2
YE Dec 17p	93	16	4	3	89	15	68	14	35	11	23	7	9	5	1	1	21	6	2	2	6	2

Table 4 International Passenger Survey (IPS) estimates of long-term international migration - Rolling annual data for the United Kingdom, year ending December 2017

Former immigrants - Formal Study are designated as Experimental Statistics. This follows a report from the Office for Statistics Regulation recommending this until ONS has a more complete and coherent picture of former student emigration

Our latest student update report 'What's happening with international student migration?' was published 24 August 2017

United Kingdom
thousands

Outflow of migrants by citizenship and, for former immigrants[1], previous main reason for immigration

Migration status and, for former immigrants[1], Previous main reason for immigration	All citizenships		British (Including Overseas Territories)		Non-British		European Union[2]		European Union EU15		European Union EU8		European Union EU2		European Union Other		Non-European Union[3] All		Other Europe[4]		Asia All	
	Estimate	+/-CI	Estimate	+/-CI	Estimate	+/-CI	Estimate	+/-CI	Estimate	+/-CI	Estimate	+/-CI	Estimate	+/-CI	Estimate	+/-CI	Estimate	+/-CI	Estimate	+/-CI	Estimate	+/-CI
Former immigrants - Looking for work																						
YE Dec 12	15	4	1	1	14	4	8	3	5	3	3	2	0~	0~	.		6	2	0~	0~	3	1
YE Mar 13	12	3	1	1	11	3	6	2	3	2	2	2	0~	0~	.		5	2	0~	0~	2	1
YE Jun 13	12	3	1	1	11	3	6	3	2	1	3	2	0~	0~	.		6	2	0~	0~	2	1
YE Sep 13	14	3	1	1	12	3	6	3	2	2	3	2	1	1	.		6	2	0~	0~	2	1
YE Dec 13	16	4	2	1	14	4	8	3	2	2	5	3	0~	0~	.		6	2	0~	0~	1	1
YE Mar 14	16	4	2	1	14	4	8	3	2	2	5	3	0~	1	.		6	2	0~	0~	2	1
YE Jun 14	18	5	2	1	15	5	9	4	3	2	5	4	1	1	.		6	2	0~	0~	2	1
YE Sep 14	17	5	3	2	14	5	8	4	3	2	5	4	0~	0~	.		6	2	0~	0~	2	1
YE Dec 14	16	5	3	2	14	5	8	5	3	2	5	4	0~	0~	.		4	2	0~	0~	2	1
YE Mar 15	18	6	3	2	15	6	10	5	5	4	5	3	0~	0~	.		3	2	0~	0~	1	1
YE Jun 15	22	6	3	2	19	6	12	6	6	4	6	3	1	2	.		3	2	0~	0~	1	1
YE Sep 15	22	6	3	1	19	6	16	6	9	5	6	3	1	2	.		2	1	0~	0~	0~	1
YE Dec 15	22	6	4	2	19	6	16	6	9	5	6	3	1	2	.		4	2	0~	0~	1	1
YE Mar 16	21	6	3	2	18	5	15	5	8	4	4	3	2	2	.		4	2	0~	0~	1	1
YE Jun 16	18	5	3	2	15	4	11	4	7	3	3	2	2	1	.		5	2	1	1	1	1
YE Sep 16	19	5	2	1	18	5	13	5	6	3	6	3	1	1	.		5	2	1	1	1	1
YE Dec 16	20	5	1	1	19	5	15	5	6	3	7	3	2	2	.		4	2	0~	0~	1	1
YE Mar 17p	22	6	1	1	20	5	18	5	7	3	8	3	3	2	.		3	1	1	1	1	1
YE Jun 17p9	21	6	2	2	20	5	17	5	7	3	8	3	3	3	.		2	1	0~	0~	1	1
YE Sep 17p9	28	8	3	2	26	8	23	8	8	3	9	4	6	5	0~	0~	2	1	0~	0~	1	1
YE Dec 17p	30	10	3	2	28	10	26	10	10	4	11	4	5	5	0~	1	2	1	0~	1	1	1
Former Immigrants - Accompany / Join																						
YE Dec 12	16	4	5	2	11	3	5	3	2	2	1	1	1	2	.		6	2	0~	0~	3	1
YE Mar 13	17	5	4	1	13	5	6	4	4	3	1	2	1	2	.		7	2	0~	0~	3	1
YE Jun 13	18	5	5	2	13	5	7	5	5	4	1	2	1	2	.		6	2	0~	0~	3	1
YE Sep 13	17	5	4	1	13	5	6	5	6	4	1	1	0~	0~	.		6	2	0~	0~	3	1
YE Dec 13	17	5	4	1	13	5	6	4	5	4	0~	1	0~	0~	.		7	2	1	1	3	1
YE Mar 14	16	4	4	1	12	4	6	4	5	3	1	1	0~	0~	.		7	2	1	1	3	1
YE Jun 14	14	4	3	1	11	4	5	4	4	3	1	1	0~	0~	.		7	2	0~	1	3	1
YE Sep 14	14	3	5	2	9	3	3	3	3	2	1	1	1	1	.		6	2	0~	1	2	1
YE Dec 14	13	3	5	2	8	3	3	3	2	1	1	1	1	1	.		6	2	1	1	1	1
YE Mar 15	12	3	5	2	7	2	4	2	2	2	1	1	1	1	.		4	1	0~	1	2	1
YE Jun 15	13	3	5	2	7	3	3	2	2	1	1	1	0~	0~	1		4	2	0~	0~	2	1
YE Sep 15	15	4	5	2	10	3	3	2	2	2	1	1	0~	0~	1		5	2	0~	0~	2	1
YE Dec 15	15	4	6	2	10	3	4	3	3	2	1	1	0~	0~	.		6	2	0~	1	3	1
YE Mar 16	16	4	5	2	10	3	5	3	3	2	2	1	0~	0~	.		5	2	0~	1	3	1
YE Jun 16	15	4	5	2	10	3	4	2	4	2	0~	0~	0~	1	1		5	2	0~	1	3	1
YE Sep 16	17	5	4	2	12	5	5	3	4	2	1	1	0~	0~	1		9	4	0~	0~	3	2
YE Dec 16	18	6	3	1	15	5	5	3	3	2	1	1	1	1	.		10	5	0~	0~	3	2
YE Mar 17p	18	6	3	1	15	5	4	3	2	2	2	2	2	2	.		10	5	0~	0~	4	2
YE Jun 17p9	17	6	2	1	15	5	3	2	2	2	1	2	2	2	.		10	5	0~	0~	4	2
YE Sep 17p9	15	5	3	2	12	4	4	3	3	3	2	2	1	1	.		6	2	1	1	3	1
YE Dec 17p	13	5	4	1	9	3	1	0	2	2	2	2	2	2	.		5	2	0~	1	3	1

Table 4 International Passenger Survey (IPS) estimates of long-term international migration - Rolling annual data for the United Kingdom, year ending December 2017

Former immigrants - Formal Study are designated as Experimental Statistics. This follows a report from the Office for Statistics Regulation recommending this until ONS has a more complete and coherent picture of former student emigration

Our latest student update report 'What's happening with international student migration?' was published 24 August 2017

Outflow of migrants by citizenship and, for former immigrants[1], previous main reason for immigration

Previous main reason for immigration	All citizenships Est.	+/-CI	British (Incl. Overseas Territories) Est.	+/-CI	Non-British Est.	+/-CI	European Union[2] Est.	+/-CI	EU15 Est.	+/-CI	EU8 Est.	+/-CI	EU2 Est.	+/-CI	Other Est.	+/-CI	Non-EU[3] All Est.	+/-CI	Other Europe[4] Est.	+/-CI	Asia All Est.	+/-CI
Former immigrants - Formal study (experimental statistics)[6]																						
YE Dec 12	67	9	3	3	64	9	15	6	10	4	4	5	1	1	1	1	49	6	2	2	38	5
YE Mar 13	68	9	3	3	65	9	17	6	12	4	4	5	1	1	1	1	49	6	2	2	38	5
YE Jun 13	70	10	3	3	67	9	16	7	12	5	2	4	0~	0~	0~	0~	50	6	3	3	39	5
YE Sep 13	72	10	4	2	69	10	20	8	14	6	3	4	1	2	1	1	49	5	4	4	35	4
YE Dec 13	72	9	4	2	68	9	18	7	14	6	1	1	2	2	2	2	50	6	4	4	36	5
YE Mar 14	74	11	4	2	70	11	20	10	16	10	1	1	2	2	2	2	50	6	3	3	35	5
YE Jun 14	72	11	4	2	68	11	18	9	14	9	2	1	2	1	2	2	51	6	3	3	36	6
YE Sep 14	70	11	3	2	67	11	19	9	16	9	3	1	0~	1	0~	1	48	6	2	2	37	6
YE Dec 14	65	11	2	2	63	11	19	9	15	9	3	3	0~	0~	0~	0~	44	6	2	2	35	6
YE Mar 15	59	8	2	2	56	8	15	5	12	4	3	3	0~	0~	0~	0~	41	6	2	2	33	5
YE Jun 15	57	8	3	2	54	8	16	5	12	4	3	3	0~	0~	0~	0~	38	5	1	1	32	5
YE Sep 15	57	8	3	2	54	7	14	5	10	4	2	3	0~	1	1	1	40	6	1	1	30	5
YE Dec 15	61	8	4	3	57	8	15	5	11	4	1	2	1	1	1	1	43	6	1	1	31	5
YE Mar 16	66	9	4	3	62	9	17	6	14	5	2	2	1	2	2	1	45	7	1	1	32	6
YE Jun 16	67	10	4	3	63	9	18	6	14	5	3	3	2	2	1	1	45	7	1	1	32	6
YE Sep 16	62	10	3	2	59	10	18	6	13	5	2	3	1	2	1	1	41	7	1	1	28	6
YE Dec 16	63	10	2	1	61	10	21	7	16	6	3	2	1	2	1	1	40	8	1	1	28	6
YE Mar 17p	59	10	2	1	57	9	19	6	15	6	2	3	1	2	0~	0~	37	7	1	1	26	5
YE Jun 17p9	58	9	1	1	57	9	21	7	18	6	3	2	1	1	0~	0~	37	7	1	1	26	5
YE Sep 17p9	66	10	1	1	64	10	21	10	18	6	3	2					44	8	2	2	33	6
YE Dec 17p	59	9	1	1	58	9	18	6	13	5	4	3					40	7	2	2	31	6
Former immigrants - Other reason or no reason stated																						
YE Dec 12	26	5	3	2	23	5	10	4	5	3	5	3	0~	0~	0~	0~	13	3	0~	0~	4	2
YE Mar 13	24	5	3	1	21	5	9	4	4	2	6	3			0~	0~	11	3	0~	0~	5	2
YE Jun 13	26	5	5	2	21	5	10	4	4	3	6	3	0~	0~	1	2	11	3	1	1	5	2
YE Sep 13	28	6	6	2	22	5	9	4	5	3	4	3	0~	0~	0~	0~	13	3	1	1	5	2
YE Dec 13	31	6	7	3	25	6	10	5	6	4	4	4	0~	0~	1	1	14	4	1	1	6	2
YE Mar 14	33	6	9	3	24	6	10	5	6	3	4	3	0~	0~	1	1	14	3	1	1	5	2
YE Jun 14	33	7	8	2	25	6	12	6	7	4	5	4	0~	0~	0~	0~	13	3	0~	0~	5	2
YE Sep 14	31	7	8	2	24	6	10	5	5	3	5	3	0~	0~	1	1	13	3	1	1	5	2
YE Dec 14	31	6	8	2	23	5	10	5	6	3	4	3	0~	0~	1	1	13	3	1	1	5	2
YE Mar 15	31	6	8	2	23	6	11	5	7	4	3	4	1	1	1	1	12	3	1	1	4	2
YE Jun 15	31	7	10	4	21	5	10	4	6	3	3	3	1	1	1	1	12	3	1	1	5	2
YE Sep 15	34	7	11	5	23	5	11	5	6	3	5	3	0~	0~	1	1	11	3			5	2
YE Dec 15	33	8	11	5	23	6	11	5	6	4	5	3	0~	0~	1	1	12	3			5	2
YE Mar 16	35	8	14	5	21	6	10	5	6	4	4	3	0~	0~	1	1	11	3			5	2
YE Jun 16	40	8	15	4	24	7	14	6	8	5	5	4	0~	0~	1	1	11	3			5	2
YE Sep 16	41	8	19	5	22	6	12	6	8	5	5	4	0~	1	1	1	10	3	0~	0~	4	2
YE Dec 16	43	8	24	6	18	5	10	5	5	3	5	3	0~	1	1	1	8	3	0~	0~	4	2
YE Mar 17p	44	8	23	6	21	6	12	6	6	4	6	5	1	1	1	1	8	3	0~	0~	4	2
YE Jun 17p9	39	7	19	5	20	5	10	5	4	2	5	4	2	2	0~	0~	10	3	1	1	5	2
YE Sep 17p9	40	8	17	5	23	6	14	7	7	5	5	4	2	2	1	1	10	3	1	1	5	2
YE Dec 17p	39	8	13	4	26	6	16	8	8	6	4	4	4	3	1	2	9	3	1	1	4	2

Table 4 International Passenger Survey (IPS) estimates of long-term international migration - Rolling annual data for the United Kingdom, year ending December 2017

Former immigrants - Formal Study are designated as Experimental Statistics. This follows a report from the Office for Statistics Regulation recommending this until ONS has a more complete and coherent picture of former student emigration

Our latest student update report 'What's happening with international student migration?' was published 24 August 2017

Outflow of migrants by citizenship and, for former immigrants[1], previous main reason for immigration

United Kingdom
thousands

Migration status and, for former immigrants[1], Previous main reason for immigration	All citizenships		British (Including Overseas Territories)		Non-British		European Union[2]		European Union EU15		European Union EU8		European Union EU2		European Union Other		Non-European Union[3] All		Other Europe[4]		Asia All	
	Estimate	+/-CI	Estimate	+/-CI	Estimate	+/-CI	Estimate	+/-CI	Estimate	+/-CI	Estimate	+/-CI	Estimate	+/-CI	Estimate	+/-CI	Estimate	+/-CI	Estimate	+/-CI	Estimate	+/-CI
Former immigrants - UK born - not asked[7]																						
YE Dec 12	30	10	29	10	1	1	1	1	.	.	.	.	.	.	.	.	1	1	0~	0~	0~	0~
YE Mar 13	28	10	27	10	1	1	1	1	.	.	.	.	.	.	.	.	1	1	0~	0~	0~	0~
YE Jun 13	18	5	17	5	1	1	1	1	.	.	.	.	.	.	.	.	1	1	0~	0~	0~	0~
YE Sep 13	9	3	9	3	0~	0~	0~	0~	.	.	.	.	.	.	.	.	0~	0~	.	.	.	.
YE Dec 13	3	2	3	2	z	z	z	z	.	.	.	.	.	.	.	.	z	z	.	.	.	.
YE Mar 14	z	z	z	z	z	z	z	z	z	z	z	z	z	z	z	z	z	z	z	z	z	z
YE Jun 14	z	z	z	z	z	z	z	z	z	z	z	z	z	z	z	z	z	z	z	z	z	z
YE Sep 14	z	z	z	z	z	z	z	z	z	z	z	z	z	z	z	z	z	z	z	z	z	z
YE Dec 14	z	z	z	z	z	z	z	z	z	z	z	z	z	z	z	z	z	z	z	z	z	z
YE Mar 15	z	z	z	z	z	z	z	z	z	z	z	z	z	z	z	z	z	z	z	z	z	z
YE Jun 15	z	z	z	z	z	z	z	z	z	z	z	z	z	z	z	z	z	z	z	z	z	z
YE Sep 15	z	z	z	z	z	z	z	z	z	z	z	z	z	z	z	z	z	z	z	z	z	z
YE Dec 15	z	z	z	z	z	z	z	z	z	z	z	z	z	z	z	z	z	z	z	z	z	z
YE Mar 16	z	z	z	z	z	z	z	z	z	z	z	z	z	z	z	z	z	z	z	z	z	z
YE Jun 16	z	z	z	z	z	z	z	z	z	z	z	z	z	z	z	z	z	z	z	z	z	z
YE Sep 16	z	z	z	z	z	z	z	z	z	z	z	z	z	z	z	z	z	z	z	z	z	z
YE Dec 16	z	z	z	z	z	z	z	z	z	z	z	z	z	z	z	z	z	z	z	z	z	z
YE Mar 17[p]	z	z	z	z	z	z	z	z	z	z	z	z	z	z	z	z	z	z	z	z	z	z
YE Jun 17[p9]	z	z	z	z	z	z	z	z	z	z	z	z	z	z	z	z	z	z	z	z	z	z
YE Sep 17[p9]	z	z	z	z	z	z	z	z	z	z	z	z	z	z	z	z	z	z	z	z	z	z
YE Dec 17[p]	z	z	z	z	z	z	z	z	z	z	z	z	z	z	z	z	z	z	z	z	z	z
New emigrants[8]																						
YE Dec 12	92	9	90	9	2	2	1	1	1	1	1	1	.	.	.	.	1	1	0~	0~	0~	0~
YE Mar 13	93	9	91	9	2	2	1	1	0~	0~	1	1	.	.	.	.	1	1	0~	0~	0~	0~
YE Jun 13	98	10	96	10	2	2	1	1	1	1	1	1	.	.	.	.	1	1	0~	0~	0~	0~
YE Sep 13	98	11	97	10	1	1	0~	0~	0~	0~	0~	0~	.	.	.	.	1	1	0~	0~	0~	0~
YE Dec 13	100	11	98	11	1	1	1	1	1	1	1	1	.	.	.	.	1	1	0~	0~	0~	0~
YE Mar 14	95	10	92	10	2	2	2	2	1	1	1	1	.	.	.	.	1	1	0~	0~	0~	0~
YE Jun 14	100	12	96	12	3	3	3	3	1	1	1	1	1	1	.	.	2	2	1	1	1	1
YE Sep 14	103	12	98	12	5	3	3	3	2	2	2	2	1	1	.	.	2	2	1	1	1	1
YE Dec 14	101	12	97	12	4	3	2	2	2	2	2	3	1	1	.	.	2	2	1	1	1	1
YE Mar 15	98	12	93	12	5	4	3	3	2	2	2	2	2	2	.	.	2	1	1	1	1	1
YE Jun 15	94	11	89	11	5	4	4	4	3	3	2	2	2	2	1	1	1	1	1	1	1	1
YE Sep 15	89	11	85	10	3	3	3	3	2	2	1	1	1	1	1	1	1	1	0~	0~	1	1
YE Dec 15	85	11	80	11	4	3	3	3	2	2	2	2	1	1	1	2	1	1	0~	0~	0~	0~
YE Mar 16	86	12	83	11	3	2	2	2	0~	0~	1	1	0~	0~	1	2	2	1	.	.	.	.
YE Jun 16	85	11	83	11	2	1	0~	0~	0~	0~	1	1	.	.	1	2	2	2	.	.	.	.
YE Sep 16	88	11	85	11	2	1	0~	1	0~	1	1	1	.	.	.	.	2	1	.	.	.	.
YE Dec 16	89	11	88	11	1	1	0~	0~	0~	0~	0~	1	.	.	.	.	1	1	0~	0~	0~	0~
YE Mar 17[p]	87	11	86	10	2	1	1	1	0~	0~	1	1	.	.	.	.	1	1	0~	0~	0~	0~
YE Jun 17[p9]	82	11	79	10	3	3	3	3	2	2	1	1	.	.	.	.	1	1	0~	0~	0~	0~
YE Sep 17[p9]	86	11	81	11	5	4	3	3	2	2	2	2	.	.	.	.	2	2	1	1	1	1
YE Dec 17[p]	86	12	81	11	5	4	3	3	2	2	2	2	0~	1	.	.	2	2	1	1	1	1

Table 4 International Passenger Survey (IPS) estimates of long term international migration - Rolling annual data for the United Kingdom, year ending December 2017

Former immigrants - Formal Study are designated as Experimental Statistics. This follows a report from the Office for Statistics Regulation recommending this until ONS has a more complete and coherent picture of former student emigration

Our latest student update report 'What's happening with international student migration?' was published 24 August 2017

United Kingdom
thousands

Outflow of migrants by citizenship and, for former immigrants[1], previous main reason for immigration

Migration status and, for former immigrants[1], Previous main reason for immigration	Non-European Union[3] (contd.)																						
	Asia (contd.)								Rest of the World													Stateless	
	Middle East and Central Asia		East Asia		South Asia		South East Asia		All		Sub-Saharan Africa		North Africa		North America		Central and South America		Oceania			
	Estimate	+/-CI	Estimate	+/-CI	Estimate	+/-CI	Estimate	+/-CI	Estimate	+/-CI	Estimate	+/-CI	Estimate	+/-CI	Estimate	+/-CI	Estimate	+/-CI	Estimate	+/-CI	Estimate	+/-CI

Outflow

All emigrants

YE Dec 12	4	2	20	2	24	4	10	3	34	5	7	2	1	1	10	3	4	2	12	3	.	.
YE Mar 13	4	2	21	2	24	4	9	2	32	5	6	2	1	1	10	2	4	2	11	3	.	.
YE Jun 13	4	2	20	2	24	4	8	2	32	5	6	2	1	1	9	2	4	2	12	3	.	.
YE Sep 13	3	1	18	1	24	3	8	2	38	6	6	2	1	1	12	4	5	3	13	3	.	.
YE Dec 13	4	2	20	2	22	4	7	2	38	6	7	2	2	1	13	4	4	2	13	3	.	.
YE Mar 14	4	2	21	2	21	4	8	3	37	6	8	2	1	1	13	4	3	2	12	3	.	.
YE Jun 14	4	2	22	2	20	4	9	3	37	6	8	2	1	1	12	4	3	2	12	3	.	.
YE Sep 14	5	2	27	2	17	8	8	3	31	5	6	2	1	1	9	3	3	2	12	3	.	.
YE Dec 14	4	2	26	2	18	8	7	3	26	4	5	2	1	1	8	3	1	1	11	3	.	.
YE Mar 15	4	2	24	2	16	8	7	3	26	5	4	2	1	1	9	3	1	1	11	3	.	.
YE Jun 15	4	2	24	2	17	7	6	3	25	4	4	2	1	1	9	3	1	1	10	3	.	.
YE Sep 15	4	2	21	2	17	4	7	3	27	5	5	2	1	1	9	3	4	2	7	2	.	.
YE Dec 15	4	2	20	2	18	4	8	3	32	5	6	2	1	1	10	3	5	2	9	3	.	.
YE Mar 16	5	4	20	4	19	4	9	4	32	5	6	2	1	1	12	3	5	2	8	3	.	.
YE Jun 16	4	4	21	4	18	4	8	4	33	5	5	2	2	2	11	3	5	2	11	3	.	.
YE Sep 16	5	4	18	4	18	4	8	3	38	7	6	3	2	2	16	5	4	2	11	3	.	.
YE Dec 16	6	4	17	4	16	4	8	3	34	7	4	3	2	2	16	5	3	2	9	3	0~	0~
YE Mar 17p	6	2	18	2	16	4	7	3	33	7	3	3	2	2	15	5	4	2	9	3	0~	0~
YE Jun 17pg	6	2	17	2	15	4	8	3	34	8	4	3	2	2	15	5	4	2	9	3	0~	0~
YE Sep 17pg	9	4	21	4	13	4	7	3	29	6	4	3	2	1	10	4	3	2	9	3	0~	0~
YE Dec 17p	8	4	20	4	10	3	6	3	29	7	4	3	2	1	10	5	3	3	9	3	0~	0~

Former immigrants - All reasons

YE Dec 12	4	2	19	2	24	4	10	3	33	5	7	2	1	1	10	2	4	2	12	3	.	.
YE Mar 13	4	2	20	2	24	4	9	2	32	5	6	2	1	1	9	2	4	2	11	3	.	.
YE Jun 13	4	2	20	2	24	4	8	2	32	5	6	2	1	1	9	2	4	2	12	3	.	.
YE Sep 13	3	1	18	1	24	3	8	2	37	6	6	2	1	1	12	4	5	2	13	3	.	.
YE Dec 13	4	2	20	2	22	4	7	2	37	6	7	2	2	1	13	4	4	2	13	3	.	.
YE Mar 14	4	2	21	2	21	4	8	3	36	6	7	2	1	1	13	4	3	2	12	3	.	.
YE Jun 14	4	2	22	2	20	4	9	3	36	6	8	2	1	1	12	4	3	2	12	3	.	.
YE Sep 14	5	2	27	2	17	8	8	3	30	5	6	2	1	1	9	3	2	1	12	3	.	.
YE Dec 14	4	2	26	2	18	8	8	3	25	4	5	2	1	1	8	3	1	1	10	3	.	.
YE Mar 15	4	2	24	2	16	8	7	3	25	4	4	2	1	1	9	3	1	1	11	3	.	.
YE Jun 15	4	2	24	2	17	7	6	3	25	4	4	2	1	1	9	3	1	1	11	3	.	.
YE Sep 15	4	1	21	1	17	4	7	3	27	5	5	2	1	1	9	3	4	2	10	3	.	.
YE Dec 15	3	1	20	1	18	4	8	3	31	5	6	2	1	1	10	3	5	2	7	2	.	.
YE Mar 16	4	4	20	4	19	4	9	3	31	5	6	2	1	1	11	3	5	2	9	3	.	.
YE Jun 16	4	4	21	4	18	4	8	4	32	5	5	2	2	2	11	3	5	2	10	3	.	.
YE Sep 16	4	4	18	4	18	4	8	3	33	7	5	3	2	2	15	5	4	2	10	3	.	.
YE Dec 16	6	4	17	4	16	4	8	4	33	7	4	3	2	2	16	5	3	2	9	3	.	.
YE Mar 17p	6	2	18	2	16	4	7	3	32	7	3	3	2	2	14	5	4	2	9	3	0~	0~
YE Jun 17pg	6	2	17	2	14	4	8	3	33	8	3	3	2	2	15	5	4	2	9	3	0~	0~
YE Sep 17pg	9	4	21	4	13	4	7	3	28	6	4	3	2	1	10	3	3	2	9	3	0~	0~
YE Dec 17p	8	4	20	4	10	3	6	3	28	7	4	3	2	1	9	4	3	3	9	3	0~	0~

Table 4 International Passenger Survey (IPS) estimates of long-term international migration - Rolling annual data for the United Kingdom, year ending December 2017

Former immigrants - Formal Study are designated as Experimental Statistics. This follows a report from the Office for Statistics Regulation recommending this until ONS has a more complete and coherent picture of former student emigration
Our latest student update report 'What's happening with international student migration?' was published 24 August 2017

United Kingdom
thousands

Outflow of migrants by citizenship and, for former immigrants, previous main reason for immigration

Migration status: Non-European Union[3] (contd.)

Previous main reason for immigration	Middle East and Central Asia Estimate	+/-CI	East Asia Estimate	+/-CI	South Asia Estimate	+/-CI	South East Asia Estimate	+/-CI	Rest of the World: All Estimate	+/-CI	Sub-Saharan Africa Estimate	+/-CI	North Africa Estimate	+/-CI	North America Estimate	+/-CI	Central and South America Estimate	+/-CI	Oceania Estimate	+/-CI	Stateless Estimate	+/-CI
Former immigrants - Work related[5]																						
YE Dec 12	1	1	3	2	7	2	2	1	13	3	1	1	0~	1	3	2	2	1	6	2		
YE Mar 13	1	1	3	1	6	2	2	1	13	3	1	1	0~	0~	4	2	2	1	6	2		
YE Jun 13	1	1	3	2	6	2	2	1	14	3	1	1	0~	0~	3	1	2	1	7	2		
YE Sep 13	1	1	2	1	6	2	2	1	17	4	1	1	.	.	5	3	2	1	9	3		
YE Dec 13	0~	1	3	2	5	2	2	1	16	4	2	1	0~	1	5	3	1	1	8	2		
YE Mar 14	1	1	3	2	6	2	2	1	14	4	2	1	0~	1	4	3	1	1	7	2		
YE Jun 14	1	1	3	2	6	2	2	1	12	4	2	1	0~	1	4	3	1	1	7	2		
YE Sep 14	1	1	6	6	4	2	2	1	10	3	1	1	0~	1	2	1	0~	0~	6	2		
YE Dec 14	1	1	6	6	5	2	2	2	8	3	1	1	0~	0~	2	1	0~	0~	6	2		
YE Mar 15	1	1	5	6	5	2	2	1	9	3	1	1	0~	0~	2	1	0~	0~	5	2		
YE Jun 15	1	1	5	6	6	2	2	1	10	3	2	2	0~	0~	3	1	0~	0~	5	2		
YE Sep 15	0~	1	2	1	7	2	2	1	9	3	2	1	0~	0~	3	1	1	1	3	1		
YE Dec 15	0~	0~	2	1	8	3	3	1	12	3	2	1	0~	0~	4	2	1	1	4	2		
YE Mar 16	0~	0~	1	1	9	4	4	1	12	3	2	1	0~	0~	4	2	1	1	5	2		
YE Jun 16			3	1	7	3	3	1	12	3	1	1	0~	0~	4	2	1	1	5	2		
YE Sep 16	1	1	2	1	9	4	4	1	12	3	1	1	0~	0~	5	2	1	1	6	2		
YE Dec 16	1	1	3	1	8	3	3	1	11	3	0~	0~	0~	0~	4	2	0~	1	6	3		
YE Mar 17p	1	1	3	1	7	2	2	1	11	4	0~	0~	0~	0~	4	2	0~	0~	6	3		
YE Jun 17p9	1	1	2	1	7	2	2	1	13	4	1	1	1	1	4	2	1	2	7	3		
YE Sep 17p9	1	1	2	1	5	2	2	0~	13	4	1	1	1	1	3	2	2	2	7	3		
YE Dec 17p	0~	0~	2	1	4	2	2	0~	15	5	1	1	1	1	5	4	2	2	6	3		
Former immigrants - Definite job																						
YE Dec 12	1	1	2	1	6	2	0~	0~	10	3	1	1	0~	1	3	1	2	1	4	2		
YE Mar 13	1	1	3	1	5	2	1	1	10	3	1	1	0~	0~	3	1	2	1	5	2		
YE Jun 13	1	1	2	1	5	2	1	1	10	3	1	1	0~	0~	2	1	2	1	5	2		
YE Sep 13	0~	1	2	1	5	2	1	1	13	4	1	1	0~	1	5	3	1	1	6	2		
YE Dec 13	0~	0~	2	2	5	2	1	1	11	4	1	1	0~	1	4	3	1	1	4	2		
YE Mar 14	0~	0~	2	1	5	2	1	1	10	4	1	1	0~	1	4	3	0~	0~	4	2		
YE Jun 14	0~	1	2	1	5	1	1	1	6	4	1	1	0~	1	1	1	0~	0~	4	2		
YE Sep 14	1	1	5	6	4	1	1	1	6	2	2	1	0~	1	1	1	0~	0~	3	2		
YE Dec 14	1	1	5	6	5	2	1	1	6	2	1	1	0~	0~	2	1	0~	0~	3	2		
YE Mar 15	1	1	5	6	5	2	1	1	7	2	1	1	0~	0~	2	1	0~	0~	3	2		
YE Jun 15	1	1	5	6	6	2	1	0~	8	2	2	1	0~	0~	3	1	0~	0~	3	1		
YE Sep 15	0~	0~	2	1	6	2	1	1	8	2	2	2	0~	0~	3	2	1	1	2	1		
YE Dec 15	0~	0~	2	1	8	3	1	0~	9	3	2	2	0~	0~	3	2	1	1	3	2		
YE Mar 16	0~	0~	1	1	8	3	1	0~	9	3	2	1	0~	0~	4	2	1	1	3	2		
YE Jun 16	1	1	3	1	7	3	1	1	9	3	1	1	0~	0~	4	2	1	1	4	2		
YE Sep 16	2	1	2	1	8	3	1	1	10	3	1	1	0~	0~	4	2	1	1	4	2		
YE Dec 16	1	1	2	1	7	2	1	1	9	3	0~	0~	0~	0~	4	2	0~	0~	3	2		
YE Mar 17p	1	1	2	1	7	2	1	1	10	3	0~	0~	0~	0~	4	2	0~	0~	4	3		
YE Jun 17p9	1	1	2	1	7	2	1	0~	12	4	1	1	0*	1	4	2	1	1	5	3		
YE Sep 17p9	0~	0~	1	1	5	2	0~	0~	12	4	1	1	0~	1	3	2	1	2	6	3		
YE Dec 17p			2	1	4	2	0~	0~	13	5	1	1	0~	1	5	4	2	2	5	2		

Table 4 International Passenger Survey (IPS) estimates of long-term international migration - Rolling annual data for the United Kingdom, year ending December 2017

Former immigrants - Formal Study are designated as Experimental Statistics. This follows a report from the Office for Statistics Regulation recommending this until ONS has a more complete and coherent picture of former student emigration

Our latest student update report 'What's happening with international student migration?' was published 24 August 2017

United Kingdom
thousands

Outflow of migrants by citizenship and, for former immigrants[1], previous main reason for immigration

Migration status and, for former immigrants[1], Previous main reason for immigration	Non-European Union[3] (contd.)								Rest of the World												Stateless	
	Asia (contd.)								All		Sub-Saharan Africa		North Africa		North America		Central and South America		Oceania			
	Middle East and Central Asia		East Asia		South Asia		South East Asia															
	Estimate	+/-CI	Estimate	+/-CI	Estimate	+/-CI	Estimate	+/-CI	Estimate	+/-CI	Estimate	+/-CI	Estimate	+/-CI	Estimate	+/-CI	Estimate	+/-CI	Estimate	+/-CI	Estimate	+/-CI
Former immigrants - Looking for work																						
YE Dec 12	0~		1	1	2	1	0~	1	3	1	0~	0~			1	1	0~	0~	2	1	1	1
YE Mar 13	0~	0~	0~	1	1	1			3	1	1	1			1	1	0~	1	2	1	1	1
YE Jun 13			0~	1	1	1			4	2	1	1			1	1	0~	1	2	1	1	1
YE Sep 13	0~	0~	0~	0~	1	1			4	2	1	1	0~	0~	1	1	0~	1	3	1	1	2
YE Dec 13	0~	0~	1	1	0~	0~	0~	0~	5	2	0~	0~	0~	0~	0~	1	0~	1	3	1	1	2
YE Mar 14	0~	1	1	1	1	1	0~	1	4	2	0~	0~	0~	0~	1	1			2	1	1	1
YE Jun 14	0~	1	1	1	1	1	0~	1	3	2	0~	0~	0~	0~	0~	0~			3	1	1	2
YE Sep 14	0~	1	1	1	1	1	0~	1	3	2	0~	0~	0~	0~	0~	0~			3	1	1	2
YE Dec 14			1	1	1	1	0~	1	3	1	0~	0~			0~	1	0~	0~	2	1	1	1
YE Mar 15					0~	1	0~	0~	2	1					0~	0~	0~	1	2	1	1	1
YE Jun 15			0~	0~	0~	0~	0~	0~	2	1	0~	0~			0~	0~	0~	1	2	1	1	1
YE Sep 15			0~	0~	0~	0~	0~	0~	2	1	0~	0~			1	1	0~	1	2	1	1	1
YE Dec 15			0~	0~	0~	0~	0~	0~	2	1	0~	0~			1	1	0~	1	2	1	1	1
YE Mar 16					1	1	0~	1	3	1	0~	0~			1	1	0~	1	2	1	1	1
YE Jun 16					1	1	0~	0~	3	1	0~	0~			0~	0~	0~	1	1	1	1	1
YE Sep 16	0~	0~	0~	0~	1	1	0~	0~	3	2	0~	0~			0~	1	0~	1	1	1	1	1
YE Dec 16	0~	0~	0~	0~	1	1	0~	1	2	1	0~	0~	0~	0~	0~	1	0~	1	1	1	1	1
YE Mar 17[p]	0~	0~	0~	0~	0~	0~	0~	0~	2	1	0~	0~	0~	0~			0~	1	1	1	1	1
YE Jun 17[p9]	0~	0~	0~	0~	0~	0~	0~	0~	1	1	0~	0~	0~	0~			0~	1	1	1	1	1
YE Sep 17[p9]	0~	0~	0~	0~	0~	0~	0~	0~	1	1	0~	0~	0~	0~			0~	1	1	1	1	1
YE Dec 17[p]	0~	0~	0~	0~	0~	0~	0~	1	1	1	0~	0~	0~	0~			0~	1	1	1	1	1
Former Immigrants - Accompany / Join																						
YE Dec 12	0~	0~	0~	0~	1	1	1	1	4	1	1	1	0~	0~	2	1	0~	0~	1	1	1	1
YE Mar 13	0~	0~	0~	0~	1	1	1	1	4	1	1	1	0~	0~	2	1	0~	0~	1	1	1	1
YE Jun 13	0~	0~	1	1	1	1	1	1	4	1	1	1	0~	0~	2	1	0~	0~	1	1	1	1
YE Sep 13	0~	0~	1	1	1	1	0~	1	3	1	1	1	0~	0~	1	1			1	1	1	1
YE Dec 13	0~	0~	1	1	2	1	0~	1	3	2	1	1	0~	0~	2	1	0~	0~	1	1	1	1
YE Mar 14	0~	0~	1	1	2	1	0~	1	3	2	1	1	0~	0~	2	1	0~	0~	1	1	1	1
YE Jun 14	0~	0~	1	1	2	1	1	1	3	1	1	1	0~	0~	2	1	0~	0~	1	1	1	1
YE Sep 14	0~	0~	0~	1	2	1	1	1	3	2	1	1	0~	0~	2	1	0~	0~	1	1	1	1
YE Dec 14	0~	0~	0~	1	1	1	1	1	2	1	1	1	0~	0~	1	1	0~	0~	1	1	1	1
YE Mar 15	0~	0~	0~	1	0~	1	0~	1	2	1	1	1	0~	0~	1	1	0~	0~	1	1	1	1
YE Jun 15	0~	0~	1	1	1	1	0~	1	2	1	0~	0~	0~	0~	1	1			1	1	1	1
YE Sep 15	0~	1	1	1	1	1	0~	1	2	1	0~	0~	0~	0~	1	1			1	1	1	1
YE Dec 15	0~	1	1	1	1	1	0~	1	2	1	0~	0~	0~	0~	1	1			1	1	1	1
YE Mar 16	0~	0~	1	1	1	1	0~	0~	2	1	0~	0~	0~	0~	1	1	0~	0~	1	1	0~	1
YE Jun 16	0~	0~	0~	1	1	1	0~	0~	2	1	0~	0~	0~	0~	1	1	0~	0~	1	1	0~	1
YE Sep 16	0~	0~	0~	1	2	1	1	1	7	4	0~	1	0~	0~	5	4	0~	0~	1	1	0~	1
YE Dec 16	0~	0~	0~	1	1	1	1	1	7	4	0~	1	0~	0~	6	4	0~	1	1	1	0~	1
YE Mar 17[p]	1	1	1	1	2	1	1	1	7	4	0~	0~	0~	0~	5	4	0~	1	1	1	0~	1
YE Jun 17[p9]	1	1	1	1	2	1	1	1	6	4	0~	0~	0~	0~	5	4	0~	1	1	1	0~	1
YE Sep 17[p9]	1	1	1	1	1	1	0~	0~	2	1	0~	0~	0~	0~	1	1	0~	0~	0~	1	0~	1
YE Dec 17[p]	0~	1	1	1	1	1	0~	1	2	1	0~	0~	0~	0~	0~	1	0~	0~	1	1	1	1

Table 4 International Passenger Survey (IPS) estimates of long-term international migration - Rolling annual data for the United Kingdom, year ending December 2017

Former immigrants - Formal Study are designated as Experimental Statistics. This follows a report from the Office for Statistics Regulation recommending this until ONS has a more complete and coherent picture of former student emigration

Our latest student update report 'What's happening with international student migration?' was published 24 August 2017

Outflow of migrants by citizenship and, for former immigrants[1], previous main reason for immigration

Migration status and, for former immigrants[1], Previous main reason for immigration	Middle East and Central Asia Estimate	+/-CI	East Asia Estimate	+/-CI	South Asia Estimate	+/-CI	South East Asia Estimate	+/-CI	All Estimate	+/-CI	Sub-Saharan Africa Estimate	+/-CI	North Africa Estimate	+/-CI	North America Estimate	+/-CI	Central and South America Estimate	+/-CI	Oceania Estimate	+/-CI	Stateless Estimate	+/-CI
Former immigrants - Formal study (experimental statistics)[6]																						
YE Dec 12	3	0~	15	3	13	3	7	2	8	3	4	2	0~	0~	2	1	2	1	0~	0~	..	..
YE Mar 13	3	0~	15	3	14	3	7	2	8	3	3	2			2	1	2	1	1	1	..	..
YE Jun 13	3	1	15	3	15	3	6	2	9	3	3	2	1	1	3	1	2	1	0~	0~	..	..
YE Sep 13	2	1	13	3	14	3	6	2	10	2	3	1	1	1	4	2	2	1	1	1	..	..
YE Dec 13	3	1	15	3	12	3	6	2	11	3	3	1	1	1	4	2	2	1	0~	0~	..	..
YE Mar 14	3	0~	16	3	10	3	6	2	11	3	4	2	0~	1	4	2	2	1	0~	0~	..	..
YE Jun 14	3	0~	17	3	9	2	6	3	12	3	4	1	0~	1	5	2	2	1	1	1	..	..
YE Sep 14	3	0~	19	4	8	2	6	3	9	3	3	1	0~	0~	3	2	1	1	1	1	..	..
YE Dec 14	3	1	17	4	9	2	5	3	8	2	3	1	0~	0~	3	2	1	1	1	1	..	..
YE Mar 15	3	1	17	4	8	2	5	3	6	2	1	1	0~	0~	3	2	1	1	0~	0~	..	..
YE Jun 15	3	2	16	4	8	2	4	2	6	2	2	2	0~	0~	2	1	1	1	0~	0~	..	..
YE Sep 15	3	1	14	3	8	2	5	2	9	3	3	2	1	1	3	2	3	2	0~	0~	..	..
YE Dec 15	2	1	14	3	8	2	7	2	11	3	3	2	1	1	3	2	3	2	0~	0~	..	..
YE Mar 16	4	4	15	3	7	2	7	2	12	3	4	2	1	1	4	2	3	2	0~	1	..	..
YE Jun 16	4	4	15	3	7	2	6	2	12	3	3	2	1	1	4	2	4	2	0~	0~	..	..
YE Sep 16	4	4	14	3	6	2	5	2	12	4	4	3	2	2	4	2	2	2	0~	0~	..	..
YE Dec 16	5	4	13	3	6	3	5	2	11	5	3	3	1	2	5	3	2	1	0~	0~	..	..
YE Mar 17[p]	3	2	13	3	6	3	4	2	10	4	3	3	1	2	4	3	2	2	0~	0~	..	..
YE Jun 17[p9]	4	2	12	3	4	2	5	3	10	4	3	3	1	1	4	2	1	1	0~	0~	..	..
YE Sep 17[p9]	7	4	16	4	4	2	6	3	8	4	3	3	1	1	4	2	1	1	0~	0~	..	..
YE Dec 17[p]	7	4	16	4	3	2	5	2	7	3	3	3	1	1	3	1	0~	1	0~	0~	..	..
Former immigrants - Other reason or no reason stated																						
YE Dec 12	0~	0~	1	1	2	1	1	1	8	2	2	1			2	1	0~	0~	4	1	..	..
YE Mar 13	0~	1	1	1	3	1	1	1	6	2	2	1			2	1	0~	0~	3	1	..	..
YE Jun 13	1	1	1	1	3	1	0~	0~	5	2	1	1			1	1	0~	1	3	1	..	..
YE Sep 13	0~	0~	1	1	3	1	0~	0~	6	2	1	1			1	1			3	1	..	..
YE Dec 13	0~	0~	2	1	3	1	0~	0~	7	2	1	1			2	1	1	1	4	1	..	..
YE Mar 14	0~	0~	2	1	3	1	0~	0~	8	2	2	1	0~	0~	2	1			4	2	..	..
YE Jun 14	0~	0~	2	1	3	1	0~	1	8	2	2	1	0~	0~	2	1	1	1	4	2	..	..
YE Sep 14	0~	0~	2	1	3	1	0~	1	8	2	1	1	0~	0~	2	1	0~	0~	4	2	..	..
YE Dec 14	0~	0~	2	1	3	1	0~	1	7	2	1	1	0~	0~	2	1	0~	0~	4	2	..	..
YE Mar 15	0~	0~	2	1	3	1	0~	1	7	2	1	1	0~	1	3	2			3	1	..	..
YE Jun 15	0~	0~	2	1	2	1	1	1	7	2	1	1	0~	0~	3	2	0~	0~	3	2	..	..
YE Sep 15	0~	0~	3	1	2	1	1	1	6	2	0~	0~	0~	0~	2	1	0~	0~	3	2	..	..
YE Dec 15	0~	0~	2	1	2	1	1	1	6	2	0~	0~	0~	1	2	1	0~	1	3	2	..	..
YE Mar 16	0~	0~	3	1	2	1	1	1	6	2	1	1	0~	0~	1	1	0~	1	4	2	..	..
YE Jun 16	0~	0~	2	1	2	1	1	1	6	2	1	1	0~	0~	1	1	0~	0~	3	2	..	..
YE Sep 16	0~	0~	2	1	2	1	1	1	6	2	1	1	0~	0~	1	1	0~	0~	2	2	..	..
YE Dec 16	0~	0~	2	1	1	1	1	1	4	2	1	1	0~	0~	1	1	0~	0~	2	1	..	..
YE Mar 17[p]	0~	1	1	1	1	1	1	1	4	2	0~	0~	0~	0~	1	1	0~	0~	2	1	0~	0~
YE Jun 17[p9]	0~	1	2	1	1	1	1	1	4	2	0~	0~	0~	1	1	1	0~	0~	2	1	0~	0~
YE Sep 17[p9]	0~	1	2	1	2	1	1	1	4	2	0~	0~	0~	1	1	1	1	1	1	1	0~	0~
YE Dec 17[p]	0~	1	2	1	2	1	1	1	5	2	0~	0~	0~	1	1	1	1	1	2	1	0~	0~

Table 4 International Passenger Survey (IPS) estimates of long-term international migration - Rolling annual data for the United Kingdom, year ending December 2017

Former immigrants - Formal Study are designated as Experimental Statistics. This follows a report from the Office for Statistics Regulation recommending this until ONS has a more complete and coherent picture of former student emigration

Our latest student update report 'What's happening with international student migration?' was published 24 August 2017

United Kingdom
thousands

Outflow of migrants by citizenship and, for former immigrants[1], previous main reason for immigration

Migration status and, for former immigrants[1], Previous main reason for immigration	Non-European Union[3] (contd.)								Rest of the World												Stateless	
	Asia (contd.)								All		Sub-Saharan Africa		North Africa		North America		Central and South America		Oceania			
	Middle East and Central Asia		East Asia		South Asia		South East Asia															
	Estimate	+/-CI	Estimate	+/-CI	Estimate	+/-CI	Estimate	+/-CI	Estimate	+/-CI	Estimate	+/-CI	Estimate	+/-CI	Estimate	+/-CI	Estimate	+/-CI	Estimate	+/-CI	Estimate	+/-CI
Former immigrants - UK born - not asked[7]																						
YE Dec 12									1	1					0~	1			0~	0~		
YE Mar 13									1	1					0~	1			0~	0~		
YE Jun 13									1	1					0~	1			0~	0~		
YE Sep 13							0~	0~	0~	0~									0~	0~		
YE Dec 13																						
YE Mar 14	N	N	N	N	N	N	N	N	N	N	N	N	N	N	N	N	N	N	N	N	N	N
YE Jun 14	N	N	N	N	N	N	N	N	N	N	N	N	N	N	N	N	N	N	N	N	N	N
YE Sep 14	N	N	N	N	N	N	N	N	N	N	N	N	N	N	N	N	N	N	N	N	N	N
YE Dec 14	N	N	N	N	N	N	N	N	N	N	N	N	N	N	N	N	N	N	N	N	N	N
YE Mar 15	N	N	N	N	N	N	N	N	N	N	N	N	N	N	N	N	N	N	N	N	N	N
YE Jun 15	N	N	N	N	N	N	N	N	N	N	N	N	N	N	N	N	N	N	N	N	N	N
YE Sep 15	N	N	N	N	N	N	N	N	N	N	N	N	N	N	N	N	N	N	N	N	N	N
YE Dec 15	N	N	N	N	N	N	N	N	N	N	N	N	N	N	N	N	N	N	N	N	N	N
YE Mar 16	N	N	N	N	N	N	N	N	N	N	N	N	N	N	N	N	N	N	N	N	N	N
YE Jun 16	N	N	N	N	N	N	N	N	N	N	N	N	N	N	N	N	N	N	N	N	N	N
YE Sep 16	N	N	N	N	N	N	N	N	N	N	N	N	N	N	N	N	N	N	N	N	N	N
YE Dec 16	N	N	N	N	N	N	N	N	N	N	N	N	N	N	N	N	N	N	N	N	N	N
YE Mar 17[p]	N	N	N	N	N	N	N	N	N	N	N	N	N	N	N	N	N	N	N	N	N	N
YE Jun 17[p9]	N	N	N	N	N	N	N	N	N	N	N	N	N	N	N	N	N	N	N	N	N	N
YE Sep 17[p9]	N	N	N	N	N	N	N	N	N	N	N	N	N	N	N	N	N	N	N	N	N	N
YE Dec 17[p]	N	N	N	N	N	N	N	N	N	N	N	N	N	N	N	N	N	N	N	N	N	N
New emigrants[8]																						
YE Dec 12									1	1					0~	0~			0~	0~		
YE Mar 13			0~	0~	0~	0~			0~	0~	0~	0~			0~	0~	0~	0~	0~	0~		
YE Jun 13			0~	0~	0~	0~			0~	0~	0~	0~			0~	0~	0~	0~	0~	0~		
YE Sep 13					0~	0~			1	1	0~	0~			0~	0~	0~	0~	0~	0~		
YE Dec 13			0~	0~	0~	0~			0~	0~	0~	0~			0~	0~	0~	0~	0~	0~		
YE Mar 14			0~	0~	0~	0~			1	1	0~	0~			0~	0~	0~	0~	0~	0~		
YE Jun 14					0~	0~			1	1	0~	0~	0~	0~					0~	0~		
YE Sep 14			0~	0~	1	1			1	1	0~	0~	0~	0~					0~	0~		
YE Dec 14			0~	0~	0~	0~			1	1	0~	0~	0~	0~					0~	0~		
YE Mar 15			0~	0~	1	1			1	1	0~	0~	0~	0~					0~	0~		
YE Jun 15	0~	0~			0~	0~	0~	0~	0~	0~					0~	0~	0~	0~	0~	0~		
YE Sep 15	1	1	0~	0~	0~	0~			1	1	0~	0~			0~	0~	0~	0~	0~	0~		
YE Dec 15	1	1	0~	0~	0~	0~			1	1	0~	0~			0~	0~	0~	0~	0~	1		
YE Mar 16	1	1	0~	0~	0~	0~			1	1	0~	0~			0~	1	0~	1	0~	0~		
YE Jun 16	0~	1	0~	0~	0~	0~			1	1	0~	0~			0~	0~	0~	1	0~	0~		
YE Sep 16					0~	0~			1	1	0~	0~			0~	0~	0~	0~	0~	0~		
YE Dec 16					0~	0~			1	1	0~	0~			0~	0~			0~	0~		
YE Mar 17[p]					0~	0~			1	1	0~	0~			0~	0~	0~	0~	0~	1		
YE Jun 17[p9]					0~	0~			1	1	0~	0~			0~	0~	1	1	0~	1		
YE Sep 17[p9]					0~	0~			1	2	0~	0~			1	1	1	1	0~	1		
YE Dec 17[p]					0~	0~			1	2	0~	0~			1	1	1	1	0~	1		

Table 4 International Passenger Survey (IPS) estimates of long-term international migration - Rolling annual data for the United Kingdom, year ending December 2017

Source: Office for National Statistics (ONS).

Totals may not sum due to rounding.

"z" - Not applicable, " " - No contact, "0~" - Rounds to zero. Please see the Notes worksheet for more information.

YE = Year Ending

p = Year includes provisional estimates for 2017

Estimates of emigration by previous main reason for immigration are only available from year ending December 2012 onwards.

1 Former immigrants are those who previously entered the UK as long-term international immigrants and are now leaving the UK as long-term international emigrants. Please see the Notes worksheet for more information.

2 European Union estimates are for the EU15 (Austria, Belgium, Denmark, Finland, France, Germany, Greece, Republic of Ireland, Italy, Luxembourg, Netherlands, Portugal, Spain and Sweden) up to 2003, the EU25 (the EU15 and the EU8 groupings plus Malta and Cyprus) from 2004 to 2006, the EU27 (the EU25 plus Bulgaria and Romania) from 2007 and the EU28 (the EU27 plus Croatia) from July 2013. Estimates are also shown separately for the EU15, the EU8 (Czech Republic, Estonia, Hungary, Latvia, Lithuania, Poland, Slovakia and Slovenia), the EU2 (Bulgaria and Romania) and EU Other (Malta, Cyprus and Croatia). British citizens are excluded from all citizenship groupings and are shown separately.

3 Excludes British and other European Union citizens as defined in footnote 2.

4 From July 2013 onwards, Other Europe excludes Croatia which joined the EU in July 2013.

5 "Work related" includes "Definite job" and "Looking for work".

6 Former immigrants - Formal Study are designated as Experimental Statistics. This follows a report from the Office for Statistics Regulation recommending this until ONS has a more complete and coherent picture of former student emigration. Please see the Notes worksheet for more information.

The estimated numbers of long-term emigrants whose previous main reason for immigration was study are consistently lower than the estimated numbers of long-term immigrants whose main reason for migration is study in tables 2 and 3. There are several reasons for these differences. Please see the downloadable document "International student migration - what do the statistics tell us?"

7 Former immigrants originally born in the UK migrating before 1 April 2013 were not asked their previous main reason for immigration. Please see the Notes worksheet for more information. All former immigrants in the year ending March 2014 and later were asked their previous main reason for immigration.

8 New emigrants are those who have never lived outside the UK long enough to establish usual residence elsewhere and are therefore leaving the UK for the first time as long-term international emigrants. Please see the Notes worksheet for more information.

9. Please see the correction notice on the Contents and Notes page for information relating to YE Jun 17p and YE Sep 17p

This table uses 95% confidence intervals (CI) to indicate the robustness of each estimate. Please see the Notes worksheet for more information.

Statistically Significant Increase

Statistically Significant Decrease

The latest estimates (year ending December 2017) have been compared with the corresponding estimates for the period one year earlier. Where changes have been found to be statistically significant, the relevant pair of estimates have been highlighted by setting their background colour. Please see the Notes worksheet for more information.

Published on 16 July 2018 by the Office for National Statistics. Email: migstatsunit@ons.gsi.gov.uk

© Crown copyright. You may re-use this information (not including logos) free of charge in any format or medium, under the terms of the Open Government Licence.

To view this licence, go to: http://www.nationalarchives.gov.uk/doc/open-government-licence/

or write to the Information Policy Team, The National Archives, Kew, London TW9 4DU. Email: psi@nationalarchives.gsi.gov.uk

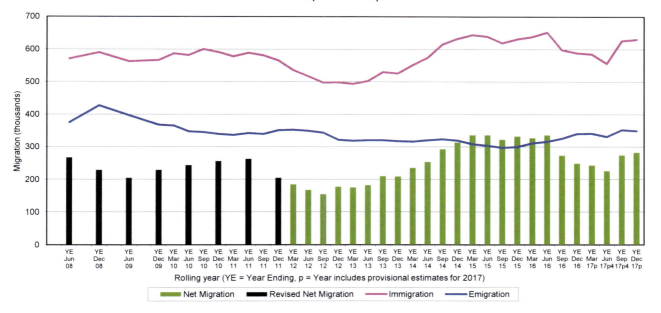

Chart 1 TS: Times series chart of LTIM estimates by selected citizenship group

Long-Term International Migration into and out of the United Kingdom. YE Jun 08 to YE Dec 17
Citizenship: All citizenships

Long-Term International Migration estimates by citizenship are only available for calendar years and mid years up to YE Dec 2009.
Net migration ("Balance") figures for the United Kingdom for calendar years 2001 to 2011 and mid years 2001-2002 to 2010-2011 have been revised in light of the results of the 2011 Census. These revisions are shown as black bars in the chart.
Please see the Notes worksheet for more information.
It is not possible to offer a chart for stateless migrants due to the very small numbers involved.

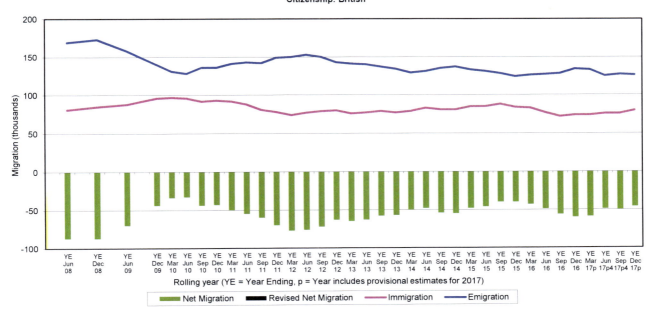

Long-Term International Migration into and out of the United Kingdom. YE Jun 08 to YE Dec 17
Citizenship: British

Long-Term International Migration estimates by citizenship are only available for calendar years and mid years up to YE Dec 2009.

It is not possible to offer a chart for stateless migrants due to the very small numbers involved.

Chart 1 TS: Times series chart of LTIM estimates by selected citizenship group

Long-Term International Migration into and out of the United Kingdom. YE Jun 08 to YE Dec 17
Citizenship: Non-British

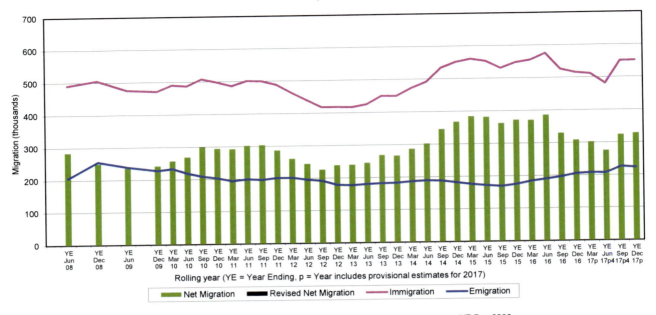

Long-Term International Migration estimates by citizenship are only available for calendar years and mid years up to YE Dec 2009.

It is not possible to offer a chart for stateless migrants due to the very small numbers involved.

Long-Term International Migration into and out of the United Kingdom. YE Jun 08 to YE Dec 17
Citizenship: European Union as constituted in relevant time period (other than British)

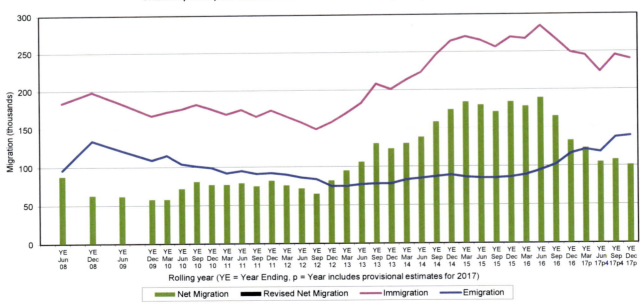

Long-Term International Migration estimates by citizenship are only available for calendar years and mid years up to YE Dec 2009.

It is not possible to offer a chart for stateless migrants due to the very small numbers involved.

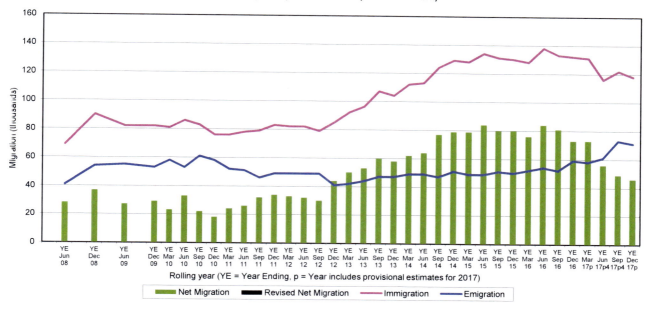

Long-Term International Migration into and out of the United Kingdom. YE Jun 08 to YE Dec 17
Citizenship: European Union EU15 (other than British)

Long-Term International Migration estimates by citizenship are only available for calendar years and mid years up to YE Dec 2009.

I is not possible to offer a chart for stateless migrants due to the very small numbers involved.

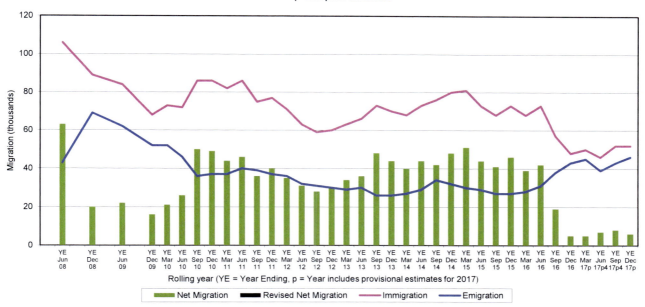

Long-Term International Migration into and out of the United Kingdom. YE Jun 08 to YE Dec 17
Citizenship: European Union EU8

Long-Term International Migration estimates by citizenship are only available for calendar years and mid years up to YE Dec 2009.

It is not possible to offer a chart for stateless migrants due to the very small numbers involved.

221

Long-Term International Migration into and out of the United Kingdom. YE Jun 08 to YE Dec 17
Citizenship: European Union EU2

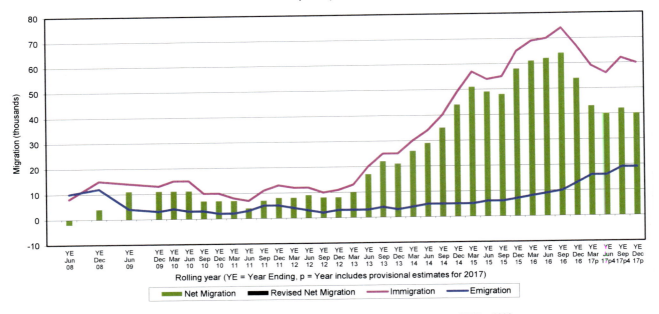

Long-Term International Migration estimates by citizenship are only available for calendar years and mid years up to YE Dec 2009.

It is not possible to offer a chart for stateless migrants due to the very small numbers involved.

Long-Term International Migration into and out of the United Kingdom. YE Jun 08 to YE Dec 17
Citizenship: European Union Other (Malta, Cyprus, Croatia)

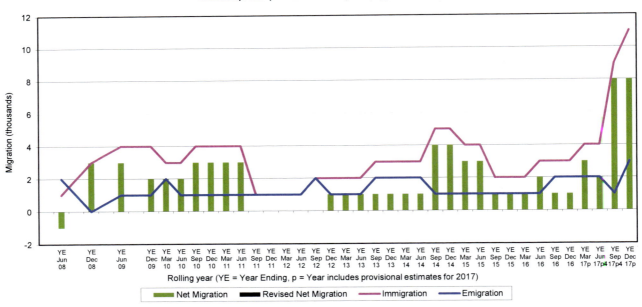

Long-Term International Migration estimates by citizenship are only available for calendar years and mid years up to YE Dec 2009.

It is not possible to offer a chart for stateless migrants due to the very small numbers involved.

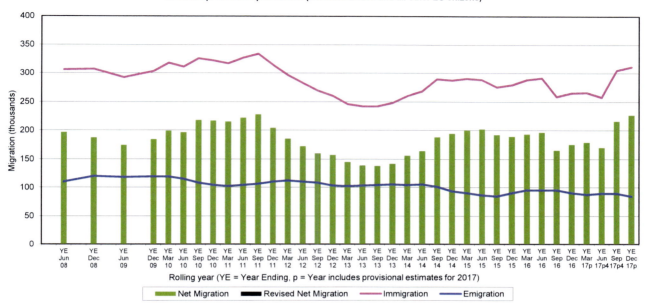

Long-Term International Migration into and out of the United Kingdom. YE Jun 08 to YE Dec 17
Citizenship: Non-European Union (excludes British and all other EU citizens)

Long-Term International Migration estimates by citizenship are only available for calendar years and mid years up to YE Dec 2009.

It is not possible to offer a chart for stateless migrants due to the very small numbers involved.

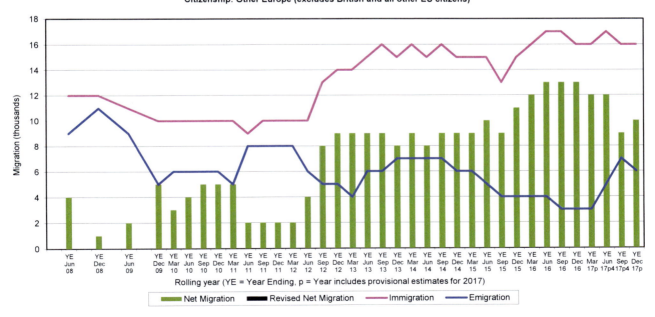

Long-Term International Migration into and out of the United Kingdom. YE Jun 08 to YE Dec 17
Citizenship: Other Europe (excludes British and all other EU citizens)

Long-Term International Migration estimates by citizenship are only available for calendar years and mid years up to YE Dec 2009.

It is not possible to offer a chart for stateless migrants due to the very small numbers involved.

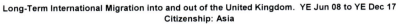

Chart 1 TS: Times series chart of LTIM estimates by selected citizenship group

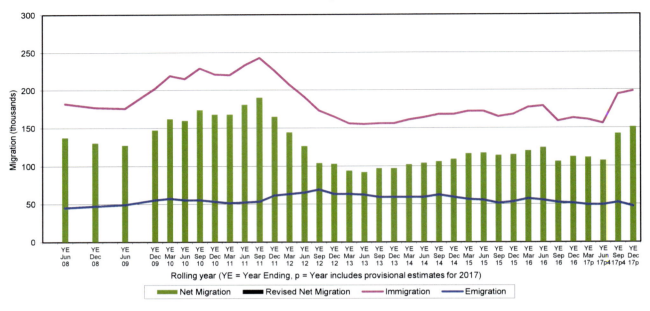

Long-Term International Migration into and out of the United Kingdom. YE Jun 08 to YE Dec 17
Citizenship: Asia

Long-Term International Migration estimates by citizenship are only available for calendar years and mid years up to YE Dec 2009.

It is not possible to offer a chart for stateless migrants due to the very small numbers involved.

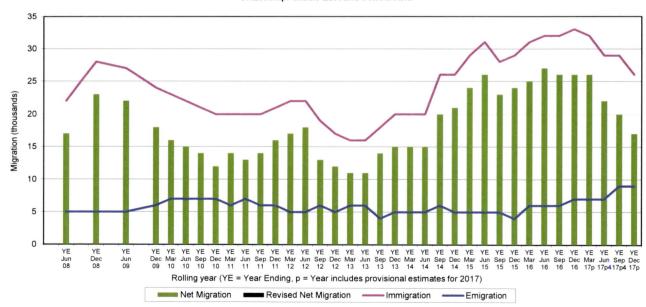

Long-Term International Migration into and out of the United Kingdom. YE Jun 08 to YE Dec 17
Citizenship: Middle East and Central Asia

Long-Term International Migration estimates by citizenship are only available for calendar years and mid years up to YE Dec 2009.

It is not possible to offer a chart for stateless migrants due to the very small numbers involved.

Long-Term International Migration into and out of the United Kingdom. YE Jun 08 to YE Dec 17
Citizenship: East Asia

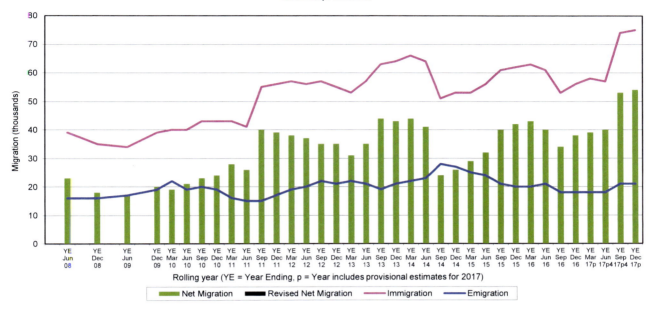

Long-Term International Migration estimates by citizenship are only available for calendar years and mid years up to YE Dec 2009.

It is not possible to offer a chart for stateless migrants due to the very small numbers involved.

Long-Term International Migration into and out of the United Kingdom. YE Jun 08 to YE Dec 17
Citizenship: South Asia

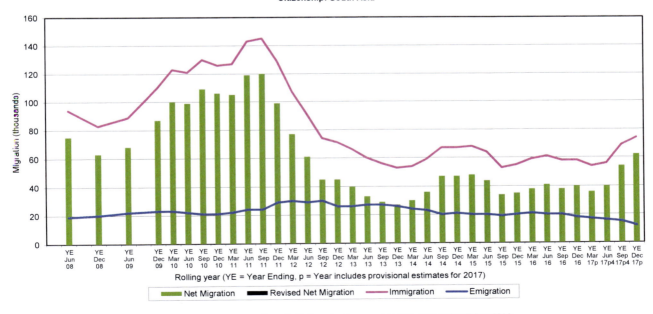

Long-Term International Migration estimates by citizenship are only available for calendar years and mid years up to YE Dec 2009.

It is not possible to offer a chart for stateless migrants due to the very small numbers involved.

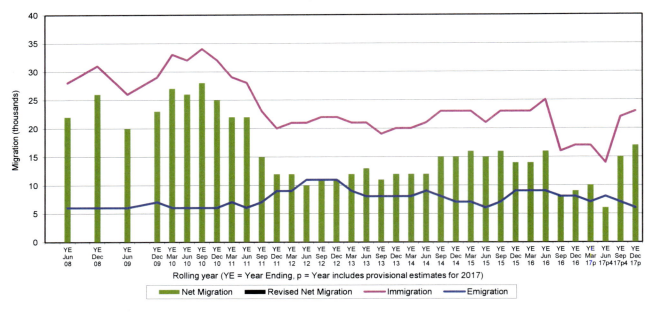

Chart 1 TS: Times series chart of LTIM estimates by selected citizenship group

Long-Term International Migration into and out of the United Kingdom. YE Jun 08 to YE Dec 17
Citizenship: South East Asia

Long-Term International Migration estimates by citizenship are only available for calendar years and mid years up to YE Dec 2009.

It is not possible to offer a chart for stateless migrants due to the very small numbers involved.

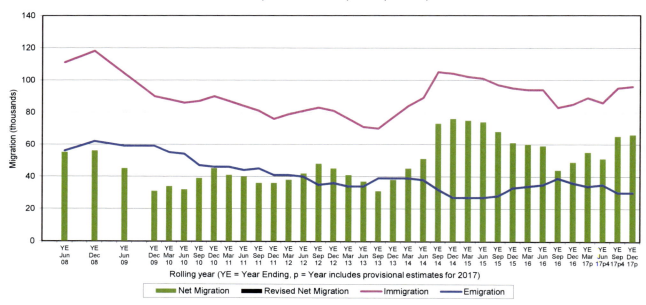

Long-Term International Migration into and out of the United Kingdom. YE Jun 08 to YE Dec 17
Citizenship: Rest of the world (not Europe or Asia)

Long-Term International Migration estimates by citizenship are only available for calendar years and mid years up to YE Dec 2009.

It is not possible to offer a chart for stateless migrants due to the very small numbers involved.

Long-Term International Migration into and out of the United Kingdom. YE Jun 08 to YE Dec 17
Citizenship: Sub-Saharan Africa

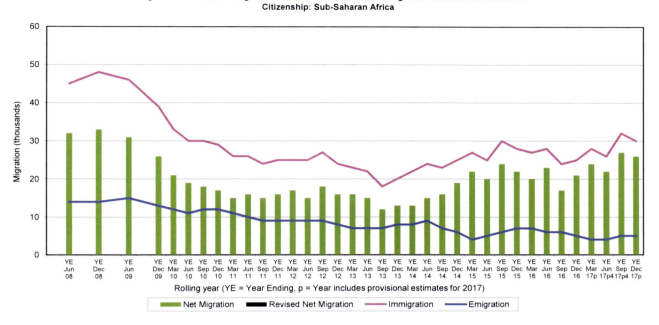

Long-Term International Migration estimates by citizenship are only available for calendar years and mid years up to YE Dec 2009.

It is not possible to offer a chart for stateless migrants due to the very small numbers involved.

Long-Term International Migration into and out of the United Kingdom. YE Jun 08 to YE Dec 17
Citizenship: North Africa

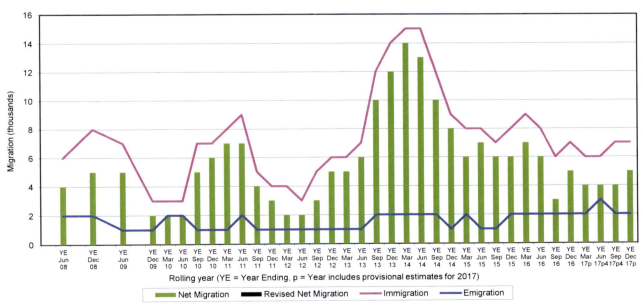

Long-Term International Migration estimates by citizenship are only available for calendar years and mid years up to YE Dec 2009.

It is not possible to offer a chart for stateless migrants due to the very small numbers involved.

Chart 1 TS: Times series chart of LTIM estimates by selected citizenship group

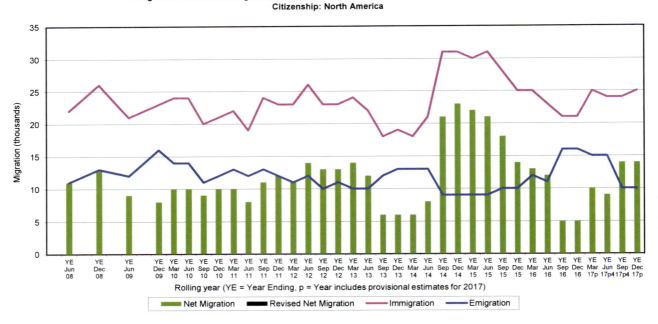

Long-Term International Migration into and out of the United Kingdom. YE Jun 08 to YE Dec 17
Citizenship: North America

Long-Term International Migration estimates by citizenship are only available for calendar years and mid years up to YE Dec 2009.

It is not possible to offer a chart for stateless migrants due to the very small numbers involved.

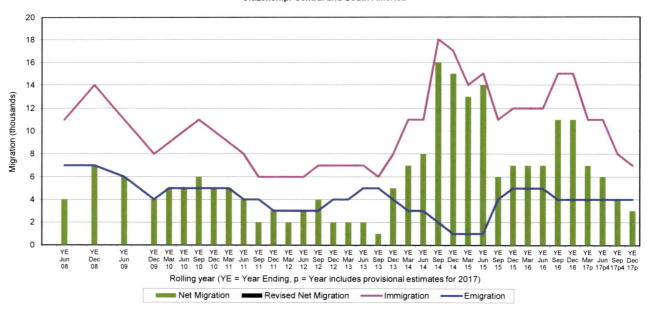

Long-Term International Migration into and out of the United Kingdom. YE Jun 08 to YE Dec 17
Citizenship: Central and South America

Long-Term International Migration estimates by citizenship are only available for calendar years and mid years up to YE Dec 2009.

It is not possible to offer a chart for stateless migrants due to the very small numbers involved.

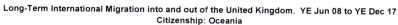

Chart 1 TS: Times series chart of LTIM estimates by selected citizenship group

Long-Term International Migration into and out of the United Kingdom. YE Jun 08 to YE Dec 17
Citizenship: Oceania

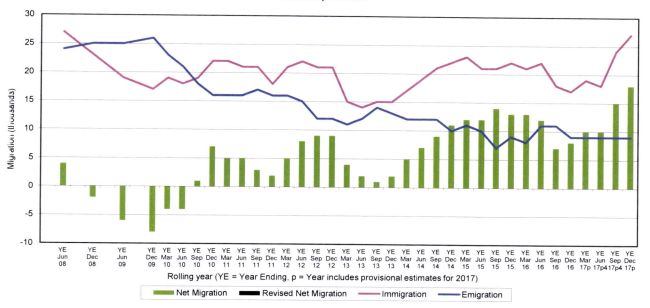

Long-Term International Migration estimates by citizenship are only available for calendar years and mid years up to YE Dec 2009.

It is not possible to offer a chart for stateless migrants due to the very small numbers involved.

Chart 1 Net: Composition of net long-term international migration by citizenship group, YE Mar 17 - YE Dec 2017

The Overall Composition of Long-Term International Migration by Citizenship. YE December 2017 (Provisional)
Net migration: 282 thousand

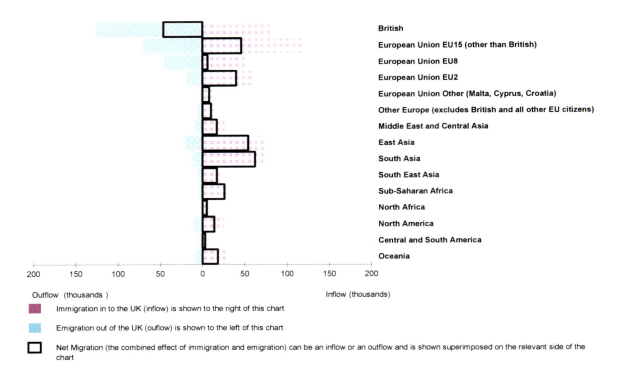

Outflow (thousands)   Inflow (thousands)

Immigration in to the UK (inflow) is shown to the right of this chart

Emigration out of the UK (ouflow) is shown to the left of this chart

Net Migration (the combined effect of immigration and emigration) can be an inflow or an outflow and is shown superimposed on the relevant side of the chart

Chart 1 Net: Composition of net long-term international migration by citizenship group, YE Mar 17 - YE Dec 2017

The Overall Composition of Long-Term International Migration by Citizenship. YE September 2017 (Provisional)
Net migration: 274 thousand

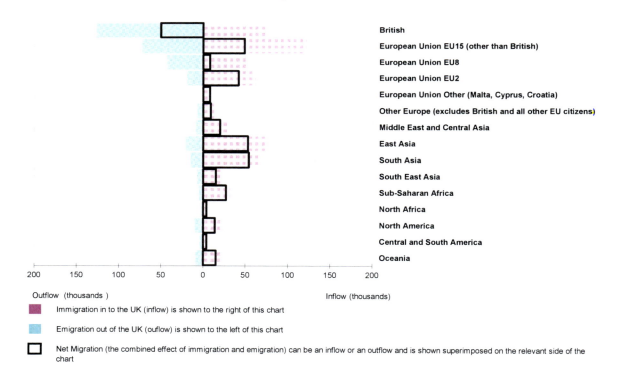

Outflow (thousands)   Inflow (thousands)

Immigration in to the UK (inflow) is shown to the right of this chart

Emigration out of the UK (ouflow) is shown to the left of this chart

Net Migration (the combined effect of immigration and emigration) can be an inflow or an outflow and is shown superimposed on the relevant side of the chart

Chart 1 Net: Composition of net long-term international migration by citizenship group, YE Mar 17 - YE Dec 2017

The Overall Composition of Long-Term International Migration by Citizenship. YE June 2017 (Provisional)
Net migration: 226 thousand

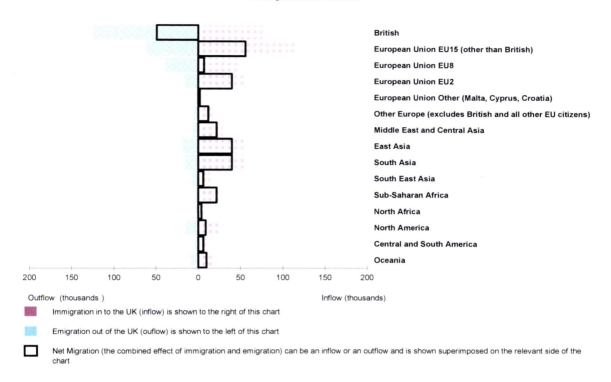

Outflow (thousands)   Inflow (thousands)

Immigration in to the UK (inflow) is shown to the right of this chart

Emigration out of the UK (ouflow) is shown to the left of this chart

Net Migration (the combined effect of immigration and emigration) can be an inflow or an outflow and is shown superimposed on the relevant side of the chart

Chart 1 Net: Composition of net long-term international migration by citizenship group, YE Mar 17 - YE Dec 2017

The Overall Composition of Long-Term International Migration by Citizenship. YE March 2017 (Provisional)
Net migration: 243 thousand

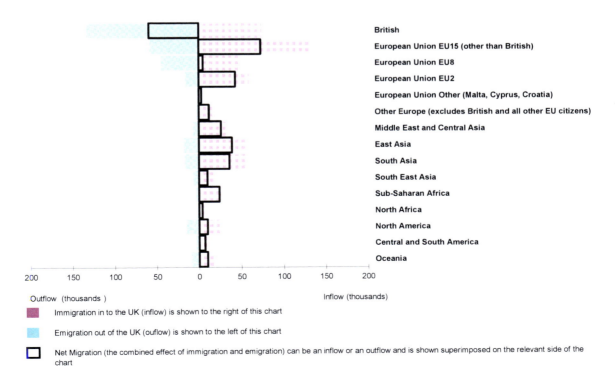

Outflow (thousands)   Inflow (thousands)

Immigration in to the UK (inflow) is shown to the right of this chart

Emigration out of the UK (ouflow) is shown to the left of this chart

Net Migration (the combined effect of immigration and emigration) can be an inflow or an outflow and is shown superimposed on the relevant side of the chart

231

Chart 2a: Times series chart of LTIM estimates by main reason for migration groups by selected flow direction

Long-Term International Migration into the United Kingdom. YE Dec 08 to YE Dec 17
Immigration by Main Reason for Migration

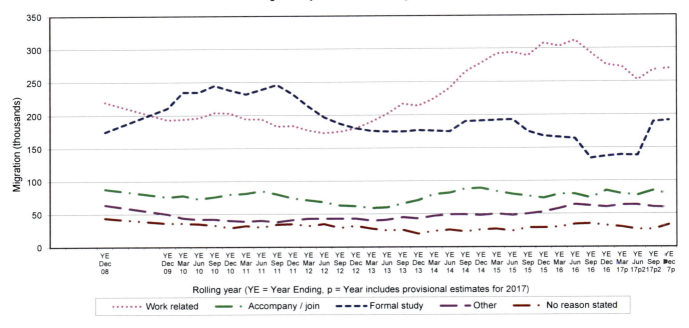

Long-Term International Migration estimates by reason for migration are only available for calendar years up to YE Dec 2009.

Chart 2a: Times series chart of LTIM estimates by main reason for migration groups by selected flow direction

Long-Term International Migration out of the United Kingdom. YE Dec 08 to YE Dec 17
Emigration by Main Reason for Migration

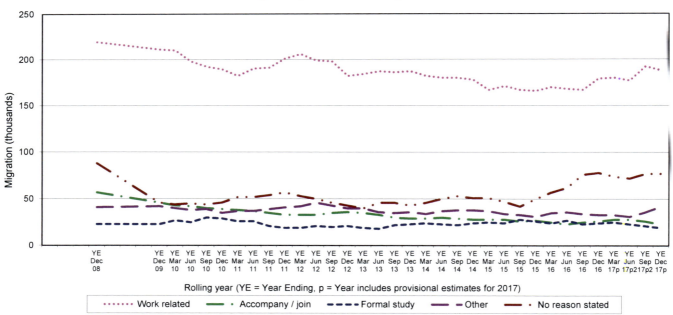

Long-Term International Migration estimates by reason for migration are only available for calendar years up to YE Dec 2009.

Chart 2b: Times series chart of LTIM estimates by selected main reason for migration group

Long-Term International Migration into and out of the United Kingdom. YE Dec 08 to YE Dec 17
Main Reason for Migration: All reasons

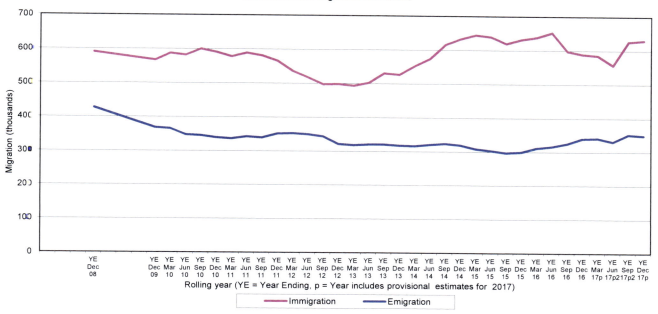

Long-Term International Migration estimates by reason for migration are only available for calendar years up to YE Dec 2009.

Chart 2b: Times series chart of LTIM estimates by selected main reason for migration group

Long-Term International Migration into and out of the United Kingdom. YE Dec 08 to YE Dec 17
Main Reason for Migration: Work related (definite job or looking for work)

Long-Term International Migration estimates by reason for migration are only available for calendar years up to YE Dec 2009.

Care should be taken when comparing inflow and outflow by main reason for migration. The outflow estimates in this chart are for emigrants' main reason for leaving the UK. A former immigrant's main reason for leaving the UK may well differ from their previous main reason for immigrating into the UK. Because of this, no balance estimates are displayed. Please see the Notes worksheet for more information.

233

Chart 2b: Times series chart of LTIM estimates by selected main reason for migration group

Long-Term International Migration into and out of the United Kingdom. YE Dec 08 to YE Dec 17
Main Reason for Migration: Definite job

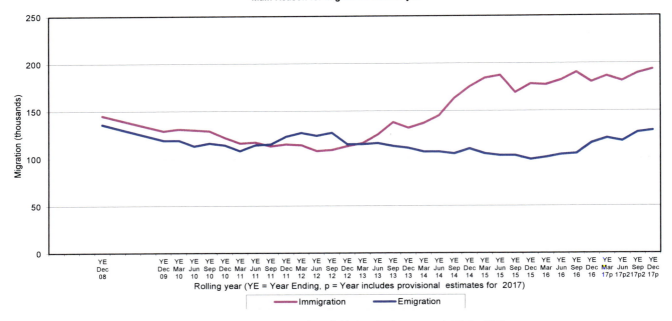

Long-Term International Migration estimates by reason for migration are only available for calendar years up to YE Dec 2009.

Care should be taken when comparing inflow and outflow by main reason for migration. The outflow estimates in this chart are for emigrants' main reason for leaving the UK. A former immigrant's main reason for leaving the UK may well differ from their previous main reason for immigrating into the UK. Because of this, no balance estimates are displayed. Please see the Notes worksheet for more information.

Chart 2b: Times series chart of LTIM estimates by selected main reason for migration group

Long-Term International Migration into and out of the United Kingdom. YE Dec 08 to YE Dec 17
Main Reason for Migration: Looking for work

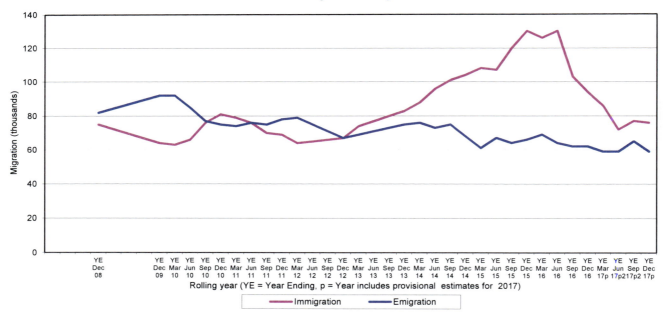

Long-Term International Migration estimates by reason for migration are only available for calendar years up to YE Dec 2009.

Care should be taken when comparing inflow and outflow by main reason for migration. The outflow estimates in this chart are for emigrants' main reason for leaving the UK. A former immigrant's main reason for leaving the UK may well differ from their previous main reason for immigrating into the UK. Because of this, no balance estimates are displayed. Please see the Notes worksheet for more information.

234

Chart 2b: Times series chart of LTIM estimates by selected main reason for migration group

Long-Term International Migration into and out of the United Kingdom. YE Dec 08 to YE Dec 17
Main Reason for Migration: Accompany/join

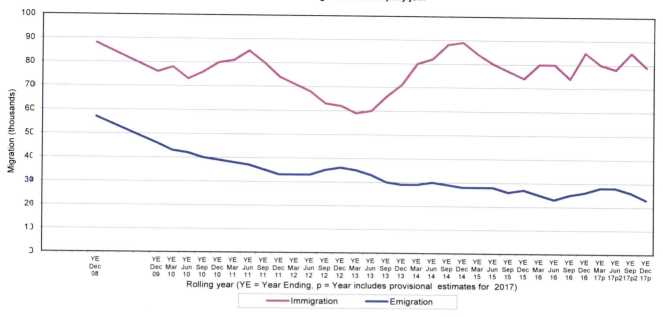

Rolling year (YE = Year Ending, p = Year includes provisional estimates for 2017)

— Immigration — Emigration

Long-Term International Migration estimates by reason for migration are only available for calendar years up to YE Dec 2009.

Care should be taken when comparing inflow and outflow by main reason for migration. The outflow estimates in this chart are for emigrants' main reason for leaving the UK. A former immigrant's main reason for leaving the UK may well differ from their previous main reason for immigrating into the UK. Because of this, no balance estimates are displayed. Please see the Notes worksheet for more information.

Chart 2b: Times series chart of LTIM estimates by selected main reason for migration group

Long-Term International Migration into and out of the United Kingdom. YE Dec 08 to YE Dec 17
Main Reason for Migration: Formal study

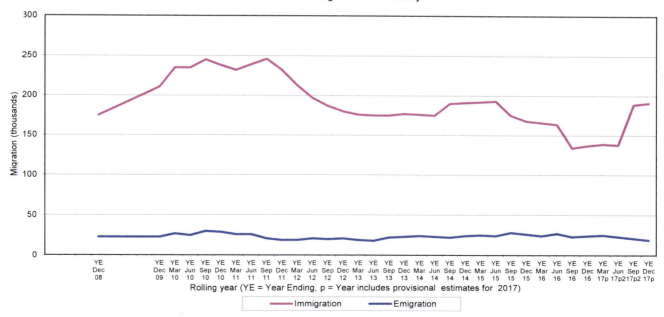

Rolling year (YE = Year Ending, p = Year includes provisional estimates for 2017)

— Immigration — Emigration

Long-Term International Migration estimates by reason for migration are only available for calendar years up to YE Dec 2009.

Care should be taken when comparing inflow and outflow by main reason for migration. The outflow estimates in this chart are for emigrants' main reason for leaving the UK. A former immigrant's main reason for leaving the UK may well differ from their previous main reason for immigrating into the UK. Because of this, no balance estimates are displayed. Please see the Notes worksheet for more information.

235

Chart 2b: Times series chart of LTIM estimates by selected main reason for migration group

Long-Term International Migration into and out of the United Kingdom. YE Dec 08 to YE Dec 17
Main Reason for Migration: Other stated reason (not work related, accompany/join or formal study)

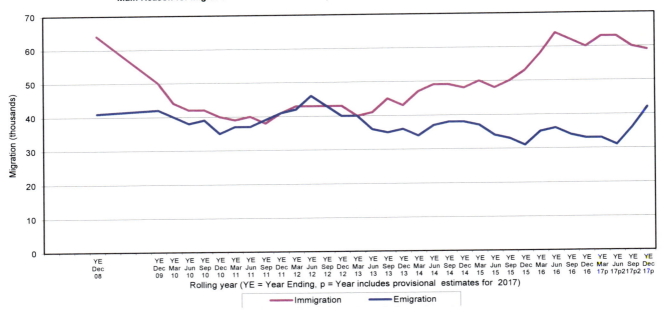

Long-Term International Migration estimates by reason for migration are only available for calendar years up to YE Dec 2009.

Care should be taken when comparing inflow and outflow by main reason for migration. The outflow estimates in this chart are for emigrants' main reason for leaving the UK. A former immigrant's main reason for leaving the UK may well differ from their previous main reason for immigrating into the UK. Because of this, no balance estimates are displayed. Please see the Notes worksheet for more information.

Chart 2b: Times series chart of LTIM estimates by selected main reason for migration group

Long-Term International Migration into and out of the United Kingdom. YE Dec 08 to YE Dec 17
Main Reason for Migration: Not stated

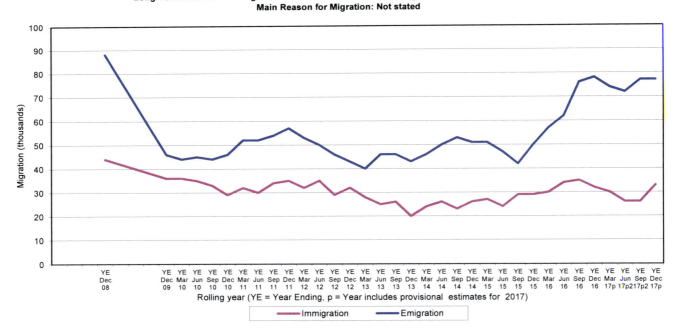

Long-Term International Migration estimates by reason for migration are only available for calendar years up to YE Dec 2009.

Care should be taken when comparing inflow and outflow by main reason for migration. The outflow estimates in this chart are for emigrants' main reason for leaving the UK. A former immigrant's main reason for leaving the UK may well differ from their previous main reason for immigrating into the UK. Because of this, no balance estimates are displayed. Please see the Notes worksheet for more information.

Chart 3: Times series chart of IPS estimates by all citizenships and all main reasons for migration.

International Passenger Survey estimates of long-term international migration into and out of the United Kingdom. YE Jun 08 to YE Dec 17
Citizenship: All citizenships
Main Reason for Migration: All reasons

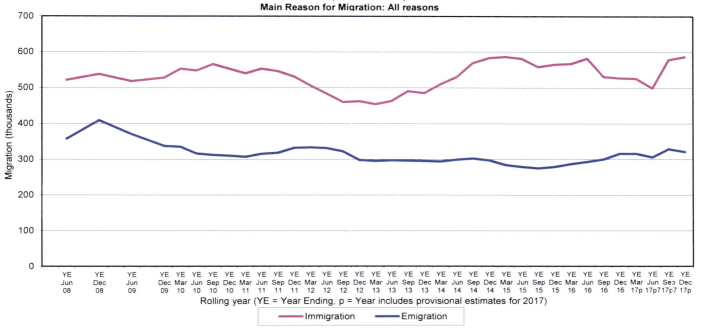

Migration between the UK and the Republic of Ireland is included in IPS estimates for 2008 onwards but excluded for previous years.
All estimates are calibrated. Calibrated IPS estimates of migration are only available for calendar years and mid years up to YE Dec 2009.

It is not possible to offer a chart for stateless migrants due to the very small numbers involved.